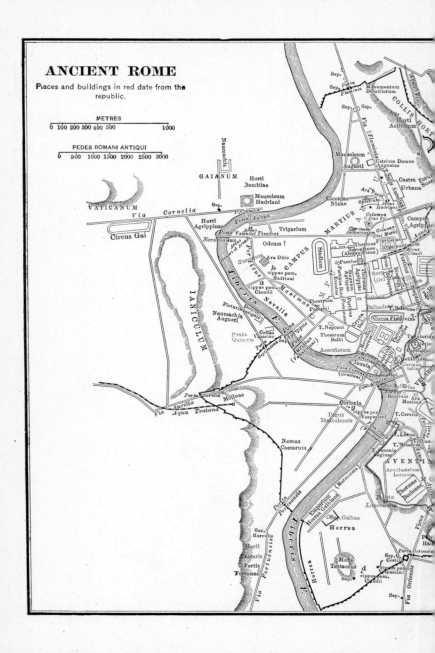

# ANCIENT ROME

Places and buildings in red date from the republic.

METRES
0  100 200 300 400 500          1000

PEDES ROMANI ANTIQUI
0   500  1000 1500 2000 2500 3000

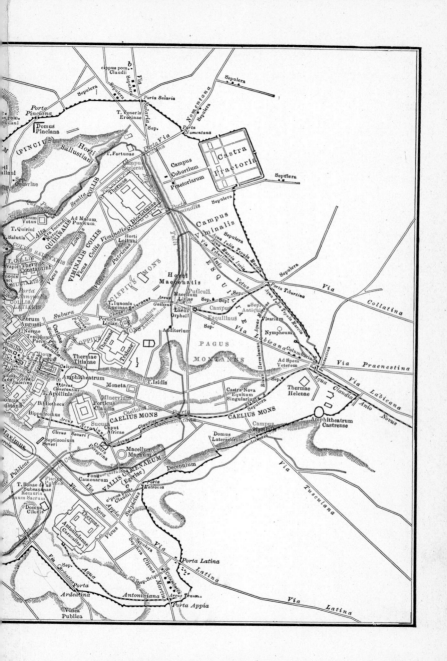

ALLYN AND BACON'S COLLEGE LATIN SERIES

# THE

# TOPOGRAPHY AND MONUMENTS OF

# ANCIENT ROME

BY

## SAMUEL BALL PLATNER
WESTERN RESERVE UNIVERSITY

*SECOND EDITION*
*REVISED AND ENLARGED*

## ALLYN AND BACON

BOSTON    NEW YORK    CHICAGO
ATLANTA    SAN FRANCISCO

COPYRIGHT, 1904 AND 1911,
BY SAMUEL BALL PLATNER.

EAP

Norwood Press
J. S. Cushing Co. — Berwick & Smith Co.
Norwood, Mass., U.S.A.

CHRISTIANO  HVELSENO

TOPOGRAPHIAE  VRBIS  ROMAE  ANTIQVAE

MAGISTRO  PERITISSIMO

S.

# PREFACE.

WHILE the actual excavations in Rome during the past six years have not been so important as those of the preceding five, the study of their results has been continuous and fruitful, so that it has seemed best to issue a revised edition of this manual which should be, so far as possible, brought down to date.

It is especially unfortunate that the official reports of much of the work done in the Forum have not yet appeared, so that many essential facts are still unknown; and that the excavations on the Palatine have lagged so sadly. The partial excavations of 1906–1908, and some new investigations based on them that have recently been undertaken, may, when completed, revolutionize some of the accepted views about the history and topography of that hill.

The most important contribution to the topography of Rome since 1904 has been the publication of the third part of the first volume of Jordan's *Topographie der Stadt Rom*, written by Professor Hülsen, to whom I wish to acknowledge again my deep obligations; the minor literature on the subject has increased so greatly that the references in this edition are considerably more numerous than in the first. This increase seems both justifiable and desirable, in spite of the fact that Professor Hülsen intends to issue a new edition of his *Nomenclator Urbis Romae* before long. Some of the categorical statements of the first edition have been modified, and errors corrected so far as discovered. In general, reference is made to views in conflict with those stated in the text.

Besides the acknowledgments made in the preface to the first edition, I wish to express my indebtedness to Comm. G. T. Rivoira for information concerning the temple of Venus and Roma, and for the use of one of his own illustrations; to Dr. Esther B. Van Deman for many valuable suggestions and criticisms in general, and in particular for the material contained in her work on the Atrium Vestae; and to Herr Baedeker of Leipzig for permission to use his latest map of the Forum.

S. B. P.

CLEVELAND, July, 1911.

v

# FROM THE PREFACE TO THE FIRST EDITION.

THIS book is intended to serve as an introduction to the study of the topography of ancient Rome for students of Roman antiquities and history, and incidentally as a book of reference for those who have any special interest in the monuments which still remain. It contains an outline of the successive stages in the growth of the city, a discussion of the topography of each region and the position of its buildings so far as this is known, and a somewhat detailed description of the more important structures.

To facilitate further study, references of two classes have been added: first, to the sources of information in ancient literature and inscriptions, and second, to the most important material in current periodicals and the standard works on topography.

This handbook makes no claim to exhaustiveness or originality; it is only a compilation from various sources, which, it is hoped, will form a useful addition to the working library of the student of Roman antiquities. It will be evident at once to those who know the literature of the subject that I have drawn continually upon the labors of others, especially upon Richter, — whose *Topographie der Stadt Rom* has been practically the basis of the present work, — Lanciani, Hülsen, Jordan, Gilbert, Borsari, Boni, and Ashby. As it is manifestly impossible to indicate in each case the precise amount and kind of indebtedness, I trust that I may be regarded as having discharged my duty by this general acknowledgment of obligation. I desire, however, to express my special gratitude to that master of Roman topography, Professor Christian Hülsen of the German Archaeological Institute, whose discussions of the subject during the past fifteen years have been definitive in almost every case, and whose generosity in the present instance has been most marked.

vi

In explanation of the usage adopted in this book with respect to capitals and small letters, attention is called to the fact that in the Latin names of places and monuments such ordinary words as *via, domus, pons, porta, hortus, templum,* etc., occur with great frequency, and that it is very undesirable to write them everywhere with capitals. Therefore, in the interest of consistency, these words are written regularly with small letters, and the distinguishing attributive words usually with capitals, as *Sacra via, domus Augustana.* Certain names, which have become identified in modern usage with one place or building, are written with capitals to distinguish them from others of the same class, as the *Forum,* the *Rostra,* the *Curia.* In view of its prevalence in ordinary use, the expression "Aurelian wall" has been adopted, although, strictly speaking, it is incorrect.

It has also been found convenient in many cases to describe the location of some monument or place in ancient Rome by later or even modern topographical references, in spite of the somewhat violent anachronisms involved.

My thanks are due to Professors Hülsen and Richter, to the C. H. Beck Publishing Company of Munich, and to Messrs. Adam and Charles Black of London, for permission to use illustrative material.

In conclusion I wish to acknowledge my special obligations to the editor-in-chief of this Series, Professor John C. Rolfe of the University of Pennsylvania, and to Professor Grant Showerman of the University of Wisconsin, both of whom have read all the proof and have made many helpful criticisms and suggestions. They are, however, in no way responsible for any errors either of fact or of citation.

S. B. P.

CLEVELAND, April, 1904.

# CONTENTS.

# MAPS AND PLANS.

# ILLUSTRATIONS.

# ABBREVIATED TITLES USED IN FOOTNOTES.

AJA. . . . . . . *American Journal of Archaeology*, First Series, 1885–1896 ; Second Series, 1897–.

AJP. . . . . . . *American Journal of Philology*, 1880–.

Altmann, *Rundbauten* . W. Altmann, *Die Italischen Rundbauten*, Berlin, 1906.

Ann. d. Ist. . . . . *Annali dell' Istituto di Corrispondenza Archeologica*, Rome, 1829–1885.

Antike Denkmäler . *Antike Denkmäler herausg. vom kais. Deutschen Archäologischen Institut*, Berlin, 1887–.

Arch. Anz. . . . . *Archäologischer Anzeiger; Beiblatt zum Jahrbuch des Archäologischen Instituts*, Berlin, 1889–.

Atti . . . . . . *Atti del Congresso Internazionale di Scienze Storiche*, vol. v, Rome, 1904.

Babelon, *Monnaies* . E. Babelon, *Monnaies de la République Romaine*, 2d ed., 2 vols., Paris, 1885–1886.

BC. . . . . . . *Bullettino della Commissione Archeologica Comunale di Roma*, Rome, 1872–.

Bull. Crist. . . . . *Bullettino di Archeologia Cristiana*, Rome, 1863–.

Bull. d. Ist. . . . . *Bullettino dell' Istituto di Corrispondenza Archeologica*, Rome, 1829–1885.

Chronogr. a. 354 . . *Chronographus anni 354*, in : *Monumenta Germaniae Auctorum Antiquissimorum*, vol. ix., 2d ed. (Mommsen), pp. 143–148, Berlin, 1892.

CIL. . . . . . . *Corpus Inscriptionum Latinarum*, Berlin, 1863–.

Cohen . . . . . . H. Cohen, *Monnaies Frappées sous l' Empire*, 2d ed., 8 vols., Paris, 1880–1892.

Cohen, *Méd Cons.* . Cohen, *Monnaies de la République Romaine, communément appelées Médailles Consulaires*, Paris, 1857.

CP. . . . . . . *Classical Philology*, Chicago, 1906–.

CQ. . . . . . . *The Classical Quarterly*, London, 1907–.

CR. . . . . . . *The Classical Review*, London, 1887–.

EE. . . . . . . *Ephemeris Epigraphica*, Berlin, 1872–.

GA. . . . . . . *Gazette Archéologique*, Paris, 1875–1889.

Gilbert . . . . . O. Gilbert, *Geschichte und Topographie der Stadt Rom im Altertum*, 3 vols., Leipzig, 1883–1890.

Hülsen-Carter . . . Ch. Hülsen, *The Roman Forum*. Translated from the second German edition by Jesse Benedict Carter, 2d ed., Rome, 1909.

xiii

# TOPOGRAPHY AND MONUMENTS OF ANCIENT ROME.

## CHAPTER I.

### SOURCES OF INFORMATION.

THE chief sources of information about the topography and monuments of ancient Rome, besides the monuments themselves, may be divided into two classes, the ancient and the medieval. The ancient sources are: Greek and Latin literature, inscriptions, the Capitoline Plan of the city, the Regionary Catalogues, and coins and reliefs. The medieval sources are: the Einsiedeln Itinerary, the Mirabilia Romae, and drawings, sketches, and views, although most of these belong to the Renaissance.

**Literary Evidence.** — The references in Latin literature are of primary importance in giving information as to the position and history of buildings and monuments of every kind. Such references are found in more or less abundance in the writings of every Latin author, but there are some of especial value, — the *Fasti* of Ovid, the *Naturalis Historia* of Pliny, the *De Architectura* of Vitruvius, the *De Aquis* of Frontinus, the *De Lingua Latina* of Varro, and the histories of Livy and Tacitus. Among Greek authors, the most useful are Dionysius of Halicarnassus and Dio Cassius.

**Inscriptions** afford much topographical information both by their content and by their position. Besides the ordinary dedicatory and honorary inscriptions which regularly state the

1

purpose of the monument, the name of its builder or restorer, and the date, there are others of great importance, — for example, the so-called **Capitoline Base**, [1] a pedestal now standing in the palazzo dei Conservatori. This pedestal and the statue which it supported were dedicated to the emperor Hadrian in 136 A.D. by the *vicomagistri* of five of the city regions, and on the sides of the base are cut the names of the various officials of the *vici*, together with the names of the *vici* themselves. The **Monumentum Ancyranum**, [2] the bronze tablets placed by Augustus on his mausoleum in Rome, which were reproduced at Ancyra in Asia Minor and also at Apollonia, contains an invaluable list of the buildings which Augustus either erected or restored. The fragments of Roman calendars, [3] in their announcements of festivals and religious observances, contain much information with regard to the relative position of temples and shrines. Finally, the inscriptions stamped on tiles and bricks [4] are exceedingly valuable and trustworthy evidence in determining the date of structures in which they are found.

**The Capitoline Plan** (*Forma Urbis Romae*). — North of the Sacra via and a short distance east of the forum of Augustus, are the remains of a structure, now sometimes called **templum Sacrae Urbis**, which was probably erected by Vespasian and seems to have been used as a repository for municipal records and archives, particularly the results of the census and survey of the city made in the years 73–75. [5]

Whether erected originally by Vespasian or not, the building seems to have been restored by Severus, [6] and its north wall covered with marble blocks on which was engraved a map or plan of the whole city. This was probably a restoration of that previously existing, which in its turn may have been a

---

[1] *CIL.* vi. 975.

[2] *CIL.* iii. pp. 769–799; Mommsen, *Res Gestae divi Augusti*, 1883.

[3] *CIL.* i². *passim.*          [4] *CIL.* xv. pt. i.

[5] *BC.* 1892, 93–111; *Mitt.* 1897, 148–160; Pl. *NH.* iii. 66–67.

[6] *CIL.* vi. 935; Jordan, I. 3. 5–7.

copy made by Vespasian of an original by Agrippa. The structure itself was incorporated with the temple of Romulus, the son of Maxentius, and made over into the church of SS. Cosma e Damiano between the years 526 and 530. During the years 1559–1565, a large number of fragments of this plan were found at the foot of the wall of the temple, and came into the possession of the Farnese family. In 1742 they were transferred

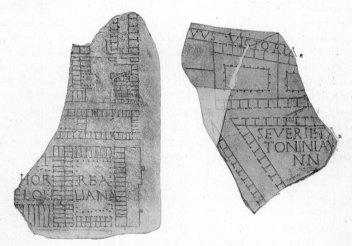

FIG. 1. — FRAGMENTS OF THE MARBLE PLAN.

to the Capitoline Museum, where they were fastened to the walls of the main stairway. Soon after the discovery of these fragments, drawings were made of ninety-two of the principal pieces, and as many of the pieces themselves were lost in the transfer to the Capitoline Museum, restorations made from these drawings were put up in their place. These restorations were marked with a star.

In 1867 a few more fragments were found on the same spot. In 1882 a piece containing a plan of the vicus Tuscus [1] was

---

[1] *NS.* 1882, 233–238.

found in the Forum; in 1884 another fragment,[1] also in the
Forum; and in 1888 more than one hundred and eighty pieces,[2]
mostly small and insignificant, were found behind the palazzo
Farnese, which may have belonged to those discovered in the
sixteenth century, but they do not appear on any of the drawings made at that time.   In 1891 about twenty-five fragments [3]
were discovered at the foot of the wall of the temple; and
recent excavations in the Forum (1899–1901) have brought
to light about four hundred pieces [4] more, mostly very
small.

In 1903 the fragments were removed to the palazzo dei Conservatori where the larger part of the plan was reconstructed
on the north wall of the garden on its original scale.   Of the
one thousand and forty-nine fragments that had been found,
only one hundred and sixty-seven could be identified with
certainty.[5]

The wall on which the plan was fastened is still standing,
and measures 22 metres in length and 15 in height, and the
surface covered by the plan has been estimated at 266 square
metres.   The blocks of marble varied from 0.70 to 1.18 metres
in height, and from 1.70 to 2.25 metres in width, their thickness also being unequal.   The scale [6] on which the map is
drawn varies even within the limits of the same structure, but
seems to have been in general 1 to 250.   If this scale had been
employed throughout, the whole city could not have been represented on this wall, whereas in fact the plan embraces some
of the suburbs.   This plan was not set up with the north at
the top, as is now the custom, but at the bottom.   It seems
probable that most of the plan was placed so that the southeast

    [1] NS. 1884, 423.

    [2] NS. 1888, 391–392, 437, 569; BC. 1888, 386.            [3] Mitt. 1892, 267.

    [4] NS. 1900, 633–634; BC. 1901, 3–21; CR. 1899, 234; 1901, 330; 1902, 96.

    [5] Atti del Congresso Internazionale di Scienze Storiche, Rome, 1903, i. 111–
122; Lanciani, Golden Days of the Renaissance in Rome, Boston, 1906, 132;
BC. 1902, 347–348; 1903, 380.

    [6] BC. 1886, 270–274; Ann. d. Ist. 1883, 5–22.

was at the top.[1] This arrangement was not carried out with
perfect consistency, and a variation of as much as 45° must be
allowed in some of the fragments. Names of public buildings
are given, but not always those of streets and squares. The
details of buildings are not accurately given, nor is the proper
proportion always preserved. Notwithstanding these defects,
however, the plan served its purpose well, and its fragments
have been of great assistance in identifying existing ruins.[2]

**The Regionary Catalogues.** — These are two interpolated
forms of the same original document, which was a catalogue
of the buildings contained in each of the fourteen regions established by Augustus. One, which bears no name in the manu-
scripts, is known as the **Notitia,** and the other is called the
**Curiosum Urbis Romae Regionum XIV cum Breviariis suis.**[3] The
common original was probably compiled between 312 and 315
A.D. and was itself based on a similar document of the first
century. The *Notitia* dates from some time later than 334, the
*Curiosum* from about 357 A.D.

These catalogues differ slightly in details of statement,
but are arranged in the same way. They fall into three
parts : —

(1) An enumeration of the principal buildings and monuments of each region, beginning with the number and name
of the region, followed by the verb *continet.* After the names
of the buildings, follow statistics of the number of *vici, aedi-
culae, vicomagistri, curatores, insulae, domus, horrea, balnea,
lacus,* and *pistrina,* and finally a statement of the number of
feet in the region. It is still uncertain whether this number
refers to the circumference of the region, or to the sum of the

---

[1] *BC.* 1893, 128–134; 1901, 5; *Mitt.* 1889, 79, 229; 1892, 267; *RhM.* 1894, 420.

[2] H. Jordan, *Forma Urbis Romae regionum xiv,* Berlin, 1874; A. Elter,
*De forma urbis Romae . . .* diss. i. ii. Bonn, 1891; Hülsen, *Piante icnografiche incise in marmo, Mitt.* 1890, 46–63.

[3] Preller, *Die Regionen der Stadt Rom,* Jena, 1846; Jordan, II. 1–178, 546–
582; Richter, *Top.*[2] 371–391; Merrill, *CP.* 1906, 133–144.

street distances within the region, but it probably refers to the former, although the figures are incorrect.

In some regions, as the eighth, the list of buildings is complete, or nearly so ; but in others it is quite incomplete, so that there has been much dispute as to whether it was intended to include all the noteworthy structures in the regions, or only those along the boundaries. The former is undoubtedly the true hypothesis, but the catalogue seems to have been made up from a map of the city, and not by a man who was actually exploring each district. Most of the omissions can be explained in this way.

(2) An appendix without special title, beginning with the number of *bibliothecae* and *obelisci*, with their size and situation. This is followed by a list of the *pontes, montes, campi, fora, basilicae, thermae, aquae, viae*, with their number and names.

(3) A second appendix, called *Horum Breviarium*, which is a concise statement of the number of buildings and monuments in the whole city.

In the case of those classes of buildings the numbers of which are given under each region, the totals in the appendix do not agree with the sum of the numbers in the regions. These discrepancies, however, are probably due to the ordinary errors of manuscript tradition.

**Coins and Reliefs.** — The frequent representations of buildings on coins [1] are of value in identifying and dating existing remains. The same thing is true of many reliefs, like that of the Haterii (Fig. 2) [2] in the Lateran Museum, on which are depicted various structures at the upper end of the Sacra via, and the relief representing the Rostra of Domitian, on the arch of Constantine.

---

[1] E. Babelon, *Monnaies de la République Romaine*, 2 vols., Paris, 1885–1886; H. Cohen, *Monnaies frappées sous l'Empire Romaine*, 2d ed. 8 vols., Paris, 1880–1892.

[2] *Ann. d. Ist.* 1894, 465–510; *Mon. d. Ist.* v. 7; Helbig, *Führer durch die Museen Roms*, i[2]. 462–466; G. Spano, *Sul rilievo sepolchrale degli Aterii*, Naples, 1906.

**The Einsiedeln Itinerary.**[1] —
As early as the eighth century,
the need was felt of something
in the nature of a guide-book for
pilgrims visiting Rome, which
should describe the routes
through the city to the principal churches and to the ceme-
teries outside. An epitome of
such an itinerary is contained
in a manuscript (No. 326) preserved in the library of the
monastery of Einsiedeln in
Switzerland. This manuscript
also contains the first known
collection of Latin inscriptions.
The inscriptions appear to have
been copied with care, but the
topographical information is
full of inaccuracies. The original itinerary appears to have
been based on a map representing the city as a circle, and the
method of the author is to give
the names of the monuments on
the right and left of the travel-
ler as he passes along certain
streets, which are designated
by their terminals.

[1] Lanciani, *L'Itinerario di Einsiedeln e l'ordine di Benedetto Canonico.
Monumenti Antichi pubblicati per
cura della Reale Accademia dei Lincei*,
i. 1891, 437–452; Jordan, II. 329–356,
646–663; Hülsen, *La Pianta di Roma
dell' Anonimo Einsidlense*, Rome, 1907.

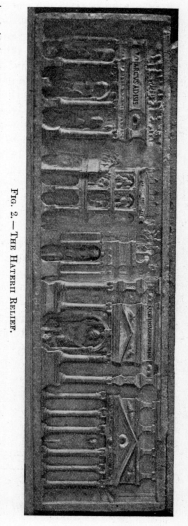

FIG. 2.—THE HATERII RELIEF.

Eleven routes through the city are described, but there is no mention of the temples of heathen divinities, and in the collection of inscriptions there are none containing the names of these divinities. A map representing the city as elliptical, but probably similar to that which accompanied this Itinerary, is still in existence,[1] and there is no reason to doubt that others like it were in use much earlier.

After the Itinerary is a description[2] of the wall of Aurelian, giving the number of its towers, bulwarks, posterns, windows, etc., and these numbers correspond in general with the evidence of the ruins themselves. This description seems to have been taken from one written in the fifth century, and appears, with some variations, in a work by William of Malmesbury, entitled *De numero portarum et sanctis Romae*, of the twelfth century, and in the *Mirabilia* of the twelfth.

**Mirabilia Romae**. — This is a description of the city,[3] compiled about 1150, consisting of three parts : —

I. A classified enumeration of the various monuments, viz., *de muro urbis, de portis, de miliaribus, nomina portarum*, etc.

II. Five legends: (1) *De visione Octaviani imperatoris et responsione Sibillae;* (2) *Quare factus est caballus marmoreus;* (3) *Quare factus est equus qui dicitur Constantini ;* (4) *Quare factum sit Pantheon ;* (5) *Quare Octavianus vocatus sit Augustus et quare dicatur ecclesia S. Petri ad vincula.*

III. A *Periegesis*, or description of the principal monuments and marvels met with in walking from the Vatican through the city and back to Trastevere.

This third part was written by the unknown compiler of the whole work ; while the first was taken from some guide-book like the Einsiedeln Itinerary, and the second was a selection

---

[1] *Cod. Vat.* 1960 ; Höfler, *Deutsche Päpste*, i. 324 ; Hülsen, *l.c.* 387.

[2] Jordan, II. 578–582.

[3] F. M. Nichols, *Mirabilia Urbis Romae.* An English version, London, 1889 ; Jordan, II. 357–536, 605–643.

from current legends. The chief purpose of the compiler seems to have been to identify the ancient temples, and was one of the consequences of that desire for a reëstablishment of the old republic which animated so many Romans in the twelfth century. This book had a very considerable vogue, was issued in a second edition a century later, and incorporated in several other works.

The Graphia Aureae Urbis Romae is a somewhat later recension of the same original, in which the legends, omitting the fifth, have been inserted in the third part, and various additions have been made.

Selections [1] from the *Graphia* are found in Martin of Troppau's (Martinus Polonus) Chronicon, 1268; Fazio degli Uberti's Dittamondo, about 1360; Nicolaus Signorili's De iuribus et excellentiis urbis Romae, 1417–1437; and in a manuscript called the Anonymus Magliabecchianus,[2] 1410–1415.

**Drawings and Views.** — Scattered through the libraries of Italy and elsewhere in Europe are many drawings and sketches of the ruins of the ancient buildings of Rome, made by the Italian architects of the fifteenth, sixteenth, and seventeenth centuries. These have been found very useful in identifying or locating monuments which have been nearly or completely destroyed since the time when the drawings were made. The same is true of engravings and, in some cases, of paintings of this period.[3]

There are also numerous views [4] of the whole city or portions

---

[1] Jordan, II. 387–400; *Bull. d. Ist.* 1871, 11–17; *CIL.* vi. pp. xv–xvi.

[2] Ed. Mercklin, Dorpat, 1852.

[3] *PBS.* ii.; Hülsen-Carter, 35–46; Jordan, I. 3, notes, *passim*.

[4] List of those known in *BC.* 1892, 38–40, notes; de Rossi, *Piante icnografiche e prospettiche di Roma anteriori al secolo xvi,* Rome, 1879; Rocchi, *Le piante icnografiche e prospettiche di Roma del secolo xvi,* Turin, 1902; Ashby, *Un Panorama de Rome par Antoine van den Wyngaerde, Mélanges,* 1901, 471–486; Egger, *Codex Escurialensis, Ein Skizzenbuch aus der Werkstatt*

thereof, both engraved and painted, beginning with those of
Cimabue in the thirteenth century, which have considerable
topographical value, in spite of their inaccuracies.

*Domenico Ghirlandaios*, Vienna, 1906; Hülsen, *La Roma Antica di Ciriaco
d'Ancona*, Rome, 1907; Ehrle, *La Pianta di Roma du Perac-Lafrery del
1577*, Rome, 1908; *Mitt.* 1896, 213–226; *BC.* 1900, 28–32; *CR.* 1906, 236.

# CHAPTER II.

## GENERAL TOPOGRAPHY OF ROME AND THE CAMPAGNA.

**The Campagna.** — The city of Rome is situated in the middle of an undulating plain, called the Campagna.[1] It is bounded on the north by the Sabatine mountains, lying north of lake Bracciano and forming the southern limit of the ancient Ciminian forest; on the east by the high range of the Sabine Apennines; on the southeast by the Alban mountains; and on the west by the sea. Directly south of Rome this plain stretches on between the Alban and Volscian mountains and the Mediterranean to Tarracina (Anxur), where the mountains run into the sea. The southern part of this district is covered by the great Pontine Marshes, paludes Pomptinae. The term Campagna is sometimes used to include all of this plain, but it properly belongs only to that portion which lies north of Lanuvium and Ardea.

---

[1] R. Burn, *Rome and the Campagna*, London, 1876, 346–444; E. Abbate *Guida della provincia di Roma*, 2d ed. 2 vols., Rome, 1894, i. 1–175; T. Ashby *Classical Topography of the Roman Campagna*, *PBS.* i. 127–285; iii. 1–212 iv. 1–158; v. 215–432; G. Tomassetti, *La Campagna Romana*, i. ii., Rome 1909, 1910; G. Brocchi, *Dello stato fisico del suolo di Roma*, Rome, 1820 Raffaele Canevari, *Cenni sulle condizioni altimetriche ed idrauliche dell' agr romano*, Rome, 1874 (Annali del Ministero di Agricoltura); Felice Giordano *Condizioni topografiche e fisiche di Roma e della Campagna Romana*, Mono grafia della città di Roma e della Campagna Romana presentata all' Es posizione universale di Parigi, 1878; Paolo Mantovani, *Descrizione geologic della Campagna Romana*, Rome, 1874.

Maps: in Abbate's *Guida*, vol ii., and in Ashby's papers (*vid. sup.*). Those issued by the Istituto Geografico Militare are in sheets 1 : 100,000, 1 : 50,000, and 1 : 25,000.

The distance from the Sabatine to the Alban mountains is about 60 kilometres; from Rome to the foot of the Apennines is 25 kilometres, and the distance to the seacoast is about the same. This width decreases as one goes south. From Rome to Tarracina, the southern extremity of this plain, is 95 kilometres.

**Geological Formation**. — This plain is of volcanic origin, and was covered during the tertiary period by the sea. The eruption of submarine volcanoes covered the Pliocene clay and marl with a layer of volcanic products to an average depth of more than 30 metres, and this, being more or less stratified by the action of water, formed what is known as *tufa*. Volcanic forces then elevated the land very considerably, and the sea receded to its present limits.

The centre of volcanic activity during this first period is thought to have been at the northern extremity of the plain, around lake Bracciano. After the sea had receded, another centre of volcanic disturbance was formed in the Alban hills, and from their craters igneous products were poured forth which formed deposits of conglomerate at various points, especially near Albano, where the rock is called lapis Albanus, and near Gabii, where it is called lapis Gabinus. From this Alban volcano there issued also streams of lava, the course of one of which can be traced almost to the city of Rome. The surface thus formed was cut and eroded in all directions by the action of the river Tiber, flowing through it from the north, and of the many affluents which streamed into it from the surrounding mountains.

The general appearance of the Campagna is that of an undulating plain, abounding in hillocks and crossed in all directions by deep ravines and steep cliffs, the height of which averages about 30 metres. It is estimated that four-fifths of the Campagna consists of hills and one-fifth of valleys.

The erosion of the water has produced two types of elevation, one that of a tongue projecting from a plateau between

two streams which flow together at its end, the other that of
an entirely isolated hill with steep cliffs on all sides, due to
its having been completely surrounded by water courses.
These isolated points afforded exceedingly advantageous sites
for the fortified hamlets of the earliest settlers.

Whether the volcanoes of this region were active in historical times is still a matter of dispute. Alleged discoveries,
beneath volcanic deposits, of material which can be dated as
late as the third or fourth century B.C. lack convincing evidence of authenticity; but that the slopes of the hills were
inhabited before the total extinction of the volcanoes is proved
by the discovery of a necropolis near Albano, entirely covered
by a layer of peperino.[1]

It is probable that all the volcanoes of this district were
practically extinct before the date assigned by tradition to the
founding of the city of Rome. Some of the craters of these
extinct volcanoes are now lakes, notably lake Bracciano (*lacus
Sabatinus*) and lake Martignano (*lacus Alsietinus*) in the north;
and lake Albano (*lacus Albanus*) and lake Nemi (*lacus Nemo-
rensis*) in the south.

As these lakes are very deep, much of the water which they
contain is forced under high pressure through the sides of the
crater, and collects in subterranean reservoirs formed between
the strata of volcanic deposit. Part of this water is drained
off into the Tiber, but much of it, being unable to flow through
the impermeable strata, accumulates near the surface of the
ground, and can be carried off only by evaporation.

In classical times, a complete system of artificial drainage
seems to have been provided to dispose of this accumulated
water. Remains of the ancient *cuniculi*, or drains, have been
found in many parts of the Campagna. This system of drainage, and the careful cultivation of the soil, must have rendered
the whole region comparatively healthy,[2] and accounts for the

---

[1] Abbate, *Guida*, i. 83–84; *Bull. d. Ist.* 1871, 34–40; *Ann. d. Ist.* 1871, 239–279.
[2] Jordan, I. 1  148–152.

fact that the Campagna was thickly covered with villas, even in those districts where now the fever is most dangerous. As is now well known, the germs of this fever are disseminated by a mosquito which breeds in marshy districts.

**The Tiber.** — The chief factor in the process of erosion was the Tiber, the principal river of the peninsula, 393 kilometres in length, which rises near Arezzo (*Arretium*) in Etruria, and flows southward to Rome, where it turns westward to the sea. In the period following that of greatest volcanic activity, its channel was many times as wide as at present and its volume of water enormous. At its mouth, some 11 kilometres farther inland than at present, the stream appears to have been nearly 2 kilometres wide. Its course is in general parallel to the main range of the Apennines, and its banks are marked by cliffs and hills of the two types described above (p. 12). At the last great bend of the river toward the sea, its eroding force produced that combination of these two formations which conditioned the material development of the city of Rome.

Here the river flowed between the edge of a tableland on the east and a ridge of hills of marine formation on the west. The width of its bed varied greatly, from 2 kilometres at the campus Martius to less than a quarter of that distance between the Aventine and the southern point of the Janiculum. This gradual narrowing of the channel produced a swifter current, and increased the amount of erosion. During the formative period, the river filled the whole space between the tableland on the one side and the hills on the other. As the width of the river grew less, the eroding action of the water which flowed down into it from the higher ground was greatly increased.

Certain of the hills of Rome, therefore, which now appear completely isolated, like the Palatine and Aventine, or nearly so, like the Capitoline and Caelian, are so because during this period they were entirely surrounded by the river and exposed to its action on all sides; while the eastern hills, projecting like tongues of land, were not thus surrounded.

**The Site of Rome.**[1] — The present topography of the city is in its main features almost the same as when the first settlements were made upon that site.

The Tiber, now 100 metres in width, flows through the city from north to south, in five reaches: from the point where the Aurelian wall approached the stream, southeast for about 800 metres to the Tarentum; then almost due west for 1 kilometre to a short distance beyond the mausoleum of Hadrian (the castle of S. Angelo); then southeast for 2 kilometres to a point opposite the Palatine hill; then southwest for 1.5 kilometres to the Emporium; and finally south again for 1 kilometre to the angle of the Aurelian wall. Where the river approaches most nearly to the Capitoline, it divides and flows round an island about 270 metres in length and 70 metres in greatest breadth.

The great bend to the west inclosed the meadows, nearly 1.5 kilometres wide, to which the name of campus Martius was given, and the smaller bend to the east left space on the right bank of the stream for that part of the city which was known as trans Tiberim (*Trastevere*). East and south of the campus Martius rise the hills which are the characteristic features of the city.

The central point is marked by the Palatine, an irregular quadrilateral, about twenty-five acres (10 hectares) in extent, surrounded by steep cliffs except at its eastern angle, where a spur, the Velia, connected it with the Esquiline. The western angle of the hill approaches to within about 300 metres of the river.

---

[1] All previous maps of the ancient city of Rome have been superseded by the following great work: *Forma Urbis Romae, consilio et auctoritate Regiae Academiae Lincaeorum . . . edidit Rodolphus Lanciani*, forty-six sheets, Milan, Hoepli, 1893–1901. The best wall-map is Hülsen, *Romae veteris tabula in usum scholarum descripta*, 1 : 4250, Berlin, 1901.

South and southwest of the Palatine lies the **Aventine**, a hill of similar formation, but somewhat larger. North of the Palatine, the **Capitoline** now appears as an entirely isolated elevation, and seems always to have been such, although the shoulder of the Quirinal may have approached nearer to it. (See p. 285.) It corresponds closely with the Palatine and Aventine.

The remaining hills are quite different, and are all spurs of the eastern plateau, projecting out toward the river, and separated from each other by depressions of varying length and breadth. The southernmost of these, **mons Caelius**, directly east of the Palatine, preserves more of the appearance of an independent hill, being connected with the high land behind it only by a narrow neck. North of the Caelian is the **Esquiline**, a large hill consisting of two parts, the main southern portion called **mons Oppius**, and the smaller northern spur, **mons Cispius**. North of the Esquiline is another small tongue of land, **collis Viminalis**; and beyond this and almost inclosing it, the **collis Quirinalis**. This long ridge was originally divided into four parts : the **collis Latiaris**, the southern elevation above the forum of Trajan ; the **collis Mucialis**, from the via di Magnanapoli to monte Cavallo ; the **collis Salutaris**, from monte Cavallo to the church of S. Andrea ; and the **collis Quirinalis**, from this point east. The first three names passed out of use at an early date, and collis Quirinalis became the proper designation of the whole hill. North of the Quirinal is the **collis hortorum**, the modern Pincian, which marked the latest stage in the growth of the city, and was never reckoned among the "Seven Hills." The term *mons* was very rarely applied to the Viminal and Quirinal, which were known as *colles* (p. 41).

On the right bank of the Tiber, the ridge of the Janiculum, in its modern sense, runs almost due north and south for 2 kilometres, coming to an abrupt end at the point where the river makes its great bend to the southeast. Here the hill approaches to within 100 metres of the river. The ridge is separated from the plateau behind by a long depression. At the northern end of the Janiculum, the level between the river and the hill stretches out for 1.5 kilometres, and is bounded on the west by the continuation of the high ground behind the Janiculum.

There are now in the city three elevations of artificial origin. One, mons Testaceus (*monte Testaccio*), southwest of the Aventine and close to the river and ancient warehouses, is composed entirely of fragments of earthen vessels in which grain and stores of various sorts were brought to Rome, and rises to a height of 43 metres above the Tiber. Inasmuch as the first of these warehouses (*horrea*) dated from the last century of the republic, the accumulation of these fragments probably began as early as that date.

The two other artificial hills or mounds are in the campus Martius, the monte Giordano and the monte Citorio,[1] respectively 6 and 9 metres in height. Both mounds are formed by the ruins of imperial buildings. (See pp. 365, 370, 379.)

The following table[2] gives the altitude of the different hills above the level of the Tiber, which is 6.7 metres above the sea-level at the Ripetta: —

| | |
|---|---|
| Aventine (S. Alessio) . . . . . | 39.22 metres. |
| Capitoline (Aracoeli) . . . . . | 39.30 " |
| Caelian (Villa Mattei) . . . . . | 41.15 " |
| Palatine (S. Bonaventura) . . . . | 43.30 " |
| Esquiline (S. Maria Maggiore) . . . . | 47.75 " |
| Viminal (R.R. station) . . . . . | 50.78 " |
| Quirinal (Porta Pia) . . . . . | 56.35 " |
| Pincian (Porta Pinciana) . . . . . | 56.35 " |
| Vatican (Pope's Gardens) . . . . | 67.30 " |
| Janiculum (Villa Savorelli) . . . . | 82.30 " |

The highest point within the Aurelian wall is on the Janiculum at the porta Aurelia (*Porta di S. Pancrazio*), 75 metres above the river.

Between the hills are valleys, or rather depressions, which

---

[1] Richter, *Top.*[2] 254; Jordan, I. 3. 595, 603.    [2] Lanciani, *Ruins*, 3.

form well-defined topographical units. The most important is
that lying between the Palatine, the Esquiline, the Quirinal,
and the Capitoline, which became the Forum. North of the
Forum is a narrow valley, which runs between the ends of
the Oppian and Quirinal and then widens. This valley was
called the Subura, and was one of the most thickly settled and
disreputable quarters of the city. From it three depressions
run eastward and northward between the projecting spurs of
the hills.

Through the Subura, with affluents from the slopes on each
side, ran a brook [1] which crossed the Forum, traversed the low
ground between the Forum and the river, and emptied into
the latter below the island. This brook was walled in at an
early date, and became the famous Cloaca Maxima.

The low district between the Forum, the Palatine and Capitoline, and the river comprised the Velabrum and the cattle
and vegetable markets (forum Boarium, forum Holitorium). Whatever may be the correct derivation of the word Velabrum, there
is no doubt that when the first settlements were made on the
surrounding hills, this region was very marshy and to some
extent under water, besides being continually subject to inundations from the Tiber.

After the Forum and the Subura, the most important valley in
Rome was that between the Palatine and the Aventine, through
which ran a brook called in the middle ages the Marrana, which
had its source near the seventh milestone on the via Tusculana, and flowing from the southwest, passed under the line of
the Aurelian wall near the porta Metrovia, and through the
depression between the Esquiline and the Caelian. The valley
between the Palatine and Aventine was called the vallis Murcia,
and in late republican and imperial times was completely filled
by the Circus Maximus.

Still another long valley lies between the Pincian and the

---

[1] Perhaps the Spinon. Cic. *de nat. deor.* iii. 52; Lanciani, *Ruins*, 29; Pinza,
*Mon. d. Lincei*, 1905, 275.

Quirinal, and through it ran a stream which emptied into one of the two principal swampy ponds of the campus Martius,[1] the Caprae palus. Another brook flowed from the western slope of the Quirinal, near the porta Salutaris, westward across the campus Martius. Topographers are not entirely agreed as to which of these last two streams is the Petronia amnis,[2] which had its source in the Cati fons. The probability is that the southernmost of the two is the original Petronia amnis, and that it may be identified with a stream that now flows underground from a source, the Cati fons, beneath a courtyard in the royal palace, just east of the via della Panetteria.

North of the Caprae palus lay the second pond, similar but much smaller, known as the Tarentum. West of the Caelian, and at a higher elevation than the others, was another pool, called the Decenniae.

**Geology of the City.** —There are three principal formations visible within the circuit of the city itself. The most important is the volcanic tufa rock, already mentioned, which forms the hills on the left bank of the Tiber and the stratum underlying the whole region. The low ground and the depressions between the hills themselves and between the hills and the river are covered to a considerable depth with a quaternary alluvial deposit of sand, clay, and gravel, brought down by the Tiber during the period of its greatest activity and volume. This deposit is found also upon the lower slopes of the hills. On the right bank, on the Janiculum and mons Vaticanus, there is a marine formation belonging to the Older Pliocene period, and consisting mainly of a bluish gray marl, much used for making pottery, and of yellow sea sand, of great value for building purposes. In all of these strata, except the tufa, fossils are found in considerable abundance.

---

[1] For another view, cf. *BC.* 1883, 244–258.

[2] Fest. 250; *Epit.* 45; *RhM.* 1894, 401 ff.; Richter, *Top.*[2] 225, 285; Jordan, I. 3. 472–474.

**Changes in Level**. — It is certain, from the evidence of actual excavations and from the testimony of classical literature, that some changes in the altitude of the hills and valleys of the city have taken place since early times.[1] These changes have resulted from the tremendous building activity of the empire, on the one hand; and on the other, from the falling into decay of most of the ancient city during the middle ages, the dumping of rubbish in certain localities during long periods, and the building activity of the renaissance.

With regard to the changes under the empire, all excavations in Rome show clearly that we have to do, not with structures of one period, but of successive periods, and that it was customary to erect the later building upon the ruins of the earlier. It is not unusual to find the remains of three or even four structures, one above another. The recent excavations in the Forum have shown this in a most striking way. The level of the Comitium, or open area in front of the senate house, in the time of Diocletian, was 4 metres higher than the earliest level of the ground at this point; and in some parts of the Forum the variation is still greater.

With the earth removed by Diocletian in clearing a space for his enormous baths, a mound was formed on the Viminal some 20 metres high, the highest point within the Aurelian wall east of the Tiber, and the construction of the great agger across the Viminal and Esquiline, and its subsequent conversion into part of the gardens of Maecenas must have brought about considerable changes in level in that region. During this period, however, the relative height of hills and valleys does not appear to have been materially altered except at a few points.

During the centuries between the fall of the empire and the renaissance, the history of the city is one of steady destruction, and changes in level were due almost entirely to the accumulation of the ruins of ancient structures. These ruins, produced

---

[1] Lanciani, *Ruins*, 99–104; *Destruction of Ancient Rome*, chapters ii. xix, and *passim*.

either by natural decay or intentional destruction during this long period, must have raised the level of the soil in some parts of the city very considerably. The renewed building activity just before and during the renaissance caused further changes in two ways, — by the clearing away of existing ruins for new structures, and by the dumping of vast amounts of rubbish in certain localities. Thus Cardinal Farnese, when building the church of the Gesù in the campus Martius, removed great quantities of earth to the Palatine hill. From the tenth to the sixteenth centuries so much rubbish had been emptied into the Forum that its level was raised nearly 10 metres above the pavement of the empire.

The excavations which have been carried on in the city show that the depth of the debris, which has accumulated in these different ways, varies from a few inches to nearly 20 metres. The foundations of the new treasury building on the Quirinal had to be sunk through 12 metres of loose soil, and similar conditions have been found in other parts of the city.

# CHAPTER III.

## BUILDING MATERIALS AND METHODS.

**Building Materials.** — The principal building materials [1] employed in Rome were the following: —

**Tufa** (*Tofus ruber et niger*). This volcanic product,[2] already mentioned in connection with the formation of the Campagna, is a mechanical conglomerate of scoriae, ashes, and sand, and of varying density. In some districts it presents few signs of stratification, being either loose and friable like earth, or hardened into a solid mass by time and pressure. Elsewhere it shows distinct evidence of having been deposited in water and stratified by its action. The color varies from reddish brown to yellow and sometimes gray. Even the hardest varieties make poor building stone when left exposed to the atmosphere, but are sufficiently durable when covered with stucco or cement. Tufa is characteristic of the first centuries of Rome's existence, being the only stone employed during the earliest period.

**Peperino** (*lapis Albanus*). This,[3] like tufa, is a conglomerate of volcanic ashes and sand, together with fragments of stone, but formed in a somewhat different way, apparently by the action of hot water upon ashes. Thickly scattered through its mass are scoriae in large quantities, which from their resemblance to peppercorns (*piper*) have given the current name to the stone. It was quarried in the Alban hills, hence its ancient name, lapis Albanus. It is a much harder and better building stone than tufa, and was very largely employed during the later republic and empire in structures where greater dura-

---

[1] Middleton, *Remains*, i. 1–26.       [3] Vitr. ii. **7. 1.**
[2] Vitr. ii. 7. 1–2; Pl. *NH.* xxxvi. 166.

bility and strength were required than could be furnished by tufa.

**Sperone** (*lapis Gabinus*). This stone was quarried near Gabii, and is similar in formation to peperino, but it is still harder and more durable. It contains many fragments of lava of varying sizes. It was used like peperino,[1] but apparently not so extensively.

**Travertine** (*lapis Tiburtinus*). This is the famous limestone[2] of the Sabine hills, the principal quarries of which were, as the name indicates, near Tibur. It also lies in large beds all along the Anio and some other smaller streams in the vicinity. Travertine "is a pure carbonate of lime, very hard, of a beautiful creamy color which weathers into a rich golden tint. It is a deposit from running water, and is found in a highly stratified state, with frequent cavities and fissures, lined with crystallized carbonate of lime."[3] Travertine was not introduced into general use in the city until the second century B.C., but after that time it was one of the principal materials employed by the Romans, especially for large and magnificent structures like the Colosseum.

**Lava** (*silex*). Four lava streams[4] had flowed down from the Alban crater, one of which approached within three miles of the city itself, close to the tomb of Caecilia Metella on the via Appia. From these beds the lava was quarried in large blocks for the pavement of streets, while the smaller pieces were mixed with pozzolana and lime to make concrete and rubble-work.

**Pozzolana** (*pulvis Puteolanus*). This volcanic sand[5] derives its name from Puteoli, near Naples, where great beds of it exist, although it is also found in large quantities all round Rome. It consists chiefly of silica, magnesia, potash, lime, and alumina, and when mixed with lime in the proportion of about

---

[1] Tac. *Ann.* xv. 43.
[2] Vitr. ii. 7. 1–2.
[3] Middleton, *Remains*, i. 7.
[4] Pl. *NH.* xxxvi. 168.
[5] Vitr. ii. 6. 1.

two to one, forms an hydraulic cement of remarkable strength. The concrete made of this cement and fragments of different sorts of stone was one of the most important materials employed by the Romans, as it rendered possible the enormous vault and dome construction which is so conspicuous in the buildings of the empire.

**Brick** (*later, testa, tegula*).    The Romans made two kinds of brick,[1] the one dried in the sun (*later*) and the other dried in a kiln (*testa, tegula*), the principal material in their manufacture being the clay (*creta figulina* [2]) which was found in abundance in several places in the vicinity, but especially on the slopes of the Vatican.    No examples of unburnt brick now exist, but it was used almost exclusively down to the time of Augustus, and was reasonably durable while carefully protected from the action of the atmosphere.    Kiln-dried bricks and tiles (*testa, tegula*) exist in vast numbers, having been most extensively used in buildings of every description throughout the empire.    The bricks proper are of different shapes, — square, oblong, round, and triangular, — but the last is the prevailing type, as it suited best the ordinary method of use.    Walls and foundations, when not constructed of solid stone, were regularly built of concrete faced with a lining of small stones, tiles, or bricks, which were tailed into the mass behind.    The triangular shape was therefore especially convenient.    Tiles (*tegulae*), which were used in this way in such quantities, were broken or sawed into irregular or triangular pieces.

So far as we know bricks proper were never made larger than 22 centimetres square, but the tiles were considerably larger. They were frequently stamped with a round or rectangular seal,[3] which contain some or all of the following indications : the name of the owner or superintendent of the clay-pits or kilns, the actual maker of the brick, the person in charge

---

[1] Vitr. ii. 3.                          [2] Varro, *RR*. iii. 9. 3.
[3] Marini, *Iscrizioni doliari*, Rome, 1884 ; H. Dressel, in *CIL*. xv. 1.

of the sale of the manufactured product, and the names of the consuls for the year or of the ruling emperor. By means of these dates, the time of construction or restoration of many Roman buildings has been determined, and it has been possible to arrive at criteria for fixing the period of manufacture of different kinds of bricks.

**Marble.** The use of marble,[1] both native and foreign, began in Rome in the first decade of the first century B.C., and spread with great rapidity. Augustus boasted that he had found the city brick and left it marble;[2] and under the succeeding emperors the amount of marble of all possible varieties which was brought to Rome surpasses our belief. The number of kinds mounts up to about one hundred and fifty, and in spite of centuries of destruction the amount still visible in churches and palaces is almost incredible. With the exception of that quarried at Luna near Carrara, practically all the marble used in Rome was imported. It was rarely used in solid blocks in the construction of an entire wall, but in slabs of varying thickness, with which a wall of other material was lined. These slabs were fastened to the wall with clamps or pins.

The term marble, in connection with Roman buildings, is ordinarily not restricted to its exact scientific application, but includes many other stones of a decorative character, such as serpentine, alabaster, and fluor spar, which with granite, basalt, and porphyry, were imported into Rome from every part of the known world, in enormous quantities.

**Methods of Building.**[3] — These may be classified as follows: —

**Opus quadratum.**[4] There are no traces of the so-called

---

[1] Corsi, *Delle pietre antiche*, Rome, 1845; H. W. Pullen, *Handbook of Ancient Roman Marbles*, London, 1894; M. W. Porter, *What Rome was built with*, London, 1907. [2] Suet. *Aug.* 28.

[3] Middleton, *Remains*, i. 27–91; A. Choisy, *L'Art de bâtir chez les Romains*, Paris, 1873; J. Durm, *Die Baukunst der Römer*, 2d ed., Stuttgart, 1905; Jordan, I. 1. 3–24. [4] Vitr. ii. 8. 5–8.

polygonal masonry in Rome, and the earliest walls were built of rectangular blocks of tufa, laid in regular courses.    To this form of construction the term *opus quadratum* was applied, whatever the nature of the stone itself.    Where brown or yellow tufa or peperino were used, the blocks were usually 2 Roman feet in height and in thickness.    The length varied, but in the most perfect examples it is usually 4 feet, just twice the height, and the blocks are laid in alternate courses of headers and stretchers, one course running lengthwise and the next being laid endwise (*emplecton*).    In the earliest *opus quadratum* of gray tufa the blocks were smaller.    Where travertine was the material employed, the blocks were not all cut of the same size, as that would have involved too great a loss.

Mortar or cement was used during the earliest period, but only in a thin bed or skin, not to bind the blocks together, but simply to make a more perfect joint.    At the close of the republic and under the empire this use of mortar became infrequent, and the surfaces of the stone were worked so smooth that the joints are barely discernible.    This can be seen in the wall of the podium of the temple of Faustina.    At that time it was usual to fasten the blocks together with iron clamps or wooden dowels.    The native tufa was the stone first and most extensively employed for this sort of construction, but at a comparatively early date the Romans introduced the custom of using peperino at points where greater strength and durability were required.

After the second century B.C. travertine was used for this purpose ; and sometimes alone, to form the whole wall, as in the podium of the temple of Vespasian.    Some of the walls of the Colosseum and of the forum Pacis are of tufa, travertine, and peperino.    In such cases, the harder stones are regularly used for keystones, springers, voussoirs, jambs, and points where the pressure is greatest.

Concrete (*structura caementicia*).    Roman concrete was made of pozzolana and lime, with fragments of stone (*caementum*) scattered through the mass irregularly or in layers. During republican times these fragments were regularly of tufa, rarely of peperino; but later, broken brick, travertine, bits of marble, and pumice stone were used, the last in making the great vaults where lightness was especially desirable. This concrete is so remarkable for its cohesiveness that when firmly set it is like solid rock. From the beginning of the first century B.C. it was the principal material used in building walls and foundations, sometimes without, but usually with, a facing of brick or stone. Unfaced concrete was used in foundations and substructures which were not to be seen. It must have been laid in a sort of mould, — cast, in other words, — while in a semifluid state. Planks were arranged so as to form a wooden box of the required size and shape, and in this successive layers of semifluid cement and fragments of stone were placed. When the mass had hardened, the planking was removed. Traces of these wooden supports are plainly visible in many places, — for example, on the massive foundations beneath the Flavian palace on the Palatine.

Far more frequently concrete was faced with stone or brick, and the relative structural value of the two parts varied according to the total thickness of the wall. Construction of this sort is named according to the kind of facing employed, and the terms which properly refer only to the facing itself are applied to the whole structure.

**Opus incertum.**[1] The concrete is faced with irregular bits of tufa, 6 to 10 centimetres across, with smooth outer surface and cut in conical or pyramidal shape so as to tail easily into the concrete backing. This was the oldest method of facing, and was in vogue during the second and first centuries B.C. A good example of opus incertum of the second century can be seen in the wall at the foot of the scalae Caci on the Palatine.

**Opus reticulatum.**[2] This is similar to opus incertum, except

---

[1] Vitr. ii. 8. 1. Cf. *The Nation*, 1904, 202.    [2] Vitr. ii. 8. 1.

that the small stones are carefully cut with square or lozenge-shaped ends, and are arranged in rows corner to corner, so as to present a perfectly symmetrical appearance, resembling the meshes of a net.   This displaced opus incertum almost entirely,

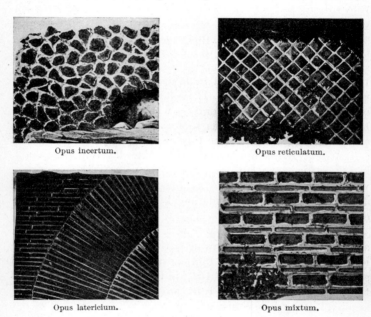

Opus incertum.                    Opus reticulatum.

Opus latericium.                    Opus mixtum.

Fig. 3. — Methods of Construction.

and was used from the beginning of the first century b.c. to the middle of the second century.   Examples are very numerous, one of the most accessible being in the house of Germanicus on the Palatine.

Opus testaceum or latericium.  This is concrete faced with kiln-dried brick.   Therefore, when the term *latericium* is used, it is to be understood as referring to *lateres cocti*, equivalent to *testae*, and not to *lateres crudi*.   There are no examples of facing with sun-dried brick. This method of construction with brick facing was the one most extensively employed throughout the imperial period.

The bricks [1] vary in size, the ordinary dimensions being from 0.20 to 0.62 metre in length, and from 2 to 6 centimetres in thickness. They are either square, rectangular, triangular, or, when made from broken tiles, irregular. (See p. 24.) In simple facings the triangular shape was regularly employed, but at intervals single courses of large square tiles were introduced, apparently to strengthen the cohesiveness of the mass. In vaults, arches, and corners, square or rectangular bricks were most frequently used.

While it is true that a wall was rarely, if ever, built of solid brick, but always with a concrete filling, the structural value of each part varied widely. For instance, in a wall 60 centimetres thick, the structural importance of the facing would be very slight, while in a wall 30 centimetres thick, a facing of the same dimensions would amount to about half the total volume of the wall, and be an extremely important element. The most perfect opus testaceum belongs to the time of Nero and the first years of the Flavian emperors, and is characterized by the thinness of the cement bed and the thickness of the bricks. After this time the deterioration in the work may be traced by a gradual increase in the thickness of the cement bed and a decrease in that of the bricks. The relative dimensions of the two and the character of the brick itself make it possible to date construction of this sort with a considerable degree of accuracy, even without the direct evidence of the stamps. One of the finest examples of brickwork in Rome is to be seen in the arches of Nero's extension of the aqua Claudia (p. 99) on the Caelian, although this seems to be later than Nero.

**Opus mixtum.** This modern term is used to describe a method of construction which came into use at the end of the third century, in which the ordinary facing of opus testaceum is

---

[1] Vitr. ii. 3; ii. 8. 9–20.

interrupted at intervals by courses of rectangular tufa blocks, about 26 centimetres long and 10 deep. The earliest example of this work in Rome is said to be in the wall of the circus of Maxentius, built about 310 A.D.; but frequent examples have been found in Pompeii.[1]

All these facings were covered with plaster, so that there was no visible indication of the character of the wall behind.

As the tufa or brick had to be laid at the same time as the semifluid concrete backing, it was often necessary, where the wall was of any considerable thickness, to build a wooden casing to prevent the facing from being pushed outward by the pressure of the concrete. This was done in somewhat the same manner as in the case of the massive unfaced foundations, but on a much smaller scale and more easily.

The foundations of temples were usually made of a massive outer wall of opus quadratum, and the inner space was then filled solid with concrete. In such cases the stone wall was in itself strong enough to resist the pressure of the concrete until it had set. In many cases this concrete core was entirely unnecessary, as it had ordinarily nothing but the floor of the cella to support.

The most striking feature of Roman architecture during the imperial period was the use of the vault or dome in such enormous structures as the baths or the basilica of Constantine. The great strength of Roman concrete was the principal reason for the development of this method of covering very large halls, but it is a mistake to eliminate entirely, as has sometimes been done, the importance of the brick relieving arches which form, as it were, the skeleton of the vault. It is manifestly almost impossible to arrive at complete architectural analyses of these vaults in most cases, and hence their precise character has been the subject of much dispute. Very strong complicated scaffolding and centring must have been necessary in building

---

[1] Mau-Kelsey, *Pompeii, its Life and Art*, New York, 1899, 37–38.

the system of brick arches and in supporting the concrete until it had set. After this had taken place, the whole vault was practically a solid mass, and lateral thrust and pressure were reduced to a minimum.

Sun-dried brick (*lateres crudi*[1]). While this material has no present importance, since nothing remains of buildings so constructed, it should not be forgotten that during the republic and even later the ordinary houses in Rome, as well as some public buildings, were built of crude brick and wooden framing. Their unsubstantial character is plainly shown by the reports in classical writers of the great destruction wrought by fire, water, slight earthquake shocks, and natural decay.

Plaster or stucco (*tectorium*[2]). As has been said, concrete walls faced in these various ways were regularly covered with plaster or stucco of varying thickness. Not infrequently walls of opus quadratum were treated in the same way, and in later times even marble surfaces were coated with a marble stucco, in order that pigments might be more easily applied. The finest kind of stucco was called *opus albarium* or *caementum marmoreum*, and was made of lime and powdered white marble, water or milk, and some albuminous substance. When properly applied it produced a surface in no way inferior to that of marble itself. Other kinds of cement were made of inferior materials, one of them, which was much used for lining water channels on account of its hardness, being made of pozzolana and pounded pottery (*testae tunsae*) and called opus signinum.

---

[1] Vitr. ii. 3.     [2] Vitr. vii. 2–6.

# CHAPTER IV.

## HISTORY OF THE DEVELOPMENT OF THE CITY.

By comparing the testimony of classical literature with archaeological evidence and physical conditions, the growth of the city of Rome has been traced from its beginning through certain stages. According to the view that has been generally held six periods are to be distinguished in the topographical history of the city; namely, (1) the **Palatine** city, (2) the **Septimontium** or "City of the Seven Hills," (3) the city of the **Four Regions,** (4) the so-called **Servian** city, (5) the open city of the **Fourteen Regions,** and (6) the city of **Aurelian.** Recently, however, objections have been raised against the existence of the first two of these stages, and a different theory of the origin of the city has been brought forward, which will be stated on p. 44.

**The Palatine City.** — The current view,[1] based on the unanimous testimony of ancient literature, assigns to the Palatine[2] hill the first settlement of that part of the Latin stock which afterward assumed the name of Romans. Physiographically this hill was better adapted for such a settlement than any other in the neighborhood, for its complete isolation made its defence easy, and the nearness of the Tiber gave its settlers all the advantages of river communication with the sea and with the interior. Its area was about 10 hectares (25 acres), which corresponded closely to that of the other Latin settlements in the Campagna. In shape the hill is an irregular rectangle, but at first it was probably more nearly square. The length of the sides averages about 450 metres.

---

[1] For the most recent review of the whole question of the Palatine and earlier stages in the city's growth, cf. Binder, *Die Plebs*, Leipzig, 1909, 1–170.
[2] Schneider, *Mitt.* 1895, 160–175.

The first settlers came from the north, and while they were already divided politically into the three tribes of Ramnes, Tities, and Luceres, their settlement, and then the hill itself, was called Palatium.[1] This substantive form of its name differentiates this hill from all the others on the left bank of the Tiber, except the Capitolium. This latter name, however, was of comparatively late origin, and was applied to the hill after it had really become the capitol of the extended city. The word *Palatium*, probably connected with the root *pa* which appears in *pasco* and *Pales*,[2] seems to have been applied in its earliest and narrowest sense to the settlement on the eastern half of the hill, while the western part was called Cermalus,[3] which would seem to indicate that originally the Palatine community was divided into two hamlets, occupying the two parts of the hill. However this may be, in its historical development the community is to be regarded as a unit, although the name Cermalus was used in the days of Cicero and Livy.[4] As a part of the Palatine city, although outside its wall, must be reckoned also the ridge or spur stretching out from the middle of the north side of the Palatine toward the Oppian. This was called the Velia,[5] and always retained its distinctive name, although more frequently referred to in literature as the summa Sacra via.[6] At some time, either in this first period or that which followed, the settlement came to be known as Ruma, Roma, probably from the Etruscan gentile name *ruma*,[7] and its inhabitants as Romani.

---

[1] *BC.* 1881, 63–73; Jordan, I. 1. 180–183; Varro, *LL.* v. 53; Fest. 220; Serv. *ad Aen.* viii. 51; Dionys. i. 32; ii. 1.

[2] This etymology is disputed. Cf. *JJ.* 1907, 345; Walde, *Lat. Etymolog. Wörterbuch.*

[3] Gilbert, I. 40–41, notes; Jordan, I. 3. 35–36; Plut. *Rom.* 3; Varro, *LL.* v. 54.

[4] Cic. *ad Att.* iv. 3. 3; Liv. xxxiii. 26.

[5] Liv. ii. 7. 6; Asc. *in Pis.* 52; Gilbert, I. 38–39, 101–109; Jordan, I. 2. 416.

[6] Solin. i. 23.

[7] Schulze, *Zur Geschichte lateinischer Eigennamen*, Berlin, 1904, 218 ff., 580; *CR.* 1906, 411; Pais, *Legends*, 55.

The fortification of such a hill was an easy matter. Where the cliff was at all abrupt, — and it was decidedly so at almost every point, — it was scarped down for about 13 or 14 metres, and there an artificial shelf was cut. On this shelf, and resting against the side of the hill, a tufa wall of opus quadratum was built, which rose somewhat above the top of the hill, so as to form a sort of breastwork. It is possible that some fragments of this earliest wall are still standing (p. 110).

To the Palatine settlement all Roman and Greek legends[1] of the founding of the city go back. On this hill were the casa Romuli,[2] or hut of the mythical founder; the Lupercal,[3] or cave of the she-wolf which suckled him; the sacred cornel cherry tree,[4] which sprang from the lance cast by Romulus from the Aventine to the Cermalus; and the Mundus, or augural centre of the city-templum. All these, although of later origin, bore witness to the antiquity and validity of the legend which assigned the beginning of Rome to this spot. In the primitive Roman conception of a city, two things were essential, the dwelling of the king and a shrine where the sacred fire could be kept. In the Palatine city, the casa Romuli was naturally the representative of the former, and although we are distinctly told that the temple of Vesta was outside of the pomerium of the early city, it is at least a plausible hypothesis that a primitive Italian deity, Caca,[5] perhaps a goddess of the hearth, had a shrine on the hill, and was displaced by Vesta at a later period (p. 133).

In ritual, the festival of the Lupercalia, celebrated on the fifteenth of February, continued to keep the beginnings of the city before the minds of the Romans down to the end of the

---

[1] Pais, *Legends*, 43–59.

[2] Plut. *Rom.* 20; Dionys. i. 79; *Notit.* Reg. x.; Gilbert, I. 48.

[3] Dionys. i. 32, 79; Serv. *ad Aen.* viii. 90; Ov. *Fast.* ii. 421; Cic. *ad Fam.* vii. 20. 1; Gilbert, I. 53–59.

[4] Plut. *Rom.* 3.

[5] Serv. *ad Aen.* viii. 190; Roscher, *Lexikon der Mythologie*, i. 842; *Mitt.* 1895, 163; Wissowa, *Religion der Römer*, 144; *CR.* 1905, 233; De Sanctis, *Storia dei Romani*, ii. 524–525. Cf., however, *University of Michigan Studies*, iv. 234.

western empire.[1]  At this festival the Luperci, a college of
priests whose institution dated back to the earliest times,
dressed in goatskins and waving leather thongs, ran round the
Palatine along a line said to be that of the ancient pomerium,
thus performing the ceremony of purification.  The rules of
augural procedure required that the site destined for a city
should be inaugurated as a *templum*,[2] or rectangular area,
marked off from the ager publicus, or outside territory under
the control of the city-state.  Within this templum the
auspices could be taken, and the civil authority, in distinction
from the military, was supreme.  The formal founding of a
city is thus described by Varro : [3] —

Oppida condebant in Latio Etrusco ritu ut multa, id est iunctis bobus
tauro et vacca interiore aratro circumagebant sulcum.  Hoc faciebant
religionis causa die auspicato, ut fossa et muro essent muniti.  Terram
unde exsculpserant *fossam* vocabant et introrsus iactam *murum* : post ea
qui fiebat orbis, urbis principium, qui quod erat post murum, *postmoerium*
dictum, eoque auspicia urbana finiuntur.

The furrow represented the moat; and the earth thrown up
by the plough, the wall of the city.  The line *urbis principium*,
or pomerium, behind (*i.e.* within) the *murus*, marked the limit
of the inaugurated district within which auspices could be
taken.  The word pomerium,[4] which first meant the boundary
line itself (*certis spatiis interiecti lapides*),[5] was soon transferred

---

[1] Dionys. i. 80; Jordan, I. 1. 162; Marquardt, *Römische Staatsverwaltung*,
iii. 438–446; Gilbert, I. 83–88.

[2] Liv. v. 52; Varro, *LL.* vi. 53; v. 33; Gell. xiii. 14; Nissen, *Templum*, 6 ff.

[3] *LL.* v. 143.

[4] Mommsen, *Das Begriff des Pomeriums, Hermes*, 1876, 24–50; *Röm. For-
schungen*, ii. 23–41; F. Wehr, *Das Palatinische Pomerium*, Brüx, 1895;
O. Richter, *Die älteste Wohnstätte des Röm. Volkes. Prog.*, Berlin, 1891;
Becker, *Topographie*, 92–108; Jordan, I. 1. 163–175; Gilbert, I. 114–134; Hülsen, *Mitt.* 1892, 293; Platner, *The Pomerium and Roma Quadrata, AJP.*
1901, 420–425; Pais, *Legends*, 224–234; Carter, *Roma Quadrata and the
Septimontium, AJA.* 1908, 172–183, and *The Pomerium*, Rome, 1909; *Mélanges*,
1908, 278–280.

[5] Tac. *Ann.* xii. 24.

to the strip of land between this line and the actual city wall, and was then used in both senses.[1] At a later period it seems to have been still further extended in application and to have been incorrectly used of the strip on both sides of the wall. This is plainly the understanding of Livy when he writes:[2] —

Pomerium, verbi vim solam intuentes, postmoerium interpretantur esse: est autem magis circamoerium, locus, quem in condendis urbibus quondam Etrusci, qua murum ducturi erant, certis circa terminis inaugurato consecrabant, ut neque interiore parte aedificia moenibus continuarentur, quae nunc vulgo etiam coniungunt, et extrinsecus puri aliquid ab humano cultu pateret soli. Hoc spatium, quod neque habitari neque arari fas erat, non magis quod post murum esset, quam quod murus post id, pomerium Romani apellarunt.

These discrepancies may be due to a very natural confusion of the ceremonial *murus* with the actual city wall at various periods.

In the case of the Palatine city, existing remains of later date show that the first wall must have been built on the slope of the hill, but Tacitus describes in the following passage[3] the line which in his day was regarded as that of the original pomerium, marked out by Romulus: —

Sed initium condendi et quod pomerium Romulus posuerit, noscere haud absurdum reor. Igitur a foro boario, ubi aereum tauri simulacrum aspicimus, quia id genus animalium aratro subditur, sulcus designandi oppidi coeptus, ut magnam Herculis aram amplecteretur; inde certis spatiis interiecti lapides per ima montis Palatini ad aram Consi, mox curias veteres, tum ad sacellum Larum ; forumque Romanum et Capitolium non a Romulo, sed a Tito Tatio additum urbi credidere.

The site of the ara Herculis (p. 397) is known to have been within a very short distance of the present church of S. Maria in Cosmedin, northwest of the northwest end of the Circus Maximus. The ara Consi (p. 404) is also known to have stood at the eastern end of the spina of the circus. With al-

---

[1] Dionys. i. 88; Jordan, I. 1. 163; Gilbert, I. 114–134; *Mitt.* 1892, 293.
[2] i. 44.  [3] *Ann.* xii. 24.

most equal certainty the Curiae veteres (p. 130) is to be placed
at the northeastern corner of the Palatine, and the sacellum
Larum (p. 131) near the northwestern corner.   This can hardly
have been the line of an original Palatine pomerium, which can
only be a matter of conjecture, and Tacitus is evidently describing the course followed by the Luperci in his day.[1]

At three points in the circuit,[2] the plough was carefully lifted
up and carried for a few feet.   These breaks in the furrow
marked the position of the three gates required for every
settlement by Etruscan ritual.   Varro[3] says that one of these
gates of the Palatine city was the porta Mugonia, or vetus porta
Palati, on the north side of the hill, near the site of the temple of Iuppiter Stator.   This is shown to have been its real
position by the contour of the ground as well as by the remains
of the pavement of a street (p. 165) leading up the hill at this
point, which, although of a much later period, probably represented the early road.   It is clear that cattle would have
been driven in and out at this gate, and Varro derives the name
from their lowing (*mugitus*).   The location of the second gate is
unknown, but it may have been somewhere on the south side,
perhaps near the scalae Caci.   The third gate is described by
Varro[4] as follows : —

Alteram Romanulam ab Roma dictam, quae habet gradus in nova via
ad Volupiae sacellum ;

and by Festus,[5] who says, —

Porta Romana instituta est a Romulo infimo clivo Victoriae qui locus
gradibus in quadram formatus est.

A gate[6] at the foot of the clivus Victoriae (p. 138) must have

---

[1] Platner, *The Pomerium and Roma Quadrata, AJP.* 1901, 420–425.

[2] Varro, *LL.* v. 142; Serv. *ad Aen.* i. 422.

[3] *LL.* v. 164; Dionys. ii. 50; Fest. 144; Solin. i. 24.

[4] *LL.* v. 164.                [5] Fest. 262.

[6] Jordan, I. 1. 176; Gilbert, I. 112, 121; II. 114–116; *BC.* 1881, 69–70; *Ann.
d. Ist.* 1884, 203–204; *Mélanges,* 1908, 256–258.   The old explanation of *porta
Romanula* as the river-gate, based on a connection between Roma and a supposed *rumon*, a river, must probably be given up (cf. p. 33).

been on the west side of the hill, probably not far from the church of S. Teodoro, and this was undoubtedly the **porta Romanula** or **Romana**.

The Palatine city was called in later times **Roma quadrata**, a name which is explained by Solinus [1] (from Varro) as follows: —

> Dictaque primum est Roma quadrata, quod ad aequilibrium foret posita. Ea incipit a silva quae est in area Apollinis, et ad supercilium scalarum Caci habet terminum, ubi tugurium fuit Faustuli.

The line *a silva . . . ad supercilium* [2] was the northeast and south-west diagonal of a trapezoidal area which Varro evidently thought had been that inclosed within the walls of the Palatine city.    Roma quadrata was also, and first, perhaps, used in the sense of **Mundus**, or the receptacle at the centre of the templum, for Festus [3] states, on the authority of Ennius : —

> Quadrata Roma in Palatio ante templum Apollinis dicitur, ubi reposita sunt quae solent boni ominis gratia in urbe condenda adhiberi, quia saxo munitus est initio in speciem quadratam.

This Mundus [4] is supposed to be represented upon a fragment of the Marble Plan, where a small four-sided structure of stone, raised above the ground and approached by steps on two sides, stands in the *area Apollinis*.

**The Septimontium, or City of the Seven Hills**. — The direction in which the Palatine [5] city should expand was indicated by political and topographical conditions.    There were other small settlements on some of the surrounding hills, and the second period of the city's history was that of union with such hamlets on the adjacent spurs of the Esquiline and the Caelian.    Topo-graphical conditions rendered it almost certain that the control

---

[1] i. 17.   Cf. also *Mélanges*, 1908, 271–278.

[2] *Mitt.* 1896, 210–212; *AJP.* 1901, 420–425; Pais, *Legends*, 223–234, 257–263.
[3] 258.

[4] *Mitt.* 1896, 202–204; Pais, *Legends*, 229–234; Binder, *Die Plebs*, 43–71.

[5] For a hypothetical *urbs trimontialis* between the Palatine city and the Septimontium, see *Mélanges*, 1908, 249–282.

of the inhabitants of the Palatine should extend along the ridge of the Velia and across the eastern end of the Forum valley, and that further expansion should take place up the slopes of the Esquiline. The same conditions obtained with respect to the Caelian, but to a somewhat less marked degree.

Aside from the direct testimony of these topographical conditions, evidence as to the extent of this second city is derived from the festival of the Septimontium itself, and the scattered passages in Latin literature which refer to it or to the city. As the Lupercalia preserved in ritual a reminiscence of the first Rome, so the Septimontium is believed to have

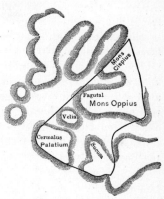

FIG. 4. — THE SEPTIMONTIUM.

preserved one of the succeeding stage. This festival,[1] in some calendars marked simply as Agonia or Agonalia, was celebrated on the 11th of December, even during the empire, and consisted in part of a lustral procession round the Palatine and Esquiline hills, thus corresponding to the Lupercalia.

Varro[2] states that the name Septimontium was given to the city before it was called Rome, but says that the hills were those which the Servian wall afterward inclosed. The real extent of this city is supposed to be described by Festus[3] and Paulus Diaconus,[4] who tell us that the seven *montes* were the three parts of the Palatine: Palatium, Cermalus, and Velia; the two spurs of the Esquiline: Oppius and Cispius; the north-

---

[1] Fest. 340; Macrob. i. 16. 6; Jordan, I. 1. 199; Mommsen, *Römisches Staatsrecht*, iii. 1. 113–114; *CIL*. i.² p. 336.

[2] *LL*. v. 41; Wissowa, *Satura Viadrina*, Breslau, 1896, 1–19; Platner, *CP*. 1906, 69–80; Pais, *Legends*, 234–241.

[3] 348.   [4] 341.

ern spur of the Caelian, which was called Sucusa; and the
Fagūtal.

Fagūtal is a substantive form from *fagutalis*, and designated
a part of the Esquiline ridge, between the Oppius proper and
the extreme western slope, which was known at a later period
as the Carinae (Fig. 4). Here was a grove of beech trees, the
lucus Fagutalis,[1] in which was a shrine of Jupiter, worshipped
under the name of Iuppiter Fagutalis. Sucusa was confused
with Subura, and so appears in our sources. The etymology[2]
and origin of the words Oppius and Cispius is obscure, but they
may have been derived from the clans dwelling at these points.
They were displaced in ordinary usage by the collective term
Esquiliae, which, as its form indicates, was a settlement-name,
perhaps equivalent to *ex-quiliae*. The common adjective *esquilinus*, in *mons esquilinus*, would then be analogous to *inquilinus*,
'an inhabitant,' and it is a plausible hypothesis that the inhabitants of the Palatium, *inquilini*, applied the term *Esquiliae*
to the settlements on the opposite hills, which afterward became
a part of the city. Sucusa is probably also an ancient Italian
settlement-name.

The city formed by the union of these topographical units
was undoubtedly surrounded by fortifications; that is, the
existing wall of the Palatium was connected with the walls of
the newly annexed hamlets. No remains of these connecting
walls have been found, and it would be remarkable in the
highest degree if they had survived the great changes of
centuries in the very centre of the city. An obscure passage
in Varro[3] mentions a murus terreus Carinarum, evidently an
embankment of earth on the Carinae, and this has been
thought by some[4] to be the wall of the Septimontium; and
on the supposition that it ran along the bank of the brook

[1] Varro, *LL.* v. 152; *BC.* 1905, 199–201.
[2] Jordan, I. 1. 183–188; 3. 254; Gilbert, I. 166–169.        [3] *LL.* v. 48.
[4] Schneider, *Mitt.* 1895, 167–178; Richter, *Top.*[2] 38 n. Cf. also *Mélanges*,
1908, 274–276.

to the Forum valley, the temple of Janus (p. 191), which has been the subject of much discussion, has been explained as the **portae belli** in this wall. Further evidence that the second period in the city's development was the union of the Palatine and Oppius-Cispius group of settlements, is sometimes thought to be found in the annual struggle for the October horse, described by Festus,[1] in which the Sacravienses represent the Palatini, and the Suburanenses their early neighbors and rivals.

**The City of the Four Regions**. — Between the Septimontium and the city that, having been inclosed by the Servian wall, became the Rome of the republic, intervened a period of development to which it has been found convenient to give the name of the Four Regions, from its most distinctive feature. In consequence of the reforms which tradition ascribes to Servius Tullius, the inhabitants of the city of Rome were divided into four tribes (*tribus*), which, although purely political divisions so far as our knowledge of them extends, were doubtless based on the local division into four regions,[2] belonging to the previous period. This local division remained in force until the time of Augustus.

The expansion of the Septimontium took place in two directions, north and south. On the north the added area comprised the small Viminal [3] hill, next to the Cispius, and the much larger Quirinal immediately beyond, with the adjacent Capitolium. It is to be noted that these two hills were not properly called *montes*,[4] but *colles*, the distinguishing adjectives Quirinalis and Viminalis being added afterward, and that the settlers in this district were called *collini*, not *montani*. The **collis Quirinalis** derived its name [5] from a shrine of the god

---

[1] 178.       [2] Varro, *LL*. v. 56.       [3] Jordan, I. 3. 372, 394.

[4] For apparent exceptions cf. Florus, i. 7 (13), 16; Eutropius, i. 7 (6); Claudian, *de sext. cons. Hon.* 543; *CP*. 1907, 463–464.

[5] Jordan, I. 1. 180.

Quirinus, who appears to have been worshipped there as
well as on the Palatine. The settlement on this hill has
usually been regarded as largely made up of Sabine elements,
but this traditional view has been vigorously combated.[1] Vimi-

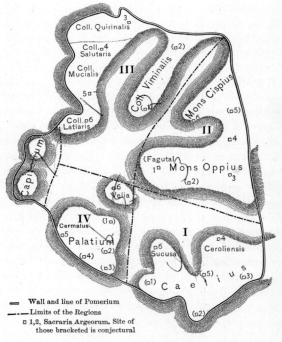

FIG. 5. — THE CITY OF THE FOUR REGIONS.

nalis is of course derived from *vimina* 'osiers,' which grew
abundantly in this region.

On the south the rest of the Caelian, comprising the Caelius
proper and the Ceroliensis, was added to the area of the Septi-

[1] Binder, *Die Plebs*, 139–170; Mommsen, *History of Rome*, i. 85.

montium.  A line of fortification must have surrounded the
city of the Four Regions, and its probable course may be
traced by the contour of the ground.  Beginning at the southwest corner of the Capitoline, it ran northeast along the edge
of the cliffs of this hill and of the Quirinal to a point where,
bending at a right angle, it ran southeast and south across the
Quirinal, the Viminal, and the Esquiline, just where the valleys begin which descend between these hills.  At the southeast corner of the Caelian it turned to the southwest round
the hill, and thence ran northwest to the Palatine and back
to the Capitoline (Fig. 5).

The four regions are described by Varro[1] as the Suburana,
the Esquilina, the Collina, and the Palatina.  Regio I, Suburana, comprised the Sucusa, the Ceroliensis, and the Caelius;
Regio II, Esquilina, the Oppius and the Cispius; Regio III,
Collina, the Quirinal and the Viminal; Regio IV, Palatina, the
Palatium, the Cermalus, and the Velia.  These four regions met
at a common point, probably near the Velia.  The Capitoline,
although a part of the city, seems not to have been included in
any one of the regions, perhaps because it was from the beginning regarded as the citadel and religious centre of the whole
city, and not as a local division or part.[2]  This is implied by
the very name Capitolium, which was deliberately given to the
hill as the Capitol, and was not derived from any existing
settlement.  The pomerium coincided with the wall, having
been extended with each enlargement of the city's area, but
after this time it was not extended again until Sulla's dictatorship.

Varro[3] is the chief authority for this division into regions,
and in the same connection he describes the shrines known as
the sacraria Argeorum,[4] and the ceremonial festival connected

---

[1] LL. v. 45.        [2] Jordan, I. 1. 180.  Cf. also *Mélanges*, 1908, 272-274.
[3] LL. v. 45-54.

[4] Richter, *Top.*[2] 9-10, 38-40; Gilbert, II. 329-375; Jordan, II. 237-290, 599-
604; Mommsen, *Staatsrecht*, iii. 122-126; Marquardt, *Staatsverwaltung*, iii.

with them. His incomplete and somewhat obscure account distributes twenty-seven of these sacraria among the four regions, and describes the position of twelve with such minuteness that all but one of them can be located with reasonable certainty. These eleven, and also the conjectural sites of thirteen others, are marked on Fig. 5, making twenty-four in all, or six in each region. There are no means of determining the location of the remaining three. The shrines themselves were called Argei, *a principibus qui cum Ercule Argivo venerunt Romam*, and the word is evidently a Latinization of Ἀργεῖοι. The festival at these shrines took place on March 16th and 17th, and on May 14th. On the latter date, the procession of priests, Vestals, and the city praetor, after visiting all the shrines in order, halted on the pons Sublicius, and twenty-seven straw puppets, one for each shrine, were solemnly cast into the Tiber. These puppets were also called Argei, and it is supposed that at the festival in March they were consecrated in the sacraria, to be collected at the ceremony in May.

Whatever the meaning and origin of this festival may have been, it was probably introduced into Rome in the third century B.C., and the topographical details belong to that period. It is this topographical information which gives Varro's description its great importance.

**Another Theory of the Origin of the City.** — In opposition to this view of the organic development of Rome from a nucleus on the Palatine, another theory[1] has recently been brought forward, according to which the origin of the organized city was due to the union of hamlets situated on the different hills. These hamlets had been entirely autonomous, and no one was

---

190–194; Roscher, *Lexikon der Mythologie*, i. 496–500; Studemund, *Phil.* 1889, 168–177; Hülsen, *RhM.* 1894, 414–416; Wissowa, Pauly's *Real-Encyclopädie* (art. Argei); Diels, *Sibyllinische Blätter*, 43; *BC.* 1905, 196–199.

[1] Degering, *Berl. Phil. Wochenschrift*, 1903, 1646; Kornemann, *Klio*, 1905, 88–91; Pinza, *Mon. d. Lincei*, 1905, 746–778; Carter, *AJA.* 1908, 172–183, and *The Pomerium*, Rome, 1909.

distinguished above the others because of priority of settlement or the exercise of any sort of hegemony.   The festival of the Septimontium was a celebration carried out by seven of these communities in a state of mere alliance with each other, rather than as parts of one *urbs*.   Under pressure from outside these allied settlements finally united, probably before the end of the seventh century B.C., losing their autonomy, and constituting the *urbs Roma*, corresponding in extent with that which has been described as the city of the Four Regions.   This was the Rome of history down to the Gallic invasion, when the so-called Servian wall was built round an enlarged area.   The belief in a Palatine city was of very late growth, due entirely to the inventive imagination of poets and historiographers, Greek and Roman, and without any foundation in native tradition.

While there is much to be said in support of this view, it still seems on the whole less probable than the other.

**The Servian City.**[1] — Tradition ascribes to Servius Tullius the building of the famous wall which surrounded Rome during the historical period, the remains of which are still to be seen.   These remains, however, are in large part (pp. 112 ff.) not earlier than the fourth century B.C., belonging to the period after the invasion of the Gauls.   It is probable, therefore, that this wall of the fourth century was a complete rebuilding of much weaker fortifications that had existed for a long time, and that it followed in the main the earlier line, but with some variations.   The evidence of literature and inscriptions and the remains of the wall itself enable us to trace this line[2] in its final course with certainty at almost every point.   It coincided with the probable wall of the city of the Four Regions from the southwest corner of the Capitoline along the edge of the

---

[1] Jordan, I. 1. 201–295; Gilbert, II. 258–456; III. 1–57.

[2] *Ann. d. Ist.* 1871, 40–85; Jordan, I. 1. 201–245; *BC.* 1872, 225–226; 1876, 29–30, 34–38, 121–128; 1888, 12–22; 1909, 119–121; Merlin, *L'Aventin dans l'Antiquité*, Paris, 1906, 114–132; *NS.* 1907, 504–510; 1909, 221–222.

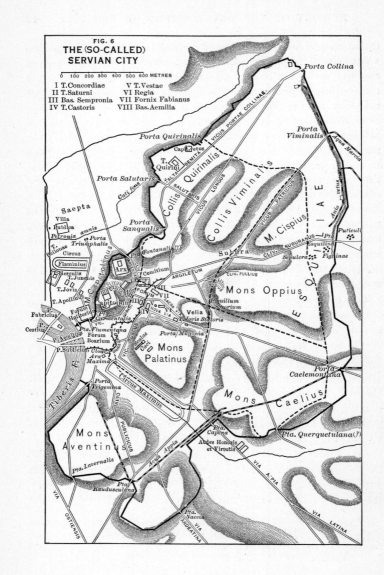

FIG. 6

## THE (SO-CALLED) SERVIAN CITY

0 100 200 300 400 500 600 METRES

I T.Concordiae     V T.Vestae
II T.Saturni        VI Regia
III Bas. Sempronia  VII Fornix Fabianus
IV T.Castoris     VIII Bas. Aemilia

Porta Collina

Porta Quirinalis

Porta Viminalis

Aqua Marcia

Capi Vetus

T. Quirini

VICUS PORTAE COLLINAE

ALTA SEMITA

Porta Salutaris

Collis Quirinalis

Cati fons

VICUS SALUTARIS

VICUS LONGUS

Collis Viminalis

Anio vetus

E S Q U I L I A E

Porta Sanqualis

VICUS PATRICIUS

M. Cispius

Puticuli

Saepta

Villa Publica

Subura

Esquiliae

Petronia amnis

Porta Triumphalis

Porta Fontanalis(?)

CLIV. SUBURANUS

Pta Figlinae

Sepulcra

T. Bellona
Circus

Arx

Comitium

ARGILETUM

CLIV. PULLIUS

Flaminius

Capitolinus

Herculis
T.Junonis

T.Jovis

FORVM

VIII

VII

SACRA

Mons Oppius

T.Apollinis

VI

V

III

II

I

Pantilium
aratorium

P. Fabricius

Forum
Holitorium

Pta
Carmentalis

NOVA VIA

Velia
T.Jovis Statoris

Velia

P. Cestius

Pta.Flumentana
Forum
Boarium

Scalae
Caci

Porta Mugonia

P.Sublicius
Ara
Maxima

Cloaca

Mons
Palatinus

Mons
Caelius

Porta
Trigemina

Circus Maximus

Porta
Caelemontana

Mons
Aventinus

CLIVUS PUBLICIUS

Aedes Honoris
et Virtutis

Pta
Capena

Pta. Querquetulana(?)

Pta.Lavernalis

Arx Appia

VIA A.PIA

Pta
Raudusculana

VIA OSTIENSIS

Pta.
Naevia

VIA ARDEATINA

VIA LATINA

Quirinal, but extended almost a kilometre farther northeast, to a point near the junction of the tableland behind the Quirinal and the collis hortorum, the present Pincian hill.    Thence it ran southeast and south until it again approached the line of the city of the Four Regions on the Oppius.    Following closely, or coinciding with, this line round the Caelian, it diverged at the porta Capena, and inclosed the Aventine, passing along its slope to the northern corner, where it bent at right angles and continued in a straight line to the Tiber, here only about 125 metres distant from the hill.    From the southwestern corner of the Capitoline, it was also built in a direct line to the river.[1]    This left a distance of about 300 metres along the river bank where there was no wall like that which surrounded the rest of the city.    Recent excavations have brought to light the remains of stone quays built along the bank, and doubtless provided with a sort of parapet, which would prevent an enemy from making a landing.

The area added to the city was in two sections, that on the northeast tableland, stretching back from the Quirinal and Esquiline to the new wall,[2] and that on the south, the whole region of the Aventine and the low ground between the Palatine, the Forum, and the Capitoline.    A large part of this newly acquired district was covered with woods, and continued to be so until the later days of the republic, as is shown by Varro's[3] description of the situation of the sacraria Argeorum, which in certain parts of the city, as on the Aventine and the Esquiline, are described as being near this or that grove.

For much the greater part of its course this wall was built along the edge of the cliffs in the manner of the Palatine fortifications, an independent wall being necessary only where low ground or the end of a valley had to be crossed, as between the

---

[1] For a presentation of the view that the wall ran directly across from the Capitoline to the Aventine, see *Mélanges,* 1909, 103–144.

[2] Liv. i. 44.   Cf. p. 48, note 4.

[3] *LL.* v. 50.   For the *luci* of Rome, cf. *BC.* 1905, 189–232.

hills and the river or between the Caelian and the Aventine, except for the long stretch across the plateau of the Quirinal and the Esquiline. Here, instead of an ordinary wall, the famous agger[1] was erected.

Dionysius[2] states that the length of the Servian wall was the same as that of the wall of Athens, 43 stadia, or 5⅜ Roman miles, and this corresponds very closely with the line as it can now be traced. Communication with the opposite bank of the Tiber was secured by the pons Sublicius. This wooden bridge was the only one in existence until 179 B.C., and is usually supposed[3] to have spanned the river close by the forum Boarium, within the limits of the Servian fortifications.

The city inclosed within this wall marked a most important departure from the earlier conception of the city, or *urbs*, in that the line of the pomerium, and therefore the city-templum, was not extended to coincide with the new wall, but remained as it had been during the previous period. The new Esquiline and Aventine regions remained without the sacred precinct. The reason for this condition is unknown,[4] but from the time of Sulla the political fiction[5] was developed that no one who had not increased the area of Roman territory by actual conquest[6] had the right to extend the pomerium of the city.

Latin literature speaks of many gates in the Servian wall, and gives the names of sixteen which are accepted as authentic. Of these, the site of some can be made out with certainty, of the others with more or less probability.

Those the location of which may be regarded as certain, are : —

1. **Porta Carmentalis,**[7] with two openings, at the southwestern corner of the Capitoline.

---

[1] For the description of this wall and agger, see pp. 112–115.

[2] iv. 13.                        [3] For the discussion of this question, see p. 78.

[4] Cf., however, *CP*. 1909, 420–432; *AJA*. 1908, 183.

[5] Gell. xiii. 14; *CIL*. vi. 1231–1233.

[6] For further extensions of the pomerium, see pp. 67–69.

[7] Dionys. i. 32; Solin. i. 13.

2. **Porta Sanqualis,**[1] on the collis Mucialis (p. 16), in the via di Magnanapoli.
3. **Porta Salutaris,**[2] on the collis Salutaris (p. 16), in the piazza del Quirinale, near the via della Dateria.
4. **Porta Quirinalis,**[3] on the Quirinal, close to the line of the via delle Quattro Fontane.
5. **Porta Collina,**[4] at the extreme northeastern corner of the wall, over the via Nomentana.
6. **Porta Viminalis,**[5] on the Viminal, north of the present railroad station.
7. **Porta Esquilina,**[6] over the via Labicana, northwest of the piazza Vittorio Emanuele.
8. **Porta Caelemontana,**[7] on the Caelian, near the Lateran.
9. **Porta Capena,**[8] over the via Appia.
10. **Porta Trigemina,**[9] between the Aventine and the Tiber.

Those the situation of which is highly probable, although not so certain, are:—

11. **Porta Naevia,**[10] between S. Saba and the baths of Caracalla.
12. **Porta Raudusculana,**[11] at the junction of the viale Aventino and the via di porta S. Paolo.
13. **Porta Lavernalis,**[12] in the via del Priorato,—all three on the southern slope of the Aventine.

---

[1] Fest. 343; *BC.* 1876, 35–36; *RhM.* 1894, 411; Jordan, I. 1. 213; 3. 399.
[2] Fest. 326–327; *RhM.* 1894, 405, 411; *BC.* 1876, 123.
[3] Fest. 254; *Hermes*, 1891, 137; Jordan, I. 3. 399, 411.
[4] *BC.* 1876, 165–167; Strabo, v. 234; Dionys. ix. 68; Jordan, I. 3. 399.
[5] Fest. 376; *BC.* 1876, 168–170.
[6] Liv. ii. 11; *BC.* 1875, 191.
[7] Cic. *in Pis.* 55, 61; Liv. xxxv. 9; Lanciani, *Mon. d. Lincei,* i. 536.
[8] Ov. *Fast.* vi. 192; Juv. iii. 11; Mart. iii. 47; *Bull. d. Ist.* 1882, 121–127.
[9] Solin. i. 8; Frontin. 5; *Arch. Zeit.* 1873, 9–11; *Mélanges,* 1909, 129–132.
[10] Varro, *LL.* v. 163; Liv. ii. 11.
[11] Varro, *LL.* v. 163; Fest. *Epit.* 275; Val. Max. v. 6. 3.
[12] Varro, *LL.* v. 163; Fest. *Epit.* 117; Jordan, I. 1. 168; Merlin, *L'Aventin,* 119–121.

14. **Porta Flumentana**,[1] between the porta Carmentalis and the
    river.

Somewhat more doubtful are the sites of the following:—

15. **Porta Fontinalis**,[2] at the northeastern extremity of the Capi-
    toline, and belonging originally to the collis Latiaris.
    A road from the Forum into the campus Martius cer-
    tainly crossed between the Capitoline and Quirinal at
    this point, and passed through a gate, but whether it
    was the porta Fontinalis or not, is uncertain.
16. **Porta Querquetulana**,[3] probably on the Caelian, where a road
    passed out to the vallis Egeriae.[4]

The relation of the district on the right bank of the Tiber to
the city proper during the early period has been much discussed. According to tradition, Ancus Marcius[5] united the
Ianiculum, or Janus-city, to the city by the pons Sublicius and
by a wall from this bridge to the top of the hill. We are also
told that while the comitia centuriata was meeting in the campus Martius,[6] flag-signals were interchanged between the Capitol and the Janiculum, where a watch was being kept for the
approach of an enemy.

It is probable that shortly before or after the beginnings of
the Servian city, it became customary from time to time to
station an outpost on the Janiculum,[7] whenever there was any
reason to fear the sudden approach of an enemy, and that

---

[1] Varro, *RR*. iii. 2; Liv. vi. 20; xxxv. 9 and 21; Fest. 89; *CIL*. vi. 9208. Cf.
*Mélanges*, 1909, 140–141.

[2] Liv. xxxv. 10; Fest. 85; *CIL*. vi. 9514, 9921; *RhM*. 1894, 411; *BC*. 1906,
209–223.          [3] Pl. *NH*. xvi. 37; Fest. 260, 261; *BC*. 1905, 201.

[4] The **porta Ratumena**, mentioned by Festus, 274, was probably a gate in
the Capitoline inclosure; cf. Jordan, I. 1. 210; Hülsen, *RhM*. 1894, 412.

[5] Liv. i. 33; Dionys. iii. 45.          [6] Liv. xxxix. 15; Dio Cass. xxxvii. 28.

[7] For the discussion of the Janiculum, its derivation and meaning, cf.
Richter, *Befestigung des Janiculum*, Berlin, 1882; Gilbert, II. 174–179; Jordan, I. 1. 241–245; Elter, *RhM*. 1891, 112–138; Mayerhöfer, *Gesch.-topo-
graphische Studien*, Munich, 1887, 7–21.

some time afterward a small fort of some sort was erected, which, however, does not appear to have been connected with the river by any line of fortification. All necessity for such an outpost ended when Rome became mistress of the peninsula, and thenceforth the district *trans Tiberim* underwent a normal development, first as the pagus Ianiculensis, belonging to the ager Romanus, and afterward as a part of the city itself.

By the time of Sulla, the wall had been destroyed in many places, and houses had been built over and against it. A little later, Dionysius says that it was difficult to trace its course, and Maecenas included the agger in a park (p. 71). From these and other indications, we may infer that the wall was kept in reasonably good repair down to the second century B.C.; but that from that time on it fell more and more rapidly into decay, so that it could practically be disregarded by Augustus in his reorganization of the city.

Along the river, the spread of the city beyond the line of the walls began at a very early date. The importance of the Tiber for the development of Rome was greatest during the first four centuries of the republic, and more room upon its bank was needed than that included within the wall. The first extension, therefore, of business and population beyond the fortifications was northward from the porta Flumentana and southward from the porta Trigemina. Ships from Ostia began to discharge their cargoes along the bank under the Aventine, where later stood the Emporium, or market place for foreign goods, and in imperial times the enormous horrea, or warehouses. The forum Boarium, or cattle market, was near the river within the walls; but the forum Holitorium, or vegetable market, was outside the porta Carmentalis : and still further up the river were the Navalia, or shipyards. It is probable that the population in the district between the Palatine, the Capitoline, the Forum, and the Tiber was more dense than anywhere else in the city, except possibly in the Subura, and an early overflow into the campus Martius was natural.

The names of at least three suburban districts north of the
Servian wall are known to us, although their respective limits
cannot accurately be defined: namely, the campus Flaminius,[1]
where Flaminius built a circus for the plebs in the year
221 B.C., a distinctly plebeian quarter, sometimes called the
prata Flaminia;[2] the region called extra portam Flumentanam;[3]
and that known as the Aemiliana.[4]

As the city underwent an almost complete transformation
under Augustus and his successors, and as existing remains
with few exceptions date from this later period, it is difficult
to form any definite and exact idea of the appearance of the
Rome of the republic. Temples and public buildings were
built of opus quadratum of tufa, or of concrete faced with
opus incertum, extremely simple in style, and with no preten-
sion to beauty. The dwellings of most of the citizens were
built of wooden framing, sun-dried bricks (lateres crudi), and
wattled work of mud and osiers, unsubstantial in character and
unattractive in appearance. These houses furnished excellent
material for the frequent conflagrations[5] which swept through
the city, and which were at the same time the cause and the
result of this worthless style of construction. The constant
danger of inundations in the districts along the river was
another reason for the persistence of a cheap method of
building.

A marked change in the character of the houses of the rich
began, apparently, about the year 100 B.C., and we are told of
the magnificence of many of the palaces of wealthy Romans,
erected on the Palatine after that date (p. 134).

Comparatively little was done, however, in the way of restoring existing temples and public buildings, or erecting new

---

[1] Varro, *LL.* v. 154; Gilbert, III. 66–69; Jordan, I. 3. 484.

[2] Liv. iii. 54, 63.                    [3] Liv. xxxv. 9. 21; Jordan, I. 1. 240.

[4] Varro, *RR.* iii. 2; Gilbert, III. 378; Jordan, I. 3. 490.

[5] For seven great fires, recorded in this period, see Jordan, I. 1. 482 note,
and Friedländer, *Sittengeschichte*, i[6]. 31; i[7]. 20.

edifices of any remarkable character, the Tabularium (78 B.C.) and the theatre of Pompey (55 B.C.) being almost the sole exceptions, so that we may accept without doubt the statements of Cicero and Augustus, as describing justly the appearance of the chief city of the world at the end of the republic.[1]

That temples in large numbers had been erected during the republic is known from the statement[2] of Augustus that he had restored eighty-two at his own expense; but there is no reason to suppose that many of them were architecturally successful or beautiful. The spoils of Sicily and Greece, gathered by Roman generals during two centuries of conquest, which had been placed in the temples and public buildings, must have served in general to emphasize the artistic poverty of their surroundings.

More important than the buildings themselves was the general plan of the Servian city, for this was followed in its main lines in the succeeding periods. To speak of a "plan" is somewhat misleading, for the city of Rome was not laid out according to any plan whatsoever. We are told[3] that after its burning by the Gauls the city was rebuilt without regard to previous boundaries, in an absolutely haphazard fashion. Although considerable doubt attends this alleged burning by the Gauls,[4] it is evident that the lines of the city were dependent upon the contour of the ground and the conditions of settlement, and not at all upon conscious purpose. The first settlements were on the hills, — the Palatine, the Esquiline, the Quirinal, and the Caelian, — and consisted of peasants' huts grouped together with no idea of symmetry. When these settlements were united into one city, the valleys between the hills were made use of for meeting-places, markets, public games, and similar

---

[1] Cic. *de Div.* ii. 99: in latere aut in caemento ex quibus urbs effecta est. Varro *ap.* Non. 48. 9; Suet. *Aug.* 28: urbem neque pro maiestate imperii ornatam et inundationibus incendiisque obnoxiam excoluit adeo ut iure sit gloriatus marmoream se relinquere quam latericiam accepisset.

[2] *Mon. Anc.* 21.        [3] Liv. v, 55.        [4] Thouret, *JJ.* iv. Suppl. Bd. 164 ff.

purposes.   Paths were trodden along these valleys to the various points on the hills, along the paths buildings were erected, and they afterward became the main streets of the city.   First in time and importance was the Sacra via, between the Palatine and the Esquiline, which, beginning near the present site of the Colosseum, crossed the ridge of the Velia and extended to the east end of the Forum.   Its continuation passed through the Forum valley to the foot of the Capitoline (p. 171).   From this point it was called the clivus Capitolinus, and ascended the Capitoline to the depression between the Capitol and the Arx, where it divided and continued to each summit.

Probably the second street to receive a name was the Nova via (so called to distinguish it from the Sacra via), which extended from the northeast corner of the Palatine, along its north and west sides, to the Velabrum.   This coincides with part of the line which Tacitus describes as having been that of the Palatine pomerium (p. 36).

These were the only two streets within the Servian city which were called *viae*, this term being elsewhere applied only to the great roads which ran from Rome to the various parts of Italy, and at a later period to a few streets in the campus Martius[1] and on the Aventine.[2]

In the city of the Four Regions, the main streets, besides the two already mentioned, must have been the Subura, and its extension, the clivus Suburanus, and the two leading from the end of the Sacra via in the Colosseum valley along the north and west sides of the Caelian.   In the Servian city this list of principal streets was increased by those which ran from the Subura up the slopes of the Quirinal and Viminal to the gates in the Esquiline wall and agger, the vicus portae Collinae, which ran across the Quirinal, and three which led out from the Forum, — the vicus Tuscus southwest along the north side of the Palatine, the vicus Iugarius round the southwest slope of the Capi-

---

[1] Via Tecta (p. 377), via Lata (p. 125), via Fornicata (p. 342).

[2] Via Nova sub thermis Antoninianis (p. 414).

toline to the porta Carmentalis, and that which connected the northeast corner of the Forum with the campus Martius, between the Capitoline and the Quirinal.

These streets, with such open spaces as the Forum, the forum Boarium, and the forum Holitorium, formed the framework, so to speak, of the city of the republic, and from them branched off a constantly increasing number of less important cross-streets and alleys. The average width of these streets was about 4 metres, although the broadest were 2 or 3 metres wider. Down to the beginning of the third century B.C. it is probable that the Sacra via and the Nova via were the only streets which were paved, but after that date [1] there was great improvement in this respect, although records of paving are for the most part still later.

The regular name for a city street was *vicus*[2]: that of a side street or alley, *pergula*[3] or *semita* if open at both ends, and *angiportus* if a cul-de-sac. But *vicus* was also regularly used to include a main street, the side streets and alleys opening into it, and the houses standing upon them, so that the term was equivalent to ward or quarter. The names of about one hundred[4] of these *vici* have been handed down, but their situation is not always certain.

By the laws of the Twelve Tables each house must be surrounded by a narrow passage, to guard against the danger of fire. Hence such a dwelling was called an *insula*,[5] and there was a considerable number of these *insulae* in each vicus. Toward the end of the republic this regulation was disregarded, and a distinction arose between *domus* and *insula*, the former term being applied to the separate mansions of the

---

[1] Liv. xxxviii. 28; xli. 27.

[2] *Arch. f. Lat. Lex.* 1905, 301–316.     [3] *Mitt.* 1887, 214–220.

[4] Kiepert and Hülsen, *Nomenclator Topographicus*, Berlin, 1896.

[5] Richter, *Hermes*, 1885, 91 ff.; Attilio dei Marchi, *Ricerche intorno alle "insulae" o case a pigione di Roma antica*, Milan, 1891; Hülsen, *Mitt.* 1892, 279–284.

rich Romans, while the latter was restricted to the tenements in which the bulk of the population lived.[1]  Later, another transfer of meaning took place, in consequence of which *insula* was the name given to an apartment of one or more rooms, of which one building might contain many.  It is in this sense that the word is used in the *Notitia.*

During the republic the population was most dense in the Subura and Velabrum.  The Palatine became the residence quarter of the rich, while the Aventine was distinctly plebeian.

Attention has already been called to the overflow of population beyond the porta Carmentalis and the porta Flumentana, but it should be borne in mind that the campus Martius and the campus Flaminius were in no sense within the city until the time of Augustus.  They formed part of the public domain, and we have no record of any sale to private individuals before Sulla.[2]  Shrines to various divinities had been erected in this district from very early times, but almost no buildings of distinction before Pompey's magnificent structures.

Within the six centuries of the existence of the city of the republic certain periods in its development stand out as especially marked.  The last years of the kings witnessed the beginning of the Cloaca Maxima, and the draining of the Forum and the Comitium.  The censorship of Appius Claudius Caecus, in 312 B.C., marked a second stage, for the building of the via Appia from the porta Capena south, and of the aqua Appia, the first Roman aqueduct, by which water was brought across the Aventine down to the porta Trigemina, must have contributed greatly to the development of the districts affected.

The third notable epoch was the first forty years of the second century B.C., when the results of the Punic and Macedonian wars were making themselves felt in attempts to adorn the city with the spoils of Greece, and to improve the condition of streets and sewers by systematic paving and rebuilding.  At this time

---

[1] Cf. Jordan, I. 3. 280.          [2] Oros. v. 18.

also the erection of basilicas in and round the Forum marked a new departure in Roman architecture ; and the erection of a second bridge, the pons Aemilius, begun in 179 B.C., stimulated the growth of intercourse with the opposite bank of the Tiber.

The dictatorship of Sulla marks the last epoch in the republican city, for, besides the actual construction and restoration effected at that time, new ideas of architectural beauty and municipal symmetry were becoming current, to be formulated by Caesar and carried out by Augustus and his successors.

The last century of the republic also witnessed that change in building materials, — from crude to kiln-dried brick, from tufa to travertine, — and the introduction of marble and granite from the East, which in the years to come revolutionized the appearance of the city.

**Urbs Regionum XIV, or the Open City of the Fourteen Regions.** — The plans of Augustus for administrative reform included every part of the Roman world, especially the city itself, which had far outgrown its previous limits, and had no longer need of walls of any sort. He therefore reorganized it in the year 8 B.C.[1] on an entirely different basis, dividing the whole city into fourteen regiones, or wards, which were still further subdivided into vici.[2] The number of vici in the different regions varied somewhat.

Two objects were attained by this new arrangement. In the first place, the police and fire service was organized on a scale commensurate with its importance ; and secondly, the cult of the emperor was introduced in a manner cleverly devised to impress the minds of the mass of the population. The Lares compitales had long been worshipped at shrines set up at the compita throughout the city, and to these two deities a third was now added, the Genius Augusti.[3]

---

[1] Suet. *Aug.* 30 ; Dio Cass. lv. 8 ; Preller, *Die Regionen der Stadt Rom*, Jena, 1846.     [2] *BC.* 1890, 121 ff. ; Jordan, II. 585–598.

[3] Suet. *Aug.* 31 ; Preller, *Römische Mythologie*, ii.[3] 113 ; Carter, *The Religion of Numa*, London, 1906, 177–180.

A new set of magistrates, chosen from the common citizens, was instituted, who were called *magistri vicorum*,[1] originally four from each vicus, but afterward forty-eight in each region, regardless of the number of vici, and two *curatores*. These magistrates seem to have had to do mainly with the religious ceremonies of the regions, the regular municipal administration being in the hands of the higher officials.

From the Regionary Catalogue[2] it is possible to determine with sufficient exactness, in most cases, the limits of these regions in the fourth century; but it is somewhat more difficult to do this for the Augustan division, inasmuch as it is certain that the outer boundaries at least had been extended at some points during the intervening three hundred years. The only sources of information with regard to the original regions are certain passages in literature[3] and a few inscribed terminal stones of the pomerium (pp. 68–69) and of the customs-boundary which have been found.

The number of the regions, fourteen, was twice the traditional number of the hills of the Servian city, *i.e.* the Palatine, Capitoline, Aventine, Caelian, Esquiline, Viminal, and Quirinal. These regions were originally known only by number, and the names found in the Regionary Catalogue became current at various later periods, doubtless as a result of popular usage. Thus the name templum Pacis, applied to region IV, could not have antedated the erection of this temple by Vespasian in 75 A.D.[4]

It has usually been supposed[5] that the Servian wall formed a general boundary for these regions, II, III, IV, VI, VIII, X, XI being entirely within, and I, V, VII, IX, XIV entirely

---

[1] Marquardt, *Staatsverwaltung*, iii. 203–207; Mommsen, *Staatsrecht*, ii. 1035–1037; iii. 119–122; *CIL.* vi. 975; *BC.* 1906, 198–208.

[2] Jordan, II. 540–574.

[3] Notably Pl. *NH.* iii. 66–67; Preller, *Regionen*, 69.

[4] Dio Cass, lxvi. 15; Joseph. *Bell. Iud.* vii. 5. 7; Pl. *NH.* xxxvi. 102.

[5] Jordan, I. 1. 296–339; *BC.* 1890, 115–137.

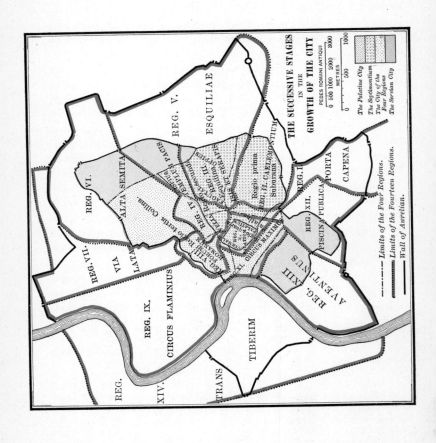

THE SUCCESSIVE STAGES
IN THE
GROWTH OF THE CITY

PEDES ROMANI ANTIQUI
0   500 1000  2000    3000
METRES
0    500       1000

The Palatine City
The Septimontium
The City of the
Four Regions
The Servian City

........... Limits of the Four Regions.
━━━━━ Limits of the Fourteen Regions.
━━━━━ Wall of Aurelian.

REG. V.

ESQUILIAE

REG. VI.

ALTA SEMITA

REG. IV. TEMPLUM PACIS

Regio Prima
REG. II. CAELEMONTIUM
Suburana

REG. I.

PORTA
CAPENA

REG. XII.
PISCINA PUBLICA

REG. VII.
VIA LATA

CIRCUS MAXIMUS

REG. XIII.
AVENTINUS

REG. IX.
CIRCUS FLAMINIUS

TIBERIM

REG.
XIV.
TRANS

without its circuit; while XII and XIII were perhaps always exceptions, including territory on both sides of the wall. It seems probable, however, that regions I, II, and VI, also included territory on each side of the wall, at least in the fourth century, but the determination of their exact limits is very difficult, if not impossible.[1]

It has also been assumed that the Aurelian wall was built on the outer boundary of the regions, but it has been shown that this was not always the case.[2] Hülsen's sketch (Fig. 7) shows some of the probable limits of the city in the time of Pliny.[3] In the year 73 A.D. Vespasian had a new survey of the city made and maps drawn, and he probably placed the famous Marble Plan (p. 2) on the wall of the templum Sacrae Urbis. This survey and plan were perhaps based on similar work of Agrippa's,[4] but as Claudius had meanwhile extended the pomerium (p. 67), it is possible that either he or Vespasian also extended the boundaries of some of the regions, but not to any great extent. Augustus inclosed the fourteen regions with a customs-barrier, which was enlarged somewhat by Vespasian.

Hülsen has shown[5] also that the thirty-seven singulae portae[6] mentioned by Pliny were not gates in the Servian wall, as was once the general opinion, but gates in this customs-barrier,

---

[1] *RhM.* 1894, 416–23. Cf. map of ancient city on opposite page, for the latest view as to the division.

[2] *BC.* 1892, 93–104.                     [3] *Mitt.* 1897, 148–160.

[4] Jordan, I. 1. 301.                      [5] *Mitt.* 1897, 154–156.

[6] Pliny, *NH.* iii. 66–67: Moenia urbis collegere ambitu imperatoribus censoribusque Vespasianis, anno conditae DCCCXXVI millia passuum XIII CC, complexa montes septem. Ipsa dividitur in regiones quattuordecim, compita Larum CCLXV. Eiusdem spatium, mensura currente a milliario in capite Romani fori statuto ad singulas portas, quae sunt hodie numero XXXVII ita ut duodecim semel numerentur, praetereanturque ex veteribus septem, quae esse desierunt, efficit passuum per directum XXMDCCLXV. Ad extrema vero tectorum cum castris praetoriis ab eodem milliario per vias omnium vicorum mensura colligit paulo amplius XX millia passuum.

which was marked by stone cippi. Four of these inscribed[1] cippi (Fig. 7) have been found *in situ*, but they belong to the time of Commodus. Three of them were close to the Aurelian wall.

This number, thirty-seven, is large enough to provide for a gate where each of the thirteen principal *viae* — the Flaminia, Salaria, Nomentana, Gabina, Tiburtina, Labicana, Asinaria, Latina, Appia, Ostiensis, Portuensis, Aurelia, and Triumphalis[2] — passed out of the city, and for an average of two others between these, separated from each other by about 500 metres.

The fourteen regions established by Augustus, with their later names, were the following : —

I. **Porta Capena**, so called from the gate in the Servian wall whence the via Appia issued. It was an irregularly shaped district, beginning at the east corner of the Palatine, bounded on the west by that hill, and running south to some distance beyond the porta Capena between two almost parallel lines, not more than 150 metres apart on the average. Beyond the Aventine it widened considerably and extended to the bank of the Almo, a stream some distance beyond the line of the Aurelian wall. It is probable that regions I, II, III, IV, and X all met at one point near the Meta Sudans.

II. **Caelemontium**. This region[3] included the greater part of the Caelian, and extended east to the Aurelian wall.

III. **Isis et Serapis**, so called because of the temples to these two Egyptian deities, erected within its boundaries. It included the Colosseum valley and the part of the Oppius within the Servian wall.

IV. **Templum Pacis**, including the Sacra via from its beginning to the atrium Vestae, the Subura, and the Cispius within the Servian wall.

---

[1] *CIL*. vi. 1016 a, b, c ; *EE*. iv. 787 ; *CIL*. vi. 31227.
[2] Hülsen's list, *Mitt*. 1897, 156 ; but cf. pp. 125–128.　　　[3] *Mitt*. 1892, 270.

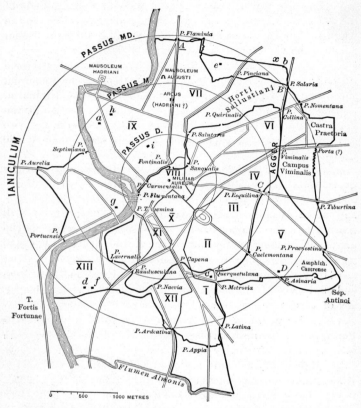

TERMINAL STONES OF THE POMERIUM.

TERMINAL STONES OF THE CUSTOMS-
BARRIER.

a, b, c, d, x :  Claudius.
e, f, g :  Vespasian.
h, i :  Hadrian.

A.   *CIL*. vi. 1016 *c*.
B.   *CIL*. vi. 1016 *b*.
C.   *CIL*. vi. 1016 *a*.
D.   *CIL*. vi. 31227.

FIG. 7.—MAP SHOWING TERMINAL STONES OF THE POMERIUM AND
CUSTOMS-BARRIER.

V. **Esquiliae,** the eastern district of the city, lying outside of
the Servian wall and north of the via Asinaria.   In the time of
Augustus the campus Viminalis, and probably all the district
between the via Tiburtina and the via Salaria, lay outside the
city,[1] and none of it was included in region V until after the
time of Vespasian.   The boundary of this region was at a
short distance beyond the Aurelian wall on the south, but in
the fourth century coincided with it from a point south of the
via Labicana to the south side of the castra Praetoria.

VI. **Alta Semita,** so called from a street which crossed the
Quirinal, on the line of the modern via Quirinale.   This
region[2] included the Quirinal from the imperial fora to the
Servian wall between the porta Viminalis and the porta Collina,
and extended west far enough to take in the horti Sallustiani,
and north even beyond the Aurelian wall.   In the fourth
century, after the castra Praetoria had been made a part of the
city, the boundary of this region coincided with the Aurelian
wall from the porta Salaria south round the castra.

VII. **Via Lata,** so called from the name given to the southern
end of the via Flaminia, between which and the western boundary of VI this region lay.

VIII. **Forum Romanum vel Magnum.**   This region included the
Forum, the imperial fora, the Capitoline and the district south
of it, extending to a line drawn north of the forum Boarium,
through the Velabrum and back to the Forum.

IX. **Circus Flaminius,** all the territory between the via Flaminia, the Servian wall, and the Tiber.

X. **Palatium,** the Palatine, within the lines described by
Tacitus[3] (p. 36) as those of the first pomerium.

XI. **Circus Maximus,** another very irregular region, comprising the Circus Maximus and all that part of the city between
the limits of VIII and X and the Tiber.

---

[1] Pl. *loc. cit.*        [2] *Mitt.* 1892, 307–308; *RhM.* 1894, 422; Jordan, I. 3. 418.
[3] *Ann.* xii. 24.

XII. **Piscina Publica,** so called from a large artificial pool for washing and similar purposes, near the site of the baths of Caracalla. This region included the eastern part of the Aventine, and the districts south of the via Appia as far as the Aurelian wall.

XIII. **Aventinus.** This region extended from the boundaries of XI and XII to the river, including the larger half of the Aventine.

XIV. **Trans Tiberim** (*Trastevere*). This was the name given to all that part of the city on the right bank of the Tiber, but whether its limits corresponded with the line of the Aurelian wall is entirely uncertain.[1] The insula Tiberina (p. 83) was also included in this region.

Augustus organized the fire and police service on the basis of this new division into regions. During the republic, similar services had been performed by a corps of *publici*, or slaves of the municipality, under the command of the *tresviri nocturni*.[2] The new body consisted of seven *cohortes vigilum*,[3] numbering seven thousand men, under the command of a *praefectus vigilum*, who was subordinate to the *praefectus urbi*. These guards were garrisoned in seven barracks, called **stationes**,[4] and fourteen smaller posts, **excubitoria**.

From actual remains and inscriptions[5] found *in situ*, the location of five of these barracks has been determined, namely, statio 1 in region VII, 2 in V, 3 in VI, 4 in XII, and 5 in II. According to the *Notitia*, statio 6 was in region VIII, and 7 in XIV.

All these inscriptions are later than the time of Augustus, and the location of some of these barracks may have been changed during the interval. This was certainly true of No. 2,

---

[1] *Mitt.* 1897, 153.  [2] Mommsen, *Staatsrecht,* i. 328–329; ii. 594–595.
[3] Mommsen, *Staatsrecht,* ii. 1054–1058; Marquardt, *Staatsverwaltung,* ii. 484–487.  [4] *Ann. d. Ist.* 1858, 265–297, 391–392.
[5] *CIL.* vi. 2959–3090.

which could not have been so far out at first. All the barracks which can be definitely located, except this No. 2, were close to the Servian wall, and so arranged that each cohort had charge of two adjacent regions. The natural combinations were I and II, III and V, IV and VI, VII and IX, VIII and X, XI and XIV,[1] XII and XIII.

**The City of Aurelian**. — The last stage in the development of the city was marked by its being inclosed again within walls. For nearly six hundred years there had been practically no fear of foreign invasion, but in the latter half of the third century the northern barbarians became so threatening that the open capital of the world was converted into a fortified city.

The wall was begun by the emperor Aurelian (270–275 A.D.), and finished by his successor Probus (276–288).[2] It must have been very imperfectly constructed or else strangely neglected, for it had to be extensively restored in the reign of Honorius, under the supervision of Flavius Macrobius Longinianus, prefect of the city in the year 403. This is known from three famous inscriptions[3] which are built into the wall over the porta Tiburtina, the porta Praenestina, and the porta Portuensis. Serious breaches were also made by the Goths under Totila in the sixth century,[4] and repaired by Belisarius. This wall, commonly known as the Aurelian wall, is the fortification of the modern city, except on the right bank of the river. Its usefulness is entirely past, and as a result of many centuries of injury and decay, it presents the appearance of a ruin.

In consequence of the invasion of the Saracens in 846 A.D., Pope Leo IV built a wall which inclosed the Vatican, St. Peter's, and the Borgo, and extended to the river. This section of the city was then known by the name of civitas Leonina, or the city of Leo. In 1642 Urban VIII began the construction

---

[1] Richter, *Top.*[2] 54 n.

[2] Zos. i. 49; Vop. *Vit. Aur.* 21; Jordan, I. 1. 340–392.

[3] *CIL.* vi. 1188–1190.     [4] Procop. *Bell. Goth.* iii. 22.

of another wall which extended from the Castle of St. Angelo round the Leonine City, and along the western slope of the Janiculum to the Tiber, opposite the Aventine. This wall is still kept in repair for military purposes.

The length of the wall as restored by Honorius, according to Lanciani's[1] latest measurements, was 18,837 metres, and there is no doubt that this restoration was made on exactly the line of the original structure of Aurelian and Probus. Its course probably coincided in general with the customs-barrier (p. 59), being determined primarily by the necessity of inclosing the territory actually covered by the city at the time; and if this had been the only consideration, the line of the wall would have coincided with the outer boundary of the regions. On the other hand, military and engineering considerations made it necessary to take advantage of the character of the ground, and to make use of such structures already existing as could become a part of the fortifications. This is clearly seen at many points, but especially where the line does not coincide with the limits of the regions. This difference, however, seems on the whole to have been comparatively slight.

Appended to the Einsiedeln Itinerary is a description of the wall, evidently made by the official in charge of the restoration of Honorius, which gives the names of the gates, and the number of the *turres, propugnacula, posternae, fenestrae*, etc., throughout its whole extent.[2]

Beginning on the north at the bank of the Tiber, the wall extended east beyond the limits of regions IX and VII, in order to make use of the enormously strong retaining wall already built round the Pincian hill, then occupied by the horti Aciliorum ; and from this point, in the same general direction, to the northwest corner of the castra Praetoria. These barracks were already inclosed by strong fortifications which became a part of the new wall. From the castra Prae-

---

[1] *Ruins*, 68; *BC.* 1892, 87–111.

[2] Jordan, II. 155–178, 578–582; Richter, *Top.*[2] 393–394.

toria the wall ran southeast to the point where the via Labicana and the via Praenestina divided, which was the meeting-place of seven aqueducts.  For several hundred yards the magnifi- cent Claudian aqueduct formed the wall, it being necessary only to close the open arches.  Turning sharply to the south- west it followed, with many changes in direction, the slopes of the Caelian and the Aventine to the extreme southwest point of the latter hill, where it crossed the via Ostiensis. Thence the line ran directly to the Tiber and north along its bank to the Emporium in order to inclose the enormous store- houses of region XII.  On the right bank, the course of the wall seems to have been determined solely by military considerations, as it was built in two almost straight lines from the fortified top of the Janiculum to the nearest points on the river, and probably did not include all of region XIV. The southernmost of these two lines ran to the river opposite the Emporium.  The circuit was completed by continuing the wall along the left bank, from the porta Flaminia to a point opposite the end of the northern line from the Janiculum, and the passage of the river itself seems to have been barred by chains stretched across the stream between the opposite ends of the wall.  There were at this time several bridges across the river, but the exact method of uniting them with the wall so as to form a part of the system of fortification is unknown.

It frequently happened that tombs stood directly in the way of the wall, especially where it crossed the roads leading out from the city.  In such cases the tombs were not destroyed, but carefully built into the masonry of the wall (pp. 420, 505).

The description in the Einsiedeln Itinerary gives the names of fourteen gates, as follows: Flaminia, Salaria, Pinciana, Nomentana, Tiburtina, Praenestina-Labicana, Asinaria, Latina, Metrovia, Appia, Ostiensis, Portuensis, Aurelia, and Cornelia.[1]

---

[1] For the description of the wall, gates, and roads, see chap. vii.

**Extensions of the Pomerium.** — The Pomerium[1] of the city of the Four Regions probably coincided with the line of its fortifications (p. 43), but this condition afterward ceased to exist, for the Aventine was within the later Servian wall, although outside the pomerium.[2] For unknown reasons no further extension of the pomerium was made until the time of Sulla, who based his action on the following principle, then appearing for the first time, *habebat autem ius proferendi pomerii qui populum Romanum agro de hostibus capto auxerat.*[3] In Sulla's time this referred to territory in Italy,[4] but later[5] the idea was expanded to cover the *ager barbaricus.* Nothing definite is known with regard to the line of Sulla's pomerium, except that it did not include the Aventine. Elsewhere it probably coincided in general with the Servian wall.

Roman writers[6] speak of extensions of the pomerium by Caesar, Augustus, Claudius, Nero, Trajan, and Aurelian, but more or less doubt has been cast upon this testimony in the case of all except Claudius. Such action on his part has been proved by unimpeachable literary testimony, and also by the discovery of five of the terminal stones, *cippi*, which he set up, and the inscriptions recording the fact.[7] Claudius finally included the Aventine within the city.

The pomerium was again extended by Vespasian in connection with his new survey of the city, and of the terminal stones set up in the years 73–75 A.D. three have been found, although there is no reference to this action in extant literature.

---

[1] Richter, *Top.*[2] 64–66; Jordan, I. 1. 319–336; Gilbert, III. 3–5, 9–13; Detlefsen, *Das Pomerium Roms und die Grenzen Italiens, Hermes,* 1886, 497–562; Hülsen, *Das Pomerium Roms in der Kaiserzeit, ib.,* 1887, 615–626.

[2] Cf., however, p. 48, note 4.  [3] Gell. xiii. 14. 3.

[4] Sen. *de Brev. Vit.* 13. 8.  [5] Vop. *Vit. Aur.* 21.

[6] Gell. xiii. 14; Dio Cass. xliii. 50; Vop. *loc. cit.;* Tac. *Ann.* xii. 24; *CIL.* vi. 930.

[7] *CIL.* vi. 1231; Ti. Claudius | Drusi f. Caisar | Aug. Germanicus | pont. max. trib. pot. | VIIII imp. XVI cos. IIII | censor p. p. | auctis populi Romani | finibus pomerium | ampliavit terminavitque.

Under Hadrian the line of the pomerium was again marked
out, and two of the stones have been discovered, but they
record only a restoration and not an extension.

The five stones of Claudius's pomerium are (Fig. 7) : —

(a) *CIL.* vi. 1231a, found in the campus Martius near S. Lucia
della Chiavica.

(b) *CIL.* vi. 31537c, found just outside the porta Salaria.

(c) *CIL.* vi. 1231b, 31537b, found near the porta Metrovia,
inside the Aurelian wall, not far from its original site. According to Ficoroni, this stone when found still bore the
number XXXV.

(d) *CIL.* vi. 31537a, found *in situ* southeast of monte Testaccio, with the number VIII.

(x) *BC.* 1909, 130, found *in situ* just outside the porta Salaria
near b, with the number CIIX.

Of Vespasian's pomerium, three terminal stones have been
found : —

(e) *CIL.* vi. 31538a, found outside the porta Pinciana, with
the number XXXI.

(f) *CIL.* vi. 1232, 31538b, found near the porta Ostiensis, just
inside the Aurelian wall, and 60 metres from d, with the
number XLVII.

(g) *NS.* 1900, 15–17; *BC.* 1899, 270–279; found under the
church of S. Cecilia in Trastevere, without numbering, and
probably not exactly in its original position.

Finally, two stones of Hadrian's restoration have been found,
both *in situ :* —

(h) *CIL.* vi. 1233a, under the house No. 18 in the piazza
Sforza, with the number VI.

(i) *CIL.* vi. 1233b, near S. Stefano del Cacco.

It is probable that even in the cases where the stones were
not found precisely *in situ*, they had not been removed to any
considerable distance.

A comparison of the positions of these terminal stones shows
(1) that north of the Pincian the pomerium of Vespasian, and
therefore that of Claudius, lay beyond the line of the Aurelian
wall; (2) that near the porta Metrovia pomerium and wall
probably coincided; (3) that the monte Testaccio was still
outside the pomerium; and (4) that as late as the time of
Hadrian a large part of the campus Martius had not been
included within the pomerium. Compare the position of the
stones *a*, *h*, *i*.

We are told that in Vespasian's time the porticus Octaviae
was also outside the pomerium, and it is probable that the
campus Martius proper (p. 340) was never within it, for this
district must always have been regarded as the real meeting-
place for the army of Rome, and outside of the civil jurisdic-
tion. The one stone (*g*) found in region XIV furnishes no
data sufficient to warrant any inference as to the line of the
pomerium on the right bank of the river. The inscription
on one stone (*h*) gives 480 Roman feet as the distance between
it and the next; that on another, 347 feet; and some of the
stones are marked with numbers; but all attempts to combine
these figures so as to derive any information as to the rest of
the pomerium line have proved abortive.

**Rome during the Empire.** — The appearance which the city
of Rome presented in the fourth century was the result achieved
by systematic effort on the part of nearly all the emperors
from Augustus to Constantine, ably seconded by their wealthy
courtiers. Only a detailed study of the methods employed
in construction and of the ruins now visible, as well as of the
gradual destruction of the city which was going on for twelve
centuries, and a comparison of the wealth of decorative material still displayed in Roman churches and palaces, can suffice
to give any adequate idea of the magnificence of Rome at the
period of its highest development.

As has been remarked (p. 57), the substitution of traver-

tine for tufa, the introduction of the newly worked Luna marble, and the importation of all kinds of marble, granite, and
decorative stone from the East, added to the countless spoils of
Greek and Sicilian cities which had been flowing to Rome ever
since the days of Marcellus, had already begun to affect the
architecture and appearance of the city in the half century
before Caesar's dictatorship.  Not until Caesar, however, do
we hear of any definite plans for the embellishment of the
capital.  Of these plans we get some hints in the literature[1]
of the period.  They included the removal of the squalid
quarter north of the Forum, the widening of the depression
between the Capitoline and the Quirinal, and the utilization of
part of the campus Martius for distinctively municipal purposes.  Caesar himself made a beginning by building the
forum Iulium directly adjoining the Forum proper, but his
scheme was not completely carried out until a century and a
half later.  Caesar had also thought of diverting the Tiber
from its course at a point near the pons Mulvius, and carrying
it in a new channel to the west of the Vatican and Janiculum, thus joining the two parts of the city and eliminating
all danger of inundation; but this great work was never
actually undertaken.

Whether Augustus only carried out the plans of his adoptive
father or supplemented them with his own, it is to him that
the chief glory of transforming Rome must be assigned.  Following his example, able coadjutors like Maecenas and Marcus
Agrippa took part in the same work, and to Agrippa especially
no small share of the credit for its accomplishment is due.
The activity of the Augustan period was most strikingly displayed in the Forum, in the forum of Augustus, in the district
north of the Servian wall near the Tiber, where the theatre
of Marcellus and the porticus Octaviae were erected, and on the
Palatine, where Augustus built the famous temple of Apollo

---

[1] Cic. *ad Att.* iv. 16. 14;  xiii. 20. 1;  33a. 1;  35. 1.

and the domus Augustana, which, with its successive additions, became from that time the residence of the emperors.

Maecenas reclaimed the gruesome region on the Esquiline along the Servian wall, and made it a public park; while Agrippa erected the first public baths and the original Pantheon in the campus Martius, and spanned the Tiber with a new bridge, the pons Agrippae.

No better *résumé* of what was accomplished can be given than that which Augustus himself caused to be inscribed in bronze on his own mausoleum in the campus Martius (p. 382):[1] —

Curiam et continens ei chalcidicum, templumque Apollinis in Palatio cum porticibus, aedem divi Iuli, lupercal, porticum ad circum Flaminium, quam sum appellari passus ex nomine eius qui priorem eodem in solo fecerat Octaviam, pulvinar ad circum maximum, aedes in Capitolio Iovis Feretri et Iovis Tonantis, aedem Quirini, aedes Minervae et Iunonis Reginae et Iovis Libertatis in Aventino, aedem Larum in summa sacra via, aedem deum Penatium in Velia, aedem Iuventatis, aedem Matris Magnae in Palatio feci. Capitolium et Pompeium theatrum utrumque opus impensa grandi refeci sine ulla inscriptione nominis mei. Rivos aquarum compluribus locis vetustate labentes refeci, et aquam quae Marcia appellatur duplicavi fonte novo in rivum eius inmisso. Forum Iulium et basilicam, quae fuit inter aedem Castoris et aedem Saturni, coepta profligataque opera a patre meo perfeci et eandem basilicam consumptam incendio ampliato eius solo sub titulo nominis filiorum meorum incohavi et, si vivus non perfecissem, perfici ab heredibus iussi. Duo et octoginta templa deum in urbe consul sextum ex decreto senatus refeci, nullo praetermisso quod eo tempore refici debebat. Consul septimum viam Flaminiam ab urbe Ariminum feci et pontes omnes praeter Mulvium et Minucium. In privato solo Martis Ultoris templum forumque Augustum ex manibiis feci. Theatrum ad aedem Apollinis in solo magna ex parte a privatis empto feci, quod sub nomine M. Marcelli generi mei esset.

Augustus introduced the systematic use of travertine, either alone, as in the theatre of Marcellus, or in combination with other materials, as in Tiberius' restoration of the temple of Castor; and also the practice of covering concrete and brick

---

[1] *Mon. Anc.* iv. 1–23. Cf. *AJA.* 1905, 427–440.

masonry with marble slabs, which produced such remarkable results.

During the lifetime of Augustus, Tiberius had actively engaged in the work of restoring and building; but after he became emperor, his natural disposition toward economy prevented the continuance of this policy, almost the only buildings the erection of which can be assigned to him being the domus Tiberiana on the Palatine, the temple of the deified Augustus, and an arch in the Forum.

Caligula added to the imperial palace on the Palatine, and connected it with the temples of Castor and Iuppiter Capitolinus, but the freaks of this madman left few permanent traces in the city. His successor Claudius is remembered for having brought to a successful completion the two largest aqueducts of Rome, the Anio vetus and the Claudia, and for the enlargement and restoration of the Circus Maximus, one of the most wonderful monuments of Rome.

In the principate of Nero occurred the greatest fire in the history of the city, which lasted, according to Tacitus,[1] nine days, destroyed three regions entirely and seven others partially, and left only four uninjured. This report is probably somewhat exaggerated,[2] although the district between the Palatine, the Esquiline, and the Caelian was burned over so far as to offer Nero a pretext for taking possession of it and building there his famous domus Aurea. This park and palace occupied an area 1.5 kilometres square, extending from the Palatine to the gardens of Maecenas on the Esquiline, and changing completely the appearance of this quarter of the city.

The domus Aurea was destroyed by the Flavian emperors, and its site restored to the use of the public, notably by the erection of the Colosseum and the baths of Titus. To the

---

[1] *Ann.* xv. 38.

[2] Profumo, *Le Fonti ed I Tempi dello Incendio Neroniano*, Rome, 1905; Emery, *Western Reserve University Bulletin*, 1897, 22–28; *Mitt.* 1891, 94–97; Gilbert, III. 34–36.

Flavians Rome owed the arch of Titus on the summa Sacra via, the palace on the Palatine, the Stadium, the completion of the temple of Claudius on the Caelian, the forum Pacis, the third of the imperial fora, the templum Sacrae Urbis, and the temple of Vespasian in the Forum, besides a vast amount of restoration which was carried out principally by Domitian.

The forum Transitorium, the fourth of the imperial fora, was begun by Domitian and finished during the short reign of Nerva, but it remained for Trajan to complete the series with his own forum, by far the largest and most magnificent of all. Space was obtained for the construction of this forum by cutting away the adjacent slopes of the Capitoline and the Quirinal. This united the old Forum and the campus Martius, and successfully completed Caesar's plan outlined one hundred and fifty years before.

The reign of Hadrian was preëminently a period of restoration and rebuilding ; yet this emperor, with the help of his Greek architects, erected at least three remarkable structures : the double temple of Venus and Roma on the summa Sacra via ; the Pantheon in its present proportions; and his own mausoleum on the right bank of the Tiber, the present castle of S. Angelo, with the bridge, pons Aelius, which connected it with the left bank of the river.

The double temple of Venus and Roma, the largest in the city, not only marked a new departure in temple-building, but necessitated a change in the general topography of the imme-diate neighborhood ; the Pantheon still remains the most won-derful creation of Roman architectural genius, and almost as strong terms might be used in describing the mausoleum. Hadrian also enlarged very considerably the palace on the Palatine.

Under the Antonines less was done, the principal new struc-tures being the column and temple of Marcus Aurelius, and the temple of Faustina in the Forum. Severus and Caracalla dis-played great energy in repairing the ravages of time and of

the terrible fire of Commodus in the year 191 A.D., and during
their reigns almost as much was done in the way of restoration as by Hadrian.  Severus built the most striking part of
the Palatine palace, the so-called Septizonium, a seven-zoned
structure at the south angle of the palace, and the first building of the city visible to one approaching by the via Appia.
The decadent taste of the period is shown by the arch of
Severus, which destroyed the symmetry of the western part of
the Forum.

Just south of the Aventine, Caracalla built his famous baths,
which were exceeded in size only by those afterward erected
by Diocletian on the Viminal.   These *thermae* formed one of
the most striking features of the city, there being no less than
eleven in the time of Constantine, enormous in extent and
imposing in appearance.

During the hundred years from Caracalla to Maxentius, with
the exception of the baths of Alexander and Diocletian, and
the temple on the Quirinal, which has often been called
Aurelian's temple of the Sun, no remarkable works were added
to those already in existence.  The Heroon of Romulus, the
son of Maxentius, in the Forum, and the arch and basilica of
Constantine were the last great triumphs of Roman architecture, and with them the development of imperial Rome may
be said to have ceased.

The result of Caesar's plans and the initiative of Augustus
had been the creation of the most magnificent city which the
world has ever seen,[1] for it must be remembered that these
countless marvellous buildings of all descriptions, as well as
the streets and squares, were completely filled with treasures
of art which for five centuries had been flowing in a steady
stream from all parts of the world to enrich its capital.

---

[1] See Bühlmann und Wagner, *Das Alte Rom.  Rundgemälde von Rom mit
dem Triumphzuge Constantins in Jahre 312* A.D.  Munich, 1892: a photo-
graphic reproduction of a panorama, painted by these artists, representing a
restoration of the Rome of the fourth century, taken from the Capitol.

# CHAPTER V.

## THE TIBER AND ITS BRIDGES.

**The Tiber.**— The Tiber flows through Rome in a channel which in classical times varied in width from 60 to 100 metres. So great is the amount of sand and mud which the river has always carried down, — according to recent calculations 4,000,000 cubic metres annually, — that the seashore at its mouth has steadily advanced, and the site of the original town of Ostia is now 6600 metres inland. The continual formation of bars at the mouth of the river and the consequent obstruction of navigation, as well as the increase in the danger of inundation as far up as Rome, made it necessary for the Roman engineers to spend much labor on the harbor at Ostia in dredging the old channels and in cutting new ones. Inscriptions[1] of Claudius and Trajan record measures of this sort. At Rome, the result of this alluvial deposit has been to raise the bed of the river 1 metre since the fall of the empire.

The inundations of the Tiber have always been a source of great danger to large sections of the city, not only near the river, where the water actually overflows, but as far away as the Pantheon, where the water sets back through underground channels. One hundred and thirty-two of these inundations[2] have been recorded since the traditional one when Romulus and Remus were exposed to the flood, one hundred and six of them since the Christian era. The highest was that of 1598, when the river rose 19.56 metres above its ordinary level. To guard in some measure against the dangers of inundation, especially the cutting away of the banks,

---

[1] *CIL*. xiv. 85.     [2] Lanciani, *Ruins*, 10.

the Romans began to build protecting walls at various points [1] at least as early as the second century B.C., and it is probable that the opus quadratum which surrounds the mouth of the Cloaca Maxima is older still.

Toward the end of the republic, the general oversight of the river and its banks was intrusted to certain *curatores* appointed by the senate, and in the year 15 A.D. they were organized into a standing board, the *curatores alvei Tiberis et riparum* (later, *et cloacarum urbis*).[2] To this board was intrusted the dredging of the channel, the building and repairing of the river walls, and the determination of the width of the strip of land on each side of the stream which technically formed the ripae. This strip was marked off by a line of terminal stones, at irregular intervals, which formed the boundary between public and private domain. The width of these *ripae* is unknown, but judging from the position of those terminal stones which have been found, they must have extended in length from the pons Mulvius to the church of S. Paolo fuori le mura, 3 kilometres below the city. Inscribed cippi [3] have been found dating from 54 B.C. to the reign of Hadrian.

Remains of walls of tufa, travertine, and brick have been found at various points along the river, which date from the earlier empire, but there is no definite reference in literature or inscriptions to such embankments before the third century.[4] The present government has been engaged for many years in building a magnificent embankment along both sides of the river for the whole extent of its course through the city, and this great undertaking has now been practically completed. The channel provided for the river is 100 metres in width,

---

[1] *BC.* 1889, 165–172 ; *Mitt.* 1889, 285.

[2] *BC.* 1889, 185–205 ; 1894, 39–51, 354–359.

[3] *CIL.* vi. 1234–1242 ; 31540–31557 ; *Mitt.* 1891, 130–136 ; 1892, 328–329 ; 1893, 319–320 ; *BC.* 1904, 88–90 ; 1906, 117.

[4] Vop. *Vit. Aur.* 47 ; *CIL.* vi. 1242.

except where it divides in flowing round the island, and the old line of the banks has been very materially altered by this process of straightening.

While this work was in progress near the pons Aelius, the embankments of the empire were discovered, and it was found that the bed was not made of equal width to the full depth of the stream, but that its section was triple, thus providing a suitable channel for the river at all stages of low or high water.[1]

**Bridges.** — The development of the relations between the left and the right banks of the Tiber is illustrated by the history[2] of the successive bridges from the earliest times down to the fifth century. If *pontifex* is really derived from *pons-facere*,[3] the authority of this college in matters of state religion may have been partly due to the importance of the bridge to the earliest settlers.

The bridges over the Tiber were constructed in the following chronological order.

(1) **Pons Sublicius.** Tradition agrees[4] in ascribing to Ancus Marcius the erection of the first bridge. It was called the pons Sublicius, from *sublica*,[5] a pile, and was constructed wholly of wood without metal of any sort whatsoever.[6] This bridge was invested with a sacred character, so that its preservation became a matter of religion, and after having been rebuilt many times, it was still in existence in the fifth century. Its antiquity is vouched for by its method of construction,

---

[1] For the literature, mostly Italian, bearing on the Tiber, its peculiarities, inundations, embankments, etc., see Lanciani, *Ruins*, 10, 12, 13.

[2] Jordan, I. 1. 393–430; Mayerhöfer, *Die Brücken im alten Rom, Gesch.-topographische Studien*, 1–63; Zippel, *JJ.* 1886, 481–499; Lanciani, *Ruins*, 16–26.

[3] Cf., however, *Archiv f. lat. Lex.* 1908, 221; Walde, *Lat. etym. Wörterb.*

[4] Liv. i. 33; Dionys. iii. 45; Plut, *Numa*, 9.

[5] Fest. 293.        [6] Pl. *NH.* xxxvi. 100.

which seems to have belonged to the period before the inhabitants of Latium had developed the working of metal far enough
for use in bridge-building; and we shall probably not be far
out of the way in assigning its first erection to the second stage
of the city's growth when the construction of the Nova via
points to a connection between the old Sacra via and the bridge
across the Tiber.[1]  The earliest form of this bridge was doubtless very simple, perhaps a series of floats which could easily
be disconnected at the approach of an enemy.

The position of the pons Sublicius is uncertain.[2]  The early
settlers of Rome might have taken advantage of the island as
a natural means of connection between the banks of the river,
and might have preferred to build two short bridges from it to
either side, rather than a long one below or above.  The first
reference to bridges to and from the island occurs in Livy's[3]
history of the year 192 B.C., where they are called duos pontes,
and later the island itself was spoken of as inter duos pontes.[4]
It is certain that a bridge was built from the left bank to the
island as early as the year 291 B.C., when the worship of
Aesculapius was established there, and by no means improbable that it was built long before that date.  As these early
bridges were probably of wood, some have maintained that the
first pons Sublicius consisted of the two which crossed at the
island.   From the island as an extreme northern point,
the pons  Sublicius has been placed in various positions, as far
down as the Aventine below the porta Trigemina.   The
strongest evidence seems to indicate a point between the porta

---

[1] *Mitt*. 1895, 160–162.

[2] Gilbert, II. 171–183, 217–223; Richter, *Die Befestigung des Janiculum*,
14 ff.; Mommsen, *Ber. d. k. sächs. Gesell. d. Wiss.* 1850, 320–326; Urlichs,
*Sitzungsb. d. k. bayr. Akad.* 1870, 459–499; Wecklein, *Hermes*, 1872, 178–184;
Jordan, I. 1. 402–407; 3. 632; Besnier, *L'Île Tibérine dans l'Antiquité*, Paris,
1902, 123–132.

[3] xxxv. 21. 5.

[4] Jordan, *FUR.* 42; Macrob, *Sat.* iii. 16. 14–17.

Trigemina and the ruined ponte Rotto, and very probably close to the latter.

(2) **Pons Mulvius,** the modern ponte Molle. This was the next in order of time after the pons Sublicius and the island-bridges, and carried the great via Flaminia across the Tiber, 3 kilometres north of the city. As this road was built in 220 B.C., the bridge must be at least as old, and may very probably be older, but the first reference to it is in the year 207 B.C.[1] Who Mulvius was is unknown. Twice[2] Aemilius Scaurus, censor in 110 B.C., is spoken of as its builder, and it needed no restoration[3] by Augustus. Of the six arches of the present structure, — restored for the last time in 1808, — four are ancient, but whether they belong to the bridge of 110 B.C. is uncertain. The material of the bridge is peperino, with travertine facing.

(3) **Pons Aemilius,** probably the ruined ponte Rotto, although some uncertainty[4] attaches to the history and identification of this bridge. The evidence is very scanty,[5] but seems to indicate that this was the name given to the first stone bridge within the limits of the city, which was begun in 179 and finished in 142 B.C. It crossed the river from the forum Boarium, just above the pons Sublicius, and was known in the fourth and fifth centuries as the **pons Lapideus** and **pons Lepidi** ;[6] in the middle ages as the **pons Senatorum**[7] and **pons Sanctae Mariae.** In 1598 part of the bridge was carried away by a flood, and not being repaired, it was thenceforth called the ponte Rotto. One arch only now stands in mid-stream. By some this is thought to be the bridge which was restored by the emperor Probus, and which is called pons Probi in the *Notitia.*

---

[1] Liv. xxvii. 51; Delbrück, *Hellenistische Bauten in Latium*, Strassburg, 1907, 3–12.

[2] Auct. *Vir. Ill.* 72; Amm. Marc. xxvii. 3. 9.   [3] *Mon. Anc.* iv. 20.

[4] *Ber. d. k. sächs. Gesell.* 1850, 320–326; Gilbert, III. 257–260; Delbrück, *op. cit.* 12–22.

[5] Plut. *Numa*, 9; Liv. xl. 51. 4; *CIL.* i.[2] p. 325; Lamprid. *Vit. Elag.* 17.

[6] Aethicus, *Cosmog.* 54.   [7] *Mirabilia*, 11.

(4) **Pons Fabricius**, the modern ponte dei Quattro Capi.   This stone bridge[1] still joins the left bank of the river with the island.   Inscriptions over the arches state that the bridge was built by L. Fabricius, *curator viarum*, in 62 B.C., and restored by M. Lollius and Q. Lepidus in 21 B.C.   This structure is the one now standing, no further restorations of importance having been necessary.   It is built of tufa and peperino with travertine facing, and has two semicircular arches, with a smaller one in the pier between.   The present parapet is modern, but the original was divided into panels by pilasters supporting four-headed hermae, and connected by a metal balustrade. The two hermae at the east end of the bridge are original, and from them the modern name is derived.   During the middle ages the bridge was known as the **pons Iudaeorum**, as it crossed the river directly from the Ghetto.

(5) **Pons Cestius**, the modern ponte di S. Bartolomeo.   This bridge leads from the island to the right bank of the river.   It is first mentioned in the *Notitia*, but its identification with the bridge restored by Symmachus in 370 A.D. and thenceforth known as **pons Gratiani**,[2] is certain.   Its original construction dates from the same period as the pons Fabricius, probably between 72 and 44 B.C., when the Cestii were in close relation with the leading statesmen of Rome.   Further restoration was made in the eleventh century and recently in 1886–1889.[3]   Of the three arches of the present structure, the central one alone contains some of the original material.

(6) **Pons Agrippae.**   Our knowledge of the existence of this bridge rests upon the inscription[4] on a stone cippus discovered in 1877, and upon the discovery, a dozen years later, of the

---

[1] Dio Cass. xxxvii. 45; Porph. *ad.* Hor. *Sat.* ii. 3. 36; *CIL*. i. 600; vi. 1305; *Mitt.* 1891, 135; Besnier, *L'Île Tibérine*, 94–105.

[2] Pol. Silvius, 545; *CIL*. vi. 1175; Besnier, *op.cit.* 107–119.

[3] *Mitt.* 1889, 282–285.

[4] *CIL*. vi. 31545.

remains of sunken piers,[1] 160 metres above the ponte Sisto. There is no other information in regard to the building, purpose, or history of this bridge, but its existence seems to be an assured fact.

(7) **Pons Neronianus.** In the *Mirabilia* mention is made of the pons Neronianus, which is further described, in a later edition of this *Mirabilia*,[2] as *pons ruptus ad S. Spiritum in Sassia.* The remains of its piers are about 100 metres below the ponte S. Angelo, and can still be seen at low water. As this bridge[3] is not mentioned in the *Notitia*, it must have been destroyed before the time of Constantine. It connected the campus Martius with the Vatican meadows where were the gardens of Agrippina and the circus of Nero, in which that emperor was especially fond of indulging in all manner of sports and orgies, and it was probably built between 60 and 64 A.D., to facilitate communication between this district and the city. The later pons Aelius rendered Nero's bridge unnecessary.

(8) **Pons Aelius,** the modern ponte S. Angelo. This bridge was built by Hadrian[4] in connection with his great mausoleum, and finished in 134 A.D. It was afterward called **pons Hadriani** and **pons Sancti Petri.**[5] As originally built,[6] it consisted of three main arches in the centre, with three smaller ones on the left and two on the right, making eight in all. From the central part, over the three main arches, the bridge sloped in each direction to the banks, more steeply on the left than on the right. The material is peperino with travertine facings. With the exception of the balustrade, which was mostly a restoration of the middle ages, the ancient structure

---

[1] *NS.* 1887, 323; *BC.* 1887, 306–313; 1888, 92–98; *Mitt.* 1889, 285–286; 1891, 135–136.

[2] *Anon. Magliabecchianus,* 158.     [3] Gilbert, III. 261.

[4] Spart. *Vit. Hadr.* xix. 11; *CIL.* vi. 973; Dio Cass. lxix. 23.

[5] *Anon. Magliab.* 158.

[6] *BC.* 1888, 129–131; 1893, 14–26; *NS.* 1892, 411–428; *Mitt.* 1893, 321–324.

of Hadrian was preserved until 1892, although two of the arches at the left end had been covered up by the embankment and were not visible.

The building of the new embankment has rendered it necessary to rebuild completely the ends of the bridge, so that only the three central arches of the original structure remain.

(9) **Pons Aurelius**, the modern ponte Sisto. In the list of bridges in the *Notitia*, we find the pons Aurelius. This name does not occur in the guide-books of the middle ages, but in its place a pons Antonini,[1] or pons Ianicularis,[2] which was partially destroyed in 772 and called *pons ruptus* until 1475, when it was rebuilt in its present shape by Sixtus V, and known thenceforth as the ponte Sisto.

In 1878, immediately below the first arch of the ponte Sisto, were found [3] fragments of an earlier bridge and also of a memorial arch which stood at its entrance. On some of these fragments are inscriptions which record the rebuilding of arch and bridge by the emperor Valentinian in the years 365-366 A.D.[4] The identification of this bridge of Valentinian with the pons Antonini and the pons Aurelius is now regarded as certain; and while nothing is known as to the time when it was first erected, the fact that it bore the names of Aurelius and Antoninus makes it certain that it was built by one of the emperors who belonged to both these families. It is usually attributed to Caracalla, who thus brought the buildings erected by Severus in Trastevere [5] into closer connection with the campus Martius. It may, however, with equal probability be assigned to Marcus Aurelius.

(10) **Pons Probi**. In the *Notitia* the list of bridges then existing in Rome reads thus: *pontes octo, Aelius Aemilius Aurelius Mulvius Sublicius Fabricius Cestius Probi*. The identification

---

[1] *Mirabilia*, 11.     [2] *Anon. Magliab.* 158.     [3] *BC.* 1878, 241; 1881, 11.
[4] *CIL.* vi. 31402–31412; *EE.* iv. 799, 800; Amm. Marc. xxvii. 3. 3; *NS.* 1892, 50, 234–235.     [5] Spart. *Vit. Sev.* 19.

of this last is still very doubtful. The name occurs only once elsewhere, in an *enarratio fabricarum urbis Romae,* taken from the *Curiosum* and inserted in the calendar published by Polemius Silvius in the year 448 A.D. In the *Mirabilia* we find mention of the pons Theodosii,[1] — also called pons Marmoreus and pons in ripa Romaea, — and to this bridge there are several references in the letters of Symmachus,[2] from which it appears that, although begun in 381, it was not finished until 387 A.D. It was the last of the bridges of the city, and the farthest down-stream, as it crossed the river under the Aventine near the Marmorata. It was partially destroyed in the eleventh century, and completely in 1484. The bases of the piers still exist beneath the level of the river. The identification of this pons Theodosii with the pons Probi depends upon the answer given to the question whether or not Theodosius erected an absolutely new structure where none had previously existed. Decisive evidence is lacking,[3] and scholars are quite equally divided. If the pons Probi is not the pons Theodosii, then the former name must have belonged to one of the other bridges, probably the pons Aemilius, which may have been restored by Probus.

**Insula Tiberina.** — The island [4] in the Tiber seems to be the extremity of the ridge of which the Capitoline is a part. Owing perhaps to the harder character of its tufa, the river did not cut it away entirely, but divided and flowed on either side. The island thus formed is 269 metres long and its greatest width is 67 metres. According to tradition,[5] its formation was due to the great quantity of grain which was cut from the estates of the Tarquins in the campus Martius after

---

[1] *Mitt.* 1893, 320; Gilbert, III. 262.

[2] *Epist.* iv. 70. 1; v. 76. 3.     [3] *BC.* 1877, 167; 1878, 243–247.

[4] Besnier, *L'Île Tibérine dans l'Antiquité* (Bibliothèque des Écoles françaises d'Athènes et de Rome), Paris, 1902.

[5] Liv. ii. 5; Dionys. v. 13; Plut. *Popl.* 8.

the expulsion of the kings, and thrown into the river just
above this point.   Whether the first bridge built by the Romans crossed the island or not (p. 78), there is no allusion
to any connection between it and the city until 291 B.C., and
it formed no integral part of the city until some time after
that date.   In the reorganization of Augustus, it was included
in region XIV.

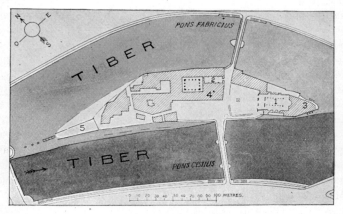

FIG. 8. — THE INSULA TIBERINA.

| | |
|---|---|
| 1. S. Bartolomeo. | 4. Mosaic of Iuppiter |
| 2. S. Giovanni. |    Iurarius. |
| 3. Morgue. | 5. Modern Mole. |

In the year 292 B.C., in consequence of a pestilence in Rome,
an embassy was sent to Epidaurus [1] to bring back the statue
of the god Aesculapius.   The embassy returned the next year,
bringing, not the statue, but a serpent from Epidaurus, which
abandoned the ship and swam to the island.   A temple to
Aesculapius [2] was at once erected and the whole island conse-

---

[1] Liv. x. 47; *Epit.* xi; Ov. *Met.* xv. 739; Val. Max. i. 8. 2.
[2] Plut. *Quaest. Rom.* 94; Gilbert, III. 72–73; Jordan, *Commentarii in hon.
Mommsen,* 356–396; *CIL.* vi. 9–12.

crated as its temenos. It became therefore *sacra,* and did not pass into private possession. The island was also known as insula Aesculapii,[1] insula serpentis Epidauri,[2] and inter duos pontes.[3] The temple was restored,[4] probably about the time when the pons Fabricius was built, and its site is now occupied by the church of S. Bartolomeo. Some of the columns of the nave belonged probably to the temple or to the neighboring porticus.

Two other temples were afterward erected within the original temenos of Aesculapius. (1) The temple of Faunus, which was vowed in 196 and dedicated in 194 B.C.[5] It was built with money received in fines, and is described as prostyle in form.[6] (2) The temple of Iuppiter, which was vowed by L. Furius Purpureo in 200 B.C. and dedicated January 1, 194.[7] It is probable that the cult here celebrated was that of Iuppiter Veiovis,[8] and that this temple stood in some relation to that of Iuppiter Veiovis on the Capitoline.

Besides these three temples, there was a shrine to the river god Tiberinus,[9] to whom a sacrifice was offered on December 8, and an altar, or shrine, to Semo Sancus[10] or Deus Fidius, which gave rise to the belief among the early Christians that Simon Magus was worshipped here.

As a result of the legend that the serpent had been brought by ship from Epidaurus, the island itself was made to resemble a ship. A stone platform was built round it, and upon this a wall was erected which in shape exactly reproduced the

---

[1] Suet. *Claud.* 25.

[2] Sidon. Apoll. *Epist.* i. 7.

[3] Jordan, *FUR.* 42; *Chronogr. a. 354*, p. 145.

[4] Varro, *LL.* vii. 57; *CIL.* vi. 6, 7, 12.

[5] *CIL.* i.[2] p. 309; Liv. xxxiii. 42; xxxiv. 53; Ov. *Fast.* ii. 193.

[6] Vitr. iii. 2. 3.

[7] Ov. *Fast.* i. 293; Liv. xxxi. 21.

[8] Gilbert, III. 82–84; Jordan, I. 3. 635. Cf. for opposite view, Besnier, *op. cit.* 249–272.

[9] *CIL.* i.[2] p. 336.

[10] *CIL.* vi. 567; Justin. Martyr. *Apol.* i. 26; Jordan, I. 3. 636.

sides of a Roman ship.[1]   Before the great changes in the river-
bed caused by the building of the new embankments, a considerable portion of the travertine stern could still be seen at
the east end of the island.   An obelisk, fragments of which
are in the museum at Naples, is thought to have represented
the mast.   We have no information as to the time when this
curious idea was carried out, but the remains of the walls
point to the same period as that of the construction of the pons
Fabricius, and it is quite possible that the erection of the two
stone bridges was part of the same plan as the building of the
ship.

Suetonius [2] says that sick slaves were brought to the temple
of Aesculapius and left there to be cured, and in general it
appears that there was some attempt to reproduce the effect of
the great sanitarium at Epidaurus.

A statue of Julius Caesar [3] was erected on the island, and we
know of a *vicus Censorius*.[4]   In the middle ages the island was
called insula Lycaonia,[5] for some unknown reason.

**The Emporium.** — The first traffic with the seacoast in which
Rome engaged was in salt, which was brought by boat from
Ostia to the Salinae,[6] or salt warehouses just outside the porta
Trigemina, and thence by the via Salaria [7] into the interior.

In time other commodities, as wood, wine, corn, and oil, began to be imported by ship, and the Salinae formed the nucleus
from which was developed the harbor and warehouse system
of Rome.   After the city became a metropolis and goods of all
descriptions were imported from all parts of the world, the
business of this region increased most remarkably.   Comparatively few of the ships that brought wares from over sea sailed
up to the city, their cargoes being transferred at Ostia.

---

[1] *Ann. d. Ist.* 1867, 389 ff.                        [2] *Claud.* 25.
[3] Tac. *Hist.* i. 86.          [4] *CIL.* vi. 975.     [5] Jordan, I. 3. 631.
[6] Pl. *NH.* xxxi. 89; Solin. i. 8.                     [7] Fest. *Epit.* 327.

The character of the river banks is such that something in the way of wharves or landing-places must have been provided at an early date; but the first record of anything of this sort is in the year 193 B.C.,[1] when the aedileship of M. Aemilius Lepidus and L. Aemilius Paulus was signalized by the building of the porticus Aemilia beyond the porta Trigemina, *emporio ad Tiberim adiecto.*

The term *Emporium*,[2] mentioned here for the first time, was applied to the bank itself and to the ground stretching back from it for some little distance, which was used as a landing-place, storehouse, and market. In the year 174 B.C. this open Emporium,[3] which extended down the river from the southwest corner of the Aventine, was paved, inclosed with barriers, and provided with flights of steps leading down to the water's edge. These steps rendered a river wall necessary, which was extended as the demands of commerce increased, until the whole bank, for 1 kilometre down-stream from the porta Trigemina, had been converted into one long quay.

The name portus,[4] in its widest meaning, was applied to the entire harbor, but it was also applied, with limiting adjectives, to different sections of the quay, which were assigned to different kinds of goods, as portus vinarius [5] and lignarius [6] (perhaps). Some of these sections seem to have been under the control of private individuals, and to have been called by their names, as the portus Licinii, etc.[7] It is, however, not entirely certain that all these sections of quay were in this region.

Excavations [8] carried on along the river since 1868 have brought to light fragments of the wall and quay and of the steps and paved inclines which led down to the water to facili-

---

[1] Liv. xxxv. 10. 12.    [2] Gilbert, III. 240–243; Jordan, I. 1. 429–434; 3. 171–173.
[3] Liv. xli. 27. 8; Jordan, *FUR.* 44.
[4] Jordan, I. 1. 429–430; 3. 174.    [5] *CIL.* vi. 9189–9190.
[6] Liv. xxxv. 41.
[7] Cassiod. i. 25; *CIL.* xv. 408–412; *NS.* 1892, 347.
[8] *Bull. d. Ist.* 1872, 134–135; *BC.* 1886, 34–35.

tate unloading, and a few of the stone corbels, sometimes in the shape of lions' heads, which projected out from the quay and were pierced with holes for mooring-rings. Part of the masonry of this quay is of opus quadratum and belongs to the last century of the republic, but the greater portion is of brickwork[1] and dates from the time of Hadrian.

Under the empire, one of the chief articles of import was marble, and a long stretch of quay, beneath the Aventine and above the Emporium proper, was devoted to its reception. This part was called the **Marmorata**, a name still preserved in the via della Marmorata. There was also an **officina marmoraria**,[2] where the stone was worked.

In the years of 1868–1870, more than six hundred blocks[3] of unused marble were found scattered over the Marmorata and the Emporium, some of which are still to be seen. Many of them had Greek inscriptions. Besides the Marmorata, another wharf, built for the landing of marbles, was discovered in 1891, about 150 metres above the ponte S. Angelo.[4] This was not a quay, but a stone platform, 26 metres long and 14 wide, projecting into the river at an angle of 40°. The convenience of having a landing-place for marble and granite in the upper part of the city is obvious. Outside the porta Trigemina was a column or statue of L. Minucius Augurinus,[5] *praefectus annonae* in 439 B.C., erected by popular subscription.

**Navalia**. — The Navalia, or docks for ships of war,[6] were beyond the porta Flumentana in the campus Martius, opposite the prata Quinctia (p. 508), just west of the modern palazzo Farnese. We do not know when they were first constructed,

---

[1] *Ber. d. k. sächs Gesell.* 1848, 137 ff.        [2] *BC.* 1891, 23–36.

[3] *Ann. d. Ist.* 1870, 106–204 ; *NS.* 1886, 22.

[4] *BC.* 1891, 45-60; 1892, 175-178; *Mitt.* 1892, 322–326.

[5] Pl. *NH.* xviii. 15; xxxiv. 21.

[6] Liv. iii. 26 ; Plut. *Cato Min.* 39; Gilbert, III. 146–150; Richter, *Top.*[2] 200-203; Jordan, *FUR.* 45–46; Jordan, I. 3. 485–486.

but it was prior to 338 B.C., for in that year the ships captured at Antium[1] were moored at these docks.   The mooring of captured ships here continued to be the custom for nearly two centuries, as those taken from the Macedonians were also brought here in 167.[2]  In the middle of the second century B.C. the docks were burned, and rebuilt by the Greek architect Hermodorus.[3]  References to them after this date are infrequent, but in the sixth century Procopius[4] speaks of them as ἐν μέσῃ τῇ πόλει, which probably means that they were within the line of the fortifications of Aurelian.  The Navalia included an arsenal, which seems to have become a sort of museum, and other buildings for various purposes, and must have covered a considerable area.  Whether ships were actually built at these docks[5] is a disputed point.  In any case, their importance must have declined very rapidly after the second Punic war, as it would no longer have been necessary for Roman ships to sail up the river.  In 147 B.C. the Carthaginian hostages were detained[6] in the Navalia.

A porta Navalis, mentioned by Festus,[7] has been thought by some to be the gate into the inclosure, but without good reason. In 179 B.C. the censor Fulvius built a porticus *extra portam Trigeminam et aliam post navalia et ad fanum Herculis*,[8] and on fragment 61 of the Marble Plan is the inscription NAVALEM-FER. . . .   This evidence, together with the passage in Procopius already cited, and a bronze of Antoninus Pius,[9] have been used in an attempt[10] to prove the existence of other earlier docks, Navale inferius, just north of the porta Trigemina, and, while this seems probable, no general agreement has been reached.

---

1 Liv. viii. 14.

2 Liv. xlv. 42.

3 Cic. *de Or.* i. 62.

4 *Bell. Goth.* iv. 22.

5 Serv. *ad Aen.* xi. 326.

6 Polyb. xxxvi. 3.

7 *Epit.* 179; Jordan, I. 3. 486.

8 Liv. xl. 51.

9 Cohen, *Méd. Imp.* ii. 271, No. 17.

10 Hülsen, *Dissertazioni dell' Accademia Pontificia*, ser. ii. vol. vi. ; *Zeitschr. f. Numismatik*, 1899, 32; Jordan, I. 3. 143–145; Merlin, *L'Aventin*, 121–123.

# CHAPTER VI.

## AQUEDUCTS AND SEWERS.

**Rome's Water Supply**. — Before the building of the first
aqueduct in 312 B.C., the Romans depended for their water
supply upon the Tiber and upon wells, springs, and rain water
caught and stored in cisterns.[1] The soil was so rich in springs
and underground streams that wells could be sunk successfully
at any point, and the average depth necessary was only about
5 metres.[2] Such wells (*putei*) were common from the earliest
period, and the recent excavations in the Forum (p. 273) have
brought to light upward of thirty, some of which date from
the republic. It is therefore improbable that the water of the
Tiber itself was ever used very extensively for drinking purposes, although certain of the popes of the sixteenth century
have left a record of their preference for this substantial
beverage.[3] The word *fons* was employed by the Romans to
denote, not only natural springs, but also artificial fountains.
The *Notitia* states that in the fourth century there were in the
city twelve hundred and twelve public fountains, of which the
great majority must have been of the artificial kind. These
fountains were ordinarily in the form of basins (*lacus*), large
and small, or of spouting jets (*salientes*).

The most famous natural springs were the following: fons
Camenarum,[4] the spring of the Muses, which, together with a
sacred grove and shrine, was in the vallis Egeriae (p. 432)

---

[1] Frontinus, *de Aq*. i. 4.   [2] Lanciani, *Acque*, 6.   [3] Lanciani, *Acque*, 3–4.
[4] Vitr. viii. 3. 1; Front. *de Aq*. i. 4; Lanciani, *Acque*, 11–13; Herschel,
*Frontinus*, 131–132; Jordan, I. 3. 206–208.

outside the porta Capena, northeast of the via Appia. This valley is marked by the via della Mola and the brook Marrana, and the fountain itself is usually identified with a spring near the villa Fonseca. Considerable changes have taken place in this region, and there are several springs near by, so that a positive identification seems rather hazardous. Fons Apollinis,[1] the position of which is unknown, but which has been identified with a spring now flowing in the villa Mattei on the Caelian, not far from the fons Camenarum, and also with one near the west end of the Circus Maximus. Fons Iuturnae, perhaps the most celebrated of all Roman springs, which was discovered in the year 1900 just behind the temple of Castor. Its site and the ruins of the lacus are described on page 214. Aqua Mercurii,[2] a spring which is thought to be one of those now flowing in the gardens of the villa Mattei. Its waters were conducted in an artificial channel through the valley of the Circus Maximus to the Cloaca Maxima.

Among the other springs mentioned in literature, which seem to have had a special claim to celebrity, are the Lautolae (p. 192) or hot springs *ad Ianum geminum*, still a puzzle to topographers, and the fons Lupercalis,[3] the earliest of all, which gushed forth from the Lupercal (p. 130) on the slope of the Cermalus. The porta Fontinalis in the Servian wall was named from a spring which may be that now visible in the cortile di S. Felice in the via della Dateria, sometimes called the aqua Fontinalis.[4] Beneath the Carcer on the slope of the Capitoline is a spring, which perhaps supplied the Arx in the earliest days of the city, and from which the lower part of the Carcer, the Tullianum, is generally supposed to have derived its name (*tullius* = 'a spring'?). This derivation has lately been disputed (p. 252).

[1] Front. *loc. cit.* ; Lanciani, *Acque*, 13.

[2] Ov. *Fast.* v. 673; Lanciani, *Acque*, 9–11. Cf. *BC.* 1904, 217–230.

[3] Lanciani, *Acque*, 21.

[4] Cf., however, p. 50, note 2.

Rain water was caught in the *compluvia* of the houses, but there was probably less necessity for its use in Rome than in most cities. Many large cisterns (*piscinae*) have been found in different parts of the city; but it is usually difficult to tell whether they were intended only for rain water, or were reservoirs fed by small pipes from a spring or aqueduct. A series of underground cisterns has been found on the Pincian,[1] which were made for the villa of the Acilii Glabriones and consist of galleries cut in the tufa rock and intersecting each other at right angles (p. 482). All other cisterns, so far discovered, are constructed in a similar manner.

**Aqueducts.** — Springs and cisterns must have proved inadequate to supply the rapidly growing city, for in 312 B.C. the first of that long series of aqueducts was constructed which has justly been regarded as among the most remarkable and distinctive features of ancient Rome.[2] Our knowledge of their history and general administration is chiefly due to the fortunate preservation of a treatise on the subject, the *De Aquis Urbis Romae*, by Sextus Julius Frontinus, who was appointed *curator aquarum* in 97 A.D. and signalized his tenure of office by a complete reform of the system. This work of Frontinus is amply illustrated by the many remains of arches, channels (*specus*), distributing reservoirs (*castella aquae*), and pipes of all sizes, which have been preserved.

The first of these aqueducts, the **Appia**,[3] was built in 312 B.C. by the censors Appius Claudius Caecus and C. Plautius Venox. It was fed by springs situated east of Rome, 780 passus

---

[1] Lanciani, *Acque*, 29–30.

[2] The most authoritative works on the water supply and aqueducts of Rome are: Lanciani, *I Commentarii di Frontino intorno le Acque e gli Acquedotti*, Rome, 1880; Herschel, *The Two Books on the Water Supply of the City of Rome of Sextus Julius Frontinus*, Boston, 1899; and Ashby, *The Builder*, 1908, 37, 64, 89, 111, 142, 174, 203, 234; *JJ.* 1909, 246–260.

[3] Front. 5, 7, 18, 22, 65, 79, 126; Lanciani, *Acque*, 34–43; Herschel, 143–146.

(1153 metres) to the left of the via Collatina, between the sixth and seventh milestones, near the Anio.[1] The channel (*specus*) was subterranean, and entered the city more than 15 metres below the surface, near the temple of Spes vetus, **ad Spem veterem** (p. 462), just inside the porta Praenestina (Maggiore). Thence it ran along the south slope of the Caelian, across the depression on the Aventine, to a point approximately halfway between S. Saba and S. Prisca ; then, making a sharp turn to the northwest, it crossed the Aventine and ended at the Salinae, just outside the porta Trigemina. The total length of the channel was 11,190 passus (16.47 kilometres), entirely underground except for a distance of 60 passus (89 metres), where it was carried on arches across the via Appia, outside the porta Capena. Remains of this specus have been discovered at various points on the Aventine along the via di S. Paolo, especially in the old quarries near S. Saba. Augustus increased the amount of water brought to the city by this aqueduct by building a branch, the **aqua Appia Augusta**, from some springs a little more than 1 kilometre north of the sixth milestone on the via Praenestina. This joined the old Appia *ad Spem veterem*. The specus of this branch was entirely subterranean, and 6360 passus (9.18 kilometres) in length.

The **Anio vetus**[2] was begun in 272 B.C. by the censor M'. Curius Dentatus, and finished in 270 by M. Fulvius Flaccus, who with Dentatus had been created *duumvir aquis perducendis*. The original cost was paid out of spoils taken from Pyrrhus. Its source was the river Anio, 1 kilometre above the monastery of S. Cosimato near Mandela, 17 kilometres above Tivoli. Its course can be traced from the source to Gallicano, but from there to Rome it is uncertain. This aqueduct entered the city *ad Spem veterem*, at about the present ground level, struck the Servian wall and followed it

---

[1] Cf., however, *BC*. 1903, 243–248 ; 1904, 215–232.

[2] Front. 6, 7, 9, 18, 21, 92, and freq.; *CIL*. vi. 1243, 2345; Lanciani, *Acque*, 43–58; Herschel, 146–150.

to the porta Esquilina. For part of this distance it was built
in the agger, and during the modern building operations around
the railroad station it was often exposed to view. The specus
was subterranean, except for a distance of 221 passus (327
metres) outside the porta Praenestina, where it was carried
above ground. Its total length was 43,000 passus (63.64
kilometres).[1] At the second milestone outside the city, a
branch, built by Augustus and called the specus Octavianus, led
off from the Anio vetus and ran toward the via Latina and
the horti Asiniani, probably near the porta Metrovia.

The Marcia[2] was begun in 144 B.C. by the praetor Q. Marcius
Rex, who had been ordered by the senate to repair the two
existing aqueducts, Appia and Anio, and to build a third, as
the supply of water was insufficient. The completion of the
Marcia required five years, and the water was successfully
brought to the top of the Capitoline in 140 B.C.

This was the first of the high-level aqueducts, its source
being about 275 metres above Rome in the Sabine mountains.
This source was two or three — perhaps those known as the
second and third Serena — of a series of eight springs which
extend along the north side of the Anio, between Arsoli and
Agosta, at the base of monte della Prugna and near the thirty-
sixth milestone of the via Valeria. The water of all these
springs is remarkably clear and cold, and the water of the
aqua Marcia was the best brought into Rome in antiquity.[3]

The course of the Marcia can be traced from its source to
Gallicano, as it winds down the hills, following the Anio to
Tivoli, and then bending to the south, crossing the valleys on
bridges and passing through the hills in tunnels. This part
of its course is practically the same as that of the Anio vetus,
the Claudia and the Anio novus. At one point a single bridge,

---

[1] Cf., however, *CR.* 1902, 336.

[2] *CIL.* vi. 1244–1251; Pl. *NH.* xxxvi. 121; Front. *passim;* Lanciani, *Acque,*
58–81, 86–102; Herschel, 150–162.

[3] Vitr. viii. 3. 1; Pl. *NH.* xxxi. 41.

the ponte Lupo, carries all four. From Gallicano the Marcia ran underground to the sixth milestone on the via Latina, and thence to the porta Praenestina on arches which continued to the porta Tiburtina (porta S. Lorenzo), and to the distributing station on the Viminal.

The later aqueducts, Julia and Tepula, ran on these same arches as far as the porta Tiburtina, above the specus of the Marcia, and the stretch between this gate and the porta Praenestina was afterward incorporated into the Aurelian wall. Where these arches began at Roma Vecchia, their ruins are still visible.

Within the city the Marcia was carried in pipes from the Viminal to the Capitoline, and above ground to the Caelian. During the reign of Nero, a branch called the rivus Herculaneus[1] was built, which ran underground from the main aqueduct, a little south of the porta Tiburtina, across the Caelian to the porta Capena.[2] In the villa Wolkonsky some remains of an aqueduct have been found, consisting of tufa blocks pierced with a circular channel, which probably belonged to this branch.[3] This was extended by Trajan to the Aventine. In 212 A.D. Caracalla built another branch, the aqua Antoniniana,[4] nearly 7 kilometres long, from a point near the porta Furba (3 kilometres from the porta S. Giovanni), to carry water to his baths. This crossed the via Appia on the so-called arch of Drusus (p. 434), and near by are ruins of other arches. In 284 A.D. Diocletian restored the Marcia; and afterward the name Iovia[5] was applied either to the whole aqueduct, or to the branch Antoniniana.

Augustus increased the volume of water of the Marcia by building a short branch[6] from its head to another spring about 1200 metres farther from Rome. This additional supply was

---

[1] Front. 19. Cf. also p. 101.   [2] Cf. Juv. iii. 11.

[3] BC. 1886, 406; 1888, 400; Mitt. 1889, 235.

[4] Not., appendix, 1; CIL. vi. 1245; Lanciani, Acque, 103–106.

[5] Lanciani, Acque, 106–107.   [6] Mon. Anc. iv. 11.

for use in time of drought, and could be turned into the Claudia instead of the Marcia, if necessary. The total length of the Marcia was 91.3 kilometres. Its specus was underground from its source to the point where it emerged at Roma Vecchia, except at a few places where it was carried across valleys on arches.

The Tepula [1] was built in 125 B.C. by the censors Cn. Servilius Caepio and L. Cassius Longinus. It was fed by volcanic springs in the Alban hills between Frascati and Rocca di Papa, 2000 passus (2960 metres) west of the tenth milestone on the via Latina. These springs are now called the Sorgenti dell' Acqua Preziosa. Their temperature is about 63° Fahrenheit, hence the name Tepula. Until the building of the Julia, the Tepula flowed in its own channel, but its course is wholly unknown.

The Julia [2] was built in 33 B.C. by Marcus Agrippa. Its source was 2000 passus (2960 metres) west of the twelfth milestone on the via Latina, 3 kilometres farther up the Alban hills toward Rocca di Papa than that of the Tepula. The springs are now called Il Fontanile degli Squarciarelli di Grotta Ferrata. About 16 kilometres from the city, Agrippa caused the waters of the Tepula and Julia to unite in the proportion of one to three, and they flowed in one specus for nearly 7 kilometres. The resultant temperature of the mixture was about 53°. At the sixth milestone this aqueduct was again divided into two channels, — one having three times the capacity of the other, — and so brought to the city. The point of division was close to the Marcia where it emerged from its subterranean specus, and all three aqueducts were conducted thence to the city on the same arches. The line may easily be traced, for the piers of the original arches now serve as founda-

---

[1] Front. 8, 9, 19, 68–69, and *passim;* Lanciani, *Acque*, 81–83, 86–98, 101–102; Herschel, 163–164.

[2] Front. 9, 18–19, 69, 76, 83, and *passim;* Lanciani, *Acque*, 83–98, 102–103; Herschel, 164–170.

tions for the acqua Felice, which was constructed in the sixteenth century. The length of the channel of the Tepula is
estimated at 17.745 kilometres; that of the Julia is stated to
have been 15,426 passus (22.83 kilometres).

From the porta Tiburtina, the Marcia and Tepula were carried to the main distributing station on the site of the present
treasury building, with a branch leading off to another station
near the porta Viminalis. The Julia branched off near the
porta Tiburtina and was carried to the Esquiline, where in
the piazza Vittorio Emanuele can still be seen the remains of
the castellum built by Alexander Severus (p. 463). Some
of the piers of this branch are still standing in the piazza
Guglielmo Pepe, and the foundations of others have been
found during excavations in the neighborhood. Most of those
now standing measure 2.90 by 2.95 metres at the base.

The Virgo [1] was built by Agrippa to supply his baths in the
campus Martius, and was finished June 9, 19 B.C. Its source
was several springs near the eighth milestone on the via Collatina, and near the present railroad station of Salone. It is said
that the name Virgo was given to this aqueduct because its
source was pointed out to the soldiers by a girl. As the springs
were in a swampy region, their waters were first collected in a
stone basin, part of which is still in existence. The course of
the aqueduct was toward the porta Praenestina, like so many of
the others; but about 1 kilometre from this gate, it bent
sharply and ran north for some distance, entering the city
under the villa Medici on the Pincian. The first piscina was
just east of the piazza di Spagna. Thence it was conducted to
the baths of Agrippa. The Virgo was restored by Claudius in
52 A.D. and is now in use, having been rebuilt by Pius V in
1570. At various points in the city portions of the original
structure still remain,[2] as in the garden of the palazzo Castel-

---

[1] Front. 10, 18, 22, 70, and *passim;* Pl. *NH.* xxxi. 42 ; xxxvi. 121; Dio Cass.
liv. 11 ; *CIL.* vi. 1252–1254; Lanciani, *Acque*, 120–130 ; Herschel, 170–172.
[2] *BC.* 1881, 61–67; 1883, 6–7, 51–52; *Mitt.* 1889, 269.

lani, at No. 12 via Nazareno (p. 480), and in the court of the palazzo Sciarra. The length of the Virgo was 14,105 passus (20.88 kilometres), of which 12,865 passus (19 kilometres) were underground. Of the part above ground, not quite half was on masonry substructures, and 700 passus (1036 metres) on arches, for the most part within the city limits.

The Alsietina,[1] or Augusta, was built by Augustus about 10 A.D., to supply his naumachia (p. 513) on the right bank of the Tiber. Its source was the lacus Alsietinus, the modern lake Martignano, 33 kilometres from Rome. The water was worthless for drinking purposes, and was only so used in time of drought. No remains of this aqueduct have been found, with the possible exception of one inscription.[2] Its length was 22,172 passus (32.8 kilometres).

The Claudia[3] was begun in 38 A.D. by Caligula, and finished in 52 by Claudius. This was the most magnificent of all Roman aqueducts, although not as long as the Anio novus or the Marcia. Its sources were three of the springs in the valley of the Anio, near those of the Marcia, and its course was down this valley to Tivoli, and round monte Ripoli to a point near Gallicano, following closely the line of the Anio vetus. Thence it skirted the hills to a point below Frascati, and crossed the Campagna to the distributing station *ad Spem veterem*. Domitian shortened the course by cutting a tunnel, 5 kilometres long, through monte Affliano. From the springs to the point (Le Capannelle) about 12 kilometres from Rome where the specus finally emerged, the channel was subterranean, except at various points in the mountains where it was carried across deep valleys on arches. Where this subterranean specus ended, — *intra septimum miliarium*, — a small reservoir was erected, and from here the Claudia ran above ground for 1 kilometre on substruc-

---

[1] Front. 11, 18, 22, 71, 83; Lanciani, *Acque*, 130–132; Herschel, 173–175.

[2] *Mitt.* 1889, 289.

[3] Front. *passim; CIL.* vi. 1256–1259, 3866. Cf. Tac. *Ann.* xi. 13; xiv. 22; Lanciani, *Acque*, 133–137, 144–162; Herschel, 175–183.

tures, and for about 10 kilometres on the most magnificent arches to be found near Rome. They have an average span of 5.5 metres and a thickness at the crown of nearly 1 metre. The piers are about 2.4 metres thick in elevation, and the height of the whole structure is more than 27 metres. The original construction of this aqueduct must have been very faulty, for after ten years it fell into disuse and was afterward restored by Vespasian,[1] and ten years later by Titus. For 300 metres south from the porta Praenestina, these arches were made a part of the Aurelian wall.

From the castellum, 250 metres northwest of the porta Praenestina, the water of this aqueduct was distributed throughout the city in pipes. Nero built a branch specus from the angle near the porta Praenestina to the great buildings of Claudius on the Caelian. This branch was over 2 kilometres long, and was carried on arches, — the arcus Caelemontani or Neroniani,[2] — some of which, as afterward restored, are among the finest specimens of brickwork in the city. These arches have a span of 7.75 metres, and the piers are 2.30 by 2.10 metres in thickness and 16 metres high. Domitian carried the water of the Claudia from the Caelian to the Palatine by means of a lead siphon 30 centimetres in diameter. This Severus replaced by a line of arches across the intervening valley, 43 metres high in the centre and 430 metres long, the ruins of which are still visible. The length of the Claudia was 46,406 passus (68.7 kilometres),[3] of which 53.6 kilometres were underground. Some ruins of the castellum of the Claudia and Anio novus have been found near the three arches of the railroad tracks.

The Anio novus [4] was built at the same time as the Claudia. Its source was the river Anio at Subiaco, near the forty-

---

[1] CIL. vi. 1257–1258.     [2] CIL. vi. 1259 ; Lanciani, Acque, 152–162.
[3] Cf., however, CIL. vi. 1256 = 45,000 passus.
[4] Front. passim ; Pl. NH. xxxvi. 122; CIL. vi. 1256; ix. 4051; Lanciani, Acque, 138–162; Herschel, 183–184.

Fig. 9. — Arches of the Claudia and Anio Novus.

second milestone on the via Sublacensis, but this water was frequently muddy and unfit to drink. A *piscina limaria,* or basin in which the mud might be deposited, was therefore built at the beginning of the aqueduct; and four miles below this point, a small auxiliary stream, the rivus Herculaneus (cf. p. 95), was admitted into the main specus. Trajan improved the quality of the water more effectively by

FIG. 10. — THE JUNCTION OF SEVEN AQUEDUCTS AT THE PORTA PRAENESTINA.

drawing it from one of the three lakes above Subiaco, which Nero had constructed by building a dam across the Anio, close by his famous villa.

The Anio novus paralleled the Claudia throughout its course to Le Capannelle, where both emerged from the ground. From here the Anio novus was carried on the Claudian arches above the specus of the Claudia to the castellum, where the water of the two was mixed before being distributed. The length of its specus was 58,700 passus (86.8

kilometres), 49,300 passus (72.9 kilometres) being underground.

The Traiana[1] was built by Trajan in 109 A.D., to supply
region XIV, trans Tiberim, with drinking water, as the
Alsietina was unfit for that purpose.  Its sources were sev-
eral springs lying to the north and west of the lacus Sabatinus, the modern lake Bracciano, in the district between
Oriolo Bassano and the lake.  The water was collected at
a point near Vicarello, where the aqueduct proper began.
Its length from this point to Rome was 57.7 kilometres.
The specus was wholly subterranean, and terminated on the
Janiculum in a castellum, which is represented on coins[2] of
Trajan.  During the later empire it supplied motive power
for mills[3] which were built on the slope of the hill.  This
aqueduct was injured in 537 A.D. by the Gothic general,
Vitiges, restored by Belisarius, and afterward by several of
the popes.  In 1611 Paul V restored it again, increased its
volume by admitting the water of lake Bracciano itself, and
built the famous Fontana Paolina on the site of the original
castellum.  It is now called the acqua Paola.

The Alexandrina[4] was built in 226 A.D. by Alexander Severus
to supply his baths in the campus Martius.  The springs
which fed this aqueduct, and which partially supply the
modern acqua Felice, are situated east of monte Falcone on
the via Praenestina, between Gabii and lake Regillus, and
about 20 kilometres from Rome.  The total length of the
channel was 22 kilometres.  In 1585 Sixtus V built the acqua
Felice in the same region and along nearly the same line.
There are many remains of the original Alexandrina up to a
point 3 kilometres from the city, but from there its course
cannot be traced accurately.  It is probable, however, that
a piscina, the ruins of which have been found in what was

---

[1] *CIL.* vi. 1260; Pol. Silv. 545–546; Lanciani, *Acque*, 162–168.
[2] Cohen, *Trai.* 20–25.           [3] Procop. *Bell. Goth.* i. 19.
[4] Lamprid. *Vit. Alex.* 25; Pol. Silv. 545–546; Lanciani, *Acque*, 168–177

| | Date | Source | Destination | Altitude of Spring | Altitude at Rome | Length of Channel | | | Size of Specus |
|---|---|---|---|---|---|---|---|---|---|
| | | | | | | Under-ground | Above ground | Total | |
| Appia | B.C. 312 | Latomie della Rustica, Via Latina* | Porta Trigemina | 30 m. (about) | 20 m. (about) | 11130 p. 15.6 km. | 60 p. 89 m. | 11190 p. 16.5 km. | 1.5×.75 m.[1] (about) |
| Anio vetus | 272–219 | The Anio above Vicovaro | Porta Esquilina, Porta Capena | 280 m. | 48 m. | 42779 p. 63.3 km. | 221 p. 327 m. | 43000 p. 63.64 km. | 2.4×1.1 m.[1] (about) |
| Marcia | 144–140 | Springs north of the Anio near Agosta | Capitol, Viminal, Baths of Caracalla | 318 m. | 58.63 m. | 54247.5 p. 80.3 km. | 7463 p. 11 km. | 61710.5 p. 91.3 km. | 1.74×2.53 m.[1] .9×1.74 m. |
| Tepula | 125 | Alban Hills | Quirinal | 151 m. | 60.63 m. | 7.38 km. | 7000 p. 10.36 km. | 17.745 km. | 1×.9 m.[1] |
| Julia | 33 | Alban Hills | Esquiline and Viminal | 350 m. | 63.73 m. | 8426.5 p. 12.47 km. | 7000 p. 10.36 km. | 15426 5 p. 22.83 km. | 1.4×.7 m.[1] |
| Virgo | 19 | Salone on the via Collatina | Baths of Agrippa, Campus Martius | 24 m. | 20 m. | 12865 p. 19 km. | 1240 p. 1.84 km. | 14105 p. 20.88 km. | 2×.49 m.[1] |
| Alsietina | 10(?) | Lake Martignano | Trastevere | 209 m. | 16.50 m. | 21814 p. 32.3 km. | 358 p. 530 m. | 22172 p. 32.8 km. | 1.78×2.67 m.[2] |
| Claudia | A.D. 38–52 | Springs north of the Anio | Spes vetus, Caelian and Palatine | 320 m. | 67.40 m. | 38230 p. 56.6 km. | 10176 p. 15.1 km. | 46406 p. 68.7 km. | 1×2 m.[1] (below intake) |
| Anio novus | 38–52 | The Anio at Subiaco | Spes vetus | 400 m. (about) | 70.40 m. | 49300 p. 72.9 km. | 9400 p. 13.9 km. | 58700 p. 86.8 km. | 1×2.74 m.[1] |
| Traiana | 109 | Springs at Trevignano | Janiculum | 300 m. (about) | 71.16 m. | 57.7 km. | | 57.7 km. | 2.32×1.3 m.[2] |
| Alexandrina | 226 | Monte Falcone on via Praenestina | Baths of Alexander | 65 m. | 43 m. | 12 3 km. | 9.7 km. | 22 km. | 1.71×.73 m.[2] |

[103]

The altitudes are taken from Lanciani; the length of the channels is computed from Frontinus's statements (passus = 1.48 m.) except in the case of the Tepula, Traiana, and Alexandrina, where Lanciani is followed; the size of the specus varied somewhat, but the figures given are those of Herschel [1] and Lanciani [2]. Abbreviations: p. = passus, m. = metre, km. = kilometre.

* See p. 93, note 1.

formerly the vigna Conti, between the porta Maggiore and S. Croce in Gerusalemme, belonged to this aqueduct. According to measurements [1] taken in the seventeenth century, more than a third (9.7 kilometres) of its channel was above ground. Its ruins are to be seen in the valley of the acqua Bollicante on the via Praenestina.

Of the other aqueducts [2] mentioned in the Regionary Catalogue — Annia, Attica, Herculea, Caerulea, Augustea, Ciminia, Aurelia, Damnata, and Severiana — nothing certain is known, but they were probably branches, mostly outside the city, or else these names were corruptions of earlier forms, as Herculea for rivus Herculaneus. Two others, Dotraciana and Drusia,[3] are mentioned elsewhere, and two, the Pinciana[4] and Conclusa,[5] occur in inscriptions.

The estimates which are usually given of the amount of water supplied to Rome by these aqueducts have been very greatly exaggerated.[6] They are based upon statements of Frontinus, but these involve many unknown factors, and there is no way of determining the value of his unit, the *quinaria,* with anything like exactness.

**The Sewers**. — The sewerage system[7] of Rome conformed to the natural lines of drainage, and fell therefore into three divisions. The northern division comprised the campus Martius, the Pincian, and the north and west slopes of the Quirinal and the Capitoline. The principal stream of this section, the Petronia amnis (p. 19), and other less important water courses, came down from the hills and emptied into the

[1] Lanciani, *Acque*, 176.

[2] Jordan, I. 1. 479–480; II. 223–225; Gilbert, III. 277; Richter, *Top.*[2] 381.

[3] Pol. Silv. 545–546.

[4] *CIL.* xv. 7259; Lanciani, *Acque*, 225 n.        [5] *BC.* 1880, 55.

[6] Cf. Herschel, 200–215; and Morgan, *Water Supply of Ancient Rome, Transactions of Am. Phil. Assoc.* 1902, 30–37, and literature there cited.

[7] Narducci, *Sulla Fognatura della Città di Roma*, Rome, 1889; Borsari, *Topografia di Roma Antica*, 90–96; Jordan, I. 1. 441–452; Gilbert, II. 410–415.

swamps of the campus. The central division comprised the south and east slopes of the Capitoline and Quirinal, the Viminal, the north and west slopes of the Palatine, the Forum, and the Velabrum, — a section drained by the brook (p. 18) which came down through the Subura. The third division comprised the southern part of the city, drained mainly by the streams on either side of the Caelian, which united at the east end of the vallis Murcia. In each of these divisions there was probably one principal collecting sewer, into which others emptied.

There is no doubt that the earliest attempts at artificial drainage date from the regal period. The first part of the city to be drained was the Forum valley, and later, as the city grew in that direction, the Subura and the slopes of the Quirinal, the Viminal, and the Esquiline. The system was developed with considerable rapidity, and the statement made by Livy, that after the invasion of the Gauls the city was rebuilt so as not to interfere with the existing sewers, is probably true. After the censorship of Appius Claudius and the building of the first aqueduct, renewed activity was displayed in the construction of sewers, and almost none of the existing remains are of earlier date.

The rapid growth in population during the first two centuries of the empire, the construction of the great baths and new aqueducts, together with the countless small baths and public fountains, and such enormous buildings as the Colosseum and Circus Maximus, necessitated a corresponding increase in the provision for drainage. The system became so elaborate that the city was called *urbs pensilis subterque navigata*.[1] Remains[2] of this great system have been found everywhere throughout the city. In some cases the old channels have been worked into the modern sewers, and in a few cases the old sewers themselves are in actual use. It is out of the question here to do more than speak briefly of the matter.

---

[1] Pl. *NH*. xxxvi. 104.  [2] Gilbert, III. 291–292; Narducci, *op. cit. passim.*

The earliest Roman sewer consisted undoubtedly of a natural watercourse, the channel of which was widened and deepened. Later the banks were walled up and the bed of the stream paved, and then the channel was sometimes covered. At a still later period, many sewers were built which did not follow a stream. The dates of the successive steps in construction varied in the case of different sewers. The earliest remains show that the roof was not vaulted, but consisted of flat stones placed on walls which gradually approached each other as they rose. The vaulted roof was probably not used before the fourth century B.C. Existing remains of Roman sewers exhibit two distinct types of construction, those of the republican period being built of opus quadratum of tufa or peperino, with or without a vaulted roof, and those of the imperial period being built of concrete lined with tiles, and with a gable roof formed of large tiles.

Various remains of republican sewers have been found in the campus Martius, all of which appear to have emptied into the main collecting sewer,[1] which has been discovered between the piazzetta Mattei and the Tiber. This is a distance of about 450 metres, and the course of the sewer is a little west of south. The construction points to the same time as that of the circus Flaminius, where this sewer is formed by the union of smaller branches. It is highly probable, therefore, that when the city had extended to this point, a large part of the drainage from the district to the north and east which had flowed into the palus Caprae (p. 19) and thence into the Tiber was provided for by the construction of this system of sewers. The collecting sewer empties into the river opposite the west end of the island, but its mouth was destroyed at the beginning of the last century. Beneath the piazzetta Mattei it is built of peperino with a vaulted roof, and is 3.21 metres high, 1.40 in width, and 9.27 below the street level. Other

---

[1] Narducci, *op. cit.* 36–37.

remains of republican sewers have been found in the Corso near S. Carlo and in the via del Seminario. Remains of the sewers built by Agrippa and restored by Hadrian have been discovered round the Torre Argentina and the Pantheon, those of the Antonines in the piazza di Pietra, and some of a later date round the baths of Diocletian.

The main sewer of the south section of the city began in the valley of the Colosseum, following a stream, perhaps the Nodinus,[1] and, passing through the valley between the Palatine and the Caelian, united with the Marrana (p. 18). This brook, which had flowed in an irregular course through the Circus Maximus, was converted into a straight sewer, which turned sharply to the left at the west end of the circus and emptied into the Tiber about 50 metres below the Cloaca Maxima. Its channel[2] has been found at various points, especially at the west end of the circus at the corner of the via della Salara and the via della Greca, in the piazza and via di S. Gregorio, and under the arch of Constantine. In the via della Greca the specus of the sewer is 10.50 metres below the present level. It is built of tufa and vaulted, is 3.40 metres in height, and into it open two smaller sewers, one 1.10 metres and the other 0.86 metre in height, dating from the third century B.C. At a depth of 2.89 metres beneath the modern pavement of the via di S. Gregorio is the pavement of an ancient street of the later empire (p. 322), and about 5 metres below this is a much earlier street. Just beneath the pavement of this lower street is the top of the channel of this sewer, which near the arch of Constantine is 1.80 metres high and 1.40 wide, with a vaulted tufa roof (Fig. 67).

**The Cloaca Maxima.** — According to tradition,[3] this sewer was constructed by Tarquinius Superbus to drain the Forum. Beginning in the Argiletum, where it collected the waters of

[1] Cic. *de Nat. Deor.* iii. 52.

[2] Narducci, *op. cit.* 61–63; *BC.* 1892, 279–282.

[3] Liv. i. 38, 56; Dionys. iii. 67.

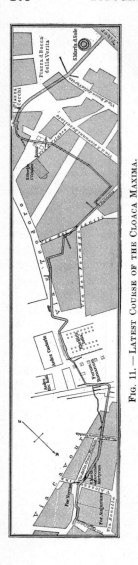

FIG. 11. — LATEST COURSE OF THE CLOACA MAXIMA.

the Esquiline, the Viminal, and the Quirinal, it flowed through the Forum and the Velabrum to the Tiber. The upper part was the line of a natural watercourse, probably the Spinon, and it is undoubtedly true that the first regulation of its flow, and perhaps the protection of its banks by walls, dated from the regal period. Of the existing sewer, however, the oldest part is not earlier than the third century B.C., while some of it consists of restorations of imperial times. Its earlier form, therefore, is only a matter of conjecture.

The Cloaca Maxima [1] proper appears to have begun at a point near the northwest corner of the forum of Augustus, in the via di Torre dei Conti. Its extreme crookedness is explained principally by the fact that it represents the natural course of the stream ; but at some points, its line seems to have been changed during the empire, on account of the erection of buildings. This apparent condition is sometimes very perplexing. For instance, the bend in the cloaca in the via della Croce Bianca seems to have been necessitated by the erection of the temple of Minerva (p. 283), not earlier than 90 A.D., and yet this

[1] Narducci, *op. cit.* 39–49; *Antike Denkmäler*, i. 25–28, pl. 37; *BC.* 1890, 95–102; *Mitt.* 1891, 86–88.

portion of the work seems to be earlier than the part nearer the Forum. This whole section, from the beginning to the Forum, is about 200 metres long, and exhibits two forms of construction. From the beginning to the via Alessandrina, it is built entirely of blocks of peperino, laid without mortar, vaulted, and paved with pentagonal blocks of lava, — the characteristic style of the republican cloaca. Between the via Alessandrina and the Forum, the side walls of the sewer are of peperino, but the roof is of brick-faced concrete. The specus is here 4.20 metres high and 3.20 wide. Eight smaller sewers empty into this section of the Cloaca Maxima, and near its beginning the main sewer from the Quirinal flowed into it from the north.

Between the Forum [1] and the river, the best view of the sewer can be had near the church of S. Giorgio in Velabro. The larger part of this section belongs to the republican period, with restorations of later times. The mouth of the sewer, 4.50 metres wide and 3.30 high, is close to the round temple (p. 401) in the forum Boarium.

---

[1] For a description of the Cloaca Maxima within the limits of the Forum, see p. 271.

# CHAPTER VII.

## WALLS, GATES, AND ROADS.

**The Walls of the Palatine**. — Current views in regard to the early fortifications of Rome have been considerably modified in recent years, and of the existing remains of walls only a very small part, if any, can be assigned to the regal period. Probably the oldest fragment now visible on the Palatine is at the southwest corner of the hill (*k*, Fig. 17) where two small sections of opus quadratum, one of seven courses and one of four, are *in situ*. The stone is a gray-green tufa, known as *cappellaccio*, and the blocks vary in size somewhat, those in one section measuring 0.60–0.77 metre in length, 0.25–0.27 in height, and 0.25–0.40 in depth, while those in the other section measure only 0.35 metre in length, and 0.30 in height. The finish is not perfect, and no mortar or cement is employed. Two courses of stretchers appear to alternate with one of headers. This wall has been assigned by some [1] to the pre-Servian period; by others [2] to the end of the regal period, as it corresponds so closely to the masonry in the foundations of the temple of Jupiter on the Capitoline (p. 297) that were undoubtedly laid by the last Tarquin; and by still others [3] to a somewhat later date in the fifth century B.C. In any case it seems most reasonable to suppose that this was, if not the original, at least a restoration of the original Palatine wall, after this had passed the earliest stage of a mere rampart of earth. The method of construction employed in this, as well

---

[1] Jordan, I. 3. 37.
[2] Delbrück, *Der Apollotempel auf dem Marsfeld*, Rome, 1903, 13–14.
[3] *Mon. d. Lincei*, xv. 787–788.

as in the later walls, is that ordinarily found in central Italy at the same period. At about two-thirds of the distance from base to summit, an artificial shelf was cut into the slope, and the cliff above scarped off. On this ledge, and backing against the cliff, the wall was erected, usually projecting high enough above the summit to form a breastwork. Where the cliff was quite vertical, nothing more than a breastwork was needed.

Outside of this earlier wall, at a distance of 0.75 metre, and covering it completely, was a later wall, of which some remains exist at various points on the south and west sides of the hill. The material of this wall is a friable brown tufa, quarried on the spot, and cut into blocks about two Roman feet in height and width (0.59–0.60 metre), and from 1 to 1.5 metres in length. On these blocks are masons' marks, and the workmanship is much more careful than in the earlier wall. When the slopes of the Palatine were built over in later times with the enormous substructures of the imperial palace above, and with rows of barracks and storerooms, the wall itself was either destroyed or covered up. It was evidently built to replace the earlier wall when stronger fortifications were needed. Its structure corresponds very closely to that of the later Servian wall (see below), and it seems to belong to the same general period, either that immediately following the Gallic invasion, or a somewhat earlier date in the fifth century. The latter is the more probable, for after 390 B.C., when the magnificent structure of the city wall was in process of being completed, it is difficult to understand why the Palatine should have been so strongly fortified.

**Gates.** — As Etruscan ritual required (p. 37), three gates gave access to the Palatine city, the porta Mugonia or Cattlegate, which stood near the arch of Titus, but of which it is impossible to indicate the exact site; the porta Romanula (pp. 37, 38) on the west side of the hill, probably where the clivus Victoriae began its ascent to the Nova via; and a third, unknown by name, which was probably on the southern side, in connection with the approach to the hill by the scalae Caci. These gates undoubtedly maintained their original position as long as the walls themselves, but all traces of them have been completely obliterated.

**The Wall of Servius.**[1] — During the last sixty years, considerable portions of this great fortification have been discovered, and then destroyed. Especially was this the case during the vast improvements carried on in the eastern quarter of the city, when almost the whole line of the agger was uncovered. Of the wall of this agger, the largest portions still standing are in the yard of the freight station and in the piazza Fanti. Of the rest of the wall, the most extensive remains are on the Aventine.

In different parts of the city different methods of construction were followed, which depended largely upon the nature of the ground traversed. Where the wall followed the slopes of the hills, — as it did for most of the distance except between the porta Collina and the porta Esquilina and along the bank of the Tiber, — the method was similar to that of the Palatine wall just described. On a ledge cut in the slope, and against the scarped side of the hill, are laid blocks of brown tufa in alternate courses of headers and stretchers, a method known to the Romans as *emplecton*, without mortar. The edges of the stone are carefully worked, and the blocks are very regular, measuring about 1.50 metres in length, by 0.62 in width, and from 0.55 to 0.59 in height. The thickness of the wall varies from 2 to 3.5 metres. This is illustrated (Fig. 12) in the ruins[2] in the via di porta S. Paolo on the Aventine, where, however, the existing arch has nothing to do with the original wall. This same kind of masonry is also employed in the outer wall

---

[1] See p. 45, Note 2.
[2] *Ann. d. Ist.* 1871, 81 ff.; *Mon. d. Ist.* 1871, 11; Merlin, *L'Aventin*, 116, 130.

of the agger, and is the most characteristic of the whole fortification in its final shape.

A second kind of masonry, which has been found at various

Fig. 12. — The Wall of Servius, with Late Additions.

points along the northwest slope of the Quirinal, is illustrated
by a section (Fig. 13) excavated in 1909 at the head of the via
delle Finanze.[1]   This section is 35 metres long, and of varying

---

[1] *NS*. 1907, 504–510; 1908, 348, 382; 1909, 221–222; *BC*. 1909, 119–121.

height, from nine to seventeen courses being preserved. The wall is built in a somewhat irregular *emplecton*, of blocks of gray-green tufa, 0.55–0.60 metre wide, 0.20–0.27 high, and

FIG. 13. — THE WALL OF SERVIUS.

0.80–0.90 long. It stands on the native rock, and the lower courses, which were covered up, are roughly bossed, while those above are carefully finished. The upper courses are also laid with a slight batter. Against the back of this wall was an embankment, and perhaps an inner retaining wall.

Where there was an embankment of any sort behind the outer wall, the style of fortification approximated slightly to that employed on the eastern side of the city, between the porta Collina and the porta Esquilina, where the line of the wall crossed the plateau. This was a combination of trench, embankment, and wall, and was called an agger. A very large part of this agger was discovered[1] in the years 1876–1879, and

---

[1] *BC.* 1874, 199–202; 1876, 129–133, 171–172.

destroyed during the building of the railroad station and the laying out of the new quarters on the Esquiline and Viminal. The description of Dionysius[1] was borne out by these excavations. A trench was dug, 30 Roman feet deep and 100 wide, and the earth, thrown up on the inside, formed an embankment of corresponding magnitude, the agger proper. A supporting wall of opus quadratum was then built from the bottom of the trench to the top of this agger, and a second but lower wall on the inside. A paved road ran round the city, just within this inner wall, and also one on the outer edge of the trench. The average thickness of the main wall was about 3.7 metres, that of the wall and the agger together upwards of 15 metres, and the total length about 1300 metres. The best preserved remains of the walls of this agger are in the freight yard of the railroad station, although all traces of the agger itself have disappeared. The outer wall is the characteristic opus quadratum of brown tufa.[2] Fifteen metres behind it are the remains of the inner retaining wall, consisting of ten courses of gray-green tufa, cut in blocks measuring 0.27–0.30 by 0.60 by 0.75–0.90 metre when laid in stretchers, and somewhat less in length when laid as headers. This inner wall is very similar to that used as an outer wall in the section on the Quirinal just described. Neither the inner nor outer walls were integral parts of the original agger.

What method, if any, the Romans adopted in early times to protect the bank of the river between the ends of the Servian wall, we do not know. Many fragments have been found of an embankment of peperino, about 8 metres in height, divided into two parts by a landing-step about 3 metres wide and 3 metres above low-water mark. This embankment may have replaced an earlier parapet of some sort.

Servius Tullius is credited by tradition with having surrounded Rome with a wall, and this system of fortification has

---

[1] ix. 68.    [2] Delbrück, *Der Apollotempel auf dem Marsfeld*, 14–16.

always been called by his name, but in the course of recent investigation it has become clear that, in its final shape at least, it is much later than the regal period.[1]  In regard to the relative age of the different parts of the wall, it is generally agreed that the characteristic opus quadratum of brown tufa is later than that of smaller blocks of gray tufa, which in its turn is probably later than the agger proper.

In regard to the question of absolute age, there is also a general agreement that the masonry of brown tufa, as it is laid up in the existing remains, is not older than the fourth century B.C.  This conclusion is based principally on the character of the workmanship, the presence of masons' marks, and the date of similar construction in Rome and other Latin towns. Attempts have also been made[2] to draw evidence for the date of the work from the height of the blocks, some of which measure 0.59 metre or 2 Roman feet on the scale of the Attic-Roman foot (0.296 metre), and others 0.55–56 metre or 2 feet on the scale of the earlier Italic foot (0.278 metre), but these attempts cannot be regarded as conclusive in either direction.

So far as there is any evidence, the gray tufa wall might be dated anywhere in the fifth century B.C. or in the early part of the fourth, and there is no valid reason why the agger itself should not be as early as the sixth.  Those who believe in the reality of a Servian city (p. 45) with some kind of a wall, assume that this original fortification was rebuilt from time to time, and that some of the existing gray tufa, and perhaps the brown also, belonged to the fifth century work, but that, as a result of the Gallic invasion, the whole structure was enormously enlarged and strengthened, the original line being for the most part preserved.  To this reconstruction the later ma-

---

[1] Richter, *Ueber antike Steinmetzzeichen*, 39–42; *BRT.* I. 15–17; *Top.*[2] 43; Delbrück, *loc. cit.* ; Pinza, *Mon. d. Lincei*, xv. 746–754.

[2] Richter, *BRT.* I. 15–17; *Berl. Phil. Wochenschrift*, 1908, 1421–1422; *Arch. Anz.* 1908, 442–443. Cf. *Hermes*, 1886, 411–423; 1887, 17–27, 79–85; Richter, *Top.*[2] 43.

sonry belongs, and to it such passages in literature as that in Livy [1] in regard to the work of 379 B.C. refer.

On the other hand, those who believe that there was no permanent wall round the whole city before the Gallic invasion, assign the construction of the whole so-called Servian wall to the fourth century B.C. and to the early part of the third, and date even the agger and earliest tufa to the beginning of that period. As stated already (p. 45) the first seems the more reasonable view.

**Gates.** — Under the palazzo Antonelli in the via Nazionale is a gate,[2] consisting of a single archway, 1.9 metres wide, which may have been a sort of postern in the so-called Servian wall, and just where this wall crossed the via Appia, the recent construction of the Zona Monumentale has again brought to light remains of opus quadratum which are quite probably part of the famous porta Capena. No traces of any other gates have been found.

**The Wall of Aurelian.** — This wall,[3] after having been largely rebuilt by Honorius and having been restored many times during the intervening centuries, is still the wall of the modern city, although at present little attempt is made to keep it in repair. It was built on a strip of land 19 metres wide, and was so placed that the part inside was 5 metres wide, and that outside 10, thus providing space for two roads round a large part of the circumference of the city. Aurelian incorporated into this line of fortification certain structures already existing, like the supporting wall of the horti Aciliorum round the Pincian, the castra Praetoria, the arches of the Julia, Marcia, Tepula, Claudia, and Anio novus aqueducts, and the amphi-

---

[1] vi. 31. 1.

[2] *BC*. 1876, 35–36, 123–124; 1887, 52–56; *RhM*. 1894, 411.

[3] *BC*. 1892, 87–111. For a study of the stamped bricks used in this wall, see *Supplementary Papers of the American School of Classical Studies in Rome*, i. 1–86.

theatrum Castrense, and was thereby spared the labor and expense of constructing anew about one-sixth of the entire circuit.

These existing structures were rendered serviceable [1] by the addition of battlements, loopholes, and similar members, while the new wall itself was of two sorts, the quay wall and the

FIG. 14.— THE WALL OF AURELIAN, NEAR THE SESSORIUM.

wall with an inner gallery. Of the original quay wall nothing remains; but Procopius says that it was low and difficult to defend.

All the new wall on the east side of the Tiber was built of

---

[1] *BC.* 1886, 341; 1892, 104–105.

brick-faced concrete, 3.50 to 4 metres in thickness.   The height
varied from 8 to nearly 16 metres, according to the configura-
tion of the ground.   Where the wall was built on a slope, the
height outside was often much greater than that inside.   At a
height of from 2.5 to 3 metres above ground, inside, a gallery

FIG. 15. — THE WALL OF AURELIAN, NEAR THE PORTA PINCIANA.

or passage for the soldiers ran through the entire length of the
wall, which opened inward by a series of high arches, six between each pair of towers.   The thick curtain wall between
this passage and the outside was pierced with narrow slits
through which missiles could be thrown.   The top of the wall
was protected by battlements, *propugnacula*, of which nothing

remains.  At intervals of about 29 to 30 metres square towers
were built, which projected about 4 metres from the outer face
of the wall and rose to a considerable height above the battlements.  In these towers were rooms, 3.20 metres in breadth,
the lowest of which was usually on the same level as the gallery, of which it formed, in each case, a part.  The outer walls
of these rooms were pierced by loopholes.  The upper rooms,
on the level of the top of the wall, contained five embrasures,
three in front and one on each side, thus commanding the wall
between each tower and the next.

A survey of this wall, the so-called *Descriptio Murorum*
(p. 8), made in 403 A.D. after the restoration by Honorius, gives
the number of these towers as three hundred and eighty-one, of
which only one, the sixth to the left of the porta Salaria, is
still wholly intact.  The massive Bastione del Sangallo, a short
distance west of the porta S. Sebastiano, was built about the
middle of the sixteenth century, when 400 metres of the Aurelian wall were removed to make room for it.

**Gates.** — The gates[1] in the Aurelian wall, beginning at the
north, were the Flaminia, Pinciana, Salaria, Nomentana, an
unnamed gate just south of the castra Praetoria, the Tiburtina,
Praenestina, Asinaria, Metrovia, Latina, Appia, Ardeatina, Ostiensis, Portuensis, Aurelia, and Septimiana.  Of these original
gates the following have been destroyed at various dates: the
Flaminia[2] in 1561, replaced by the modern porta del Popolo;
the Salaria in 1871, replaced by the present gate of the same
name; the Ardeatina[3] in 1539, to make way for the Bastione del
Sangallo; the Portuensis[4] in 1643, when the city limits were
moved 500 metres farther north; the Aurelia[5] in 1643, replaced

---

[1] Jordan, I. 1. 353–383.

[2] *B C.* 1877, 207–213; 1880, 169–182; 1881, 174–188.

[3] *Mitt.* 1894, 320–327.          [4] *CIL.* vi. 1190.

[5] A second porta Aurelia (Procop. *Bell. Goth.* i. 19), identical with the porta
S. Petri of the *Descriptio Murorum*, and also called porta Cornelia, is placed
by some in the quay wall at the east end of the pons Aelius, and by others in

by the present porta S. Pancrazio; and the Septimiana [1] in 1498, when the present porta Septimiana was built. There was probably a gate at or near the point where the Marrana flowed under the wall, and an archway in the angle of the wall at this place is usually identified with the porta Metrovia.

The porta Nomentana was closed in 1562; the gate just south of the castra Praetoria some time before the ninth century; and the Asinaria about 1574. The porta Latina, after having been closed since 1827, has just been opened again.

The Nomentana and Asinaria are very much alike in construction, both consisting of a central arch, flanked by semicircular towers, and dating from the restoration by Honorius. Only one of the towers of the Nomentana remains standing. The porta Latina [2] is also of the same form, but the central arch is of travertine and the towers stand upon octagonal bases. Over the archway is a row of five windows, and the keystone is ornamented with the monogram of Christ. The gate dates from Honorius, but additions were made to it in Byzantine times.

Four other ancient gates are still in use, the Tiburtina, Praenestina, Appia, and Ostiensis, and one postern (posterula), the modern porta Pinciana. The Tiburtina, the modern porta S. Lorenzo, spans the via Tiburtina. Its central arch is built of travertine, and over it is a row of six windows. The arch was flanked by two square towers, but one of them was removed by Pius IX in 1869. The towers and arch are the work of Honorius,[3] but the foundations of the towers may belong to the time of Aurelian. Just inside this gate is a second arch, carrying the specus of the three aqueducts, Marcia, Tepula, and Julia, which entered the city here. This arch, built by Augustus,[4] is much injured; and even in the fourth century the

---

the fortifications of the mausoleum of Hadrian on the right bank of the river. See Tomassetti, La Campagna, ii. 473; Jordan, I. 1. 375–387; II. 166, 580; Richter, Top². 72; Hülsen, Romae veteris tabula.

[1] Spart. Vit. Sev. 19.

[2] PBS. iv. 13.          [3] CIL. vi. 1188.          [4] CIL. vi. 1244.

contour of the ground had been so changed at this point that
the bases of the towers of the gate of Aurelian are almost on a
level with the spring of the arch of the aqueducts.

The porta Praenestina, the modern porta Maggiore, is a double
arch of the aqueducts Anio novus and Claudia (p. 99), built
by Claudius over the via Praenestina and the via Labicana,

FIG. 16.— PORTA PRAENESTINA (MAGGIORE).

and afterwards incorporated in the wall of Aurelian. It is 32
metres wide and 24 high, and built of travertine, with two
principal archways, each 14 metres high and 6.35 wide, and
three small gateways, between and on each side of the larger.
The piers on each side of the arches have niches with engaged
Corinthian columns and an entablature. On the attic, which
has three compartments, are three inscriptions,[1] one by

---

[1] *CIL.* vi. 1256–1258; *Mélanges,* 1906, 305–318.

Claudius, and the other two commemorating restorations by Vespasian and Titus. The via Praenestina passed through the north gateway, and the via Labicana through the south. This latter was walled up by Honorius, and a tower erected on each side of the other passage. These towers stood until 1838, and beneath one of them the tomb of Eurysaces (p. 474) was found.

The **porta Appia**, the modern porta S. Sebastiano, consists of an arch of marble, built of blocks taken from some other edifice, perhaps the temple of Mars (p. 432). On each side of the arch are semicircular towers standing on double square bases, the lower one of which is of marble. In the towers are two rows of windows, and over the arch two rows of five windows each. On the keystone is the monogram of Christ, with Greek inscriptions. Above the towers and arch are crenelated battlements.

The **porta Ostiensis**, the modern porta S. Paolo, as built originally by Aurelian, was double;[1] that is, there were two passages, one on each side of the pyramid of Cestius (p. 420), through which passages the two roads — that from the porta Trigemina and the vicus Piscinae Publicae — passed before uniting. Honorius closed up the gate on the west of the pyramid, and remodelled the other, making it double by erecting outside the existing passage the present arch of travertine, with five windows above and a semicular tower on each side. The whole gate is surmounted by crenelated battlements.

The **porta Pinciana**, originally not a *porta*, but a *posterula*,[2] enlarged and rebuilt at a later date, perhaps by Honorius, consists of an arch of travertine, flanked by two semicircular towers, of which the bases only are of travertine. The threshold of the gate is formed of slabs of travertine, taken from some earlier building, on one of which is a fragmentary inscription.

---

[1] *Mon. d. Lincei*, i. 511–513.     [2] *BC.* 1892, 102.

**Roads**. — As early as the fourth century B.C., the Romans began to carry out their policy of connecting the different parts of Italy with the capital by means of a system of great roads, or *viae*. Some of these lines of communication had already existed for a long time, as, for instance, the early road into the Sabine territory, by which the salt trade was carried on, which afterwards became the via Salaria ; but the actual building of stone highways began in the censorship of Appius Claudius. These roads were regarded as beginning at the gates in the Servian wall, and gates in the Aurelian wall were afterwards built where the roads crossed its line.

The ordinary pavement of these roads consisted of polygonal blocks of lava, of which a stream had flowed down from the Alban hills to within 5 kilometres of the city. These blocks were usually set on a foundation composed of three strata : first, a layer of broken stone (*statumen*[1]) ; second, a layer of smaller stones mixed with lime in the proportion of three to one (*rudus*) ; and third, a layer of cement (*nucleus*). Where the bed rock was close to the surface of the ground, the *statumen* was dispensed with, and on marshy soil it was replaced with piles.

The width of these roads varied from 3 to 5 metres, and sometimes, as in the via Appia, there were paved sidewalks on each side of the road itself. This pavement is practically indestructible, and therefore, except where it has been intentionally removed or built over, it exists to a greater or less extent along all the roads, so that their line can usually be determined. In general, the ancient level in Rome and the immediate vicinity was lower than the present, and the old pavement is buried beneath modern streets or buildings.

---

[1] Cf. Vitr. vii. 1. 5–7 ; Stat. *Silv*. iv. 3. 1–3, 40–53.

The principal roads[1] leading out of Rome at the time when the Aurelian wall was built, were the following: —

(1) The via Flaminia leading to Ariminum, was built by C. Flaminius,[2] consul in 223 B.C. It began at the porta Fontinalis and ran north by east through the porta Flaminia. The first part of this road, f.om the Capitol to the porticus Agrippae, was called the via Lata, and corresponded with the modern Corso. The ancient pavement has been found both within and without the wall.

(2) The via Salaria led into the territory of the Sabines, and derived its name from the salt trade. The earliest road, the via Salaria vetus, probably left the city by one of the gates on the Quirinal, the porta Salutaris or the porta Quirinalis, and crossed the line of the Aurelian wall at the porta Pinciana, but it seems to have lost its importance and to have been displaced in ordinary use during the republic by the via Salaria nova, which began at the porta Collina and, passing through the porta Salaria, joined the old road northeast of the city. The line of the Salaria vetus is marked by the modern via di porta Pinciana, and that of the Salaria nova by the present via di porta Salaria, the pavement of both having been found within and without the city.

(3) The via Nomentana extended to Nomentum in the Sabine territory. It began at the porta Collina, and bending a little to the south of the present via Venti Settembre, passed through the Aurelian wall by the porta Nomentana, and crossed the line of the modern via Nomentana about 450 metres beyond

---

[1] Jordan, II. 230–236. For a complete description of the Salaria, Nomentana, and Tiburtina, beyond the city, see T. Ashby, *Classical Topography of the Roman Campagna, PBS*. iii. 1–212 ; of the Praenestina, Labicana, and Collatina, i. 127–285 ; of the Latina, iv. 3–158 ; v. 215–432. For the Appia, see Ripostelli et Marucchi, *La Via Appia*, 2d ed., Rome, 1908 ; Tomassetti, *La Campagna Romana*, Rome, 1910, ii. 1–407 ; for the Ardeatina, *ib*. 409–461 ; for the Aurelia, *ib*. 463–547.

[2] Liv. *Epit*. xx.

the porta Pia.  The ancient pavement exists both inside and outside of this gate.

(4) The via Tiburtina, earlier called the via Gabina, probably began at the porta Esquilina and ran through the porta Tiburtina to Tibur.  Outside the wall, its course corresponds closely with the modern via di S. Lorenzo, but inside the city it has been entirely built over.

(5) The via Praenestina also began at the porta Esquilina, and ran southeast to Praeneste, passing through the porta Praenestina.  Within the city its pavement has been found to coincide closely with the line of the via di Principe Umberto and via di porta Maggiore, and it also exists outside the city.

(6) The via Labicana, extending to the town of Labicum, branched off to the south from the via Praenestina just inside the porta Praenestina, and its course is easily traced by the pavement.

(7) The via Asinaria began at the porta Caelemontana and ran southeast through the porta Asinaria.  It appears to have coincided for a short distance outside the wall with the modern via Appia nuova.  About a quarter of a mile from the porta Asinaria, the pavement of an ancient road branches off to the north.  This may have been the via Tusculana.

(8) The via Latina branched off to the east from the via Appia, about half a mile south of the porta Capena, and joined it again at Casilinum.  It passed through the Aurelian wall by the porta Latina, its course within the wall coinciding with the via di porta Latina, where the ancient pavement still exists.

(9) The via Appia [1] was built in 312 B.C. by the censor Appius Claudius.  This was the oldest and most famous of Roman roads, connecting the capital with Capua and southern Italy.  It passed through the Servian wall by the porta Capena, and through the wall of Aurelian by the porta Appia.  Between

----

[1] Liv. ix. 29; Stat. *Silv.* iv. 3. 1–3, 40–55; ii. 2. 12.

these gates the old road is a little to the north of the via di porta S. Sebastiano, but its course is distinctly marked. Outside the city the road is still in use, and the ancient pavement exists, though in a fragmentary condition, for many miles, especially beyond the tomb of Caecilia Metella.

(10) The via Ardeatina,[1] extending to Ardea, branched off to the south from the vicus Piscinae Publicae, crossed the Aventine between S. Balbina and S. Saba, and passed through the porta Naevia of the Servian wall and the Porta Ardeatina.

(11) The via Ostiensis was the great highway from Rome to the seacoast at Ostia. It is a matter of dispute just where the road began to bear this name. The road which passed through the porta Trigemina skirted the west and south slopes of the Aventine, and united with the vicus Piscinae Publicae, which crossed the Aventine just beyond the pyramid of Cestius. This condition of things lasted until the time of Honorius, who caused the two roads to unite within the wall of Aurelian and to pass out through one gate, the porta Ostiensis. Whether or not the whole stretch of road from the Porta Trigemina was called via Ostiensis is uncertain. The ancient pavement exists along the line of the modern via della Marmorata, and outside the gate in the via di S. Paolo.

(12) The via Portuensis ran down the right bank of the Tiber to Portus Augusti. This road began at the pons Aemilius and extended southwest through the porta Portuensis. Its ancient pavement exists within the city, in the via di S. Cecilia and via di S. Michele, and also south of the wall, but here it does not correspond with any modern road.

(13) The via Aurelia[2] led west and north to the coast towns of Etruria. The Aurelia vetus began at the pons Aemilius, ascended the Janiculum, and crossed the line of the later Aurelian wall at the porta Aurelia. Its pavement has been

---

[1] *BC.* 1876, 144–146; *Mitt.* 1894, 318–327.
[2] Tomassetti, *La Campagna*, ii. 463 ff.; Jordan, I. 1. 378–380; II. 235.

found within the city, but it does not correspond with any modern street. Outside the gate it follows quite closely the strada Tiradiavoli. In the second century there was a via Aurelia nova, which probably coincided with the via Cornelia for a short distance, and then branched off to the left and joined the Aurelia vetus at some distance west of the city.

(14) The via Cornelia ran directly west from the pons Aelius, and then northwest into southern Etruria. Its pavement exists beneath the piazza and church of St. Peter's, but the name Aurelia nova seems to have gradually displaced Cornelia as the designation of this part of the road.

(15) The via Triumphalis [1] — as it appears to have been called after the third century at least — began at the pons Neronianus, and ran northwest, crossing the via Cornelia. After the destruction of the pons Neronianus, this road really began at the via Cornelia. Its pavement has been found between the Borgo and the piazza del Risorgimento, but does not correspond with any modern street.

(16) At the porta Tiburtina an ancient road branched off to the south, called the via Collatina, which coincided for a short distance with the modern vicolo Malabarba. It ran east to Collatia, and was of little importance except for local traffic. It is not mentioned in the Regionary Catalogue among the twenty-eight *viae*. Of these, besides those already described, the via Ianiculensis is unknown, and the rest were branch roads at greater or less distances from the city.

---

[1] For another explanation of this name, see *BC.* 1908, 125–150.

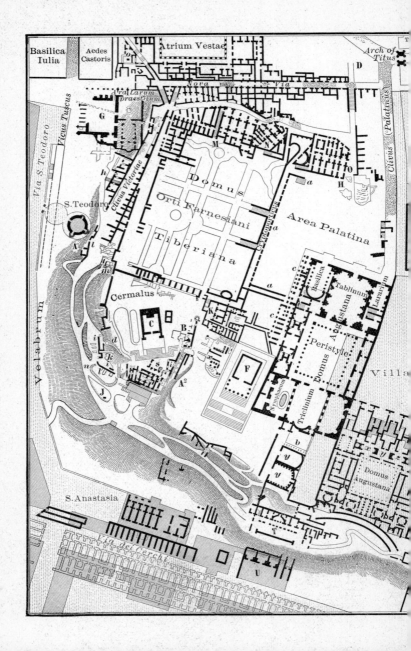

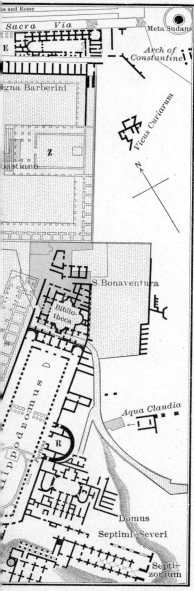

## Fig. 17
# THE PALATINE

METRES

0     25     50     75     100

▢ *Still unexcavated or built over*

A = Probable approximate site of the Porta Romanula.

$A^2$ = Ancient stairway (Scalae Caci).

B = Early cisterns and later masonry.

C = Temple of Magna Mater.

E = Temple of Iuppiter Stator.

F = Temple of Apollo (Pinza), or of Iuppiter Victor (Hülsen).

G = Augusteum.

H = Foundations built over in medieval times.

J = Altar to unknown deity.

K = House of Livia (Germanicus) or of Augustus.

N.M. = Substructures of first and second centuries.

R = Exedra of Hadrian.

T = Paedagogium.

U = Domus Gelotiana (?).

Z = Temple and Porticus of Apollo (Hülsen), or site of Adonaea.

$aa$ = Cryptoporticus.

$b$   = Foundations of Domus Augustana.

$c$   = Additions of Hadrian's time.

$d$   = Ancient cistern.

$h$   = Remains of structures built against the slope of the Palatine.

$i$   = Remains of early walls.

$k$   = Remains of earliest walls.

$m$ = Probable site of the temple of Victoria.

$n$   = Probable site of Lupercal.

$o$   = Lacus Iuturnae.

$s$   = Recent excavations (1907).

$x$   = Foundations of structure of Augustan (?) period.

$y$   = So-called Bibliotheca and Academia.

# CHAPTER VIII.

## THE PALATINE HILL.

**The Palatine Hill** (p. 32) is an irregular quadrilateral in shape, and about 2 kilometres in circuit. Its highest point is 43 metres above the Tiber level. A depression, crossing the hill in a northeast to southwest direction, which was filled up or vaulted over during the first century of the empire, divided it into two parts, the Cermalus on the west and the Palatium proper on the southeast; but the latter name was gradually extended to the whole hill. The spur which projected from the northeast side of the Palatine toward the Esquiline was called the Velia. ₁ A considerable part of this hill has not been excavated, and the excavations already made have not been exhaustively carried out.[1] Certain identification of existing ruins is therefore often impossible, and in general it may be said that the topography of the Palatine is in a very unsatisfactory state.

**The Regal Period**. — According to the well-known tradition[2] the basket containing Romulus and Remus was washed ashore at the base of the slope of the Cermalus, at the spot where there grew a fig tree, the ficus Ruminalis, which was afterward miraculously removed to the Comitium. The twins were

---

[1] Jordan, I. 3. 29–33. The latest survey and map of the Palatine is the *Rilievo Planimetrico e Altimetrico del Palatino*, prepared by the Scuola d' Applicazione per gli Ingegneri, and published in *NS*. 1904, 43–46. Good popular descriptions of the Palatine are: Haugwitz, *Der Palatin, seine Geschichte und seine Ruinen*, Rome, 1901; and Cancogni, *Le Rovine del Palatino*, Milan, 1909.

[2] Liv. i. 4; Ov. *Fast.* ii. 412; Serv. *ad Aen.* viii. 90; Pl. *NH.* xv. 77; Tac. *Ann.* xiii. 58.

suckled by a she-wolf, which had her lair in a grotto, or cave, beneath the fig tree.[1] This den was called the Lupercal, and from it issued the famous fons Lupercalis (p. 91). This cave became a sanctuary of some sort, and was at least provided with a monumental entrance, for its restoration is recorded in the *Monumentum Ancyranum*,[2] and it is mentioned in the *Notitia.* A shepherd, Faustulus, carried the children to his hut, tugurium Faustuli,[3] on the top of the hill. In later years Romulus lived in a house called the casa Romuli,[4] which may be regarded as identical with the tugurium Faustuli, and was on the southwest corner of the Cermalus, at the top of the scalae Caci. This hut of straw is described as having been preserved in its original form down to imperial times, and hence it is not possible to identify it with any of the ancient tufa buildings on this part of the hill. Varro[5] speaks, however, of an aedes Romuli, which evidently stood in some relation to the casa, and it has been conjectured that the casa may have been inside the aedes.[6] Where Romulus took the famous auspices, the spot was marked by a stone platform, the Auguratorium, and a cornel cherry tree[7] sprang from the lance which the founder of the city hurled across the valley from the Aventine. To the earliest period also belonged the curia Saliorum,[8] or assembling place of the Salii, where the sacred trumpet, the *lituus,* of Romulus was kept.

The Curiae veteres,[9] mentioned by Tacitus as one point in the Palatine pomerium (p. 37), was the earliest sanctuary of the curies. It became too small, and a second structure, the Curiae novae,[10] was built, probably in the immediate neighborhood, but

---

[1] Dionys. i. 32, 79; Jordan, I. 3. 37–39; Pais, *Legends*, 43–59, 229–234.

[2] iv. 2.    [3] Solin. i. 18.    [4] Dionys. i. 79; Plut. *Rom.* 20.    [5] *LL.* v. 54.

[6] Jordan, I. 3. 39–40; II. 268; Gilbert, I. 59; Richter, *Top.*[2] 134.

[7] Plut. *Rom.* 20.

[8] Cic. *de Div.* i. 30; Val. Max. i. 8. 11; Gilbert, I. 140; III. 424; Marquardt, *Staatsverwaltung*, iii. 427–433.

[9] Varro, *LL.* v. 155; Gilbert, I. 208–213; Jordan, I. 3. 43–44.

[10] Fest. 174; Gilbert, I. 196–199, 208–213; II. 126–127.

seven curies refused to move from the old place of assembly. This Curiae veteres was at the northeast corner of the Palatine, and probably at its foot, very near the line of the Sacra via and the later arch of Constantine.

The fourth point mentioned by Tacitus, in the line of the pomerium, was the sacellum Larum, which, in spite of certain objections, is probably identical with the ara Larum Praestitum,[1] and stood at the northwest corner of the hill, behind the temple of Vesta, where the Nova via bends sharply to the southwest. This shrine had fallen into ruins in Ovid's[2] day, but may have been restored afterward.

These monuments were carefully preserved during the republican period and even longer, but their exact location is now only a matter of conjecture.

**The Earliest Remains**. — The earliest remains on the Palatine lie on the top, and round the slope, of the southwest corner of the hill, that is, the Cermalus, to which tradition assigned them; but whether or not any of them actually belong to the pre-republican period is somewhat uncertain. Unfortunately the excavations of 1907 were not carried far enough to be decisive. Of the so-called wall of the kings, that is, the original fortification of the Palatine, it is now generally agreed that nothing remains except a few courses[3] of gray-green tufa at the southwest corner of the hill (*k*, Fig. 17). These blocks are smaller than those of brown tufa in the later Servian wall, and resemble those used in the substructures of the temple of Iuppiter Capitolinus, and in the ancient cistern on the hill (p. 132). They are laid up against the rocky slope which was cut away for the purpose (p. 110). Along the west and south sides of the hill are considerable fragments of other walls, of the

---

[1] Richter, *Top.*[2] 33 n., with literature there cited; *Mitt.* 1905, 119.

[2] *Fast.* v. 129–136.

[3] Jordan, I. 3. 37; Delbrück, *Der Apollotempel auf dem Marsfeld*, Rome, 1903, 11–12.

same character as the Servian wall (p. 111), and presumably
not earlier than that.   While these remains belong, therefore,
to a republican restoration of the Palatine fortifications, some
of them perhaps being as late as the fourth century, there is
little doubt that they occupy practically the same position as
the original wall.   Near the remains of the earliest wall is
an ancient cistern in the side of the hill, but this is not the
Lupercal, as it is commonly called.

At the top of the hill, between the temple of Cybele, the
house of Livia, and the present gardener's house (between B
and the slope of the hill above J, Fig. 17), is a complicated
network of walls, foundations, and drains, partially laid bare
by the recent excavations.[1]   No adequate plan has been published, and therefore no satisfactory description can be given.[2]
Northeast of B (Fig. 17) is a circular cistern, usually regarded
as of very early date, 2.8 metres in diameter, and built of tufa
lined with stucco.   Its top was formed of overlapping rings of
stone, and through its centre a later wall of opus quadratum
was built.   This wall of brown tufa extends southwest to the
slope of the hill, and seems to have divided the precinct of
Cybele from the higher area on the west.   Just below B (Fig.
17) is another cistern, about 6 metres in diameter, built of
thin blocks of gray-green tufa, and coated on the outside with
clay.   A circular flight of steps leads down to the bottom of
this cistern, and its roof was probably conical.

Among the remains of walls of different periods are the oldest of gray-green tufa, those of a later date of brown tufa with
masons' marks, and the most recent of composite construction.
These walls run northwest-southeast and northeast-southwest,

---

[1] *NS.* 1907, 185–205, 264–282, 444–460, 529–542; *Rendiconti dei Lincei*, 1907,
669–680; 1908, 201–210; 1909, 249–262; *CQ.* 1908, 145–147; *BC.* 1907, 202–205;
Pinza, *L'Angolo sudovest del Palatino*, reprinted from *Annali della Società
degli Ingegneri ed Architetti Italiani*, 1907.

[2] A complete discussion of these remains has been promised by Pinza, *BC.*
1910, 30.

and contain drains at different levels, corresponding to the different periods. Some of the walls seem to have served as the foundation of a building, part of which, consisting of blocks of tufa forming a rectangle, is *in situ*. This is evidently a restoration of an earlier structure and suggests the aedes Romuli (p. 130).

In the surface of the native rock are numerous circular holes, of varying depth and size, and shallow curved channels running at different angles. The variation in depth seems to be due to the fact that the surface of the rock was cut away to lower the level. Partly under one of the walls is a rectangular grave for inhumation, covered with a slab of brown tufa now broken, and dating from the fourth century B.C. These holes and channels are not cremation tombs, as has been thought, but probably were intended to support the framework of the thatched huts of the first settlers on the hill. The existence of one fourth-century grave does not prove that this point was still outside the wall at that time, for exceptions to the law of the Twelve Tables are by no means unknown.

Just below the edge of the slope are some remains of masonry of the Augustan period which seem to have formed part of a double colonnade, extending downward in a westerly direction from the higher level round the temple marked F (Fig. 17). This colonnade probably intersected the protected approach to the top of the hill at this point, which is without much doubt the scalae Caci.

Tradition[1] connected this corner with the story of the robber Cacus, whose cave was at the base of the cliff, and who was himself killed by Hercules. In reality, Cacus was an ancient Italic firegod, he and his sister Caca being worshipped as deities of the hearth. This worship of Caca[2] was after-

---

[1] *Ann. d. Ist.* 1884, 189–204; Jordan, I. 3. 41–42; Solin. i. 18; Plut. *Rom.* 20; Liv. i. 7.

[2] *Mitt.* 1895, 163–164; Roscher, *Lexikon der Mythologie*, i. 842. See p. 34.

ward displaced by that of Vesta, which may explain the absence from the Palatine city of any shrine of the latter goddess until the time of Augustus. The approach itself is cut in the rock, and appears to have been the bed of a paved road rather than a flight of steps, but this is not entirely certain. It was walled in on both sides, and where it reaches the top of the hill, the travertine foundations of a gate of the imperial period are *in situ*. This approach did not extend straight down to the valley, but curved round the southwest corner of the hill. The plausible suggestion has been made [1] that the porta Romanula (p. 38) was at the junction of this scalae and the clivus Victoriae, rather than farther north (A, Fig. 17).

**The Republican Period.** — The growth of the city, and the incorporation of the hills on the east, removed the political and business centre to the Forum valley and diminished greatly the importance of the Palatine. During the republic it became the chief residence quarter of the wealthy, especially the northeast and northwest sides, which overlooked the Forum and the Velabrum. Access to this part of the hill was given by the clivus Victoriae and the clivus Palatinus (p. 165) and by a flight of steps at the north corner, leading up from the Forum behind the temple of Castor (cf. p. 161).[2] Possibly this stairway was the scalae Anulariae mentioned by Suetonius.[3]

Mention is made in extant Roman literature of at least fifteen houses on this hill, built and inhabited by famous citizens of the last century of the republic, among them M. Fulvius,[4] consul in 125 B.C.; Q. Lutatius Catulus,[5] consul in 102; M. Livius Drusus,[6] whose house passed into the hands of M. Licinius

[1] *CQ*. 1908, 145.

[2] *NS*. 1882, 237–238, pl. xiv.

[3] *Aug*. 72.

[4] Cic. *pro Domo*, 102, 114; Val. Max. vi. 3. 1.

[5] Varro, *RR*. iii. 5; Pl. *NH*. xvii. 2.

[6] Vell. ii. 14. 3; Cic. *passim*; Gilbert, III. 418–419.

Crassus, and was afterward bought by Cicero; Quintus Cicero;[1] Catulus;[2] M. Aemilius Scaurus;[3] and Q. Hortensius.[4] The remains of one, the domus Liviae or domus Germanici, were brought

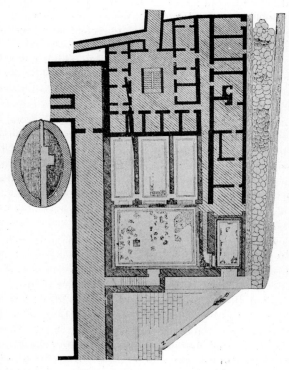

FIG. 18. — PLAN OF THE DOMUS LIVIAE.

[1] Cic. *ad Att.* iv. 3. 2.
[2] Suet. *de Gramm.* 17.
[3] Pl. *NH.* xvii. 5; xxxvi. 6; Ascon. *in Scaur.* 45.
[4] Suet. *Aug.* 72. For all the private houses on the Palatine, cf. Jordan, I. 3. 55–60, 104–105.

to light by the excavations of 1869.[1] This house is the only well-preserved example of a Roman private dwelling of this period. It has usually[2] been supposed that it belonged to Livia, the mother of the emperor Tiberius, or to her first husband, Tiberius Claudius Nero. On account of its associations it was not torn down but incorporated into the later imperial residence, while retaining its original form and modest exterior.

It stands on one side of the depression which crossed the Palatine, and its first, or ground, floor is on a much lower level than the adjoining palaces of Tiberius and Domitian, the latter of which was built on very lofty foundations. A stairway of travertine leads from the upper level to the passage from which one enters the atrium of the house. This passage is connected with a long cryptoporticus which runs to the palace of Caligula. From the upper story another cryptoporticus leads to the Flavian palace and to the chambers under the adjacent temple (F, Fig. 17).

The material out of which this house is constructed is concrete, faced with opus reticulatum. The inner walls were covered with stucco and painted. The main hall, or atrium, 13 by 10 metres, was partially roofed over, and from it, on the side opposite the entrance, open three rooms, each about 7 metres deep. The central room, 1 metre wider than the other two, is called the tablinum, or reception room, and was evidently the most richly decorated. South of the atrium is the triclinium, or dining room, 8 by 4 metres. All these rooms are paved with black and white mosaic, except the tablinum, where there is also some marble.

When this house was first excavated, the wall-paintings were remarkably fresh, but they have faded rapidly since that time.

---

[1] *GA.* 1888, 128–130; Jordan, I. 3. 60–63.

[2] For a very recent theory that this house was the original domus Augustana (pp. 143, 146), see *BC.* 1910, 30.

They belong to the second, or republican, style of Pompeian wall-paintings,[1] and consist of architectural details, columns, architraves, etc., variously enriched, and panels on which are pictures representing scenes from Greek mythology, as Galatea and Polyphemus, and Io and Argus. Back of the triclinium is a row of small bathrooms and household offices. On one side of the atrium, a narrow staircase leads to the upper floor, which was wholly occupied by small chambers, evidently intended for sleeping purposes. This part of the house seems to have been restored at various times, especially under Severus and Caracalla. Excavations now going on have disclosed a deep well behind the tablinum on the right, and also the walls of earlier buildings.

Beneath the Flavian palace, the walls of another substantial house of this period still exist, having been made use of, wherever it was possible, in the foundations of the palace. Complete excavations would doubtless show that this was the fate of many such houses on this hill. According to the Regionary Catalogue, there were eighty-nine *domus* and twenty-six hundred and forty *insulae* in region X in the fourth century, although the domus Augustana and the temples occupied so large a portion of the hill, and to provide room for so many dwellings is a most perplexing problem. They were probably crowded very closely together on the lower slopes and at the base of the hill, where many vestiges have recently been found.

The development of the Palatine as a residence quarter was accompanied by the erection of temples, the earliest of which date from the beginning of the third century B.C. According to tradition, Romulus vowed a temple to **Iuppiter Stator**[2] at the critical moment in the battle between the Romans and the Sabines, when the former had been driven across the Forum valley to the porta Mugonia; but this temple was never built.

---

[1] *Mon. d. Ist.* xi. 22, 23; Mau, *Geschichte der Wandmalerei*, 167–174, 196–205.

[2] Liv. i. 12, 41; x. 36, 37; Dionys. ii. 50; Plut. *Cic.* 16; *Hermes*, 1885, 407–429; *BC.* 1902, 35; 1903, 18; *CR.* 1902, 336; 1905, 75; Jordan, I. 3. 20–23.

In 294 B.C. the consul M. Atilius Regulus made a similar vow
under similar circumstances in a battle with the Samnites, and
erected the temple immediately afterward.  It stood on the
summa Sacra via, outside the porta Mugonia and probably just
east of the later arch of Titus.  The most recent excavations
(see p. 313) seem to show that the massive foundations on which
the medieval turris Cartularia was built, belong to a restoration of this temple, and that the early structure may possibly
have been a little farther northwest.  The temple is represented
on the relief of the Haterii (Fig. 2) as hexastyle.[1]  Near it was
a statue, either of Cloelia or Valeria.[2]

In 295 B.C., at the battle of Sentinum, the dictator Q. Fabius
Maximus Rullianus vowed a temple to Iuppiter Victor,[3] which
was completed within the next two years, but nothing further
is known of it, except that the day of dedication was April 13.
A number of inscriptions[4] have been found, which show that
on this hill there was also a temple dedicated to Iuppiter Pro-
pugnator, and this has sometimes been identified with that
of Iuppiter Victor, but without good reason.

The temple of Victoria[5] was said to be older than the city of
Romulus itself, but it was really built by L. Postumius Megel-
lus in 294 B.C.  Almost nothing is known of its subsequent
history, except that the stone which represented the Magna
Mater was deposited here during the years 204–191,[6] while the
temple of the Magna Mater was being completed.  There is no
record of any restoration,[7] and its site is a matter of dispute.
The ascent to the Palatine on the west side was by the clivus
Victoriae,[8] which evidently took its name from this temple.
This clivus[9] probably began at the porta Romanula, near the

[1] *Mon. d. Ist.* v. 7.                    [2] Pl. *NH.* xxxiv. 28; Gilbert, I. 226.
[3] Liv. x. 29; *GA.* 1888, 130; Jordan, I. 3. 50–51; *CR.* 1908, 155.
[4] *CIL.* vi. 2004–2009.       [5] Liv. x. 33; Dionys. i. 32.      [6] Liv. xxix. 14.
[7] *AJA.* 1905, 438–440.                   [8] Jordan, *FUR.* 37; Fest. 262.
[9] *BC.* 1885, 157–160; *NS.* 1882, 233–238; 1886, 51, 123; *Mitt.* 1895, 23–24.  Cf.,
however, the suggestion on p. 134.

present church of S. Teodoro. The modern path leads from the entrance north of the church toward the hill, and then turns toward the left and skirting the cliff ascends to the north corner of the hill, where it turns abruptly to the right and passes under the substructures of the domus Gaiana (p. 147). This is the line of an ancient road, of which the pavement is still in existence, and which is usually identified with the clivus Victoriae. There is no sufficient reason for doubting that this is the line of the clivus as it existed after the erection of this part of the palace; but this building must have materially altered the previous conditions and the earlier line of the road.

At the point marked *m* on the Palatine plan (Fig. 17), some fragments of inscriptions [1] were found in the early part of the eighteenth century, which belong to a Victoria. On the supposition that these fragments were found *in situ*, the temple of Victoria was placed here on the side hill,[2] near the beginning of the clivus, and the tufa masonry, found during the recent excavations, may have belonged to such a building. According to this view, the clivus took its name from a temple at its lower end, rather than from one to which it led, as was usually the case. (Cf. clivus Capitolinus, clivus Salutis, etc.)

Another temple on this hill, and one of the most famous in the city, was that of the **Magna Mater**, or **Cybele**.[3] In 204 B.C. a Roman embassy brought to Rome from the sanctuary of Cybele at Pessinus the pointed black stone which represented the goddess, and this temple, erected in her honor, was dedicated in 191 by the praetor M. Junius Brutus. It was twice burned, and restored by Metellus in 111 B.C. and by Augustus in 3 A.D., and was standing unharmed in the fourth

---

[1] *CIL.* vi. 31059–31060.

[2] *BC.* 1883, 206–212; *Mitt.* 1895, 23–24; Jordan, I. 3. 47–50; *Mélanges*, 1889, 197–199; *CR.* 1908, 155. Cf., however, p. 142.

[3] Liv. xxix. 37; xxxvi. 36; Mart.vii. 73; Cic. *de Har.* 24; Gilbert, III. 104–107; Jordan, I. 3. 51–54.

century.[1]  The stone needle itself was removed by Elagabalus
to the lararium of the Flavian palace, where it was probably
seen by Bianchini in 1725.[2]   Inscriptions[3] relating to the Magna
Mater, a portion of a colossal female figure — undoubtedly the
goddess — seated on a throne, and a fragment of a base with
the paws of lions, the regular attendants of Cybele, have been
found near the podium of the temple marked C on the plan
of the Palatine.

Other temples [4] built during this period were the aedicula
Victoriae Virginis,[5] erected by M. Porcius Cato in 193 B.C. near
the temple of Victoria; a temple to Iuno Sospita,[6] of which
nothing further is known; a third, to Luna Noctiluca;[7] and a
fourth, to Fides,[8] the erection of which is assigned to Roma, the
daughter of Ascanius, but which is otherwise unknown.   A
fifth to Fortuna Huiusce Diei (cf. p. 349),[9] known to have been on
the Palatine because of the vicus Huiusce Diei in the inscription
on the Capitoline Base, is of unknown date.   It was probably
in this temple that L. Aemilius Paulus, and afterward Q.
Lutatius Catulus, set up statues by Phidias.[10]   No trace of these
structures remains, nor of the altars or shrines to Dea Febris,[11]
Dea Viriplaca,[12] and Venus,[13] which are mentioned as having stood
on this hill.

On the southwest slope of the hill, toward the Velabrum,
is an altar [14] of primitive form, on which is the following
inscription : [15] —

---

[1] *Mon. Anc.* iv. 8; Val. Max. i. 8, 11; Ov. *Fast.* iv. 347; Obseq. 99; Vop.
*Vit. Aurel.* 1; Treb. Poll. *Vit. Claudi.* 4.   Cf. *AJA.* 1905, 438–440.

[2] *Del Palazzo dei Cesari*, Rome, 1738, 254.

[3] *CIL.* vi. 3702, 1040.                 [4] Jordan, I. 3. 45–47.

[5] Liv. xxxv. 9.                          [6] Ov. *Fast.* ii. 55.

[7] Varro, *LL.* v. 68.                     [8] Fest. 269.

[9] Jordan, I. 3. 104; Wissowa, *Religion der Römer*, 211; Richter, *Top.*[2] 142.

[10] Pl. *NH.* xxxiv. 54.

[11] Cic. *de Nat. Deor.* iii. 63; *de Legg.* ii. 28.

[12] Val. Max. ii. 1, 6.                    [13] Dio Cass. lxxiv. 3.

[14] *Mitt.* 1894, 33; *Jahreshefte d. oest. arch. Instituts*, 1903, 142.

[15] *CIL.* i. 632; vi. 110.

SEI DEO SEI DEIVAE SAC(*rum*)
C. SEXTIVS C. F. CALVINVS PR(*aetor*)
DE SENATI SENTENTIA RESTITVIT

This C. Sextius Calvinus was a candidate for the praetorship
in 100 B.C., and the altar was probably erected soon after
that date. It is of travertine, and undoubtedly a copy of the
earlier one on which was the original inscription. It had
no connection with the altar erected to commemorate the
voice heard in the grove of Vesta, announcing the approach
of the Gauls, and known as the ara Aii Locutii.[1] The altar of
Calvinus is not *in situ*, as the level of the soil at this point is
about 12 metres above that of the republic.

At a very much later date, the mad emperor Elagabalus
(218–222 A.D.) built a temple of the Sun [2] (Elagabalus) near the
domus Augustana, in which he is said to have intended to
place the image of the Magna Mater, the sacred fire of Vesta,
the *palladium* and the *ancilia*. This temple was burned, probably not long after the death of Elagabalus, and it is not mentioned in the *Notitia*.

The *Notitia* mentions a Fortuna Respiciens, evidently a temple
or shrine of this deity in the vicus Fortunae Respicientis of
the Capitoline Base.

There are on that part of the hill which lies between the domus
Augustana, the domus Tiberiana, and the southwest edge the
remains of two temples. The first (C, Fig. 17) is between the
domus Tiberiana and the scalae Caci, and its ruins [3] consist of
a massive podium, made of irregular pieces of tufa and peperino
laid in thick mortar, and fragments of columns and entablature.
The walls of the podium are 3.84 metres thick (those of the
cella were somewhat thinner) on the sides and 5.50 in the rear,
but this extraordinary thickness is due to the fact that the

---

[1] Cic. *de Div.* i. 101; Gell. xvi. 17.
[2] Lamprid. *Vit. Hel.* 1, 3, 6; Jordan, I. 3. 105–106; *Mitt.* 1892, 158.
[3] *Mitt.* 1895, 7–23.

rear wall is double, there being an air space, 1.80 metres wide, between the parts.    This wall was not faced on the outside with opus quadratum, but only with stucco.    The total length of the temple was 33.18 metres, and its width 17.10.    It was prostyle hexastyle, and was approached by a flight of steps extending entirely across the front.    From the rear wall of the cella projects the base of a pedestal, on which an image or statue probably stood.    The remaining fragments of columns, capitals, and entablature are of peperino, and belong to a building of early date, undoubtedly the oldest of which any considerable remains have been preserved, and there are no traces of any later restoration.

The ruins[1] of the other temple (F, Fig. 17) are between the scalae Caci and the domus Augustana, and consist of a podium of concrete, 44 metres long and 25 wide, faced with blocks of tufa.    On and around the podium are fragments of columns of tufa and of red granite, and of colored marbles, some of which may have belonged to the temple.    The fragment of an altar, now standing on the steps, and dedicated by Cn. Domitius Calvinus, consul in 53 B.C., has nothing to do with the temple.

It is generally agreed that of these temples, that at the southwest corner of the hill is either the temple of Victoria[2] or of the Magna Mater,[3] and the evidence now available seems to be distinctly in favor of the latter.    The other temple (F) has sometimes been assigned conjecturally to Iuppiter Victor, but the most recent investigation[4] is tending to identify it with Augustus's temple of Apollo (p. 144).    If this identification be correct, the remains of a rectangular structure (X, Fig. 17) may belong to the library of this temple.

**The Empire.** — The Palatine had been the Rome of the kings, but under the republic the political, religious, and financial

---

[1] *GA.* 1888, 130; Lanciani, *Ruins*, 138–139.

[2] Richter, *Top.*[2] 136–139.   Cf. p. 139.

[3] Hülsen, *Mitt.* 1895, 3–28; 1908, 368–374; Jordan, I. 3. 48, 51–54.

[4] *BC.* 1910, 3–41.

centre of Roman life was transferred to the Forum. One of
the outward signs of the return to monarchy was the fixing of
the abode of the emperors upon the Palatine hill.

Augustus was born on this hill, *ad capita bubula*,[1] a street or
quarter at its northeast angle, where, after his death, a shrine
was erected to his memory. After the death of Julius Caesar,
Augustus bought the house of the orator Hortensius, a modest
dwelling, which he enlarged in 36 B.C. by purchasing adjacent
property. Soon afterward it was struck by lightning, and
Augustus began to construct the temple of Apollo at the point
where the fire broke out. The house itself was again injured
by fire, and rebuilt with the aid of a popular subscription.[2]
Besides this house, the Augustan group on the Palatine comprised the temple and portico of Apollo, the library, and the
temple of Vesta.

Either before or soon after the death of Augustus, his house
was called the domus Augustana,[3] and this name continued to be
applied to the imperial residence down to the fourth century.
In modern times a distinction has frequently been made between the domus Augustana and the other parts of the completed palace, the former term being limited to that portion
which is still covered by the villa Mills; and this distinction
has sometimes been accompanied by the belief that this part
was the original house of Augustus. In reality, however, this
part dates from the time of Domitian or even later. Domus
Augustana denoted the whole imperial residence[4] except the
domus Tiberiana (see below), at any given period. Domus Flavia,
domus Commodiana, domus Severiana, are modern terms for the
parts erected by these several emperors.

After Augustus became pontifex maximus in 12 B.C., instead

---

[1] Suet. *Aug.* 5; Serv. *ad Aen.* viii. 361.

[2] Suet. *Aug.* 57. Cf. Dio Cass. lv. 12.

[3] *Mitt.* 1889, 185, 256; 1894, 3–36; *GA.* 1888, 145–147; *Mélanges,* 1889, 189–
191; Jordan, I. 3. 63–66, 74–76; *CIL.* vi. 8640–8652.

[4] Joseph. *Ant. Iud.* xix. 1, 15.

of living in the domus Publica, the official home of the pontifex maximus near the temple of Vesta in the Forum, he presented[1] this property to the Vestal Virgins, and built a new
temple to Vesta close to or within[2] his own residence on the
Palatine. This temple — doubtless of similar form to that in
the Forum — was destroyed in the fire of 363 A.D., and no certain remains of it have been found.

The most magnificent of the buildings of Augustus, on the
Palatine, was the famous temple of Apollo,[3] which was vowed
in 36 B.C., during the campaign against Sextus Pompeius, begun in the same year, and dedicated October 9, 28 B.C.[4] It was
built of solid white marble and filled with works of art and
treasures of every sort, but as almost no details of its construction are given by classical writers, it is impossible to reconstruct it, except in a general way.

It was probably either prostyle hexastyle, or peripteral and
octostyle, but in either case the intercolumniations were thrice
the diameter of the columns.[5] In the area Apollinis stood a
colossal bronze statue of Apollo Actius, pouring a libation on
an altar before him. Around this altar were grouped four
bronze oxen, the work of Myron. The temple was connected
with, and perhaps surrounded by, a porticus,[6] the main entrance of which, directly opposite the front of the temple, was
formed by an arch,[7] above which stood a famous work of
Lysias, — Apollo and Diana in a quadriga. The columns of
the porticus were of giallo antico, and between them were
statues of the fifty daughters of Danaus,[8] while before them

---

[1] Dio Cass. liv. 27; Ov. *Fast.* iv. 949; *Met.* xv. 864.

[2] *GA.* 1888, 151–152; *BC.* 1883, 198–205; *Mitt.* 1895, 28–37; Altmann, *Rundbauten*, 72.

[3] *GA.* 1888, 147–155; *Mélanges*, 1889, 191–197; *BC.* 1883, 185–198; *Mitt.*
1890, 76–77; 1896, 193–212; Richter, *Top.*[2] 148–149, and note; Jordan, I. 3.
66–74.

[4] Vell. ii. 81; Dio Cass. liii. 1; Serv. *ad Aen.* viii. 720. See references in
Richter, *Top.*[2] 147. [5] Vitr. iii. 3, 4. [6] Prop. ii. 31. 2, 9; Vell. ii. 81,
[7] Pl. *NH.* xxxvi. 36. [8] Prop. ii. 31. 3–4.

Fig. 19.—The Area Palatina Restored.

were placed equestrian statues of their unfortunate husbands, the sons of Aegyptus.[1] The façade of the temple was ornamented with bronze statues, and its doors with bas-reliefs representing the defeat of the Gauls and the death of the children of Niobe. Adjoining the porticus, or perhaps forming a part of it, was a library,[2] consisting of two sections, one for Greek and one for Latin books, with medallion portraits of famous authors on the walls.

The position of this temple and of the adjacent house of Augustus is now in dispute. According to the view[3] hitherto prevailing, the temple and its porticus stood on the northeast corner of the hill, the site now occupied by the convent and gardens of S. Sebastiano, while the library and house were probably within the area covered by the villa Mills or some part of the domus Flavia. If this be true, all traces of the four buildings have vanished entirely, with the exception of a few portions of the statues of the Danaids, and some architectural fragments which were not found *in situ*, but in the course of excavations round the villa Mills. According to the most recent theory,[4] all the buildings of Augustus are located on the southwestern part of the hill, and the temple of Apollo is identified with the existing podium (F, Fig. 17) which has been sometimes assigned to the temple of Iuppiter Victor. The house of Livia is consequently identified with the original domus Augustana, and the tufa foundations between it and the temple with the library. The porticus cannot have surrounded the temple, but is supposed to have occupied the space between it and the brow of the hill, and also to have extended a short distance down the slope until it met the scalae Caci (p. 133). Various remains of masonry of the Augustan epoch on the slope of the hill seem to have belonged to such a

---

[1] Schol. Pers. 2, 56.

[2] *Mélanges*, 1889, 199–205; Suet. *Aug.* 29; Juv. i. 128; Tac. *Ann.* ii. 37, 83; Amm. Marc. xxiii. 3. 3.

[3] *Mitt.* 1896, 193–212; Jordan, I. 3. 64–66.      [4] *BC.* 1910, 3–41.

porticus. Some grave difficulties inherent in the current view are avoided by the second, and while only a preliminary report of the investigation has as yet been published, and a final decision would be premature, the available evidence seems to point distinctly to the southwest part of the hill.

Tiberius did not live in the domus Augustana, but built another house for himself, the domus Tiberiana,[1] which adjoined the domus Germanici, and extended north and west from it.[2] This palace was built round a central court, about 100 metres square, and surrounded by a colonnade. It did not extend on the north as far as the clivus Victoriae, and its façade was probably on the east. Among the apartments which opened off from the central court there seems to have been a famous library, the bibliotheca domus Tiberianae,[3] which was in existence in the fourth century (see p. 162). The site of this house is now occupied by the Farnese gardens, and there is practically nothing visible except some substructures on the south side, which belong to the platform, partly natural, partly artificial, on which the palace stood. Between the original walls is a row of chambers of later date, which are cut back into the native tufa and finished with opus reticulatum. They were designed for the use of slaves, soldiers, and palace attendants, as is shown by many graffiti[4] scratched on the stuccoed walls. At the south corner of the domus Tiberiana is a large oval water tank, or *piscina*, of peculiar construction, which probably served to contain the fish until they were needed for the emperor's table.

Caligula added[5] a wing to the domus Tiberiana on the north, but this extended no farther than the clivus Victoriae, and the vast masses of masonry now existing at this corner of the hill, and sometimes called the domus Gaiana, belong to a much later period, — the second and third centuries. A sunken corridor

---

[1] Tac. *Hist.* i. 27; Suet. *Vit.* 15; *Otho*, 6; Plut. *Galba*, 24; *CIL.* vi. 8653-8655.        [2] *GA.* 1888, 155; Gilbert, III. 178; Jordan, I. 3. 76–79.

[3] Gell. xiii. 20, 1; Vop. *Vit. Probi*, 2.        [4] *BC.* 1894, 94–100.

[5] Suet. *Cal.* 22.

or cryptoporticus, about 140 metres long, led from the wing of Caligula along the east side of the domus Tiberiana to the house of Livia, and by a branch to the domus Augustana. Its walls were covered with slabs of colored marbles; its floor was made of mosaic; while the ceiling was adorned with mosaic and painting. This corridor still exists in a state of partial preservation; but what is left of the mosaic and marble belongs to the later restorations of the Antonines. Light was admitted through windows in the vaulted roof. It was in a corridor like this that Caligula was assassinated.[1]

In order to connect his own residence directly with the temple of Jupiter on the Capitoline,[2] Caligula built a footbridge across the intervening valley, making use of the temple of Augustus and the basilica Iulia as piers; but this ridiculous structure was removed soon after the emperor's death. Notwithstanding the great additions and restorations made by later emperors, all that part of the palace which was west of the area Palatina continued to be called the domus Tiberiana.

Of all the ruins of the imperial residence now visible on the Palatine, almost nothing[3] but some foundations and substructures belong to the ante-Flavian epoch.

The great fire of 64 A.D. destroyed the domus Augustana, and Vespasian therefore began a new palace, which was finished early in the reign of Domitian. It extended southeast from the podium F (Fig. 17), covering the space occupied by the earlier palace and including the area of the Hippodromus, or palace-gardens. The distinctive name, **domus Flavia**, however, is usually limited to the part lying west of the villa Mills. Between the domus Flavia and the Hippodromus, the ruins of the palace are buried deep beneath the gardens of the villa Mills, and but few rooms are accessible by a passage from the gardens.[4]

---

[1] Dio Cass. lix. 29; Suet. *Cal.* 58.

[2] Suet. *Cal.* 22; Joseph. *Ant. Iud.* xix. 1, 11.

[3] Unless the domus Liviae be the first domus Augustana.  Cf. p. 146.

[4] Excavations on this site are to be continued.

That Hadrian restored to some extent the imperial residence is shown by the large number of bricks bearing his stamp, and, in particular, he added the great exedra to the Hippodromus; but it was not until the destructive fire of 191 A.D. that repairs on a large scale were necessary. They were carried out by Severus and Caracalla, who enlarged the domus Augustana on the southeast by building an additional wing on enormous substructures and by erecting the Septizonium, and extended the domus Tiberiana in the same way across the clivus Victoriae to the Nova via.

**The Domus Flavia.** — The palace of Domitian [1] was built partly on a rectangular platform, about 150 metres in length and 80 in width, extending northeast and southwest over the depression which originally divided the Cermalus and the Palatium. The private houses which stood here were partly destroyed and partly used as supports for the structure above. One such dwelling of late republican or early imperial date is still accessible beneath the southwest part of the peristyle. The concrete walls of the palace foundations cut directly through the rooms of this house. Besides its walls and vaults, some of the stucco moldings and marble floors remain, but the colored decoration has mostly disappeared.

Until further excavations have been made, it will be impossible to form any idea of the character or use of the subterranean passages and chambers of the domus Flavia, and as nothing remains of the second story, only the plan of the first floor is known. The palace faced northeast, and in front of the façade was a porticus formed by twenty-two columns of cipollino, standing on the edge of the lofty podium. [2] This

---

[1] *GA.* 1888, 143–163, 211–224, pl. 21, 22, 23, 30; *Mitt.* 1895, 252–276; Jordan, I. 3. 86–94.

[2] For references to the magnificence of this palace, see Martial, i. 70; vii. 56; viii. 36, 39, 60; ix. 13, 79; xii. 15; Stat. *Silv.* i. 1. 24; iv. 2. 18–25; Plut. *Popl.* 15.

porticus also extended a considerable distance toward the south along each side. The northern part of the palace was divided into three rooms, a large *aula regia*, or throne room, in the centre, and a smaller one on each side. This throne room was 47.3 by 35.5 metres, and on each side were three niches containing colossal statues of basalt. Between these niches, and also at the ends, were sixteen columns of pavonazzetto, 8 metres in height. The main entrance was flanked by two columns of giallo antico, the bases and capitals of which were of ivory-colored marble, and the entablature of white marble. Opposite the main entrance was the apse, in which stood the throne, and on each side of it, as well as on each side of the entrance, were other niches. The walls were covered with colored marbles, the coffered ceiling was gilded, and the floor was paved with rich mosaic; but of all this magnificent decoration only insignificant fragments remain. This is true of the whole palace.

The room to the west of the throne room, about 35 by 20 metres, is called the *basilica*, and is supposed to have been the apartment where the emperor dispensed justice. It terminates at the south end in an apse, within which there are traces of a *suggestus*, or tribunal. Along each side of the hall was a row of six Corinthian columns of marble, which supported a narrow gallery and formed aisles. The original roof of this hall was of timber, but at some later period the side walls were strengthened by massive supporting pillars, and a vaulted roof of concrete constructed. It is probable that there were gilt screens between the columns, which separated the central space from that under the galleries.

The room on the east of the throne room is the smallest of the three, and in it, built against the rear wall and approached by two flights of steps, an altar [1] was found in the last century,

---

[1] Bianchini, *Del Palazzo dei Cesari*, 252. This altar is not to be confused with the stone needle, p. 140.

FIG. 20. — THE DOMUS FLAVIA RESTORED.

which has since disappeared.    Because of this altar, the name
*lararium* was given to the apartment, although there is no
further evidence to connect it with the worship of the emperor.
South of the lararium are two small chambers and two stairways.    One of these stairways leads to the upper floor, and the
other to a cellar in the unexcavated part of the palace beneath
the villa Mills.

The central open court, or peristyle, was surrounded by a
colonnade, of which the columns themselves were of Porta santa,
and the Corinthian capitals and bases of white marble.    Over
this colonnade was probably [1] an open gallery, with columns of
granite and porphyry.    A large part of the inner walls of the
corridor was covered with slabs of phengite marble,[2] which,
when polished, reflected the image of the passer-by.    The rest
of the side walls and the pavement were made of the most
magnificent colored marbles and porphyry, of which nothing
remains but a few fragments.

On the west side of the peristyle is a series of nine apartments, of which the central room, octagonal in shape, seems
to have been an entrance hall or vestibule.    The other smaller
chambers were probably used for anterooms for footmen, and
for cloakrooms.    As the eastern portion of the peristyle and
that part of the palace which lies beyond have not yet been
excavated, it is impossible to say with certainty whether or
not the rooms on the east of the peristyle correspond exactly
with those on the west.

South of the peristyle is another large and imposing apartment, which may have served as a state dining-room, commonly
called the *triclinium* or *cenatio Iovis*.[3]    This room terminates at
the south end in an apse, where perhaps the emperor's table
was set.    From the evidence of the fragments which have been
found, it is probable that this room was flanked by two rows
of six or eight granite columns, and its decoration was, if

---

[1] The restoration (Fig. 20) shows no such gallery.          [2] Suet. *Dom.* 14.
[3] Jul. Capit. *Vit. Pertin.* 11, but this identification is arbitrary.

possible, more magnificent than that of the peristyle. Some of the marble pavement of the apse is still in place, but it is of inferior workmanship and dates from a late restoration. On each side of the triclinium is a *nymphaeum*, or fountain-room. That on the east, although explored in the sixteenth century, is now hidden beneath the villa Mills, and it corresponds to that on the other side. In this room is a large oval core of concrete, which was entirely covered with alabaster. In its sides were niches containing statues, and from its top streams of water gushed out of pipes and flowed in miniature cascades into the surrounding channel. Flowers and statues were placed here and there between the streams of water and around the room, and probably caged birds also. The thick wall between this room and the triclinium was pierced with five large openings.

South of the triclinium are two rooms (Y, Fig. 17), side by side and curved into hemicycles on the east, with an orientation differing from that of the palace, and corresponding with that of the podium F, with which they may have been connected before the building of the palace. They are commonly called the *bibliotheca* and the *academia*, names suggested by their shape. In the bibliotheca, which is nearest to the palace, nothing remains but some bits of pavement; in the other, the academia, there are rows of seats at the curved end, and above them niches for statues, and between the two rooms are portions of marble pavement. The six columns now standing were arbitrarily set up by Rosa in recent years.

The platform, or first floor of the palace, rests at this south end upon substructures, which appear to be partly earlier buildings and partly walls erected for the purpose, and it is certain that there were many apartments on this lower level. Some of them were discovered and stripped of their decorations in the last century, but at present they are almost entirely inaccessible. Some remains of republican masonry may still be seen.

The larger part of the Flavian palace still lies buried beneath the villa Mills.[1] Excavations were made here in 1775
by Guattani, and from the plans and drawings which he has
left, together with the little which is now accessible, the general plan of the southern portion can be made out. The front
wall, which is exposed, is curved, and forms a species of exedra from which the sports in the circus could be viewed. This
exedra, however, has nothing to do with the Pulvinar ad Circum
Maximum (p. 405) built by Augustus. Access to the ruins of
this part of the palace is by an entrance from the Hippodromus,
where a flight of steps which led to the upper gallery has been
broken away. All that can now be seen is a few standing walls
and the three rooms north of the peristyle. Its general plan is
that of a central court, with the main entrance on the south.
This court was surrounded with a colonnade of fifty-six fluted
Ionic columns of white marble, supporting a gallery with another colonnade of Corinthian columns. From all sides of the
peristyle opened apartments of various shapes and sizes, of
which the three (x, y, z, Fig. 17) on the north have been
excavated. The two outer rooms are octagonal in shape, and
all three had domed ceilings and received light from above.
There were niches in all these rooms for statues, and the
decoration corresponded in beauty with that of the rest of
the palace. Many architectural fragments have been found
here, as well as some famous works of art.

Adjoining the domus Augustana on the southeast, and with
the same orientation, is the Hippodromus[2] which has usually,
though erroneously, been called the Stadium of Domitian. It
is a large open space, 160 metres long and 50 wide, inclosed
by a wall and nearly rectangular in shape, except at the south

---

[1] *Mitt.* 1889, 185–187; Jordan, *FUR.* 144, 163.

[2] *GA.* 1888, 216–224; *Mélanges,* 1889, 184–229; *Jahrbuch des Instituts,* 1895,
129–143; *Mon. d. Lincei,* v. 16–83, pl. i–iv; *Mitt.* 1894, 16–17; 1895, 276–283; *NS.*
1877, 79–80, 109–110, 201–204; 1878, 66, 93, 346; 1893, 31–32, 70, 117–118, 162–163,
358–360, 419; Sturm, *Das Kaiserl. Stadium,* 1888; Jordan, I. 3. 94–96.

end, where there is a slight curve. Within the wall and surrounding the entire central area, except at the north end, was a
porticus, formed by a row of pillars of brick-faced concrete
with engaged half-columns. Pilasters projected from the inside of the wall directly opposite each pillar, and arches, resting on these pilasters and pillars, supported an upper gallery,
which also surrounded the entire court. Columns and pilasters
were covered with slabs of Porta santa marble, with bases and
capitals of white marble. In the middle of the east side is an
enormous exedra with two stories. Its lower floor, which is
on a level with the central area, contained three rooms, a large
central hall, and two small chambers on either side, one of
which appears not to have been finished. In the other the
mosaic floor is still in existence. The second floor had only
one room, semicircular in shape, with a domed ceiling. The
front of this imperial box was decorated with a colonnade of
granite, and the back with one of pavonazzetto, as is shown by
the numerous fragments which remain.

At the north end of the Hippodromus, is a row of five small
chambers with coffered ceilings, which originally supported a
balcony, before the erection of the wall with three openings
that continued the colonnade on this side. At each end of
the longitudinal axis of the central area, which was not paved,
is a semicircular piscina or fountain-basin, and on a line between the basins stand the pedestals of statues. Lead pipes,
stamped with the name of Domitian, brought water into this
area at its northeast corner, about 60 centimetres above its
present level, and a stone water-channel encircles the whole
area, parallel to the porticus.

This Hippodromus was the garden of the Flavian palace,
and consisted at first of the central area surrounded by a wall,
into which one could look from the windows of the palace.
Later emperors made various changes, and it is probable that
Hadrian built the great exedra, and Severus the porticus, which
may have served to support hanging gardens. These changes

were the natural result of the additions to the palace, made by these emperors, which shut off the view to the east and south. Although only fragments of the decoration remain, the appearance of the Hippodromus must have been remarkably beautiful, on account of the combination of brilliant marbles and mosaics with flowers and plants of all descriptions.

At a much later period, perhaps as late as Theodoric, still further changes were made. Another porticus was built across the Hippodromus from the north end of the exedra, and a wall parallel to this porticus, from the south end of the exedra, thus dividing the whole area into three parts. Within the southern division an elliptical inclosure was erected, the walls of which were tangent to the cross-wall and the colonnade. The masonry of this inclosure is of the latest period, and the walls, although the remains are a metre high, have no solid foundations, but rest on the débris of the area. This elliptical wall was strengthened at certain points by spur walls extending to the colonnade. The only entrance to the inclosure was at the south end, where two pedestals from the house of the Vestals were built into the doorway. Openings, somewhat over a metre in width, were made in the wall itself at regular intervals, and within one of these openings is a basin or trough with two compartments. It is altogether probable that this inclosure was a *vivarium*, built to contain wild animals, a sort of private menagerie of the emperors.

In connection with the Flavian palace, there was also an αὐλὴ Ἀδώνιδος,[1] which has erroneously been identified with the edifice or space marked ADONAEA[2] on the Capitoline Plan. The extent of this Adonaea (apparently at least 110 by 90 metres) is so great that it seems impossible to find room for it on the Palatine except on the site now occupied by the con-

---

[1] Philostr. *Vit. Apoll. Tyan.* vii. 32; Richter, *Top.*[2] 155–156; *Mitt.* 1890, 77; 1896, 206.

[2] Jordan, *FUR.* 44; *BC.* 1910, 13.

vent and gardens of S. Sebastiano, where it may well have been if the temple of Apollo (p. 146) belongs on the southwest part of the hill. The αὐλή was probably a room in the palace, or perhaps a conservatory.

The south front of the Hippodromus, which dates from the time of Severus, seems to have contained several apartments on two floors, the purpose of the whole being apparently to afford a view over the Circus Maximus and the Campagna.

The style and material of the masonry show that Hadrian made restorations at some points in the domus Augustana, and in particular added extensive baths to the palace, to which belong the coffered hall and rooms with hypocausts just east and southeast of the exedra. It is almost impossible, however, to separate with certainty the work of Hadrian and that of Severus, who completed the palace in this direction. It is evident that much the greater part belongs to the latter emperor. As the slope of the hill began just east of Hadrian's addition, it was necessary for Severus,[1] when he wished to extend the palace in this direction, to build out an artificial platform by means of a series of enormous arches and substructures. On this platform the new part of the palace proper rose. These arched substructures extend to some distance from the edge of the hill, and at their extremity the platform is from 23 to 24.5 metres above the valley beneath. They are still among the most imposing ruins of Rome. Of the palace itself almost nothing remains, but the substructures are very complicated in their arrangement of arches, cisterns, and apartments of various sizes, the use of which cannot be made out.

At the extreme southeast corner of the hill, Severus constructed an edifice, called the Septizonium, — *ut ex Africa venientibus suum opus occurreret.*[2] This structure stood about 100

---

[1] Jordan, I. 3. 98–100.

[2] Spart. *Vit. Sev.* 24 (21); Jordan, *FUR.* 38; *CIL.* vi. 1032; Hülsen, *Das Septizonium*, Berlin, 1886; *BC.* 1888, 269–278; *Mitt.* 1889, 258–259; 1910, 56–73; Jordan, I. 3. 100–102; Durm, *Baukunst der Römer*, 2d ed., 469–474.

metres east of the end of the existing lofty platform of the palace, and some remains of its north end are beneath the level of the modern via di S. Gregorio.   The building was nothing more than a decorative façade, about 100 metres long, 31 high, and 17 deep, the back of which was a plain wall.   In this façade were three great niches, flanked by projecting towers, and it appeared to be built in three stories, each of which was ornamented with columns of marble, porphyry, and granite. We are told that Severus intended that the central niche of the Septizonium should be the principal entrance to the Palatium, but that during the absence of the emperor the prefect of the city set up a colossal statue of his master at this very point. Whatever may be the value of this story, it is quite possible that changes in the original plan of the building were introduced during its construction.   It seems certain that it served no purpose except to form a magnificent architectural member to complete the palace of Severus.

No thoroughly satisfactory explanation of the name Septizonium has been found.   The edifice was not seven stories in height, and the *septem zonae* may refer to the seven bands formed by the stylobate, the three colonnades, and the three entablatures.[1]   A recent suggestion is that Septizonium is a corruption of *Septizodium*,[2] the house of the seven planets. The main axis of the Septizonium did not correspond with that of the Palatium or of the Circus Maximus, but was perpendicular to the line of the via Appia, which began directly in front of the central niche.   Very considerable portions of this structure were standing at the close of the sixteenth century, but they were then torn down, and the material employed elsewhere.

Directly below the southwest end of the domus Flavia, about halfway up the slope of the hill, are remains of a building, con-

---

[1] *Archiv f. Lat. Lexikographie*, 1892, 272.

[2] Maass, *Die Tagesgötter in Rom und den Provinzen*, Berlin, 1902, 106–117; *CIL*. viii. 14372.   Cf. *Mitt.* 1910, 68–73.

sisting of a number of small chambers opening from the north side of a peristyle. The walls of these chambers were lined with marble and stucco, and round the peristyle ran a porticus supported by Corinthian columns of granite, one of which is *in situ*. While much of the construction is of later date, the original building was probably in existence when Domitian's palace was erected. The present porticus is entirely a modern restoration. Numerous graffiti[1] have been found, incised in the stucco of the chambers, which have been supposed to prove that the building was used as a **Paedagogium**, or training school for the pages of the imperial household,[2] but this is somewhat doubtful.

In front of this Paedagogium, at a lower level and with a slightly different orientation, are the ruins of a private house, consisting of an atrium, a tablinum, and a triclinium.[3] This house is on the same level as the Circus Maximus, and close to it. It has been identified with a **domus Gelotiana**,[4] which was incorporated into the palace by Caligula, but the evidence for this identification is inconclusive.

**The Additions to the Domus Tiberiana.** — As has been stated above, the additions made to the domus Tiberiana by Caligula did not extend beyond the later clivus Victoriae, and by far the greater part of the enormous mass of masonry at this corner of the Palatine belongs to the later building of the Antonines, especially Severus and Caracalla. These emperors adopted the same method of increasing the available area here as at the opposite corner of the hill. From the line of the Nova via great arched substructures rose to the height of the hill itself, and on the platform which they supported the additions to the

---

[1] *BC.* 1893, 248–260; 1894, 89–94.

[2] *Bull. Crist.* 1863, 72; 1867, 75; *Ann. d. Ist.* 1882, 191–220; Jordan, I. 3, 91–93; Hülsen, *Das sogenannte Paedagogium auf dem Palatin. Mélanges Boissier*, Paris, 1903.

[3] *NS.* 1892, 44; *Mitt.* 1893, 289–292.  [4] Suet. *Cal.* 18; *CIL.* vi. 8663.

palace were erected. The height of the perpendicular from the pavement of the Nova via to the summit of the hill is about 25 metres, so that the façade of the palace on the side toward the Forum was remarkably imposing. These substructures were filled with story above story of apartments, devoted

FIG. 21. — NORTHWEST CORNER OF THE PALATINE.

partly to the use of palace attendants of all grades, and partly, along the Nova via and the clivus, to shops. This complicated mass of masonry, of concrete faced with tufa and brick, comprises the remnants of the original structure of Caligula, and the restorations and additions of the two centuries following, which in some parts have a different orientation.

Three main tiers of apartments can be distinguished, the lowest opening on the Nova via, which appear to have been shops; those of the story above opening on the clivus Victoriae, perhaps shops also; and finally those at the top of the hill. Of the palace proper which towered above the platform, nothing remains. Vestiges of elaborate wall-decorations, marble lin-

ings, and mosaic pavements may still be seen in some of the
chambers and passages of the substructures, and a part of a
gallery above the clivus Victoriae.   Flights of steps connected
the different stories, of which the longest, in a good state of
preservation, leads from the clivus Victoriae to the top of the
hill.

Direct access from the Forum to this part of the palace was
afforded by a flight of steps (p. 134) that led up between the
temples of Vesta and Castor to the north corner of the hill,
and by another flight that led to the same place from a point a
little farther east on the Nova via.   Another way of approach
was by a passage, paved with opus spicatum, or herring-bone
brick,[1] which ascended in a zigzag course from behind the temple of Castor along the east side of the bibliotheca divi Augusti,
until it joined the first of these flights of steps and the clivus
Victoriae (p. 163).

**The Temple and Library of Augustus**. — Tiberius commenced
and Caligula completed the erection of a temple of Augustus,[2]
in which were placed the statues of Augustus, Livia, Claudius,
and probably of the later emperors and empresses who were
deified.   The temple was therefore called by various names, —
templum divi Augusti,[3] divi Augusti et divae Augustae,[4] templum novum,[5] templum novum in Palatio, etc., and it is altogether probable that aedes Caesarum[6] and templum divorum
in Palatio[7] refer to the same building.   It was burned in the
reign of Vespasian or Domitian,[8] and rebuilt by the latter, after
which time it was still spoken of as the templum novum[9] or

---

[1] *BC*. 1900, 74; 1903, 167–170; *Mitt*. 1902, 74; Hülsen-Carter, 177.

[2] Suet. *Tib*. 47; *Cal*. 21; Dio Cass. lvi. 46; Pl. *NH*. xii. 94; Tac. *Ann*. vi.
45; Gilbert, III. 121–123, 131–133; Jordan, I. 3. 79–86; Lanciani, *Ruins*, 122–125.

[3] Suet. *Cal*. 22.                    [5] Suet. *Tib*. 74.

[4] *CIL*. vi. 4222.                    [6] Suet. *Galba*, 1.

[7] *CIL*. vi. 2087, 2104; cf., however, Hülsen in Jordan, I. 3. 81–82.

[8] Pl. *NH*. xii. 94.                  [9] Mart. iv. 53.

templum divi Augusti ad Minervam.[1]   Coins[2] of Antoninus
Pius indicate a restoration during his reign.

Tiberius also erected a library[3] (bibliotheca templi divi
Augusti) in connection with[4] the temple, which was probably
injured in the fire which destroyed the temple, for the books
appear to have been removed by Domitian and replaced by
Trajan.[4]   This library may possibly be the same as that which
was afterwards called the bibliotheca domus Tiberianae[5] (see
p. 147).

The position of this temple is defined by the statement that
Caligula united the Capitoline and the Palatine by a bridge, —
super templum divi Augusti transmisso,[6] — and it has been generally identified with the building the ruins of which, belonging to the period of Domitian and partly known before, have
been recently uncovered by the removal of the church of S.
Maria Liberatrice.   This structure[7] filled the space between
the temple of Castor, the vicus Tuscus, and the clivus Victoriae,
at a height of about 12 metres above the level of the Forum
pavement (Fig. 40).   The main façade was toward the vicus
Tuscus, and the axis of the building was perpendicular to that
street.

The front part of the building consists of a vestibule, 32
metres wide and 6 deep, which formed the façade, and of a very
large rectangular hall behind it.   The roof of the vestibule was
lower than that of the main hall, and seems to have had no
supports originally except at the ends.   At a later period six
short cross-walls (a'a', Fig. 40) were built in the vestibule.   At
each end was a colossal semicircular niche.   The remains of
the front wall of the structure are too scanty to afford any in-

---

[1] *CIL*. iii. pp. 859, 861.                  [2] Cohen, *Ant*. 797–810.

[3] Suet. *Tib*. 74.

[4] Mart. xii. 8 (in Friedländer's ed.).    [5] Gell. xiii. 20; Vop. *Vit. Prob*. 2.

[6] Suet. *Cal*. 22.

[7] *Mitt*. 1902, 74–82; 1905, 82–83; *PBS*. I. 19–25; *CR*. 1901, 329; 1902, 95, 284;
*BC*. 1903, 199–204, 230–236; Hülsen-Carter. 161–179.

dication as to the number of doorways between the vestibule and the main hall. This hall was 32 metres wide and about 25 deep, and in its walls were rectangular and semicircular niches, arranged alternately, in which the statues of the deified persons were placed. Above the niches towered the lofty wall of brick, with several rows of sham relieving arches, and sheathed with marble. Its upper part was pierced with windows, and the roof was probably of timber.

On the north side of the building, toward the temple of Castor, was a porticus of brick piers (*b'b'*, Fig. 40) with engaged columns on their outer face, which formed a sort of second façade. From this porticus one entrance led into the great hall just described, and another, farther east, into that part of the building which was behind the temple proper. This part consists of a large rectangular hall (H), behind it a sort of peristyle (P) or quadriporticus, and back of that a series of three rooms opening into the peristyle. The first hall is about 21 metres deep by 20 wide, and its walls contain niches, alternately square and semicircular. Doors opened from this hall into the main building, and on the opposite side into a very lofty passage (A), from 3 to 4 metres wide (see p. 161), which ascends gradually, with four turns, to the clivus Victoriae. The second hall, or peristyle, was divided by four brick piers, with columns between them, into a central part and aisles. It is uncertain whether the central space was originally roofed over or not. Doorways opened from the aisles into the temple proper and into the ascending corridor. At the south end of this peristyle were three rectangular rooms, the central one being the largest, 8.5 by 7 metres, and the others smaller, 4.5 by 7, and 4.5 by 5. The south wall is built at an angle with the axis of the temple, and perpendicular to the line of the clivus Victoriae. It was perfectly solid, so as to cut off the building entirely from the hill on the south and southeast. There is little doubt that this eastern portion of the structure is the bibliotheca attached to the temple, al though this so-called temple itself is far from conforming to the normal type.

Beneath the bibliotheca are the remains of a very large piscina (B), 9 metres wide and 25 metres long, built of brick with steps at each end and niches in the sides, which dates from the time of Caligula, and seems to have belonged to the buildings by which he connected the Palatine and Capitoline. It is oriented according to the line of the clivus Victoriae and infima Nova via. Other fragments of an earlier structure with the same orientation have been found beneath the temple proper, which may have belonged to the first temple of Caligula.

The original Nova via[1] ran along the north slope of the Palatine, but probably farther north than the existing line. At the northwest corner of the hill it probably turned toward the south and joined the vicus Tuscus at some point not far from this corner. The erection of the temple of Augustus must have changed the conditions essentially, and the course of the Nova via is now exceedingly doubtful. The existing pavement[2] of this street lies along the south side of the atrium Vestae, but is blocked completely[3] at the corner of the hill by a hall (p, Fig. 40; cf. p. 219) in front of the bibliotheca. During the imperial period, therefore, it appears that the Nova via had no connection with the temple of Castor or the vicus Tuscus, except through the Forum or the clivus Victoriae.

During the Byzantine period the library of the temple of Augustus was converted into the church of S. Maria Antiqua,[4] and various changes were made in the original structure, such as the substitution of granite columns for the brick piers in

---

[1] Cic. de Div. i. 101; ii. 69; Varro, LL. v. 43, 164; vi. 59; Ov. Fast. vi. 396; Liv. i. 41; v. 32; Gilbert, II. 114–117; III. 422–423; Hermes, 1885, 428–429; Pais, Ancient Legends, 272–273.

[2] NS. 1882, 234–238, 413; 1884, 191; CR. 1905, 76.

[3] Mitt. 1902, 73–74.

[4] PBS. I. 1–119 (S. Maria Antiqua); Mitt. 1902, 82–86; 1905, 84–94; BC. 1900, 299–320; 1903, 204–230; Hülsen-Carter, 168–177.

the peristyle, the cutting of doors through the niches between the hall and peristyle, and the construction of a sort of choir in the central portion. The walls of the church were covered with frescoes, which have been brought to light by the recent excavations.

On the southwest side of the temple of Augustus these excavations [1] have also disclosed a series of chambers which are built against the side of the hill, and rise to the level of the clivus Victoriae. The lower rooms are of opus quadratum, and the upper of brickwork, and in front of them is a trapezoidal court surrounded by similar rectangular rooms. These remains form one structure and belong to the buildings represented on the Capitoline Plan as standing here, which appear to be horrea, possibly the horrea Germaniciana of the *Notitia*.[2]

The space bounded on the west and south by the domus Tiberiana and the domus Augustana, of somewhat indefinite extent and use, was called the area Palatina (Fig. 19).[3] The principal approach to it was by a street which led up from the summa Sacra via through the porta Mugonia. This street is now usually called the clivus Palatinus, but there is no ancient authority for this name. Some believe that the term Sacer clivus (p. 312) was applied to this street as well as to part of the Sacra via, and it has also been identified with the vicus Apollinis of the Capitoline Base.

South of the Nova via are traces of pavements at two levels, the earlier dating probably from the beginning of the empire and the later from the period after the fire of Nero. The later street was wider and straighter than the earlier, and was flanked on the west by structures built against the slope of the hill that appear to have been shops. Considerable portions of their walls have recently been excavated.[4]

---

[1] *CR*. 1903, 329; 1904, 139, 331; *Mitt*. 1905, 84.

[2] Reg. viii. Cf., however, p. 419.   [3] Gell. xx. 1, 1; *Mitt*. 1890, 77.

[4] *CR*. 1903, 136; 1905, 237; 1909, 61; *Mitt*. 1905, 119; *BC*. 1903, 17; *Berl. Phil. Wochenschrift*, 1905, 428.

The exact site of the porta Mugonia (p. 37) cannot be determined with certainty, although it was undoubtedly very near the intersection of the Nova via and the clivus Palatinus. Very near the centre of the area Palatina is a mass of medieval masonry, which belonged to the fortifications of the Frangipani family. Near by are traces of buildings of the earliest period, but nothing which can be identified, although it is altogether probable that the Mundus,[1] or augural centre of the city (p. 38), was just here.

---

[1] Ov. *Fast.* iv. 821; Fest. 157, 258; *EE.* viii. 283, 12; *Mitt.* 1890, 76; 1896, 202–204; Jordan, I. 3. 43.

# CHAPTER IX.

## THE FORUM.

**The Topographical Centre of Ancient Rome** was the low ground lying between the Palatine, the Velia, the Esquiline, the Viminal, and the Capitoline. When the Palatine city had extended its boundaries to the adjacent heights, this became the natural meeting-place for trade and political action. These two functions were carefully separated, the political assemblies being held on the Comitium, a small and definitely marked-out area, which lay at the northwest corner of the much larger and undetermined area where the people met for other purposes. This was called the Forum, or market-place.[1] Although there was no natural line of demarcation between Forum and Comitium, they were kept distinct in use until the middle of the second century B.C. After that date they gradually lost their separate identity, and the phrase *Comitium et Forum*[2] conveyed but one idea.

This valley was originally swampy, being the natural basin for the drainage of the surrounding hills. The principal water-course (see p. 18) came down from the Subura, and crossing the Forum flowed through the Velabrum to the Tiber. It is not possible to ascertain the exact elevation of all parts of this district, but the original level of the Comitium appears to have been 9 metres above the sea, or 2.30 metres above the mean level of the Tiber, while that of the travertine pavements in front of the temple of Julius Caesar, on which the altar was built, is 12.62 metres above the sea. This was one of the lowest

---

[1] Varro, *LL*. v. 145–146; Fest. 84.       [2] Tac. *Agr.* 2 (*ac* for *et*).

points in the Forum, in the last century of the republic.  The distance from the base of the Capitoline hill, directly in front of the steps of the temple of Saturn, to the east end of the Regia is about 210 metres.

The path or road from the ridge of the Velia down to the Forum was called the **Sacra via** (p. 54), a name that in modern times has been extended to the continuation of this road, which ran through the Forum to the base of the Capitoline.

We may distinguish four stages in the development of the Forum, the first extending to the last years of the monarchy, the second to the beginning of the second century B.C., the third to the time of Julius Caesar, and the fourth to the third century.

The end of the first period was marked by the beginning of a systematic attempt to drain the swampy ground.  This was effected by constructing sewers, and especially the Cloaca Maxima, which at this early time was made by simply walling up the banks of the brook and regulating its flow.  The date, to which tradition assigned this drainage, has been confirmed by the discovery of an ancient necropolis (p. 187) on the Sacra via, in front of the later temple of Faustina and just outside the limits of the Forum during this first period.  This necropolis ceased to be used in the sixth century.  Before this time it had been impracticable to construct any permanent buildings in the centre of the Forum, but rude booths, tabernae,[1] had been erected on both sides of the Sacra via, which were occupied by butchers and fishmongers.  There were a few sanctuaries, such as the altars of Saturn and Vulcan at the west end on the slope of the Capitoline, the double archway of Janus on the north side, and the shrine of Vesta at the corner of the Palatine.  There must also have been a building in which the senate met on the Comitium.  There were clay pits (p. 173) on the north side, from which the material for crude brick was ob-

---

[1] Liv. i. 35; Dionys. iii. 67; Non. 532.

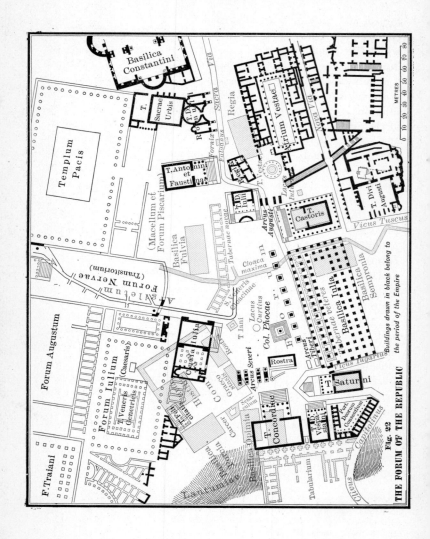

THE FORUM OF THE REPUBLIC

Fig. 22

Buildings drawn in black belong to
the period of the Empire

Basilica
Constantini

Templum
Pacis

(Macellum et
Forum Piscarium)

Atrium
Forum Nervae
(Transitorium)

Forum Augustum

Forum Iulium

F. Traiani

T. Veneris
Genetricis

T. Sacrae Urbis

T. Antonini
et
Faustinae

Basilica Fulvia

Regia

Atrium Vestae

T. Vestae

Arcus Augusti

T. D. Iulii

T. Castoris

T. Divi Augusti

Vicus Tuscus

Via Sacra

Nova Via

Cloaca maxima

Lacus Curtius

Col. Phocae

Tabernae veteres

Basilica Iulia

Basilica Sempronia

Vicus Iugarius

Rostra

Arcus Severi

T. Saturni

T. Concordiae

T. Vespasiani

Tabularium

Clivus Capitolinus

METRES
0  10  20  30  40  50  60  70  80

tained, and tufa quarries, Lautumiae (p. 172), at the base of the Capitoline. There were several springs and pools, two of which, the lacus Curtius and lacus Iuturnae, continued to exist during historical times. It is possible that the *tabernae* assumed a more permanent character toward the end of this period.

During the second period, — the first three centuries of the republic, — the Forum became an increasingly important part of the city. The temples of Saturn, of Castor and Pollux, and of Concord were erected and the Regia, or official house of the pontifex maximus, was built just outside the eastern limits of the Forum proper. The central area was paved, probably in the fourth century, and gladiatorial games and shows of all sorts were celebrated here. C. Maenius, the victor in the battle of Antium, introduced the custom of erecting galleries above the shops, from which these games could be witnessed, and which were called *maeniana*.[1] We are told that at some time before 310 B.C. the butchers were banished from these shops, and that they were occupied by money-changers and bankers, being thenceforth known as tabernae argentariae.[2] It is possible that this improvement also was due to Maenius. In 210 B.C. the shops on the north side of the Sacra via burned down, and after being rebuilt were called tabernae novae, while those on the south side were known as tabernae veteres, and the two sides of the Forum were distinguished as *sub novis* and *sub veteribus*.[3] On the Comitium, the Rostra and the Graecostasis, or platform on which foreign ambassadors were received, were built during this period.

The character and appearance of the Forum was greatly changed at the beginning of the second century B.C. by the erection of the three basilicas, Porcia, Aemilia, and Sempronia, and, fifty years later, of the Opimia. These basilicas added

---

[1] Fest. 135; Vitr. v. 1, 1.    [2] Varro, *ap.* Non. 532; Vitr. v. 1, 1.
[3] Liv. xxvi. 27; Varro, *LL.* vi. 59; Fest. 230; Cic. *Acad.* ii. 70; Jordan, I. 2. 378–383; Gilbert, III. 202–207.

greatly to the appearance of the Forum ; but their main object was to afford convenient and sheltered halls where the Romans could meet to transact the steadily increasing business of the capital.    The arch of Fabius was built at the east entrance to the Forum, and two or more arches of Janus at other points, while the area was gradually filled with statues of famous citizens. In the latter part of this period considerable changes took place in the Comitium.    On the whole, however, the appearance of the Forum in the middle of the first century B.C. must have been decidedly ugly and irregular.    In the middle of the second century B.C. the political assemblies of the people had been transferred from the small Comitium to the Forum, a transfer marked a century later by the removal of the Rostra to the Forum itself, which then became in the fullest sense the centre of Rome.

The fourth period witnessed the complete rebuilding of the Forum, a process which was just begun by Julius Caesar, and carried out by Augustus and Tiberius.    Later emperors did something ; but, with the exception of the temples of Vespasian and Faustina, the arch of Septimius Severus, the eight pedestals and columns in front of the basilica Iulia, and a few minor changes, chiefly in its central area, the Forum of the empire, which is known to us by its ruins, is the work of Augustus and Tiberius.

In its final shape,[1] the area of the Forum was surrounded by the following buildings, beginning at the northwest corner :

---

[1] For a new triangulation of the Forum, and the elevations of its various points, see *NS.* 1900, 220–229, with plan.    The best handbook for the Forum is Hülsen, *The Roman Forum*, translated by J. B. Carter, 2d ed. Rome, 1909. See also H. Thédenat, *Le Forum Romain et les Forums imperiaux*, 4th ed. Paris, 1908 ; Thédenat et Hoffbauer, *Le Forum Romain et la voie sacrée ; aspect successif des monuments depuis le IVe siècle jusqu'à nos jours*, Paris, 1905.    The best description of the excavations of 1899–1904 are by Hülsen, *Mitt.* 1902, 1–97 ; 1905, 1–119.    See also Vaglieri, *BC.* 1903, 3–239 ; Boni, *NS.* 1900—, *passim* ; Ashby, *CR.* 1900–1906, and *CQ.* 1907—, *passim* ; *BC.* 1904—, *passim* ; Boni, *Atti* v. 483–584 ; Richter, *BRT.* IV.

the Carcer, the temples of Concord and Vespasian, which abutted against the substructures of the Tabularium, the porticus Deorum Consentium in the angle of the clivus Capitolinus, and the temple of Saturn ; on the south side, the basilica Iulia, the temple of Castor and Pollux, the lacus Iuturnae, and the temple of Vesta; at the east end, the temple of Julius Caesar and the arch of Augustus, and behind them the Regia, the atrium Vestae, and the arch of Fabius ; on the north side, the temple of Faustina, the basilica Aemilia, the Curia, and the Secretarium senatus. Across the west end stretched the Rostra of the empire, and there were numerous other structures of various sorts which will be described hereafter. After the building of the imperial fora, the old Forum was sometimes distinguished from them by the epithets **Romanum** or **Magnum**.

**Streets**. — Until the time of Augustus, the **Sacra via** passed along the north side of the Regia, and then, bending to the left, continued along the south side of the Forum to the temple of Saturn, where the clivus Capitolinus began. The erection of the temple of the deified Julius necessitated a change, and thereafter the street ran in a straight line from the arch of Fabius to the north corner of the temple of Julius, then turned at a right angle and passed in front of this temple to the temple of Castor, where it turned again at a right angle and ran along the front of the basilica Iulia.[1]

Besides the Sacra via and clivus Capitolinus, six other ways led into the Forum : the vicus Iugarius, between the temple of Saturn and the basilica Iulia ; the vicus Tuscus, between the basilica Iulia and the temple of Castor ; the flight of steps (p. 161) which led up to the Nova via and clivus Victoriae, between the lacus Iuturnae and the atrium Vestae ; the street between the temple of Faustina and the basilica Aemilia, the name of which is not known ; the Argiletum, between the

---

[1] For a different view, according to which the road ran along the south side of the Regia, see *Mélanges*, 1908, 236–253.

basilica Aemilia and the Curia; and, finally, the street between the Curia and the temple of Concord, on which were the
quarries (p. 169), and which was itself called Lautumiae in
early times and clivus Argentarius[1] under the late empire.    This
street, which connected the Forum with the porta Fontinalis
(p. 50), was the direct means of communication between the
Forum and the campus Martius until the imperial fora were
built.    The ancient pavement has been found beneath what
has been until very recently a part of the via di Marforio, with
which it approximately coincided.

The vicus Iugarius is said to have received its name from an
altar of Iuno Iuga, *quam putabant matrimonia iungere*,[2] but it
is quite as likely that it was so called because it connected the
Forum with the district of the forum Holitorium, or because
the makers of yokes had their shops here.    The present pavement is not ancient,[3] but preserves the line of the street after
the building of the basilica Iulia.    Some earlier foundations,
recently discovered[4] beneath the temple of Saturn, show that
before the Augustan period this street was a little farther to
the southeast.

According to tradition,[5] the vicus Tuscus derived its name
from a settlement of Etruscans, who either had fled to Rome
after the repulse of Porsenna at Aricia or had come to the
assistance of the Romans against Titus Tatius.    A more
plausible explanation is that this settlement was composed of
the workmen who had come to Rome to build the temple of
Iuppiter Capitolinus.    This street connected the Forum and
Velabrum, and bore an unsavory reputation.[6]    On its east side,
directly behind the temple of Castor, stood the temple of

---

[1] Jordan, I. 2. 437–438.

[2] Fest. 290; *Epit.* 104; Jordan, I. 2. 468; Gilbert, I. 257–263; III. 416–417.

[3] *NS.* 1883, 14.                    [4] *CR.* 1902, 94.

[5] Liv. ii. 14; Varro, *LL.* v. 46; Tac. *Ann.* iv. 65; Serv. *ad Aen.* v. 560;
Jordan, I. 1. 273–274, 295; I. 2. 469; Gilbert, II. 101–118; III. 416.

[6] Plaut. *Curc.* 482; Hor. *Sat.* ii. 3. 228.

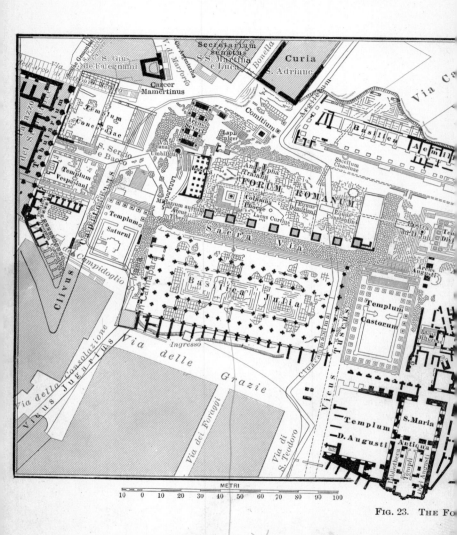

FIG. 23.  THE FO

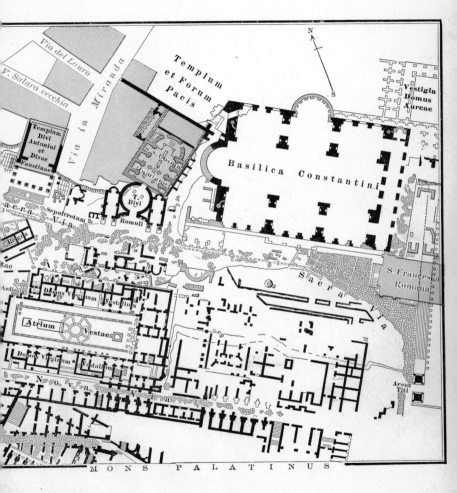

Via del Lauro

V. Salara vecchia

Templum
et Forum
Pacis

Via in Miranda

Templum
Divi
Antonini
et Divae
Faustinae

N

S

Vestigia
Domus
Aureae

S. Cosma
e Damiano

T.
Divi

S a c r a

Sepulcretum
V i a

Romuli

Basilica    Constantini

Regia

S. Francesca
Romana

Sacra
Via

ae

Aedien

Domus Virginum Vestalium

Atrium    Vestae

Domus Virginum   Vestalium

N O V A   V i a

Arcus
Titi

M O N S   P A L A T I N U S

Augustus and extensive warehouses (p. 165); and the removal of the medieval pavement between the basilica Iulia and the temple of Castor exposed to view[1] a unique specimen of street pavement of opus spicatum, or small cubes of brick. This pavement is about 15 metres in length, and is bounded on the west side by a gutter, but on the other it extends beneath the foundations of the temple, and was therefore laid before this temple was rebuilt by Tiberius. In this street stood a statue of Vortumnus,[2] which tradition assigned to Numa.

The **Argiletum**[3] connected the Forum with the Subura and the eastern section of the city, and was one of the great arteries of communication. Its general character was like that of the Subura (p. 457), but it was also a centre of the book trade. Any number of explanations were given by the Romans for the name, but the most probable is that it was derived from the clay (*argilla*) which was dug close by. The lower part of it was converted by Domitian and Nerva into the forum Transitorium (p. 282).

**The Temple of Concord.** — From the very earliest times an altar of Vulcan stood on the lower slope of the Capitoline, at the northwest corner of the Forum, and the surrounding space was called the **area Volcani** or **Volcanal**.[4] This area, a *locus substructus*, was about 5 metres above the level of the Comitium, and from it, before the building of the Rostra, the Roman officials addressed the people. At the edge of this area was also the Senaculum (p. 231), the assembling place of the senate, and a lotos tree, said to be as old as the city itself, was growing here in the time of Pliny. Some remains of very

---

[1] *CR.* 1899, 466; *BC.* 1899, 253. (This pavement is now covered.)

[2] Prop. iv. 2; Gilbert, III. 416.

[3] Varro, *LL.* v. 157; Serv. *ad Aen.* viii. 345; Mart. i. 3. 1, 117. 9; Jordan, I. 2. 345, 351; 3. 327; Gilbert, II. 87–92; *BC.* 1890, 98–102.

[4] Liv. xl. 19; Dionys. ii. 50; Fest. 290; Gell. iv. 5; Pl. *NH.* xvi. 236; Jordan, I. 2. 339–341; Gilbert, I. 248–257; *Mitt.* 1893, 87–88.

early tufa foundations have been found[1] just behind the arch
of Severus, which seem to have belonged to the Volcanal, and
traces of a sort of rock platform, 3.95 metres long by 2.80 wide,
which had been covered with cement and painted red. Its
upper surface is cut by various channels, and in front of it
are the remains of a drain made of tufa slabs. This may
possibly have been the ara Volcani. It shows signs of having
been damaged and repaired. Behind it are steps cut in the
rock and leading up to the temple of Concord. In the surface
of this rock are cuttings, round and square, which have some
resemblance to graves, and are so regarded by some[2] but probably
without reason. Although the cult of Vulcan continued here
at least down to the early empire,[3] the Volcanal must have been
much diminished in size by the encroachment of surrounding
buildings, and perhaps at last entirely buried.

The first temple of Concord was built by M. Furius Camillus in 367 B.C., to commemorate the passage of the Licinian
laws and the end of the long struggle between the orders.[4]
The space around the temple was then called the area Concordiae.
The temple was rebuilt in 121 B.C. by L. Opimius,[5] who also
erected the basilica Opimia[6] close to the temple on the north,
with probably the same orientation. The basilica was removed
and the temple entirely rebuilt by Tiberius, and dedicated in
10 A.D. in his own name and that of Drusus as the aedes Concordiae Augustae.[7] It was restored at least once afterward, but
at an unknown date. Peculiar local conditions led to the adop-
tion of a plan which made the structure unique among Roman
temples. Instead of the usual proportions, the cella of the
Augustan temple was 45 metres wide and only 24 deep, while

---

[1] CR. 1902, 94 ; BC. 1902, 25–26, 125–133 ; 1903, 159–162 ; Mitt. 1902, 10 ; 1905,
7–9.          [2] Richter, BRT. IV. 15–16.          [3] CIL. vi. 457.
[4] Plut. Cam. 42 ; Ov. Fast. i. 641 ; Jordan, I. 2. 332–336 ; Gilbert, III. 62–64.
[5] App. Bell. Civ. i. 26 ; Plut. C. Gracch. 17.
[6] Varro, LL. v. 156 ; Cic. pro Sest. 140 ; CIL. vi. 2338–2339 ; Jordan, I. 2.
338, 384 ; Gilbert, III. 214 ; Mitt. 1893, 84, 91.
[7] Suet. Tib. 20 ; Dio Cass. lv. 8 ; lvi. 25 ; CIL. vi. 89–94.

the pronaos was only 24 metres wide and 14 deep, and there-fore did not extend across the whole front of the cella. The back wall of the cella abutted against the front of the Tabu-larium (p. 307), and a very wide flight of steps led down from the pronaos to the area. The interior of the cella was sur-rounded by a row of white marble columns, standing on a low shelf which projected from the main wall. This wall con-tained eleven niches, in the central one of which, opposite the entrance, a statue of Concord must have stood.

Recent investigation[1] of the concrete foundations has brought forward evidence of four successive periods in the history of the temple, and has shown that the peculiar shape was to some extent characteristic of all of them. The earliest concrete seems to date from the third century B.C., and, together with some in the temple of Castor (see p. 180), is probably the earliest known example of its use. Its existence would indi-cate a restoration, otherwise unknown to us, before that of Opimius.

The existing remains consist of the concrete core of the podium, in which are two chambers that may have been store-rooms for treasure; the threshold of the main entrance, com-posed of two blocks of Porta santa marble 7 metres long; a very few fragments of the marble pavement of the cella and the pronaos; and a part of the magnificent cornice, now in the Tabularium, together with numerous small architectural frag-ments. The exterior of the temple was covered with marble, and the cella was a veritable museum[2] of works of art of all kinds, to which frequent reference is made in classical litera-ture. It also served as a frequent meeting-place for the senate.

Near by was an aedicula Concordiae, built by Q. Flavius in 304 B.C. This shrine[3] was made of bronze and stood *in Graecostasi*

---

[1] *CR.* 1906, 82–84, 184.

[2] Pl. *NH.* xxxiv. 73, 80, 89; xxxvii. 4; Jacobi, *Grundzüge einer Museo-graphie d. Stadt Rom zur Zeit des Kaisers Augustus*, 1884.

[3] Pl. *NH.* xxxiii. 19; Liv. ix. 46; Gilbert, III. 64.

(p. 230) *quae tunc supra comitium erat.* It must have been removed when Tiberius rebuilt the temple of Concord.

Close to the Volcanal were certain stationes municipiorum,[1] the exact object of which is not known; but for their position near the temple of Concord epigraphic evidence has recently been found.

**The Temple of Vespasian.** — The temple of Vespasian[2] was begun by Titus, completed by Domitian, and restored by Severus. Although only the name of Vespasian appeared on the temple, it is called the temple of Vespasian and Titus in documents of the fourth century, and was probably dedicated to both by Domitian. It was prostyle hexastyle, 33 metres long and 22 wide. The existing remains consist of the core of the podium, with some of its peperino lining; two fragments of the cella wall of travertine; part of the pedestal in the rear of the cella, on which stood the statues of Vespasian and Titus; and three Corinthian columns at the southeast corner of the pronaos. These columns are of white marble, 15.20 metres high and 1.57 in diameter at the base, and support a portion of the entablature on which are the last letters of the inscription[3] recording the restoration by Severus and Caracalla. A restored fragment of the cornice is in the Tabularium. The temple was covered inside and out with marble in the usual way, and there were marble columns round the interior of the cella, as in the temple of Castor.

As the available space was small and ill adapted for its purpose, this temple had to be built directly against the front of the Tabularium. It thus closed the entrance to the long flight of steps which led from the Forum through the Tabularium to the top of the Capitoline (p. 308). The existing columns and entablature were taken down in 1811, and reset.

---

[1] Pl. *NH.* xvi. 236; *BC.* 1899, 242–243; 1900, 124–134; *Mitt.* 1902, 11; 1905, 9.
[2] Jordan, I. 2. 192–193; Reber, *Die Ruinen Roms*, 81–86.
[3] *CIL.* vi. 938.

Between this temple and that of Concord are the ruins of a small building, erroneously called an aedicula Faustinae,[1] which is contemporary with the temple of Vespasian, as its left wall rests on the foundations of the temple, which were made to project for this very purpose. The building was 4.10 metres wide and 2.50 deep, and the marks of its vaulted roof are visible on the front wall of the Tabularium. The purpose of the structure is unknown, but in it was found a marble base dedicated to Faustina by the *viatores quaestorii ab aerario Saturni.*

FIG. 24. — THE PORTICUS DEORUM CONSENTIUM.

**The Porticus Deorum Consentium.** — Next to the temple of Vespasian, in the obtuse angle formed by the Tabularium and the clivus Capitolinus, are the remains of a curious structure consisting of two parts. The substructure contains seven small chambers, without light and of unknown use. Above is a plat-

---

[1] *CIL.* vi. 1019; *Mitt.* 1893, 284–285.

form, paved with blocks of marble, on which is a row of small
rooms, 4 metres high and 3.70 deep, made of brick-faced concrete.    They are built against the rock under the Tabularium,
and against the retaining wall of the clivus.    Seven have been
excavated, and the rest (probably five) are buried beneath the
houses on the west side of the clivus.    In front of these chambers, which open outward, is a porticus of Corinthian columns
supporting an entablature.    This porticus has been restored,
but most of the entablature and four of the columns are ancient.
The statues of the twelve Dii Consentes stood probably in the
intercolumniations of this colonnade, the restoration or building
of which in 367 A.D. by Vettius Praetextatus, a vigorous sup-
porter of paganism, is recorded by the inscription [1] on the architrave.    Gilded statues of these gods and goddesses [2] had stood
in this part of the Forum from very early times, but nothing is
known of any temple or shrine in which they were placed.

**The Temple of Saturn.** — Corresponding to the altar of Vulcan at the northwest corner of the Forum, there was at the
southwest corner a very ancient altar of Saturn, [3] which was
replaced at the beginning of the republic by a temple, built, it
was said, by the consuls for the year 497 B.C. [4]  The temple
was rebuilt [5] by L. Munatius Plancus in 42 B.C., and is represented on fragments [6] of the Marble Plan.    During the later
empire, it was injured by fire and restored, as the inscription [7]
on the architrave records.    The existing podium belongs to
the temple of Plancus.    It is constructed of walls of travertine and peperino, with concrete filling, and was covered
with marble facing.    It is 22.50 metres wide, about 40 long,

---

[1] *CIL*. vi. 102.

[2] Varro, *RR.* i. 1; Jordan, I. 2. 366–367; Gilbert, III. 102–103.

[3] Dionys. i. 34; Macrob. *Sat.* i. 8. 2.

[4] Liv. ii. 21; Dionys. vi. 1; Jordan I. 2. 360–363; Gilbert, III. 401–403.

[5] Suet. *Aug.* 29; *CIL*. vi. 1316; x. 6087.

[6] Jordan, *FUR.* 22, 23, 30.          [7] *CIL*. vi. 937.

and its front and east side rise very high above the Forum because of the slope of the Capitoline hill. The temple was Ionic, hexastyle prostyle, with two columns on each side, not counting those at the angles. Of the superstructure eight columns of the pronaos remain, six in front and one on each side, together with the entablature, and all date from a period of great decadence, that of the final restoration. The front columns are of gray and those on the sides of red granite, while the entablature is of white marble. The columns are 11 metres in height, and 1.43 in diameter at the base; but in some of them the drums which form the shaft have been wrongly placed, so that the shaft does not taper regularly toward the top. The bases, also, are of three different kinds — Attic, and Corinthian with and without a plinth. The entablature exhibits the same debased style, as architrave and frieze are united in one plane.[1]

The steps of this temple were of peculiar form, on account of the closeness of the clivus Capitolinus and the sharp angle which it made in front of the temple, the main flight being only about one-third the width of the pronaos. From the early years of the republic to the end of the empire, the temple of Saturn contained the aerarium Saturni or state treasury, which was presided over by quaestors and praefecti aerarii, under the control of the senate. It is possible that there may be strong rooms for the storage of money in the podium, but they have not been discovered.

The area Saturni[2] was probably in the space between the vicus Iugarius and the clivus Capitolinus, south of the temple, for there appears to have been no room for it on any other side. The offices of the treasury department may have stood on this area, and also altars of Ceres and Ops, erected in 7 B.C. *in vico Iugario*.[3]

---

[1] For recent excavations, see *NS*. 1899, 49; *Arch. Anz.* 1899, 7; *CR.* 1899, 234; *BC.* 1902, 26; *Mitt.* 1902, 9.

[2] *CIL*. i. 636; vi. 1265.    [3] *CIL*. i². p. 240; Jordan, I. 2. 364–365.

**The Temple of Castor**. — The official name of this temple was aedes Castoris [1] [ad Forum] but it was also called aedes Castorum,[2] and sometimes erroneously aedes Castoris et Pollucis.[3] It was dedicated, according to tradition, in 484 B.C.,[4] close to the spring of Juturna, to commemorate the appearance of the Dioscuri at that spot after the battle of lake Regillus. Internal evidence [5] seems to show that it was restored perhaps two hundred years later, and again [6] in 117 B.C. by L. Caecilius Metellus, but probably still in the Tuscan style, with stuccoed columns of tufa. Some repairs at least were made by Verres; [7] but the temple was completely rebuilt by Tiberius,[8] and dedicated in his own name and that of Drusus in 6 A.D. A still later restoration has usually been supposed to have been carried out by Domitian or Hadrian, but this is by no means certain,[9] and in any case it was probably not such as to materially affect the appearance of the building.

The imperial temple was Corinthian,[10] octostyle and peripteral, with eleven columns on a side, and a double row on each side of the pronaos. This pronaos was 9.90 metres by 15.80, the cella 16 by 19.70, and the whole temple about 50 metres long by 30 wide. The floor of the temple was about 7 metres above the Sacra via. The very lofty podium consisted of a concrete core enclosed in tufa walls, from which projected short spur walls. On these stood the columns, but directly beneath them at the points of heaviest pressure travertine was substituted for tufa. Between these spur walls were chambers in the podium, opening outward and closed by metal doors,

---

[1] Suet. *Caes.* 10.

[2] Pl. *NH.* x. 121.

[3] Suet. *Cal.* 22; *CIL.* vi. 2202.

[7] Cic. *in Verr.* i. 130–154.

[4] Liv. ii. 42; Ov. *Fast.* i. 706.

[5] *CR.* 1906, 77–82.

[6] Asc. *ad Scaur.* 46; Cic. *in Verr.* i. 154.

[8] Suet. *Tib.* 20; Dio Cass. lv. 27; Jordan, I. 2. 369–376; Gilbert, III. 58–62.

[9] *CR.* 1906, 77.

[10] Reber, *Die Ruinen Roms*, 136–142; *Jahrb. d. Inst.* 1898, 87–114; *CR.* 1899, 466; 1902, 95, 284; 1906, 77–84, 184; *BC.* 1899, 253; 1900, 66, 285; 1902, 28; 1903, 165; *Mitt.* 1902, 66–67; 1905, 80.

Fig. 25. — The Temple of Castor.

which seem to have been used as safe deposit vaults for the
imperial fiscus and for the treasures of private persons.[1]

From the pronaos a flight of eleven steps, extending nearly
across the whole width of the temple, led down to a wide platform, 3.66 metres above the area in front.  This platform was
provided with a railing, and formed a high and safe place
from which to address the people.  From the frequent references in literature, it is evident that there was a similar

FIG. 26. — THE TEMPLE OF CASTOR RESTORED.

arrangement in the earlier temple of Metellus.  Leading from
this platform to the ground were two narrow staircases, at the
ends and not in front.  The podium was covered with marble
facing, and decorated with two cornices, one at the top, and
another just above the metal doors of the strong chambers.
The pavement of the temple of the late republic or early em-

---

[1] Cic. *pro Quinct.* 17 ; Schol. Juven. xiv. 261.

pire was of mosaic, of which a small fragment has been preserved, but this was afterward covered by a pavement of
marble slabs.  Of the superstructure three columns on the
east side are standing, which are regarded as perhaps the finest
architectural remains in Rome.  They are of white marble,
fluted, 12.50 metres in height and 1.45 in diameter.  The entablature, 3.75 metres high, has a plain frieze and an admir-
ably worked cornice.  Those who believe in an effective
restoration of the temple after the Augustan period, assign the
existing superstructure to this later date.

In the temple of Castor were kept the standard weights and
measures,[1] and it was frequently used for meetings of the
senate,[2] as its commanding position made it comparatively safe
from attacks of the mob.

**The Temple of Julius Caesar**. — The body of Julius Caesar
was burned [3] at the east end of the Forum, in front of the
Regia, and on this very spot an altar [4] was erected and a
column of Numidian marble,[5] twenty feet high, set up; but
they were soon removed by Dolabella.[6]  In 42 B.C. Augustus
determined [7] to build here a temple to the deified Caesar (aedes
divi Iuli).  The temple was finished some years later, after the
battle of Actium, and dedicated August 18, 29 B.C.[8]  It was restored by Hadrian,[9] and there are some traces of a still later
restoration, perhaps in the fourth century.

Considerable portions of the foundation remain, and the excavations,[10] recently completed, have shown that it consisted of

---

[1] Jordan, I. 2. 374 n.;  *Mitt.* 1889, 244–245.

[2] Cic. *in Verr.* i. 129; Jul. Capit. *Vit. Maximin.* 16; Trebell. *Vit. Valerian.*
5; *CIL.* i. p. 107.                         [3] Liv. *Epit.* 116; Plut. *Caes.* 68.

[4] App. *Bell. Civ.* ii. 148; iii. 2; Dio Cass. xliv. 51.        [5] Suet. *Caes.* 85.

[6] Cic. *ad Att.* xiv. 15; *Phil.* i. 5.

[7] Dio Cass. xlvii. 18, 19; *Mon. Anc.* iv. 2; Jordan, I. 2. 406–409.

[8] Dio Cass. li. 22; *Hemer. Amit. Antiat. ad xv. Kal. Sept.*

[9] Cohen, *Hadr.* 416–419, 1388.

[10] *Jahrb. des Inst.* 1889, 137–162; *Antike Denkmäler*, i. 27, 28; *CR.* 1899,
185, 466; *Mitt.* 1902, 61–62; 1905, 75–76; *BC.* 1903, 81–83; *Atti,* 563–566.

two parts, a rectangular platform 3.5 metres high, 26 wide, and about 30 long, and on this the stylobate proper of the temple, which rose 2.36 metres above the platform and was about 17 metres in width.   In the middle of the front of the platform is a semicircular niche, 8.3 metres in diameter, of which a consid-

FIG. 27. — THE ALTAR OF CAESAR.

erable part of the peperino wall has been left in place, although elsewhere the tufa and peperino blocks have been removed and only the concrete core remains.   At a late date, a rude wall of tufa was built directly across this niche, and its removal disclosed a portion of the concrete core of a round altar standing on the travertine slabs which formed the pavement of the Forum when the temple was built.   This is shown by the fact that the slabs were cut off to allow the wall of the niche to be built. The altar appears to have been purposely demolished.   It is evident that when the temple was built the altar on the spot where Caesar's body was burnt had been restored, and that the sacred monument was preserved in the niche of the platform.

This platform projected beyond the stylobate on both sides, and in front for a distance of 7 metres. The projection in front, encircling the niche, was called the rostra aedis divi Iuli, or perhaps the rostra Iulia.[1] The wall on both sides of the niche was decorated with the beaks of the ships which were captured

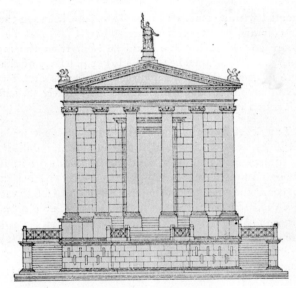

Fig. 28. — The Temple of Caesar restored.

at Actium,[2] in a style similar to that of the old Rostra. There is some evidence in support of the view, probable in itself, that Caesar had himself erected a second rostra at the east end of the Forum, which was represented by the rostra aedis divi Iuli after the building of this temple.[3]

The temple itself was of an unusual type,[4] being of the Ionic

---

[1] Suet. *Aug.* 100; Dio Cass. lvi. 34; Front. *de Aquis*, 129.    [2] Dio Cass. li. 19.
[3] Richter, *Geschichte der Rednerbühne*, 52–55; Gilbert, III. 117.
[4] Vitr. iii. 2. 2; Stat. *Silv.* i. 1. 22–24.

order, hexastyle pycnostyle, probably with *antae*. The diameter of the columns at the base was about 1.18 metres, and their height nine times the diameter. The cella occupied the whole width of the temple, about 17 metres, but was only about 6.5 metres deep. Within the cella, opposite the very wide entrance, stood a colossal statue of Caesar, the head of which was ornamented with a comet or star. The space between the two middle columns of the pronaos was wider than that between the others, so that this statue could be seen from the area of the Forum. The approaches to the lower platform of the temple were at each side of the rostra. Numerous architectural fragments have been found, and from them a fairly satisfactory reconstruction can be made.

**The Temple of Antoninus and Faustina**. — This temple was erected in 141 A.D., and dedicated to Faustina, the deified wife of Antoninus Pius; and after the death of the latter in 161, it was dedicated to both together.[1] The inscription[2] on the architrave records the first dedication, and that added afterward on the frieze records the second. In the seventh or eighth century the temple, apparently in good condition, was converted into the church of S. Lorenzo in Miranda, but since that time it has suffered great injuries. It was hexastyle prostyle, with two columns on each side, besides those at the corners, and pilasters *in antis*. The columns are of cipollino, 17 metres high and 1.45 in diameter at the base, with Corinthian capitals of white marble, and support an entablature of white marble, which probably encircled the whole building. The existing remains consist of portions of the cella wall of peperino, built into the walls of the church, extending for 20 metres on the northwest and 15 on the southeast side; the columns of the pronaos, which stand free from the church with the exception of the two nearest the *antae;* the architrave and frieze of the façade and sides as far as the cella wall extends, but only a

---

[1] Jul. Capit. *Vit. Pii*, 6, 13; *CIL*. vi. 2001.    [2] *CIL*. vi. 1005.

small part of the cornice; and the wide flight of steps [1] leading down to the Sacra via, in the middle of which are the remains of an altar. Some fragments of a colossal seated female statue,[2] and a few other bits of sculpture, have been found near by. The whole temple was covered with slabs of marble, but these have entirely disappeared. The frieze on the sides of the temple is very beautifully sculptured in relief with garlands, sacrificial implements, and griffins. On the columns are numerous inscriptions and figures.

FIG. 29. — THE REGIA AND THE TEMPLE OF ANTONINUS AND FAUSTINA.

**The Archaic Necropolis.** — The recent excavations have brought to light the original level of the Sacra via in front of

[1] *CR.* 1899, 186; *NS.* 1899, 77; *BC.* 1900, 62–63.
[2] *CR.* 1902, 285; *BC.* 1902, 30–31.

the temple of Faustina, the lower parts of its steps, and also the remains of several private houses which occupied this site before the building of the temple, each one of which was provided with a separate sewer emptying into the main cloaca under the street (p. 273). The most important discovery at this point is that of an ancient necropolis,[1] belonging to the early Palatine or Septimontium city, at a depth of 3 or 4 metres beneath the pavement of the Sacra via.

Fifty-two graves had been found up to the close of 1909. Their contents have been removed, and the whole area covered. These graves are of two kinds, those for inhumation, and those constructed as receptacles for ashes. The latter are the earlier, and are round holes sunk in the rock and covered with slabs of tufa. In them were placed large *dolia*, containing cinerary urns and various smaller vessels for sacrificial gifts. The urns are of different shapes, some of them hut-urns, representing the early Italic hut, with a door and a roof with raised bars like the rafters of a house. Others are bowl-shaped, but with a cover like that of the hut-urns. Besides ashes, fragments of bone and charred grains of wheat were found in these urns. Almost all the pottery is of clay found in the neighborhood, made without a potter's wheel, and in some cases decorated with simple scratchings.

The graves for inhumation are rectangular in shape, and belong in general to a later period, as is shown by the fact that they cut into the round graves. The larger number, however, are graves for children, and as the burial of children seems to have been often contemporaneous with the cremation of adults, the two periods may have overlapped. Some of these graves contained skeletons, and one the remnants of a wooden coffin.

---

[1] *NS.* 1902, 96–111; 1903, 123–170; 375–427; 1905, 145–193; 1906, 5–54, 253–294; *BC.* 1902, 37–53, 186–189; 1903, 33–42, 252–271; 1909, 117; *Mitt.* 1902, 92–94; 1905, 95–115; *CR.* 1902, 476–477; 1903, 328; 1904, 137–138; *Mon. d. Lincei,* 1905, 273–314; Pais, *Ancient Legends,* 34–37; *Atti,* 499–514.

FIG. 30. — THE ANCIENT NECROPOLIS ON THE SACRA VIA.

They resemble the graves found on the Esquiline and belong to the same period of civilization, the early iron age.

The funeral gifts found in all these graves, aside from the pottery, consist mostly of bronze jewellery and arms, with some ornaments of glass, amber, and ivory, but no gold, and only two bits of silver. Nothing is later than the sixth century, and the use of the necropolis probably extended from about the ninth to the sixth century. It was buried and forgotten during the republic, and the date of its abandonment corresponds with that assigned by tradition for the draining of the Forum and the beginning of its development.

**The Temple of Ianus Geminus.** — This temple is said to have been built by Numa,[1] but there is no record of any restoration or rebuilding of any sort, although the edifice was standing in the sixth century. It is therefore very unlikely that it was ever moved from its original site. Besides Geminus, the epithets Quirinus,[2] Bifrons,[3] and Biformis [4] were employed when this temple was mentioned. Its gates were opened in time of war and closed in time of peace. After the reign of Numa, such closing is said to have occurred in the year 235 B.C. after the end of the first Punic war, in 30 B.C. after the battle of Actium, and thereafter at more frequent intervals, down to the fifth century.[5]

A very brief description,[6] and coins of Nero,[7] represent this temple as a small rectangular structure, with two side walls and double doors at each end. The walls were not so high as the doors, and were surmounted by a grating. These gratings and the arches over the doors supported an entablature of two members, which extended all round the building, but there was

---

[1] Liv. i. 19; Jordan, I. 2. 345–352; Gilbert, I. 321–328.

[2] Suet. *Aug.* 22.        [3] Verg. *Aen.* xii. 198.        [4] Ov. *Fast.* i. 89.

[5] *Mon. Anc.* ii. 42; Lamprid. *Vit. Comm.* 16; Jul. Capit. *Vit. Gordian.* 26; Claudian, *de Cons. Stil.* ii. 287.

[6] Procop. *Bell. Goth.* i. 25.

[7] Cohen, *Nero*, 132–178, 183.

no roof. The ancient bronze statue of the two-faced god, of Etruscan workmanship, stood in the centre of the temple, which was no temple in the ordinary sense, but a passage (*ianus*) with gates, intended to symbolize some essential part of the Roman conception of this divinity. The whole temple, as well as the statue, was of bronze, and being so small a structure, it appears to have disappeared entirely, for no traces of it have ever been found. The numerous references in literature to its site do not furnish as exact information as might be desired. It is described as being *circa imum Argiletum*,[1] *ad infimum Argiletum*,[2] before the Curia,[3] in front of the Curia,[4] and Ovid[5] says that it was *iuncta duobus foris, i.e.* the forum Romanum and the forum Iulium.

FIG. 31. — THE TEMPLE OF JANUS.

It is clear, therefore, that it was on the north side of the Forum, near the Curia, and it has generally been supposed that it was between the Curia and the west end of the basilica Aemilia, at the end of the Argiletum, but the recent excavations have shown hardly any room here even for so small a building.[6]

The temple was also called geminae portae and portae belli,[7] and Varro,[8] in describing the gates of the Palatine, states that the third was called the porta Ianualis from Janus, and therefore a statue of Janus was placed there. According to another tradition,[9] Janus caused a flood of hot water to issue from this gate, the porta Ianualis,[10] to defend the Romans from the ad-

[1] Serv. *ad Aen.* vii. 607.  [4] Dio Cass. lxxiii. 13.  [7] Verg. *Aen.* vii. 607 ; i. 294.

[2] Liv. i. 19.  [5] *Fast.* i. 258.  [8] *LL.* v. 165.

[3] Procob. *Bell. Goth.* i. 25.  [6] *Mitt.* 1902, 47.  [9] Macrob. *Sat.* i. 9, 17.

[10] For an ingenious but unconvincing theory that the temple, identical with the porta Ianualis, was a gate in the fortification of the Septimontium, which here coincided with the brook Spinon, and that the story of a flood of hot

vance of the victorious Sabines, and from this event the
spot was called **Lautolae** (*a lavando*).[1] A porta Ianualis, however, on or near the site of this temple, can have belonged
neither to the Palatine nor the Servian wall.

**The Basilica Iulia.** — The regular appearance of the Forum
was due in large measure to the great basilicas which bounded
it on the north and south sides. In 170 B.C. Sempronius
Gracchus erected the basilica Sempronia[2] behind the tabernae
veteres, but nothing further is known of this building, and it
and the tabernae must have been removed to make room for
the basilica Iulia. This was begun by Julius Caesar in 54 B.C.,
dedicated in an unfinished state in 46, completed by Augustus,
burned soon afterward, and, having been rebuilt by Augustus,
dedicated again in 12 A.D. in the names of Gaius and Lucius
Caesar.[3] There are indications of repairs or restorations under
the Antonines,[4] and the building was restored by Diocletian
after it had been severely injured by fire. It was again restored[5] by a certain Probianus, prefect of the city, probably
in 416 A.D., who also adorned it with statues. The amount
and magnificence of the marble used in this basilica marked it
as the special prey of the vandals of the middle ages, a lime-kiln
having been found built on its very pavement. In the sixth
century the outer aisle on the west side was converted into the
church of S. Maria de Cannapara.[6]

The basilica occupied a space 101 metres long and 49 wide,

---

water was connected with this stream, see Schneider, *Mitt.* 1895, 172–178. For
other recent views, see *Mélanges*, 1908, 258–261; and Binder, *Die Plebs*, Leipzig, 1909, 61–72.

[1] Varro, *LL.* v. 156.   [2] Liv. xliv. 16; Gilbert, III. 214.

[3] Cic. *ad Att.* iv. 17. 8 (16. 14); *Mon. Anc.* iv. 13; Suet. *Aug.* 29; Jordan, I.
2. 385–391; Gilbert, III. 221–223.

[4] *BC.* 1871, 246.

[5] *NS.* 1883, 47–48; *CIL.* vi. 1156, 1658; *Mitt.* 1902, 54; *Klio*, 1902, 269–270.

[6] Cf. *BC.* 1891, 229 ff.; *Archivio Storico dell' Arte*, 1896, 164; Frothingham,
*Monuments of Christian Rome*, New York, 1908, 83.

bounded on all sides by streets, the Sacra via, the vicus Iugarius, the vicus Tuscus, and a street on the south connecting the last two, the name of which is not known. In the later restorations the material of construction, but not the form, of the Augustan basilica was changed.[1] It consisted of a central court, 82 metres long and 16 wide, surrounded on all sides by two aisles, 7.50 metres wide, over which were the galleries of a second story.[2] These aisles were formed by the pillars of the façade, which were of marble, and by inner rows of similar pillars made of brick and lined with marble. The first floor of the basilica was therefore an open arcade, divided by the marble balustrades which joined the pillars. Of these pillars there were eighteen on each of the longer sides and eight, counting the ends of the spur walls, on the shorter. The entire outside of the basilica was constructed originally of white marble, and on the outer faces of its pillars were engaged columns of the Doric order. The floor of the basilica sloped slightly toward the northeast corner, and was paved with slabs of marble, colored in the central court and white in the aisles. There is no doubt that the central area was covered with a wooden roof,[3] which rose above the roof of the side aisles, and admitted light through its side windows.

A continuous flight of three steps leads down from the floor of the central court to that of the outer aisle in front, which, being lower, forms a sort of portico. From this aisle steps again lead down to the street, but as there is a considerable grade in the Sacra via, there were seven steps at the east end and only one at the west. On the south side was a row of rooms, opening on the street, called *tabernae*, and probably used as offices. Some of these rooms, with massive tufa walls, have been partially excavated.

The existing remains consist of the foundation, with frag-

---

[1] *CR.* 1901, 136; *Mitt.* 1902, 60.      [2] Pl. *Epist.* vi. 33; Suet. *Cal.* 37.
[3] Stat. *Silv.* i. 1, 29; Mart. vi. 38. 6.

ments of the marble pavement, both white and colored, on
which are inscribed upwards of eighty *tabulae lusoriae*;[1] the
steps, with portions of the marble casing; and on the vicus
Iugarius some of the brick pillars and arches of the outer aisles
which were built into the church of S. Maria in Cannapara,
together with some fragments of the marble pillars of the
outside. Against the second column from the front on the
west end, a heavy pier of masonry was built, which formed
part of an arch across the vicus Iugarius. Of this arch nothing further is known. Some architectural fragments have
been found, but the standing column of travertine and many
of the brick piers are modern.

**The Basilica Aemilia.** — In 179 B.C. the censors M. Aemilius
Lepidus and M. Fulvius Nobilior erected a basilica[2] which was
called either the Fulvia[3] or Aemilia et Fulvia.[4] This edifice was decorated with metal shields and probably thoroughly
restored by M. Aemilius Lepidus, consul in 78 B.C.[5] Another
restoration, at Caesar's expense, was undertaken in 54 B.C. by
the aedile L. Aemilius Paullus,[6] but he seems not to have
finished the work, and the new structure was completed and
dedicated by his son in 34 B.C.[7] It was burned in 14 B.C.,
and again rebuilt at the expense of Augustus,[8] but in the name
of Aemilius. It had become a sort of family monument,
and was regularly known as the basilica Aemilia, or basilica
Pauli.

Some parts of this basilica were visible as late as the sixteenth century, but they were destroyed or buried soon afterward. As a result of the recent excavations, however, the
larger part of the building has been uncovered, and although

---

[1] *Mitt.* 1896, 227–252.          [2] Liv. xl. 51.          [3] Plut. *Caes.* 29.
[4] Varro, *LL.* vi. 4.          [5] Pl. *NH.* xxxv. 13; Babelon, *Monnaies*, i. 129.
[6] Cic. *ad Att.* iv. 16, 14, App. *Bell. Civ.* ii. 26; Stat. *Silv.* i. 1, 30; Tac.
*Ann.* iii. 72.          [7] Dio Cass. xlix. 42.
[8] Dio Cass. liv. 24; Jordan, I. 2. 391–394; Gilbert, III. 213, 221–222.

the work has not yet been completed, its general plan is now known.

The basilica [1] occupied the whole space between the temple of Faustina and the Argiletum, and the ruins which have been found in this area belong to four successive epochs, — the republican, the Augustan, the late imperial, and the medieval. The first lie beneath the second, and consist principally of massive walls of tufa, some of which have been worked into

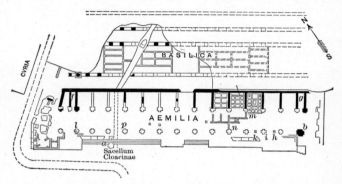

FIG. 32. — PLAN OF THE BASILICA AEMILIA.[2]

the foundations of the Augustan structure, and of a network of drains, some of them very ancient, which are at a lower level than the so-called Cloaca Maxima.

So far as can be known from the excavations up to date, the Augustan basilica consisted of three parts: the porticus, or façade toward the Forum; the tabernae, or rooms opening into the porticus; and the main hall, which was separated from the front part by a wall. Four steps lead from the Forum area to a platform 0.75 metre wide and two more to the floor of the porticus, the façade of which was formed by an

---

[1] BC. 1899, 169–204; 1900, 3–8; 1903, 87–96; *Arch. Anz.* 1900, 5–6; *Mitt.* 1902, 41–57; 1905, 53–63; *CR.* 1899, 465; 1900, 237; 1901, 136; 1902, 95; *Atti*, 566–570.

[2] The central hall has now been almost entirely excavated.

arcade of sixteen great pillars, besides the larger piers at the
ends, of white marble, with engaged half-columns on their
outer faces. Only the base of the pillar (b, Fig. 32) at the
east corner was found standing, but the travertine foundations
of all the others are *in situ*, except that of the pillar at the
west corner. Here the foundations had been removed bodily,
and the entire west end[1] of the porticus had been built over,
apparently about the beginning of the sixteenth century. The
distance between these pillars was 5.41 metres, and from 14 to
15 metres behind them was a wall of tufa which seems to have
been built originally of two courses of stone, 1.20 metres thick,
separating the porticus from the central hall. The inner
course of tufa was afterward partly replaced by a brick wall
of equal thickness, on which fragments of the decoration of the
hall were found. From this main wall, spur walls 7 metres
long projected on lines corresponding exactly with the pillars
of the façade, and formed chambers between them, 7.15 metres
in depth and 5.41 in breadth. These chambers have been
called tabernae, and doubtless served as offices of some sort.
The spur walls ended in marble pilasters, of one of which
a fragment was found *in situ*, and the walls themselves were
probably covered with marble. As they projected 7 metres
from the main wall, the space between them and the pillars of
the façade was also 7 metres wide, thus forming a corridor of
that width and about 85 metres long. In the middle taberna,
the main wall was cut through and a doorway 3.80 metres
wide made, of which the threshold is still *in situ*, and there
were also two other doorways, east and west of that in the
centre. At the east end of the row of tabernae is a smaller
room, and at the west end two, which may have contained
staircases to the upper story. The west end of the basilica
was not built at right angles to the main axis of the structure,
because of the Curia opposite. Across the east end of the

---

[1] For a discussion of the sixteenth-century drawings of this end of the
basilica, see *Mitt.* 1902, 45–49; 1905, 54–56, and literature there cited.

porticus is a sort of pavilion-like hall.  Very few remains have
been found of the architectural members of the façade of this
basilica (cf. Fig. 33).   The main hall was probably about 70
metres in length.   Its width was 27 metres, and it was divided
into a central nave 12 metres wide and three aisles 5 metres in
width, two of which were on the north side.   The pavement

FIG. 33. — FRAGMENTS FROM THE BASILICA AEMILIA.

of this main hall was composed of slabs of colored marble,
many of which are *in situ*.   Fastened to them by partial
melting are many coins and bits of metal, the evident result
of a fire about the beginning of the fifth century.   This pavement was then covered over with another.   The side aisles
were divided from the nave by rows of columns of African
marble, 0.85 metre in diameter, with Corinthian capitals and
an entablature of white marble.   Over the aisles, which had

wooden ceilings, were galleries, and an upper row of columns
stood upon the lower, of the same marble, but only 0.55 metre
in diameter.   Many fragments of these columns and entablatures have been found, and they exhibit the best form of
Roman decorative art.   We are told that one of the chief
ornaments of this basilica was twenty-four columns of Phrygian
marble,[1] but no trace of them has yet been found.   The main
entrance to this hall must have been at the west end.

At a much later period, probably in the early part of the
fifth century, the porticus underwent a complete transformation, and in place of the great marble pillars, about twenty-five
columns of red granite with Corinthian capitals were erected
on white marble pedestals, with an intercolumnar space of 3.77
metres.   These columns did not correspond with the walls of
the tabernae, and what was done with these chambers cannot be
discovered from the ruins.   One of these columns only (*l*, Fig.
32) was found *in situ*, but parts of three others (*h, i, k*) have
been set up in their proper places.

In the seventh and eighth centuries the basilica was more
or less built over, and walls of that epoch, with pavements of
white and colored marble, are visible, especially in the tabernae,
where there was evidently a sort of fortified dwelling.   The
threshold (*n*, Fig. 32) of one of the doors was formed by one
of the blocks of marble from the Regia, on which the *fasti consulares* were engraved.[2]  This block contains part of the lists
of the years 380 and 331/330 B.C., but some of the inscription
has been worn away.   It is now in the palazzo dei Conservatori.

On the north side of the Forum, near the Comitium and the
cloaca, was a shrine of **Venus Cloacina**,[3] which probably dated
from the end of the sixth century B.C.   At the edge of the low-

---

[1] Pl. *NH.* xxxvi. 102; cf. *Mitt.* 1888, 95; 1889, 242.

[2] *NS.* 1899, 384; *BC.* 1899, 204–213; *Arch. Anz.* 1900, 6.

[3] Liv. iii. 48; Pl. *NH.* xv. 119; Plaut. *Curc.* 471; Cohen, *Méd. Cons.* xxix,
*Mussidia*, 5, 6; *Mitt.* 1893, 248; 1905, 62–63; *Wiener Studien*, 1902, 418–424;
*BC.* 1900, 61–62; 1903, 97–99; *CR.* 1901, 138.

est step of the basilica, near the west end and directly over the drain that flows under the basilica, is a marble base (*a*, Fig. 32), round, except on the west side, where it has a rectangular projection, and 2.40 metres in diameter. It rests on a slab of travertine and eight courses of tufa, the character of which shows that the foundation was gradually raised as the basilica encroached upon it. Shape, position close to the Cloaca Maxima, and especially the evidence of a denarius of 43 B.C., on which the sacellum Cloacinae is represented, make the identification of this base as that of the shrine in question practically certain.

At the south corner of the basilica was found a pile of broken blocks of marble, which has not been disturbed. Some of them belong to the Augustan basilica, and the rest are of unknown origin. Most noteworthy are three very large pieces which together form an epistyle[1] 5.75 metres long and 1.75 high, on which is a dedicatory inscription to Lucius Caesar. It has been suggested that this inscription, together with another, the fragments of which were found near by, belonged to a monument erected in honor of Augustus near the east end of the basilica, and in front of the temple of Julius Caesar. It is also possible that these inscriptions were on the architrave of the pavilion-like structure that formed the east end of the basilica.

**The Temenos of Vesta.** — The temenos or precinct of Vesta contained originally the temple of Vesta, the dwelling of the Vestals, the sacred grove[2] (*lucus*), the so-called domus Publica,[3] or official residence of the pontifex maximus, which has often been confused with the Regia, and the Regia itself. Only the first three belonged to the Vestals during the republic, but in 12 B.C. Augustus, who was then pontifex maximus, removed to his new house on the Palatine, and presented the domus

---

[1] *BC.* 1899, 141ff., pl. xiii, xiv. 1; 1903, 83–86; *Arch. Anz.* 1900, 6; *Mitt.* 1905, 59–62.

[2] Cic. *de Div.* i. 101; *BC.* 1905, 208–210; *Mélanges*, 1908, 238–240.

[3] Suet. *Caes.* 46; *Jahrb. d. Inst.* 1889, 247.

Publica to the Vestals.[1] All these buildings had the same orientation, — north and south, east and west, — corresponding with that of the republican Comitium at the other end of the Forum, and formed parts of a single group. The remains[2] of a fine house of the republic, which are visible all along the north side of the atrium and below its level, are doubtless to be identified with the domus Publica, which may have been used by the Vestals in its original shape for a few years after it was given to them. The temple was probably always on the same site. The lucus, which originally extended along the Nova via to the foot of the Palatine, was encroached upon, and finally destroyed by the later buildings.

**The Temple of Vesta.** — The temple of Vesta was said to have been built by Numa,[3] but it was outside the Palatine pomerium, and cannot have antedated the second stage of the city's growth. It was perhaps the most sacred spot in Rome, although not a consecrated *templum*,[4] round in shape,[5] and contained the sacred fire,[6] the Palladium,[7] and other *sacra*, which were kept in a secret recess called the penus Vestae,[8] but no statue[9] of the goddess herself. The temple was burned in 390 and in 241 B.C.,[10] again in the fire of Nero,[11] after which it was restored by the Flavians, and finally in 191 A.D.,[12] when it was restored by Julia Domna, the wife of Septimius Severus.[13]

The existing remains[14] of the temple are the podium and

---

[1] Dio Cass. liv. 27.

[2] *BC*. 1903, 79–80.

[3] Dionys. ii. 65, 66.

[4] Gell. xiv. 7; Serv. *ad Aen.* vii. 153.

[5] Ov. *Fast.* vi. 265–296; Fest. 262.

[6] Ov. *Fast.* vi. 297.

[7] Ov. *Trist.* iii. 1. 29.

[8] Fest. 250; Serv. *ad Aen.* iii. 12.

[9] Ov. *Fast.* vi. 295–298.

[10] Liv. *Epit.* 19; Oros. iv. 11; Ov. *Fast.* vi. 437–454.

[11] Tac. *Ann.* xv. 41.    [12] Dio Cass. lxxii. 24; Herodian, i. 14.

[13] For a general discussion of this temple, see Jordan, I. 2. 293, 421–423; Gilbert, I. 301–310; III. 405–415; Altmann, *Rundbauten*, 51–60.

[14] *NS*. 1883, 434–468; 1900, 159–191; *Nuova Antologia*, fasc. 1, Aug. 1900; *BC*. 1900, 281–284; 1903, 57–69; *CR*. 1899, 185; 1901, 139; *Mitt*. 1902, 88–91; *Atti*, 525–530.

many architectural fragments. The podium consists of four strata of concrete, with facings of opus incertum and brick. The lowest stratum is a circular foundation set in the soil, 15.05 metres in diameter and 2.17 metres thick. On this rest the three others, between the second and third of which there is a very thin layer of bits of marble. On the east side, and

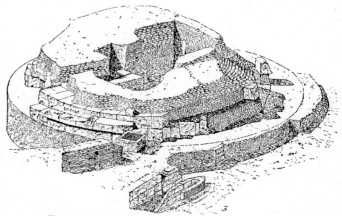

FIG. 34. — THE PODIUM OF THE TEMPLE OF VESTA.

here and there on the other sides, of these strata are some tufa blocks, which were the foundation of the marble steps. In the centre of the podium is a cavity of trapezoidal shape, extending to the bottom of the foundation, a depth of 5 metres. The sides measure between 2.30 and 2.50 metres in length. This cavity, or *favissa*, was entered from the floor of the cella, and may have been the receptacle for the *stercus*,[1] or ashes of the sacred fire, which was removed once a year and emptied out of the porta Stercoraria (p. 295). The two lowest strata, and probably the third, belong to the time of the Flavians; the uppermost, to that of Julia Domna. It is to her restoration

[1] Fest. 344.

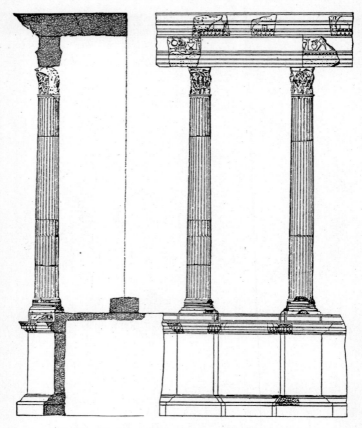

FIG. 35. — THE PERIBOLUS OF THE TEMPLE OF VESTA.

also that the remaining architectural fragments belong. These fragments, with coins [1] of the period, and a relief [2] in Florence

---

[1] Cohen, *Méd. Imp.* iii, pl. ix. p. 333, and Nos. 121–123, 205–209; Dressel, *Zeitschrift f. Numismatik*, 1899, 20–31.

[2] *Mitt.* 1892, 284–287; 1893, 285–286.

enable us to reconstruct[1] the temple with considerable accuracy.  It is not probable that the structure of Domitian's time

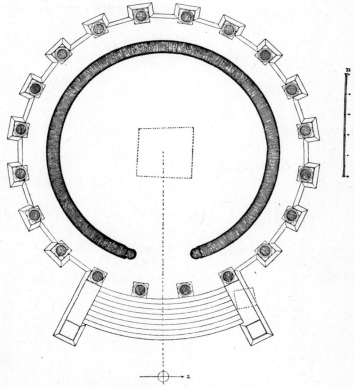

FIG. 36. — PLAN OF THE TEMPLE OF VESTA.

varied greatly from that of the time of Severus, except in the height of the podium.

---

[1] Jordan, *Der Tempel der Vesta u. das Haus der Vestalinnen*, 1886; Auer, *Der Tempel der Vesta u. das Haus der Vestalinnen*, *Denkschriften der Wiener Akademie*, 1888, 209–228; *Mitt.* 1889, 245–247; cf. Boni, *NS.* 1900, 185–189.

The temple was round, peripteral, and built of white marble, with twenty columns connected by metal gratings. The roof was dome-shaped, with an opening in the centre for the exit of the smoke of the sacred fire. This opening must have been protected by metal work of some kind, which would also allow the entrance of light. Fragments that have been found seem to indicate the existence of at least one window in the cella wall. The shafts of the columns were fluted, 0.51 metre in diameter and about 4.45 metres high, with Corinthian capitals. Near the temple were statues of an ox and a ram. A coin of Augustus [1] seems to represent the temple of his time as Ionic in style. On the north and southwest sides of the temple were found many sacrificial remains, bones, ashes, potsherds, statuettes, etc.

**The Atrium Vestae**. — Aside from the meagre evidence of coins, we are mainly dependent upon that derived from the building itself for our knowledge of the history of the atrium Vestae,[2] or house of the Vestals. Recent investigation [3] of the existing remains, which were excavated in 1883 [4] and 1889–1902,[5] has shown that there were six stages in the development of the atrium. That of the republic and early empire was immediately south of the temple and adjoined the domus Publica on the east, with the same north and south orientation. It consisted of a small court with rows of rooms on the south and west sides, and remains of its walls and pavements are still

[1] Cohen, *Aug.* 250, 251; *Zeitschrift f. Numismatik*, 1899, pl. I. Nos. 3–8.

[2] Ov. *Fast.* vi. 263; Gell. i. 12; Serv. *ad Aen.* vii. 153; Jordan, I. 2. 299, 427; Gilbert, I. 304–305; III. 408–410.

[3] Esther B. Van Deman, *The Atrium Vestae*, Washington, The Carnegie Institution, 1909.

[4] *NS.* 1883, 468–470, 480–486; Jordan, *Der Tempel der Vesta*, 25–40; Auer, *op. cit.* 209–222.

[5] *NS.* 1899, 325–333; 1900, 159–191; *BC.* 1899, 253–256; 1902, 30; 1903, 70–78; *Arch. Anz.* 1900, 8–9; *CR.* 1899, 467; 1900, 238; 1901, 139; 1902, 284; *Mitt.* 1902, 90–92; 1905, 94; *Atti*, 539–547.

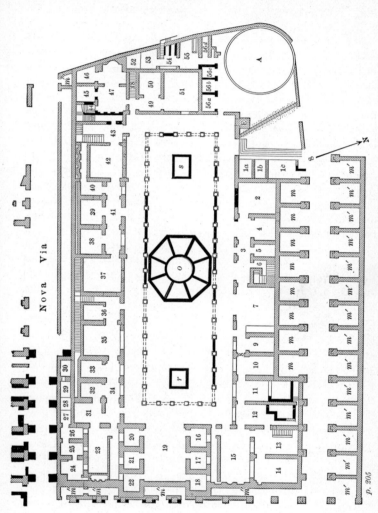

Nova Via

A

O

s

r

1a 1b 1c
2
3
4
5 5
6 5
7
8
9
10
11
12
13
14
15
16
17
18
19
20
21
22
23
24
25
26
27 28 29 30
31
32 33
34
35
36
37
38
39
40
41
42
43
44
45 46
47
48
49 50
51
52 53 54 55
56a 56b 56c
56a 56b 56c

m m m m m m m m m m m m m m m m
m′ m′ m′ m′ m′ m′ m′ m′ m′ m′ m′
m₁ m₁ m₁

N
s

Fig. 37.—Plan of the Atrium Vestae.

visible at various points beneath the northwest corner of the latest building. The remains of the domus Publica, which virtually formed a part of the original atrium, lie along the north side of the latest building, and were entirely covered up by the road that Nero built here in front of the shops (see below).

This atrium was probably destroyed in the fire of Nero, and rebuilt by him in different form and with a different orientation. It now consisted of a trapezoidal inclosure, approximately the size of the later building, with a central court surrounded with rooms on three sides and part of the fourth. This court was not so large as that of the latest period, and the eastern part of the inclosure was a garden, probably a part of the *lucus*. Outside the inclosure wall on the east and north were rows of shops, some of which (Fig. 37) were not destroyed in later restorations. This building was injured by fire and restored by Domitian, who erected a colonnade around the court, and entirely rebuilt the west end. Hadrian seems to have been the next to modify the atrium, principally by building rooms across the east end, and thereby diminishing the area of the garden by more than one-half. The fifth stage of development was reached under the Antonines, who filled in the space at the corners of the garden with rooms and erected a second and third story. This atrium was again injured in the fire of Commodus, and finally restored, probably by Julia Domna, the court being lengthened so as to occupy all the central area. Minor alterations were made in the third and fourth centuries, but in general we may say that all the changes effected after the time of Nero were merely successive steps in the development of his building.

The atrium after the last restoration consisted of an open peristyle, surrounded on all sides by rooms of various kinds, in two and three stories. The central court was rectangular, 69 metres long and 24 wide, and was surrounded by a colonnade of forty-eight Corinthian columns of cipollino. These columns stood about 4 metres from the wall, forming a corridor of that width, and leaving an open court 60 by 15 metres in length and breadth. Above these columns was an upper arcade of the same number of columns of breccia corallina, of which two have been preserved uninjured besides numerous fragments. Of the columns of the lower arcade only fragments and the travertine foundations are preserved. At a later period a brick wall, pierced with arches, was substituted for this colonnade, and the cipollino columns were sawn into slabs for other purposes. The latest pavement of the court was lava mosaic; but under it are remains of a slightly older one of opus spicatum, some of which dates from the time of Severus, and beneath that a network of brick drains has been found, which run under the various parts of the building, and finally flow into one large cloaca that passes out at the northwest corner. At the east end of the peristyle is a piscina, or water tank, about 4 metres square, and at the opposite end is another, slightly larger. Between this latter tank and the centre of the peristyle is a third, lined with marble like the other two, of about the same width, but about 13 metres long and a little more than 1 metre deep. This belonged to the earlier atrium and was filled up when the court was finally enlarged. Over one end of this piscina, in the centre of the enlarged peristyle, is a pattern in brickwork, an octagon inclosing a circle, the radii of which are prolonged from the circumference to the angles of the octagon. Whether this is all that is left of the foundation of a pavilion or summer-house, or of a sort of curb which might have inclosed a flower bed, is uncertain. The walls of the peristyle, and in general the walls of all the adjoining rooms except those which were for the most domestic uses, were magnificently decorated with linings of colored marbles, of which a little has been found in place.

At the east end of the peristyle, the corridor is paved with colored marbles instead of mosaic, and from it four steps lead up between two columns into a hall, which is also paved with magnificent marbles, and out of which six smaller rooms open, three on each side. The hall is usually called the tablinum.

South of this group is a small hall (23) in which were built in the time of the Antonines a sort of vaulted cellar, perhaps the *penus* of the household, and a large water tank. In the wall above this tank are niches, perhaps for the Penates, and a staircase leading to a series of rooms that formed a *mezzanino*. At the northeast corner are other rooms, in which are remains of the earlier tufa walls, and in one of them a square altar made of ashes and sacrificial matter, covered with stucco and surrounded by a stone gutter, which belonged to the house of the republic. Very little is left of the rooms on the north side of the peristyle; but they were large, and perhaps served as public reception rooms and offices. Outside the north wall of the building was a row of tabernae, opening on the Sacra via; and under and in front of them are the remains of several rooms of the domus Publica, with well-preserved mosaic pavements.

At the west end of the court are three rooms (49–51) of unknown use, and behind them a series of small rooms (52–55), cut off from the atrium and opening into the temple area. Many fragments of clay vessels were found in one (52) of these rooms, and they may have served as storerooms for the *instrumentum* of the cult. South of these rooms is another group (45–47) consisting of a large apartment, with an apse and adjoining rooms, which, being remote from the temple and accessible by stairways from the ramp leading up to the Palatine, may have been connected with some other cult, perhaps that of the Lares. The remains of the original building are numerous at this west end. Some of the rooms on the east, west, and north sides were heated by hypocausts, the floors being double, and the walls lined with flues. The rooms on the south side of the peristyle were especially exposed to dampness, because they were built against the cliff of the Palatine, and were cut off from the sunlight by the lofty palace on the hill. In the successive restorations inner walls were built in nearly all these rooms, and an air space, more than a metre in width, left between them and the outer wall, while hypocausts were built beneath. The floor level was also raised, 0.70 metre on the average, and the removal of this later floor has exposed to view in several of the rooms an earlier mosaic of opus sectile. In one room nearly the whole pavement of giallo antico, pavonazzetto, and Porta santa has been preserved.

The central rooms on the south side are of uncertain purpose, but the first three at the east end seem to have belonged to the culinary department of the house, as one (32) contains ovens, and another (33) a mill, although this is probably of very late date. Behind the fourth and fifth is a staircase leading to the second story, and at the west end are two other staircases. Behind the last room is a corridor, the door of which had been walled up; and in this corridor, in the opening of a brick drain, was found a hoard of three hundred and ninety-seven gold coins,[1] which had evidently been placed in a bag and thrown into this drain for concealment. These coins date from 335 to 467–472 A.D. The Vestals were driven from their house in 382 A.D.,[2] and it is supposed that the atrium then became the residence of imperial officials, who fled about 470 to escape some invasion from the North. In 1883 a hoard of eight hundred and thirty Anglo-Saxon coins, dating down to the middle of the tenth century, was found at the northwest corner of the atrium.[3]

The third story has entirely disappeared, and what remains of the second, at the southeast corner, seems to have consisted principally of elaborate baths, which were installed after the time of Severus in rooms originally belonging to the sleeping apartments. Set up round the peristyle are the fragments of the many statues[4] of the Vestals, belonging for the most part

---

[1] *NS.* 1899, 327–330.      [2] Zos. v. 38.      [3] *NS.* 1883, 487–514.
[4] Jordan, *Der Tempel der Vesta*, 44–49, and pl. VIII–X; *AJP.* 1908, 172–178; *AJA.* 1908, 324–342.

to the third century, with inscribed pedestals. The pedestals and the statues, however, do not belong together.

The main entrance to the atrium was at the northwest corner, and close by it is the podium, about 3 by 2 metres in dimensions, of an aedicula Vestae.[1] As the temple itself did not contain any statue of the goddess, the aedicula was probably erected for this purpose. Some fragments of the marble lining and plinth are *in situ;* and the entablature with an inscription of the time of Hadrian which records a restoration, together with numerous architectural fragments, have been found. The entablature has recently been placed upon a column and a brick pier.

**The Regia.** — The Regia[2] is said to have been built and dwelt in by Numa,[3] and it is also said to have been the house of the rex sacrificulus and of the pontifex maximus.[4] In historical times, however, it was a consecrated *fanum,* the official headquarters of the pontifex maximus, and is to be carefully distinguished from the house of the rex sacrificulus on the Velia, and the domus Publica (p. 199). It contained the sacrarium Martis,[5] in which the sacred spears and shields (*ancilia*) were kept, the sacrarium Opis Consivae,[6] the archives of the pontifices, and a place of assembly for various sacred colleges. The Regia was burned and restored in 210, 148,[7] and 36 B.C. This last restoration[8] was carried out by Cn. Domitius Calvinus, who erected a building which, although small, must have been of unusual beauty.

---

[1] Cf. Cic. *de Nat. Deor.* iii. 80; *de Or.* iii. 10; Liv. *Epit.* 86; Jordan, *Der Tempel der Vesta*, 25–28; *Top.* I. 2. 290–291.

[2] Jordan, I. 2. 302–304, 423–429; Gilbert, I. 225–227, 305–310, 341–352; III. 407–410.

[3] Solin. i. 21; Ov. *Trist.* iii. 1. 30; Tac. *Ann.* xv. 41.

[4] Fest. 278–279; Serv. *ad Aen.* viii. 363.

[5] Gell. iv. 6; Liv. xl. 19; Dio Cass. xliv. 17; Jordan, II. 271–278.

[6] Varro, *LL.* vi. 21; Fest. 186.          [7] Liv. xxvi. 27; Obseq. 19.

[8] Dio Cass. xlviii. 42; Pl. *NH.* xxxiv. 48.

Its site has now been completely excavated, and the existing ruins[1] belong to three periods, the republican, the imperial, and the medieval. Of the superstructure of the first two periods, almost nothing remains except the lowest courses of some of the walls and many architectural fragments. The republican remains are found only in the foundations of the later structure, and have been built over so many times that no reconstruction of the original building is possible, but it probably extended farther to the west and south than the Regia of Calvinus. After his restoration, the Regia was shaped like an irregular pentagon, filling the space between the Sacra via, the temenos of Vesta, and the temple of Julius Caesar, and consisting of parts unsymmetrically joined together.

The principal part was trapezoidal (*klmn*, Fig. 38), with a mean length of about 22 metres and a width of 8 metres. Unlike most Roman buildings, this was built of solid blocks of white marble. On the west and south sides were inscribed in four double panels the *fasti consulares,* and on the pilasters of the south side, the *fasti triumphales.* Many of the fragments of these blocks have been preserved.[2] Fig. 39 represents the architectural arrangement of these panels, and also of the building itself.

The interior was divided into three rooms, in the largest of which was found a pavement of tufa blocks, and on this a circular substructure (*d*, Fig. 38) of gray tufa, 2.53 metres in diameter, dating from the early period.[3] There was a doorway (*c*) in the original building, but it was roughly widened for the medieval house, and two rude steps placed in front of it.

The irregular space between this part of the Regia and the

---

[1] *Mitt.* 1886, 94–98, 99–111; 1902, 62–66; 1905, 77–80; *Archaeologia,* 1887, 227–250; *Jahrb. d. Inst.* 1889, 228–253; *NS.* 1899, 220–223, 384–386, 486–488; *BC.* 1899, 205–213; 1903, 42–55; *CR.* 1899, 322, 466; 1901, 139; *Arch. Anz.* 1900, 6–8; *Atti,* 518–525.

[2] *Mitt.* 1904, 117–123; 1905, 77–80; *NS.* 1904, 8–10; *BC.* 1904, 188; *Wiener Studien,* 1902, 324–335.

[3] The top layer of stone is modern.

Sacra via was occupied by an open court, with a covered ante-
chamber at the east end, where the main entrance seems to
have been.  The greatest width, north and south, of the area

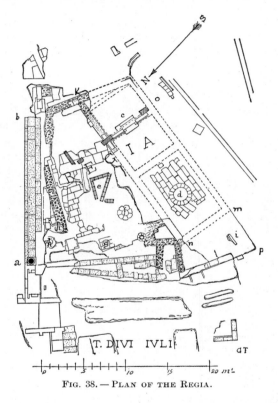

FIG. 38. — PLAN OF THE REGIA.

of the Regia was about 27 metres, and the least about 12
metres.  The court was paved with slabs of marble, and in
it are two wells and a cistern, which date from a very early
time.  One of these wells (*h*) is 14.35 metres deep and 0.69
in diameter, and contained pieces of fire-marked tufa, terra-

cotta weights, and potsherds. The other well contained nothing of interest. The cistern (*f*), shaped like a tholus, 4.36 metres deep and 3.02 in diameter at the bottom, with tufa walls and a bottom of opus signinum, contained fragments of amphorae and Arretine vases, eighty-two bone *stili*, part of an oaken writing-tablet, and a fragment of a marble curb, on which was the word REGIA in letters of republican date.

FIG. 39. — THE REGIA RESTORED.

Near this cistern is a base (*g*) of tufa blocks, on which there are traces of a circular superstructure, to which probably belongs a fragment of peperino found near by, with the inscription A. COVRI.

At the southwest end of the marble building is a small room (*nmp*) paved with black and white mosaic. Near it in the wall was found a fragment of an epistyle with part of an inscription,[1] — the other part of which was already known, — which

---

[1] *NS.* 1899, 128; *BC.* 1899, 146; *Mitt.* 1902, 65–66.

proves the existence in or near the Regia of a schola kalatorum pontificum. No identification of any of the existing divisions of the ruins with any of the ancient parts of the Regia is possible.

In the seventh or eighth century the Regia was transformed into a private house, the traces of which are visible in all parts of the area, but especially along the Sacra via, where the house was approached by a flight of two steps (*ab*), roughly made of marble and travertine and 20 metres long. Above them stood a row of cipollino columns with bases of red granite, which had been taken from some ancient building and formed the entrance to this house.

Between the south wall of the Regia and the temenos of Vesta is another well of republican date,[1] about 5 metres deep, built of tufa.

**The Lacus Iuturnae.** — The most famous spring near the Forum was that of Juturna,[2] which was known to be close to the temple of Castor. This part of the Forum has now been excavated, and the triangular space between the temple of Castor and the atrium Vestae may be called the precinct of Juturna. The existing ruins[3] belong principally to the imperial period, but there are some of earlier date. In the centre of the precinct is the lacus (*fgki*, Fig. 40), a basin 2.12 metres deep, the bottom of which measures 5.13 by 5.04 metres. In the middle of the basin is a quadrilateral base (*w*) 1.78 metres high and about 3 long by 2 wide. The basin is paved with marble slabs, beneath which are some tufa remains with a different orientation, which belong to the earlier structure. The lower walls of opus reticulatum rise to the same height

---

[1] *BC.* 1903, 56.

[2] Ov. *Fast.* i. 709; Dionys. vi. 13; Jordan, I. 2. 371; Lanciani, *Acque*, 13–14; Herschel, *Frontinus*, 132–133.

[3] *NS.* 1900, 291–295; 1901, 41–144; *BC.* 1900, 67–74, 285–295; 1903, 166–198; *CR.* 1901, 139; *Mitt.* 1902, 67–74; 1905, 81–82; *Atti*, 530–539.

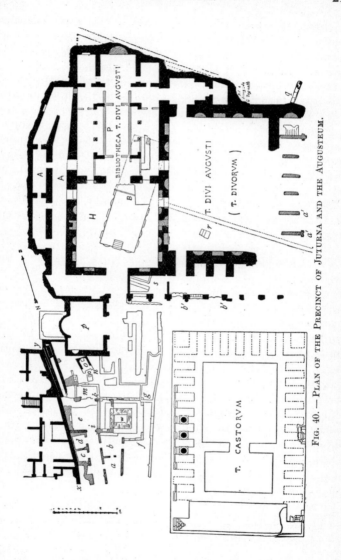

Fig. 40. — Plan of the Precinct of Juturna and the Augusteum.

on three sides as the base just mentioned, and this appears to
have been the level of the precinct in republican times, corresponding to that of the pavements in front of the temple of
Castor.   On this wall is a ledge about 1.50 metres wide, and
round this a later wall of opus incertum, 1.23 metres high, on
which is a travertine curbing.   There are indications of marble
or metal balustrades on this curbing and on the ledge below.
At the top the basin measures about 10 metres square.   At the
northeast and northwest corners of the pavement of the basin
are the two springs by which it has always been fed, which
are now flowing freely.   The whole inner surface of this basin
was lined with marble, much of which is *in situ*.   The east
side of the basin has been entirely changed by being built over
in the fourth century, in order to enlarge the room at the
east (*e*).   A number of pieces of a beautifully executed frieze
of palmettes were found in the lacus and adjacent parts of the
Forum, enough to extend a distance of 15 metres.   Other
fragments of this or a similar frieze exist elsewhere in Rome.[1]

About 4 metres south of the lacus is a group belonging to
the precinct, and composed of an altar (*n*), a well with marble
curb or puteal, and a shrine (*o*) of the goddess Juturna.   The
puteal is 0.968 metre high, with decorated plinth and cornice.
On the edge of the puteal and on its front is an inscription,[2]
which states that it was restored and dedicated by M. Barbatius
Pollio, probably the partisan of Marcus Antonius.[3]   Close to
the front of the puteal is a large slab of marble, and on this
was found a marble altar, lying on its face, on which are sculptured a male and female figure in the style of the time of
Severus.   Slab and altar had been used as steps to the puteal,
which seems to have been too high for the convenient drawing
of water at this later period.   The base of the puteal had also
been covered up with pozzolana.   The level of the spring in
this well is the same as that of those in the basin.

---

[1] *Mitt.* 1905, 81–82.          [2] *Mitt.* 1902, 70.          [3] Cic. *Phil.* xiii. 3.

FIG. 41. — THE PRECINCT OF JUTURNA.

Immediately behind and somewhat higher than the puteal is a brick foundation on which stands the aedicula Iuturnae (*o*), which consisted of a cella and pronaos, with two marble

columns. Of these columns there are no remains. A statue
of the goddess undoubtedly stood in the apse of this aedicula,

FIG. 42. — THE LACUS IUTURNAE.

and a fragment of the epistyle was found near by, with the
inscription IVTVRNAI S.

The inclined way from the Forum to the Palatine started
near the temple of Vesta, and ascended along the wall of the

atrium ($xy$), supported by a series of arches, under which are chambers ($c$, $d$) opening on the corridor. The room $e$, with three niches in the east wall, has been enlarged by taking down the wall between the two adjoining chambers, destroying the original west wall, and building out over the lacus,. as previously described. In this room and the next ($m$) there is a pavement of tiles laid over an early one of opus spicatum. On the west side of the corridor are two other rooms ($a$, $b$), and in the corridor itself are three pavements, the earliest of opus spicatum, the next of tiles, and the latest of white and black mosaic. In these rooms have been found many fragments of inscriptions [1] relating to the *curatores aquarum* and the statio aquarum, or headquarters of the water department of Rome. One of these records a restoration of the statio by Fl. Maesius Egnatius Lollianus in 328 A.D., and it is probable that the enlargement just described took place at that time, when the statio was in the precinct of Juturna. When this office was first established here is not known.[2]

Many remains of sculpture were found here, among them a marble altar in the lacus, similar to that at the shrine, with beautiful reliefs, fragments of the Dioscuri of life size,[3] and a statue of Aesculapius in front of the niche in room $e$. The large number of medieval potsherds, now stored in room $d$, shows that the springs were in use at a late date.

Immediately south of the aedicula, at a higher level, is a large hall ($p$) with an apse, which completely blocks the Nova via (p. 164) and probably dates from about the same period as the enlargement of the statio aquarum. In the middle ages this became an oratory. No trace has been found of the sacellum Larum [4] (p. 131), which is described as being one of

---

[1] *NS.* 1901, 129–131; *BC.* 1900, 72; *Mitt.* 1902, 72–73.

[2] For an ingenious suggestion as to the possible use made of these rooms before the establishment of the *statio*, see *JJ.* 1902, 370–388.

[3] *Mitt.* 1900, 338–349.

[4] Tac. *Ann.* xii. 24; *CR.* 1905, 76.

the points in the first pomerium, and is supposed to have stood at this corner of the hill.

**The Rostra.** — The Rostra [1] was the famous platform from which the Roman orators addressed the people. Such a platform must have existed from very early times, but the name *rostra* was applied to it after 338 B.C., when C. Maenius [2] decorated the *suggestus*, either that already in existence or a new one, with the rostra of the ships captured at Antium. This platform stood on the south side of the republican Comitium (p. 228), so that from it the speaker could address the people assembled either on the Comitium or in the Forum. [3] It was consecrated as a templum, [4] and on it were placed statues [5] of famous men, in such numbers that at intervals the platform had to be cleared in order to make room for new claimants for the honor. On this Rostra, or close by, was the **columna rostrata**, [6] a column ornamented with beaks of ships, and erected in honor of C. Duilius Nepos, the victor at Mylae in 260 B.C. The column and its archaic inscription were restored by Augustus or Tiberius (or possibly Claudius), and part of the restored inscription has been preserved. This Rostra kept its place on the Comitium throughout the republic, and was the most distinctive symbol of the old régime.

Caesar decided to remove the Rostra to the Forum, but his definite plan seems not to have been carried out, or at least the dedication not to have taken place, until after 42 B.C. [7] Augustus seems to have rebuilt the Rostra, incorporating in it part

[1] Jordan, I. 2. 353–356; Gilbert, III. 151–155, 172–173.

[2] Liv. viii. 14; Pl. *NH.* xxxiv. 20.

[3] Varro, *LL.* v. 155; Diodor. xii. 26; Ascon. *in Mil.* p. 37.

[4] Liv. ii. 56; Cic. *in Vatin.* 24.

[5] Liv. iv. 17; viii. 13; Cic. *Phil.* ix. 16, and freq.; cf. Jacobi, *Grundzüge einer Museographie der Stadt Rom,* 52–53.

[6] Pl. *NH.* xxxiv. 20; Quint. i. 7. 12; Serv. *ad Georg.* iii. 29; *CIL.* vi. 1300; *Ber. d. k. bayerisch. Akademie,* 1890, 293–321.

[7] Dio Cass. xliii. 49.

of the Julian structure, and most of the existing remains belong to this period. Thenceforth the Rostra of the empire was a long platform extending across the west end of the Forum. It was remodelled by Severus, lengthened in the fifth century, and is represented in a famous relief on the arch of Constantine.

The existing remains[1] seem to be divided into two parts, a rectangular structure (*gj*, Fig. 46) in front, and the so-called hemicycle behind. The rectangular structure is about 24 metres long, 10 deep, and 3 high. The front and side walls are built of opus quadratum of tufa, and the rear wall is a mass of brick-faced concrete. The travertine slabs of the platform were supported by these walls and by three rows of travertine piers, which were in later times partly replaced and partly strengthened by brick piers and walls. This was necessitated by the increasing weight of the statues and honorary columns which were set up on the Rostra. A marble balustrade extended along the sides and front of the platform, except in the centre, where there

[1] Richter, *Rekonstruktion und Geschichte der Röm. Rednerbühne*, 1884; *Jahrb. d. Inst.* 1889, 1–17; *Mitt.* 1889, 238–239; 1902, 17–20; *BC.* 1903, 158.

Fig. 43.—THE RELIEF OF THE ROSTRA, FROM THE ARCH OF CONSTANTINE.

was an opening. The façade was lined with marble, with plinth and cornice, and divided into twenty compartments by pilasters of bronze, and bronze strips above the plinth and under the cornice. In the centre of each compartment a bronze

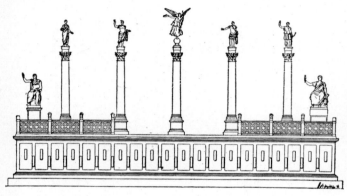

FIG. 44. — THE FRONT OF THE ROSTRA RESTORED.

beak was fixed, and a second row of beaks, below these, was fixed to the pilasters, making thirty-nine in all. These beaks were made for the purpose, and not actually taken from ships. The approach was from the rear, and the marble balustrades (p. 263) now standing on the pavement of the Forum may possibly have stood either on each side of this approach, or on the two shorter sides of the platform, in place of the marble screen.

At some later period most of the north wall (*hi*, Fig. 46) of the Rostra was removed, and the north part of the back wall (*hf*) of brick-faced concrete was cut down to the level of the pavement. At the south end, however, part of this wall and the concrete mass behind it is still standing, reduced to half its original height. The space between the east and west walls was paved with tiles laid over an earlier opus spicatum, much of which is still *in situ*. At a much later date this rectangular part of the Rostra was lengthened by a trapezoidal brick addi-

tion (*jm*) at the north end, the façade of which was also decorated with beaks.   On some of the marble blocks which took
the place of a cornice was an inscription, fragments of which
have been recovered, recording the restoration by Junius Va-
lentinus in honor of two Augusti, perhaps Leo and Anthemius.[1]

Fig. 45. — The Rear of the Rostra restored.

The so-called hemicycle[2] consists of a curved façade generally supposed to have been as long as the Rostra, although this
is open to doubt, and a flight of five travertine steps, equally
wide, which leads up from the level of the clivus Capitolinus
to the top of the façade on the inner side of the curve.   It thus
formed a retaining wall for the higher level of the area Concordiae.   The steps of the north half are well preserved, but
of the south half only the core of opus incertum is left.
The top of the hemicycle was only 2 metres wide and paved
with travertine, and on its north half at least was a colonnade.
The façade was decorated with slabs of Porta santa marble,
with a plinth of Pentelic marble, and a cornice, only fragments
of which have been found.

---

[1] *Mitt.* 1895, 59–60; 1902, 19.
[2] *Mitt.* 1902, 17–19; *CR.* 1901, 88; *BC.* 1903, 158–159.

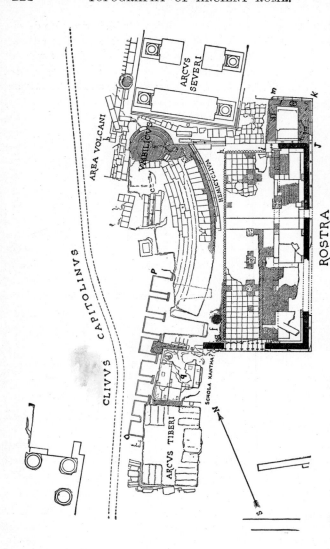

Fig. 46. — Plan of the Rostra and Surrounding Structures.

With regard to the structural history of the Rostra, and the relation of rectangle and hemicycle, two views are now held. According to one,[1] the hemicycle is the original Rostra of Julius Caesar, which preserved the curved form of the Rostra of the Comitium (p. 236). At a later time, perhaps by Trajan, the rectangle was built, which entirely concealed the façade of the hemicycle and completely changed the character of the structure.

According to the other[2] view, the Rostra of Julius Caesar was for the most part incorporated in the Rostra built by Augustus, which consisted of the rectangular portion (*gj*, Fig. 46) and the solid mass of concrete behind with its brick facing (*gh*). This concrete mass served as the foundation for the curved flight of steps on the west extending across the whole length of the Rostra and forming a monumental approach (Fig. 45) to the platform itself, which was more than 12 metres wide. This continued to be the shape of the Rostra until the end of the second century, when, in consequence of the erection of the arch of Severus, the structure was restored with very considerable changes. The north wall (*hi*, Fig. 46) was removed, and the brick-faced concrete mass (*hg*) was cut away, for at least more than half its length, so that its curve should correspond with that of the flight of steps behind. The north half of this curved wall was then decorated in the manner already described (p. 223), and a small triangular court formed, from which access was had to the platform above. At the southern end the decoration of the curved surface and the demolition of the brick facing were not completed.

Objections have been urged against each of these views, but at present the weight of evidence seems to be in favor of the second, the strongest argument against the priority of the

---

[1] Mau, *Mitt.* 1905, 230–266; Richter, *BRT.* II; IV. 11.

[2] Richter, *opp. citt.* p. 221, n.1; *Top.*[2] 242; Hülsen, *Mitt.* 1905, 16–23; Van Deman, *AJA.* 1909, 170–186.

hemicycle being found in the apparently complete structural unity of it and the rectangular section.

At the north end of the hemicycle is the core of the **Umbilicus Romae**,[1] a cylindrical brick-faced structure which rose in three stages, its diameter at the bottom being 4.60 metres and at the top 3. This was covered with marble and represented the central point of city and empire, possibly in imitation of the ὀμφαλός at Delphi. It was probably erected in the latter part of the third century. At the west end of the Forum, Augustus had erected a column, covered with gilt-bronze, which was called the **Milliarium Aureum**.[2] On it were engraved the names of the principal cities of the empire, and their distances from the capital. Part of a circular marble plinth has been found here, which may have belonged to this monument; and it is possible that the Milliarium Aureum stood in a position at the south end of the Rostra corresponding to that of the Umbilicus at the other.[3]

**Beginning** behind the south end of the hemicycle, and extending about 20 metres south, is a row (*op*, Fig. 46) of eight arched rectangular chambers[4] set on a line parallel with the major axis of the temple of Saturn and forming an angle of 15° with that of the Rostra. The two chambers at the south end were partially built over by the foundations of the arch of Tiberius. The structure is built of opus reticulatum of tufa, and is 20.80 metres long and 2.30 high. The rooms are 1.60 metres high, 1.70 broad, and from 1.50 to 2.15 deep. The inside walls are covered with opus signinum, and the pavement is of rude brick tesserae, and extended for a distance of 4 metres from the front of the row. Above these rooms is a floor of rammed tufa, edged with tufa slabs (the present upper layer is modern).

---

[1] *Not.* Reg. viii.; Jordan, I. 2. 245.

[2] Pl. *NH.* iii. 66; Tac. *Hist.* i. 27; Dio Cass. liv. 8; Gilbert, III. 173–174.

[3] *CR.* 1900, 237; *Mitt.* 1902, 20.

[4] *NS.* 1900, 627–634; *BC.* 1900, 267–269; 1903, 153–158; *CR.* 1901, 87–88; *Mitt.* 1902, 13–16; 1905, 14–15.

FIG. 47. — THE SUBSTRUCTURES OF THE CLIVUS CAPITOLINUS.

It seems clear that this row of arches was a sort of viaduct, built to support the clivus Capitolinus when the temple of Saturn was restored by Plancus in 42 B.C.[1] The enlargement of the temple at that time made it necessary to push the line

[1] For arguments in favor of assigning this substructure to the time of Sulla, see *BC.* 1902, 128; Richter, *Geschichte der Rednerbühne,* 8–9.

of the clivus farther east, and it was then carried on these
substructures. The theory at first advanced[1] that this structure was the rostra of Julius Caesar has been shown to be
untenable.

In front of these chambers, between the arch of Tiberius
and the prolongation of the south wall of the Rostra, are the
remains of a room (*q*, Fig. 46) of trapezoidal shape, with a
pavement of white marble. A marble seat encircled three
sides of the chamber, and in the middle of the north wall is
a door from which a flight of steps led up to the level of the
clivus Capitolinus. There are also marks of posts or columns
on the pavement. This may possibly have been the so-called
schola Xanthi,[2] an office of the scribae, librarii, and praecones
of the curule aediles. An epistyle[3] was found on this spot
in the sixteenth century, which recorded the erection of this
schola by Bebryx Aug. lib. Drusianus and A. Fabius Xanthus,
not later than the time of Trajan and perhaps as early as that
of Tiberius, and its restoration by a certain C. Avilius Licinius
Trosius at the beginning of the third century.

**The Comitium.** — The word *comitium*[4] means the place of
assembly (*com-eo*), and until the middle of the second century
B.C.[5] it was the political centre of Rome (p. 170). The changes
effected by Caesar and his successors destroyed its previous
topographical arrangement, but this can be reconstructed in
its main lines. The republican Comitium[6] was a *templum* or
inaugurated plot of ground, approximately 70 metres east and
west and somewhat more north and south, oriented according

[1] *NS*. 1900, 627–634; Richter, *BRT*. IV. 14.

[2] Gilbert, III. 161–162; *Mitt*. 1888, 208–232; 1902, 12–13; *BC*. 1903, 164.

[3] *CIL*. vi. 103.    [4] Varro, *LL*. v. 155.

[5] Cic. *Lael*. 96; Varro, *RR*. i. 2. 9; Gilbert, III. 138–141.

[6] Jordan, I. 2. 261, 318–322, Gilbert, II. 70–74; and esp. *Mitt*. 1893, 79–94.
Cf. also O'Connor, *The Graecostasis of the Roman Forum and its Vicinity*,
*University of Wisconsin Bulletin*, 1904, 159–203. For the view that the
orientation of the early Comitium was the same as that of the latest, see
Pinza, *Il Comizio Romano nella Età Repubblicana*, Rome, 1905.

to the cardinal points of the compass. This is also the orientation of three sides of the Carcer, of some of the so-called tabernae on the south side of the forum Iulium, the foundations of which have been found, of part of the early structures under the lapis niger, and of the early Regia and domus Publica. The east side of the Carcer and of the tabernae determines the west and north sides of the Comitium, while its extent toward the east was limited by the brook that came down through the Subura and the Argiletum. In the centre of the north side was the Curia; on the west were the basilica Porcia and the Carcer; on the south were the Rostra and the Graecostasis; and a little farther off was the Senaculum, but the exact position of these three with reference to each other is very uncertain. The area of the Comitium, undoubtedly paved at a very early date, was inclosed,[1] partly by these buildings and partly by railings.

The building of the first senate house was ascribed to Tullus Hostilius,[2] and it was regularly called the curia Hostilia. It was restored[3] by Sulla in 80 B.C., and may have been somewhat enlarged, as Sulla is said to have removed the statues[4] of Pythagoras and Alcibiades, which had stood at the corners of the Comitium. This hall was burned in 52 B.C. and rebuilt by Faustus Sulla,[5] and very possibly the enlargement just referred to was really his work. In 45 B.C. Caesar began the erection of a new Curia,[6] — the curia Iulia, — just east of the curia Hostilia and with a different orientation.[7] We are told that he removed the curia Hostilia, and erected on its site a temple of Felicitas, but this temple was completed and dedicated by Lepidus after Caesar's death, and in 45 B.C. the old Curia was

[1] Cic. *de Rep.* ii. 31.

[2] Varro, *LL.* v. 155; *Mem. d. Linc.* 1883, 3–5.

[3] Cic. *de Fin.* v. 2.                    [4] Pl. *NH.* xxxiv. 26.

[5] Cic. *pro Mil.* 90; Ascon. *in Mil.* p. 29; Dio Cass. xl. 49.

[6] Dio Cass. xliv. 5; xlv. 17; xlvii. 19.

[7] For the subsequent history of the curia Iulia, see p. 238.

still in use.   It is therefore probable that it was not entirely destroyed until the new building was at least partially ready for use, and that the temple of Felicitas occupied only a small part of its site, on its west side.   The presence of this temple, with the orientation of the old Curia, would account for the irregular shape of the tabernae of the forum Iulium at this point.   Of the later history of the temple nothing is known, nor is there any clue to the appearance of the curia Hostilia, except that it was not so large as the curia Iulia.

On the west side of the Comitium was the **basilica Porcia**,[1] the first structure of the sort of which we have any record. It was built by Cato the Censor in 184 B.C., and stood *in lautumiis* and next to the Curia, so that its site is very closely determined.   It was burned in 52 B.C., at the same time with the Curia of Sulla, and if not totally destroyed then, it must have been removed during the changes of the following years.

The Rostra (p. 220) of the republic occupied a large part of the south side of the Comitium.   West of it was the **Graecostasis**, and the relative position of these structures and the general orientation of the Comitium is further determined by the statement of Pliny [2] that the *accensus* of the consuls proclaimed the hour of noon when, from the Curia, he saw the sun between the Rostra and Graecostasis, — that is, in the south.

This Graecostasis [3] was a raised platform, without a roof, on which ambassadors from foreign states awaited their reception in the senate, and from which they could witness the assemblies of the people.

The **Graecostadium**,[4] a structure evidently of some considerable

---

[1] Liv. xxxix. 44; Ascon. *in Mil.* p. 29; Plut. *Cat.* 19; Gilbert, III. 210–212; *Mitt.* 1893, 84, 91.

[2] *NH.* vii. 212.

[3] Varro, *LL.* v. 155; Cic. *ad Q. Fr.* ii. 1.3; Jordan, I. 2. 243–244; Gilbert, III. 139–140; *Mitt.* 1893, 87, 91; O'Connor, *op. cit.* 159–169.

[4] Jul. Capit. *Vit. Ant. Pii*, 8; *Chronogr. a. 354*, p. 148; Jordan, *FUR.* 19; *Bull. Crist.* 1902, 126; *Mitt.* 1905, 11–14; O'Connor, *op. cit.* 169–178.

size, which was restored by Antoninus Pius and again after the fire of Carinus, has usually been identified with the earlier Graecostasis, but it was almost certainly another building. Part of the name occurs on a fragment of the Marble Plan, it is mentioned in the *Notitia* and *Curiosum*, and may be referred to by Plutarch.[1] It probably stood just south of the basilica Iulia, and not in the Forum itself.

The Senaculum,[2] a building in which the senators assembled, — presumably before entering the Curia itself, — was *supra Graecostasim, ubi aedes et basilica Opimia*. It must, therefore, have stood on the Volcanal, at the very edge of the Comitium and in front of the earlier temple of Concord and the basilica Opimia. Its position is thus determined within very narrow limits. It must have been removed at the latest when the temple of Concord was rebuilt by Tiberius, but it was probably moved at a still earlier date, along with the Rostra and the Graecostasis.

On the Comitium, in front of the Curia, was a puteal, or stone curb, on a spot which had been struck by lightning; but in the development of the legend of Attus Navius, the belief had become general that his razor and whetstone were buried here.[3] The statue of the famous augur stood on the left side of the steps of the Curia, and near by was the ficus Ruminalis [4] (p. 129), which he had caused to be miraculously transplanted from the Lupercal to the Comitium. This fig tree was standing in the time of Nero, when its drying up and reviving was regarded as a prodigy.

Near the basilica Porcia and the Carcer was the columna Maenia,[5]

---

[1] *De Sollertia Anim.* 19 (973 c).

[2] Varro, *LL.* v. 156; Fest. 347; Val. Max. ii. 2. 6; Gilbert, II. 70–71; III. 63; *Mitt.* 1893, 87, 91; Mommsen, *Staatsrecht*, iii. 913–915.

[3] Liv. i. 36; Cic. *de Div.* i. 33.

[4] Conon, *Narr.* 48; Dionys. iii. 71; Pl. *NH.* xv. 77; Tac. *Ann.* xiii. 58; Jordan, I. 2. 264, 356–357; *Mitt.* 1893, 92; Gilbert, III. 138–139.

[5] Pl. *NH.* vii. 212; xxxiv. 20; Cic. *Div. in Caecil.* 50; Jordan, I. 2. 345; *Mitt.* 1893, 84–85; O'Connor, *op. cit.* 188–189.

erected in 338 B.C. in honor of C. Maenius, the victor at
Antium.    Another story [1] that was current in later times about
the origin of this column is certainly false.    It is spoken
of in the fourth century by Symmachus as then standing.
Just west of the Curia were the subsellia tribunorum,[2] the wooden
benches occupied by the tribunes of the people, which seem
not to have survived the republic, being mentioned for the last
time in connection with Caesar's triumph in 45.    Near these
subsellia was the tabula Valeria,[3] usually explained as a painting
of the naval battle between the Romans and Carthaginians in
263 B.C., which was placed, we are told, by the victor, Valerius
Messalla, *in latere curiae*.    This is interpreted to mean either
the wall of the Curia, although it is somewhat difficult to explain how it survived the rebuilding by Sulla, or a sort of separate balustrade which might have surrounded the whole or
part of the Curia.    A more probable explanation [4] is that the
tabula Valeria was an inscription in bronze or marble, containing the provisions of the famous Valerio-Horatian laws concerning the office of tribune.    Such a tablet might very naturally
be set up near their subsellia.

Until the recent excavations, the Comitium was buried to a
depth of more than 9 metres, but it has now been completely
uncovered from the front of the Curia (S. Adriano) in all directions, except on the northwest side.    A stratigraphic examina-
tion [5] of the area of the Comitium has shown that there are
twenty-three strata from the latest pavement to the virgin soil,
a depth of 4.04 metres.    These twenty-three strata may, however, be assigned to about fourteen main divisions, which in
turn represent probably about six successive elevations.    These

---

[1] Pseudo-Ascon. *ad* Cic. *Div. in Caecil.* 16; Porphyr. *ad* Hor. *Sat.* i. 3. 21.

[2] Suet. *Caes.* 78; cf. Cic. *pro Sest.* 18; Plut. *Cat. Min.* 5; Gilbert, III. 165.

[3] Cic. *in Vatin.* 21; *ad Fam.* xiv. 2; Pl. *NH.* xxxv. 22; Jordan, I. 2.
330–331; *Mitt.* 1893, 93; *AJP.* 1898, 406–412.

[4] *CP.* 1908, 278–284.

[5] *NS.* 1900, 317–340; *BC.* 1900, 274–280; 1903, 125–134; Pinza, *Il Comizio
Romano nella Età Repubblicana*, Rome, 1905.

successive elevations in level are due to human agency; and while it is not possible to assign an exact duration of time to all of them, they present a vivid picture of the rapid changes which were going on continually in and round the Forum. Besides earth, gravel, sand, and broken tufa, these strata contain fragments of all sorts such as potsherds, sacrificial remains, votive offerings, and bricks, of all periods. This material, some of which came from buildings that had been burned, was evidently dumped here whenever it was necessary to raise the level of the Comitium.

The latest pavement[1] of the Comitium begins at a distance of about 11 metres from the front of the Curia, and extends in a fragmentary condition as far as the lapis niger. It consists of slabs of travertine, very roughly laid, and dates probably from the fourth or fifth century, although some of it may be the Caesarian pavement (see below) raised and relaid. Directly in front of the Curia is a pavement of blocks of Luna marble of the early imperial period. This lies about 20 centimetres below the level of the pavement just described, and represents the level of the Comitium as established by Caesar, 13.50 metres above the sea. Between this marble pavement and the later one is a travertine water-channel (1, 2, Fig. 48) 0.42 metre wide, parallel to the front of the Curia, and also a strip of gray marble (3, 4) in which are traces of the holes for marble pilasters, 1 metre apart. Between these pilasters there must have been a screen which divided the Comitium into two parts. Beyond this division the pavement of the Caesarian period was of travertine, and this still exists around the lapis niger, which is embedded in it, and westward to the arch of Severus.

Resting partly on the marble pavement and partly on the later travertine, is the circular marble basin (T) 5.26 metres in diameter, which belonged to a fountain.[2] It is made of eight

---

[1] For these pavements, see *NS.* 1900, 305–316; *BC.* 1900, 273–274; 1903, 146–149; *CR.* 1899, 233; 1900, 237; *Mitt.* 1902, 31–39.

[2] *BC.* 1900, 13–25; *CR.* 1901, 86–87; *Mitt.* 1902, 34–35.

CVRIA    IVLIA

v. 234

FIG. 48. — THE COMITIUM.

pieces, and in its centre is an octagonal space in which the foot of the fountain stood. This must have been something like a slender cantharus in shape, and was fed by a lead pipe laid in the water-channel (1, 2). It is generally supposed to date from about the fifth or sixth century, but the workmanship seems remarkably good for so late a period.

At a depth of 0.47 metre below the level of the imperial pavement is a small section of a pavement (k) of perfectly squared slabs of travertine on a foundation of broken tufa. The orientation of this pavement is not that of those above it, — which correspond with the Curia, — but is almost north and south, east and west, like that of the republican Comitium; and this is, in fact, the pavement of the last century of the republic, probably belonging to the time of Sulla. Under it are the remains of a flight of tufa steps (l), 1.24 metres high, leading down to

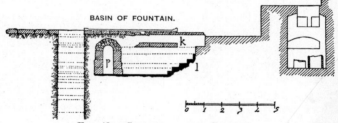

BASIN OF FOUNTAIN.

FIG. 49. — SECTION OF THE COMITIUM.

a still older pavement made of bits of broken tufa. This pavement is 2.40 metres below that of the empire, and extends southeast a distance of 2.64 metres, where it is blocked by a vaulted drain (p, Fig. 49). This drain is built of tufa, is 1.63 metres high, and runs parallel to the front of the Curia, emptying into the sewer of the Argiletum. It appears to have been built in the time of Caesar, when the lines of the Comitium were changed.

On this lower level was a straight flight of steps, extending

across the Comitium in an east and west direction, traces of
which are visible at several points (*dcba*, Fig. 48). These steps
led up to a sort of *suggestus*, which seems to have divided the
Comitium and Forum, and in which it is difficult to see anything else than the early Rostra (p. 220). Almost parallel to
these steps, and further to the south, are remains of a wall of
tufa blocks (*efghi*), quite archaic in appearance,[1] which may
have formed the front or retaining wall of the *suggestus*. The
lapis niger and adjacent monuments stand in a niche formed
in this *suggestus* by two cross walls.

This flight of steps was afterwards built over, at a higher
level, by another flight which was curved instead of straight.
Of this curved flight some portions still exist at *p'pp'm*. The
*suggestus* to which they led covered the earlier, and was paved
with tufa blocks, some of which are *in situ* at H. South of the
archaic wall (*ghi*) is a curved channel (*xz*) of tufa and opus reticulatum, which may mark the outer line of the second *suggestus*.
The four "pozzi" (I, II, III, IV, see below) were evidently built
in this second platform when it was covered by the pavement
which lies at the level of their tops. The possible relations
between these successive tribunals and the inclosed monuments
are referred to on p. 247.

Standing on a layer of earth which covered the late travertine pavement is a marble pedestal[2] (S, Fig. 48) 1.26 metres
high and 0.80 by 0.85 in width and breadth. On its top are
holes for clamps to hold a statue or column. This pedestal
was originally dedicated by the officials of a guild of carpen-
ters (*fabri tignuarii*), August 1, 154 A.D., as is shown by the
inscriptions on the north and west sides. It was afterward
dedicated in the name of Maxentius to **Mars Invictus** and the
founders — Romulus and Remus — of the eternal city, by a
certain Furius Octavianus, on the birthday of the city, April

---

[1] Delbrück, *Der Apollotempel auf dem Marsfeld*, Rome, 1903, 11–12; *Mitt.*
1905, 30–32.

[2] *BC.* 1899, 213–220; 1903, 134–138; *NS.* 1900, 303–305; *Mitt.* 1902, 31.

21, in the year 308 A.D. The two inscriptions which record this dedication are on the south and east sides. This base has some bearing on the question of the lapis niger (p. 247). On the east side of the Comitium, along the Argiletum, are three marble pedestals (PQR, Fig. 48) *in situ*, one of which (P) is broken, but which was originally of the same size as the others, 1.55 metres high and about 1.30 square. One of these (Q) bears a dedicatory inscription [1] of Memmius Vitrasius Orfitus to the emperor Constantius, and the other (R) the most meagre traces of a similar inscription, probably to the emperor Julianus. In the medieval masonry at the southeast corner of the porch of the Curia were found some inscribed cippi; and at various points on the Comitium and Forum, both built into later masonry and lying in the midst of the accumulated soil, many inscriptions [2] have come to light, which date all the way from the end of the republic to the end of the empire. At O on the late pavement is a large rectangular base of brickwork, but there is no clue to what it supported.

At various points in the Comitium, in the stratum lying beneath the republican pavement, are twenty-one small and shallow pits [3] (as I, II, Fig. 48), made of blocks of tufa, and of various shapes, — rectangular, pentagonal, and rhombo-trapezoidal. These pits are sometimes covered with stone slabs, but are usually open at the bottom. Similar pits have been found at various points in the Forum, — a line of eleven in front of the Rostra (Fig. 57), another line of nine under the Sacra via at the west end of the basilica Iulia, several between the arch of Augustus and the temple of Castor, and others south of the lapis niger. Those in the Comitium seem to belong to the Caesarian period, or possibly a few years earlier, while some of the others, like those near the arch of

---

[1] *CIL*. vi. 31395.

[2] For inscriptions found during the excavations 1899–1902, see *NS. passim*; *BC*. 1899, 205–247 ; 1900, 63–74.

[3] *NS*. 1900, 317 ; *BC*. 1900, 60 ; 1903, 149–150 ; *Mitt*. 1902, 58 ; 1905, 31–35.

Augustus, are as late as that emperor.   When discovered, most of the pits on the Comitium were filled with rubbish of the end of the republic, in which were fragments of bones, potsherds, etc.   According to one explanation, these pits are "pozzi rituali," or receptacles in which the remains of sacrifices were

FIG. 50. — SHALLOW PIT, AND VAULT OF THE CLOACA MAXIMA.

preserved; according to another, — at least as probable, — they are simply openings built to facilitate the draining away of rain-water.

The curia Iulia[1] was dedicated in 29 B.C., at which time

---

[1] *Mon. Anc.* iv. 1; Dio Cass. li. 22; Gilbert, III. 167–170; *Mem. d. Linc.* 1883, 5–26, and plates; *Mitt.* 1893, 278–281.

Augustus added to it a sort of annex, called the Chalcidicum and afterward the atrium Minervae, which seems to have been a repository for records. There was also another annex or part of the senate house, the Secretarium senatus, of which we have no direct evidence before an inscription[1] of the time of Honorius; but there is little doubt that this apartment, evidently an office for the clerks of the senate, formed part of the structure of Augustus, as it did of that of Diocletian. The first curia Iulia was restored by Domitian,[2] burned in the fire of Carinus, and finally rebuilt by Diocletian.[3] This building is the present church of S. Adriano, into which it was transformed about 630 A.D. Drawings of the sixteenth century show the condition of the building at that time and the main lines of its original construction. It occupied a rectangular space, 51.28 metres long and 27.51 wide, fronting on the Comitium, and in the rear abutting on the inclosure wall of the forum Iulium. Its east side was on the Argiletum. The building consisted of three parts. The Curia proper, or hall in which the senate met, which is the modern church, occupied the east end. This hall is 25.20 metres deep and 17.61 wide. Little of the ancient interior remains except the Corinthian pilasters of marble on each side and at the ends. The exterior can hardly have been imposing. The lower part of the brick-faced façade was covered with slabs of colored marble, some of which have been found in situ, and the upper part with painted stucco, traces of which are visible.[4] The brick cornice is supported by travertine consoles, and above it is a triangular pediment, round which the cornice was continued. The main entrance of Diocletian's Curia was at the top of a flight of steps, 1.60 metres above the imperial pavement. Only the foundation of these steps remains. The

---

[1] CIL. vi. 1718; Jordan, I. 2. 256–257.

[2] Hieronym. 161.  [3] Chronogr. a. 354, p. 148.

[4] NS. 1900, 48–49, 295–303; BC. 1899, 251–252; 1900, 271–273; 1903, 143–146; CR. 1900, 236–237; Mitt. 1902, 39–41; 1905, 47–52.

doorway itself was 5.90 metres in height from threshold to architrave, and continued in use until the latter part of the eleventh century, probably after the Norman invasion, when its lower half was walled up with fragments of all sorts, marble and porphyry columns, inscriptions, and the like, and the new threshold was laid 3.25 metres above the earlier. In 1654 the upper part of the original doorway was walled up,

FIG. 51.—CURIA AND COMITIUM.

and a new one cut through above, so that its threshold corresponded with the top of the first. This was the doorway of the church which was in use until the recent excavations. The bronze doors themselves were removed to the Lateran by Alexander VII in the seventeenth century. By means of a tunnel cut through the wall (at Y, Fig. 48) portions of the original pavement of colored marbles have been found *in situ*.

After the building had become a church, bodies were buried in niches (*loculi*) cut in the front wall, seven of which have been found, one containing a skeleton. Other tombs were cut in the foundation of the steps (Z, Fig. 48), and on this foundation and on the Comitium were found three sarcophagi. At the west end of the steps is a well of republican date (U, Fig. 48) 0.69 metre in diameter, in which, besides the usual rubbish, were fragments of stucco decoration in the second Pompeian style, which may have belonged to the curia Hostilia.

The west end of the building was occupied by the Secretarium, a hall measuring 18.17 by 8.92 metres, with an apse at the north end. This hall became the church of S. Martina, and was completely modernized in the sixteenth century. Through the centre of the building, between the Curia and Secretarium, Cardinal Bonelli cut the modern via Bonella. From the drawings it is not possible to decide with absolute certainty whether this space was taken up by one large hall, divided by rows of columns into a nave and two aisles, or by two smaller rooms, but the former is the more probable. Either this central portion, or rooms shown in the drawings behind S. Adriano, was the Chalcidicum or atrium Minervae.

**The Lapis Niger and Adjacent Monuments.**[1] — At the south edge of the Comitium is a pavement of black marble (Fig. 52), about 4 metres long by 3 wide, and 0.25 to 0.30 metre thick. It has suffered from fire and other injuries, and has been repaired in one place with a block of white marble. The centre of this pavement is 29.50 metres from the Curia, and 19.50 from the arch of Severus, and it lies on the same level as the Caesarian pavement (p. 233) of the Comitium, of which it seems to form a part. On the south and adjacent parts of the east and west sides, it is protected by a rude curb of marble slabs set in travertine sills. As excavations have been made beneath this pavement, it is now supported by an iron framework. It has the same orientation as the Curia.

---

[1] For the description of these monuments, see esp. *NS.* 1899, 129, 151–158; Comparetti, *Iscrizione Arcaica del Foro Romano*, 1900, 1–13; *Mitt.* 1902, 22–26; Richter, *Top.*[2] 363–367; *BC.* 1903, 108–114.

Underneath this pavement is a group of ancient tufa structures which rest on a pavement of broken tufa, 2 metres below
the upper surface of the black marble, and about 1.50 metres

FIG. 52. — THE LAPIS NIGER.

below the level of the travertine pavement of the later republic. This group consists of two parts. That at the east consists of a rectangular foundation of one course of tufa, on
which rest two bases (A, B, Fig. 53), 2.66 metres long and
1.31 broad, and 1 metre apart, connected at the rear (south) by
a course of the same height and 0.435 metre broad. The
height of the upper surface of these bases from the pavement
is 0.59 metre. In the centre of the rectangle, between the
bases, is an open space, 1.20 by 1 metres, where there is no
foundation, but a bottom of soil and ashes. On the edge of the
foundation, and projecting over this space, is a single tufa
block (C), measuring 0.725 by 0.52 by 0.29 metre. The rectangle formed by these two bases measures 3.64 metres in length
and 2.66 in depth. On the bases were pedestals of tufa with
curved profiles except at the south, where the ends were cut

off square. Of these pedestals, that on the west base is almost entirely preserved, but of the other only two blocks remain. There is no trace of what they supported. Directly

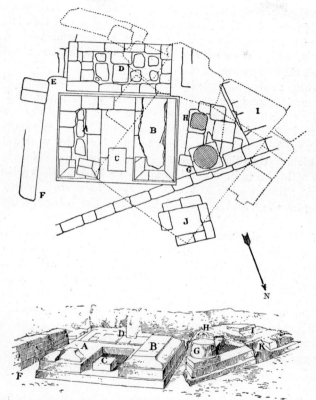

Fig. 53. — The Archaic Structures under the Lapis Niger.

behind them is another platform (D) of tufa, 3.50 metres long and 1.60 wide, with no trace of a superstructure. The orientation of this group, ordinarily called the *sacellum*, differs not

only from that of the adjacent structures and of the lapis niger,
but also from that of the Comitium of the republic, being 30°
east of north. The straight flight of steps (*abc*, Fig. 48) was
interrupted by this sacellum, the north corner of which projects just across its line. Just east of this structure, and
nearly parallel with it, is a wall of four courses of tufa blocks,
one of the two retaining walls of the *suggestus* mentioned on
p. 236, which were evidently built to inclose the niche in
which these monuments stand.

West of this rectangle is the second part of the group. The
first and second steps of the *suggestus* begin again, and extending south from them, on a level with the top of the lowest,
are several blocks of very early pavement. West of this pavement are traces of what seems to have been the west wall of
the niche. On this pavement stands the lower part of a cippus
(*H*) of brown tufa, which has also been broken off at a height
varying from 0.45 to 0.61 metre. It is four-sided, each edge
being bevelled, and tapers slightly from the bottom, where it
measures 0.47 by 0.52 metre. On the four sides and on one
of the bevelled edges is part of an archaic inscription in Greek
letters, which dates probably from about the beginning of the
fifth century B.C. The letters have suffered so little from ex-
posure that it is probable that they were covered with stucco
and painted red. As nearly as can be judged, from a half to
two-thirds of the cippus has been broken off, and as the inscription is cut in the vertical boustrophedon style, — that is, with
letters running in different directions in alternate lines, from
one end of the cippus to the other, — only a few words can be
made out with certainty, and no agreement has been reached
as to its meaning.[1] From the few words that can be read it is
probable that the inscription, perhaps a *lex sacrata*, refers to
some ceremony performed here by the *rex*, either the real

---

[1] The best discussion of this inscription is by Warren, *The Stele Inscription
in the Forum*, *AJP*. 1907, 249–272, 373–400.

king, or his successor, the *rex sacrorum*. The cippus stands
in a shallow hollow, cut for it in the surface of the pavement,
but it has been slightly displaced. Around it lie some blocks
(Fig. 54) of a second pavement, superimposed upon the
first, which cover the lower part of the cippus as far as the

FIG. 54. — THE CIPPUS AND INSCRIPTION.

beginning of the inscription. The displacement just mentioned is probably due to the laying of this second pavement.

On the corner of the second step of the *suggestus*, nearest the
pedestals, is a square base, and on it the lower part of a conical
column (G, Fig. 53) of yellow tufa, 0.77 metre in diameter at
the bottom and 0.69 at the top, which has been broken off at
a height of 0.48 metre. Cippus and cone have been broken off
at the same level, which corresponds with that of the bed of
the late republican pavement (*k*, Fig. 48). The base of this
cone projects beyond the second step, over the second pavement which has been rudely hacked away to make room for it.

North of the broken cone is a square pit (J), inclosed by walls of brown tufa which project 0.90 metre above the level on which these tufa structures stand. The filling between this level and the lapis niger was composed of a layer of sand and gravel from the Tiber, 0.55 metre thick, and above this a layer, 0.40 metre thick, of earth and ashes in which were also many fragments of bones of animals, potsherds, terra cottas, and figurines and objects of various sorts made of bronze,[1] dating from the sixth to the first century B.C., and mixed together in the utmost confusion. Although some of these objects may have been originally votive offerings, the character of the stratum in which they are found makes it improbable that we have here a *stips votiva*. The material in this layer was probably scraped together from the ruins of neighboring buildings when burned, and used with the gravel to cover the tufa structures. Above it was laid a mass of broken tufa, with bits of travertine and fragments of the black marble of which the lapis niger consists. On this was laid the concrete bed of the lapis niger itself.

The available evidence of the monuments themselves and the adjacent strata seems to show, with a considerable degree of certainty, that their chronological sequence is as follows : (1) the inscribed cippus, which is surely as old as the fifth and possibly as the sixth century ; (2) the conical column of tufa which also dates from the fifth century ; (3) the sacellum — altar and pedestals — which in its present form belongs to the period after the Gallic invasion and probably to the latter half of the fourth century ; (4) the pavement of black marble, in regard to which there are two widely divergent views. According to one,[2] it is a part of the Caesarian pavement of travertine (p. 233) which surrounds it, and therefore no later than that, although it may have been laid first in the time of Sulla on

---

[1] *NS.* 1900, 143–146; *Mitt.* 1902, 25–26; *BC.* 1903, 115–123.
[2] See Pinza, Studniczka, and Petersen, in works cited below.

the level of his pavement (*k*, Fig. 48) and afterward raised. It may also have been large enough then to cover the underlying structures. Confirmation of this view is sought in the presence of fragments of this black marble in the bed beneath. According to the second[1] view, this pavement is not an integral part of the Caesarian, and the fact that it does not correspond at all, in extent or orientation, with the monuments beneath, shows that it can not have been laid until the knowledge of their exact position had been lost. It is well known from literary and other sources that the emperor Maxentius revived the cult of Romulus, and the discovery of the base (S, Fig. 48) on the Comitium, dedicated to Mars Invictus and to Romulus and Remus, the founders of the city, in the name of Maxentius, makes it easy to suppose that he laid the pavement of black marble, to reproduce the lapis niger of the founder's tomb, as nearly as possible over its original site. Confirmation of this view is also sought in the absence of any mention in the literature of the empire to so striking a monument as this black marble pavement in the most frequented part of the Forum would have been.

From a combination of these chronological data with those derived from the walls of the Comitium (p. 236), it would appear that about the middle of the fifth century the Comitium was separated from the Forum by a low platform, on which stood the archaic cippus, the cone, and probably an earlier monument, represented by the existing sacellum of a considerably later date. After the destruction of the Curia by the Gauls, the level of the Comitium was raised, and the first platform replaced by a higher, that to which the straight flight of steps belonged (*cba*, Fig. 48). In this platform, which was called the Rostra after 338 B.C., was an irregular niche inclosing the monuments in question. Toward the end of the republic the level of the Comitium was again raised, and the

---

[1] *Mitt.* 1902, 30–31; 1905, 44–46.

straight Rostra built over by that with curved steps ($p'pm$, Fig.
48). Finally, at the end of the republic, in consequence of
the changes made either by Sulla, Faustus Sulla, or Caesar himself, the level of the Comitium was raised again, perhaps twice
in quick succession, and a new pavement laid which also covered the existing Rostra and its niche. This necessitated the
destruction of cippus, cone, and sacellum, and the filling up of
the niche. Owing to the incompleteness of the reports as yet
published, and the inadequacy of the excavations themselves,
all attempts to reconstruct the successive stages of the Comitium with greater accuracy in dates and matters of detail, such
as the shape and extent of the Rostra at different epochs, must
be regarded as purely tentative.

The attempt to explain and identify these monuments has
given rise to a vast amount of discussion and speculation.[1]
Two passages in Dionysius,[2] who wrote in the time of
Augustus, state (1) that some say that a stone lion which
stood in the chief place in the Forum, near the Rostra, marked
the tomb of Faustulus, and (2) that Hostilius was buried in
the chief place in the Forum and honored with an inscribed
stele. Festus,[3] quoting Verrius Flaccus, a contemporary of
Dionysius, says that a *niger lapis* in the Comitium marks a

---

[1] For a complete review of this literature to 1904, see G. Tropea, *La Stele
Arcaica del Foro Romano, Cronaca della discussione. Rivista di Storia
Antica*, 1899, 470–509; 1900, 101–136, 301–359; 1901, 157–184; 1902, 36–45, 425–
427; 1903, 529–534. Also *Bursian's Jahresbericht*, 1905, 257–280. Brief lists
of the more important works in *Arch. Anz.* 1900, 2 n.; *Mitt.* 1902, 26 n.; *BC.*
1903, 138–139. The most important discussions of these monuments and the
remains on the Comitium are: Studniczka, *Jahresheft d. oest. Arch. Instituts*,
1903, 129–155; 1904, 239–244; Petersen, *Comitium, Rostra, Grab des Romulus*,
Rome, 1904; *Comitium und Rostra, Mitt.* 1906, 193–210; Hülsen, *Mitt.* 1905,
29–46; Pinza, *Il Comizio romano nell' età repubblicana* (reprinted from *Annali
della Società degli Ingegneri ed Architetti Italiani*, 1905), Rome, 1905. See
also Delbrück, *Der Apollotempel auf dem Marsfeld*, Rome, 1903, 11; *AJA.*
1909, 25–29; *CR.* 1904, 140; 1905, 77–78; 1906, 134; *Mon. d. Lincei*, 1905, 753–
754; Pais, *Legends*, 15–34; Richter, *BRT.* IV. 5–13.

[2] i. 87; iii. 1.    [3] 177.

*locus funestus*, set apart according to some authorities for the grave of Romulus, but not used for him, but for Hostilius or Faustulus. Finally two passages in the scholia of Horace,[1] state (1) that Varro said that Romulus was buried *post rostra*, and (2) that in the opinion of many, Romulus was buried *in rostris*, and that the statues of two lions were set up on the spot in memory of this, according to the custom of the present day. In consequence of these statements it was natural to connect the pavement of black marble with the lapis niger, the sacellum with the tomb of Romulus or Faustulus or Hostilius, and the cippus with the inscribed stele erected in honor of Hostilius. The destruction and covering up of the monuments were attributed to the Gauls, but this can not have been the case, for the archaeological evidence shows that this covering can not have taken place before the time of Sulla at the earliest, while the sharpness of the edges of the stone proves that the fracture was soon followed by burial in the earth. Varro might therefore have seen the monuments in his youth. It is also a matter of grave doubt whether the term *lapis niger* could have been used of a pavement, *locus nigro lapide stratus*. Furthermore the shape of the sacellum is not like that of any known tomb, and there is strong evidence in support of the view that the existing bases are only the lower parts of higher bases which are to be reconstructed with profiles similar to that of the altar erected by Calvinus on the Palatine (p. 141). These bases might still have supported recumbent lions or served as altars. The rectangular structure behind these bases, evidently somewhat older than they, seems best adapted for an altar, although some regard it as part of the early Rostra.

Every explanation and identification of these monuments is open to some serious objection, but perhaps the least unsatisfactory, although incomplete, is about as follows. The

---

[1] *Epod.* 16. 13, 14; Porphyr. *ib.;* Comm. Cruq, *ib.*

cippus, with its archaic inscription referring to some sacrifice or ceremony performed by the king, stood here from a very early date, and close beside it was a shrine of some sort, both being regarded with such veneration that they were preserved in a niche when the first platforms for public speakers were built on the edge of the Comitium. In process of time the inscription became unintelligible, and the legend of Romulus, as it gradually developed, became attached to the neighboring shrine, so that it came to be regarded as his tomb, or that of one of his companions. In the fourth century the sacellum was restored or rebuilt, and consisted of two pedestals, of the shape suggested above, in front of a rectangular altar. On these pedestals were the statues of two lions, and a lapis niger formed part of the group, marking the spot as a *locus funestus*. At the end of the republic, when such notable changes were made in the Comitium, and the Rostra removed to the Forum, the meaning of this whole group had so far faded away in the mists of uncertainty that no hesitation seems to have been felt in partially destroying it and hiding it completely from view. The lions may very likely have been removed bodily, and Dionysius may have seen one of them. The site was undoubtedly marked in some way, either by the existing pavement of black marble, which took the place of the lapis niger, or by another similar pavement, perhaps of greater area. It seems very difficult at present to decide between these two possibilities.

**The Carcer.** — Between the temple of Concord and the Curia, at the foot of the Capitoline, *media urbe foro imminens*,[1] is the ancient prison of Rome, which, in part at least, is as old as any structure in the city. Above it have been built the small churches of S. Giuseppe dei Falegnami and S. Pietro in Carcere. This Carcer consists of two parts.[2] The lower and more

---

[1] Liv. i. 33.    [2] Sallust, *Cat.* 55; Abeken, *Mittelitalien*, 191–197.

ancient part was a circular chamber, about 7 metres in diameter at the bottom, which is now below the surface of the ground. The walls of this chamber were built of blocks of tufa, laid in such a way that each successive course projects farther inward than that immediately beneath it. Of the original structure only what appears to be the three lower courses of stone still exists, although it is quite possible that there may be one still lower that is now hidden. If it was ever built up to a top, this chamber must have been about 10 metres high, and have resembled a Mycenean θόλος. The upper part of the structure was removed at some later date and a straight wall of tufa about 5 metres long, differing somewhat from the earlier masonry in construction, was laid across the circle, like a chord, on the Forum side. The chamber was then covered by an exceedingly flat arch of tufa blocks fastened together with iron clamps, in the centre of which is an aperture 0.60 metre in diameter. In the floor is a well, 0.55 metre in diameter and 0.63 deep, which is fed by a spring. From this room a drain leads into the cloaca of the Forum, but it appears to be of very late, even perhaps modern, construction.

The upper room is trapezoidal in shape, its longest side, 5 metres in length, being over the straight side of the lower room. The other sides measure 4.95, 4.90, and 3.60 metres in length. The roof is a barrel-vault 5 metres high, in the centre of which is a square opening, apparently at one time the only entrance. On the outside of this chamber is a travertine string course, on which is an inscription[1] recording a restoration in the consulship of C. Vibius Rufinus and M. Cocceius Nerva. This is generally assigned to the reign of Tiberius.

The lower room was called, in classical times, Tullianum,[2] and the whole prison Carcer simply, the name Custodia Mamertini not being found until the middle ages. Tullianum[3] is usually

---

[1] *CIL.* vi. 1539.

[2] Pl. *NH.* vii. 212; Fest. 356; Varro, *LL.* v. 151; cf. also Fest. 264.

[3] Jordan, I. 1. 453–455; 2. 323–328; Gilbert, II. 74–81; Lanciani, *Acque*, 23–24.

derived from *tullius,* a spring, and this chamber has usually been supposed to have been a spring-house, built in the regal

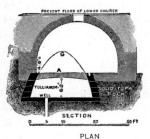

period, which was afterward made into a prison. The upper room was undoubtedly first built at an early period, but materially changed in the later restoration. Its irregular shape was made necessary by its position between two streets. Adjoining it are other chambers which have not been excavated and are not accessible. There are many difficulties connected with this explanation of the Tullianum as a spring-house, and an attempt has recently been made to prove that it was an ancient tomb.[1] However this may be, there is no doubt that this was the Carcer of the republic, where so many famous victims were executed and their bodies then thrown out on the scalae Gemoniae (p. 295), which passed close by.

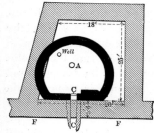

FIG. 55. — PLAN AND SECTION OF THE CARCER.

A. Opening in floor over the Tullianum.

CC. Cloaca.

FF. Front wall of Carcer with inscription.

At just this point on the slope of the hill were the stone-quarries that came to be used as a prison, especially for slaves. They were called **Lautumiae** [2] (λατομία), after those at Syracuse which were used for a similar purpose. It is possible that the unexcavated chambers next to the Carcer may belong to the prison *in lautumiis.*

[1] *BC.* 1902, 40–45; *Rendiconti dei Lincei,* 1902, 226–239.

[2] Varro, *LL.* v. 151; Fest. 117; Sen. *Contr.* ix. 27. 20; Liv. xxvi. 27; xxxii. 26; xxxvii. 3; xxxix. 44; Jordan, I. 1. 505–507; 2. 343–345; Gilbert, II. 80; for an erroneous view that the Lautumiae were near the temple of Faustina, cf. *NS.* 1902, 96; *BC.* 1902, 31–34; *Berl. Phil. Wochenschrift,* 1903, 1647.

**The Arch of Augustus.** — There were at least three so-called triumphal arches in the Forum, besides the fornix Fabianus (p. 319) at the entrance. We are told that two such arches were erected in honor of Augustus, one [1] in 29 B.C. to commemorate the victory at Actium, and the other in 19 B.C. on account of the return of the standards which had been captured by the Parthians at Carrhae.[2] This return of the standards is also recorded on a denarius of 18/17 B.C.,[3] together with a representation of a triple arch. The foundations of such an arch have been discovered between the temple of Julius and that of Castor,[4] being laid on the short axis of the former temple and close to it. These foundations consist of travertine blocks on concrete beds, and those of three of the four piers are *in situ*. The middle piers were 2.95 metres wide, and those at the sides 1.35, thus giving the arch a peculiar appearance. The width of the central archway was 4.05 metres, and that of the side arches 2.55, the breadth of the whole structure being 17.75 metres. The pavement in the central passage is still partially preserved, and some of the marble fragments of the arch have been set in brick beds on the travertine foundations. If the coin referred to above is a fairly accurate representation of this arch, the middle portion was much higher than the sides, and was surmounted by a quadriga. When the temple of Castor was rebuilt by Tiberius, the south part of the arch was largely hidden by the steps of the temple, which were very close to it. The foundations of this arch rest upon the pavement of a street, with curbstones of tufa, of the republican period, which ran north and south at this point.

Another coin [5] of the period represents a triple arch, but of a different shape; and an inscription [6] cut on a block of Parian

---

[1] Dio Cass. li. 19.　　　[2] Dio Cass. liv. 8; *Schol. Veron. Aen.* vii. 606.
[3] Eckhel, vi. 101; Cohen, *Aug.* 82.
[4] *Jahrb. des Inst.* 1889, 151–162; *Antike Denkmäler*, i. 14–15, 27–28; *Mitt.* 1889, 243–244; 1905, 76–77.
[5] Eckhel, vi. 106; Cohen, *Aug.* 544.　　　[6] *CIL.* vi. 873.

marble, about 3 metres long, which was found close to these foundations, records a dedication to Augustus in 29 B.C. This inscription may have been set in an arch, and it is therefore somewhat uncertain whether the arch which stood on the foundations that have been discovered was erected in 29 or 19. There was no corresponding arch on the other side of the temple of Julius.

**The Arch of Tiberius**. — This arch was built by Tiberius [1] to commemorate the return of the standards which had been captured by the Germans in 8 A.D. at the defeat of Varus. It stood at the northwest corner of the basilica Iulia, not spanning the Sacra via, but just north of it. The street was made narrower at this point, and the curb bent toward the south to afford room for the arch. The concrete foundations, 9 metres long by 6.3 wide, have recently been found.[2] The arch was single, and was approached by steps from the level of the Forum. Its foundations blocked up two of the arches (Fig. 46) at the southwest end of the viaduct of the clivus Capitolinus, two of the pits in the line of the street (p. 237), and also the arched opening of a drain built of tufa blocks. Into this drain at this point ran two other drains at an acute angle, and a block of tufa, set in the floor of the archway, served to regulate the flow of the currents. Some architectural fragments of this arch and part of the inscription have been recovered.[3]

**The Arch of Severus**. — As the arch of Tiberius stood at the south end of the Rostra, it has been thought probable that another arch stood at the north end;[4] but if so, it must have been removed to make room for the great arch of Severus, which was erected in 203 A.D. in honor of Severus and his two sons, Geta and Caracalla. This dedication is recorded in the

---

[1] Tac. *Ann.* ii. 41.

[2] *NS*. 1900, 632; *BC*. 1902, 26–27; 1903, 163; *CR*. 1901, 329; 1906, 133; *Mitt.* 1902, 12.

[3] *CIL*. vi. 906; Jordan, I. 2. 211–213.

[4] Perhaps that of Drusus, erected in 23 A.D. Cf. Tac. *Ann.* ii. 83; iv. 9.

inscription [1] which is repeated on both sides of the attic. The bronze letters have disappeared, but the matrices remain, and it can be seen that the name of Geta was chiselled away after he was murdered by Caracalla. This arch destroyed the

FIG. 56. — THE ARCH OF SEPTIMIUS SEVERUS (BEFORE THE RECENT EXCAVATIONS).

symmetry of the Forum, and its architecture and sculpture display the marked artistic decadence of the period.

The arch is triple,[2] of Pentelic marble, and stands on a foundation of travertine, the upper part of which was covered with

[1] CIL. vi. 1033.      [2] CR. 1899, 233; Mitt. 1902, 21–22.

marble facing.  The lower courses of this foundation are un-finished, and must have been covered either with earth or by the foundation of the steps that always formed the approach to the arch from the Forum side.  The level of the Augustan pavement was preserved in this corner of the Forum until a late period, as is shown by the massive concrete base in front of the arch on which is set the pedestal of the equestrian statue of Constantius, dedicated by Naeratius Cerialis, prefect of the city in 354 A.D.[1]  The Augustan pavement on which this base stands is 3 metres below that of the pavement of the arch, and 1.40 below that of the lowest steps to the side arches.

The arch is 23 metres high, 25 wide and 11.85 deep, the cen-tral archway being 12 metres high and 7 wide, and the side archways 7.80 high and 3 wide.   Between the central and side arches are vaulted passages, the ceilings of which are coffered, with rosettes in the coffers.   On each face of the arch are four fluted Corinthian columns, 8.78 metres high and 0.90 metre in diameter at the base.   These columns stand free from the arch on projecting pedestals, and behind them are corresponding pilasters.   An entablature surrounds the arch, and above it is the lofty attic, 5.60 metres in height, within which are four chambers.

Over the side arches are narrow bands of reliefs represent-ing the triumphs of Rome over conquered peoples ; and above these bands four large reliefs which represent the campaigns of Severus in the East.[2]   In the spandrels of the central arch are winged Victories, and in those of the side arches, river gods. On the keystones of the central arch are reliefs of Mars Victor, and on the pedestals of the columns, Roman soldiers driving captives before them.   On top of the arch, in the centre, was originally a chariot in which stood Severus and Victory, escorted by Geta and Caracalla, and on the ends four eques-trian figures ; but of these statues no traces have been found.

---

[1] *CIL.* vi. 1158.          [2] Strong, *Sculpture*, 297–300.

**The Arches of Janus**. — Besides the temple of Ianus Geminus (p. 190), a Ianus medius [1] is mentioned by Cicero and Horace and in inscriptions of the second century, and later commentators agree with the literary sources in making it the head-quarters of bankers and speculators. They also seem to locate it near the basilica Aemilia. A Ianus primus occurs in one inscription,[2] but it is doubtful whether this was in the Forum. The Horatian [3] phrase, *haec ianus summus ab imo prodocet*, can not be regarded as authority for a Ianus summus and a Ianus imus. The most probable explanation [4] of these references is that Ianus medius was a small single arch which stood in the Forum near the basilica Aemilia; but there is no means of deciding whether *medius* refers to its position in the Forum, or to its position with respect to other similar arches. Those who take the latter view suppose that these arches stood at the points where the streets entered the Forum; and, in support of this, point to the two cases of possible *iani* on the Rostra relief, the remains of an arch across the vicus Iugarius (of later date), the presence of such a *ianus* near the statue of Vortumnus [5] in the vicus Tuscus, and the statements of commentators of the later empire. Against this view may be urged the entire absence of any certain reference to other *iani* in the Forum.[6]

**The Area of the Forum**. — After the completion of the surrounding buildings, the open area between them, the Forum proper, formed an irregular quadrilateral, which was bounded

---

[1] Cic. *de Off*. ii. 87; *Phil*. vi. 15; vii. 16; Hor. *Sat*. ii. 3. 18, and Porphyrion's note; *CIL*. vi. 5845, 10027.

[2] *CIL*. vi. 12816.  [3] *Epist*. i. 1. 54.

[4] Cf. Jordan, I. 2. 214–218; Richter, *Top*.[2] 106–107.

[5] Hor. *Epist*. i. 20. 1; cf. Cic. *Verr*. i. 154 and Asconius' note; Varro, *LL*. v. 46; Prop. iv. 2. 5; cf. *Berl. Phil. Wochenschrift*, 1903, 1117.

[6] For a third but erroneous view, according to which summus, medius, and imus refer to points on a street, the vicus Ianus, which ran along the north side of the Forum, see Bentley, Hor. *Epist*. i. 1. 54, and Lanciani, *BC*. 1890, 100; *Ruins*, 253–254.

on the east and south by the continuation of the Sacra via.
The length of this area, from the foundation wall of the Rostra
to the curb of the street in front of the temple of Julius
Caesar, is 102 metres ; its width from the steps of the temple
of Castor to the basilica Aemilia, 45 metres, and from the
curb of the Sacra via in front of the basilica Iulia to the edge
of the lapis niger, 46 metres.   The Forum was paved, partially
at least, as early as the fourth or third century B.C. ; but, like
the Comitium, its level was gradually raised at successive
periods.    The present pavement of travertine is usually
assigned to the late empire, but, although some of it has undoubtedly been relaid, it probably represents in general the
level established by Augustus.   At an average depth of about
0.60 metre beneath this pavement are considerable portions
of an earlier one of travertine, which was probably laid by
Caesar,[1] and some fragments of the tufa pavement of the
republic have been found at various points, part of which is
more than 2 metres below the later level.   The pavement of
the Sacra via is separated from that of the area by a travertine
curb (crepido), the raised portion of which is 0.72 metre wide.
In this curb, at intervals of from 0.60 to 0.80 metre, are
square holes, in which it is probable that the poles which supported awnings were set.   We know that shelter of this sort
was provided in the Forum,[2] and similar holes are visible in
the latest pavement.

Like the Comitium, the Forum was incumbered with many
statues, honorary columns, and similar memorials.   As early
as 158 B.C.[3] the censors decreed that all statues of magistrates
which had been erected without the sanction of the state should
be removed, and from time to time even those that properly
belonged there disappeared to make room for others.   Almost
nothing is known from literary sources about any of the

---

[1] Cf., however, Richter, BRT. IV.      [2] Pl. NH. xix. 23, 24.
[3] Pl. NH. xxxiv. 30.

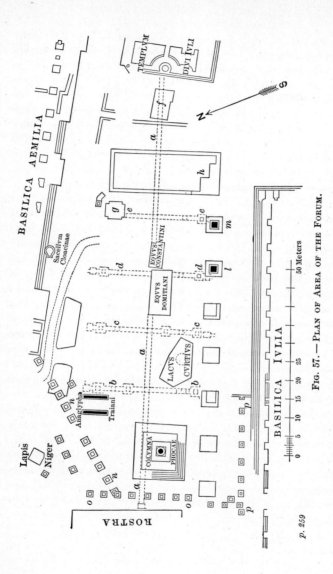

FIG. 57. — PLAN OF AREA OF THE FORUM.

individual statues; and of the inscriptions which have been recovered, only about one quarter date from a period earlier than that of the Antonines, and the same is true of the existing monuments themselves.  On the south side of the area is a row of large cubical pedestals of brick-faced concrete, once covered with marble, which date from the time of Diocletian.  These pedestals supported lofty columns of red and gray granite and pavonazzetto.  Two shafts [1] found lying near by have been set up on the two easternmost pedestals, the missing architectural members being restored in brick.

In front of the Rostra is the **columna Phocae**, a fluted Corinthian column of white marble, 1.39 metres in diameter and 13.60 high, on which was placed the statue of Phocas in gilt bronze.  The inscription [2] on the marble base states that it was erected in 608 A.D. by Smaragdus, exarch of Italy, in honor of the eastern emperor Phocas.[3]  The marble base rests on a square brick pedestal, which was entirely surrounded by flights of nine steps made of tufa blocks taken from other structures.  These steps have now been removed from the north and east sides.  As the column is far superior in style and execution to the work of so late a period, it must have been taken from some other building and set up by Smaragdus, or else it was already standing here, and the inscription refers only to the erection of the statue of Phocas.  The latter seems the more probable, as the brick pedestal is not later than the fourth century, and corresponds in general with those just mentioned.  The tufa steps belong to the latest period.

In front of the temple of Caesar, and having the same orientation, is a rectangular concrete base, measuring 8 by 5 metres, the top of which is at the level of the early imperial pavement.  At the northeast corner of this base, 1.70 metres below its upper surface, are the remains of the tufa pavement of the republican

---

[1] *Mitt.* 1902, 59–60.            [2] *CIL.* vi. 1200.
[3] Jordan, I. 2. 246; *Mitt.* 1891, 88–90; 1902, 58–59; 1905, 68; *Atti*, 577–580.

period. On the south side a covered drain of tufa blocks runs under the base. This drain is at a slightly higher level than the tufa pavement. On the base are seven large blocks of travertine, which, while probably belonging to the original superstructure, do not seem to be in their original position. This has been explained by some as the pedestal of an equestrian statue of Q. Marcius Tremulus,[1] consul in 306 B.C., which in Cicero's time stood *ante Castoris*, but had disappeared when Pliny wrote. The existing remains, however, can not have antedated the Augustan epoch, and if restored then in their present dimensions, they can hardly have disappeared in so short a time. A second explanation is that this base is the foundation of the marble monument to the family of Augustus, to which the fragments of the great epistyle, now lying in front of the basilica Aemilia (p.199), belonged.

Very near the centre of the area of the Forum is a large concrete base, 11.80 metres long and 5.90 metres wide, the top of which is 1.50 metres below the level of the latest pavement. This mass, 2.78 metres high, cuts into the main *cuniculus* (p. 266) and one of the cross-passages, and must therefore have been built after them. On the other hand, the concrete construction can not be later than the end of the first century. In the tops of this base are set three square blocks of travertine in which are holes about 0.44 metre square and 0.15 deep, which seem well adapted to hold supports of some kind, although there is in them no trace of metal or melted lead. This base is undoubtedly the foundation of the pedestal of the Equus Domitiani,[2] an equestrian statue of Domitian erected in 91 A.D. in honor of his campaign in Germany. In consequence of the *damnatio* decreed by the senate after his death, this monument was probably removed, which would explain the entire absence

---

[1] Liv. ix. 43; Cic. *Phil.* vi. 13; Pl. *NH.* xxxiv. 23; *NS.* 1904, 106; *CR.* 1904, 330; *BC.* 1904, 178–179: *Mitt.* 1905, 73–74; *Atti*, 583–584.

[2] Stat. *Silv.* i. 1. 29; *CR.* 1904, 139, 328–329; *BC.* 1904, 75–82, 174–178; *Mitt.* 1905, 71–72; *Atti*, 574–577.

of any trace of the superstructure. In the east end of the base a hollow block of travertine was found, containing five clay jars like those discovered in the necropolis of the Sacra via (p. 188). In these jars were found sand, stone, pitch, and fragments of tortoise shell, and in one of them a very small piece of quartz with a bit of gold attached to it, but nothing suggestive of funeral gifts. It is quite uncertain whether this deposit represents the contents of early graves, disturbed when this foundation was laid and therefore preserved in this way, or whether it was connected with some ritual attending the inauguration of the statue.

In the middle of the area, close to the course of the Cloaca Maxima, is the low pedestal of an equestrian statue, standing directly upon the travertine pavement. This is made of brick on which blocks of travertine and fragments of marble columns were placed, but in spite of its wretched construction it may have been the pedestal of an equestrian statue of the emperor Constantine.[1] It has also been connected with an equestrian statue of Severus [2] that stood somewhere in the Forum.

Near the southeast corner of the Rostra lies a square base [3] of white marble, with reliefs on its four sides, and the inscription *Caesarum decennalia feliciter*. This was found in front of the Curia in 1547, and in 1500 a similar base had been discovered with the inscription *Augustorum vicennalia feliciter*. These bases probably supported columns and were set up in 303 A.D. in honor of Diocletian and his colleagues. In this vicinity the remains of several monuments and inscriptions have been found, which record the struggles during the last century of the western empire. Some of them have been left in the Forum. One consists of a travertine base, supporting a marble block, itself originally the pedestal of an equestrian statue. This block had been set upon end, and the later

---

[1] *CIL.* vi. 1141; *Not.* Reg. viii.

[2] Herodian, ii. 9; *Mélanges*, 1900, 209–222; *Mitt.* 1905, 74–75.

[3] *CIL.* vi. 1204, 1205, 31262; Strong, *Sculpture*, 323.

inscription cut transversely across the field of an earlier one that had been erased. This was done in 405 A.D., by vote of the state, to commemorate the victory of Stilicho over Radagaisus.[1] Near by are some fragments of the base of a quadriga, erected in honor of Arcadius and Honorius, to commemorate their victory over the African rebel, Gildo, in 398 A.D.[2]

In 1872 the remains of a long brick structure were found, which extended across the east end of the area of the Forum, just west of the Sacra via. All that was found was destroyed, except the south end of the building, it being supposed that the structure was medieval. It is, however, probable that it belonged to the late empire.[3]

In front of the basilica Iulia, between the second and third brick bases, beginning at the east, and just beneath the travertine pavement, are the lower courses of brick walls which inclose two rectangular rooms. These rooms were originally paved with marble, but that has been covered over with a pavement of large stamped tiles [4] of the period of Diocletian, or soon after, with an orientation different from that of the building. The third brick base was built over one corner of this structure. The concrete foundation of these two rooms seems to extend south across the main *cuniculus* (p. 266) to the foundation of the equus Domitiani, and to have been covered with corresponding pavements of marble and tiles. This has been identified as a **Tribunal Principatus**,[5] but incorrectly.

A short distance northeast of the column of Phocas are the two marble **plutei**, or balustrades, frequently called the **anaglypha Traiani**, which are generally supposed to have formed part of the Rostra (p. 222), standing either on each side of the approach or at the ends of the platform. They now stand, just as they were found, on rough foundations of travertine which

---

[1] *CIL*. vi. 31987.          [2] *Mitt*. 1895, 52–58; *CIL*. vi. 1187, 31256.
[3] Richter, *BRT*. IV. 26–27.          [4] *CIL*. xv. 1569 a. 2–9.
[5] *Berl. Phil. Wochenschrift*, 1906, 221; *CR*. 1906, 132.

rest directly upon the pavement of the area, having evidently been used during the early middle ages as the foundation of some building. These balustrades date from the time of Trajan or Hadrian, and are made of several blocks of marble of unequal size.[1] A little modern restoration has been made with pieces of white marble, in order that they may stand firmly. They measure 5.37 metres in length, 1.75 in breadth, and stand parallel to each other, 2.95 metres apart. The inner surfaces of both have the same reliefs, figures of a sheep, swine, and bull, adorned with garlands and fillets, representing the sacrifice of the *suovetaurilia*. On the outer side of the west pluteus, at the left end, is a platform adorned with *rostra* in profile, upon which stands a man clad in a toga, attended by lictors. In front of the platform is a group of men, also clad in togas, in the act of applauding. Just to the right of the centre is a platform upon which sits the emperor, and before him stands a woman who seems to hold a child on her left arm, and to be leading another. Several men stand near. At the right end of the platform is a figure of Marsyas with a wine-skin, and a fig-tree on a square base. On the outer side of the other (the east) pluteus, at the left end, is a similar representation of the fig-tree and Marsyas. The central portion is occupied by figures of men who are bringing burdens on their shoulders, and throwing them down in a pile in the foreground. The right end of this pluteus has been broken, but there are traces of a platform with a seated figure. The background of each relief is formed by a succession of buildings and arches, and the general explanation is that these buildings represent the sides of the Forum, as they would appear to a speaker standing between them on the Rostra, while the scenes in the foreground represent Trajan's charity in providing for the support of the poor in various parts of Italy, and his measures for the remitting of taxes on inheri-

---

[1] *Ann. d. Ist.* 1872, 309; *Mon. d. Ist.* ix. 47, 48.

The East Pluteus

The West Pluteus.

The Suovetaurilia.

FIG. 58. — THE MARBLE PLUTEI.

tances already due the imperial treasury. The precise identification of the buildings has given rise to much discussion,[1] and
the view just stated is open to serious objections. According to
another theory, which has recently[2] been more fully developed,
the plutei formed part of some monument erected in honor of
Trajan near the tribunal praetorium (p. 268), and the two
reliefs represent the buildings on the south side only of the
Forum, the statue of Marsyas being repeated on each slab.
This explanation has much to commend it.

In the centre of the area a system of underground passages
(*cuniculi*) has been found.[3]  These passages are about 1.5
metres wide and 2.40 metres high, with tufa walls and a concrete vault, the crown of which is about 1.5 metres below the
latest pavement of the area.  These *cuniculi* themselves date
from the Caesarian period.  The longest passage, 120 metres
in length, extends from the Rostra to the front of the temple
of Caesar, and is crossed at right angles by four others.  Near
the ends of these cross-passages, and in two of them near the
middle also, are small, nearly rectangular chambers, with a
large block of travertine set in the middle of the pavement.
At the intersections of the main and cross-passages, and at
two other points in each of the latter, are square shafts in the
vaulting, surrounded by slabs of travertine, the angles of which
are much worn by ropes.  These marks, and others on the travertine blocks in the square chambers, seem to indicate the
presence of windlasses and tackle, but whether this machinery
was used to move heavy weights over the Forum, or, less probably, the apparatus of gladiatorial games, is quite uncertain.

---

[1] See the latest literature: Petersen, *Die Reliefschranken auf dem römi-
schen Forum, Abhandl. A. v. Oettingen . . . gewidmet,* 1898, 130–143; *BC.*
1900, 145–146; *Mitt.* 1897, 326–327; 1902, 21; *AJA.* 1901, 58–82; Strong, *Sculpture,* 151–157.

[2] *AJA.* 1910, 310–317.

[3] *BC.* 1902, 27–28; 1903, 101, 271–272; *CR.* 1902, 94; 1903, 328; 1904, 140;
*Mitt.* 1902, 57; 1905, 64–66.

Besides the lacus Iuturnae there were two other lacus in the Forum.  One of these, the lacus Servilius,[1] is mentioned in connection with the massacres of Sulla, and is generally supposed to have been near the vicus Iugarius.  The other, the so-called lacus Curtius, has recently been found between the column of Phocas and the equus Domitiani.  Three stories were current among the Romans as to the origin of this lacus.[2]  One was that at the beginning of the regal period a chasm suddenly opened in the centre of the Forum valley.  When the soothsayers asserted that this could be closed only by the sacrifice of that *quo plurimum populus Romanus posset*, a youth named Curtius leaped in, and the chasm closed over him.  According to the second story, the swamp was called the lacus Curtius from the Sabine Mettius Curtius, who rode his horse into it when hard pressed by the Romans, and escaped.  The third explanation was that the lacus was a spot of ground which had been struck by lightning, and then inclosed by a stone curb, or puteal, by C. Curtius, consul in 445 B.C.  The existing remains[3] of the lacus consist of a layer of blocks of brown and gray tufa, forming an irregularly trapezoidal field about 10 metres long and nearly 9 in greatest width, on which is a second layer of blocks of travertine surrounded with a curb.  Only part of this layer has been preserved.  Its upper surface is on the same level as that of the curb of the shaft of the adjacent *cuniculus*, for which it has been cut away, and it is clear that this lacus is a restoration of an earlier structure, carried out at the time of the Caesarian changes in the Forum. The level of the travertine layer is 0.60 to 0.80 metre below that of the existing travertine pavement of the Forum.  On its curb are marks that indicate the existence of a screen or balustrade, on which, as has been suggested, the famous archaistic relief of

---

[1] Cic. *pro Rosc. Am.* 89; Fest. 290; Sen. *de Prov.* 3. 7.

[2] Varro, *LL.* v. 148–150; Liv. i. 12; vii. 6; Dionys. ii. 42.

[3] *CR.* 1904, 329–330; 1905, 74; *BC.* 1904, 181–187; *Mitt.* 1905, 68–71; *Atti*, 580–582; Strong, *Sculpture*, 324–326.

Mettius Curtius, found near this spot in 1553 and now in the palazzo dei Conservatori, may have stood. On the western part of the lacus are traces of rectangular bases which suggest the *arae siccae* of Ovid.[1] Into the puteal of the lacus in the time of Augustus people of all ranks were accustomed to throw coins once a year, as an offering for the health of the emperor.[2] It is probable that there had once been a pool or fountain here, which had dried up, and its place was marked by a puteal. The lacus is not mentioned after the latter part of the first century.[3]

On the north side of the Rostra there were statues of three Sibyls, which were called the Tria Fata,[4] and, in the later centuries of the empire, gave this name to the whole area about the Curia. Still later it was called the Palma Aurea. These statues were said to have been set up originally on the Comitium in the time of Tarquinius Priscus, but they afterward disappeared, and were restored by Messalla and Pacuvius Taurus in the time of Augustus.

At the east end of the Forum, near the temple of Castor, was the puteal Libonis[5] or Scribonianum,[6] said to have been built by a certain Scribonius Libo on a spot that had been struck by lightning, and represented on a coin of the gens Scribonia.[7] Near the arch of Augustus are six blocks of travertine, with marks indicating the presence of a metal balustrade on their upper surface, which seem to form part of a circular puteal. These have been identified with the puteal Libonis, but without sufficient reasons.

Near the lacus Curtius was the tribunal praetorium, a sort of

---

[1] *Fast.* vi. 401–405.        [2] Suet. *Aug.* 57.        [3] Pl. *NH.* xv. 78.

[4] Procop. *Bell. Goth.* i. 25; Pl. *NH.* xxxiv. 22; Jordan, I. 2. 259, 349; II. 482.

[5] Schol. Pers. iv. 49; Cic. *pro Sest.* 18; Hor. *Epist.* i. 19. 8, and Porphyrion's note. Cf. *Mélanges*, 1908, 261–263.

[6] Fest. 333; Jordan, I. 2. 403; Gilbert, III. 159.

[7] Babelon, *Monnaies, Aemilia* 11, *Scribonia* 8.

wooden platform, which perhaps rested on a stone foundation, but was not a monumental structure. This was the judgment seat of the praetor, and was originally on the Comitium.[1] The date of its removal to the Forum is not known with certainty, but it was probably in the second century B.C., a period marked by the transfer of the comitia to the Forum. In the travertine pavement in front of the column of Phocas are now visible the matrices for bronze letters, 0.30 metre high, of the inscription L. NAEVIVS. L . . . DINVS PR. This is evidently the praetor, L. Naevius Surdinus, whose name occurs on the back of the archaistic relief of Mettius Curtius (p. 267), and who is probably to be identified with the *triumvir monetalis* of 15 B.C. Another inscription of a praetor was found here in 1817, so that it seems quite certain that this was the site of the tribunal,[2] and that this part of the pavement at least belongs to the Augustan period. No mention of this tribunal occurs after the time of Augustus, when all law business began to be transferred to the imperial fora. Near by was a statue of **Marsyas**,[3] of unknown origin, but it may well have been erected when the tribunal praetorium was removed to the Forum. Marsyas was regarded as a symbol of liberty,[4] and the type occurs on coins of cities which enjoyed special privileges. The statue in the Forum is represented on a coin [5] of the first century B.C., and on the marble balustrades, where the satyr is figured as standing upright with a wine-skin over his shoulder.[6] The statue was standing at the beginning of the second century.

Near the statue of Marsyas were a fig-tree and vine, which had sprung from chance seeds, and an olive-tree. The excavations have disclosed a spot of ground about 4 metres

---

[1] Liv. xxvii. 50; Jordan, I. 2. 402.

[2] *CR*. 1906, 133; *CIL*. vi. 1278; Richter, *BRT*. IV. 28.

[3] Hor. *Sat*. i. 6. 120, and Schol.; Pl. *NH*. xxi. 9; Jordan, I. 2. 265–266.

[4] Serv. *ad Aen*. iii. 20.    [5] Babelon, *Monnaies, Marcia* 42.

[6] *Arch. Anz*. 1891, 14–15; *Mitt*. 1892, 287–288.

square, between the marble plutei and the Naevius inscription, where there is no pavement, and here we may reasonably place these trees. An altar, which had formed part of the group, was removed when the last gladiatorial games were given by Julius Caesar.[1]

The increase in the number of jury trials during the last century of the republic must have necessitated the erection of other tribunals besides that of the praetor, but we know definitely of only one, the tribunal Aurelium, which is mentioned several times in Cicero,[2] and was probably built by M. Aurelius Cotta, consul in 74 B.C. The gradus Aurelii, also mentioned by Cicero,[3] was undoubtedly another name for the same structure, the gradus being the rows of steps which led up to the platform proper. The exact site of this tribunal is of course unknown.[4] According to the *Notitia* a shrine dedicated to the Genius populi Romani stood near the Rostra.

The pila Horatia[5] was a memorial of the contest between the Horatii and the Curiatii. It was probably originally a column, but is described in the time of Augustus as being the corner pillar of one of the halls at the entrance of the Forum, that is, probably, of the basilica Iulia.

**Drainage.** — The recent excavations have brought to light a complicated network of sewers, extending from the slope of the Capitoline to the Velia. They lie at various levels, and show that the drainage of this district was always a most difficult problem. Some of these sewers are undoubtedly of early republican date; but the gradual changes in level and the great building activity of the early empire necessitated the construction of new cloacae, and the consequent neglect of the old.

---

[1] Pl. *NH.* xv. 77–78.     [2] *Pro Sest.* 34; *in Pis.* 11; *de Domo*, 54.

[3] *Pro Cluent.* 93; *pro Flacc.* 66; Jordan, I. 2. 405.

[4] See, however, O'Connor, *AJA.* 1900, 303–309, and *University of Wisconsin Bulletin*, 1904, 178–182.

[5] Liv. i. 26; Dionys. iii. 22; Schol. Bob. Cic. *pro Mil.* p. 277; Gilbert, II. 67–70; Jordan, I. 2. 394.

The official reports have contained as yet little information, except with regard to the Cloaca Maxima.

Previous to the recent excavations, the supposed original Cloaca Maxima (p. 107) had been traced along the east side of the Curia and Comitium to a point not far from the sculptured plutei, where it turned sharply to the east, and, after continuing in this direction about 40 metres, turned again sharply to the south and crossed the area of the Forum. It passed under the east end of the basilica Iulia, and thence into the Velabrum. The excavation of the basilica Aemilia has shown that at least all that part of this cloaca which skirts the basilica dates from the early empire, and was probably the work of Agrippa.[1] This new course was necessitated by the enlargement of the basilica toward the west, in the year 34 B.C. The side walls of the cloaca rest partly upon the tufa pavement (p. 235) of the republican period in front of the basilica, and the top of its vault is about 1.50 metres above the level of the republican Comitium. Furthermore, the stone out of which this part of the cloaca was constructed had been taken from republican buildings (cf. Fig. 50).

Beneath the nave of the basilica an earlier channel of this sewer has been found, crossing the building obliquely in a northeast-southwest direction. The original channel has been widened and repaired, so that now the lower courses of the walls and the pavement are of travertine, and the upper part of the walls of tufa. Where the wall supporting the north row of columns of the nave crosses the line of this sewer, three large blocks of travertine lie in the channel, evidently to afford additional support for the wall above. This sewer continued originally in a straight line toward the column of Phocas, probably as far as the present west corner of the basilica; but just where it passed under the main longitudinal wall which

---

[1] *Mitt.* 1902, 29, 44, 57–58; 1905, 67; *CR.* 1901, 86, 137–138; *BC.* 1900, 60–61 279–280; 1903, 96, 99.

separates the nave from the tabernae, a branch sewer was built. This crosses the rest of the basilica in a line perpendicular to its main axis, at an angle of about 30° with the other channel, and meets the sewer of Agrippa about where it turns south to cross the area of the Forum. Although the existing masonry of these sewers is not earlier than the Augustan building of the basilica, it is clear that this was the original line of drainage. The basilica, when rebuilt in 34 b.c., was extended over the earlier Cloaca Maxima, and the new course of the sewer was constructed round the northwest end of the building. The pavement in front of the restored basilica must have rested almost directly upon the top of the cloaca. In the time of Plautus [1] the Cloaca Maxima was an uncovered *canalis,* and probably continued to be such until the Caesarian period.

The principal sewer west of the Cloaca Maxima seems to have been that which runs beneath the clivus Capitolinus. Its course [2] has been traced from the via di Marforio, through the vicus Iugarius (via della Consolazione) as far as the church of S. Maria della Consolazione. The section nearest the church is of brick, with brick pavement and concrete vaulting, and dates from the empire. The rest is of early date, being built of tufa blocks, with a tufa pavement and flat tufa top, thus having a rectangular section. The pavement of this sewer is 10 metres below the level of the via della Consolazione. In the Forum, the crown of its vault is higher than the substructures of the clivus Capitolinus. Between this sewer and the upper slope of the hill is a network of ancient drains, running at various angles and levels; and beneath the foundation of the steps of the temple of Saturn is a vaulted sewer of tufa, of very early date, and parallel to the front of the temple. [3] This sewer presents a peculiar appearance on account of a sort of

---

[1] *Curc.* 476.    [2] *NS.* 1899, 49; *BC.* 1899, 248–250; 1903, 162; *Mitt.* 1902, 9.
[3] *Mitt.* 1902, 9; *CR.* 1899, 234, 464; *BC.* 1903, 162–163.

shelf that has been cut in the side of the channel. For other drains near by, at a lower level, see p. 254.

The slope from the Velia to the Forum proper was drained into the basin of the Cloaca Maxima by means of a sewer under the Sacra via. Sections of this sewer have been excavated near the summa Sacra via, where the construction is of tufa blocks with a tile roof; in front of the basilica of Constantine,[1] where it is of opus reticulatum of tufa; and along the north side of the Regia and temple of Julius Caesar, where the work is also of opus reticulatum. It is evident that this sewer was of early date, but that it underwent considerable change in line and construction, at later periods.

During the recent excavations more than thirty wells (*putei*) of various depths and sizes have been found scattered through the Forum. Most of these wells belong either to the republic or to the middle ages, although there are a few of the intervening period. Some are fed by springs, and, after being cleaned out, have begun to flow. Their presence in such numbers is puzzling. The so-called pozzi rituali, which probably were connected with the drainage system, have been described on p. 237.

---

[1] *NS.* 1899, 266; *BC.* 1902, 34.

# CHAPTER X.

## THE IMPERIAL FORA.

By the middle of the first century B.C. the district north of the Forum, extending between the Quirinal and the Capitoline to the line of the Servian wall, had become one of the most densely populated in the city, as it contained almost no public buildings. Previous to 179 B.C. the fish-market, forum Piscatorium[1] or Piscarium, stood here ; but in that year M. Fulvius Nobilior erected for it, and for the butchers' shops that had been banished from the Forum in the fourth century, a *macellum*, or general market. In the time of Augustus an important market, known as the macellum Liviae[2] (p. 470), was erected on the Esquiline, and the earlier market seems to have been removed when the forum Pacis was built.

The rapid increase in population had made the old Forum too small, and it was with the object of providing adequate space for political and business requirements, as well as to beautify the city itself, that Caesar began the series of imperial fora. His plans were comprehensive, and included the conversion of this district into public fora, which should form a convenient and splendid thoroughfare between the Forum and the campus Martius. Communication here between these two parts of the city had hitherto been provided by a road leading past the Tullianum, along the slope of the Capitoline, to the porta Fontinalis, the via di Marforio. In the middle ages this road was called the clivus Argentarius,[3] and a basilica Argentaria

---

[1] Liv. xxvi. 27; xl. 51; Varro, *LL.* v. 145–147; Fest. 125; Jordan, I. 2. 433–435; Altmann, *Rundbauten*, 73–74.

[2] Dio Cass. lv. 8; *CIL.* vi. 1178; *Not.* Reg. v; Gilbert, III. 238.

[3] Gilbert, III. 228–229.

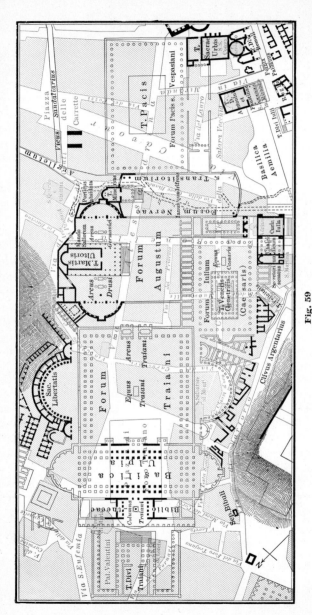

Fig. 59

PLAN OF THE IMPERIAL FORA

is mentioned in the Regionary Catalogue; but there is no doubt that the road itself dates from the time of the republic, and the ancient pavement has been found only a little beneath the level of the modern street. It is a possible hypothesis that the arcus Argentariorum,[1] or arcus Panis Aurei in Capitolio, mentioned in medieval documents, stood on this clivus, and that it was the arch erected by Marcus Aurelius in 176 A.D., from which the panels in the attic of the arch of Constantine were taken (p. 324).

We are told that Caesar intended to extend the Forum as far as the atrium Libertatis. This building,[2] which contained the offices and archives of the censors, was magnificently restored by Asinius Pollio, who established in it the first library in Rome. In the sixth century the name, atrium Libertatis, was applied by Theodoric to a part of the Curia. It is not entirely certain where this building stood, whether within the space afterward occupied by Trajan's forum, or beyond it in the campus Martius. The principal street in this region was the Argiletum (p. 173), a name also given to the district on either side of it, leading from the Subura into the Forum between the Curia and the basilica Aemilia, and afterward incorporated into the forum Transitorium of Nerva.

The first step toward carrying out the general plan was the building of the forum Iulium or Caesaris, which Caesar began in 54 B.C., and which was finished by Augustus.[3] It is said that the cost of the ground alone was a hundred million sesterces[4] (about four million dollars), but this has been thought an exaggeration. The old Forum and the new fora were essentially different. The first was an irregular open space which in the course of centuries had been surrounded with buildings of

---

[1] *PBS.* iii. 252–253; *CIL.* vi. 1014.

[2] *Hermes*, 1888, 631–633; *BC.* 1889, 362–363; *Mitt.* 1889, 240–241; Gilbert, III. 162–163; Liv. xliii. 16; xlv. 15; Cic. *ad Att.* iv. 16; *pro Mil.* 59; Fest. 241; Suet. *Aug.* 29; *Galba*, 20.

[3] Nic. Damasc. *Caes.* 22; *Mon. Anc.* iv. 12.

[4] Pl. *NH.* xxxvi. 103; Suet. *Caes.* 26.

various sorts; the latter were regular areas, inclosed by walls and containing temples and halls, symmetrically placed.

The forum Iulium[1] was a rectangular court, about 115 metres long and 30 wide, surrounded by a colonnade and wall. In the centre of this court stood the temple of Venus Genetrix. The main axis of the forum ran northwest and southeast, in the same direction as that of the Curia Iulia, which adjoined it at the south corner. The temple of **Venus Genetrix**,[2] the mythical ancestress of the Julian gens, was vowed by Caesar on the battlefield of Pharsalus, and dedicated September 26, 46 B.C. Vitruvius[3] describes the temple as pycnostyle. It was peripteral, hexastyle or octostyle,[4] and built of solid marble. Excavations in the sixteenth century brought to light portions of the foundations of peperino and travertine, and fragments of columns and a frieze. All that now remains of this forum is a part of the peperino inclosure wall on the southwest side (via delle Marmorelle 29), 12 metres high and 3.70 thick, and some small vaulted chambers or tabernae, which opened into the corridor of the Forum through a row of peperino arches with travertine imposts. In front of the temple stood a famous equestrian statue[5] of Caesar himself, and a fountain surrounded by a group of nymphs, called the **Appiades**.[6] This forum was not intended for markets or trade, but for legal business and as a general meeting-place.[7] It was injured by fire in 283 A.D. and restored by Diocletian,[8] but is not mentioned afterward.

**Forum Augustum.** — The forum Romanum and the forum Iulium did not afford sufficient room for the courts and legal business of the city, and to provide for this deficiency, Augus-

---

[1] Jordan, I. 2. 436–441; Gilbert, III. 225–227.

[2] Dio Cass. xliii. 22; Pl. *NH.* vii. 126; ix. 116; xxxv. 156; xxxvii. 11.

[3] iii. 2. 2.　　　　　　　　　　　　[4] So drawn on Palladio's plan.

[5] Suet. *Caes.* 61; *Ber. d. k. sächs. Gesell.* 1891, 99–112.

[6] Pl. *NH.* xxxvi. 33.

[7] App. *Bell. Civ.* ii. 102.　　　　　[8] *Chronogr.* a. 354, p. 148.

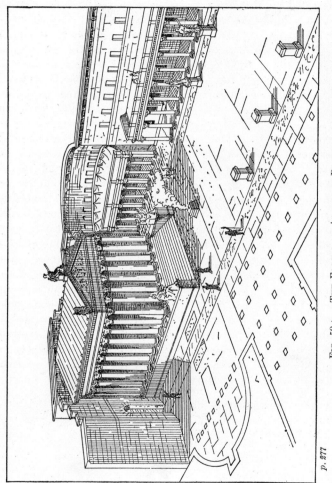

FIG. 59 A. — THE FORUM OF AUGUSTUS RESTORED.

tus erected a third,[1] in connection with the temple of Mars Ultor which he had vowed at the battle of Philippi.  This forum, known as the forum Augustum, or at a later period Martis forum, inclosed the temple of Mars, just as the forum Iulium inclosed the temple of Venus Genetrix.

FIG. 60.—THE FORUM OF AUGUSTUS.

The forum Augustum [2] was rectangular in shape, about 125 metres long and 90 wide, and joined the forum Iulium on the northeast, its longest axis being perpendicular to that of the latter.  The regularity of this rectangle was broken by two large semicircular apses or *exedrae* on the southeast and northwest sides, and also at the northeast end, where the irregularity is explained by the fact that Augustus, who was obliged to purchase all the site of this forum from private owners,[3] did not succeed in acquiring enough land to carry out his original plan.  Exactly in the middle of the northeast

---

[1] Suet. *Aug.* 29; Ov. *Fast.* v. 566–598; Jordan, I. 2. 442–447; Gilbert, III. 229–231.

[2] *Mem. d. Lincei*, xiii. 1884, 400–415; *Mitt.* 1891, 94–98.

[3] Suet. *Aug.* 56; *Mon. Anc.* iv. 21.

half of the forum stood the temple of Mars, with its end abutting against the inclosure wall. The building of temple and forum was so much delayed that the formal dedication did not take place until August 1, 2 B.C.,[1] a day which was afterward celebrated as an annual festival. The forum was surrounded by an enormous wall, which served the double purpose of protecting it against fire and shutting off the view of the squalid quarters of the city in the immediate neighborhood. A considerable part of this wall at the northeast end, and also of the southeast exedra, has been preserved. It was originally nearly 36 metres high, and was built of large blocks of peperino in alternate courses of headers and stretchers, with wooden dowels but no mortar. On the outside, two courses of travertine divided it into three sections. In the part of the wall now standing is one of the original arched gateways (arco dei Pantani), through which the modern via Bonella passes, 6 metres above the ancient level. The inner surface of the wall was covered with marble and stucco. Whether a colonnade and porticus surrounded the south part of the forum within the wall is uncertain.

Each apse was separated from the forum area by a line of four pilasters and six fluted columns of cipollino, 9.50 metres high, which supported an entablature of white marble. In the curved wall of the apse were two rows of rectangular niches, the lower about 2.50 metres, and the upper about 15, from the pavement. The wide wall-space (about 8.50 metres) between these two rows of niches, which appears to have been bare of ornament other than the lining, was probably masked by the entablature already mentioned. About 5 metres above the upper row of niches ran a cornice, and above this the wall rose again for a considerable height. In each apse, in the lower row, were fourteen niches, not counting the large one in the middle, and four between each apse and the temple, making

---

[1] Macrob. *Sat.* ii. 4. 9; Dio Cass. lx. 5.

thirty-six in all.   Whether there were more in the other portion of the wall, is not known.

In these lower niches were placed the bronze statues of all
the Roman *triumphatores,* from Aeneas down.[1]   The name and
*cursus honorum* of each general were engraved on the plinth of
the statue, and the *res gestae* on a marble slab fixed to the wall
below.   Of these inscriptions a considerable number have been
recovered.[2]   The upper niches probably contained trophies.

The temple of Mars Ultor,[3] one of the most magnificent in
Rome, was octostyle, and peripteral except at the northeast
end, where it joined the forum wall.   Three of the columns
with the architrave are still standing.   They are of white
marble, fluted, 15.30 metres high and 1.76 in diameter, with
Corinthian capitals.   It is possible that they belong to the
restoration by Hadrian,[4] and not to the structure of Augustus.
The cella wall is of peperino, lined with Greek marble.   The
ceiling of the peristyle, between the cella wall and the columns,
is coffered, with rosettes in the centre of each coffer.

The forum Augustum was intended primarily for the Roman
courts,[5] and Trajan himself sat in judgment here, although the
construction of his great forum diminished the importance of
the others.   Certain formalities [6] were regularly observed here,
*i.e.* the assumption of the toga virilis by all members of the
imperial household, the formal leave-taking of provincial gov-
ernors when setting out for their posts, and the granting of the
honor of a triumph by the senate.   The insignia of triumph
and the standards recovered from the Parthians [7] were deposited
in the temple of Mars, and the forum itself contained the
bronze statues of victorious generals [8] and many works of art.[9]

---

[1] Suet. *Aug.* 31 ; Pl. *NH.* xxii. 13; Dio Cass. lv. 10.

[2] *BC.* 1889, 26–34, 73–79, 481–482; 1890, 251–259; *Mitt.* 1889, 247–249; 1891,
99–101 ; *CIL.* i.² pp. 186–202.

[3] *Mem. d. Lincei,* xiii. 1884, 405–411.        [4] Spart. *Vit. Hadr.* 19.

[5] Suet. *Claud.* 33; Dio Cass. lxviii. 10.

[6] Dio Cass. lv. 10.

[7] *Mon. Anc.* v. 42.

[8] Tac. *Ann.* iii. 18 ; iv. 15; xiii. 8.

[9] Pl. *NH.* vii. 183; xxxv. 93.

In 19 A.D. Tiberius erected two triumphal arches,[1] one on each side of the temple, in honor of the victories of Drusus and Germanicus in Germany. By a decree of the senate a quadriga was dedicated to Augustus himself, as *pater patriae*.[2]

**Forum Pacis or Vespasiani.** — In 71 A.D., after the taking of Jerusalem, Vespasian commenced building a temple of Peace,[3] which was completed four years later. The inclosed area in the centre of which the temple stood was finished by Domitian and came to be known as the forum Pacis,[4] or forum Vespasiani.[5] It lay behind the basilica Aemilia and southeast of the forum Augustum but not directly adjoining it, as the Argiletum, the main thoroughfare to the Subura, passed between the two. The orientation of the two fora was the same. The forum Pacis was rectangular in shape, 145 metres in length and about 85 in width, and was surrounded by a lofty wall of peperino lined with marble and pierced by several gates. At its southwest corner this forum adjoined the templum Sacrae Urbis, supposed to have been built by Vespasian, on the back wall of which was the Marble Plan of the city.

The temple of **Sacra Urbs** [6] has already been discussed (p. 2). Why and when it was called a temple is not known, but possibly it was the result of the apotheosis of the city, which was common after the time of Severus. The main hall of the ancient building forms the body of the modern church of SS. Cosma e Damiano. The northwest and southeast walls exhibit the original construction of tufa of the first century, while the southwest and northeast walls are of concrete and brick by Severus. In each of the three sides, southeast, southwest, and northwest, were five large windows, and there were originally

[1] Tac. *Ann.* ii. 64.    [2] *Mon. Anc.* vi. 26.

[3] Suet. *Vesp.* 9; Dio Cass. lxvi. 15; cf. Statius, *Silv.* iv. 3. 17.

[4] Aur. Vict. *Caes.* 9; Amm. Marc. xvi. 10. 14; Gilbert, III. 135; Jordan, I. 3. 2–5.

[5] Polem. Silv. 545.    [6] Gilbert, III. 186–187; Jordan, I. 3. 4–7.

two entrances, one of which, on the southeast, is still visible.
Considerable remains of the marble pavement at the north end
are still *in situ.*

The temple of Peace contained the spoils brought from Jerusalem [1] and numerous other works of art,[2] as well as a library.
This temple, the basilica Aemilia, and the forum Augustum
were regarded as exceptionally beautiful buildings.[3]    The
temple was burned in 191 A.D.[4] and restored by Severus.
Both forum and temple were in existence in the fourth century.
In the sixth century Procopius[5] speaks of the works of art in
the forum, but says that the temple had long since been destroyed by lightning.    Only the faintest traces now remain.
Some fragments of the pavement of giallo antico and pavonazzetto were found in 1875, 10 metres below the present level of
the via del Tempio della Pace.[6]

**Forum Nervae or Forum Transitorium**. — To make a proper
connection between the forum Pacis and the forum Augustum,
Domitian transformed part of the intervening Argiletum
into a magnificent avenue, which had the form of a very narrow forum.[7]    As the work was completed during the short
reign of Nerva,[8] it was ordinarily known by his name, but also
as the forum Transitorium[9] or Pervium,[10] because it was the
main thoroughfare between the Subura and the forum Romanum
and between the other imperial fora.    It also appears to have
been called the forum Palladium,[11] on account of the temple of
Minerva within it.    Its length was about 120 metres and its
width only about 40, the walls of the fora already existing

---

[1] Jos. *Bell. Iud.* vii. 5. 7; Pl. *NH.* xxxiv. 84; xxxv. 102, 109.

[2] Gell. v. 21. 9; xvi. 8. 2.

[3] Pl. *NH.* xxxvi. 102.                    [5] *Bell. Goth.* iv. 21.

[4] Dio Cass. lxxii. 24.                     [6] *BC.* 1876, 52–53.

[7] Suet. *Dom.* 5; Stat. *Silv.* iv. 3. 9; Mart. x. 51. 12; Jordan, I. 2. 449–453;
Gilbert, III. 232–234.

[8] *CIL.* vi. 953.                          [10] Vict. *Caes.* 12.

[9] Lamprid. *Vit. Alex.* 28, 36.            [11] Mart. i. 2. 8.

being extended so as to form a continuous inclosure.[1] A part
of the wall at the northeast end is still standing, and corresponds in height and character with that of the forum Augustum,
which it adjoins.

In the centre of the northeast end of the forum Nervae
stood the temple of Minerva,[2] whose worship was especially
cultivated by Domitian. From either side of the temple
short walls stretched across to the fora of Augustus and
Vespasian. The main entrance to the forum was in one of
these short walls east of the temple, and there was a similar
gate on the west. The temple itself, as represented on the
Capitoline Plan,[3] was hexastyle prostyle, as the narrowness
of the space rendered a peristyle impossible. The apse projected beyond the limits of the forum. Considerable remains of
the temple were visible in the sixteenth century, but all have
disappeared, except a small part of the cella next to the forum
Augustum, and fragments of the inscription on the façade.
Some of the modern houses now stand directly upon the
podium of the temple.

Within the inclosure wall was a colonnade of marble columns,
two of which, together with about 11 metres of the wall itself,
are still standing at the east corner of the forum, in the via
della Croce Bianca. This ruin, one of the most beautiful
bits in Rome, is called Le Colonnacce. The wall is peperino,
and part of the marble lining is still in place. The columns
are 10 metres high and 0.90 metre in diameter, and the intercolumniations 5.30 metres in width. As the level of the modern street is much higher than that of the original pavement
of the forum, only the upper part of the columns is visible.

Above the columns are a cornice and a lofty attic, which, instead of following the line of the columns, run along the wall
itself in the intercolumnar spaces, and project and return round

---

[1] *Mem. d. Lincei*, xi. 1883, 22–26; *Mélanges*, 1889, 346–355; *Mitt.* 1891, 101–103.

[2] Suet. *Dom.* 15; Dio Cass. lxvii. 1.     [3] Jordan, *FUR.* 116.

the columns, thus breaking the entablature into sections.   The attic, which is 4.40 metres high, has a plinth and a cornice, and in the space between the columns is a relief of Minerva, 2.65 metres high.[1]   It is probable that similar reliefs, either of Minerva or of some other goddess, stood in each intercolumnar space.   The frieze is decorated with reliefs representing scenes of household life, such as spinning, weaving, and dyeing, — the arts which were especially under the protection of Minerva.

Somewhere in this forum Domitian erected a temple to Ianus Quadrifrons,[2] which was square in shape, with doors in the centre of each side.   During the reign of Alexander Severus[3] statues of all the emperors who had been deified were set up in this forum.

**Forum Traiani**. — This, the last, largest, and most magnificent of the imperial fora, consisted of the forum proper, the basilica Ulpia, the column of Trajan, and the bibliotheca, all of which were built by Trajan with the assistance of his architect, Apollodorus of Damascus, and dedicated, at least in part, about the year 113 A.D.[4]   It is possible, however, that this work may have been planned, or even begun, by Domitian.[5] The great temple of Trajan, which was added by Hadrian, did not form part of the original plan.

By cutting away the opposite ends of the ridges of the Quirinal and the Capitoline, Trajan successfully carried out Caesar's plan (p. 274) of connecting the Forum valley with the campus Martius.   The space thus levelled was 185 metres in width, and the extreme length of forum and temple was about 310 metres.   The inscription[6] on the base of the column

---

[1] *Ann. d. Ist.* 1877, 5–36; *Mon. Ined.* x. pl. 40, 41, 41 a; *Mitt.* 1889, 88, 249.

[2] Serv. *ad Aen.* vii. 607; Mart. x. 28. 3; *Mem. d. Lincei*, xi. 1883, 26–32.

[3] Lamprid. *Vit. Alex.* 28.

[4] Vict. *Caes.* 13; Dio Cass. lxix. 4; Jordan, I. 2. 453–467; Gilbert, III. 234–237; Richter e Grifi, *Ristauro del Foro Traiano*, Rome, 1839.

[5] Strong, *Sculpture*, 149; *NS.* 1907, 415; *CQ.* 1908, 144.

[6] *CIL.* vi. 960; cf. Dio Cass. lxviii. 16.

of Trajan states that it was erected *ad declarandum quantae altitudinis mons et locus tantis operibus sit egestus,* and until 1906 this was usually interpreted to mean that the height of the column was the same as that of the ridge between the Quirinal and the Capitoline that had to be cut away to provide room for the forum. Recent excavations,[1] however, have brought to light the pavement of an ancient street and remains of houses of the early empire beneath the corner of the foundations of the column, thus showing conclusively that no such connecting ridge existed.

Of the various attempts to explain the inscription that have been made, the least unsatisfactory is that *mons* was merely the shoulder of the Quirinal, that was cut back so far that the height of the excavation was approximately 100 feet.

The ancient road just mentioned seems to have crossed the forum area at an angle of about 71° with its major axis. It passes close to the northwest corner of the column, and beneath it are the remains of a sewer of republican date, and north of it are traces of a wall of opus quadratum.

While the other imperial fora consisted of a temple with its surrounding court, the forum of Trajan represented rather the idea of the old Forum, consisting as it did of a very large open area flanked on one side by a basilica and library. There was, however, a sacellum Libertatis [2] in the northeast hemicycle, which seems to indicate that this goddess was recognized as the presiding divinity of the forum, a choice significant of the liberal character of the emperor.

The orientation of Trajan's forum was the same as that of the other imperial fora, and it was probably connected directly with the forum Augustum, although the inclosure walls seem to have been separated by a short distance. In any case there

---

[1] *NS.* 1907, 389–410, 414–427; *CQ.* 1908, 142–144; *Mitt.* 1907, 187–197; Boni, *Trajan's Column* (from *Proceedings of the British Academy,* vol. iii), London, 1907; Binder, *Die Plebs,* 42–51.

[2] Jordan, *FUR.* 25.

must have been an avenue leading across the intervening space between the two.

The forum proper consisted of a rectangular area, 116 metres wide and 95 metres long,[1] inclosed by a wall of peperino faced with marble, except on the two sides, where great hemicycles, 45 metres in depth, projected outward. Around three sides was a colonnade of different kinds of marble, single on the southeast and double on the northeast and southwest. The entrance to this area was in the middle of the southeast side, where Trajan erected a magnificent arch to commemorate his victories in Dacia. This arch is represented on coins[2] with six columns in front, and above the attic a six-horse chariot driven by the emperor himself. In the centre of the area stood a bronze equestrian statue of Trajan, and in the intercolumnar spaces of the portico successive emperors erected statues of many distinguished statesmen and generals.[3]

Of the two hemicycles,[4] on either side of the forum proper, the northeastern is well preserved and has been partially excavated. It is built of brick with travertine trimmings, and consists principally of two stories of chambers, which abut directly against the side of the Quirinal hill. The rooms on the ground floor, which were doubtless shops, open on a road paved with polygonal blocks of basalt, which follows the line of the hemicycle. They are paved with black and white mosaic, and the walls are covered with stucco. Above the first story is a gallery with Tuscan pilasters, into which the rooms of the second story open. Above this gallery there was another story, the front which was not flush with the lower façade, but was pushed back on the slope of the hill. The semicircular space in front of this hemicycle was paved with

---

[1] This is the length according to Lanciani's measurements, as he traces the course of the *murus marmoreus*, or southeast wall of the forum, 25 metres farther from the forum Augustum than other topographers do.

[2] Cohen, *Trajan*, 167.     [3] Gell. xiii. 25. 1.     [4] *NS*. 1907, 414–427.

white marble and surrounded with a colonnade decorated with gilt-bronze trophies.

The northwest side of the forum proper was closed by the basilica Ulpia,[1] which was raised about 1 metre above the level of the forum, and was approached by three short flights of steps. The entrances to the basilica, at the tops of these steps, were flanked by columns of yellow marble and statues and surmounted by chariots and bronze trophies. The steps themselves were of giallo antico. The walls of the basilica were of concrete covered with marble, its roof of timber covered with gilt-bronze tiles, and its floor was paved with slabs of white marble, some of which are still *in situ*. The basilica was rectangular in shape, with large apses at each end. Its main axis was perpendicular to that of the forum. The great hall was surrounded with a double row of columns, ninety-six in all, probably of white or yellow marble, with Corinthian capitals. These columns formed two aisles, 5 metres wide, and supported a gallery on both sides of the nave and at the ends. The nave itself was 25 metres wide.

Behind the basilica Ulpia was a small rectangular court, 24 metres wide by 16 deep, formed by the basilica itself, the two halls of the bibliotheca, and the temple of Trajan. In the centre of this space, and forming, as it were, the crown of the whole forum, rose the columna divi Traiani,[2] which still stands in a state of almost perfect preservation. This column, called *columna cochlis* from its resemblance to the shell of a snail, or *centenaria* from its being exactly 100 Roman feet in height, is built entirely of Parian marble. The shaft and base, composed of eighteen blocks, 3.70 metres in diameter, with the additional block which forms the capital, and the plinth which is

---

[1] Jordan, *FUR.* 25, 26; Cohen, *Trajan*, 42–44: Lesueur, *La Basilica ulpienne, restauration executée en* 1823, Paris, 1878.

[2] Fröhner, *La Colonne Trajane*, Paris, 1874; Percier, *Restauration des monuments antiques*, pt. ii. 1878; Cichorius, *Die Reliefs der Trajans-Säule*, 2 parts, Berlin, 1896; Strong, *Sculpture*, 166–213; *CR.* 1906, 235; *PBS.* v. 435–459.

cut in the upper block of the pedestal, measure 100 Roman
feet (29.77 metres) in height.  It is this height of the shaft
which is referred to in the inscription.  The height of the column
and pedestal together is 38 metres.  On the top of the column
stood a statue of Trajan in gilt-bronze, but Sixtus V replaced
this in 1588 by the present statue of St. Peter.  The column
is hollow, and a spiral staircase, with one hundred and eighty-

FIG. 61. — THE COLUMN OF TRAJAN.

five steps, leads to the top.   Light is furnished by forty-three
narrow slits in the wall.  The base, 5.5 metres square and 5.04
metres high, is ornamented on three sides with trophies.   The
southeastern side has a door, and above it the dedicatory inscription.   Within this base are a vestibule, a hallway, and a
rectangular sepulchral-chamber, lighted by a window on the
southwest side, in which the ashes of Trajan,[1] in a golden urn,

---

[1] Eutr. viii. 5; Dio Cass. lxix. 2; Aur. Vict. *Epit.* 13.

were probably placed. This chamber had evidently been robbed, for a hole had been cut through the travertine foundation. To secure the stability of the structure, the chamber itself had afterward been filled up with concrete probably at some time in the eighteenth century. It was not excavated until 1906.[1]

The entire surface of the shaft is covered with reliefs, arranged on a spiral band, which varies in width from about 90 centimetres at the bottom to nearly 1.25 metres at the top. These reliefs represent the principal events in the campaigns of Trajan in Dacia between 101 and 106 A.D. The average height of the reliefs is 60 centimetres, and they were cut after the column had been erected, so that the joints of the blocks are almost wholly concealed. These reliefs were also colored most brilliantly.[2] They form a complete encyclopedia of the organization and equipment of the Roman army in the second century.

On either side of the column and abutting against the rear wall of the basilica were the two buildings of the library,[3] called the bibliotheca Ulpia, or the bibliotheca templi Traiani. One of these buildings contained the Greek and the other the Latin books, and in both were reading rooms, on the walls of which were placed the busts of celebrated authors.[4] State archives, such as the edicts of the praetors and the libri lintei, or acts of the emperors, were kept here.[5] At a later period, and for some unknown reason, the books were transferred to the baths of Diocletian.[6]

The forum Traiani was completed by Hadrian, who erected the temple of Trajan (templum divi Traiani) and his wife, Plotina, northwest of the column.[7] This temple was octostyle peripteral, and stood on a raised platform, round which was a

---

[1] NS. 1907, 361–401; CR. 1906, 379.    [2] Bull. d. Ist. 1833, 92; 1836, 39–41.
[3] Vop. Vit. Probi, 2; Vit. Aur. 24; Gell. xi. 17.
[4] Sid. Apollin. ix. 16.    [5] Vop. Vit. Aur. 1; Vit. Tac. 8; Vit. Numer. 11.
[6] Vop. Vit. Probi, 2.    [7] Spart. Vit. Hadr. 19; CIL. vi. 966, 31215.

porticus.   Fragments of its granite columns 2 metres in diameter, of smaller marble columns 1.80 metres in diameter, and
some corresponding capitals of the Corinthian order have been
found at various times, as well as remains of the concrete
substructures.[1]  The reliefs,[2] found within the area of the
forum, may have belonged to this temple, but more probably to
the encircling colonnade.

The portion of this forum which is now exposed to view
consists of the column, the central part of the basilica, and a
small part of the northwest end of the forum proper.   The
broken columns of granite now standing do not belong to the
basilica, but to some other part of the forum.   The remaining
fragments, comparatively numerous as they are, give little idea
of the wealth of precious marbles and decorative work of every
conceivable kind with which this most magnificent group of
buildings was adorned.   Ammianus Marcellinus[3] gives a most
vivid picture of the astonishment of the emperor Constantius
on the occasion of his first visit to this forum.   It soon out-
stripped all the others in importance, as is shown by the numerous statues of famous men set up here between the second
and fifth centuries.[4]  The history of its destruction begins with
the sixth century, and throughout the middle ages it furnished
an almost inexhaustible supply of decorative material for the
churches and palaces of Rome.[5]

---

[1] *Bull. d. Ist.* 1869, 237;  *NS.* 1886, 158 ff.

[2] *PBS.* iv. 229–257.                         [3] xvi. 10. 15.

[4] *CIL.* vi. *passim;* Jordan, I. 2. 465.

[5] Cf. Cerasoli, *La Colonna Traiana e le sue Adiacenze nei secoli xvi e xvii,*
*BC.* 1901, 300–308.

# CHAPTER XI.

## THE CAPITOLINE HILL.

**The Capitoline**[1] **hill** (mons Capitolinus) is about 460 metres in length and has an average breadth of about 150, being the smallest of the hills of the city. It was surrounded by steep cliffs on all sides except the southeast, where it was accessible from the Forum valley, and was composed of three distinct parts, the elevations at the north and south ends and the depression between them. The present height of the north summit, at the church of S. Maria in Aracoeli, is 39 metres (see p. 17) above the mean level of the Tiber; that of the south summit, via di monte Tarpeo, 38 metres; and that of the piazza del Campidoglio, 30 metres.

In the earliest period, the north elevation seems to have belonged to the Sabine settlement on the Quirinal, while the south portion of the hill may have come into the possession of the Palatine Romans. Each summit was fortified in the usual way, by escarpments and a breastwork where the cliff was steep, and elsewhere by tufa walls. This hill became a part of the city of the Four Regions (p. 43), and its inclusion at that time marked the completed union of the Palatine and Sabine elements in the population. The earlier fortifications on the west side of the hill became a part of the Servian wall, so that each summit formed a separate inclosure within the outer wall.

---

[1] Jordan, I. 2. 3–5; Gilbert, I. 244–247; II. 310–322. For the history of the hill see, E. Rodocanachi, *Le Capitole romain antique et moderne*, Paris, 1904; and the English translation by Frederick Lawton, *The Roman Capitol in Ancient and Modern Times*. London, 1906.

[2] *BC.* 1873, 138–146; 1887, 275.

The north peak became the arx or citadel of the new city, and on the south peak the Tarquin dynasty established the worship of the triad of great gods, — Jupiter, Juno, and Minerva, — thereby marking this point as the religious centre of the community.[1]  To it was given the name of Capitolium [2] (from *capitalis, caput*), and thenceforth throughout antiquity it continued to represent to the Romans the visible centre of the state.

The settlers on the Quirinal had already a temple dedicated to this triad of divinities and called Capitolium, which, after the erection of the Tarquinian temple, was known as the Capitolium vetus (p. 487).

The double nature of the Capitoline is shown by the prevalence of the double designation, *Arx et Capitolium*,[3] down to the end of the republic, although the increasing importance of the Capitolium and the decreasing necessity for a citadel led to the gradual application of the word Capitolium to the entire hill.   On the other hand, the word Capitolium [4] was also employed to designate simply the temple of Jupiter itself, as the most significant part of the whole.   The adjective *capitolinus* was derived from the noun, and mons Capitolinus became a common name for the whole hill.   The depression between the two summits was called inter duos lucos, or Asylum,[5] the latter name being explained by the story that Romulus welcomed here the refugees from other communities.

The precipitous cliff at the southwest corner of the Capitolium, from which criminals convicted of capital offences were hurled, was known from the earliest times as saxum Tarpeium,[6] and later as rupes Tarpeia.[7]   The statement that the original name of the hill itself was mons Tarpeius is false, and due to

---

[1] Gilbert, II. 448–456.          [2] Varro, *LL.* v. 41; Liv. i. 55.
[3] Liv. v. 39; Cic. *Catil.* iv. 18.     [4] Jordan, I. 2. 6–7; Gilbert, II. 423–432.
[5] Liv. i. 8; Jordan, I. 2. 115–118; Gilbert, I. 331; II. 433–434.
[6] Varro, v. 41; Sanders, *University of Michigan Studies*, i. 1–47;  Pais, *Legends*, 96–127.          [7] Tac. *Hist.* iii. 71.

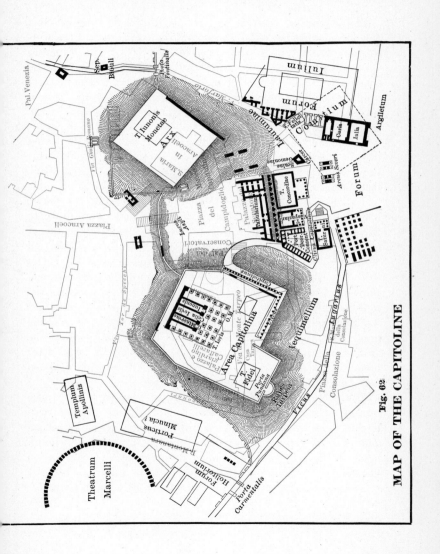

**Fig. 62**

**MAP OF THE CAPITOLINE**

Fig. 62 A. — West End of Forum and Capitolium Restored.

the imagination of the Roman antiquarians. Of the early fortifications some remains still exist, especially several courses [1] of tufa blocks at the top of the Tarpeian rock, similar in construction to the wall of the Palatine, and also above the Carcer just east of the via dell' arco di Settimio Severo. Of the Servian wall, remains [2] have been found below the palazzo Caffarelli, in the via delle Tre Pile, and on the site of the monument of Victor Emmanuel. The erection of the Tabularium, at the end of the republic, and of the medieval buildings destroyed all traces of earlier conditions on the ridge between the two summits.

The principal approach to the Arx and Capitolium was by a path from the Forum, which led first to the Asylum, and there divided. At the end of the regal period, the path to the Asylum, with the branch to the Capitolium, was made into a road suitable for vehicles, and this was henceforth known as the clivus Capitolinus.[3] It was paved by the censors Q. Fulvius Flaccus and A. Postumius Albinus, in 174 B.C., and a porticus was built on the right side of the road from the temple of Saturn to the Capitolium. It is probable, however, that this porticus did not extend below the Asylum in later times. In 190 B.C. Scipio erected a decorative arch [4] at the top of the clivus, and other arches may have been built over the road as a fornix Calpurnius [5] is mentioned in the fifth century.

The clivus Capitolinus, which is in effect a continuation of the Sacra via, begins near the arch of Tiberius, at the corner of the basilica Iulia, skirts the west side of the temple of Saturn, and making a sharp turn at the corner of the porticus Deorum Consentium, ascends to the Asylum. Part of the back

---

[1] *Ann. d. Ist.* 1871, 49–51.

[2] *Bull. d. Ist.* 1882, 227–230; *BC.* 1887, 275; 1892, 145–146; *NS.* 1889, 361; 1890, 215; 1892, 200; *Mitt.* 1889, 254–255; 1891, 104; 1893, 287.

[3] Liv. xli. 27; Pl. *NH.* xix. 23; Tac. *Hist.* iii. 71; Jordan, I. 2. 62, 78, 120–121; Gilbert, I. 313–315; II. 311–317, 445–448; *Hermes,* 1883, 104–128, 616–619; 1884, 322–324.     [4] Liv. xxxvii. 3.     [5] Oros. v. 9.

wall of the porticus serves as a foundation for the clivus, but its upper course has been changed by more recent structures. Portions of the lava pavement of the clivus still exist at various points near the bottom of the ascent, especially in front of the temple of Saturn, where one of the best specimens of republican paving in Rome may be seen. No trace remains of the upper part of the clivus or of the branch which led to the Arx, which was at first the more important of the two. Both paths probably ascended the slope in windings. It is uncertain whether the clivus entered [1] the area Capitolina on the northeast or the southeast side, but probably on the latter, directly opposite the façade of the temple.

Somewhere on the clivus, probably not far from the temple of Saturn, a passage led out through a gate, the porta Stercoraria.[2] This gate was opened only once a year, in order that the rubbish, *stercus,* from the temple of Vesta might be thrown out.

Besides the clivus, two flights of steps led to the top of the hill. One, the Centum gradus,[3] led to the Capitolium at its south corner near the Tarpeian rock; the other [4] ascended to the Asylum and Arx, between the temple of Concord and the Carcer, and may possibly be identified with the gradus Monetae mentioned by Ovid.[5] The scalae Gemoniae,[6] on which the bodies of executed criminals were thrown, either branched off from the gradus Monetae or was another name for them.

**The Arx.** — Of the exact topography of the northern part of the Capitoline hill almost nothing is known,[7] as the building of the medieval church and cloisters of S. Maria in Aracoeli [8]

---

[1] Hülsen, *Zur Topographie des Kapitols, Festschrift für H. Kiepert,* Berlin, 1898, 220–222; Richter, *Capitolium und Clivus Capitolinus,* Berlin, 1903.

[2] Fest. 344; Gilbert, II. 316.   [3] Tac. *Hist.* iii. 71.

[4] Dio Cass. lviii. 5; *Hermes,* 1883, 125–126.   [5] *Fasti,* i. 638.

[6] Gilbert, I. 327; III. 164; Jordan, I. 2. 324–325, and classical literature there cited.

[7] Gilbert, I. 267–270, 320–328.   [8] Jordan, I. 2. 112–113.

changed previous conditions completely. The excavations of recent years have brought to light on the southeast slope of the hill remains of early tufa walls, over some of which is concrete of the imperial period. These remains admit of no identification, but seem to belong to at least two different structures. It is plain, however, that the slope of the hill was protected by a retaining wall, and the top was probably artificially levelled.

There was no permanent garrison in the citadel; but in the early days sentinels were posted here while the comitia were being held in the campus Martius, to watch for the signal, displayed on the Janiculum, of an approaching enemy.[1] Another signal, *vexillum russi coloris*,[2] was at the same time raised on the Arx.

Somewhere on the east part of the Arx was the Auguraculum,[3] or open grassy spot where the omens were observed, which played an important part in some of the oldest ritual of the state. On the Arx was the house of M. Manlius Capitolinus, destroyed in 384 b.c. by order of the senate, on the site of which, forty years later, Camillus erected the famous temple of Iuno Moneta.[4] The origin of the epithet Moneta is unknown, but it was explained by the Roman antiquarians as being derived from the warning voice of the goddess which was heard in the temple on the occasion of an earthquake *ut sue plena procuratio fieret*.[5] When the coinage of silver money was begun in Rome in 269 b.c., the mint was established in this temple as an eminently safe place, and designated thenceforth as ad Monetam or Moneta. The mint appears to have been removed at the end of the first century, and nothing

---

[1] Dio Cass. xxxvii. 28.

[2] Macrob. *Sat.* i. 16. 15; Serv. *ad Aen.* viii. 1; Fest. *Epit.* 103.

[3] Fest. *Epit.* 18; Varro, *LL.* vii. 8; Cic. *de Off.* iii. 66; Vitr. ii. 1. 6; Jordan, I. 2. 104–106; Gilbert, II. 453–455; III. 401; *BC.* 1910, 132–140.

[4] Liv. vi. 20; vii. 28; Ov. *Fast.* i. 638; vi. 183–186; Solin. i. 21; Jordan, I. 2. 108–111; Gilbert, I. 333–334.   [5] Cic. *de Div.* i. 101.

further is known about the temple. L. Manlius vowed a temple to **Concord**[1] on the Arx in 218 B.C., which was completed and dedicated in 217, and the temple of **Honor et Virtus**,[2] erected by Marius, may perhaps have stood on the east slope of the citadel, although the location of this temple is wholly uncertain. There appears to have been a shrine of **Veiovis**[3] on the Arx, besides that erected *inter duos lucos* (p. 305), but whether or not this was the temple built by L. Furius Purpureo[4] in 192 B.C. we do not know.

At the foot of the northern slope of the Arx traces have been found of shrines cut in the rock, and inscriptions relating to foreign deities of a later period, like **Sebazis** and **Dea Caelestis**,[5] **Hecate**,[6] and **Mithras**.[7]

**Capitolium**. — The chief place on the south summit of the hill was occupied by the most famous of all Roman temples, the aedes Iovis Optimi Maximi or Capitolini,[8] dedicated to Jupiter and his companion deities, Juno and Minerva. It stood in the centre of the area Capitolina, a space formed by building retaining walls and substructures round the edge of the hill and leveling off the surface inclosed.[9] This temple dated from the end of the regal period, its foundation being ascribed by tradition[10] to Tarquinius Priscus and its dedication[11] to the first year of the republic. From the first it was regarded as the

[1] Liv. xxii. 33; xxiii. 21; *CIL.* i². p. 309.

[2] Cic. *pro Sest.* 116; Vitr. iii. 2. 5; vii. *praef.* 17; Val. Max. i. 7. 5; Fest. 344; Jordan, I. 2. 44; Gilbert, III. 99.

[3] Pl. *NH.* xvi. 215.                    [4] Liv. xxxv. 41.

[5] *NS.* 1892, 43, 407; *Mitt.* 1893, 288.     [6] *IGI.* 1017.     [7] *CIL.* vi. 719.

[8] *Ann. d. Ist.* 1876, 145–172; *Mon. Ined.* x. pl. xxx a; *BC.* 1875, 165–189; *Mitt.* 1888, 150–155; 1889, 249–252; *Mélanges*, 1889, 120–133; *Hermes*, 1884, 322–324; Richter, *Top.*² 121–126; *Capitolium und Clivus Capitolinus*, Berlin, 1903; Jordan, I. 2. 8–101; Gilbert, II. 416–423, 434–448; III. 382–398; Rodocanachi, *Le Capitole*, 27–40.

[9] Liv. vi. 4; Pl. *NH.* xxxvi. 104.

[10] Cic. *de Rep.* ii. 36; Liv. i. 38; Tac. *Hist.* iii. 72; Dionys. iii. 69; iv. 59.

[11] Liv. ii. 8.

symbol of the existence and greatness of Rome.   Hence Capitolium and aedes Iovis Optimi Maximi became practically synonymous terms.

The site of the temple is now occupied by the palazzo Caffarelli, which was built in the sixteenth century.   The excavations that have been carried on since that time, supplemented
by the description of the temple by Vitruvius [1] and Dionysius,[2]
enable us to form a reasonably definite idea of its size and
appearance, especially as we are distinctly told that the original foundations were preserved through all the rebuildings.

The present palazzo, while standing on the foundations of
the temple, does not coincide exactly with them.   The temple
was rectangular, almost square, and its main axis deviated 24°
to the east of the north-south line, the front being toward the
south.   So far as can be learned from the excavations, the
stylobate was not a solid mass, but consisted of a series of
parallel walls, 5.60 metres wide, of tufa blocks laid without
mortar and set deep in the ground.   The height of the stylobate was apparently from 4 to 5 metres.   From a comparison
of present measurements with the figures given by Dionysius,
it is almost certain that the temple was built by the standard
of the early Italic foot [3] (0.278 metre), instead of the later
Roman foot (0.2977 metre).   The plan of the temple is given
in Fig. 62.   The cella was divided into three chambers, the
proportion in width between the central chamber and the two
on its sides being as four to three.   The length of the shorter
sides of the stylobate, derived from actual measurements, ex-
clusive of its outer lining, of which nothing is known, was
52.50 metres, or 188.85 Italic feet, and that of the longer sides
probably 204 feet, about 60 metres.   The temple was hexastyle, with three rows of columns across the front and a row
on each side.   The intercolumniations corresponded with the

---

[1] iii. 2. 5.                              [2] iv. 61.

[3] *Hermes*, 1887, 17–28;   1888, 477–479;   Richter, *Top.*[2] 122–123;   *CR.* 1902,
335–336;   *NS.* 1907, 362.

different widths of the central and side chambers of the cella. This was probably also true of the intercolumnar spaces on the sides. As the bases of the columns were about 8 feet (2.23 metres) in breadth, the wider intercolumniations measured 40 feet (11.12 metres) and the narrower 30 feet (8.9 metres). According to this plan the cella was exactly 100 feet (27.81 metres) square. On this foundation[1] four successive edifices were erected.

1. **The temple of Tarquin.** According to the common tradition, there were shrines dedicated to other divinities on the site intended for this temple, all of whom allowed themselves to be dispossessed in the proper way except Terminus, the god of boundaries.[2] His shrine was therefore incorporated in the new temple, and this fact was regarded as a prophecy of the permanence of the cult and of Rome itself. According to the present view, however, Terminus was not a separate deity, but only an epithet of Jupiter. The original temple was probably built of the native tufa of the hill, quarried near by. As stated above, it was hexastyle, with three rows of columns across the front and one on the sides. The central chamber of the cella contained an Etruscan statue of Jupiter of terra cotta,[3] the face of which was painted red. The statue was clothed with a tunic adorned with palm branches and Victories and a toga of purple embroidered with gold, the costume afterwards worn by Roman generals when celebrating a triumph. The chamber on the right[4] was dedicated to Minerva, and that on the left to Juno. Each contained a terra cotta statue of the divinity. In the cella of Jupiter, or possibly in the pronaos, was a terminal cippus representing the god as Terminus, and in the cella of Minerva there was a small shrine of Iuventas, a deity, who, according to Dionysius, also declined to be moved from her original site. The entablature was of wood and bore

---

[1] Delbrück, *Der Apollotempel auf dem Marsfeld in Rom*, Rome, 1903, 12–13.
[2] Liv. i. 55; Fest. 162; Dionys. iii. 69.     [3] Pl. *NH.* xxxv. 157.
[4] Liv. vii. 3.

painted terra cotta statues — on the apex Jupiter in a quadriga.[1] This terra cotta quadriga was replaced in 296 B.C. by
one of bronze. The pediment was filled with terra cotta
reliefs. In 179 B.C. the walls and columns were covered anew
with stucco;[2] in 142 the ceiling was gilded, and a mosaic pavement had been laid in the cella a few years earlier.[3] This
temple became a repository for works of art of all descriptions,
the gifts of Roman generals and foreigners, as well as for
dedicatory offerings and trophies of victory. Their number
became so great that in 179 B.C. it was necessary to remove
some of the statues and many of the shields affixed to the
columns.[4]

2. The temple of Sulla and Catulus. In 83 B.C. the first temple
was burned to the ground.[5] Its rebuilding was begun by Sulla,
and finished by Q. Lutatius Catulus, by whom it was dedicated
in 69.[6] Sulla is said to have brought the white marble Corinthian columns of the Olympieion in Athens to Rome for this
temple,[7] but a denarius[8] of 43 B.C. represents the columns as
still Doric. The only difference between the first and second
temples was in the greater magnificence of the latter and the
greater height of the columns.[9] The kind of stone employed
in this rebuilding is not known. The roof was covered with
gilt bronze. In the centre of the pediment was a relief of
Roma with the wolf and twins, and on the apex was a statue of
Jupiter standing in a quadriga. The ancient terra cotta statue
of Jupiter in the cella seems[10] to have been replaced by one of
gold and ivory, made probably by some Greek artist, perhaps
Apollonius, in imitation of that of Zeus at Olympia. Augustus

---

[1] Pl. *NH. loc. cit.;* xxviii. 16.

[2] Liv. xl. 51.

[3] Pl. *NH.* xxxiii. 57; xxxvi. 185.

[4] Liv. xl. 51.

[5] Cic. *Cat.* iii. 9; Tac. *Hist.* iii. 72.

[6] Cic. *Verr.* iv. 69.

[7] Pl. *NH.* xxxvi. 45.

[8] Cohen, *Méd. Cons.* pl. xxx; *Pet.* 1. 2. For a list of coins representing this
temple at different periods, see *Arch. Zeit.* 1872, 1–8; Jordan, I. 2. 88–90.

[9] Dionys. iv. 61; Val. Max. iv. 4. 11.

[10] Brunn, *Künstlergeschichte*, i. 543.

restored[1] this temple at great expense, but we have no information as to what changes were made at that time.

3. **The temple of Vespasian.** In 69 A.D. the second temple was burned, when the Capitol was stormed by the Vitellians.[2] Vespasian rebuilt it as it was before, except that the height was again increased. Coins[3] of the period represent it as hexastyle, with Corinthian columns and a pediment surmounted by a quadriga, two chariots, two eagles, and the statues of Jupiter, Juno, and Minerva.

4. **The temple of Domitian.** Again, in 80 A.D., the temple was burned, and rebuilt by Domitian on the lines of the earlier edifices, which it surpassed, however, in magnificence.[4] The columns[5] of the portico were of the Corinthian order, and of white marble brought from Athens. The doors of the cella were covered with plates of gold, and the roof with gilt tiles. The pediment was adorned with reliefs, and its apex and gables with statues, as in the earlier temples. This temple lasted as long as the empire, and represented its spirit, as the first temple had represented that of the republic. Its destruction began in the fifth century, when Stilicho carried off the gold plates of the doors,[6] and from that time on it suffered from continual acts of vandalism, until the Caffarelli built their palace upon its foundations. Of the upper structure of this wonderful temple scarcely anything is left, except one drum of a fluted white marble column, 2.10 metres in diameter, and some fragments of the cornice and frieze, sculptured with reliefs.

**Area Capitolina.** — The open space before and round the temple of Jupiter was called the area Capitolina.[7] It was sur-

---

[1] *Mon. Anc.* iv. 9.                    [2] Tac. *Hist.* iii. 71; iv. 53.

[3] Cohen, *Vesp.* 409; *Tit.* 270, 271.    [4] Dio Cass. lxvi. 24; Suet. *Dom.* 5.

[5] *Mon. d. Ist.* v. 36; Cohen, *Dom.* 1, 69, 71.

[6] Zos. v. 38. For further references in classical literature, see Kiepert and Hülsen, *Nomenclator*, p. 82.

[7] Liv. xxv. 3; Tac. *Hist.* iii. 71; Jordan, I. 2. 37–40; Gilbert, II. 423–425; III. 388, 399; *Hermes*, 1883, 115–118.

rounded with a wall, and the principal entrance was probably on the south side, opposite the façade of the temple. The porta Pandana,[1] which according to tradition was always open, may have been at the top of the Centum gradus, and have opened out on to the Tarpeian rock. This area was the meeting place of the comitia calata and occasionally of the comitia tributa, while the cella of the temple itself served on certain occasions for the assembly of the senate. Beneath the surface of the area were subterranean passages, called *favissae*,[2] which were entered from the cella of the temple. In these favissae were stored the old statues which had fallen from the temple, and various dedicatory gifts. The Sibylline books were kept in the cella of the temple itself.

In the area was the aedes Thensarum,[3] where the carriages of the gods were kept; the curia Calabra,[4] where the pontifex minor proclaimed the calendar for each month; and the casa Romuli,[5] which was probably a replica of that on the Palatine (p. 130). Other temples were here, among them that of Fides,[6] which was traditionally assigned to Numa and was next in size to the great temple; that of Iuppiter Feretrius,[7] which was said to have been founded by Romulus to commemorate the first winning of the *spolia opima*, and was restored by Augustus; and of Iuppiter Custos,[8] built by Domitian in recognition of his concealment in the house of a porter in the area Capitolina, when the Capitol was stormed by the Vitellians. He had first built a sacellum Iovis Conservatoris.

---

[1] Varro, *LL.* v. 42; Solin. i. 13; Fest. 220; Dionys. x. 14.

[2] Gell. ii. 10; Fest. 88; Gilbert, II. 419.

[3] *CIL.* iii. p. 845, 22; Suppl. p. 1963, 29.

[4] Varro, *LL.* vi. 27; Macrob. *Sat.* i. 15. 9; Fest. 49; Gilbert, II. 451–452.

[5] Vitr. ii. 1. 5; Seneca, *Controv.* ii. 1. 4.

[6] Liv. i. 21; Dionys. ii. 75; Cic. *de Off.* iii. 104; *de Nat. Deor.* ii. 61; *CIL.* iii. Suppl. p. 2034.

[7] Liv. i. 10; iv. 20; Dionys. ii. 34; Nepos, *Att.* 20; *Mon. Anc.* iv. 5; Fest. 92.

[8] Tac. *Hist.* iii. 74; Suet. *Dom.* 5.

The exact extent of the area Capitolina is not known, but its east wall appears to have been about 30 metres from the great temple, and the south wall about 40 metres. It is probable that certain other temples, which stood on the Capitolium, were within its limits.[1] These were the temple of **Mens** and that of **Venus Erycina**,[2] which were vowed after the disastrous battle of the Trasimene lake in 217 B.C; the temple of **Ops in Capitolio**,[3] first mentioned in 186 B.C., restored between 123 and 114 B.C. by L. Metellus, and famous as the place where Caesar stored his vast wealth; the temples of **Mars Ultor** and **Iuppiter Tonans**, which were built by Augustus, the first,[4] a circular domed structure, in 20 B.C., to receive the standards recovered from the Parthians, which were afterwards transferred to the forum Augustum; and the latter[5] between 26 and 22 B.C., in commemoration of the emperor's narrow escape from being struck by lightning while engaged in a campaign against the Cantabrians. This temple was famous for its magnificence and for the statues which it contained. As it stood in front of the great temple, Iuppiter Tonans was called the *ianitor* of Iuppiter Capitolinus.

Besides these temples, the area contained several altars. The most famous was the great ara Iovis[6] in the centre, where solemn sacrifices were offered at the beginning of the year, at the celebration of triumphs, and on some other occasions, and there were others of Ζεὺς σωτήρ, mentioned once,[7] the **Gens Iulia**,[8]

---

[1] Hülsen, *Zur Topographie des Kapitols*, 209–220; *Mitt.* 1892, 290–291.

[2] Liv. xxii. 10; xxiii. 30, 31; Cic. *de Nat. Deor.* ii. 61; Suet. *Cal.* 7.

[3] Liv. xxxix. 22; Pl. *NH.* xi. 174; *CIL.* vi. p. 507; Cic. *Phil.* ii. 93; *EE.* iii. 64–73; *CIL.* i². p. 327; Gilbert, I. 248; III. 399.

[4] Dio Cass. liv. 8; *Mon. Anc.* iv. 5; Cohen, *Aug.* 189–205; Altmann, *Rundbauten*, 50.

[5] *Mon. Anc.* iv. 5; Suet. *Aug.* 29, 91; Pl. *NH.* xxxiv. 78, 79; xxxvi. 50; Dio Cass. liv. 4; Jordan, I. 2. 47–49; Gilbert, III. 399.

[6] Jordan, I. 2. 38–39.

[7] Serv. *ad Aen.* viii. 652.

[8] *CIL.* iii. pp. 847–851, 1958–1959.

Isis and Serapis, Bellona,[1] and Nemesis.[2] There were also many statues of divinities, — Hercules, Liber,[3] and others,[4] — especially one of Jupiter,[5] which was struck by lightning in 65 B.C. and replaced by another standing on the top of a high column. Equally numerous were the statues of famous men,[6] among which the most conspicuous must have been those of the seven kings of Rome.[7]

So numerous were the shrines and statues of the gods, that it was said without exaggeration *in Capitolio . . . deorum omnium simulacra colebantur.*[8] In addition to those already mentioned, we know of shrines of Fortuna Primigenia,[9] ascribed to Servius Tullius; Indulgentia,[10] built by Marcus Aurelius; the triad Genius Populi Romani, Felicitas, and Venus Victrix;[11] Felicitas[12] alone; Iuppiter Victor[13] and perhaps Valetudo.[14] Trophies of victory, like those of Marius[15] and the tropaea Germanici, and votive monuments[16] were also thickly strewn about, and a wholesale removal of these objects was ordered in the year 179 B.C. and again in the time of Augustus.[17] Countless bronze tablets containing treaties and laws and military diplomas were preserved on the Capitol, being ordinarily fastened to the walls of the temples and to the bases of statues and monuments.[18] We are told that three thousand such tablets were melted in the fire of 69 A.D.[19]

---

[1] Tertull. *ad Nat.* i. 10; *Apol.* 6; Dio Cass. xlii. 26.

[2] Pl. *NH.* xi. 251; xxviii. 22.        [3] Liv. ix. 44; *CIL.* iii. p. 849.

[4] Gilbert, III. 102, 387–388.

[5] Dio Cass. xxxvii. 9; Cic. *Cat.* iii. 20.

[6] Gilbert, III. 386; Rodocanachi, *Le Capitole*, 46.

[7] Pl. *NH.* xxxiii. 9–10; xxxiv. 22–23; Gilbert, I. 24–25; Jordan, I. 2. 56–58.

[8] Serv. *ad Aen.* ii. 319.

[9] Plut. *de Fort. Rom.* x; *CIL.* xiv. 2852.

[10] Dio Cass. lxxi. 34; Wissowa, *Religion d. Römer*, 279.

[11] *CIL.* i.² p. 331.        [12] *CIL.* i.² p. 248.        [13] Dio Cass. xlvii. 40.

[14] Petron. 88 (cf. however, Wissowa, *op. cit.* 255).

[15] Plut. *Caes.* 6; Suet. *Caes.* 11; Jordan, I. 2. 44–45; *Mélanges*, 1908, 354–361.

[16] Gilbert, III. 384–387; *Mitt.* 1889, 252–253.        [17] Suet. *Cal.* 34.

[18] Cf. *BC.* 1896, 187–190; Jordan, I. 2. 52–56.        [19] Suet. *Vesp.* 8.

Of the masonry of the area itself, a part of the east wall was found in 1875. Of the numerous structures within it, only the most meagre remains have been discovered, the most noticeable of which was a mass of concrete south of the great temple.[1] This mass, so far as it was excavated, measured 14.80 metres on the east and 16 metres on the north side. It dated from the republican period, but had itself been built over earlier structures. It was probably the foundation of some one of the temples, but no identification was possible.

**The Asylum or Inter Duos Lucos.**— The level of the depression between the two summits of the Capitoline hill has remained practically unchanged, as was shown when the foundations were laid for the equestrian statue of Marcus Aurelius, which now stands in the centre of the piazza del Campidoglio. The whole area was called inter duos lucos,[2] the duo luci being the groves that originally stood on the two summits of the hill. The Asylum was represented at the beginning of the empire by an inclosed space,[3] within which was probably a small grove, or perhaps a shrine.[4]

The importance of this part of the hill arose from the fact that it formed the thoroughfare between the two summits and the city. So far as known, only one temple stood here, that of Veiovis inter duos lucos,[5] which is said to have been of peculiar shape and to have contained a statue of a youthful Jupiter, holding arrows in his hand. This — probably ancient — temple was rebuilt by Augustus, and was in existence in the time of Hadrian. In 62 A. D. Nero erected a triumphal arch[6] and a trophy of victory, of which nothing further is known.

---

[1] *BC.* 1896, 116–120; Hülsen, *Zur Topographie des Kapitols*, 215–219.
[2] Liv. i. 8; Vell. i. 8. 5; Dionys. ii. 15; Prop. iv. 8. 31; *BC.* 1905, 211–214.
[3] Liv. i. 8.
[4] Liv. i. 30; Ov. *Fast.* iii. 431; Flor. i. 1; Serv. *ad Aen.* ii. 761.
[5] Gell. v. 12; Ov. *Fast.* iii. 429–430, 437–438; Vitr. iv. 8. 4; Jordan, I. 2. 116; Gilbert, III. 83–84, 401.
[6] Tac. *Ann.* xiii. 41; xv. 18; Cohen, *Nero*, 306.

During the first centuries of the republic, private dwellings were erected to some extent on the Capitoline hill, for in the year 380 B.C. there was a guild of those who dwelt *in Capitolio atque arce*;[1] and after the treason of M. Manlius, a law was passed which forbade any patrician to live on either summit.[2] In spite of such prohibitions, the gradual destruction of the fortifications and the demands of a rapidly increasing population led to continual encroachments upon this quasi-sacred hill. In 93 B.C. a considerable tract, which had belonged to the priests, was sold and came into private possession.[3] By the middle of the first century the whole hill, with the exception of the area Capitolina, the actual sites of the temples, and the steepest parts of the slopes, was occupied by private houses.[4] Remains[5] of these houses have been found on the Arx near the church of S. Maria in Aracoeli, and at the foot of the stairway leading from the piazza del Campidoglio to the church. On the east slope, below the Asylum, there still remains a considerable portion of a noble republican structure, the Tabularium, which formed an imposing façade, as it were, for the whole hill from the Forum side.

**The Tabularium.**— This building,[6] trapezoidal in shape, filled the entire space between the clivus Capitolinus and the flight of steps (gradus Monetae?) which led up past the Carcer to the Arx. It is not mentioned in literature; but an inscription[7] found in it states that in 78 B.C. Q. Lutatius Catulus erected *substructionem et tabularium*. As the plan of this building seems to be that of a repository of archives, and as the style of masonry indicates precisely this period, there is no difficulty in identifying it with the tabularium of Catulus,

---

[1] Liv. v. 50.   [2] Liv. vi. 20.   [3] Oros. v. 18.   [4] Tac. *Hist.* iii. 71.

[5] *NS.* 1888, 497; 1889, 68; *Mitt.* 1889, 255; *BC.* 1873, 111–122, 143–146; 1888, 331.

[6] *Ann. d. Ist.* 1858, 206–212; 1881, 62–73; Jordan, I. 2. 135–154; Gilbert, III. 165–167; Delbrück, *Hellenistische Bauten in Latium*, Strassburg, 1907, 23–46.

[7] *CIL.* vi. 1313–1314; cf. 916.

although there were other tabularia in Rome. No changes were made in it during the empire, and it remains by far the most interesting, as well as the best preserved, specimen of republican architecture. Nothing is known of its history until the reign of Boniface VIII (about 1300 A.D.), when the present tower at the north end was erected. Later, Michelangelo destroyed the entire upper and western part, and built the present palazzo del Senatore directly upon the ancient structure.

The front of the Tabularium is 85 metres long. The slope of the hill was first scarped away, and the front wall of the building was begun on the level of the area Volcani. Above this substructure, on the Forum side, there were three stories. The first consists of a long passage between the tufa rock of the hill itself and the wall of the building. This wall is here 3.43 metres thick, with a series of six recesses 1.68 metres high, from which narrow windows open. This corridor is now blocked at both ends, and may always have been so.

Immediately above this corridor is another, 5 metres wide and 10 high, extending the whole length of the building, and originally open at both ends. The arched doorway on the clivus is still in use. The front of this corridor was an arcade of the Doric order, with engaged columns of peperino. There were eleven arches, 7.50 metres in height and 3.70 in width, all but one of which have been walled up. This arcade afforded an excellent means of communication between the two portions of the Capitoline, and formed a striking architectural terminus for the Forum. Its effect, however, was sadly marred by the erection of the temple of Vespasian and the porticus Deorum Consentium, and by the restoration and enlargement of the temple of Concord. Above this arcade the palazzo is built, but there is little doubt that originally there was a second arcade above the first, probably of another order.

We can tell very little about the arrangement of the upper and west part of the building; but some rooms and passages still remain, especially one large hall behind the existing arcade and at a somewhat higher level, flanked with a row of chambers cut in the rock.   In the wall of the substructure, at the ground level, is a fine arched doorway, and from it a long flight of sixty-seven steps, partly cut in the rock, leads up to the hall just mentioned.   These steps have no connection with any other part of the building, and afforded direct access from the Forum to the upper part of the Tabularium and the Asylum. When the temple of Vespasian was built, its podium effectually blocked the entrance to this staircase.

The masonry of the Tabularium shows the very best republican workmanship.   It is wholly of opus quadratum, the blocks being uniformly two Roman feet in height and width, and averaging four in length.   They are laid in alternate courses of headers and stretchers (*emplecton*), with a thin layer of cement.   The outer walls are of peperino, the bases and capitals of the half-columns and the imposts of the arches of travertine, and the inner walls of tufa.   As the building was once used as a storehouse for salt, the inner walls have suffered much from corrosion.[1]

---

[1] For the later history of the Capitoline, see Lanciani, *Il Monte Tarpeio nel secolo xvi, BC.* 1901, 245–269; Hülsen, *Bilder aus der Geschichte des Kapitols,* Rome, 1899; and Rodocanachi, *op. cit.*

# CHAPTER XII.

## THE SACRA VIA AND THE VELIA.

**The Sacra via,**[1] the oldest and most famous street in Rome, began at the sacellum Streniae — a shrine mentioned only in this connection, and undoubtedly near the lucus Streniae [2] — in the Colosseum valley, and ran northwest to the summit of the Velia, which it crossed near the arch of Titus. This was the summa Sacra via, and from here the street curved toward the north and entered the Forum at the fornix Fabianus. Its course from this point to the Capitol has been described (p. 171). Originally the name Sacra via was given only to that part of the street which was between the Velia and the Forum, but it was soon made to include the whole extent from the Colosseum to the Forum, and in modern times even the part within the Forum. The part from the Forum to the Velia was also called the Sacer clivus.[3]

The origin of the name has been the subject of much discussion.[4] The Romans themselves were not agreed in their explanations, some saying that the street was *sacra* because it was the scene of the famous treaty between Romulus and Titus Tatius, and others believing that it was so called because of the religious processions which took place there. The explanation now generally accepted, though not altogether satisfactory, is that this name was given to the street because on it were the house of the *rex sacrificulus* and the temples of Vesta and the

---

[1] Varro, *LL.* v. 47; Fest. 290; Jordan, I. 2. 274–286, 415–416; 3. 14–15; Gilbert, I. 214–220, 236–238, 300–335; Richter, *Top.*[2] 369–370. For another view of its course see *Mélanges*, 1908, 233–253.

[2] Sym. *Ep.* x. 35 (46); *BC.* 1905, 210.     [3] Hor. *Od.* iv. 2. 35.

[4] See literature cited above, and Binder, *Die Plebs*, 62–64.

Lares.   It may be that the street itself, from its very position
and early importance, was regarded as something intrinsically
sacred.[1]

During the recent excavations,[2] the medieval pavement 23
metres wide, including the sidewalks, which was laid along the
front of the basilica of Constantine to S. Francesca Romana,

FIG. 63. — PAVEMENT OF THE SACRA VIA.

was removed, and that of the Augustan period was found,
2 metres below the medieval.   This imperial pavement is 5
metres wide; and in front of the basilica it makes a bend
southward toward the arch of Titus.   A part of this curve lay
beneath massive concrete foundations which run in parallel

[1] *Mitt.* 1895, 162.
[2] *NS.* 1899, 265–266; *BC.* 1900, 10–11; 1902, 34; 1903, 19–23; *Arch. Anz.*
1900, 9; *CR.* 1899, 322, 467; 1900, 239; 1902, 96, 286; *Mitt.* 1902, 94–95.

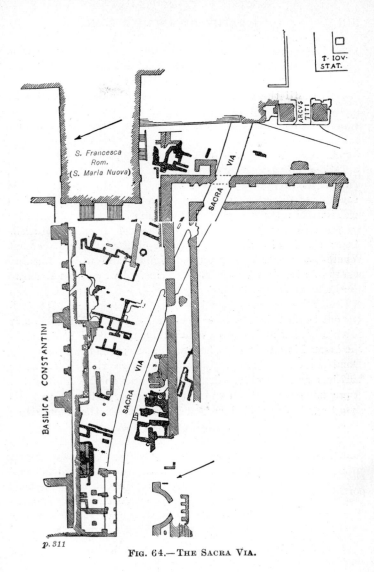

Fig. 64.—The Sacra Via.

lines first southeast, and then turning at a right angle southwest; but the imperial pavement has been found farther east,
beyond the arch of Titus, and this was the line of the street,
at least until the time of Nero.[1]  From the Sacra via another
street branched off to the south, crossed the Nova via, and
ascended the Palatine.   This is the street which is generally
called the clivus Palatinus, and its ancient pavement[2] has been
found beneath the arch of Titus and south of the Nova via.
Whether the name Sacer clivus[3] was also applied to this street,
as well as to the Sacra via between the Velia and Forum, is
a matter of dispute.   The north end of the foundations of the
arch stands upon the pavement of this street, which with its
travertine curbs is still *in situ* on the west front of the arch.
After the level was raised here, and the earlier pavement
covered, the new clivus was straighter and wider, forming
a sort of avenue which was the principal way of approach to
the Palatine (see p. 165).

Under the east end of the basilica of Constantine, and projecting out toward the south, are the foundations and walls of older
private houses and also of a building, usually identified with
the horrea Piperataria, or pepper warehouse, which was built by
Domitian on the north side of the Sacra via.   The visible
portions are, however, oriented according to the line of the
Augustan pavement, on which they border, and seem to ante-
date the Flavian period, so that it is probable that Domitian's
horrea, destroyed by the building of the basilica of Constantine,
were entirely within its area, and that changes in the width,
line, and elevation of this part of the Sacra via had taken
place during the reign of Nero, when the massive concrete
foundations mentioned above were built.   After these changes
the Sacra via from the arch of Fabius east appears to have

---

[1] See Miss Van Deman, quoted by Ashby in London *Times*, Mar. 26, 1910.

[2] *CR*. 1903, 136; 1905, 237; 1909, 61; *Mitt*. 1905, 119; *BC*. 1903, 17–18.

[3] Mart. i. 70; iv. 78; *CR*. 1902, 336; Gilbert, III. 423–424; Richter, *Top*.[2]
160 n.

been an avenue, about 20 metres wide, flanked on both sides by porticoes and shops, those on the north side being finally destroyed by the erection of the basilica of Constantine.

On the summa Sacra via stood the house of the rex sacrorum,[1] where this priest dwelt after the expulsion of the kings, and the temple of the Lares,[2] which, although very ancient, is not mentioned in literature before 106 B.C. This temple was restored by Augustus. Some tufa walls and travertine fragments found recently just southwest of the arch of Titus, on the opposite side of the clivus Palatinus, have been identified with this temple, but they probably belong to shops.

Just east of the arch of Titus are the ruins of a building which is probably to be identified with the temple of Iuppiter Stator (p. 137).[3] These ruins consist of a large rectangular platform of concrete, on which are some enormous blocks of peperino and travertine. On this foundation the medieval turris Cartularia was built, which served as a refuge for the popes in the eleventh and twelfth centuries. Very recently some tufa walls have been excavated, close to the northeast side of the arch of Titus and beneath its foundations, and it is perhaps possible that these may belong to the temple at an earlier period when its position was slightly different.

Near the temple of the Lares was the fanum Orbonae,[4] which is mentioned only once. A temple of Bacchus and a tholus of Cybele are also once mentioned together.[5] They stood on the summa Sacra via, near its junction with the clivus Palatinus and near the arch of Titus. On the Haterii relief is a representation of a statue of the Magna Mater, seated under an arch

---

[1] Varro, *LL.* v. 47; Fest. 291; Gilbert, I. 225.

[2] Solin. i. 23; *Mon. Anc.* iv. 7; Ov. *Fast.* vi. 791; Obseq. 41; *CIL.* vi. 456; Jordan, I. 2. 420; Gilbert, III. 424; *CR.* 1905, 75–76, 237, 328; 1909, 61; *Mitt.* 1905, 118–119.

[3] Lanciani, *Ruins*, 200; *BC.* 1903, 18; Jordan, I. 3. 20–23; *CR.* 1909, 61.

[4] Cic. *de Nat. Deor.* iii. 63.

[5] Mart. i. 70. 9–10; Altmann, *Rundbauten*, 71–72.

at the top of a flight of thirteen steps, and this may be in
tended for the tholus of Cybele.[1] During the recent excavations in the Sacra via, a part of a curved epistyle was found,
which bears a dedicatory inscription to Bacchus and is therefore supposed to have belonged to the first of these two temples.[2]

Farther down the street, perhaps on the site afterward occupied by the Heroon Romuli, was the temple of the **Penates**,[3]
which tradition ascribed to Tullus Hostilius. It was restored
by Augustus, but was probably removed by Vespasian when he
built the forum Pacis.

On the Velia was a shrine of **Mutunus Tutunus**,[4] a deity of
fertility, which was said to have been removed to make room
for the house of Cn. Domitius Calvinus; and another of **Vica
Pota**,[5] apparently identical with Victoria, which stood on the
site originally occupied by the house of the **Valerii**.[6] In regard
to this house, tradition varied widely. According to one account,[7] Valerius Poplicola lived, at the beginning of the republic, *in summa Velia*, but was forced by the people to tear this
house down and build again *infra Veliam*, because his first
dwelling seemed too much like a stronghold. According to
another account,[8] this house, *in summa Velia* or *in Palatio*, was
given to Valerius or to his brother Marcus by the people as an
especial honor. It is, however, probably true that the early
home of the gens Valeria was on this ridge, and also their sepulchre.[9] Tullus Hostilius [10] was believed to have lived here

---

[1] *Mitt.* 1895, 25–27.          [2] *Mitt.* 1902, 98; *BC.* 1903, 27–29.

[3] Varro, *LL.* v. 54; Solin. i. 22; Liv. xlv. 16; Dionys. i. 68; Obseq. 13;
*Mon. Anc.* iv. 7; Gilbert, II. 81–84.

[4] Fest. 154; Gilbert, I. 156; II. 369–370.

[5] Cic. *de Legg.* ii. 28.

[6] Jordan, I. 2. 416; Gilbert, I. 106–109; *EE.* iii. 1–4; *CIL.* i[2]. pp. 189–190;
*Mélanges*, 1908, 241.

[7] Liv. ii. 7; Plut. *Popl.* 10; cf. Dionys. v. 19; Val. Max. iv. 1. 1.

[8] Cic. *de Har. Resp.* 16; Asc. *in Pis.* 52; Pl. *NH.* xxxvi. 112.

[9] Cic. *de Legg.* ii. 58; Dionys. v. 48; Plut. *Quaest. Rom.* 79.

[10] Cic. *de Rep.* ii. 53.

and other kings, Numa, Ancus Marcius, and Tarquinius Superbus, near by on the Sacra via.[1]

There were many private houses [2] on and near the Sacra via, of which many remains of the period of the republic have recently been found. Those who lived in this district were called *Sacravienses*.[3] Their dwellings gradually disappeared before the increasing demands of business, but a house on the Sacra via was given to P. Scipio Nasica [4] at the end of the third century B.C., and the domus Domitiana [5] apparently continued to be the residence of that family throughout the republic. In the last years of the republic, the houses of a certain Tettius Damio [6] and of Octavius [7] were on the Sacra via. The most extensive remains are in the angle formed by the Nova via and the clivus Palatinus, where the recent excavations have brought to light a very complicated series of walls of tufa and opus reticulatum, with pavements of mosaic and herring-bone brick, which date from the republic and the time of Augustus. The earliest of these walls lie at least 12 metres below the level of the arch of Titus. They were built at successive periods, but finally cut through by the concrete walls mentioned on p. 310, and covered up to the later level.

Like all the first streets in great cities, the Sacra via became in process of time largely a street of shops.[8] At the beginning of the empire it is probable that these shops stood on both sides of the way, from the entrance to the Forum (fornix Fabianus) to the Velia, but in consequence of the great transformations wrought by the erection of the forum Pacis, the templum Sacrae Urbis, and the temple of Faustina, they were gradually restricted for the most part to the south side

---

[1] Solin. i. 22; Pl. *NH.* xxxiv. 29.

[2] Gilbert, III. 360; *Mitt.* 1902, 94–95; 1905, 118.   [3] Fest. 178.

[4] Pomp. *Dig.* i. 2. 2. 37.   [5] *CIL.* vi. p. 487.

[6] Cic. *ad Att.* iv. 3. 3.   [7] Sall. *Hist. Frag.* ii. 45.

[8] Ov. *Ars Am.* ii. 265–266; *Amor.* i. 8. 100; Prop. ii. 24. 14–15; Richter, *Top.*[2] 163–164.

of the street between the atrium Vestae and the arch of Titus.
Here it seems probable that as early as the first century a
great porticus was planned and at least partly built, in which
all the shops should be gathered, and that for this porticus
the existing republican buildings were destroyed and covered
up. This porticus was evidently rebuilt at various times, as
after the fire of 191 A.D., and it is quite possible that it is
to be identified with the porticus Margaritaria,[1] which stood
here in the fourth century. As many inscriptions [2] have been
found which relate to the tradesmen of the Sacra via, especially jewellers of all sorts, it is evident that these shops
were largely devoted to this business. There were also
shops [3] where flowers, fruit, and the chief articles of luxury
of the capital were sold.

Beneath the pavement in front of the temple of Romulus
and extending to the temple of Faustina are remains of houses
of the republican period, and a series of rooms opening off from
a corridor, which were incorporated into the foundations of the
temple. These rooms are built of tufa and paved with opus
spicatum, and may have served as storerooms for the shop-
keepers of the Sacra via.[4]

**The Temple of Venus and Roma.**— This double temple, the
largest and most magnificent in Rome, was built by Hadrian [5]
and dedicated to Venus Felix, the ancestress of the Roman
people, and to the genius of the city, Roma Aeterna. In ac-

---

[1] *BC.* 1882, 228; Jordan, I. 2. 288; *CR.* 1900, 238; 1905, 75–76; *Arch. Anz.*
1900, 9; 1902, 51; *Mitt.* 1902, 98.

[2] *CIL.* vi. 9207, 9221, 9239, 9418, 9419, 9545–9549.

[3] *CIL.* vi. 9795, 9283, 9935, 9418–9419.

[4] *Mitt.* 1902, 94; *NS.* 1902, 96; *BC.* 1902, 31–34; 1903, 30–32. The identification in these last two journals of these rooms with the *carcer in lautumiis* is
erroneous.

[5] Dio Cass. lxix. 4; *Chronogr. a. 354,* p. 146; Prud. *c. Symm.* i. 214; Jordan,
I. 3. 17–20; Rivoira, *Lombardic Architecture. Its Origin, Development, and
Derivatives,* London, 1910, vol. ii. 100–102, and *Nuova Antologia*, 1910, 631–
638.

cordance with Roman theory in such matters, it was necessary
to build a separate cella for each goddess, and in this case the
cellae were not erected side by side, but back to back, one facing east and the other west. The temple was injured by fire
in 307 A.D. and restored by Maxentius.[1]

The temple proper was built on an enormous podium of concrete faced with travertine, 145 metres long and 100 wide, on

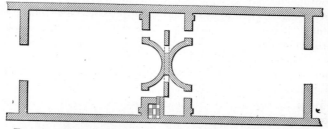

FIG. 65. — PLAN OF CELLAE OF TEMPLE OF VENUS AND ROMA.

the north side of the Sacra via, between the Velia and the Colosseum. This necessitated the removal [2] of the Colossus Neronis
(p. 335), which was then set up nearer the Colosseum, where
its base still remains visible. Owing to the slope of the ground,
the height of the podium at the east end is very considerable,
and chambers were constructed in it for the storage of the
machinery and apparatus of the amphitheatre. On this podium
was a peribolus formed of a colonnade consisting of an outer
wall and a single row of enormous columns of gray Egyptian
granite on the sides, and probably of a double row of columns
only on the ends. Many fragments of these still lie on the
podium. This colonnade had projections like propylaea at
the corners and at the middle of the long sides. At the
west end of the podium a wide flight of steps led down to
the paved area in front of the temple; but at the east end
there were only two small flights. A wide flight here would

[1] Aur. Vict. *Caes.* 40.　　　[2] Spart. *Vit. Hadr.* 19.

have encroached too much upon the area round the Colosseum. The temple proper was raised on a platform, seven steps high, in the centre of the peribolus. The two cellae ended in apses placed back to back ; but, as the side walls of the cellae were prolonged so as to meet, the external appearance was that of one long rectangular building. This temple[1] was decastyle and pseudodipteral, the columns of the peristyle being of white marble, about 1.8 metres in diameter. The cellae were narrower than the façade, and each pronaos had only four columns between the antae. The building was constructed of concrete and brick, and covered entirely with marble. Within the cellae, on each side, were rows of porphyry columns supporting an entablature. In the apses were five niches, alternately square and semicircular, with columns and entablatures in front of them. In the central niche of each apse was the statue of the goddess herself, — Venus in one and Roma in the other, — and there were also other works of art in the temple.[2] A single staircase,[3] between the apses on the south side led to the top of the temple. The roof was covered with gilt tiles, and the pediments were sculptured in relief. A part of the west front of the temple is represented on two fragments of a relief,[4] which, although in separate museums, the Lateran and the Museo delle Terme, belong together. One of these fragments shows that on the west pediment there were reliefs of Mars visiting Rhea Silvia and of the she-wolf suckling the twins. The greater part of the west cella has been destroyed, and its area partly covered by the cloisters of the church of S. Francesca Romana, which was built in 1612 on the site of an earlier church. The apse and part of the wall of the other cella still stand in ruins, with portions of the

---

[1] Cf. Cohen, *Pius*, 698–703, 1074–1076 ; *BC.* 1903, 19.

[2] Treb. Pol. *Vit. Tyr. Trig.* 32 ; Dio Cass. lxxi. 31.

[3] Rivoira, *opp. citt.*

[4] *Mitt.* 1895, 248 ; Matz-Duhn, *Antike Bildwerke*, 3519 ; Strong, *Sculpture*, 238–240.

pedestals of columns and bits of mosaic pavement made of colored marbles and porphyry.

It has been remarked that this temple with its enormous peribolus really falls into the same category of buildings as the imperial fora, of which it formed a virtual continuation.

**Arches.** — The first honorary arch in the Forum was the fornix Fabianus or arcus Fabiorum,[1] erected by Q. Fabius Allobrogicus in 121 b.c. to commemorate his victory over the Allobroges. This small and single arch stood on the Sacra via, a little to the east of the Regia. Some portions of it were found in 1882,[2] and others during the recent excavations, among them all the blocks of the arch proper, the span of which is about 4 metres. These blocks are of travertine and the core of the arch was of peperino and tufa. Its exact site is still somewhat uncertain, as no trace of its foundations has been discovered.[3]

On the line of the present via Labicana, east of the Colosseum, was an arch known to us only from the Haterii relief (Fig. 2), on which it is represented as triple, with the inscription arcus ad Isis on the attic.[4] This is generally supposed to have been only the popular name for the arch.

The arch of Titus is the most celebrated as well as the oldest now standing and the smallest of the so-called triumphal arches in Rome. It was erected *in summa Sacra via* by Domitian, in honor of the deified Titus and in commemoration of his siege of Jerusalem. It suffered serious damage in the middle ages, especially during the twelfth and thirteenth centuries, when it formed part of the city stronghold of the Frangipani family. In 1822 it was taken down and rebuilt. The

---

[1] Cic. *pro Planc.* 17; *in Verr.* i. 19; *de Or.* ii. 267; Schol. pp. 133, 393, 399, ed. Orelli; Sen. *Dial.* ii. 1. 3; *CIL.* i². p. 198; vi. 1303–1304; Jordan, I. 2. 209; Gilbert, I. 310–312; *AJA.* 1904, 15; Hülsen, *Festschrift zu Hirschfeld's 60tem Geburtstag,* Berlin, 1903, 427–428.

[2] *NS.* 1882, 222–226.     [3] *Mitt.* 1902, 94; *Mélanges,* 1908, 89–95.
[4] Gilbert, III. 193–194.

central portion alone, of Pentelic marble, is original, the two ends being restorations in travertine. The archway is 8.30 metres high and 5.35 metres wide.[1] Above it is a simple entablature, and an attic 4.40 metres in height, on which is

FIG. 66. — THE ARCH OF TITUS.

the inscription.[2] On each side is an engaged and fluted Corinthian column, standing on a square pedestal. The capitals of these columns are the earliest examples of Composite style.

---

[1] *CR*. 1902, 286.          [2] *CIL*. vi. 945.

On the inner jambs of the arch are the two famous reliefs,[1] that on the south representing the spoils from the temple at

FIG. 67. — THE ARCH OF CONSTANTINE.

Jerusalem, the table of shewbread, the seven-branched candlestick, and the silver trumpets, which are being carried in

[1] *PBS.* iii. 276–279; v. 178; Strong, *Sculpture*, 105–122.

triumph into the city; and that on the north representing
Titus standing in a quadriga, the horses of which are led by
Roma, while Victory crowns the emperor with laurel as he
passes through a triumphal arch.

In the centre of the ceiling of the archway, which is finished
in soffits (*lacunaria*), is a relief of the apotheosis of Titus, representing him as being carried up to heaven by an eagle.   The
frieze is ornamented with small figures representing sacrificial
scenes, and in the spandrels are the usual winged Victories.
On the keystones are figures of Roma and the Genius Populi
Romani (or Fortuna) with a cornucopia.   Since the foundations of the arch rest upon the pavement of the clivus Palatinus
(cf. p. 312), it has been supposed by some that the arch stood
originally farther north and was moved when the temple of
Venus and Roma was built, a rather doubtful hypothesis.[1]

Southwest of the Colosseum, at the entrance to the valley
between the Palatine and the Caelian, near the point where the
ancient road through this valley joined the Sacra via, stands
the arch of Constantine, which was built by Constantine to commemorate his victory over Maxentius at the pons Mulvius in
312 A.D.[2]   This arch, the largest and best preserved in Rome,
stands at the beginning of the modern via di S. Gregorio, which
coincides with the line of the ancient street, and is now often
called the via Triumphalis.   The arch was erected, however, at
a higher level,[3] for the marble pavement of the area in which
it stood, is just below the present level, while the pavement
of the street, belonging apparently to the later empire (p. 107),
lies more than 2 metres lower still.   The arch is built of white
marble, is 21 metres high, 25.70 wide, and 7.40 deep, and has
three archways.   That in the centre is 11.50 metres high and
6.50 wide, those at the sides 7.40 metres high and 3.36 wide.

---

[1] *Mitt.* 1905, 118; *Berl. Phil. Wochenschrift*, 1908, 1034; *Mélanges*, 1908,
247–248.

[2] *CIL.* vi. 1139; Jordan, I. 3. 25–28.          [3] *Mitt.* 1891, 92.

Between the archways and at the corners are eight fluted Corinthian columns, 7 metres high and 0.75 in diameter. These
columns are monoliths of giallo antico, except one, which is of
white marble and replaces the original, which has been removed
to the Lateran. Above the arches is an entablature, and an attic
6.60 metres high. Above the columns are projecting pedestals
round which the cornice runs. These pedestals support statues
of barbarian prisoners, sculptured in the round. In the central part of the attic, on both sides of the arch, is the dedicatory inscription. The arch is richly decorated with reliefs,
some of which are of the period of Constantine and exhibit the
characteristic decadence of that era, while the others are of
earlier date and were removed from their original position by
Constantine. To this latter class belong: —

(1) The round medallions [1] over the side arches, representing
the emperor in alternate sacrificial and hunting scenes. The
four on the south façade belong to the Flavian period and have
not been altered; those on the north are Flavian or Hadrianic,
and in two of them the head of Constantine has been substituted
for the original. In the other two the original heads have
been worked over into portraits of an emperor of the third
century, probably Claudius Gothicus. The Flavian medallions
may perhaps have belonged to the temple of the gens Flavia
(p. 504).

(2) The two reliefs at the ends of the arch and the two on
the jambs of the central archway, representing combats between
Romans and Dacians and scenes of victory.[2] These date from
the time of Trajan, and appear to have been parts of a long
band which belonged to some structure quite different from an
arch, perhaps the inclosing wall of his Forum.

(3) The eight rectangular reliefs [3] in the attic over the side

---

[1] *Mitt.* 1889, 314–339; 1891, 93; 1907, 345–360; *PBS.* iii. 229–251; Strong,
*Sculpture,* 131–141; *CR.* 1905, 183–184.

[2] *PBS.* iii. 225–228; Strong, *op. cit.* 158–164.

[3] *BC.* 1900, 75–116; *PBS.* iii. 251–268; Strong, *op. cit.* 291–294, 392–394.

archways, which represent the emperor entering Rome, engag-
ing in sacrifice, receiving an address from his soldiers and
addressing them, receiving Dacian captives and kings who are
paying homage, dispensing charity, dismissing praetorians who
had served out their time, and taking part in a *lustratio*.   These
reliefs belong to the period of the Antonines, but are an evident
imitation of the style of the preceding half-century.   Three
other reliefs[1] of the same series are now in the palazzo dei
Conservatori, and it has been plausibly suggested that they
belonged to an arch[2] erected in 176 A.D. to commemorate the
victories of Marcus Aurelius in the Sarmatian and German
wars (p. 275).

To the same period as the arch itself belong the remaining
decorations, — the sculptured band[3] above the side arches and
on the ends representing a battle at a river, the siege of a city,
triumphal processions, a largess to the people, and the Rostra;
the statues on the columns; the two round medallions at the
ends representing the setting of the moon and the rising
of the sun;[4] the barbarian captives on the pedestals of the
columns; and the Victories and river-gods in the spandrels.

Near the arch of Constantine, on the Sacra via, was a statue
of Cloelia (p. 138), and also one of Romulus, while the corresponding statue of Titus Tatius was at the other end of the
street near the Rostra.[5]

**Amphitheatrum Flavium**. — Gladiatorial combats[6] are said to
have been introduced into Rome in 264 B.C., and *venationes*,[7] or
fights with wild animals, twelve years later.   During the
republican period these performances usually took place in the
Forum, where temporary platforms, *maeniana* (p. 169), were

---

[1] Helbig, *Führer durch die Museen Roms*, 2d ed. 559–561.

[2] *CIL*. vi. 1014.

[3] *Bull. Crist.* 1907, 55–61; *Atti d. Pont. Accad. di Archeologia*, 1901, 107–
134; 1904, 3–23; *PBS*. iv. 270–276; *CR*. 1906, 235: Strong, *op. cit.* 331–337.

[4] Strong, *op. cit.* 330–331.         [5] Serv. *in Aen.* viii. 641; Gilbert, I. 24–25.

[6] Liv. *Epit.* xvi.         [7] Pl. *NH*. viii. 16–17.

erected for the spectators. In 59 B.C. Curio is said to have devised the strange plan of building two theatres [1] back to back, which were supported on pivots, and could therefore be turned round, so as to form together a circular structure in which a show of this sort could be held. This new kind of spectacular building was called by the Greek name, *amphitheatrum*.

The first permanent stone amphitheatre was erected in the campus Martius by Statilius Taurus in 30 B.C. (p. 364); but the great amphitheatre of Rome, one of the most remarkable buildings in the world, belongs to a much later time. It was begun by Vespasian, and opened and dedicated by Titus in 80 A.D.[2] This wonderful structure was called the amphitheatrum Flavium, but since the middle ages it has been commonly known as the Colosseum. The low ground between the Velia, the Esquiline, and the Caelian had been included within the domus Aurea, and here Nero had constructed an artificial pond, or stagnum, *maris instar circumsaeptum aedificiis ad urbium speciem*.[3] When Vespasian destroyed so much of the domus Aurea, he built the amphitheatre on the site of the stagnum, — one of the most accessible in the city.

Although the amphitheatre was opened by Titus, it is uncertain whether it was entirely finished during his reign or during that of Domitian,[4] and it was afterward restored by Trajan and Antoninus Pius.[5] In 217 A.D. it was struck by lightning,[6] and so seriously damaged that no more gladiatorial combats could be held in the building until 222–223, when the repairs begun by Elagabalus [7] were completed by Alexander Severus [8] (or perhaps by Gordianus III). Again, in 250, the building was restored by Decius,[9] after a fire caused by another stroke

---

[1] Pl. *NH*. xxxvi. 117–120.

[2] Suet. *Vesp.* 9; *Tit.* 7; Vict. *Caes.* 9. 7; Dio Cass. lxvi. 25; Jordan, I. 3. 282–298.

[3] Suet. *Nero*, 31; Mart. *de Spect.* 2. 5.     [4] *Chronogr. a. 354*, p. 146.

[5] Jul. Cap. *Vit. Pii*, 8.  [6] Dio Cass. lxxviii. 25.  [7] Lamprid. *Vit. Elagab.* 17.

[8] Lamprid. *Vit. Alex.* 24.                  [9] Hieron. *Chron.* p. 181.

FIG. 68.—THE INTERIOR OF THE COLOSSEUM.

of lightning.  It was injured by the earthquake of 442, and
probably again a few years later, for restorations are recorded
which were carried on by Theodosius II and Valentinian III
in 442,[1] and by Anthemius between 467 and 472.[2]  Still later

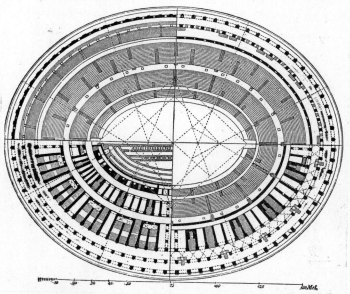

FIG. 69. — SECTIONAL PLAN OF THE COLOSSEUM.

repairs were made by Basilius in 508,[3] and by Eutharich in
519.

The last gladiatorial combats[4] took place in the amphitheatre in 404 A.D., and the last recorded venationes[5] in 523.
In the sixth century began the gradual destruction of the great
structure, which suffered from all the causes which combined
to wreck the imperial city.  The greatest destruction, however,

---

[1] *CIL*. vi. 1763.        [2] *CIL*. vi. p. 860, n. 100.        [3] *CIL*. vi. 32094.
[4] Theodoretus, v. 26.                    [5] Cassiodor. *Var*. v. 42.

was wrought by those who regarded the building as a travertine quarry. Out of it were built many medieval palaces, among them the Cancelleria, the Farnese, and the Venezia. No other Roman building has had so interesting and varied a history.[1]   During the last century various attempts were made to preserve the remaining portions from further ruin,

FIG. 70. — THE COLOSSEUM.

especially by the popes between 1805 and 1852, when great buttresses were built to support the ends of the walls.

Under the direction of Canina (1850–1852), thirteen of the arches on the third story and seven of those on the fourth were restored, the outer wall strengthened, new stairways erected, and the marble columns and pediment of the main entrance, which had been taken away, were replaced by

---

[1] Cf. Babucke, *Geschichte des Kolosseums*, Königsberg, 1899.

travertine. These restorations, however, were carried too far, and have rendered much of the original construction some-what obscure. In spite of these injuries, enough of the Colosseum is left to make it one of the most imposing buildings in the world. The north side of the outer wall still stands, comprising the arches numbered XXIII to LIV, with that part of the building which is between it and the inner wall supporting the colonnade (p. 331). Of that part of the building between this inner wall and the arena, practically the whole skeleton remains, — that is, the encircling and radiating walls on which the cavea with its marble seats rested. These marble seats, and everything in the nature of decoration, have long since disappeared.

The amphitheatre[1] is elliptical in form. Its main axis, running northwest-southeast, is 188 metres in length, and its minor axis 156. The whole exterior is constructed of large blocks of travertine; the inner walls are of concrete, with and without brick facing, strengthened by piers of peperino and travertine at the points of greatest pressure. The general plan of the building may be seen by a glance at the cross-section (Fig. 71). The outer wall, or façade, is 48.50 metres high, and stands upon a stylobate, which is raised two steps above a pavement of travertine. This is 17.50 metres wide, and extended round the whole building. Its outer edge is marked by a row of stone cippi — some of which are *in situ* — provided with bronze rings through which wooden bars were run, to serve the purpose of a fence. The outer wall itself is divided into four stories, of which the lower three consist of rows of open arcades. The arches of the lower arcade are 7.05

---

[1] For plates and description, see *Beschreibung der Stadt Rom*, iii. 1. 319–336; Canina, *Edifizi di Roma antica*, iv. 164–177; Reber, *Die Ruinen Roms*, 407–421; Cresy-Taylor, *Architectural Antiquities of Rome*, London, 1874, 114–129; Dreger, *Das flavische Amphitheater in seiner ersten Gestalt, Allgemeine Bauzeitung*, 1896, 40–60. For restorations, see Knapp in *Beschreibung der Stadt Rom, Bilderheft*, 2 (the better), and Uggieri, *Giornate pittoriche degli Edifizi di Roma*, xxiii. (1816); *Mitt.* 1897, 334.

metres high and 4.20 wide ; the pillars between them are 2.40
metres wide and 2.70 deep.   In front of these pillars are
engaged columns of the Doric order, which support an entablature 2.35 metres high, but without the distinguishing characteris-
tics of this order.   There were eighty arches in the lower arcade,
of which the four at the ends of the two axes formed the main
entrances to the amphitheatre, and were unnumbered.   The
remaining seventy-six were numbered, the numbers being cut

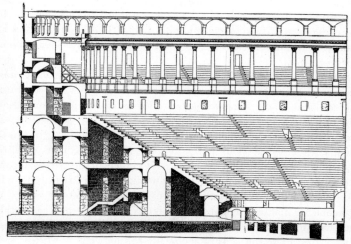

FIG. 71.—SECTION OF THE COLOSSEUM.

on the façade just beneath the architrave.   Above the entablature is an attic of the same height, with projections above the
columns, which serve as pedestals for the engaged columns of
the second arcade.   This arcade has the same dimensions as the
lowest, except that the arches are only 6.45 metres high.   The
half-columns are of the Ionic order, and in turn support an
entablature 2.10 metres in height, but not in perfect Ionic
style.   Above this is a second attic, 1.95 metres high, on which
the columns of the third arcade rest.   This last is of the

Corinthian order, and its arches are 6.40 metres high. Above this is a third entablature and attic. In each of the arches of the first and second arcades was a statue.

The three lower arcades of the outer wall belong to the original work of Vespasian and Titus. Coins of the latter emperor, however, show a fourth story as already existing at that time, and it is the current view that this was at first constructed of wood, and not replaced by stone until the third century. The existing upper division of the façade dates from this later period.

The attic above the third arcade is 2.10 metres high, and is pierced by small rectangular windows over every second arch. On it rests the upper division of the wall. This is solid, and is adorned with flat Corinthian pilasters in place of the half-columns of the lower arcades. Above these pilasters is an entablature, and between every second pair of pilasters is a window cut through the wall. Above these openings is a row of consoles, — three between each pair of pilasters. In these consoles are sockets for the masts which projected upward through corresponding holes in the cornice and perhaps supported the awnings (*velaria*) that protected the cavea.

Within this outer wall, at a distance of 5.80 metres, is a second wall with corresponding arches; and 4.50 metres inside of this a third, which divides the building into two main sections. On the lower floor, between these three walls, are two lofty arched corridors or ambulatories, encircling the entire building; on the second floor, two corridors like those below, except that the inner one is itself divided into two, an upper and a lower; and on the third floor two more. In the inner corridor on the second floor, and in both on the third, are flights of steps very ingeniously arranged, which lead to the topmost story, and afford access to the upper part of the second tier of seats.

Within the innermost of the three walls just mentioned are other walls parallel to it, and radiating walls, struck from certain points within the oval and perpendicular to its circumference. These radiating walls correspond in number to the piers of the lower arcade, and are divided into three parts, so as to leave room for two more corridors round the building. This system of radiating walls supported the sloping floor (*cavea*) on which the rows of marble seats (*gradus*) were placed. Underneath, in corridors and arches, are other flights of steps which lead to all parts of the cavea, through openings called *vomitoria*.

The arena is itself elliptical, the major axis being 86 metres long and the minor 54. All round the arena was a wall, built to protect the spectators from the attacks of the wild beasts, and behind it a narrow passage paved with marble. Behind this passage was the podium, a platform raised about 4 metres above the arena, on which were three rows of marble seats for the emperor and his family, ambassadors, and high officials of state. The names of the corporations or officials to whom these chairs belonged were inscribed on the steps or pavement of the podium. When a seat passed from one owner to another, the old name was erased and a new one substituted. More than two hundred such inscriptions have been found.[1] In the fourth century these seats began to be assigned to families and individuals. Some of these marble seats have been preserved, having been converted into bishops' thrones in the Roman churches, as in S. Stefano Rotondo and S. Gregorio. The front of the podium was protected by a brass balustrade.

From the podium, the cavea sloped upward as far as the innermost of the three walls described above. It was divided into sections (*maeniana*) by aisles and low walls (*praecinctiones*); the lower section (*maenianum primum*) contained about twenty rows of seats (*gradus*) and the upper section (*maenianum secundum*, further subdivided into *maenianum superius* and *inferius*) about sixteen. These *maeniana* were also divided

---

[1] *BC.* 1880, 211–282.

into *cunei*, or wedged-shaped sections, by the steps and aisles from the *vomitoria*. Each individual seat was exactly designated by its gradus, cuneus, and number. These seats were assigned according to wealth and rank, and by the famous lex Roscia of 67 B.C., which was revived by Domitian, the first fourteen rows were reserved for the equites. Behind the *maenianum secundum* the wall rose to a height of 5 metres above the cavea, and was pierced with doors and windows which afforded communication with the corridor behind. On this wall was a Corinthian colonnade, which, together with the outer wall, supported a flat roof. The columns were of cipollino and granite, and dated from the Flavian period. Behind them, protected by the roof, was the *summum maenianum in ligneis*, which contained wooden seats for women. On the roof was standing room for the *pullati*, or poorest classes of the population. It is probable that this upper part was built entirely of wood until the third century.

Of the four principal entrances, those at the north and south ends of the minor axis were for the imperial family, and the arches here were wider and more highly ornamented than the rest. The entrance [1] on the north seems to have been connected with the Esquiline by a porticus. A wide passage led directly from this entrance to the imperial box (*pulvinar*) on the podium. A corresponding box on the opposite side of the podium was probably reserved for the praefectus urbi. The entrances at the ends of the major axis led directly into the arena.

The floor of the arena rested on lofty substructures, consisting of walls, some of which follow the elliptical curve of the building, while others are parallel to the major axis. The east half of the arena has been excavated so that these substructures are visible. They are entered by four subterranean passages, on the lines of the major and minor axes. Commodus

---

[1] For 16th century drawings of the decoration of this entrance see *Wiener Studien*, 1902, 437–440.

constructed another subterranean passage, a sort of crypto-porticus, which starts a little to the east of the state entrance on the south side, and leads to the buildings of Claudius on the Caelian. This was for his own use, when he visited the amphitheatre. In the substructures are traces of dens for wild beasts, elevators, and mechanical appliances of various sorts, but their principal object must have been to provide for the drainage of the water, which flows so abundantly into this hollow, and which was carried off in a sewer[1] connecting with that beneath the modern via di S. Gregorio (p. 322). The masonry of these substructures dates all the way from the first century to the end of the fifth.

The total seating capacity of the Colosseum was probably from forty to forty-five thousand, and there was standing room on the roof for some five thousand more.[2]

Near the amphitheatre were several other buildings, used for purposes connected with the sports in the arena. Among them were four training schools for gladiators, the ludus Magnus, ludus Dacicus, ludus Gallicus, and ludus Matutinus. The first two, in region III, are spoken of on pp. 450 f. The ludus Gallicus[3] was a training school for Gallic gladiators; but the name ludus Matutinus[4] has not been satisfactorily explained. Both of these schools were in region II, as well as the Arma-mentarium or armory, and the Samiarium,[5] apparently a place for the repairing and sharpening of weapons. The Summum Choragium,[6] or storehouse for stage settings and scenery, was in region III, and in II the Spoliarium[7] where the bodies of dead gladiators were exposed to view. All these annexes were probably built by Domitian, when he completed the amphi-theatre itself.

---

[1] For the sewerage system of the Colosseum, see Narducci, *Sulla Fogna-tura della Città di Roma*, 65–72.

[2] *BC*. 1894, 312–324.          [3] *CIL*. vi. 9470.

[4] *CIL*. vi. 352, 10172; Jordan, I. 3. 299.     [5] *CIL*. vi. 10164; Jordan, II. 18.

[6] Jordan, *FUR*. 7; *CIL*. vi. 776, 10083–10087.     [7] Lamprid. *Vit. Com.* 18, 19

Nero erected a colossal bronze statue of himself (Colossus Neronis), 31.5 metres high, in the vestibule of the domus Aurea on the summit of the Velia.[1] This statue was the work of a Greek, Zenodorus. It was changed by Vespasian[2] into a statue of the sun. Hadrian[3] moved it nearer to the Colosseum, in order to make room for the temple of Venus and Roma. This removal was effected without taking the statue down. Commodus[4] converted it into a statue of Hercules; but at his death it was restored as the sun, and so remained. The last mention of this statue in antiquity is in the fourth century.[5] Part of the pedestal which was built by Hadrian still exists, between the Colosseum and the temple of Venus and Roma. This pedestal is 7 metres square, and is constructed of brick-faced concrete, originally covered with marble.

Just south of the Colossus was the Meta Sudans,[6] a great fountain said to have been built by Domitian in 97 A.D. In shape it resembled a goal (meta), and sudans described the appearance of the jets and streams of water. It stood at the point of meeting of five regions, I, II, III, IV, and X. The core still stands, conical in shape, 9 metres high and 5 metres in diameter at the bottom. Around its base is a great basin, which probably dates from the time of Constantine. The whole fountain was originally covered with marble.

**Basilica Constantini**. — This great building, also called the basilica Nova, was begun by Maxentius, but completed by Constantine.[7] It was erected on the north side of the Sacra via, partly on the site of the horrea Piperataria, on an enor-

---

[1] Suet. Nero, 31; Pl. NH. xxxiv. 45; Mart. de Spect. 2. 1; i. 70. 7; Dio Cass. lxvi. 15; Jordan, I. 3. 320; II. 510; Gilbert, III. 195.

[2] Suet. Vesp. 18.    [3] Spart. Vit. Hadr. 19.

[4] Lamprid. Vit. Com. 17; Dio Cass. lxxii. 22.    [5] Not. Reg. iv.

[6] Chronogr. a. 354, p. 146; Cohen, Alex. Sev. 468; Jordan, I. 3. 24–25.

[7] Chronogr. a. 354, p. 146; Vict. Caes. 40. 26; Mélanges, 1893, 161–167; Mitt. 1892, 289; Jordan, I. 3. 11–14. See Forum Plan.

mous rectangular platform of concrete, 100 metres long and 65 wide. The basilica itself was of peculiar form, consisting of a central nave, 80 metres long, 25 wide, and 35 high, and two side aisles, each 16 metres wide. These aisles were divided into three sections by walls, pierced by wide arches and ending on each side of the nave in massive piers. In front of these piers and at the corners of the nave were eight monolithic columns of marble. On these piers rested the roof of the nave, divided into three bays with quadripartite groining.

The façade of the basilica as built by Maxentius was toward the east, and at this end was a corridor or vestibule, 8 metres deep, which extended across the whole width of the building. From this vestibule there were five entrances into the basilica, three into the nave, and one into each of the aisles. A flight of steps led up from the street in front to the vestibule, which was adorned with columns. At the west end of the nave was a semicircular apse, 20 metres in diameter.

Constantine constructed a second entrance from the Sacra via in the middle of the south side, where he built a porch with porphyry columns and a long flight of steps. Opposite this new entrance he constructed a second semicircular apse in the north wall, as large as that at the west end of the nave. Thenceforth the basilica produced the same impression — of three parallel halls — whether one entered it from the south or from the east.

The material employed in the whole structure was brick and concrete, and the great thickness of the walls — 6 metres at one point at the west end — and the enormous height and span of the vaulted roof, made it one of the most remarkable buildings in Rome.

Besides the foundation, which has been almost wholly uncovered, the north wall and the north aisle — or, as it rather appears, the north sections of the three halls regarded as running north and south — are still standing. The semicircular apse in the central hall contains sixteen rectangular niches in

two rows, with a pedestal or *suggestus* in the centre.  A marble
seat with steps runs round the apse, which was separated from
the rest of the hall by two columns and marble screens, thus
forming a sort of tribunal for the emperor when holding court.

All of the monolithic marble columns of the nave have been
destroyed except one, which was removed by Paul V in 1613
to the piazza di S. Maria Maggiore, where it now stands.  This
column, with base and capital, measures 19.25 metres in height.
The vaulted roof of the basilica is constructed with deep hexagonal and octagonal coffers.  Some very large fragments of
the roof, which have fallen down within comparatively recent
years, lie on the floor.  Nothing of the nave remains except the
bases of the great piers.  The core of the porch and of the
flight of steps leading down to the Sacra via is still visible, and
several fragments of the porphyry columns have been set up,
but not *in situ*.  Of the pavement of slabs of marble considerable fragments [1] have been found.  The building, resembling a
loggia, which projects over the line of the Sacra via at the west
end of the basilica, is medieval.

The northwest corner of the basilica joined the wall of the
forum of Vespasian, thereby cutting off the previously existing thoroughfare between the forum Romanum and the district
of the Carinae.  Maxentius therefore constructed a passageway under the northwest corner of the building, about 4 metres
wide and 15 long.  In the sixth century one end of this passage was walled up, but the interrupted communication was
afterward restored.  In the middle ages this passage was
known as the arco di Latrone, from its dangerous associations.

Just west of the basilica of Constantine, on the Sacra via, is
the **Heroon Romuli**, or temple of Romulus, which was begun by
Maxentius in honor of his son Romulus, who, having died at
an early age, had been deified.[2]  The temple was finished by

---

[1] *Mitt.* 1905, 117.
[2] *CIL.* vi. 1147; *Bull. Crist.* 1867, 66–69; *BC.* 1882, 29–54; Jordan, I. 3.
10–11.

Constantine.   It adjoined the templum Sacrae Urbis in the rear, and with this latter edifice was converted into the church of SS. Cosma e Damiano in the sixth century.   The original structure, which has been almost completely preserved, consists of a central circular hall 17 metres in diameter, and on each side a narrow rectangular hall, terminating in an apse at the rear.   These halls open toward the Sacra via, and the doorways of the smaller rooms are flanked with cipollino columns, two of which are still standing.   In front of the circular hall is a sort of curved porch, and the main entrance is flanked by columns of red porphyry.   The original bronze doors are still in place, and above them is a richly decorated architrave of white marble, which belonged to another building.   The temple is built of concrete with brick and tufa facing, but nothing remains of the marble and stucco lining.

# CHAPTER XIII.

## THE CAMPUS MARTIUS.

THE term campus Martius was used at different times with somewhat varying signification. In its widest sense it embraced the district outside the Servian wall between the Capitoline, the Quirinal, and the Pincian hills, and the Tiber. This is a level plain, extending a little more than 2 kilometres from the Capitoline to the porta Flaminia, and being nearly 2 kilometres wide in its widest part between the Quirinal and the river. As early as the fifth century B.C. the south portion of this district was probably known as the prata Flaminia,[1] and campus Martius was the ordinary designation for what lay beyond. After Augustus had divided the city into fourteen regions, the name campus Martius was restricted to that portion of region IX (circus Flaminius) which was west of the via Lata, the modern Corso, and here again there seems to have been a further distinction. A cippus[2] found in the via del Seminario, near the Pantheon, proves that this campus Martius of the time of Augustus was divided into two parts, — the open meadow to the north, and the district between the cippus and the circus Flaminius, which had been more or less built over. A little later this line of separation was marked by a street[3] running west from the modern piazza Colonna to the Tiber. The original pavement of this street has been uncovered for most of this distance, and its line corresponds in general with the modern via di S. Agostino and via dei Coronari. The original pavement

---

[1] Liv. iii. 54, 63; Gilbert, III. 66–69; Jordan, I. 3. 484.    [2] *CIL*. vi. 874.

[3] This street is called by Lanciani, following the earlier topographers, the via Recta, but this is based on a probable misreading for *via tecta* in Sen. *Apoc.* 13. Cf. p. 377, and Jordan, I. 3. 503.

There were several swamps or ponds in this low-lying district, as well as streams, the largest of which, the Petronia amnis, came from a spring on the Quirinal, called the Cati fons (p. 19), and flowed into the largest swamp, the palus Caprae, or Capreae,[1] where were afterward the pool and baths of Agrippa. In the northwest part of the campus Martius, near the great bend in the river, there were hot springs, probably sulphurous, and other traces of volcanic action. This part was called the Tarentum [2] and perhaps campus Ignifer.[3]

The name campus Martius was derived from an ancient altar of Mars,[4] ascribed to the earliest period, which probably stood east of the Pantheon near the via del Seminario. The whole district belonged to the community,[5] part of it being cultivated as domain land. We are told that Sulla,[6] under the financial pressure of the impending war with Mithridates, was the first to sell to private owners any part of this public domain; but the very name, prata Flaminia, which is quoted as early as 449 B.C., seems to indicate some private ownership at a very early date. It is probable, however, that these prata had become public property but retained their original name. The campus Martius was entirely outside of the pomerium during the republic and probably down to the reign of Claudius (p. 69). By the time of Hadrian the pomerium had been extended so as to include the prata Flaminia; but the campus Martius in its narrower sense was not included until the wall of Aurelian was built. Because it was public domain and outside the pomerium, the campus was used as the place of assembly [7] for the citizens, in their military capacity as an army and in their

---

[1] Liv. i. 16; Ov. *Fast.* ii. 491; Gilbert, I. 290–291; Jordan, I. 3. 473–474.

[2] Fest. 329, 350.          [3] Zos. ii. 3: πυροφόρον πεδίον.

[4] Liv. ii. 5; Dionys. v. 13; Plut. *Popl.* 8; Schol. Juv. ii. 132; Liv. xxxv. 10; xl. 45; Ov. *Fast.* ii. 860; Fest. 189; Gilbert, I. 289; Jordan, I. 3. 475–477; *CP.* 1908, 65–73.

[5] Gilbert, III. 6–7, 67–68.

[6] Oros. v. 18.          [7] Liv. i. 44; Dionys. iv. 22; Gell. xv. 27.

civil capacity as the comitia centuriata. Audience was given here by the senate to foreign ambassadors who could not enter the city, and foreign cults were allowed to be domiciled in temples erected here. Finally public buildings of all sorts were built in the south half of the campus, while private houses did not begin to multiply to any extent before the time of the empire.[1]

Besides those already mentioned, other parts of this extensive district bore distinctive names. The forum Holitorium, or vegetable market, was just outside the Servian wall, close to the Tiber. Between the modern ponte Garibaldi and the theatre of Pompeius was a grove called the Aesculetum,[2] where the comitia met in 287 B.C. to pass the famous Hortensian laws. Fragments of the pavement of the vicus Aescleti have been found in the modern via della Regola di S. Bartolommeo. The suburb that in process of time extended from the porta Flumentana along the bank of the river to the Navalia, was known as extra portam Flumentanam ;[3] and within the limits of this precinct there had been, as late as 342 B.C., a grove called the lucus Petelinus.[4] Another suburb, the Aemiliana,[5] is more difficult to locate with certainty, but it was perhaps the district between the porta Fontinalis and the Saepta Iulia. The Trigarium,[6] where horses were exercised, was in the northwest part of the campus, between the modern piazza Navona and the Tiber. Just east of this Trigarium was probably the place where chariot races, *equiria*,[7] were held in honor of Mars. On

---

[1] Cic. *ad Att.* xiii. 33. For the history of the campus Martius see Jordan, I. 3. 493–506.

[2] Varro, *LL.* v. 152; Pl. *NH.* xvi. 37; *Mitt.* 1889, 265–267; Jordan, I. 3. 479, 521.

[3] Varro, *RR.* iii. 2. 6; Liv. vi. 20.

[4] Plut. *Camil.* 36; Liv. vii. 41; *BC.* 1905, 222–223.

[5] Varro, *loc. cit.;* Tac. *Ann.* xv. 40; Suet. *Claud.* 18; Gilbert, III. 378; Jordan, I. 3. 490.

[6] Pl. *NH.* xxviii. 238; xxix. 9; *CIL.* vi. 31545.

[7] Fest. *Epit.* 81; Varro, *LL.* vi. 13; Ov. *Fast.* ii. 860; iii. 519; Richter, *Top.*[2] 223; Gilbert, II. 97; *CP.* 1908, 70–71.

the bank of the river, not far south of the mausoleum of
Augustus, were storehouses for wine; and, to judge from the
somewhat uncertain evidence, this part seems to have been
called Ciconiae nixae or Nixae,[1] apparently from some statue or
relief representing storks with crossed bills.

Besides the three principal streets in the campus Martius,
— the via Lata, the via Tecta (p. 377), and the so-called via
Recta, — fragments of the pavement of some others have been
found.[2]  One of them ran southwest from the theatre of
Pompeius to the river, along the line of the modern via dei
Pettinari; another ran north from this theatre along the via
dei Sediari; a third extended from the theatre of Balbus to a
point near the Tarentum, where it joined the via Tecta, its
course being nearly that of the via S. Paolina, vicolo dei Venti,
and via del Montserrato.  The pavement of a fourth lies in a
line between the via degli Astalli and the Corso, and may be
that of the vicus Pallacinae,[3] which derived its name from the
balineae Pallacinae near the circus Flaminius.  Another stretch
of pavement has been discovered just north of the thermae
Alexandrinae, in the via di Ripetta; and there are also traces
of two cross-streets between the via Flaminia and the Tiber,
one north (via dei Pontefici), and the other south of the
mausoleum of Augustus.  In 216 B.C. there was a via Fornicata,
*quae ad campum erat,* but this street is mentioned only once.[4]

**The Earliest Structures.** — If the ara Martis was the first altar
in the campus Martius, the ara Ditis et Proserpinae in Tarento [5] was
undoubtedly the second.  The springs and pool of the Tarentum

---

[1] *Not.* Reg. ix; *CIL.* i[2]. p. 332; vi. 1785; Gilbert, I. 290; Jordan, I. 3. 601;
*CP.* 1908, 70–71.

[2] Cf. Gilbert, III. 378–379.

[3] Cic. *pro Rosc. Amer.* 18, 132, and Schol.; Jordan, II. 592–593; *Hermes,*
1867, 76; *PBS.* iii. 261; *BC.* 1908, 280–282.

[4] Liv. xxii. 36.

[5] Fest. 329.  Cf. Val. Max. ii. 4. 5; Serv. *in Aen.* viii. 63; Ov. *Fast.* i. 501;
Mart. x. 63. 3.

naturally suggested an entrance to Hades, and hence the worship of the gods of the lower world was established at this spot. This ara Ditis is said to have been 6 metres beneath the surface of the ground. Upon it were offered the sacrifices at the *ludi Tarentini,* games which were afterward merged with the *ludi saeculares.* The altar [1] of the time of the empire was discovered in 1886–1887, behind the palazzo Cesarini, 5 metres below the level of the Corso Vittorio Emanuele. Two blocks of the altar itself were found, resting upon a pedestal which was approached by three steps. The altar was 3.40 metres square. Behind it was a massive wall of tufa, and round it a triple wall of peperino. Not far away, in a medieval wall, were found large portions of the marble slabs containing the inscriptions which record the celebration of the *ludi saeculares* by Augustus in 17 B.C. and by Severus in 204 A.D. [2] The altar is not visible, but the inscription is in the Museo delle Terme.

The oldest temples in this district were those dedicated to Bellona and Apollo. The temple of **Bellona** [3] was vowed by Appius Claudius Caecus in 296 B.C., and dedicated somewhat later. This temple is mentioned as existing [4] in the second century, but no trace of it has been found. Its location [5] is uncertain, but from it Sulla [6] heard the cries of the prisoners who were massacred in the Villa Publica (p. 345). It is also said to have been at the opposite end [7] of the circus Flaminius from the temple of Hercules Custos (p. 347). On the whole it is probable that it was north of the east end of the circus Flaminius. Considerable importance attached to

---

[1] *Mitt.* 1891, 127–129; *BC.* 1887, 276–277; *Mon. d. Lincei,* i. 540–548.

[2] *NS.* 1890, 285; *BC.* 1896, 191–230; *EE.* viii. 225–309; *CIL.* vi. 32323–32337.

[3] Pl. *NH.* xxxv. 12 (where the reference to the Appius Claudius of 495 B.C. is now regarded as an interpolation. Wissowa, *Religion der Römer,* 137); Liv. x. 19; Ov. *Fast.* vi. 203.

[4] Dio Cass. lxxi. 33.

[5] Jordan, I. 3. 552–554; Richter, *Top.*[2] 215; Gilbert, III. 75.

[6] Plut. *Sulla,* 30.        [7] Ov. *Fast.* vi. 209.

this temple during the republic, as it was used for sessions of the senate at which victorious generals presented their claims for a triumph.[1] This could not be done within the pomerium. Near the temple was a *senaculum*, or place of assembly for the senators, and a small area which a soldier of Pyrrhus had been forced to buy in order that it might represent foreign soil. In this area was the so-called columna bellica,[2] representing a boundary stone, over which the *fetialis* cast his spear when declaring war in due form against a foreign foe. The aedes Bellonae Pulvinensis mentioned in inscriptions,[3] was a temple of the Cappadocian goddess, Mâ-Bellona, whose worship seems to have displaced that of the Latin Bellona during the empire. This temple was probably not built before the third century, and its location is unknown. Any connection with a supposed pulvinar of the circus Flaminius is unfounded.

The earliest worship of Apollo in Rome was connected with the Apollinare,[4] an altar or grove that was situated just west of the Capitolium, between it and the porticus Octaviae. On this spot a temple was built in 431 B.C.,[5] which had been vowed two years before in consequence of a plague. This was the only temple of Apollo in Rome until Augustus erected that on the Palatine.[6] It was restored in 32 B.C.,[7] and possibly [8] much earlier, in 353 B.C. Portions of the foundation wall of opus quadratum have been found beneath the houses on the south side of the piazza Campitelli, and a few fragments of the entablature with reliefs.[9] This temple was frequently

---

[1] Fest. 347; Liv. xxvi. 21, and freq.; cf. Richter, *Top.*[2] 215.

[2] Serv. *in Aen.* ix. 52; Fest. *Epit.* 33; Ov. *Fast.* vi. 205–209; Dio Cass. l. 4; lxxi. 33.

[3] *CIL.* vi. 490, 2232–2233; Jordan, I. 3. 554; Wissowa, *Religion der Römer,* 291.

[4] Liv. iii. 63.        [5] Liv. iv. 25, 29.        [6] Asc. *in Or. in Tog. Cand.* 115.

[7] Pl. *NH.* xiii. 53; xxxvi. 28.        [8] Liv. vii. 20.

[9] *Bull. d. Ist.* 1878, 218; *BC.* 1893, 46–60; Delbrück, *Der Apollotempel auf dem Marsfelde in Rom,* Rome, 1903.

used for extra-pomerial sessions of the senate,[1] and it contained many works of art, among them the famous Niobe group, and treasures of various kinds.[2] There was also a shrine of the goddess Feronia[3] in the campus Martius, which probably antedated the Punic wars; and a lucus Feroniae is vouched for by an inscription[4] recently found, but we know nothing of its location.

Not far from the ara Martis, and just north of the modern piazza del Gesù, was the Villa Publica,[5] which was said to have been built in 435 B.C. It was the only public building in the campus Martius proper before the end of the republic. Although no remains have been found, its approximate position is certain.[6] It consisted of a walled inclosure, within which was a square building, represented on a coin[7] of the end of the republic as having two stories, the lower one opening outward with a row of arches. It served as the headquarters for state officials when engaged in taking the census or levying troops.[8] Foreign ambassadors and generals who desired a triumph were also lodged here.[9] The Villa was restored in 194 B.C.,[10] and probably again in 34 by P. Fonteius Capito. If, as seems probable,[11] it is represented on some fragments of the Marble Plan, it existed as late as the second century, although much reduced in size, and simply as a monument of antiquity. Within the walls of the Villa, in 82 B.C., Sulla[12] massacred the four thousand prisoners taken in the battle of the Colline gate. Adjoining the building was the inclosed area, called the Saepta,[13] where the comitia centuriata assembled to

---

[1] Liv. xxxiv. 43 and freq.; Cic. ad Q. Fr. ii. 3.

[2] Pl. NH. xxxv. 99; xxxvi. 34.

[3] Wissowa, op. cit. 231; Jordan, I. 3. 483 ; CIL. i². p. 335.

[4] NS. 1905, 15.　　　　　　　　　　[5] Liv. iv. 22; Gilbert, III. 144–145.

[6] Varro, RR. iii. 2; Plut. Sulla, 30; cf. Berl. Phil. Wochenschrift, 1903, 575.

[7] Babelon, Monnaies, Fonteia, 18.　　　[8] Varro, loc. cit.

[9] Liv. xxx. 21; xxxiii. 24.　　　　　[10] Liv. xxxiv. 44.

[11] Mitt. 1903, 47–48.　　　　　　　[12] Liv. Epit. 88; Val. Max. ix. 2. 1.

[13] Liv. xxvi. 22; Juv. vi. 529; Serv. ad Ecl. i. 33.

vote. The division of this inclosure into smaller sections, for tribes and centuries, caused it to resemble a sheepfold, and hence it was often called Ovile.

Near the Villa Publica stood the porta Triumphalis,[1] an arched gateway, which took its name from the fact that the general who was celebrating a triumph began his march into the city at this point. We are not informed as to the date of its erection, but it was probably as early as the second century B.C. No vestiges of this arch have been found. Domitian[2] either built a second triumphal arch in this immediate neighborhood, or restored the existing porta Triumphalis.

The forum Holitorium, forming as it did an almost totally distinct section of the campus Martius, will be described on pp. 389–392, and the remaining buildings of region IX will be taken up by groups, in chronological order.

**Temples.** — (1) The temple of Fons. In 231 B.C. Cn. Papirius Maso[3] dedicated a temple to Fons from the booty that he had taken in Corsica. This was undoubtedly near the porta Fontinalis, and therefore near the northeast corner of the Capitoline.

(2) The temple of Neptune. Livy[4] mentions an altar of Neptune as existing in 206 B.C. This altar was probably replaced by the temple[5] built by some member of the gens Domitia, perhaps Cn. Domitius Ahenobarbus about 30 B.C., which contained a masterpiece of Skopas. Northwest of the

---

[1] Cic. *in Pis.* 55; Jos. *Bell. Iud.* vii. 5. 4; Gilbert, III. 157–158; Jordan, I. 3. 495, 501. For a recent theory that the porta Triumphalis was merely the name given to any gate through which the victorious general entered the city, or to a temporary arch erected at any point along the line of his march through the city, see *BC.* 1908, 109–150.

[2] Suet. *Dom.* 13; Dio Cass. lxviii. 1; Richter, *Top.*[2] 227; cf. Mart. viii. 65. 8; Gilbert, III. 157, 190–191; *BC.* 1908, 121–122; *PBS.* iii. 259–260, 269 (cf. arcus Manus Carneae, p. 480).

[3] Cic. *de Nat. Deor.* iii. 52; Fest. *Epit.* 85; *CIL.* vi. 32493; Jordan, I. 3. 483.
[4] xxviii. 11.

[5] Pl. *NH.* xxxvi. 26; Babelon, *Monnaies,* i. 466, *Domitia* 20.

piazza S. Salvatore, the remains of the substructures and of six columns of a pycnostyle temple have been found, which are usually identified with this temple of Neptune, and there are some fragments[1] of reliefs from an altar belonging to the temple in Munich and Paris.

(3) The temple of Vulcan. A temple of Vulcan existed in 214 B.C. and as late as the first century.[2] Its exact site is not known, but from the evidence of a fragmentary inscription, it may possibly have been near the temple of Juturna (p. 350) at the north end of the Saepta. The reason why this temple was outside the pomerium is given by Vitruvius:[3] (*ut*) *Volcani vi e moenibus religionibus et sacrificiis evocata ab timore incendiorum aedificia videantur liberari.*

(4) The temple of Hercules Custos. This temple was built to Hercules in his capacity as guardian of the circus Flaminius, sometime between the date of erection of the circus, 221 B.C., and 189 B.C.[4] It was restored by Sulla, and is mentioned in the first century. Its exact site is unknown, but from indications in one of the calendars it seems to have been near the porticus Minucia, and therefore at the west end of the circus. It may possibly be identified with the round temple near S. Niccoló ai Cesarini (p. 362).

(5) The temple of Hercules and the Muses. This temple was close to the southwest part of the circus Flaminius, and is shown on the Capitoline Plan.[5] It was built by M. Fulvius Nobilior after his campaign in Aetolia, about 187 B.C. In it

---

[1] *BC.* 1873, 212–221; *Sitz.-Ber. d. bayr. Akad.* 1876, 344; Bursian's *Jahresbericht*, 1873, 787–789; Strong, *Sculpture*, 33–38; Furtwängler, *Intermezzi*, Leipzig, 1896, 35; Jordan, I. 3. 522–524.

[2] Liv. xxiv. 10; Plut. *Quaest. Rom.* 47; *CIL.* i². p. 326; *EE.* i. p. 230; Gilbert, I. 252; *Neue Heidelberger Jahrbücher*, 1899, 116–117; Jordan, I. 3, 481–482.

[3] i. 7. 1.

[4] Ov. *Fast.* vi. 209; Liv. xxxviii. 35; *Comm. in hon. Mommsen*, 266–267; *CIL.* i². pp. 319, 324; Gilbert, III. 80–81.

[5] Jordan, *FUR.* 33.

was a statue of Hercules playing on the lyre, and terra cotta statues of the Muses, the work of Zeuxis.[1]  In 29 B.C. L. Marcius Philippus restored the temple[2] and built a colonnade, the porticus Philippi (p. 376), round it.  This composite structure is mentioned as late as the fourth century,[3] and some remains have been found in the piazza Mattei.[4]

(6) The temple of **Fortuna Equestris**.  This temple stood *ad theatrum lapideum*,[5] that is near the theatre of Pompeius.  It was vowed in 180 B.C. by Q. Fulvius Flaccus during his campaign in Spain,[6] and dedicated in 173.  Fulvius is said to have stolen the marble tiles from the temple of Iuno Lacinia *in Bruttiis*, but to have been forced to restore them.[7]  As we are told that there was no temple to Fortuna Equestris in Rome in 22 A.D.,[8] it must have been destroyed before that date, and never rebuilt.

(7) The temple of the **Lares Permarini**.  This temple, consecrated to the Lares who protect sailors, was vowed by L. Aemilius Regillus during the naval battle with the forces of Antiochus in 190 B.C., and dedicated in 179.[9]  As it is said to have stood *in campo Martio* and also *in porticu Minucia*, its location depends upon that of the porticus (p. 373).

(8 and 9) The temples of **Diana** and **Iuno Regina**.  These temples were vowed by M. Aemilius Lepidus in 187 B.C., and dedicated in 179.[10]  They were near the circus Flaminius, but no traces of them have been found.  A porticus[11] connected the temple of Iuno Regina with a temple of Fortuna, but we do not know whether this was Fortuna Equestris or not, as there must have been a considerable distance between the two.

---

[1] Serv. *in Aen.* i. 8; Pl. *NH.* xxxv. 66; Ov. *Fast.* vi. 797–812; *Bull. d. Ist.* 1869, 3–12; *Comm. in hon. Mommsen*, 262–268.

[2] Suet. *Aug.* 29.       [3] Macrob. *Sat.* i. 12. 16.       [4] Rosa, *Relazione*, 75.

[5] Vitr. iii. 3. 2.               [6] Liv. xl. 40, 44; xlii. 10.

[7] Liv. xlii. 3; Val. Max. i. 1. 20.

[8] Tac. *Ann.* iii. 71; but cf. *Berl. Phil. Wochenschrift*, 1903, 1648; Jordan, I. 3. 487.

[9] Liv. xl. 52; Macrob. *Sat.* i. 10. 10; *CIL.* i². p. 338; Gilbert, III. 149.

[10] Liv. xxxix. 2; xl. 52.               [11] Obseq. 75.

(10 and 11) The temples of **Iuno** and **Iuppiter Stator.** After 146 B.C. Q. Caecilius Metellus Macedonicus inclosed these two temples within his porticus (p. 371). It is not clearly stated that he built both the temples, but this is the natural inference from the passage, in which he is also said to have been the first Roman to construct a temple entirely of marble.[1] Both temples were probably restored by Augustus when he replaced the porticus Metelli by the porticus Octaviae (p. 372), and were standing in the fourth century. They were parallel to each other, and faced southwest. Both are represented on the Marble Plan,[2] the temple of Juno being hexastyle prostyle, and the temple of Jupiter hexastyle and peripteral, with ten columns on a side, although Vitruvius[3] says it had eleven. The exact site of each temple is known, that of Jupiter being mainly beneath the church of S. Maria in Campitelli. The ruins of these temples are concealed for the most part by modern houses in the via di S. Angelo in Pescheria, and consist chiefly of substructures and walls of travertine and opus reticulatum, with fragments of marble columns and entablatures. Three fluted columns of white marble belonging to the temple of Juno, 12.50 metres in height and 1.25 metres in diameter, with Corinthian capitals and entablature, may be seen in No. 11 of the street just mentioned.

(12) The temple of **Mars.** This temple[4] also was near the circus Flaminius, but its exact site is unknown. It was built by D. Junius Brutus Callaicus in 138 B.C., and contained a colossal statue of Mars and a Venus by Skopas.

(13) The temple of **Fortuna Huiusce Diei.** In 101 B.C. Q. Lutatius Catulus[5] built and dedicated a temple to this goddess, which he had vowed at the battle of Vercellae. Certain

---

[1] Pl. *NH.* xxxvi. 35, 40, 42, 43; Vell. i. 11; Macrob. *Sat.* iii. 4. 2; *Ann. d. Ist.* 1868, 108–132; Gilbert, III. 86–87; Jordan, I. 3. 538–540.

[2] Jordan, *FUR.* 33.  [3] iii. 2. 5.

[4] Priscian, viii. 17; Pl. *NH.* xxxvi. 26; *BC.* 1887, 302.

[5] Plut. *Mar.* 26; *CIL.* i². p. 323; Jordan, I. 3. 104, 491.

statues set up *ad aedem Fortunae huiusce diei*[1] may have stood in this temple rather than in that on the Palatine (p. 140).

(14) The temple of Iuturna. This temple[2] was erected by Q. Lutatius Catulus, but whether the builder of the Tabularium, or the victor in the battle at the Aegatian Islands in 241 B.C., is uncertain. It was standing in the first century, but its exact site is unknown, although it must have been near the north end of the Saepta. This temple may be identical with a temple of the Nymphs,[3] which contained many documents relating to the census, and was burned by Clodius.

(15) The temple of Minerva Chalcidica. In the year 62 B.C. Pompeius built a temple to Minerva from the spoils of his campaigns in the East.[4] Domitian[5] is said to have erected a temple to Minerva Chalcidica between the Pantheon and the temple of Isis and Serapis. It is possible that the latter was a restoration of the former, which may have been destroyed in the fire of 80 A.D. The temple of Domitian was standing in the early part of the sixteenth century, but it was destroyed then, and the modern church of S. Maria sopra Minerva was built over part of its foundations.[6] No satisfactory explanation has been found for the epithet Chalcidica.

(16 and 17) There were two other temples in the region of the circus Flaminius, of which the exact position and date of erection are unknown, but which probably belong to the last century of the republic; the temple of Pietas[7] (16) which was struck by lightning in 91 B.C.; and the temple of Castor (17) which was standing in the time of Augustus, and was built on unusual lines.[8]

---

[1] Pl. *NH.* xxxiv. 60; Procop. *Bell. Goth.* i. 15.

[2] Cic. *pro Clu.* 101; Ov. *Fast.* i. 463–464; Serv. *in Aen.* xii. 139; *Bull. d. Ist.* 1871, 136–145; *CIL.* i². p. 326.

[3] *CIL.* i². pp. 215, 326; Cic. *pro Mil.* 73; *Parad.* iv. 31; Gilbert, III. 162–163; Jordan, I. 3, 481.

[4] Pl. *NH.* vii. 97.    [5] *Chronogr. a. 354*, p. 146; *Cur.* Reg. ix.

[6] *Berl. Phil. Wochenschrift*, 1903, 575.

[7] Obseq. 114; Cic. *de Div.* i. 98; *CIL.* i². pp. 335–336.    [8] Vitr. iv. 8. 4.

(18) The Pantheon. The Pantheon[1] was built by Agrippa in 27 B.C., and with the thermae, stagnum, and Euripus formed the group of monuments which he constructed in this part of the campus Martius. This temple contained the statues of many divinities, among them those of Mars, Venus, and the deified Julius, and was probably dedicated particularly to these ancestral deities of the Julian family. Statues of Augustus and Agrippa himself stood in the pronaos. The Pantheon was burned[2] in 80 A.D. ; restored by Domitian ;[3] struck by lightning and again destroyed about 110 A.D. ;[4] rebuilt by Hadrian ;[5] and again restored by Severus in 202 A.D. On the frieze of the pronaos of the existing structure is the inscription M. AGRIPPA L. F. COS. TERTIVM FECIT ; on the architrave below, another inscription recording the restoration by Severus and Caracalla.[6] In consequence of the first of these inscriptions, the present structure was regarded until very recently as the original building of Agrippa, restored[7] but not greatly changed by later emperors ; but the investigations carried on in 1892 by Chedanne have proved this belief to be entirely erroneous.[8] The discovery of bricks of Hadrian's time in every part of the edifice proves conclusively that it was wholly constructed between the years 120 and 124 A.D.

The building[10] consists of three parts, the rotunda or drum,

---

[1] Dio Cass. liii. 27 ; Pl. *NH*. xxxvi. 38 ; Macrob. *Sat*. iii. 17. 17 ; Amm Marc. xvi. 10. 14.

[2] Dio Cass. lxvi. 24.     [3] *Chronogr. a. 354*, p. 146.     [4] Oros. vii. 12.

[5] Spart. *Vit. Hadr*. 19.   [6] *CIL*. vi. 896.   [7] *NS*. 1881, 255–276 ; 1882, 341–347.

[8] *NS*. 1892, 88–90 ; *BC*. 1892, 150–159 ; *Arch. Anz*. 1893, 1–5 ; *Mitt*. 1893, 305–318.

[9] *Mitt*. 1893, 312–315 ; *CIL*. xv. 276, 362, 811, 1406, etc.

[10] For the recent literature on the Pantheon, see Richter, *Top*.[2] 239. Most important are Michaelis, *Das Pantheon, Preussische Jahrbücher*, 1893, 208–224 ; Guillaume, *Le Pantheon d'Agrippa, Revue des deux mondes*, 1892, 562–581 ; L. Beltrami, *Il Pantheon*, Milan, 1898 ; Durm, *Baukunst der Römer* 2d ed. Darmstadt, 1904, 275–280, 343, 550–575 ; Rivoira, *Lombardic Architecture*, II. 100–101   *Nuova Antologia*, 1910, 631–633. See also Altmann *Rundbauten*, 60–63 ; Jordan, I. 3. 581–590.

the vestibule, and the pronaos. The rotunda is an enormous circular structure, containing a single hall. The walls, composed of eight hollow piers, 6.20 metres thick, and of connecting masonry of lesser thickness, support a vast dome, at the top of which is a circular opening 9 metres in diameter, through which light is admitted. The inner diameter of the drum is the same as the height from the pavement to the opening in the dome, 43.50 metres. Directly opposite the entrance, and in the middle of the east and west sides, are semicircular niches, and between these are trapezoidal niches, making seven in all besides the entrance. An entablature runs round the hall, supported by pilasters flanking each niche and by marble Corinthian columns in front of the niches. Between the niches are rectangular projections flanked by small columns, which have been converted into altars. The pavement is composed of slabs of granite, porphyry, and colored marbles, and the walls of the hall were once covered with magnificent marble linings. The ceiling of the dome is coffered and was originally gilded.

The walls are built of brick and brick-faced concrete, with a somewhat complicated system of brick relieving arches. Thus above each of the four trapezoidal niches in the perpendicular wall is an arch spanning the entire width of the niche, resting on the piers on each side of the niche and reaching nearly to the impost of the dome. This arch is composed of three concentric rings of brick (*tegulae bipedales*), and extends through the whole thickness of the wall. Beneath each of these arches are three small flat arches, and beneath them three others still smaller and flatter. Within the space of each large arch are two walls of brick, perpendicular to the circumference of the drum, and between them is a series of arched chambers each with two or three connecting sections. This method of construction serves to distribute the vast weight of the dome.

The investigation of the dome itself has been carried as far as the second row of coffers, and has shown that it is constructed, so far at least, of horizontal rings of brick, constantly

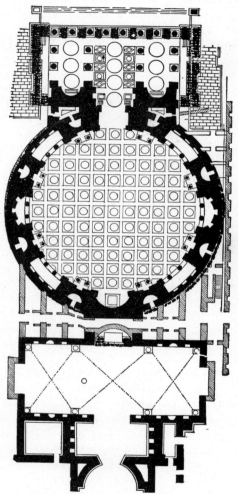

FIG 72. — THE PLAN OF THE PANTHEON.

diminishing in diameter, and of a series of arches which correspond to those just described. The walls of the drum rest
upon foundations of concrete, which project 15 centimetres beyond the drum on the outside and 70 centimetres on the inside.
This foundation is itself surrounded on the outside by a ring
of opus reticulatum, which is thought by some to be earlier

FIG. 73. — THE PANTHEON.

than Hadrian's building and perhaps to have belonged to the
thermae of Agrippa.

The vestibule, 34 metres wide and 7.40 deep, is connected
with the rotunda, rests upon the same foundations, and was
built at the same time. In front, on each side of the entrance,
are semicircular niches, which formerly contained the statues
of Augustus and Agrippa. These niches are flanked with
Corinthian pilasters, and there are similar pilasters on the
east and west side walls of the vestibule, between which runs
a double frieze with reliefs of garlands and candelabra. The

threshold of the rotunda is an enormous slab of Porta santa marble ; but the bronze doors date from the sixteenth century. The exterior of the building is faced with small triangular bricks, with courses of *tegulae bipedales* at regular intervals, and is divided into three zones by cornices. In the central zone are sixteen sham windows. This whole surface of the drum and the vestibule was covered with marble and stucco, while that of the dome was covered with tiles of gilt bronze.

The portico or pronaos is rectangular, 34 metres wide and 13.60 deep, and has three rows of columns, eight in the front row and four in the second and third, making sixteen in all. These columns are of red and gray granite, 12.50 metres in height and 1.50 in diameter, and are surmounted by Corinthian capitals of white marble. Two of them now standing at the east end of the portico were taken from the thermae Alexandrinae and set up by Alexander VII in 1662, to replace two of the original columns which had been injured. These columns support an entablature and a triangular pediment, which was adorned with reliefs and statues. The inscriptions on the frieze and architrave have already been mentioned. The entablature is continued on both sides of the portico and vestibule as far as the wall of the drum, thus cutting the central zone of the latter directly in the middle. The pavement of the portico is composed of slabs of marble and granite. There is no connection between the portico and the main structure, but an open space 55 millimetres wide, and the foundations of the portico were built after those of the rotunda. It is therefore certain that the portico was built after the rest of the structure, but probably immediately afterward, for its construction seems to date from Hadrian's time, and we can hardly conceive of the rotunda and vestibule standing by themselves with no proper front. It is possible, however, that the façade of Hadrian's structure was entirely replaced by the existing portico at some time between Hadrian and Severus, old material being used in its construction.[1] The roof of the portico was supported by a system of trusses and was ornamented with gilding. The columns rest upon two sorts of foundation; those of the second and third rows upon parallel walls of concrete of Hadrian's time, and those of the front row on a travertine wall which belonged to an earlier rectangular structure, 43.76 metres wide and 19.82 deep, the short axis of which

FIG. 74. — THE INTERIOR OF THE PANTHEON.[2]

coincides with the north-south axis of the rotunda. This travertine wall, being longer than the width of the portico, projects beyond it on each side, and could have supported ten instead of eight columns. The side wall on the west can be traced, and is 19.82 metres long. These walls belonged to a travertine and peperino podium; and surrounding them, at an average distance of 1 metre, was a marble stylobate. The

[1] Cf. Durm, *Baukunst der Römer*, 2d ed., 557.

[2] The proportions of the building have been changed in this illustration, in order to show more of the interior.

space between the stylobate and the podium appears to have been filled with rubble. On the south side of this early building was a projection — evidently a pronaos — 21.26 metres wide, showing that the building was a temple fronting south, in form similar to the temple of Concord, much wider than deep, with a pronaos which did not extend across the entire front. The level of this travertine podium is about 2.50 metres below the present pavement of the portico.

Beneath the pavement of the rotunda, at a depth of 2.15 metres, there is an earlier pavement, consisting of a bed of rubble on which were laid slabs of marble, of which fragments of pavonazzetto and giallo antico have been found. This pavement extends everywhere under the rotunda, and originally covered a greater area, for it was cut off when the circular foundations of the drum were laid. It is highest in the middle and slopes away in all directions, a condition which is probably due to the great pressure of the walls of the drum. There are no traces of walls crossing this pavement, and therefore it is probable that it was the pavement of an open area, in front of the earlier structure which is beneath the portico. Traces of a third pavement have been found beneath that just described. The marble pavement has also been found under the portico, between the travertine podium and the present pavement.

The result of these discoveries is to show that the existing Pantheon is entirely the work of Hadrian, and that it was built over an earlier building, which is probably the Pantheon of Agrippa, restored by Domitian. The presence of the inscription recording Agrippa's building may be explained by the statement of Hadrian's biographer that that emperor never inscribed his own name on monuments which he restored, nor even on those which he himself erected, with but one exception.[1] The inscription may therefore be either the original one of

---

[1] *AJA*. 1905, 425-449.

Agrippa, preserved through the vicissitudes of one hundred and fifty years, or one cut by Hadrian.

The restoration by Severus was probably confined to a redecoration of the interior. Portions of this marble ornamentation existed until the eighteenth century, when the present system was substituted. The gilt tiles of the roof of the dome were carried off by Constans II, and the bronze trusses and roof of the portico were converted into cannon by the Barberini Pope, Urban VIII, in 1625.

In 609, Boniface IV brought to the Pantheon the bones of several hundred martyrs from the catacombs, and dedicated the temple as the church of S. Maria ad Martyres. In later times it has been known as S. Maria Rotonda, and has been made the burial-place of the kings of Italy.

In front of the Pantheon was an open space surrounded by the usual porticus, which extended north as far as the present via delle Copelle and via del Collegio, and on the east and west coincided with the line of the modern houses. Its columns were of gray granite, and its level somewhat below the present. Flights of five steps led from the portico of the Pantheon to the travertine pavement of this area. Some fragments of the pavement and columns have been discovered.

(19) Iseum et Serapeum. The great temple of Isis and Serapis stood between the Saepta and the temple of Minerva. We are told that the triumvirs voted in 43 B.C. to erect a temple to these divinities,[1] but it was probably[2] not built until the reign of Caligula, about 39 A.D. It was burned in 80 A.D.,[3] and afterward rebuilt by Domitian[4] on a magnificent scale. It was restored still later by Alexander Severus,[5] about the time when this cult reached the height of its popularity. The last restoration was under Diocletian.[6]

---

[1] Dio Cass. xlvii. 15.    [2] Wissowa, *Religion der Römer*, 292–296.

[3] Dio Cass. lxvi. 24; cf. Jos. *Bell. Iud.* vii. 5. 4.    [4] Eutrop. vii. 23.

[5] Lamprid. *Vit. Alex. Sev.* 26.    [6] *Chronogr. a. 354*, p. 148.

The recent rearrangement and study of the Marble Plan (p. 4) has shown that this structure was not one double temple, like that of Venus and Roma, but that it consisted of two distinct parts.[1] The Iseum was toward the north, and while it cannot be reconstructed with any certainty, it seems to have consisted of a long, narrow temple, standing at one end of an inclosure, also long and narrow. The porticus which made this inclosure seems to have resembled the forum Transitorium in form and architecture. It is not clear whether the entrance to this temple was on the north, or on the south toward the Serapeum. The two small obelisks,[2] now set up in the piazza dei Cinquecento and the piazza della Minerva, and probably that of the piazza della Rotonda, were found on the site of the Iseum, and may have stood in front of it. Within the porticus were statues of sphinxes and lions. The Serapeum is shown on the existing fragments of the Marble Plan. Its south end was formed by a large semicircular apse, about 60 metres in diameter, in the outer wall of which were several small exedrae. The inner side of this apse was adorned with columns, and a colonnade formed its diameter. Immediately north of this apse was a rectangular area, of the same width as the apse, and about 20 metres deep, with three entrances on its north side.

Within the temple and porticus were gathered together countless works of art, many of which have been recovered, among them the statues of the Tiber (Louvre), the Nile (Vatican), the Ocean (Naples), the lions[3] in the Vatican, the obelisks already mentioned and probably others. Parts of six of the columns of the Iseum have been found *in situ*, and of eight of the Serapeum.

---

[1] Lanciani, *L'Iseum et Serapeum della regione IX*, *BC*. 1883, 33–131; 1887, 377; Hülsen, *Porticus Divorum und Serapeum*, *Mitt.* 1903, 17–57, pl. I, II; Jordan, I. 3. 567–571.

[2] Marucchi, *Gli obelischi egiziani di Roma*, 2d ed., Rome, 1898.

[3] *BC*. 1890, 321–324; *Mitt.* 1891, 125.

(20) The temple of **Fortuna Redux**. This temple[1] was built by Domitian immediately after his triumphal entry into Rome in 93 A.D. It was probably near the porta Triumphalis, and is mentioned in the fourth century.

(21) The temple of the deified **Hadrian**, or **Hadrianeum**.[2] This temple, erected by Antoninus Pius, probably stood northeast of the Pantheon, and is probably to be identified with the ancient temple that is now incorporated in the Bourse (Fig. 75), and which has usually been called the basilica of Neptune (p. 378).

A part[3] of the northeast side is still standing and consists of eleven fluted columns of white marble with Corinthian capitals, and a richly decorated entablature. The columns are 15 metres in height and 1.44 in diameter. The cornice has been so badly restored as to appear now in three patterns. The wall of the cella behind the columns is of peperino, and the original marble lining has entirely disappeared. Cella and columns stand upon a lofty stylobate, which is now buried beneath the surface of the ground. This stylobate was adorned with reliefs,[4] those beneath the columns representing the provinces, and those in the intercolumnar spaces trophies of victory. In all, sixteen statues of provinces and six trophies are in existence, but they are scattered in five different collections in Rome and Naples.

An exact restoration of this building is perhaps impossible, but it is quite probable that the temple was octostyle, peripteral, with fifteen columns on a side. If we suppose that a wide flight of steps occupied the whole front of the stylobate, there would be space for thirty-six reliefs beneath the remain-

---

[1] Mart. viii. 65; Claud. *de Sext. Cons. Honorii*, 1; *PBS.* iii. 259–262. For a theory that this temple stood outside the porta Capena, see *BC.* 1908, 122–124.

[2] Jul. Cap. *Vit. Ant.* 8; *Vit. Veri*, 3; *Cur.* Reg. ix; *BC.* 1885, 92–93; Jordan, I. 3. 608–610; Lucas, *Zur Geschichte der Neptunsbasilica in Rom*, Berlin, 1904.

[3] *NS.* 1879, 68, 267, 314; 1880, 228; 1883, 81; *BC.* 1878, 10–27; 1883, 14–16; Strong, *Sculpture*, 243–246; 388–392.

[4] *Jahrb. d. Inst.* 1900, 1–42.

ing columns of the peristyle, and this is exactly the number of the provinces in the time of Hadrian. Other remains have been found, among them pieces of travertine pavement within the cella, and fragments of columns and cornice and a granite threshold 4 metres below the present floor level. This temple was inclosed by a rectangular porticus of which some ruins

FIG. 75. — THE HADRIANEUM.

have been found — namely, portions of a travertine pavement 4 metres below the present level of the soil, peperino blocks, a Corinthian column of yellow marble, and various architectural fragments.

With these temples may be counted the **ara Pacis Augustae.** After the return of Augustus from Spain and Gaul in 13 B.C., the Senate voted to erect an altar to the Pax Augusta,[1] on which

---

[1] *Mon. Anc.* ii. 37–41; Ov. *Fast.* i. 709.

the magistrates, priests, and Vestals should offer sacrifices once a year. This decree was dated July 4, 13 B.C., but the dedication did not take place until January 30, 9 B.C. The altar[1] stood on the via Flaminia, under the modern palazzo Fiano at the corner of the Corso and the via in Lucina, where many of its fragments have been found. These fragments are now scattered in various collections in Rome, Florence, and Paris. The altar stood within an inclosing wall of white marble, about 6 metres high, which formed a rectangle about 11.50 metres east and west, and about 10.50 metres north and south. In the middle of the east and west sides were entrances flanked with pilasters, and other pilasters stood at each angle of the inclosure. The inside of the inclosing wall was decorated with a frieze of garlands and ox-skulls above a maeander pattern, beneath which was a panelling of fluted marble. A frieze of flowers and palmettes adorned the outside of the inclosure, and above this on the north and south sides were reliefs representing the procession in honor of the goddess. On each side of the east entrance were sacrificial scenes, while that on the west was flanked by a relief of Tellus, and by what seems to have been an allegorical representation of the Senate.

The church of S. Niccoló ai Cesarini, just east of the porticus Pompeia, stands upon the foundations of a rectangular peripteral hexastyle temple of tufa. Parts of six columns of the front of the pronaos and of three of the left side, together with a part of the angle of the cella, are *in situ* beneath the church. In the garden of the same church, close to the south wall, are the remains of a circular peripteral temple,[2] with a concrete

---

[1] *Mitt.* 1894, 171–228; 1903, 164–176; *Ann. d. Ist.* 1881, 302–329; *Mon. d. Ist.* xi. pl. xxxiv–xxxvi; *NS.* 1899, 50–51; 1903, 549-574; *CR.* 1899, 234; 1904, 331; Petersen, *Ara Pacis Augustae*, Vienna, 1902; *Jahreshefte des oesterr. Arch. Instituts*, 1902, 153–164; 1903, 57–66; 1906, 298–315; Sieveking, *ibid.* 1907, 175–190; *Beiblatt*, 107; *Wiener Studien*, 1902, 425–436; Strong, *Sculpture*, 39–68; *Bollettino d'Arte*, 1907, 1–16; *PBS.* v. 176–178.

[2] *BC.* 1893, 191; Altmann, *Rundbauten*, 38–40.

podium and fluted columns of tufa. These columns, sixteen in number, were covered with stucco and stood on bases of travertine. Fragments of seven have been preserved.

Both these temples are represented on the Marble Plan [1] and in drawings of the end of the fifteenth century, but they cannot be identified with any certainty, although some [2] regard the round temple as that of Hercules Magnus Custos (see above, p. 347, No. 4).

Another result of the recent study of the Marble Plan has been the discovery that eleven of its fragments, eight of which are new, represent a large building between the Saepta Iulia and the baths of Agrippa.[3] This structure covered a considerable part of the area now occupied by the palazzi Venezia, Grazioli, and Altieri, and the church of the Gesù, and it was hitherto known to us only as Divorum, from its mention in the Regionary Catalogue [4] and Chronograph. A porticus Divorum is also said to have been built by Domitian.[5] It is now almost certain that Divorum is an abbreviation for templum Divorum, that is, aedes divi Vespasiani et aedes divi Titi, a temple erected by Domitian in memory of his father and brother, and that the porticus Divorum was the usual porticus attached to this double temple. The building is represented as a rectangle about 200 metres long and 55 wide, containing a grove and an altar, with something over thirty columns on the long sides and sixteen on one short side. The entrance, on the north, was formed by a triple arch; and just within this entrance, on either side, was a small tetrastyle shrine. It is entirely probable that one of these was the aedes divi Vespasiani and the other the aedes divi Titi.[6] In front of the entrance is a *lavacrum*, to which belonged the famous bronze cone (*pinea pigna*)

---

[1] Jordan, *FUR*. 110.  [2] Lanciani, *Ruins*, 457–458.

[3] *Berl. Phil. Wochenschrift*, 1903, 574–575; *Mitt*. 1903, 17–57, pl. I, II; Jordan, I. 3. 564–566.

[4] *Not*. Reg. ix; Gilbert, III, 133.  [5] Eutrop. vii. 23.

[6] *CIL*. vi. 10234, lines 8, 23.

of the Vatican that in the middle ages gave its name to that region of the city.

**Buildings for Theatrical Representations and Games.** — The circus Flaminius. As early as 221 B.C., C. Flaminius Nepos, while censor, erected in the south part of the campus Martius his famous circus,[1] which was for many years the most conspicuous building in this section of the city, and gave its name first to the immediate neighborhood and afterward to the whole ninth region. Its site is now entirely covered with modern houses, and no traces of the circus itself are visible; but its exact position is known from the descriptions of writers of the sixteenth century, at which time large portions of the first story were still standing. The length of the circus was about 297 metres, its width about 120,[2] and its main axis ran nearly east and west. It appears to have been built according to the plan adopted in later structures of a similar nature, and its lower story opened outward through a series of travertine arcades, between which were Doric half-columns. In this circus the *ludi plebeii*[3] and the *ludi Taurii*[4] were celebrated, and its proximity to the centre of the city made it a favorite place for holding assemblies of the people[5] and for markets.

**Amphitheatres.** The amphitheatre, or edifice consisting of concentric rows of rising seats which entirely inclose a central arena, seems to have been a purely Roman invention, adapted for shows of various kinds, but especially for gladiatorial combats and fights with wild beasts. The most conspicuous example of this class of buildings is the Colosseum, but there were at least two that were earlier in the campus Martius.

The first stone amphitheatre in Rome was built in 30 B.C.

---

[1] Liv. *Epit.* xx; Varro, *LL.* v. 154; Jordan, *FUR.* 27; *CIL.* vi. 9713; E. Caetani-Lovatelli, *Passegiate nella Roma Antica*, Rome, 1909, 108–128.

[2] Lanciani, *Ruins*, 454. Cf., however, Jordan, I. 3. 551.

[3] Val. Max. i. 7. 4.    [4] Fest. 351.

[5] Cic. *ad Att.* i. 14; *pro Sest.* 33; Dio. Cass. lv. 2.

by L. Statilius Taurus.[1] It belonged to the family of the builder, and seems to have been of small size.[2] It was burned[3] in the great fire of 64 A.D., but Nero immediately erected a wooden amphitheatre, perhaps on the site of that of Taurus.[4] No traces of either amphitheatre have been found, but the slight elevation in the campus Martius, called monte Giordano, is thought by some[5] to have been caused by the ruins of the building of Taurus (see also page 370).

Stadium Domitiani. The athletic contests of the Greeks were introduced into Rome in the last century of the republic, and Caesar and Augustus[6] erected temporary structures in which they might be held, but Nero[7] seems to have been the first to put up a permanent building. This Gymnasium, as it was called, which was attached to Nero's baths, was regarded as one of the most wonderful edifices in the city.[8] It was struck by lightning[9] and burned to the ground in 62 A.D., and there is no record of its restoration; but the stadium built by Domitian[10] probably occupied the same site. This stadium was probably restored by Alexander Severus,[11] and was known in the middle ages as the stadium Alexandrinum. It was spoken of in the fourth century[12] as one of the most beautiful buildings in Rome. Curiously enough, the modern piazza Navona, the longest in the city, preserves almost exactly the shape and size of the stadium of Domitian. The piazza corresponds with the arena of the stadium, the length of which seems to have been about 250 metres, and the surrounding

---

[1] Suet. *Aug.* 29; Dio Cass. li. 23.

[2] *CIL.* vi. 6226–6228; Dio Cass. lix. 10.     [3] Dio Cass. lxii. 18.

[4] Suet. *Nero*, 12; Tac. *Ann.* xiii. 31. See O'Connor, *Bulletin of the University of Wisconsin*, 1904, 176–178.

[5] Lanciani, *Ruins*, 369–371.     [6] Suet. *Caes.* 39; Dio Cass. liii. 1.

[7] Tac. *Ann.* xiv. 47. Hülsen (Jordan, I. 3. 590) regards this as merely a part of the baths of Nero (p. 388).

[8] Philost. *Vit. Apoll.* iv. 42.     [9] Tac. *Ann.* xv. 22.

[10] Suet. *Dom.* 5; Eutrop. vii. 23.     [11] Lamprid, *Vit. Alex. Sev.* 24.

[12] Amm. Marcell. xvi. 10. 14.

buildings stand on the ruins of the cavea. Under some of these buildings, especially the church of S. Agnese in the middle of the west side, brick and concrete walls and fragments of the travertine seats may still be seen.

The theatre of Pompeius. This, the first permanent theatre of Rome, was built by Cn. Pompeius in 55 B.C., and from its construction was frequently called theatrum lapideum or marmoreum.[1] The results of excavations at various periods, compared with the outlines of the theatre on the Marble Plan, enable us to determine its location with accuracy, just northwest of the circus Flaminius. Some remains of walls of travertine and opus reticulatum still exist beneath the modern houses. The façade of the semicircular cavea resembled that of the theatre of Marcellus, consisting of three series of arcades, adorned with half-columns, those of the lowest arcade being of the Doric order, the second of the Ionic, and the third of the Corinthian. The whole building was magnificently embellished with stucco and marble. It was always the most important[2] theatre in the city, as well as the largest, seating, according to the most careful estimate, about ten thousand spectators.[3] Even after the erection of all the wonderful structures of the empire, it was regarded in the fourth century as *inter decora urbis aeternae*.[4]

In order to avoid censure for having built a permanent theatre, Pompeius is said[5] to have erected a temple to Venus Victrix at the top of the central part of the cavea, so that the rows of seats might appear to be the steps leading up to the temple, and to have dedicated the whole as a temple and not as a theatre. From a notice in one of the calendars,[6] it appears that there were at least three other temples, dedi-

---

[1] Asc. *in Pis.* 1; Vell. ii. 48; Plut. *Pomp.* 52; Dio Cass. xxxix. 38; Vitr. iii. 3. 2; Gilbert, III. 322–327; Jordan, *FUR.* 30; Jordan, I. 3. 524–530.

[2] Tac. *Ann.* xiii. 54; Dio Cass. lxiii. 6; Pl. *NH.* xxxiii. 54.

[3] *BC.* 1894, 321; Pl. *NH.* xxxvi. 115.

[4] Amm. Marcell. xvi. 10. 14.      [5] Tertull. *de Spect.* 10; Gell. x. 1. 6–10.

[6] *Hemerol. Amitern.* Aug. 12; *CIL.* i². p. 324. Cf. also Suet. *Claud.* 21.

cated to Honor, Virtus, and Felicitas, similarly placed within the theatre.

Augustus [1] restored this theatre in 32 B.C.; and it was afterward frequently injured by fire, but always rebuilt, — by Tiberius, Caligula, and Claudius,[2] by Titus and Domitian,[3] by Septimius Severus,[4] by Diocletian perhaps,[5] and by Honorius and Arcadius.[6]

The theatre of Balbus. This theatre was built by L. Cornelius Balbus, a friend of Augustus, and dedicated in 13 B.C.[7] It was burned in 80 A.D., restored,[8] probably by Domitian, and is mentioned as existing in the fourth century. It was smaller than the theatre of Pompeius and held about eight thousand spectators.[9] The ruins of this theatre formed in the middle ages the slight elevation known as the monte dei Cenci, and some remains of walls are now hidden by the houses in the piazza dei Cenci. From data afforded by earlier excavations and by notes and drawings of the renaissance, it has been possible to fix the exact site of the theatre, and it is probable that its main axis ran about northwest-southeast.[10] Its exterior was like that of the theatres of Pompeius and Marcellus, being built of travertine with three series of arcades with engaged columns, Doric below, and Ionic and Corinthian on the second and third stories. It contained four columns of onyx, which excited the utmost wonder and admiration in Rome.[11]

The Crypta Balbi [12] was probably built by Balbus in 15 B.C., at the same time as his theatre. The name is best explained

---

[1] *Mon. Anc.* iv. 9.

[2] Tac. *Ann.* iii. 72; vi. 45; Suet. *Tib.* 47; *Cal.* 21; *Claud.* 21; Dio Cass. lx. 6.

[3] Dio Cass. lxvi. 24.

[4] *CIL.* viii. 1439.

[5] Vop. *Vit. Carin.* 19.

[6] *CIL.* vi. 1191; *Mitt.* 1899, 251–259.

[7] Suet. *Aug.* 29; Dio Cass. liv. 25.

[8] Dio Cass. lxvi. 24.

[9] *BC.* 1894, 320.

[10] Jordan, I. 3. 519–521.

[11] Pl. *NH.* xxxvi. 60.

[12] *Not.* Reg. ix; Jordan, I. 3. 521; II. 534; Gilbert, III. 329.

as a term used for a vaulted passage lighted from above.[1]  It
may have been a sort of ambulatory round the cavea of the
theatre.    Until recently the ruins described on p. 374 have been
identified with this Crypta, which was supposed to be a two-
storied porticus.

The theatre of Marcellus.  The building of this theatre was
planned by Julius Caesar, but carried out by Augustus, who
purchased the site from private owners at great expense.[2]
The temple of Pietas in the forum Holitorium and other
shrines and temples were removed to make room for the
new theatre, which was named after Marcellus, the adopted
son of Augustus, who died in 23 B.C., and dedicated in 13
B.C. (or, according to Pliny, in 11 B.C.).[3]   The stage portion
was restored by Vespasian,[4] and Alexander Severus is said to
have wished to restore the whole building;[5] but the destruction of the edifice must have begun as early as 370 A.D., for
some of its stone blocks were then taken out to be used in repairing the pons Cestius.[6]   From 1086, for nearly two centuries,
the structure was occupied by the Pierleoni family as a medieval stronghold.    In 1368 it came into possession of the
Savelli, and in 1712 into that of the Orsini.[7]  The present
palazzo Orsini stands upon the stage and a large part of the
cavea of the old theatre.

The theatre is near the Tiber, between it and the southwest
end of the Capitoline, the stage being toward the river, and
the main axis running north-northeast and south-southwest.
It was built of travertine for the most part, but the inside
was covered with stucco and marble.   This same method may

---

[1] Pauly-Wissowa, *Real-Encyclopädie,* iv. 1732; Jordan, I. 3. 521, 545.

[2] Dio Cass, xliii. 49; liii. 30; Suet. *Aug.* 29; *Mon. Anc.* iv. 22; Jordan,
*FUR.* 28; *EE.* viii. 233, 285.

[3] *NH.* viii. 65.                        [5] Lamprid. *Vit. Alex. Sev.* 44.

[4] Suet. *Vesp.* 19.                      [6] *NS.* 1886, 159.

[7] *BC.* 1901, 52–70 (*Le vicende del teatro.   Il teatro nei libri di topografia*) ;
E. Caetani-Lovatelli, *Passegiate nella Roma Antica,* Rome, 1909, 53–88.

have been employed on portions of the exterior also. Part of the masonry of the interior was of opus reticulatum. Just off the piazza Montanara, in the via del Teatro di Marcello, a considerable portion of the semicircular façade is still standing, and in spite of the disreputable surroundings it forms one of the most imposing ruins in Rome.

As in the Colosseum, the exterior of the cavea was built with three series of open arcades, one above another. The existing ruins comprise a little less than one-third of the total semi-circumference. The half-columns between the arches of the lower arcade are of the Doric order. Above them is a Doric entablature with triglyphs and an attic, 1.20 metres high, the projections of which form the bases of the half-columns of the second Ionic arcade. The entablature above these columns consists of an architrave of three projecting ledges, with a plain frieze and a cornice. The masonry above the second story is modern, but there was undoubtedly an original third story, decorated with Corinthian pilasters.

The original level of the ground was about 5 metres beneath that of the modern street, and about one-third of the lower arcade is therefore buried. There are thirteen piers of this lower arcade now standing, with their engaged columns. The piers themselves are 3 metres wide and 2 thick. Immediately within these piers was an ambulatory that ran entirely round the cavea, and from it spur walls were built on radial lines, which supported the tiers of seats. The construction of walls, seats, etc., as well as of the exterior, seems to have been quite like that of the Colosseum. The modern palace covers most of the inner portion of the theatre, but a considerable section of the ambulatories and chambers between the spur walls has recently been made accessible, and there the construction may be conveniently studied. Some parts of the stage lie beneath the houses in the via monte Savelli. From the statement of the *Curiosum*, it is estimated that this theatre contained seats for from ten to fourteen thousand persons, — more than the theatre of Pompeius, although that was a larger building, — but considerable doubt attaches to these estimates of seating capacity.[1]

Somewhere in region IX, Domitian erected a building for theatrical performances called the Odeum,[2] in imitation of similar buildings in Greece. This was the only building in the city which bore this name. It was restored by Trajan,[3] and ranked in the fourth century as one of the most conspicuous monuments of Rome. No trace of it has ever been discovered, but it may be under Monte Giordano (pp. 17, 365).

We may mention here the Athenaeum,[4] a building somewhat in the style of an amphitheatre, which was erected by Hadrian for readings, lectures, and similar purposes. It is not known definitely whether this building was in the campus Martius,[5] on the Capitoline, or in the Velabrum.[6]

**Porticoes.** — The level plain of the campus Martius was particularly well adapted to this characteristic form of Roman architecture, — the *porticus*, — which conformed to a general model, while varying in proportions and details. The porticus consisted of a covered colonnade, formed by two or more rows of columns, or a wall on one side and columns on the other. Its chief purpose was to provide a place for walking and lounging which should be sheltered from storm and sun, and for this reason the intercolumnar spaces were sometimes filled with glass or hedges of box. Within the porticoes or in apartments connected closely with them, were collections of statuary, paintings, and works of art of all kinds, as well as shops and bazaars. In some cases the porticus took its name

---

[1] *BC.* 1894, 320; Jordan, I. 3. 516.      [2] Suet. *Dom.* 5; Jordan, I. 3. 594.

[3] Dio Cass. lxix. 4; Amm. Marcell. xvi. 10. 14.

[4] Vict. *Caes.* 14; Jul. Cap. *Vit. Pertin.* 11; *Vit. Gord.* 3; Lamprid. *Vit. Alex. Sev.* 35; Sid. Apoll. ix. 11.

[5] Richter, *Top.*[2] 249.

[6] Jordan, I. 2. 61; Gilbert, III. 337; O'Connor, *Bulletin of the University of Wisconsin*, 1904, 170, 170–178.

from some famous statue or painting, as the porticus Argonautarum (p. 376).

While the erection of the first porticus in the campus Martius dates from the early part of the second century B.C., the period of rapid development in their numbers and use did not begin until the Augustan era. The earliest of these structures seem to have been devoted exclusively to business purposes. By the time of the Antonines, there were upwards of a dozen in region IX,[1] some of them of great size, and it was possible to walk from the forum of Trajan to the pons Aelius under a continuous shelter. They were usually magnificently decorated and embellished, and provided with beautiful gardens. Lanciani[2] estimates the total area covered by porticoes and gardens in the campus Martius at about 100,000 square metres. The modern continuation of the porticus idea may be seen in some European cities, especially Bologna, Munich, and in the Rue de Rivoli in Paris.

Within the limits of region IX there were the following porticoes : —

(1) The porticus Octavia, built by Cn. Octavius in 168 B.C., to commemorate a naval victory over Perseus of Macedonia.[3] It was also called the porticus Corinthia, from its bronze Corinthian capitals, which may have been the first instance of the use of this order in Rome. Augustus restored[4] this porticus in 33 B.C. and placed within it the standards which he had taken from the Dalmatians. It stood between the theatre of Pompeius and the circus Flaminius.

(2) The porticus Metelli, built in 147 B.C. by Q. Caecilius Metellus Macedonicus,[5] and situated between the circus Flaminius and the theatre of Marcellus. It inclosed the temples of Iuppiter Stator and Juno (p. 349) and contained many famous works of art brought by Metellus from the east.

---

[1] *Ann. d. Ist.* 1883, 5–22.   [2] *Ruins*, 448.   [3] Fest. 178; Pl. *NH.* xxxiv. 13.

[4] *Mon. Anc.* iv. 3; Dio Cass. xlix. 43; Appian, *Illyr.* 28.

[5] Vell. i. 11; ii. 1.

Some time after 27 B.C.[1] Augustus removed this porticus and erected in its place the porticus Octaviae,[2] at the same time restoring the inclosed temples.

The porticus Octaviae was burned[3] in 80 A.D. and restored, probably by Domitian, and again, after a second fire, by Severus and Caracalla in 203 A.D.[4] It inclosed a rectangular area

FIG. 76. — THE PORTICUS OCTAVIAE RESTORED.

135 metres long and 115 wide, and is represented on the Marble Plan. It consisted of a colonnade formed by a double row of granite columns, twenty-eight in each row in front and about forty on each side. The main axis ran northeast-southwest, and the principal entrance was in the middle of the southwest side. At the four corners of the porticus were small vaulted pavilions. Within the inclosure was a bibliotheca,[5] erected by

[1] Vitr. iii. 2. 5.                [2] Suet. *Aug.* 29; Jordan, I. 3. 541–544.
[3] Dio Cass. lxvi. 24.           [4] *CIL.* vi. 1034; Jordan, *FUR.* 33.
[5] Plut. *Marc.* 30; Suet. *de Gramm.* 21; *CIL.* vi. 2347–2349, 4431–4433, 4435.

Octavia in memory of the youthful Marcellus, a curia Octaviae,[1] where the Senate sometimes met, and a so-called schola;[2] but it is uncertain whether these different names were applied to the same building, to different parts of the same building, or to entirely distinct structures.

Of this porticus some ruins[3] still remain, especially of the main entrance, which had the form of a double pronaos, projecting outward and inward. Across each front of this pronaos, between the side walls, were four Corinthian columns of white marble, which supported an entablature and a triangular pediment. The entablature and pediment and two of the columns of the outer front still exist, but the remaining columns were replaced in the fifth century by a brick arch. Of the inner front two columns and part of a third are standing, with portions of entablature and pediment. On the architrave is the inscription which records the restoration in 203 A.D. The height of the shaft of the columns of the pronaos is 8.60 metres, and their diameter at the bottom 1.10, and at the top 0.96 metre. Parts of a number of the columns of the south colonnade are also standing, but their bases are below the present level of the ground. Some of the capitals of these columns are built into the walls of houses in the via del Teatro di Marcello.

(3) The porticus Minucia, built by M. Minucius Rufus[4] (cos. 110 B.C.). This porticus was double, and seems to have consisted of two parts; for, at a later period, we are told that there were two buildings, — the porticus Minucia vetus and the porticus Minucia frumentaria.[5] In the latter, under the empire, the distribution of grain tickets to the proletariat took place; while the former was a place for lounging and for political assemblies. The relation between the porticus vetus and the porticus

[1] Pl. *NH.* xxxvi. 28; Dio Cass. lv. 8.

[2] Pl. *NH.* xxxv. 114; xxxvi. 22, 29.

[3] *Bull. d. Ist.* 1878, 209–219; *BC.* 1887, 332; 1890, 66–67; *Mitt.* 1889, 264–265.

[4] Vell. ii. 8.    [5] *Not.* Reg. ix; *Chronogr. a. 354*, p. 146.

frumentaria has never been satisfactorily explained,[1] as it is
expressly stated that they were both built by the same man
at the same time.   In the second century the porticus seems
to have served as one of the offices of the water works of
the city, as we read of *curatores aquarum et Miniciae.*[2]   Between the piazza Montanara and the vicolo della Bufala
are some remains of a colonnade that has been identified
with the porticus Minucia.[3]   Hülsen,[4] however, rejects this
view, and thinks that the remains hitherto universally regarded
as belonging to the Crypta Balbi (p. 367) are not parts of
that structure at all, and may very probably belong to the
porticus Minucia.   Two travertine pilasters, with engaged
columns and the entablature, are built into the front of
a house in the via dei Calderari, No. 23, and there are traces
of a second row of columns and a wall behind.   In the
sixteenth century much more of this building was standing, and drawings of that period show that the colonnade
had an upper story, with columns standing on the centre
of the arches below.   Blocks of the travertine pavement
have also been found.[5]

(4) The porticus Pompei,[6] built in 55 B.C. by Pompeius,[6] at the
same time as his theatre.   The porticus adjoined the *scena* of
the theatre[7] and inclosed a large rectangular court in which
were four parallel rows of columns, its purpose being to provide shelter for the spectators in case of sudden showers.
The same provision was made in the case of the theatre of
Marcellus, but no trace of that porticus has been found.   The

---

[1] *Phil.* 1870, 63–67; Hirschfeld, *Römische Verwaltungsgeschichte,* i. 134,
166; Gilbert, III. 144, 286; *BC.* 1901, 182–183.

[2] *CIL.* v. 7783; vi. 1532; Mommsen, *Staatsrecht,* ii[3]. 1053–1054.

[3] Lanciani, *FUR.* sheet 28; Delbrück, *Die drei Tempel am Forum Holitorium,* Rome, 1903, 1.

[4] Jordan, I. 3, 515, 545–547.

[5] *NS.* 1891, 336; 1892, 265; *Mitt.* 1892, 321; 1893, 318.

[6] Cic. *de Fato,* 8; Ov. *Ars Am.* iii. 387; Catull. lv. 6; Gilbert, III. 325–326.

[7] Vitr. v. 9. 1.

porticus Pompei must have suffered in the conflagrations which destroyed the theatre, and have been restored by Domitian, and by Arcadius and Honorius [1] in 418–420 A.D. After a fire in the reign of Carinus, it was restored by the prefect of the city, Aulus Helvius Dionysius, who called one part of the restored structure **porticus Iovia** [2] and the other **porticus Herculea,** in honor of the emperors Diocletian and Maximian. The central area was laid out as a garden with shady walks, and contained many works of art.[3] The curia Pompei,[4] in which Caesar was murdered, was probably an exedra in this porticus, or possibly an adjoining building.[5] The statue of Pompeius which stood there was removed by Augustus,[6] who walled up the curia as a *locus sceleratus.* In connection with this porticus was one built by Augustus, and called the **porticus ad Nationes,**[7] because it contained statues representing all the nations of the earth. It is possible, however, that this was not a separate porticus, but only a portion added to the porticus Pompei. No remains of the latter exist above ground, but its lines are known from earlier discoveries, and some fragments have been found in recent years.[8]

(5) The **Hecatostylon.** Very near to the porticus Pompei was a similar structure, called the Hecatostylon, or porticus of the hundred columns. This is not mentioned until the end of the first century,[9] but it may have been built by Pompeius. It is represented on the Marble Plan as a row of columns on each side of a long wall, on the north side of the porticus Pompei. It is therefore very doubtful whether the long piece of peperino wall and travertine pavement, which has been found between

---

[1] *CIL.* vi. 1191, 1676.

[2] *Chronogr. a. 354,* p. 148; *CIL.* vi. 255, 256; *Ann. d. Ist.* 1883, 11–12.

[3] Mart. ii. 14. 10; Pl. *NH.* xxxv. 59, 114, 126, 132.

[4] Cic. *de Div.* ii. 23; Asc. *in Mil.* 67; Gell. xiv. 7, and often.

[5] *Mélanges,* 1908, 225–228.     [6] Suet. *Caes.* 88; *Aug.* 31.

[7] Serv. *in Aen.* viii. 721; Pl. *NH.* xxxvi. 41; Suet. *Nero,* 46.

[8] *BC.* 1892, 146–148; *NS.* 1892, 348.

[9] Mart. ii. 14. 9; iii. 19. 1; Gilbert, III. 327; Jordan, I. 3. 533; *FUR.* 31.

the piazza del Gesù and the via dell' Arco dei Ginnasi, can belong to the Hecatostylon.[1]

(6) The porticus Philippi, built as the peribolus of the temple of Hercules and the Muses (p. 348), by L. Marcius Philippus, the stepfather of Augustus, at the same time that he rebuilt the temple. The exact date is not known. This porticus is represented on the Marble Plan, and is mentioned in the fourth century. It contained some famous pictures, and hair-dressers' shops.[2] A few of its ruins have been found in the piazza Mattei.[3]

(7) The porticus Argonautarum, built by Agrippa in 25 B.C. probably north of the Saepta. The name was given to the porticus because the adventures of the Argonauts were painted on its walls,[4] and it has sometimes been identified[5] with the basilica Neptuni (p. 378).

(8) The porticus Europae, situated near the Saepta, of which the exact location and date of building are unknown. Its name was derived from a famous painting of Europa on its wall.[6] In Martial's time this was one of the most popular lounging places in Rome.

In the fourth century a porticus Meleagri[7] is mentioned, but it is uncertain whether this was a separate porticus or only a part of the Saepta, so named from a statue or painting.

(9) The porticus Boni Eventus, either constructed or restored in 374 A.D. round the temple of Bonus Eventus,[8] probably just west of the thermae Agrippae. The date of this temple is un-

---

[1] NS. 1884, 103–104; BC. 1893, 122, 189–193.

[2] Pl. NH. xxxv. 66, 114, 144; Ov. Ars Am. iii. 168.

[3] Ann. d. Ist. 1869, 3–12; BC. 1890, 67; Mon. d. Lincei, i. 506; Jordan, FUR. 33.

[4] Dio Cass. liii. 27; BC. 1883, 14, 16.     [5] Jordan, I. 3. 574–575.

[6] Mart. ii. 14. 3, 5, 15; iii. 20. 12; vii. 32. 11; xi. 1. 11; Hülsen (Jordan, I. 3. 458) regards this as only another name for the porticus Vipsania (p. 477).

[7] Not. Reg. ix.

[8] Amm. Marcell. xxix. 6. 19; BC. 1878, 212–213; 1891, 224–227; Archivio della R. Società romana di storia patria, ix. 471.

known, but it may have formed a part of Agrippa's buildings, and some remains of an ancient peperino wall, evidently of a temple, found on the site of the church of S. Maria in Monterone, have been thought to belong to it. At different times since the sixteenth century, five capitals of white marble of great size, 1.70 metres in height and 1.44 in width, have been found in an almost straight line 100 metres in length, between the church of S. Maria in Monterone and the Teatro della Valle. These capitals were lying at an equal depth beneath the surface of the ground, and undoubtedly belonged to the porticus.

(10) The porticus Maximae. One of the most important streets in region IX was that which led from the neighborhood of the theatre of Balbus to the pons Aelius. During the reign of Gratian, Valentinian, and Theodosius, about 380 A.D., this street was provided with a colonnade, the porticus Maximae,[1] which extended from the Aelian bridge to the theatre of Pompeius and connected several of the other porticoes in this region. Its ruins have been found in the piazza del Pianto and the via della Reginella, — fragments of granite columns with Corinthian capitals, and bases, 3.10 metres below the present level of the ground. The pavement of the street has also been found at various points, and its line is followed closely by the modern vie di Pescheria, del Pianto, de' Giubbonari, de' Cappellari, and del Banco di S. Spirito.

Several times in classical literature a via Tecta is mentioned,[2] which seems to have connected the region of the circus Flaminius with the Tarentum. This direction corresponds with that of the street just described, and it may be that this street was protected in some way long before the porticus Maximae were built, and was therefore called the via Tecta. The street described on p. 339, called via Recta on Lanciani's map, is sometimes identified with the via Tecta.

---

[1] *CIL*. vi. 1184; *BC*. 1890, 67–68; *Ann. d. Ist*. 1883, 7, 20 ff.

[2] Mart. iii. 5. 5; viii. 75. 2; Seneca, *de Morte Claudii*, 13; Jordan, **I. 3.** 485, 503; II. 378; Gilbert, III. 378.

(11) The *porticus Divorum* (divi Vespasiani et Titi ?).   See p. 363.

**Basilicas.** — The basilica Neptuni, which was restored by Hadrian,[1] was probably the Ποσειδώνιον[2] that was burned in 80 A.D., and it has also been identified with the porticus Argonautarum (p. 376) of Agrippa.[3] This identification is plausible but by no means certain, as both porticus Argonautarum and basilica Neptuni occur in the *Curiosum*.

Basilica Matidiae, basilica Marcianae.   These two basilicas were between the Pantheon, the north end of the Saepta, and the column of Aurelius.   One of them was named from Matidia, the mother-in-law of Hadrian, and the other from Marciana, the sister of Trajan.[4] They probably formed one group with the temple of Hadrian (p. 360).   Some cipollino columns that have been found just north of the via dei Pastini, between the Pantheon and the vicolo della Spada d' Orlando, perhaps belong to one of them.   A **templum divae Matidiae**[5] seems to have stood in the immediate vicinity.

**Arches.** — Arcus Tiberii, arcus Domitiani.   In the campus Martius were many so-called triumphal arches.   Claudius erected one in honor of Tiberius near the theatre of Pompeius, which is mentioned only once,[6] and Domitian another, which was either near the porta Triumphalis or was a restoration of this gate itself (p. 346).

Arcus Pietatis.   On the north side of the Pantheon, probably in the line of the inclosing porticus, was an arch adorned with reliefs that represented the provinces, personified, in the act

---

[1] Spart. *Vit. Hadr.* 19.          [2] Dio Cass. lxvi. 24.

[3] Dio Cass. liii. 27; Jordan, I. 3. 574; Lucas, *Zur Geschichte der Neptunsbasilica in Rom*, Berlin, 1904.

[4] *Not.* Reg. ix; Pol. Silv. 545; *BC.* 1883, 5–16; *Mitt.* 1899, 141–153; Gilbert, III. 127; Jordan, I. 3. 575.

[5] Jordan, I. 3. xxiv.          [6] Suet. *Claud.* 11.

of asking favor of the emperor. This arch was called arcus Pietatis in the middle ages, but its original name is unknown.[1]

**Arcus Gratiani Valentiniani et Theodosii.** This arch[2] stood directly in front of the pons Aelius, spanned the principal street of region IX which led to this bridge from the circus Flaminius, and formed the north end of the porticus Maximae (p. 377). It was quite customary to erect such an arch at the approach to a bridge. This arch was built between 379 and 383 A.D., and seems to have stood until the fourteenth century.

**Arcus Arcadii Honorii et Theodosii.** This arch was erected in 405 A.D. to commemorate the victories[3] won by Stilicho under Arcadius, Honorius, and Theodosius. It was certainly near the arch just mentioned, and probably spanned the approach to the pons Neronianus. (For the arches on the via Lata, see p. 479.)

**Columns.** — There were two columns like that of Trajan in region IX. The first, **columna Antonini Pii**, was erected in memory of Antoninus Pius by his two adopted sons, Marcus Aurelius and Lucius Verus. It stood[4] a little west of the present House of Parliament, on the edge of the slight elevation known as monte Citorio (p. 17). It had the same orientation as the Ustrinum, from which it was separated by a distance of 25 metres. The column was a monolith of red granite, 14.75 metres high, and stood on a pedestal of white marble. As represented on a coin[5] of Antoninus, it was surrounded by a grating. Previous to the eighteenth century the base of the column was entirely buried, but the lower part of the shaft itself projected about 6 metres above the ground. In 1703 the base was excavated, but the shaft lay in the piazza Colonna for many years, until it was used to repair the obelisk in the piazza di monte Citorio. Three of the sides of the pedestal, now in the Vatican gardens, are covered with reliefs.[6] The

---

[1] Jordan, 1. 3. 590.     [2] *CIL.* vi. 1184; Jordan, I. 3. 598; II. 413.
[3] *CIL.* vi. 1196; Jordan, II. 413; Richter, *Top.*[2] 257.
[4] *Mitt.* 1889, 41–48; Jordan, I. 3. 603.     [5] Cohen, *Ant. Pius,* 353.
[6] Strong, *Sculpture,* 270–273.

principal one, representing the apotheosis of Antoninus and Faustina, was turned toward the Ustrinum. The other two represent soldiers on the march. The fourth side bears the dedicatory inscription.[1]

In close connection with the column was the **Ustrinum Antoninorum**, or crematory of the Antonines. There is no mention of this building in ancient literature; but the excavations of 1703 brought enough of its ruins to light to afford a satisfactory idea of its character.[2] It consisted of three square inclosures, one within another. The two inner inclosure walls were of travertine; the outer consisted of a travertine curb, on which stood pillars of the same material with an iron grating between them. The innermost inclosure, which formed the base of the pyre, was 13 metres square, the second inclosure 23, and the outer 30 metres square. A free space, 3 metres wide, was left between the first and second walls and between the second and third. The entrance was on the south. Remains,[3] which are probably of a similar *ustrinum*, have recently been found a little to the northeast in the via delle Missione.

The other column, **columna M. Aurelii Antonini**, which was also called *columna cochlis* and *columna centenaria divi Marci*, or *divorum Marci et Faustinae*, stood on the west side of the via Lata, opposite the campus Agrippae, and was erected sometime before 193 A.D. to commemorate the victories of Marcus Aurelius over the Dacians and Marcomanni in 172–175 A.D.[4]

It is a direct imitation of the column of Trajan, the height of shaft and capital being the same, 100 Roman feet. The shaft itself, 26.50 metres in height and 3.96 in diameter, is composed of twenty-six rings of Luna marble. It is hollow,

---

[1] *CIL*. vi. 1004. 　　　　　[2] *Mitt.* 1889, 48–64.

[3] *NS.* 1907, 525–528; 1909, 10–11; *CQ.* 1908, 148; *BC.* 1907, 326–329; 1908, 86; 1909, 113.

[4] Vict. *Caes.* 16; *Epit.* 16; *Not.* Reg. ix; Petersen, von Domaszewski, Calderini, *Die Marcussäule auf Piazza Colonna in Rom*, Munich, 1896; Jordan, I. 3. 605–607; Strong, *Sculpture*, 273–291; *Arch. Anz.* 1896, 2–18; *PBS.* v. 181

and contains a spiral staircase of two hundred and three steps. The interior is lighted by fifty-six rectangular loopholes. The capital is of the Doric order, and was surmounted originally by statues of Marcus Aurelius and Faustina. These disappeared at some unknown date, and the present bronze statue of St. Paul was erected by Sixtus V. The pedestal of the column is of great height, for a considerable part of it still rises above the present level of the ground, which in turn is 4.75 metres above the ancient travertine pavement.

The exterior of the column is adorned with reliefs, arranged on a spiral band which returns upon itself twenty-one times. These reliefs represent scenes in the campaigns of Aurelius and correspond to those on the column of Trajan, but are far inferior to them in execution, and have been much injured by fire and earthquake. The remains of the original reliefs of the pedestal were chiselled off by Sixtus V, who added the present marble decoration, some of which was taken from the Septizonium.

It is probable that the temple of Aurelius, templum divi Marci, stood just west of this column, in the same relation to it as the temple of Trajan to his column, and that temple and column were surrounded by a porticus; but no traces of this temple have been found. Near the column was a lodge, built in 193 A.D. by Adrastus, *procurator columnae centenariae divi Marci*, at the expense of the government. The inscription [1] which records this transaction has been preserved.

**The Obeliscus Augusti.** — Augustus brought two obelisks [2] from Heliopolis to Rome, one of which was set up in the Circus Maximus and the other in the campus Martius, between the ara Pacis Augustae and the columna Antonini Pii. The latter is the one now standing in the piazza di monte Citorio. The

---

[1] *CIL*. vi. 1585 a, b.

[2] Amm. Marcell. xvii. 4. 12–23; Jordan, II. 181–184; Marucchi, *Gli obelischi egiziani di Roma*, 2d ed., Rome, 1898.

inscriptions [1] on the pedestals of the two obelisks are identical, and show that they were set up in the year 10 B.C.

The obelisk of the campus Martius is of red granite, 21.79 metres in height and covered with hieroglyphics. The travertine base has been much restored, and the column itself repaired with fragments of stone from the columna Antonini.

Augustus employed this obelisk as the *gnomon*, or needle, of a great sun-dial, or solarium,[2] formed by laying an extensive pavement of white marble on the north side of the obelisk, on which pavement the lines were indicated by strips of gilt metal inlaid in the marble. Portions of this pavement, of the gilt lines, and of figures of animals representing the signs of the Zodiac, were found at various times in the fifteenth and sixteenth centuries, but they were again covered and are still buried beneath the modern buildings. The obelisk itself was thrown down at some unknown date, and although it was discovered under the ground in 1512,[3] it was not excavated until 1750, nor set up until 1789. The marble pavement must have extended about 110 metres in an east and west direction, and something more than half that distance north and south.

**The Mausoleum Augusti**. — During the first century B.C.[4] it had become customary to grant the privilege of burial in the campus Martius to persons of distinction, by special decree of the senate. With this precedent in view, Augustus erected in 28 B.C., in the most northerly part of the campus, a mausoleum for the imperial family, the remains of which still exist.[5] This mausoleum, called also the tumulus Caesarum, or tumulus Iuliorum,[6] consisted of a circular drum, and above this a tumulus or cone-shaped mound, planted with evergreens and surmounted

---

[1] *CIL*. vi. 701–702.        [2] Pl. *NH*. xxxvi. 72.        [3] *PBS*. ii. 3.

[4] Richter, *Top*.[2] 249–250; Gilbert, III. 305–307.

[5] Strabo, v. 3. 8 (236); Suet. *Aug*. 100; Jordan, I. 3. 614–621; II. 435–436; Altmann, *Rundbauten*, 46–49; Sabatini, *Il Mausoleo di Augusto*, Rome, 1907.

[6] Tac. *Ann*. iii. 9; xvi. 6.

by a colossal bronze statue of Augustus. The circular portion, 66.55 metres in diameter, was composed of concentric ring-walls of concrete, faced with opus reticulatum and covered with stucco or white marble. The entrance was on the south, and the passageway led directly to a central chamber, which was the tomb of Augustus himself. Between the outer and the second wall was a row of twelve chambers, designed for other members of the imperial family.[1] On the outer wall of the mausoleum, on each side of the entrance, were fastened the two bronze tablets[2] on which were inscribed the *Res Gestae* (p. 2), and in front was a portico flanked by two obelisks.[3] One of these obelisks was dug up in 1527, and in 1587 it was set up in the piazza dell' Esquilino. The other was found in 1781 and erected in the piazza del Quirinale. The latter is 14.40 metres in height, the former somewhat less.

In this mausoleum[4] were placed the ashes of Augustus, his nephew Marcellus, Lucius and Gaius Caesar, Germanicus, Livia, Tiberius, Claudius, and some other members of the family. The remains of Vespasian, Titus, and the latter's daughter Julia, which were placed here first, were afterward removed to the temple of the gens Flavia (p. 504) on the Quirinal.

In 410 Alaric plundered the mausoleum, and in the middle ages it was used as a fortress by the Colonna. In the sixteenth century the Soderini converted it into a sort of terrace garden. The outer wall of the drum, about 72 metres in diameter, now forms part of a concert hall, and the rest of the structure has been almost entirely transformed or built over.[5] Whether this drum stood on a square foundation, like that of the mausoleum of Hadrian, is uncertain.

---

[1] *BC.* 1882, 152–154; 1885, 89; 1895, 301–308.

[2] Suet. *Aug.* 101.      [3] Amm. Marcell. xvii. 4. 16.

[4] Cf. Richter, *Top.*[2] 250–251, and Hirschfeld, *Die Kaiserlichen Grabstätten in Rom, Abhandlungen der kaiserl. Akad. zu Berlin*, 1886, 1149 ff., for classical references. Inscriptions, *CIL.* vi. 884–895.

[5] *BC.* 1895, 301–308.

**The Saepta Iulia.** — We are told [1] that Julius Caesar planned to replace the existing Saepta (p. 345) by a marble structure inclosed by a porticus one mile in extent. This work, which Caesar only began, was continued by Lepidus and finished by Agrippa in 26 B.C. [2] It is probable, however, that the building, as completed, was not built exactly on the lines laid down by Caesar, for a part at least of the area had been taken up by the thermae of Agrippa. The new Saepta was injured by fire in 80 A.D., restored by Domitian, and afterward by Hadrian. [3]

The diminishing importance of the comitia, and the final transfer of elections from the people to the senate during the reign of Tiberius, must have brought about great changes in the use, and perhaps in the form, of the restored Saepta. Agrippa adorned it with statues; Caligula and Claudius exhibited gladiatorial shows in the building; [4] and the former also constructed a naumachia [5] within its precincts. In Domitian's time it contained a bazaar, where the most expensive luxuries in Rome were for sale. [6] It is mentioned at the beginning of the third century, [7] but of its later history nothing is known.

The Saepta is partly represented on the Marble Plan, [8] and from this and the remains which have been discovered, a reconstruction of the building in its main lines is possible. It was a rectangular porticus, [9] extending along the west side of the via Flaminia, from the aqua Virgo on the north to the modern via di S. Marco on the south, a distance of 440 metres (1500 Roman feet). Its depth was 60 metres. This porticus was built of travertine and was septuple in form, — that is, there

---

[1] Cic. *ad Att.* iv. 16. 14.

[2] Dio Cass. liii. 23.

[3] Dio Cass. lxvi. 24; Spart. *Vit. Hadr.* 19.

[4] Suet. *Cal.* 18; *Claud.* 21.

[5] Dio Cass. lix. 10.

[6] Mart. ii. 14. 5; ix. 59; x. 80.

[7] Lamprid. *Vit. Alex. Sev.* 26.

[8] Jordan, *FUR.* 34–36.

[9] *BC.* 1893, 119–142: Gilbert, III. 174–176; *Mon. d. Lincei*, i. 471–473; Jordan, I. 3. 558–562.

were eight longitudinal rows of columns and piers. The first row along the via Flaminia was ornamented with a balustrade. Remains of this porticus have been found at various points, especially beneath S. Maria in via Lata, the palazzo Doria, and the palazzo Bonaparte, the most southerly traces being beneath the palazzo Venezia and S. Marco. Whether the porticus extended as far south as the via di S. Marco is disputed, Lanciani asserting that its limit in this direction is marked by the pavement of an ancient street found just south of the remains which are beneath the church of S. Marco. If the porticus extended as far as the via di S. Marco, there was room for eighty latitudinal aisles between the short rows of columns, a number which suggests the eighty centuries of the first class of the comitia centuriata.

It is evident from the Marble Plan that this porticus constituted the Saepta in the third century; but whether it is the porticus which Lepidus built, or whether it represents in any considerable degree the original Saepta of Agrippa, is an open question. Manifestly no naumachia could be

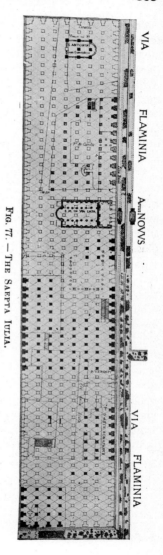

FIG. 77. — THE SAEPTA IULIA.

constructed within this porticus, nor could gladiatorial shows
have been exhibited here.   We must, therefore, assume that
west of it was an open area belonging to the Saepta, which
may or may not have been inclosed, but which after the fire in
80 A.D. was used for entirely different purposes.   Even remains
of private houses have been found within its limits under the
church of S. Ignazio.

**The Diribitorium**. — Agrippa also began the erection of a
building in which the votes cast by the people in the Saepta
could be counted (*diribere* = *dis-habere*), and which was therefore called the Diribitorium.   This building was finished by
Augustus in 7 B.C., and was famous for the construction of
the roof of its central hall, which rested on beams more than 100
feet long, without pillars or supports of any kind.[1]   For many
years it was the widest roof of this sort in Rome, but it fell during Caligula's reign and could not be restored in the same form.
In 80 A.D. the Diribitorium was burned, but it must have
been rebuilt, for it is mentioned as existing in the third
century.

It has usually been supposed that while the exact location
of the Diribitorium was unknown, it was a separate building[2]
near the Saepta; but there is much to be said in support of a
recent theory, according to which Diribitorium was the name
applied to the second story of the Saepta.[3]

**Thermae**. — The first of the thermae, or great public baths of
Rome, were the thermae Agrippae, built by Agrippa[4] in 25 B.C.,
at the same time with the Pantheon; but as the aqua Virgo
which supplied these baths with water was not completed until 19 B.C., the baths themselves can hardly have been opened
before that date.   Agrippa seems to have called these thermae

---

[1] Dio Cass. lv. 8; lix. 7; Pl. *NH.* xxxvi. 102; xvi. 201.

[2] Dio Cass. lxvi. 24; Suet. *Claud.* 18.

[3] *BC.* 1893, 119–141; Jordan, I. 3. 562–564.     [4] Dio Cass. liii. 27; liv. 29.

by the name Laconicum (sc. *balineum*), and he adorned the structure with many works of art.[1] They were burned in 80 A.D., and restored[2] either by Titus or Domitian, and afterward by Hadrian[3] between 115 and 125. A later restoration was carried out by Constans and Constantius[4] in 344–345 A.D.

From a fragment of the Marble Plan recently found, the excavations[5] of recent years, and the drawings and notes of architects of the sixteenth century, when much of the building was still standing, it seems clear that the main part of the original thermae of Agrippa occupied a rectangular area, from 100 to 120 metres north and south and from 80 to 100 east and west. Just north of the centre of the building was a circular hall, about 25 metres in diameter, part of the roof of which, called the Arco della Ciambella, is standing and may be seen above the houses in the street of the same name. This original structure was then extended toward the north, possibly by Agrippa himself, and a series of halls built that reached the Pantheon. Of these halls the only one still visible is that directly adjoining the Pantheon, rectangular in shape, 45 metres long and 19 wide, with an apse 9 metres in diameter in the north wall. Along each of the longer sides stood four columns of pavonazzetto and red granite. Between the first and second and the third and fourth columns on each side were three niches, two rectangular and one semicircular. Round the hall ran a remarkably well executed frieze. Fragments of this and also of the marbles with which the hall was lined are still *in situ.* The hall was paved with slabs of marble, especially pavonazzetto and nero Africano. The walls are only 1.75 metres in thickness, and hence it is probable that the hall

[1] Pl. *NH.* xxxiv. 62; xxxv. 26; xxxvi. 189.

[2] Dio Cass. lxvi. 24; Mart. iii. 20. 15.

[3] Spart. *Vit. Hadr.* 19.     [4] *CIL.* vi. 1165.

[5] *NS.* 1881, 276–281; 1882, 347–359; 1900, 633; *BC.* 1901, 3–19; *Mitt.* 1905, 75; Jordan, I. 3. 576–580; Rivoira, *Lombardic Architecture*, I. 66; and especially Hülsen, *Die Thermen des Agrippa*, Rome, 1910.

had only a wooden roof or none at all.   The cross-walls
which have been found between the drum of the Pantheon
and the north wall of this hall date from Hadrian's time, and
as they are not connected with either structure, but simply
abut against them, it is clear that they were intended to serve
as buttresses, perhaps in order that a heavy roof might then
be put over the hall.

Adjoining the thermae, Agrippa constructed a stagnum,[1] or
artificial pool, of considerable size, which probably extended
west from the thermae as far as the present palazzo Capranica.
This stagnum was bordered by the horti Agrippae, gardens in
which were many treasures of art.   An open channel, called
the Euripus, flowed through the gardens to the Tiber and doubtless served as an outlet for the stagnum.   The total area thus
occupied by baths, gardens, and pool, must have measured
about 250 metres north and south and about 200 east and west.

The second bathing establishment in Rome, the thermae
Neronianae, was built by Nero[2] in 64 A.D., after the great fire.
It was near the Pantheon and is spoken of as remarkable for
its magnificence.[3]   For some unknown reason these baths were
entirely rebuilt by Alexander Severus about 228 A.D., and were
henceforth known also as the thermae Alexandrinae.[4]   They
occupied a rectangular area extending from the northwest
corner of the Pantheon to the stadium of Domitian (piazza
Navona), and although nothing remains above ground except
a few portions of walls built into the palazzo Madama, excavations[5] made at various times within this area have brought
to light architectural fragments of great beauty and value.

---

[1] Tac. *Ann.* xv. 37; Ov. *ex Pont.* i. 8. 37–38; Strabo, xiii. I. 19 (590); Sen.
*Epist.* 83. 5; *NS.* 1881, 281–282; Gilbert, III. 293–294.

[2] Suet. *Nero*, 12.   Hülsen identifies the *thermae* with the *gymnasium*, and
therefore assigns their erection to 62 B.C. (Jordan, I. 3. 590–592).

[3] Stat. *Silv.* i. 5. 62; Mart. vii. 34. 5.

[4] Lamprid. *Vit. Alex.* 25; *Chronogr. a. 354*, p. 147; Cassiodor, *Var.* ii. 39;
Gilbert, III. 298.

[5] *NS.* 1881, 270–273; 1882, 412–413; 1883, 81, 130; 1892, 265; *BC.* 1907, 330.

Among them are four columns of red granite, two of which were used in the restoration of the pronaos of the Pantheon; an enormous basin for a fountain, 6.70 metres in diameter, cut from a single block of red granite, with fragments of several others; white marble capitals; and fragments of columns of porphyry, pavonazzetto, and gray granite.

Julius Caesar constructed an artificial lake, the naumachia Caesaris[1] in the campus Martius, *in minore Codeta*, and exhibited there sham naval battles on a great scale. This lake was filled up[2] in 43 B.C. in consequence of an epidemic in the city, and no traces have been found to indicate its exact position.

Stabula IV factionum. Near the circus Flaminius were the stables[3] of the different racing companies (*factiones*) of charioteers. In the first century of the empire there were four of these *factiones*, distinguished by their colors, *albata, russea, veneta*, and *prasina*. Two more, *aurata* and *purpurea*, were added by Domitian, but did not last long. According to the *Notitia*, there were eight stables in the fourth century, while the *Curiosum* gives the number as six. Without doubt they were all in the same region and near each other, but the certain traces thus far discovered — a dedicated pedestal and an inscribed water pipe — belong to the stable of the green (*prasina*) company, situated close to the church of S. Lorenzo in Damaso.[4]

**The Forum Holitorium.** — Just outside of that part of the Servian wall which connected the Capitoline and the Tiber was the forum Holitorium, or vegetable market, within the limits of region IX. Originally an open market-place,[5] this area was

---

[1] Dio Cass. lxiii. 23; Suet. *Caes.* 39; Gilbert, III. 334. Cf. Appian, *Bell. Civ.* ii. 102.

[2] Dio Cass. lxv. 17; Suet. *Caes.* 44.

[3] Cf. Suet. *Cal.* 55; Tac. *Hist.* ii. 94; Dio Cass. lix. 14.

[4] *BC.* 1886, 343; 1887, 10, 263–264; 1900, 333–334; *CIL.* vi. 10058; xv, 7254; Gilbert, III. 321; *Mon. d. Lincei*, i. 545.

[5] Varro, *LL.* v. 146.

inclosed in process of time by various public buildings — the
theatre of Marcellus on the west, a building[1] sometimes identified with the porticus Minucia (p. 373) on the north, and at
least four temples, which were built on the side toward the
river. Thus its original area, which had extended to the Tiber,
was considerably diminished. It was connected with the vicus
Iugarius and the forum Boarium by the porta Carmentalis and
the porta Flumentana. By the second century B.C. this market-
place had been paved, and considerable fragments of its travertine pavement[2] have been found between the church of S. Nicola
in Carcere and the piazza Montanara, extending over a distance
of some 90 metres. On one side of this pavement some remains
of a porticus have also been found.[3] The porta Carmentalis
probably took its name from a shrine or altar of Carmenta,[4]
originally a divinity of the fountains and therefore sometimes
confused with the Camenae. This altar was probably in or
near the forum Holitorium.

Four temples are spoken of as having been built in this
forum.

(1) The temple of Ianus,[5] erected in 260 B.C. by C. Duilius,
and restored in 17 A.D. by Tiberius. The senate was forbidden
to meet here, because the decree of the senate authorizing the
ill-fated Fabii to march against Veii was passed in a temple of
Janus.

(2) The temple of Spes,[6] built by A. Atilius Calatinus during
the first Punic war, burned in 213 B.C., rebuilt in 212,[7] burned
again in the time of Augustus, and restored by Germanicus in
17 A.D.[8]

(3) The temple of Iuno Sospita,[9] vowed in 197 B.C. by C. Cor-

---

[1] Jordan, I. 3. 515    [2] BC. 1875, 173.    [3] NS. 1879, 314.
[4] Solin. i. 13; Serv. in Aen. viii. 337; Dionys. i. 32; Jordan, I. 3. 507.
[5] CIL. i.[2] p. 325; Tac. Ann. ii. 49; Fest. 285; Gilbert, I. 260–265; III. 380.
[6] Cic. de Legg. ii. 28; de Nat. Deor. ii. 61; Tac. Ann. ii. 49.
[7] Liv. xxiv. 47; xxv. 7.    [8] Dio Cass. l. 10; Tac. loc. cit.
[9] Liv. xxxii. 30; xxxiv. 53.

nelius Cethegus, dedicated in 194, and restored [1] by L. Julius Caesar in 90 B.C.

(4) The temple of Pietas, vowed in 191 B.C.[2] by M'. Acilius Glabrio, dedicated in 181, and destroyed by Augustus in order to make room for the theatre of Marcellus.[3]

Beneath the present church of S. Nicola in Carcere are the ruins of three temples [4] which stand side by side and have the same orientation. Their façades are toward the east, — that is, toward the forum, — and the architectural fragments are of travertine, tufa, and peperino, with no traces of marble, except in the late restorations. They must therefore be assigned to the period of the republic.

The central and largest temple is about 30 metres long and 10 wide, of the Ionic order and peripteral. Three of its fluted columns of travertine, 8.70 metres in height and 0.90 metre in diameter, are built into the façade of the church; while portions of the cella wall and of other columns with their architrave have been built into other parts of the church. The temple north of this is also Ionic, hexastyle, and peripteral except at the back, and of its columns six are standing, 0.70 metre in diameter, also built into the church walls.

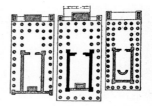

FIG. 78. — PLAN OF THE THREE TEMPLES BENEATH S. NICOLA IN CARCERE.

The third temple, the smallest of the three, is of the Doric order, hexastyle and peripteral. Some of its columns are also standing. It is probable that these existing temples are three of the four

---

[1] Cic. *de Div.* i. 99; Gilbert, III. 82, 430.

[2] Liv. xl. 34; Fest. 209; Pl. *NH.* vii. 121; Val. Max. ii. 5. 1 (v. 4. 7).

[3] Dio Cass. xliii. 49.

[4] Cf. Lanciani, *Ruins*, 513–514; Delbrück, *Die drei Tempel am Forum Holitorium*, Rome, 1903; Hülsen, *Der dorischer Tempel bei S. Nicola in Carcere, Mitt.* 1906, 169–192; Jordan, I. 3. 507–514.

described above and that the smallest, built as it is of travertine, is the latest, that of Iuno Sospita. The central temple then would be assigned to Spes, and the third to Ianus.

Extending south from these temples, under the modern via della Bocca della Verità, almost to the Cloaca Maxima, the ancient pavement of a street has been found, which seems to have been the principal thoroughfare in a north-south direction, and to have connected the circus Flaminius with the forum Boarium.

# CHAPTER XIV

## THE DISTRICT BETWEEN THE FORUM, THE TIBER, AND THE CIRCUS MAXIMUS.
## REGIONS VIII AND XI.

BETWEEN the Forum, the Capitoline, the Servian wall, the Tiber, the valley of the Circus Maximus, and the Palatine lay an irregularly shaped district, which belonged for the most part to the eleventh region of Augustus, but also included a small part of the eighth. In this district were two open market-places, the Velabrum and the forum Boarium.

The Velabrum [1] was bounded approximately by the Forum on the north, the slope of the Palatine and the vicus Tuscus on the east, and the district traversed by the vicus Iugarius on the west, while the line of separation between it and the forum Boarium passed through the present church of S. Giorgio in Velabro.

The forum Boarium [2] was originally the open meadow where cattle were bought and sold, extending from the Velabrum to the Tiber, and from the valley of the Circus Maximus on the east to a line which was approximately indicated by the road leading from the pons Sublicius or the pons Aemilius to the Velabrum. In process of time the building of dwelling-houses and of public edifices greatly diminished the size of the open markets, and the names Velabrum and forum Boarium were applied not only to them, but to the immediately adjacent districts, which became densely populated. The great fires in the city were usually particularly disastrous in this crowded region.[3]

---

[1] Varro, *LL.* v. 43; vi. 24; *CIL.* vi. 1035.

[2] Ov. *Fast.* vi. 477–478; *CIL.* vi. 919, 31574.     [3] Liv. xxiv. 47; xxxv. 40.

**The Velabrum.**[1] — The etymology[2] of the word is uncertain. Varro derived it *a vehendo* and thereby supported the traditional view, which there seems to be no good reason to doubt, that this district was very swampy until it was drained, toward the close of the regal period. A distinction appears to have been made between the Velabrum maius and the Velabrum minus,[3] but we do not know what it was. In historical times the Velabrum was a most important centre of industrial and commercial activity, being especially frequented by dealers in all kinds of food-stuffs, oil, and wine.[4] Its position made it a *locus celeberrimus urbis*,[5] for all the traffic between the part of the city about the Forum and the pons Sublicius passed through its principal streets, the vicus Tuscus and the vicus Iugarius. The character of the life and population of the Velabrum was such as to make it one of the most unsavory parts of the city.

It contained almost no monumental buildings. The only temple was that of Felicitas,[6] built by L. Licinius Lucullus about 150 B.C., which was burned in the time of Claudius and was probably not rebuilt. Its site is unknown, and, in fact, it may have been in the forum Boarium rather than in the Velabrum. A sacellum, or ara, Accae Larentiae,[7] stood at the point where the Nova via entered the Velabrum, and near it a sacellum Volupiae,[8] with a statue of Diva Angerona. A structure called the atrium Caci, and a fountain called[9] *aquam cer-*

---

1 Jordan, I. 1. 194–195; 2. 473–474; Gilbert, I. 69–70; III. 439; Richter, *Top.*[2] 181–183.

2 Varro, *LL.* v. 44; Prop. iv. 9. 5; Tib. ii. 5. 33.

3 Varro, *LL.* v. 156; Ov. *Fast.* vi. 405.

4 Plaut. *Capt.* 489; Hor. *Sat.* ii. 3. 229–230; Mart. xi. 52. 10; *CIL.* vi. 467, 9184, 9259, 9671, 9993.

5 Macrob. *Sat.* i. 10. 15.

6 Strabo, viii. 6. 23 (381); Dio Cass. xliii. 21; Cic. *Verr.* iv. 2. 4; Pl. *NH.* xxxiv. 69; xxxvi. 39; Jordan, I. 2. 486; Gilbert, III. 106–107.

7 Cic. *ad Brut.* i. 15. 8; Varro, *LL.* vi. 24; *CIL.* i². p. 338.

8 Varro, *LL.* vi. 23–24; Pl. *NH.* iii. 65; Macrob. *Sat.* i. 10. 7; *CIL.* i². p. 337; Gilbert, I. 57–58; *Not.* Reg. viii.

9 *Not.* Reg. viii; Jordan, I. 2. 472; II. 19; *Mitt.* 1896, 223.

*nentem* (Jordan *ferventem,* Hülsen *pendentem*) *quatuor scaros sub aede,* were in this region, but nothing further is known about them. Between the vicus Iugarius and the Capitoline was a district called the Aequimelium,[1] but even Cicero did not know the correct explanation of the name.

**The Forum Boarium.**[2] — Next to the forum Romanum, this was perhaps the most frequently traversed section of the city. It was the thoroughfare for all traffic between the Forum and the Tiber; into it ran the clivus Publicius, the main street of the Aventine; the valley of the Circus Maximus connected it with the via Appia; through the porta Trigemina came all the travel and traffic from Ostia; the porta Carmentalis and the porta Flumentana formed the direct connection with the campus Martius and the country to the north and east, while communication with Etruria was effected by means of two bridges, the pons Sublicius and pons Aemilius. Between the street leading to the Velabrum from the pons Aemilius and the Servian wall was a thickly settled district, and a line of buildings of various sorts probably stretched along the river bank. The district south of the church of S. Maria in Cosmedin was not regarded as a part of the forum Boarium.

This forum lay outside of the pomerium until the time of Claudius, and therefore human sacrifices took place there as late as the first century.[3] Its distinctive sign was a famous bronze statue of a bull,[4] said to be the work of Myron and to have been brought from Aegina in the third century B.C. Somewhere within its limits was a spot called the Doliola,[5] where earthenware pots were buried. It was not lawful to

---

[1] Varro, *LL.* v. 157; Liv. iv. 16; xxiv. 47; xxxviii. 28; Cic. *de Domo,* 101; *de Div.* ii. 39; Dionys. xii. 4; Jordan, I. 2. 62; Gilbert, I. 257–258.

[2] Gilbert, I. 74–80. For another view of the topography of this forum, see *Mélanges,* 1909, 103–144.

[3] Liv. xxii. 57; Pl. *NH.* xxviii. 12.      [4] Pl. *NH.* xxxiv. 10.

[5] Varro, *LL.* v. 157; Fest. *Epit.* 69; Placid. 32; Gilbert, I. 78–79; *Bull d Ist.* 1879, 76–77.

pollute this spot, and the jars were said to contain either
the bones of corpses, or *quaedam religiosa* of Numa, or the
sacred utensils of the Vestals which they buried when the
Gauls sacked the city.   At the southwest corner of the arch
of Ianus Quadrifrons (p. 403), and also at a distance of 22
metres from it, there have recently [1] been discovered the remains of small chambers arranged on both sides of narrow
corridors which form subterranean galleries.   These chambers
were vaulted over, and each contains a seat built across one
side.   They are of small size, 1.95 by 1.80 metres in width
and depth, and 1.80 high.   The floor is 3.25 metres below
the ancient pavement of the forum Boarium, which has been
found, and this is 4.50 metres below the present level of the
via del Velabro.   The construction of the galleries is that of the
last centuries of the republic, and they seem to be especially
adapted for an underground prison, suggesting the *locus saxo
consaeptus*,[2] in which two Gauls were buried alive in 215 B.C.
This may have been the place where such human sacrifices
were performed, and also the mysterious Doliola as well.
Fragments of jars and of the bones of animals were found
here.

It is usually supposed that the **Busta Gallica**,[3] or burial-place
of the Gauls who were killed at the sack of Rome, was also
somewhere in the forum Boarium, but there is no evidence to
support this view, except that they were *media in urbe*.

Outside the limits of the forum Boarium were three statues,
**Hercules Olivarius**,[4] **Apollo Caelispex**,[5] and **Elephas Herbarius**.[6]   The
first two were probably between the forum Boarium and the
porta Trigemina, while the Elephas Herbarius was very near
the forum Holitorium.   The *vicus* or district named from this

---

[1] *BC.* 1901, 141–145, 283–284; *NS.* 1901, 354–355, 422, 481–483.
[2] Liv. xxii. 57.
[3] Varro, *LL.* v. 157; Liv. v. 48; xxii. 14.
[4] *Not.* Reg. xi; *NS.* 1895, 459; *Diss. d. Accad. Pontif.* II, vi. 1896, 261.
[5] *Not. ib.*          [6] *Not.* Reg. viii; Jordan, I. 2. 476.

statue was evidently the resort of *herbarii*, as that of Hercules Olivarius was occupied by dealers in oil.

The Cloaca Maxima (p. 109) runs through the forum Boarium in its original course, and at some points the masonry of the early republican period is still visible. Another ancient sewer,[1] which drained the valley of the Circus Maximus (p. 107), entered the forum Boarium at the corner of the via della Greca and the via della Salara, and emptied into the Tiber about 50 metres below the Cloaca Maxima. Its course has been traced from the Colosseum. Just west of the corner of these two streets two smaller sewers flow into it from the southeast, and between their channels remains of early republican masonry [2] have been found, which, however, cannot be identified with any certainty.

The most ancient cult in the forum Boarium was that of Hercules, represented by two, and perhaps three, sanctuaries. The oldest of these was the **ara Herculis Maxima**,[3] erected, according to tradition, by Hercules himself. This altar was standing in the fourth century,[4] but has left no trace.[5]

The oldest temple was that of **Hercules Invictus** or **Victor**,[6] a round temple said to have been built by Hercules himself. In 168 B.C. it was restored by L. Aemilius Paulus, at whose command the poet and painter Pacuvius decorated its interior.[7] After the fire of Nero, it was restored by Vespasian. In form it was undoubtedly very like the existing round temple in the forum Boarium (p. 401). While the exact site of ara and temple cannot be marked out,[8] there is no doubt that the altar stood

---

[1] *BC.* 1892, 261–262, 281–283.

[2] *NS.* 1885, 527.

[3] Liv. i. 7; Ov. *Fast.* i. 581–582; Tac. *Ann.* xii. 24; xv. 41; Serv. *in Aen.* viii. 269–271; Gilbert, I. 78–82.     [4] *CIL.* vi. 312–319.

[5] Cf., however, *Mélanges*, 1909, 107–117.

[6] Tac. *Ann.* xv. 41; Liv. x. 23; Pl. *NH.* xxxiv. 33.

[7] Fest. 242; Pl. *NH.* xxxv. 19.

[8] *Mon. d. Ist.* 1854, 28–38; Richter, *Top.*[2] 188–189; Gilbert, III. 433–434; Jordan, I. 2. 480–483.

a little to the north of S. Maria in Cosmedin, and therefore a
short distance from the *carceres* of the Circus Maximus, and
that the temple was very near the altar.   A third temple of
Hercules, the aedes Herculis Pompeiani,[1] stood *ad circum maximum,*
but its site is a matter of dispute (p. 402).

Near the temple of Hercules Invictus was the sacellum Pudicitiae Patriciae,[2] mentioned for the first time under the date
of 296 B.C., and connected with the struggle between the two
orders in the state.   Near the pons Aemilius was the Portu-
nium,[3] or temple of Portunus, and near this temple were fish
and flower markets.

On the north side of the forum Boarium were two temples,[4]
that of Fortuna and that of Mater Matuta.   The erection of the
first was ascribed to Servius Tullius.[5]   It was burned in
213 B.C.[6] and restored by a special commission, but it is not
mentioned after the first century.   In this temple was a statue,
covered with two togas,[7] which was thought by some Romans
to be a statue of Servius Tullius, and by others to be that of
the goddess Fortuna herself.

The temple of Mater Matuta[8] was also ascribed to Servius
Tullius.   It was restored in 395 B.C. by Camillus; and burned
and again restored in 213–212, at the same time as the temple
of Fortuna.   In this temple Ti. Sempronius Gracchus placed
a bronze tablet,[9] which recorded his campaigns in Sardinia,
together with a map of the island.   In 196 B.C. two arches
(*fornices*) with gilded statues were set up by L. Stertinius in

---

[1] Vitr. iii. 3. 5; Pl. *NH*. xxxiv. 57; Gilbert, III. 434; Jordan, I. 3. 148.

[2] Liv. x. 23; Fest. 242; Jordan, I. 2. 483; Gilbert, III. 435.

[3] Varro, *LL*. vi. 19; Fronto, i. 7, p. 19 (Naber) ; Jordan, I. 2. 485–486; II. 199,
257; Gilbert, I. 263.

[4] Jordan, I. 2. 484–485; Gilbert, II. 390–393; III. 438–439; *Mélanges*, 1909,
123–127.

[5] Dionys. iv. 27.                    [6] Liv. xxiv. 47; xxv. 7.

[7] Pl. *NH*. viii. 194; Wissowa, *Analecta Romana Topographica*, 1897, p. 5.

[8] Ov. *Fast*. vi. 480–481; Liv. v. 19; xxiv. 47; xxv. 7.

[9] Liv. xli. 28.

front of these two temples.[1] If, as is probable, these arches
were part of a colonnade surrounding the two temples, the
temples themselves must have been close together, and perhaps
had the same orientation. Another arch stood directly in
front of the pons Aemilius, near these temples, the inscription[2]

Fig. 79. — S. Maria Egiziaca.

on which, recording a restoration of the bridge by Augustus,
was in existence in the middle ages.

**Existing Remains in the Forum Boarium.** — (1) S. Maria
Egiziaca. This church is an ancient temple, which was converted into its present form in 872 A.D. The temple is Ionic,
20 metres long and 12 wide, with north-south orientation par-

---

[1] Liv. xxxiii. 27.    [2] *CIL.* vi. 878; cf. *Anonymus Magliabecchianus*, p. 57.

allel to the river, tetrastyle prostyle, and stands on a podium 2.50 metres in height and originally 26 metres long. It was pseudo-peripteral, having five engaged columns in the side walls of the cella, and a pronaos. The two free columns of

FIG. 80. — S. MARIA DEL SOLE.

the pronaos were walled up to increase the size of the church. The cella walls and engaged columns, except those at the angles, are of tufa; the columns of the pronaos, the capitals of all the columns, the architrave and cornice, and the facing of the podium, of travertine. The frieze was decorated with ox-skulls and garlands, but most of this decoration has disappeared. This temple faced toward the street leading up from the pons Aemilius, and not toward the forum proper. It is generally identified with the temple of **Fortuna**, sometimes with that of **Mater Matuta**, but if either identification is correct, the temple must have been entirely restored about the middle of the first century B.C., to which period the construction seems to point.[1]

(2) **S. Maria del Sole.** This church, which stands near the river in the piazza di Bocca della Verità, is an ancient round temple, very like the temples of Vesta. It is built of white marble, the blocks of the cella being solid, with a peristyle of twenty Corinthian columns. The cella is 10 metres in diameter and stands on a podium 2 metres high. This podium is of tufa and belongs to the period of the republic, but its marble covering and the whole marble superstructure date from the early empire. The entablature is missing, and the roof is modern. Eight steps led up to the top of the podium, and the entrance is on the east, toward the forum.

This structure has been called by ten different names,[2] but it is usually identified either with the temple of **Portunus** or that of **Mater Matuta**, as there is no possibility of its being a temple of Vesta. No certainty attaches to either of these identifications.

(3) **S. Maria in Cosmedin.** Recent excavations[3] have shown that the present church occupies the site of an early republican temple and of some structure of the fourth century.

Of the temple nothing remains except tufa blocks belonging to foundations and walls. This temple appears to have existed, although in a ruined state, until the eighth century, when it

---

[1] *Mitt.* 1906, 220–279.

[2] Lanciani, *Ruins*, 518; Altmann, *Rundbauten*, 33–36.

[3] G. B. Giovenale, *Annuario dell' Associazione artistica frai cultori di architettura*, v. 1895.

was entirely destroyed, and the church, which up to that time had extended only to its wall, was enlarged so as to cover a considerable part of its foundations. There is complete uncertainty as to the name of this temple. It is sometimes identified with that of Ceres, Liber, and Libera (p. 409), sometimes with that of Hercules Pompeianus (p. 398), but there is no convincing proof in either case.[1]

Directly in front of this temple is part of a structure of the fourth century, in which the original church was built. This

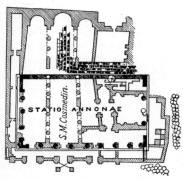

FIG. 81. — PLAN OF THE STATIO ANNONAE.

building was a rectangular porticus, 30 metres long and 15 wide, consisting of a brick wall at the rear and a colonnade on the front and sides. Eleven of the columns of this porticus are built into the wall of the present church. They appear to have stood, not on the pavement of the porticus, but on a low inclosure wall. The question of the roof of the porticus is a perplexing one, as the columns do not seem strong enough to have supported a roof without additional help. As it is known that this space at the corner of the Aventine was largely occupied with buildings which belonged to the *Annona urbis,* it is a plausible conjecture that this particular building may have been the statio Annonae,[2] or headquarters of the administration of the corn-supply.

Near the church of S. Giorgio in Velabro is a four-way arch

---

[1] For an identification with the ara Maxima, see *Mélanges*, 1909, 107–117.

[2] *Ann d. Ist.* 1885, 223–234; *BC.* 1889, 358; *Mitt.* 1891, 107; Jordan, I. 3. 146–147.

of marble,[1] consisting of four piers connected by quadripartite vaulting.  It stands directly over the Cloaca Maxima and probably marked the line of separation between the forum Boarium and the Velabrum.  It is of late date, — third or fourth century, — and is without much doubt the arch which is called in the *Notitia* arcus Constantini.  It is now usually known as Ianus quadrifrons.  The whole structure is 12 metres square and 16 high, while the arches themselves are 10.60 metres high and 5.70 wide.  Round all four sides run two rows of niches for statues, forty-eight in all, of which sixteen are unfinished. There are traces of sculpture on the keystones of the arches, but the workmanship is very poor and the whole structure illustrates the extreme decadence of the time of Constantine.

The so-called arcus Septimi Severi, or monumentum Argentariorum, is an arch which stands at the southwest angle of the church of S. Giorgio in Velabro; in fact, the campanile of the church rests partly upon one pier of the arch, concealing two of its sides.  It was erected in 204 A.D. by the *argentarii et negotiantes boarii*[2] in honor of Septimius Severus, his wife, and sons.  It is not a true arch, but a flat lintel resting on two piers, and is wholly of marble, except the base, which is of travertine.  It is 6.15 metres in height and the archway is 3.30 metres wide. At the corners of the piers are pilasters with Corinthian capitals, and the whole surface of the structure is adorned either with coarse decorative sculpture or reliefs which represent sacrificial scenes.  On the inside of the gateway the figures of some members of the imperial family are cut in relief.  The ceiling of this gateway is carved in soffits, and on the architrave is the dedicatory inscription.  The rest of the entablature exhibits the rich but superfluous decoration so characteristic of the decadence.

**The Circus Maximus.** — From the earliest times the Romans celebrated their games with races and public spectacles in the

---

[1] Jordan, I. 2. 471–472.          [2] *CIL*. vi. 1035.

valley between the Palatine and the Aventine, which was well
adapted by nature for this purpose, being 600 metres long and
150 wide, while the slopes of the hills afforded convenient
places for the spectators.[1]   This valley was called the **vallis
Murcia, ad Murciam,** or ad **Murciae,**[2] from an altar of Murcia, a
goddess sometimes identified with Venus.   Roman etymolo-
gists derived the word from *myrtea,* and supposed that the
valley was originally overgrown with myrtle.   It must have
been somewhat swampy, and a brook, called in medieval and
modern times the Marrana, flowed through it, which drained
the valleys of the Caelian and the adjacent districts.   In process of time the brook was confined within walls of masonry
for a part of its course, and became one of the great cloacae of
Rome (p. 107).

The earliest cult in this valley was that of Consus, an ancient Italic deity of agriculture and the under-world, whose
altar, the **ara Consi,**[3] stood at the southeast end of the valley
and was hidden beneath the earth except at festivals.   Of the
three festivals in honor of this deity, the principal one, the
*Consualia,* was accompanied with horse and chariot races.
After a permanent *spina* was built, the altar appears to have
been at its southeast extremity.

In this valley the first and greatest of all Roman *circi* was
gradually developed.[4]   During the regal period, while there
was nothing in the way of a permanent building, special places
were assigned to the different curiae, where they could erect
their temporary seats.   In 329 B.C. permanent *carceres*[5] were
first built, and considerably later, in the first half of the second
century, the activity displayed in so many other forms of mu-

---

[1] Liv. i. 35, 56; Dionys. iii. 68.

[2] Liv. i. 33; Varro, *LL.* v. 154; Serv. *in Aen.* viii. 636.

[3] Varro, *LL.* vi. 20; Tac. *Ann.* xii. 24; Dionys. ii. 31; Tertull. *de Spect.* 5.
Cf., however, *Mélanges,* 1908, 279.

[4] Gilbert, II. 454–456; III. 313–319; Jordan, I. 3. 120–144; Pauly, *Real-Encyclopädie,* iii. 2572–2581.

[5] Liv. viii. 20.

nicipal life made itself felt in the circus. It was at this time that the open Marrana was probably transformed into a closed cloaca, which would have allowed a permanent spina to be built. The decorative arches and statues [1] (*e.g.* fornix Stertinii, signum Pollentiae) erected at this time presuppose the existence of some permanent structure, and we may assume that by the third century B.C. the purely temporary character of the circus had passed away.

The history of the circus as one of the great buildings of the world begins with Caesar.[2] As rebuilt by him, it consisted of three bands of seats, the lowest of masonry and the upper two of wood. Just inside the lowest tier of seats, encircling the arena, was a water-channel 3 metres wide called the Euripus, the object of which was to protect the spectators from attacks of the wild beasts. In 31 B.C. the wooden part of the circus was burned, and restored by Augustus,[3] who erected the pulvinar ad circum maximum, a sort of box on the Palatine side, from which the imperial household could view the games. Augustus also set up on the spina the obelisk [4] from Heliopolis, which is now in the piazza del Popolo. The circus was partially destroyed by fire in 36 A.D., and enlarged and restored by Claudius,[5] who constructed carceres of marble and goals of gilt bronze. The great fire in 64 A.D. broke out in the circus,[6] and must have destroyed it so completely that the restoration following was practically a rebuilding. Again during Domitian's reign the edifice suffered from fire,[7] but to what extent is not known. It was once more enlarged and restored by Trajan, and then reached its greatest size and magnificence.[8] While the uppermost seats were always of wood and subject to not infrequent conflagrations, the main structure was of solid masonry and covered inside and outside with white marble. The size of this

---

[1] Liv. xxxiii. 27; xxxix. 7; xl. 2.

[2] Suet. *Caes.* 39; Dionys. iii. 68.

[3] *Mon. Anc.* iv. 4.

[4] Pl. *NH.* xxxvi. 71.

[5] Tac. *Ann.* vi. 51; Suet. *Claud.* 21.

[6] Tac. *Ann.* xv. 38.

[7] Suet. Dom. 5.

[8] Pl. *Paneg.* 51; Dio Cass. lxviii. 7.

circus and its wealth of decoration of every description made
it the most magnificent building, not only in Rome, but probably in the whole world. Later emperors [1] did something in
the way of restoration and decoration, but added little or nothing to its splendor.

From coins, fragments of the Marble Plan, the description
of Dionysius, and other evidence,[2] we can reconstruct the edifice in the main in its final shape. It was probably about 625
metres long, the arena itself being 568 metres long and 87 metres wide at the end of the spina. The cavea proper was about
27 metres in depth, but during the empire this was so much increased by additions on the slopes of the Palatine and Aventine that the total width of the whole structure seems to have
been nearly 200 metres.[3] The exterior was formed of three
stories, with arches and engaged columns of the Doric order,
like the Colosseum, but all covered with marble. The cavea
was divided into three bands or zones of seats, separated by
corridors, and the arrangement of approaches and stairways
was probably similar to that in the Colosseum. As in the latter building, a podium or raised platform surrounded the arena,
between the seats and the Euripus, and on this were the chairs
of the imperial family and high officials. The west end rose
in several stories with towers and battlements, in such a manner as to suggest the appearance of a walled town, and this
part of the circus was called sometimes *oppidum*.[4] This end
was not straight, but curved, and the ground level toward the
arena was occupied by the carceres, probably twelve in number. These carceres were closed by barriers, and this fact
probably explains the use of the name Duodecim portae [5] to des-

---

[1] Vict. *Caes*. 40.

[2] *Abhandlungen d. Berl. Akademie*, 1873, 67 ff. ; Jordan, *FUR*. 38–40 ; *Ann. d. Ist*. 1870, 232–261 ; *NS*. 1876, 101, 138–139, 184 ; 1877, 8, 110, 204 ; 1888, 191, 226–227 ; *Mitt*. 1892, 295 ; 1893, 289.

[3] *Mélanges*, 1908, 229–231 ; *BC*. 1908, 241–253.

[4] Varro, *LL*. v. 153 ; Fest. *Epit*. 184.     [5] Obseq. 130 ; *Not*. Reg. xi.

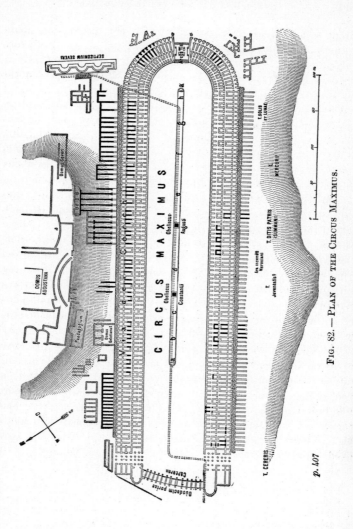

FIG. 82. — PLAN OF THE CIRCUS MAXIMUS.

p. 407

ignate this end of the building. Above the carceres were two boxes, one for the presiding magistrate and the other for the judges.

On the spina stood the obelisk of Augustus (p. 405) and a second erected by Constantius in 357 A.D.[1] and now in front of the Lateran; the altar of Consus (*h*, Fig. 82); a small shrine near each end, on one of which (*g*) were sets of seven marble eggs (*ovaria*)[2] used to indicate the laps of the race, and on the other (*b*) sets of dolphins[3] for the same purpose. At each end (*a, a'*) of the spina were the *metae*, or goals, three cones of gilt bronze. There were also other shrines (*c, d, e, f*) and statues on the spina.[4] The east end was semicircular in form and broken in the centre by a gateway, the porta Pompae, through which the procession seems to have usually entered at the beginning of the games. This gateway was formed by an arch, the arcus Vespasiani et Titi, erected by the senate[5] in 81 A.D. in honor of Titus and in commemoration of the capture of Jerusalem. The open arcades in the exterior of the circus on the ground level and the chambers above them were used for shops and especially for brothels, so that this district was one of the most disreputable in the city.[6]

The size[7] and seating capacity of the Circus Maximus have given rise to much discussion. The *Notitia* states that it contained three hundred and eighty-five thousand *loca*. The most probable explanation of this statement is that there were three hundred and eighty-five thousand running feet of seats, and therefore capacity for about two hundred thousand spectators. Others have estimated the capacity all the way from one hundred and forty thousand (Hülsen)[8] to three hundred and

---

[1] Amm. Marc. xvii. 4. 12.    [2] Liv. xli. 27.

[3] Dio Cass. xlix. 43.    [4] Tertull. *de Spect.* 8.    [5] *CIL.* vi. 944.

[6] Hor. *Sat.* i. 6. 113; Juv. vi. 588; Cic. *pro Mil.* 65; *de Div.* i. 132; Lamprid. *Vit. Elag.* 26.

[7] Dionys. iii. 68; Pl. *NH.* xxxvi. 102; Pauly, *Real-Encyclopädie*, iii. 2578; Richter, *Top.*[2] 178; Jordan, I. 3. 132–140.

[8] *BC.* 1894, 321–324.

eighty-five thousand. In any case, the enlargement after the time of Augustus was very considerable.

Throughout the republic the circus was used for gladiatorial combats and fights with wild beasts, as well as for races; but after the building of the amphitheatre of Statilius Taurus, and still more after the erection of the Colosseum, the first species of entertainment was largely, although not entirely, removed from the circus. The last recorded games took place under Totila in 549 A.D.[1] In that century the destruction of the circus began, and has continued until the present day. In the sixteenth century nothing remained except some fragments of the arcades, spur walls, and spina. The city gas-works, which have hitherto occupied the site, are being removed, and the development of the Zona Monumentale promises to result in the eventual excavation of all the remains of the circus.

Numerous divinities were worshipped within the circus, and their shrines or altars were either on the spina or in the cavea. Tertullian[2] enumerates a long list, — Castor and Pollux, the Sun, Magna Mater, Neptune, and Venus Murcia, together with various minor deities. The temple of the Sun is mentioned by Tacitus[3] and in the Regionary Catalogue as the templum Solis et Lunae.

Close by the circus were several temples, which were variously designated as *ad circum maximum, in circo maximo,* or *prope circum,* but of which no certain traces are left. The most important of these was the temple of Ceres Liber Liberaque,[4] which was said to have been vowed in 496 B.C. and dedicated three years later. It was burned in 31 B.C., rebuilt by Augustus, and dedicated by Tiberius in 17 A.D.[5] It was Tuscan in style, with wide intercolumniations, and its façade was decorated

---

[1] Procop. *Bell. Goth.* iii. 37.      [2] *De Spect.* 8.

[3] *Ann.* xv. 74. Cf. Tertull. *de Spect.* 9; Hülsen, *Diss. d. Accad. Pontif.* II. vi. 1896, 267.

[4] Dionys. vi. 17, 94; Gilbert, II. 242–250; Jordan, I. 3. 115–117.

[5] Dio Cass. l. 10; Tac. *Ann.* ii. 49.

with statues of terra cotta and gilt bronze.[1] The worship of Ceres was essentially plebeian, and the political importance of this temple was very great, as it was the headquarters of the plebeian aediles, and within it were stored the plebeian archives.[2] It was near the west end of the circus on the Aventine side, but how far up the slope of the hill is uncertain.

The other temples were those of Mercurius,[3] on the slope of the Aventine above the circus, dedicated in 495 B.C., and restored by Marcus Aurelius; Summanus,[4] built at some unknown date, and restored during the war with Pyrrhus; Venus,[5] dedicated in 295 B.C., and mentioned as standing in the first century; Iuventas,[6] near that of Summanus, dedicated by L. Licinius Lucullus in 193 B.C., burned in 16 B.C., restored by Augustus, and mentioned as existing in the first century; Flora,[7] near the temple of Ceres, built in 240 or 238 B.C., and rebuilt and dedicated by Tiberius in 17 A.D.; Salus,[8] built in 65 A.D. to commemorate Nero's escape from the conspiracy of Piso, and mentioned only once. The temple of Dis Pater, mentioned only in the *Notitia*, is perhaps to be identified [9] with that of Summanus. On the west side of the circus, at the foot of the slope of the Aventine, within the present limits of the Jewish cemetery, stood one of the arae incendii Neroniani [10] (p. 493), erected by Domitian, of which some remains have been found.

Between the porta Trigemina and the statio Annonae was the arcus Lentuli et Crispini,[11] erected by Lentulus and Crispinus, con-

---

[1] Vitr. iii. 3. 5; Pl. *NH.* xxxv. 154.

[2] Liv. iii. 55; x. 23; Dionys. vi. 89.

[3] Liv. ii. 21, 27; Ov. *Fast.* v. 669; Apul. *Met.* vi. 8; Gilbert, II. 251; Altmann, *Rundbauten*, 21.

[4] Ov. *Fast.* vi. 731; *CIL.* i². p. 320.

[5] Liv. x. 31; xxix. 37; Fest. 265; *CIL.* i². p. 320.

[6] Pl. *NH.* xxix. 57; Liv. xxxvi. 36; *Mon. Anc.* iv. 8; Dio Cass. liv. 19.

[7] Tac. *Ann.* ii. 49.       [9] Jordan, I. 3. 119.

[8] Tac. *Ann.* xv. 74.       [10] *CIL.* vi. 826; Jordan, I. 3. 128.

[11] Gilbert, III. 188; Lanciani, *Acque*, 100–101.

suls in 2 A.D. This arch stood during the early middle ages, and its inscription,[1] which has been preserved, is exactly like that [2] on the arch of Dolabella and Silanus (p. 440). The arches themselves were probably alike, and while it is not known whether they stood alone or were parts of the rivus Herculaneus (p. 95), the latter is probably the case.

---

[1] *CIL*. vi. 1385.    [2] *CIL*. vi. 1384.

# CHAPTER XV.

## THE AVENTINE. REGIONS XII AND XIII.

**The Aventine** [1] is the southernmost of the hills of Rome, and stretches southeast from the Tiber. It is trapezoidal in form, and its sides, beginning with that toward the river, measure respectively about 500, 600, 750, and 600 metres in length. Like the Palatine and the Capitoline, it is divided into two portions by a depression which crosses the hill from northeast to southwest. The western portion is much the larger, and the other is frequently called the Pseudo-Aventine, but there was no such distinction in antiquity. It is uncertain how much of the hill was originally called mons Aventinus, but it seems probable that this name belonged at first to the western part, which continued to bear that official designation. At a comparatively early period, however, perhaps as a result of the building of the Servian wall, this name was extended in ordinary usage to include the eastern portion also.[2] The hill rises abruptly from the bank of the river and is steep on the north and southwest, but slopes gradually toward the east and southeast. According to the traditional view, the Aventine [3] did not become a part of the city until the Servian wall was built, when it was included for purposes of fortification, while it remained without the pomerium until the time of Claudius, its exclusion being due to religious scruples connected with the tradition of the founding of the city.[4] The line of the Servian

---

[1] A. Merlin, *L'Aventin dans l'Antiquité. Bibliothèque des Écoles françaises.* Paris, 1906.

[2] Jordan, I. 3. 149–151; Merlin, *op. cit.* 5–14.     [3] Gilbert, II. 144–257.

[4] Aul. Gell. xiii. 14. For a forcible presentation of the view that the Aventine was not included within any wall before that of the fourth century, and was therefore outside the pomerium, see Merrill, *CP.* 1909, 420–432.

wall, its gates, and the existing remains, have been described (pp. 46, 49, 112–117).

The name **Aventinus** is still unexplained, in spite of the many etymologies offered by Roman antiquarians.[1] It is, however, a plausible suggestion that the word represents the name of an ancient Italian, or perhaps Ligurian, settlement, especially as the term pagus Aventinus [2] continued in use in historical times. According to tradition, the Aventine was public domain until 456 B.C., when by the lex Icilia a portion of it was handed over to the plebeians for settlement.[3] It continued to be an essentially plebeian quarter until the empire, when many wealthy Romans built their residences there, but it was always an unimportant part of the city, comparatively speaking, and few remains of interest have been found within its limits.

The principal streets on and about the Aventine were : the two great roads, the **via Appia**, which formed the northeast boundary of region XII, and the **via Ostiensis**, which was virtually the extension of the street which skirted the hill on the southwest ; the **vicus Piscinae Publicae**,[4] which led from the eastern end of the Circus Maximus across the depression to the porta Raudusculana, and its continuation to the via Ostiensis, which was probably the **vicus portae Raudusculanae** ;[5] the **clivus Publicius**,[6] which began at the west end of the Circus Maximus in the forum Boarium, and extended in a southerly direction to the temple of Diana and on to the vicus Piscinae Publicae (this street was paved about 238 B.C., and as it is said to have been burned over in 203 B.C., it must have been closely

---

[1] Varro, *LL.* v. 43; Liv. i. 3; Verg. *Aen.* vii. 657; Serv. *ad loc.*; Jordan, I. 1. 183–185 ; 3. 151–153 ; Merlin, *op. cit.* 26–36.

[2] (Or *Aventinensis*) *CIL.* xiv. 2105.

[3] Dionys. iii. 43; x. 31–32; Liv. iii. 31.

[4] *Bas. Capit.* Reg. xii.; cf. Amm. Marc. xvii. 4. 14; *CIL.* vi. 167; Jordan, I. 3. 183–185.

[5] *BC.* 1891, 211 n.

[6] Varro, *LL.* v. 158; Fest. 238; Ov. *Fast.* v. 293–294; Liv. xxvi. 10; xxvii. 37; xxx. 26; Gilbert, III. 441; Jordan, I. 3. 153–156; Merlin, *op. cit.* 95, 247.

built up by that time); the via Ardeatina,[1] which from very early times led through the later porta Ardeatina, that portion between the vicus Piscinae Publicae and the Servian wall being called the vicus portae Naeviae;[2] and the via Nova,[3] built by Caracalla to connect his new baths with the Circus Maximus. The clivus Delfini [4] was probably a street that ran from the via Nova, north of the baths of Caracalla, to the via Ardeatina; the area Radicaria, an open space at the northeast corner of the baths; and the campus Lanatarius perhaps not far from their northwest corner. On the western part of the hill was an ancient grove, probably afterwards an open square, called the Loretum,[5] said to have been the burial-place of Titus Tatius, from which two streets were named, the vicus Loreti maioris and the vicus Loreti minoris.[6] Here too was another open space, the Armilustrium,[7] where the festival of the same name was celebrated on the 19th of October. This also was said to have been the burial-place of Tatius. At a later time it was largely built up, but there was a vicus Armilustri [8] which probably followed the general line of the modern via di S. Sabina and via del Priorato. The Mappa Aurea [9] was probably a street on the hill above the Circus Maximus. Platanonis of the *Notitia* was also probably a vicus, and Nymphea tria a fountain. It would be natural to have long flights of steps to the top of the hill on the river side, and the Scalae Cassii of the *Notitia* was probably one of these.

Augustus divided the Aventine between two regions, making

---

[1] *Mitt.* 1894, 320–327.          [2] *Bas. Capit.* Reg. xii.

[3] Spart. *Vit. Carac.* 9; Vict. *Caes.* 21; Gilbert, III. 443; *CIL.* vi. 9684.

[4] *Not.* Reg. xii.

[5] Varro. *LL.* v. 152; Dionys. iii. 43; Pl. *NH.* xv. 138; Fest 360; Serv. *ad Aen.* viii. 276; Gilbert, II. 236–237; Jordan, I. 3. 161–163; *BC.* 1905, 215–216.

[6] *Bas. Capit.* Reg. xiii.

[7] Varro, *LL.* v. 153; vi. 22; Fest. *Epit.* 19; Plut. *Rom.* 23. For a false identification with the Circus Maximus, cf. Gilbert, I. 131–132.

[8] *CIL.* vi. 802, 31069; *Bull. d. Ist.* 1870, 88; Merlin, *op. cit.* 313–315.

[9] *CIL.* xv. 7182; *Not.* Reg. xiii; Jordan, I. 3. 170; Merlin, *op. cit.* 320.

the vicus Piscinae Publicae the boundary. The west part of
the hill and the level ground to the south where the warehouses stood, formed region XIII, called Aventinus; the east
part of the hill and the site afterward occupied by the baths
of Caracalla constituted region XII, called **Piscina Publica**.[1]
This was a public reservoir situated just outside the porta
Capena and first mentioned in 215 B.C. It had ceased to exist
in the fourth century.

## REGION XIII.

**Temples and Altars.** — According to tradition, the oldest
shrines in this region were on the slope of the hill above the
porta Trigemina, where the Cacus legend was localized and
Hercules was said to have built an altar to **Iuppiter Inventor**.[2]
Near by was an altar of **Evander**[3] of like antiquity.

The oldest and by far the most important temple was that of
**Diana**,[4] ascribed by tradition to Servius Tullius, who assembled
here the representatives of the surrounding Latin towns and
built this temple as the common sanctuary of the league. It
was rebuilt by Cornificius in the reign of Augustus, and is
probably represented on a fragment of the Marble Plan,[5] where
it is drawn as octastyle and dipteral, surrounded by a double
colonnade. Its site was west of S. Prisca on the clivus Publicius.[6]

At the extreme northern point of the Aventine was the
temple of **Luna**,[7] also ascribed to Servius Tullius. It was destroyed in the fire of Nero, and is mentioned only infrequently.
Near the temple of Diana was a group of three temples, dedicated to the three divinities of the Capitoline triad, Jupiter,

---

[1] Fest. 213; Liv. xxiii. 32; Cic. *ad Q. Fr.* iii. 7; Jordan, II. 106–107.

[2] Solin. i. 7–8.      [3] Dionys. i. 32.

[4] Liv. i. 45; Fest. 343; Oros. v. 12; Dionys. iv. 26; Suet. *Aug.* 29; Gilbert,
II. 236–241 ; Jordan, I. 3. 157–159.

[5] *BC.* 1891, 210–216; Jordan, *FUR.* 2.      [6] Mart. vi. 64. 12.

[7] Tac. *Ann.* xv. 41; Liv. xl. 2; App. *Bell. Civ.* i. 78; Auct. *de Vir. Ill.* 65;
Vitr. v. 5. 8; Ov. *Fast.* iii. 883; Jordan, I. 3. 160–161.

Juno, and Minerva.  Of these three, that of Iuno Regina stood
near the present church of S. Sabina.  It was dedicated in
392 B.C. by Camillus,[1] who placed within it a wooden statue of
Juno, which he had brought from the captured city of Veii.
The temple was afterward rebuilt by Augustus.  The temple
of Minerva[2] is first mentioned in the time of the second Punic
war, as being the sanctuary and headquarters of the guild of
*scribae* and *histriones* established by Livius Andronicus.  It
was restored by Augustus, and is represented on the Marble
Plan[3] as peripteral, hexastyle, with thirteen columns on each
side.  The temple of Iuppiter Libertas is mentioned only twice,[4]
but it probably dated from the early republican period.

In the vicus Loreti maioris stood a temple of Vortumnus,
and near it a temple of Consus.[5]  The first contained a portrait
of M. Fulvius Flaccus, in the robes of a *triumphator*, and the
second a similar portrait of L. Papirius Cursor.  It is probable,
therefore, that the temple of Vortumnus was built by Fulvius
in 264 B.C., and that of Consus by Papirius in 272, on the
occasion of their triumphs.

The place of the temple of Libertas,[6] built by Ti. Sempronius
Gracchus in 238 B.C., is unknown, and this temple has been
identified by some with that of Iuppiter Libertas, mentioned
above.  The site of the only remaining temple on this part of
the hill, that of Iuppiter Dolichenus,[7] a deity whose cult was introduced from Doliche in Syria, is shown by inscriptions to

---

[1] Liv. v. 22, 23, 31; Dionys. xiii. 3; *Mon. Anc.* iv. 6; *CIL.* vi. 364–365;
Jordan, I. 3. 165–167.

[2] Fest. 257, 333; *Mon. Anc.* iv. 6; Ov. *Fast.* vi. 728; Gilbert, II. 233–235,
238; Jordan, I. 3. 159–160; *BC.* 1891, 216; *CIL.* i². p. 312.

[3] Jordan, *FUR.* 2.

[4] *Mon. Anc.* iv. 6; Jordan, I. 3. 167.

[5] Fest. 209; *CIL.* i². p. 326; Gilbert, II. 191, 234–238; III. 445; Richter,
*Top.*² 206 n.

[6] Fest. *Epit.* 121; Liv. xxiv. 16; Gilbert, III. 97; Jordan, I. 3. 167.

[7] *Not.* Reg. xiii; *CIL.* vi. 366, 406–413; Gilbert, III. 113–114; Jordan, I. 3.
167–168; *BC.* 1893, 5–7, 223–244.

have been near the church of S. Alessio. The lucus Stimulae,[1] a
deity afterward confused with Semele, was probably near the
river between the horrea Galbiana and the hill.

**Baths**. — Aside from temples, the only buildings of importance on the west Aventine appear to have been baths. The
first of these, the thermae Suranae or balnea Surae,[2] were built
either by Licinius Sura, a friend of Trajan, or by Trajan himself in honor of this friend, who lived on the Aventine.
These baths are represented on fragments of the Marble Plan,[3]
and occupied the site of the modern restaurant Cesarini, north
of S. Prisca, where some remains have been found. With the
thermae Suranae there are mentioned in the *Notitia* the thermae
Decianae,[4] which were built by the emperor Decius about 250 A.D.
Plans of the thermae Decianae, drawn by Palladio about 1600,
have recently been found, and some remains of the buildings [5]
under the casino of the vigna Torlonia. These thermae evidently occupied a large space midway between S. Prisca and
S. Alessio.

**Horrea**. — All along the bank of the Tiber below the porta
Trigemina docks and wharves had been built, and south of
the Aventine the Emporium (p. 86) had been constructed.
During the empire, the level ground between the Emporium,
the southwest slope of the Aventine, and the line of the
Aurelian wall was gradually occupied by a series of enormous
*horrea*, or warehouses, in which were stored goods of every
description.

---

[1] Liv. xxxix. 12, 13; Schol. Juv. ii. 3; Ov. *Fast.* vi. 503; *CIL.* vi. 9897;
Jordan, I. 3. 171.

[2] Dio Cass. lxviii. 15; Vict. *Caes.* 13; *Epit.* 13; Spart. *Vit. Hadr.* 2; *CIL.*
vi. 1703; Jordan, I. 3. 156–157.

[3] Jordan, *FUR.* 41.

[4] Eutrop. ix. 4; Cassiod. *Chron. a. 252;* *CIL.* xv. 7181; *Chronogr. a. 354,*
p. 147; Jordan, I. 3. 163.

[5] *BC.* 1878, 253; 1887, 266; 1893, 240–241; Lanciani, *Ruins,* 545.

In the second century B.C. the Sulpicii possessed large estates in this district, which were called the praedia Galbiana. Here Ser. Sulpicius Galba, consul in 144 or 108 B.C., was buried; and at some time before the end of the republic the horrea Galbiana, Galbae, or Sulpicia, were built here,[1] which afterward came into the possession of the government, as in the reign of Augustus they were directly under imperial control. The emperor

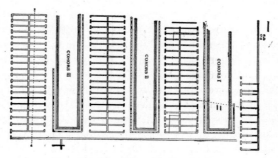

FIG. 83. — THE HORREA GALBIANA.

Galba enlarged their capacity,[2] but great care was taken not to disturb the tomb of the consular which was discovered just in front of the horrea. To meet the increasing demands of commerce other horrea[3] were built, so that in the fourth century there were at least fourteen general warehouses, named after individuals, besides the large number which Alexander Severus caused to be erected in all parts of the city, and doubtless other special storehouses. These horrea were the horrea Galbae, Vespasiani,[4] Nervae,[5] Caesaris,[6] Agrippiana et Germaniciana,[7] Aniciana,[8]

---

[1] Hor. *Od.* iv. 12. 18, and Porphyr. *ad loc.;* Gilbert, III. 285; Jordan, I. 3. 176.

[2] *Chronogr. a. 354*, p. 146.

[3] Gilbert, III. 284–285; Jordan, I. 3. 176–177.

[4] *Chronogr. a. 354*, p. 146.      [6] *CIL.* vi. 4240.

[5] *CIL.* vi. 8681.      [7] *CIL.* vi. 9972.

[8] *Not.* Reg. xiii.

Leoniana,[1] Lolliana,[2] Petroniana,[3] Postumiana,[4] Seiana,[5] Sempronia,[6] Q. Tinei Sacerdotis,[7] Volusiana.[8] Of these the Sempronia were the oldest, dating from the time of the Gracchi. The horrea Germaniciana were perhaps those of which the ruins have been found at the foot of the Palatine, next to the temple of Augustus (p. 165), but nearly all the rest were probably in region XIII.

Recent excavations,[9] occasioned by the laying out of new streets in this quarter, have brought to light many of the foundation walls of these horrea, especially of the horrea Galbae, which were the largest and most important of all, being the storehouses of the grain which belonged to the government (*annona publica*). They were directly back of the Emporium, parallel to the river bank, and formed a rectangle 200 metres long and 155 wide, inclosed by a wall. The warehouses were divided symmetrically into sections separated by courts. These courts were surrounded by travertine colonnades, through which opened the chambers of the warehouses.

In this quarter were probably the porticus Fabaria,[10] a sort of produce exchange, the vicus Frumentarius,[11] and the forum Pistorum.[12]

South of the horrea Galbiana is a remarkable hill, the mons Testaceus [13] (*monte Testaccio*), 35 metres high and about 1 kilometre in circumference, composed entirely of fragments of earthen jars (*amphorae, doliola*) in which corn and produce of all kinds had been brought to the horrea from Africa and Spain. Many of these jars had inscriptions upon the handles or necks, and a large number of them have been recovered.

---

[1] *CIL.* vi. 237.

[2] Jordan, *FUR.* 51; *CIL.* vi. 4226.

[3] *CIL.* vi. 3971.

[4] Marini, *Iscrizioni Doliari*, 279.

[5] *CIL.* vi. 238.

[6] Fest. 290.

[7] Marini, *loc. cit.*

[8] *CIL.* vi. 9973.

[9] *BC.* 1885, 51–53, 110–129; *Mitt.* 1886, 42–44, 62, 65–78; *Ann. d. Ist.* 1885, 223–231; *NS.* 1885, 224, 251.

[10] *Not.* Reg. xiii.

[11] *Bas. Capit.* Reg. xiii; *CIL.* vi. 814.

[12] *Not.* Reg. xiii; Jordan, I. 3. 179.

[13] *Ann d. Ist.* 1878, 118–192; 1885, 232–234; Jordan, I. 3. 177–178.

They date from 140 to 251 A.D., but it is certain that the dumping of débris on this spot began as early as the time of Augustus, and that the hill had reached its present height by the middle of the first century. Beneath the surface on one side of the hill a tomb of the Rusticelii has been discovered, which was covered up by a sort of land-slide. The distribution of débris shows that this hill stood in the midst of the horrea.

**Private Houses.** — On the southwest side of the Aventine, above the porta Lavernalis, there were probably many houses of wealthy Romans, among them that of the Caecinae Decii,[1] and especially the privata Traiani.[2] This was the house of Trajan, while still a private citizen, and its ruins have been found beneath the Benedictine monastery of St. Anselm. During the empire private residences multiplied rapidly on all parts of the Aventine, but our knowledge of them is in most cases confined to the names of their owners.[3]

**Tomb of Cestius.** — Close to the porta Ostiensis is a pyramidal tomb, the burial-place of a certain C. Cestius,[4] who died before 12 B.C. When the wall of Aurelian was built, the pyramid was utilized in such a way that it stands directly in the line of the wall. Inscriptions[5] on the two sides record the name and titles of Cestius, and a third inscription on the east side describes the circumstances of the erection of the monument. The pyramid itself is of brick-faced concrete, covered with white marble. It is about 35 metres high and rests upon a base of travertine 30 metres square. In the interior is the burial chamber, 5.95 metres long and 4.10 wide.

Outside of the porta Ostiensis, a necropolis like that on the via Salaria has been found, containing many cinerary urns of slaves and freedmen, with fragments of sarcophagi and skeletons.[6]

---

[1] *CIL.* xv. 7420; vi. 1192.　　　　[2] *Not.* Reg. xii; Jordan, I. 3. 168.
[3] For all the available evidence on this point, see Merlin, *op. cit.* 333–361.
[4] Cic. *Phil.* iii. 26.　　　[5] *CIL.* vi. 1374.　　　[6] *B C.* 1897, 310–316.

## Region XII.

The eastern portion of the Aventine was connected in legend
with Remus,[1] and it was here that he observed the auspices at
the founding of the city, while Romulus did the same on the
Palatine.   The spot was called the **Remoria** and was near the
church of S. Balbina, but whether it was always an open space
or was marked by some monument, we do not know.   It was
also called **Saxum**,[2] ' the Rock,' and just below it, on the northwest slope of the hill toward the Circus Maximus, was the temple of **Bona Dea Subsaxana**.[3]   The date of the founding of this
temple is unknown, but it was probably in the regal period.
It was restored by Livia, the wife of Augustus, and afterward
by Hadrian, but no traces of it have been found.   The story
told by Ovid that it was dedicated by a Vestal Virgin of the
Claudian family is probably based on an erroneous identification of this temple with an **aedicula**[4] which a Vestal, Licinia,
dedicated in 123 B.C.

It was on this part of the hill that the **ara Iovis Elicii**[5] stood,
the erection of which was ascribed to Numa for the purpose
of drawing (*elicere*) information from Jupiter, and a shrine of
**Silvanus**.[6]

The **horti Serviliani**[7] were probably in the south part of this
region, beyond the line of the wall of Aurelian, and west of
the via Ardeatina.   Like most of the great parks (p. 464),
they had become part of the imperial domain, and were a
favorite resort of Nero and Vitellius.   They contained some

---

[1] Fest. 276; Dionys. i. 85–87; Plut. *Rom.* 9, 11; Ov. *Fast.* v. 148–150; Gilbert, II. 201–204.

[2] Cic. *pro Domo*, 136.

[3] Macrob. *Sat.* i. 12. 21; Spart. *Vit. Hadr.* 19; Gilbert, II. 206–211; III. 445;
Jordan, I. 3. 181–183.

[4] Ov. *Fast.* v. 155–156; Cic. *pro Domo*, 136.

[5] Liv. i. 20; Varro, *LL.* vi. 95; Ov. *Fast.* iii. 327–331; Gilbert, II. 153.

[6] *CIL.* vi. 543.

[7] Tac. *Ann.* xv. 55; *Hist.* iii. 38; Suet. *Nero*, 47; Pl. *NH.* xxxvi. 23, 25, 36;
*CIL.* vi. 8673, 8674.

famous works of art.   In the same district was a vinea publica, which is mentioned only in one inscription.[1]  This states that Vespasian recovered it from private individuals who had wrongfully taken possession of it.   The barracks of the cohors IV vigilum was on this part of the hill just north of S. Saba, where inscriptions relating to the establishment have been found.[2]

Of the private houses in this quarter special mention should be made of the domus Cilonis,[3] or house of Cilo, a distinguished citizen of the time of Severus, who lived near S. Balbina, and of the privata Hadriani,[4] which is supposed to have been situated northeast of the porta Ostiensis.

**Thermae Antoninianae** or **Caracallae**. — The most magnificent monument in region XII was the baths of Caracalla,[5] south of the Aventine, between the via Appia and the via Ardeatina.   These baths were the largest ever built in Rome except those of Diocletian (p. 493), and their ruins are among the most imposing in the city.   They were begun about 212 A.D., opened by Caracalla about 216, and finished by Elagabalus and Alexander Severus.   They were restored by Aurelian, and by Theodoric at the beginning of the sixth century, and accommodated sixteen hundred bathers at once, — half the number provided for in the baths of Diocletian.

The ruins[6] of the thermae Antoninianae are better preserved

---

[1] *CIL.* vi. 933; *BC.* 1882, 155.

[2] *Ann. d. Ist.* 1858, 285–289; *CIL.* vi. 219; *BC.* 1902, 204–206; Jordan, I. 1. 308–309; Gilbert, III. 197.

[3] Jordan, *FUR.* 43; Vict. *Epit.* 20; *CIL.* xv. 7447; *Bull. d. Ist.* 1859, 164; *NS.* 1884, 223.

[4] Jul. Capit. *Vit. Aur.* 5; *Bull. d. Ist.* 1859, 15.   (For other private houses in this region, see p. 420, n. 3.)

[5] Spart. *Vit. Sever.* 21; *Carac.* 9; Lamprid. *Vit. Elagab.* 17; *Alex.* 25; Vict. *Caes.* 21; *Chronogr. a. 354*, pp. 147–148; *CIL.* vi. 794, 1170–1173, 9232; Gilbert, III. 298; Jordan, I. 3. 189–196.

[6] *NS.* 1878, 346; 1879, 15, 40, 114, 141, 314; 1881, 57, 89; *CR.* 1902, 286; *Mitt.* 1893, 294–295.   The latest and most complete description and restoration of these thermae is by Hülsen in Iwanoff's *Architektonische Studien*, Heft. III, herausgeg. vom kais. deutsch. arch. Institut, 1898.

than those of any other Roman baths, and furnish considerable
information as to the arrangements and service of this most
characteristic Roman institution. They are divided into two
parts, — the group of buildings which form the baths proper,
and a vast peribolus with annexes of various sorts. The whole
area covered by the establishment is quadrangular, 353 metres

Fig. 84. — Ruins of the Baths of Caracalla. The Frigidarium.

by 335, with semicircular projections on the east and west
sides. To provide so large a level space, it was necessary to
make an artificial platform at a high level, and thereby to
destroy or cover up many existing buildings. Excavations
at the south corner of the area have disclosed the peristyle
and adjoining rooms of a private house of Hadrian's time, with

mosaic pavements and the ordinary decorations. The walls of these earlier buildings were utilized in supporting the platform of the baths. Covering a part of this site, and adjacent to it, were the gardens of Asinius, horti Asiniani,[1] which are mentioned at the beginning of the second century.

The front of the thermae was parallel with the via Appia, but some distance back from it, so that Caracalla built a new street, the via Nova, directly from the Circus Maximus to the main entrance of the baths in the middle of the northeast side. The central building is 216 metres long and 112 wide, rectangular except in the middle of the southwest side, where the caldarium projects. The arrangement of parts is that common to all thermae, and consists of three main divisions, frigidarium, so-called tepidarium, and caldarium, with many smaller apartments for dressing, anointing, private bathing, service, and the various performances which took place within a Roman bath. The frigidarium is in the centre of the northeast front of the building, and is a rectangular hall divided by two rows of columns into three sections, a vestibule at each end and a great swimming pool in the centre. This pool is 53 metres long and 24 wide, and had a capacity of 1430 cubic metres of water. Wide flights of steps led down into it from each end. The very lofty ceiling of this hall was flat, and supported by eight monolithic columns of granite, four on each side. Between these columns were smaller columns, placed in pairs, which supported an entablature running round the hall. Between the monoliths on the southwest side were two niches. The walls of this hall are standing, but of columns and decoration nothing but fragments and débris remain. This frigidarium has usually been identified with the *cella soliaris*,[2] which is mentioned as having excited the wonder of architects because of its enormous ceiling, which was supposed to have been supported by concealed girders. There are no traces of these

---

[1] Front. *de Aquis*, 21.      [2] Spart. *Vit. Carac.* 9.

girders, but several iron hooks about a metre long have been found, which evidently pierced the concrete ceiling and perhaps attached it to the beams above. According to the most recent explanation [1] *cella soliaris* was a term applied to an apartment containing several hot baths (*solia*) — in these thermae the circular caldarium (see below) — and the greater part at least of its vaulted ceiling was supported by a system of trusses of bronze or wood.

Behind the frigidarium is a middle hall, ordinarily called the tepidarium. This has the same dimensions as the main part of the frigidarium, and at each end are two similar vestibules. The ceiling was formed by three quadripartite vaults, resting on eight monolithic columns of gray granite. Only one of these columns still exists, and that is in the piazza S. Trinità in Florence. Each of the long sides of this hall has three niches, or recesses, in two of which were marble baths. Directly in front of the entrance from the frigidarium is a circular basin about one metre deep and eleven metres in diameter, which was also lined with marble.

The third great hall, the caldarium, connected with the tepidarium by a large vestibule, is circular in shape, and projects for half its diameter beyond the line of the rectangle. This hall is 35 metres in diameter, and was surmounted by a domed ceiling resting on eight massive pilasters. Between the pilasters are the niches which contained the hot baths. In the pilasters spiral staircases were built, and the floor and side walls were lined with tiles communicating with hypocausts beneath. The greater part of the walls of this hall has been destroyed, only two pilasters having been left standing in anything like their original form, and of the decoration nothing remains but insignificant fragments.

On either side of the caldarium are three large apartments for various purposes of toilet and attendance, and at each end of the building is a very large rectangular peristyle, usually called a palaestra.    The two main entrances of the baths opened into these peristyles, which were surrounded by a colonnade supporting an entablature and a gallery.    The frieze was covered with reliefs representing scenes from the chase.    One fragment of this frieze remains *in situ*, in the south peristyle.    In the rear of each peristyle is a large apse.    A considerable

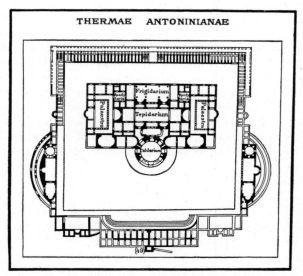

FIG. 85.— PLAN OF THE BATHS OF CARACALLA.

portion of the mosaic pavement from one of these peristyles, representing athletes, is now in the Lateran museum.    Other fragments of this pavement, and some of the capitals of the colonnades, are still to be seen in the peristyles.

In some parts of the building there were upper stories, and in general these thermae illustrate in a most striking way the characteristic methods of Roman construction, especially in the enormous concrete vaults.

The space between this central block of buildings and those which formed the inclosure was laid out as a park and adorned with works of art. The whole northeast side of the peribolus and the adjacent parts of the northwest and southeast sides were inclosed with a wall, against which on the outside were built rows of small vaulted chambers opening outward. In front of these chambers was a porticus. The west halves of the northwest and southeast sides of the peribolus were occupied by semicircular projections, like enormous apses, in each of which was a central open hall with a colonnade, flanked on one side by a swimming pool and on the other by an octagonal room. The central and larger part of the southwest side was occupied by a stadium, or rather half a stadium, as there was never an inner half. This stadium had tiers of marble seats, and behind it was the reservoir of the baths, built in the form of a rectangle and consisting of sixty-four small chambers arranged in parallel rows and in two stories. The capacity of this reservoir was 33,000 cubic metres, and the water was supplied by a branch of the aqua Marcia, the aqua Antoniniana, which was built by Caracalla and crossed the via Appia by the so-called arch of Drusus (p. 434).

These thermae were magnificently decorated and filled with works of art. It was here that the Farnese Bull and the Hercules in Naples were found.

Near these baths were the septem domus Parthorum,[1] — some of the numerous houses which Septimius Severus built and presented to his friends.

---

[1] *Not.* Reg. xii; Vict. *Epit.* 20.

# CHAPTER XVI.

## THE CAELIAN. REGIONS I AND II.

**The mons Caelius** stretches west from the tableland which forms the east part of the city, in a long and irregular tongue which ends in two promontories, so to speak, — an eastern, where the church of SS. Quattro Coronati now stands, and a western, the site of SS. Giovanni e Paolo. Part of the northern end of this tongue seems to have been called Sucusa (p. 40), but whether on the eastern or western side is a matter of dispute.[1] The same uncertainty attaches to the exact limits of that part of the hill which was called Caeliolus[2] or Caeliolum, but this was probably near SS. Quattro Coronati. The earliest name for the whole hill is said to have been mons Querquetulanus,[3] from the oak groves which covered it; but this was perhaps an invention of the antiquarians to explain the porta Querquetulana of the Servian wall. Caelius was connected by them with the settlement of Caeles Vibenna and his Etruscan companions.[4] In the Regionary Catalogues region II is called Caelemontium.[5] In the reign of Tiberius the senate voted to name this hill Augustus in his honor,[6] but this designation, if ever adopted, did not survive the emperor's lifetime. The valley between the Caelian and the Carinae is spoken of as a

---

[1] Wissowa, *Satura Viadrina*, 15; Jordan, I. 3. 224; Richter, *Top.*[2] 37.

[2] Varro, *LL.* v. 46; Cic. *de Har. Resp.* 32; Mart. xii. 18. 6; Gilbert, I. 163; II. 32; Jordan, I. 3. 220–224.

[3] Tac. *Ann.* iv. 65.

[4] Claud. *Or. de Lugdun.;* Fest. 355, *Epit.* 44; Gilbert, II. 18, 32–41; Jordan, I. 1. 186–188.

[5] *Not.* Reg. ii; *CIL.* vi. 10099; *Mitt.* 1892, 270.

[6] Tac. *Ann.* iv. 64; Suet. *Tib.* 48.

*locus Ceroliensis,* or *Ceroniensis,*[1] from which we may infer the substantive Cerolia, or Ceroniae.

All of the Caelian was included within the Servian wall except the eastern part, where the hill joins the tableland. Whether it also had its own line of fortification, like the Palatine and the Capitoline, and whether the remains of opus quadratum which have been found under S. Gregorio opposite the Palatine, resembling in construction the old Servian wall, belong to it, is a disputed question.[2]

In Augustus's division of the city, the Caelian hill fell into three regions, — the western and southern slopes into region I, the main portion into II, and the extreme eastern part into V. The hill was thickly populated during the republic, and we are told of an apartment house belonging to Ti. Claudius Centumalus[3] which the owner was ordered to demolish because it was so high as to cut off the view of the augurs. In 27 A.D. it suffered severely from a fire,[4] and afterward it became a favorite place for the residences of the rich, which, with their gardens, seem to have occupied a considerable part of the whole hill.

**Streets and Squares.** — The general plan of regions I and II can be made out with some degree of certainty, because of the fact that the modern streets have not infrequently followed the line of the ancient, the pavement of imperial times being still preserved beneath the present level.[5] The west boundary (p. 107) of region I was the street leading from the Colosseum to the Circus Maximus, the modern via S. Gregorio, beneath which the old cloaca has been found, and over that the pavement of the republican period, 6.70 metres above the mean level of the Tiber. The later pavement, somewhat above which the arch of Constantine stands, is about 12 metres above the

---

[1] Varro, *LL.* v. 47; Jordan, I. 3. 221.

[2] *Ann. d. Ist.* 1871, 47; cf. Varro, *LL.* v. 46; Jordan, I. 1. 206; 3. 224.

[3] Cic. *de Off.* iii. 66.  [4] Tac. *Ann.* iv. 64.  [5] *Mon. d. Lincei,* i. 516–518.

river, and the modern pavement about 15 metres.   The ancient
name of this street is not known.   The via Appia, which formed
the southwest boundary of region I from the porta Capena to
the northeast corner of the baths of Caracalla, was a little distance to the north of the modern via di porta S. Sebastiano.

From the four sides of the hill, — north, south, east, and
west, — streets led to a common meeting-place just a little
north of the church of S. Maria in Navicella, thus forming
two main arteries of travel across the hill in each direction.
That on the west, starting from the street between the Circus
Maximus and the Colosseum, just north of the church of S. Gregorio, is probably the street which was known in the middle
ages as the clivus Scauri.[1]   The ancient pavement follows in
general the via di SS. Giovanni e Paolo.   From the north, the
vicus Capitis Africae [2] — a name derived probably from some
statue — ascends from the east end of the Colosseum, in the
valley between the two spurs of the hill, the ancient pavement
joining the line of the via della Navicella.   A continuation of
this street must have led south to the gate in the Servian wall
(porta Querquetulana?) and to the corresponding gate in the
Aurelian wall (porta Metrovia?).   The fourth street led from
the common junction east to the porta Caelemontana, along
the line of the via di S. Stefano, where many remains of the
old pavement have been found.   The names of these last two
streets are not known with certainty, but the name Caelemontium [3] may also have been applied to one of them.

From the via Appia a street — perhaps the vicus Drusianus —
ran northeast over the hill to the Lateran, which can be traced
by its pavement for the first part of its course, and corresponds
to the via della Ferratella, although the latter is much more
crooked.   The north boundary of region II seems to have been

---

[1] Jordan, I. 3. 231; II. 594–595.

[2] *Not.* Reg. ii; *CIL*. vi. 8982–8987; *Ann. d. Ist.* 1882, 191–220; Jordan, I. 3
238; *BC.* 1906, 69–70.

[3] *Bull. Crist.* 1874, 41; *BC.* 1891, 342–344; *Mitt.* 1892, 270.

the street represented by the via dei SS. Quattro (see p. 444), thought by some to be the Tabernola mentioned by Varro.[1]

Other streets, the position of which may be approximately determined, are the vicus Fabricii, evidently running into the compitum Fabricii,[2] west of the buildings of Claudius; the vicus Trium Ararum,[3] on the slope of the Caelian, north of the porta Capena; the vicus Honoris et Virtutis,[4] running north from the via Appia near the temple of Honos et Virtus; and the vicus Camenarum, probably south of the via delle Mole. There were two other streets, the vicus Sulpicius citerior and the vicus Sulpicius ulterior,[5] which branched off from the via Appia near the baths of Caracalla, but just where is not known. From the *Notitia* and Capitoline Base we know the names of a few other streets and of various squares or open piazzas,[6] such as the vicus Fortunae Obsequentis and the vicus Pulverarius, the area Calles, area Carruces, and area Pannaria, but their exact location is uncertain. The east portion of the Caelian, outside the Servian wall, was probably the campus Caelemontanus,[7] or Martialis,[8] called in the middle ages campus Lateranensis.

Southwest of the Lateran, and outside the Aurelian wall, was a swampy district, called the Decennium,[9] or Decenniae; and the hill was crossed by two aqueducts, the rivus Herculaneus of the aqua Marcia and the arcus Neroniani of the aqua Claudia. On the western slope of the Caelian were two springs, fons Lollianus and fons Pal(atinus?), which were the centres of local cults.[10]

---

[1] *LL.* v. 47; cf., however, Jordan, I. 3. 227.

[2] *Bas. Capit.* Reg. i; Fest. 174; Placidus, 45; Gilbert, II. 126.

[3] *CIL.* vi. 453; *BC.* 1892, 65; Jordan, I. 3. 201, 231.    [4] Lanciani, *Acque*, 56.

[5] *Bas. Capit.* Reg. i; Lamprid. *Vit. Elagab.* 17; Lanciani, *loc. cit.*; Richter, *Top.*[2] 341–342; Jordan, I. 3. 196, 208–209.

[6] Gilbert, III. 346–347; Richter, *Top.*[2] 342, 344–345.

[7] *CIL.* vi. 9475; *Mon. d. Lincei*, i. 534–536; Gilbert, II. 96–97.

[8] Ov. *Fast.* iii. 519–523; Fest. *Epit.* 131; Jordan, I. 3. 225; *BC.* 1906, 66–68. For an attempt to identify the campus Martialis with the campus Minor of Catull. 55. 3, and to locate it outside the porta Capena, see *BC.* 1906, 209–223.

[9] *BC.* 1891, 343, 355–356; *CIL.* vi. 31893.    [10] *CIL.* vi. 157, 162.

## Region I.

**Temples and Shrines**. — The earliest cult in this region was that of the ·Camenae,[1] dating from the early regal period. According to tradition, Numa met his mistress, the nymph Egeria, in a grove just outside the later Servian wall at the foot of the Caelian, in the valley which was traversed by the vicus Camenarum. This valley was called vallis Egeriae or Camenarum (p. 90); the grove, lucus Egeriae or Camenarum; and the spring, fons Egeriae or Camenarum. Directed by Egeria, Numa built here a shrine to the Camenae,[2] which was afterward replaced by a temple. The grotto containing the spring was also adorned with marble. (For another spring, the aqua Mercurii, see p. 91.)

The next oldest sanctuary in this region was the temple and grove of Mars, situated at the left of the via Appia, 2 kilometres from the porta Capena and just outside the Aurelian wall. It stood on high ground, and the rise of the via Appia to the temple was called the clivus Martis.[3] At a later time the grade of the road was removed, or at least very much diminished. The temple was probably dedicated[4] in 388 B.C.; and in 296 B.C. a pavement[5] was laid from the porta Capena to it. This pavement was relaid[6] in 189 B.C., and the road provided with a porticus, so that it was afterward known as the via Tecta.[7] This temple is frequently mentioned,[8] but nothing is known of its history after the fourth century, and its approximate site is determined only by the discovery of inscriptions.[9] An in-

---

[1] Liv. i. 21; Juv. 3. 10–17; Plut. *Numa*, 13; Gilbert, I. 109–111; II. 152–158; Jordan, I. 3. 206–208; *BC.* 1905, 220–222.

[2] Serv. *ad Aen.* i. 8; Pl. *NH.* xxxiv. 19.

[3] *CIL.* vi. 1270.      [4] Liv. vi. 5.      [5] Liv. x. 23.      [6] Liv. xxxviii. 28.

[7] Ov. *Fast.* vi. 191–192. (This street is to be distinguished from the via Tecta in the campus Martius, p. 377.)

[8] Cic. *ad Q. Fr.* iii. 7; Dionys. vi. 13; App. *Bell. Civ.* iii. 41; Gilbert, II. 96–99.

[9] *CIL.* vi 473–474; Jordan, I. 3. 213–215; II. 110.

scription [1] is also the only evidence of the existence of a shrine of Aesculapius and Hygia near the temple of Mars. The lapis manalis,[2] a miraculous stone which, if brought into the city during a drought, caused rain, was also near this temple. Probably between the temple of Mars and the porta Capena was the temple of the Tempestates,[3] built in 259 B.C. by L. Cornelius Scipio, and a temple of Minerva which was in existence in the fourth century.

The temple of Honos et Virtus was situated on the north side of the via Appia, a short distance south of the porta Capena. The original part of this temple was built in 234 B.C. by Q. Fabius Maximus, and dedicated to Honos.[4] In 208 B.C. M. Claudius Marcellus attempted to rededicate it to Honos et Virtus in pursuance of a vow which he had made at the battle of Clastidium.[5] As this was forbidden by the pontifices, he restored the temple of Honos, and built a new part for Virtus. This temple was afterward restored [6] by Vespasian. It contained many of the treasures which Marcellus brought from the sack of Syracuse.[7] Near it was an ara Fortunae Reducis,[8] erected by the senate in 19 B.C. in honor of the return of Augustus from the East.

To the Almo at the southern boundary of this region, the sacred stone of the Magna Mater was brought once a year for the ceremony of *lavatio*,[9] but there was probably no temple built here, only a sacred temenos.

---

[1] *CIL*. vi. 10234.

[2] Fest. 128; Serv. *ad Aen*. iii. 175; Varro, *ap*. Non. 637; Gilbert, II. 154–155.

[3] *CIL*. i. 32 = vi. 1287; Ov. *Fast*. vi. 193–194; *Not*. Reg. i; Gilbert, III. 100.

[4] Cic. *de Nat. Deor*. ii. 61; Gilbert, III. 97–98; *Bull. d. Ist*. 1873, 89–91.

[5] Liv. xxvii. 25; Val. Max. i. 1. 8; Plut. *Marc*. 28; Symm. *Epist*. i. 20.

[6] Pl. *NH*. xxxv. 120.

[7] Liv. xxv. 40; Cic. *Verr*. iv. 120–121; Plut. *Marc*. 21; *CIL*. i. 530, note.

[8] *Mon. Anc*. ii. 29; Dio Cass. liv. 10; *CIL*. i.² p. 332; Cohen, *August*. 102-108.

[9] Ov. *Fast*. iv. 337–340; Jordan, I. 3. 215.

**Other Buildings**. — Mention is made of other buildings in this region of which little or nothing is known, such as the **Mutatorium Caesaris**,[1] an imperial property of unknown use, represented on the Marble Plan[2] and situated perhaps near the porta Capena; the **thermae Commodianae**,[3] erected by Cleander, a favorite of Commodus, and the **thermae Severianae**,[4] built probably by Severus, both of which existed in the fourth century and were somewhere south of the baths of Caracalla; the **lacus Promethei**, probably a large fountain; and six **balnea**, *i.e.* **Abascantis, Mamertini, Bolani, Antiochiani, Torquati, Vespasiani**.[5] The senate met regularly *ad portam Capenam* during the year 216 B.C., and there was here a **senaculum**,[6] as well as on the Comitium and near the temple of Bellona (p. 344).

**Arches**. — The via Appia was spanned by three and perhaps four arches within the limits of this region.

(1) The **arcus Drusi**,[7] erected after 9 B.C. in honor of the elder Drusus. It was of marble and adorned with trophies, and probably stood a short distance north of the point where the via Latina branches off from the via Appia, but no trace of it has been found.

(2) The **arcus divi Traiani**,[8] erected in 113 A.D. by the senate to commemorate the victories of Trajan over the Dacians. This arch is represented on coins, and was standing in the fourth century.

(3) The arch now standing just inside the porta S. Sebastiano, and called the **arco di Druso**. This supported the aqua Antoniniana (p. 95) where it crossed the via Appia. It is of

[1] *Not.* Reg. i; Gilbert, III. 350–351; Jordan, I. 3. 205.

[2] Jordan, *FUR.* 3.

[3] Herodian. i. 12. 3; Lamprid. *Vit. Commodi*, 17; *Not.* Reg. i; *Chronogr. a. 354*, p. 148; Gilbert, III. 298; *BC.* 1887, 323–324.

[4] Spart. *Vit. Sev.* 19; *Chronogr. a. 354*, p. 148; Jordan, I. 3. 217–218.

[5] *Not.* Reg. i; Jordan, I. 3. 219.        [6] Liv. xxiii. 32; Fest. 347.

[7] Suet. *Claud.* 1; Jordan, I. 1. 365; Lanciani, *Acque*, 55.

[8] *Not.* Reg. i; Gilbert, III. 191; Cohen, *Traian.* 547.

travertine, lined with marble, and has a single passageway, 7.21 metres high and 5.50 wide, flanked on each side by two Corinthian columns of yellow marble with white marble capitals, of which two are still standing. The origin of this arch is unknown, but it has been identified with each of those already mentioned.[1]

(4) The arcus divi Veri,[2] erected in honor of the emperor Lucius Verus, probably over the via Appia, of which nothing further is known.

According to Tacitus [3] the same honors were decreed to the younger Drusus after his death in 23 A.D., that had been paid to Germanicus in 19 A.D., and a strict interpretation of this statement would include the erection of an arch, of which, however, there is no other record.

**Tombs and Columbaria.** — Roman law forbade burial within the city, and therefore it became customary from very early times to erect tombs and monuments outside the gates along the roads leading into the country. As the city grew, many of these tombs were included within its limits, especially in region I, where the distance between the porta Capena and the outer boundary of the region was so great. The two roads, Appia and Latina, were lined with the sepulchres of great families. Many of these tombs still exist, extending for several miles outside the present city limits.

Cicero [4] speaks of four such families as having their tombs on the via Appia, — the Calatini, Servilii, Metelli, and Scipiones. Of these four, one at least was within the later city limits, for the tomb of the Scipios, sepulchrum or hypogaeum Scipionum, still exists. This tomb [5] was discovered in 1780, and is at the southeast corner of the via Appia and a road

---

[1] Cf. Gilbert, III. 189; Jordan, I. 3. 216.      [3] *Ann.* ii. 83; iv. 9.
[2] *Not.* Reg. i.      [4] *Tusc.* i. 13.
[5] Jordan, I. 3. 210–211; Ripostelli-Marucchi, *La Via Appia*, Rome, 1908, 27–41.

which crossed from it to the via Latina, the entrance being on this cross-road. It had originally two stories, but only the lower now remains. It consists of a series of irregular chambers excavated in the tufa rock and connected by passages. The entrance is formed by an arched doorway of peperino, with engaged columns. The roof is now supported by modern piers.

As the Scipios were buried and not burned,[1] the sepulchre was filled with sarcophagi, many of which were broken and their remains scattered when the tomb was opened.[2] One, however, that of L. Cornelius Scipio Barbatus, consul in 298 B.C. and the first to be buried here, has been preserved and is now in the Vatican, together with portions of several others, on which are inscriptions. The sarcophagus of Barbatus is elaborately decorated with a Doric entablature, while the lid has Ionic volutes. The inscriptions[3] in Saturnian metre upon this and the other sarcophagi are extremely valuable for the history of Latin literature and phonology, but they are probably much later than the date which has usually been assigned to them, the earliest being no earlier than the second Punic War. Ennius is said to have been buried in this tomb,[4] and his statue to have stood here in Cicero's time, while just outside the porta Capena the tomb of Horatia[5] was still visible at the end of the republic.

The space between the via Appia, the via Latina, and the Aurelian wall, now included for the most part in the vigna Sassi and the vigna Codini, was occupied in process of time by tombs of all sorts, and upward of sixteen hundred sepulchral inscriptions[6] have been found here.

---

[1] Cic. de Legg. ii. 57.    [2] Cf. CIL. i. pp. 11–12.

[3] CIL. i. 29–39 = vi. 1284–1294.

[4] Suet. de Poet.; Pl. NH. vii. 114; Liv. xxxviii. 56; Cic. pro Arch. 22.

[5] Liv. i. 26.

[6] In vigna Sassi CIL. vi. 5539–5678; in vigna Codini CIL. vi. 4418–5538, 5676–5886; Ripostelli-Marucchi, op. cit. 68–87.

With the increasing frequency of cremation, the growth of the population of the city, and the difficulty of securing space for burial purposes, the custom arose, about the beginning of the empire, of building chambers, mostly subterranean, the walls of which contained many rows of niches, arched or square, where hundreds of cinerary urns could be set. These rows of niches gave the tomb-chambers the appearance of dove-cotes, and hence they were called columbaria. They were

FIG. 86. — COLUMBARIUM IN THE VIGNA CODINI.

built by the wealthy for their slaves and freedmen, by members of these *familiae* themselves by subscription, by guilds and fraternities of various kinds, or by speculators who sold places to any who chose to buy.

This method of tomb-building was very economical and became extremely common. Many such columbaria have been discovered in the last three centuries in this district, but only four have been preserved, that of Pomponius Hylas in the vigna Sassi near the porta Latina, discovered in 1831, and three in the vigna Codini, between the sepulchrum Scipionum and the porta Appia, discovered between 1840 and 1853.[1]

All four of these columbaria date from the first century, and while they differ in some respects, they resemble each other in the main. They are beneath the ground level and approached by steep flights of steps. That discovered in 1840 is 7.50 metres long, 5.65 wide, and 6.24 high, and contains four hundred and fifty niches. The sepulchral inscriptions in these columbaria were written on tablets affixed to the wall below the niche; and as niches often passed from one owner to another, there are sometimes two inscriptions for one niche.

There were sometimes as many as nine rows of niches; and as it was impossible to reach the upper rows from the floor, provision was made for a temporary wooden scaffolding, which usually rested on stone corbels set in the wall. At a later period, after these columbaria had been filled with cinerary urns, they seem to have been opened and the uncremated bodies of the dead were thrown into them in a most promiscuous fashion. Other columbaria, as that of the slaves and freedmen of Livia,[2] the wife of Augustus, have been found outside the walls, but they are of the same general character as those just described.

## REGION II.

**Temples and Shrines.**— On that part of the Caelian afterward included in region II there were three sanctuaries devoted to very ancient cults. These were : —

(1) The sacellum Minervae Captae,[3] also called Minervium, on the north slope of Caeliolus, which derived its name from the statue of Minerva brought from Falerii when that town was

---

[1] *Bull. d. Ist.* 1840, 135–138; 1847, 49–51; 1852, 81–83; *Ann. d. Ist.* 1856, 8–24; cf. Lanciani, *Ruins*, 329–337; Jordan, I. 3. 211–213; *PBS.* v. 463–471.

[2] *CIL.* vi. 3926–4326.

[3] Ov. *Fast.* iii. 835–838; Varro, *LL.* v. 47; *CIL.* vi. 524; Gilbert, II. 26–27; *Ann. d. Ist.* 1849, 377; *Mon. d. Ist.* v. 7; Jordan, I. 3. 226.

captured; it was near the arcus ad Isis (p. 319), and was standing
in the fourth century ; (2) the sacellum Deae Carnae,[1] built by
Brutus in the first year of the republic, for the goddess who,
according to Macrobius, was believed *vitalibus humanis praeesse;*
and (3) the sacellum Dianae,[2] *maximum et sanctissimum*, situated
on the Caeliolus and removed by L. Calpurnius Piso, consul in
58 B.C. No traces of these shrines have been found, nor of the
shrines (or statues) of Iuppiter Caelius and the Genius Caelimontis,
which are represented on a relief[3] found near the baths of
Diocletian.

The only temple[4] in this region of which anything definite
is known was that of the deified Claudius, which was begun
by Agrippina. After her death Nero destroyed, *prope funditus*,
a considerable portion of what had been erected, and built in
its place a nymphaeum for the branch of the aqua Claudia
which he brought over the hill. Vespasian rebuilt the temple,
and dedicated it as the templum divi Claudi. It stood on the
north spur of the Caelian opposite the Colosseum, the site now
occupied by the gardens of the Passionist Fathers.

The temple itself stood on a lofty and extensive podium, and
was surrounded by a colonnade, the porticus Claudia.[5] Of the
temple and porticus nothing remains, but the substructures of
the podium are still visible. These substructures are different on
the different sides of the podium, those on the west consisting
of double rows of travertine arches with engaged columns and
entablature ; those on the north containing what seem to be reservoirs for water ; and those on the east consisting of square
and semicircular recesses, which are separated from the podium

---

[1] Macrob. *Sat.* i. 12, 31; Tertull. *ad Nat.* ii. 9; Ov. *Fast.* vi. 101 ff.; Gilbert,
II. 19–22.

[2] Cic. *de Har. Resp.* 32; Jordan, II. 257; Gilbert, II. 22–26.

[3] *BC.* 1887, 314.

[4] Suet. *Vesp.* 9; Front. *de Aquis*, 20, 76; Vict. *Caes.* 9; *CIL.* vi. 10251 a;
*Ann. d. Ist.* 1882, 205; *NS.* 1880, 463; 1909, 427; Lanciani, *Acque*, 159; Gilbert,
III. 124; Jordan, I. 3. 232–234.

[5] Mart. *de Spect.* ii. 9; Jordan, *FUR.* 33.

by a narrow passage. This difference in style and construction is probably due to the combination of temple and nymphaeum which was the result of Vespasian's restoration. The building existed in the fourth century, but there are indications that its destruction began about that time.

**Other Buildings.** — On the Caelian were the castra Peregrina,[1] or barracks of the *frumentarii*, originally a corps of foreign troops employed as military couriers, and in the second and third centuries as a sort of special police. Within this camp was a shrine of Iuppiter Redux,[2] erected by the soldiers of Alexander Severus and Mammaea. In 1905 some fragmentary inscriptions, and the remains of a building that may have been the castra, were found just southeast of S. Stefano Rotondo,[3] and this is now regarded as its site. South of S. Maria in Navicella, in the grounds of the villa Mattei, part of a mosaic pavement and two inscribed pedestals mark the site of the barracks of the cohors V vigilum.[4] At the north corner of the site of the castra Peregrina stands the arcus Dolabellae et Silani,[5] erected in 10 A.D. by the consuls P. Cornelius Dolabella and C. Junius Silanus. This arch is of travertine without ornamentation, and is ordinarily supposed to have been built to support a branch of the aqua Marcia and to have been utilized afterward by Nero in his extension of the aqua Claudia. Corroborative evidence for this theory is found in the similar construction and inscription[6] of the arcus Lentuli et Crispini (p. 410) at the foot of the Aventine.

According to the Regionary Catalogue the Lupanarii were near the barracks of the vigiles and the frumentarii. As the

---

[1] Amm. Marcell. xvi. 12. 66; *CIL.* vi. 230–231, 354; *Bull. d. Ist.* 1851, 113; 1884, 21–29; Jordan, I. 3. 234–236.

[2] *CIL.* vi. 428.

[3] *CR.* 1905, 328–329; *BC.* 1905, 108; Hülsen, *Atti. d. Accad. Pont.* viii. 410.

[4] *CIL.* vi. 221, 222, 1057, 1058; *Ann. d. Ist.* 1858, 289–294; Gilbert, III. 196.

[5] *CIL.* vi. 1384; Lanciani, *Acque*, 101; Gilbert, III. 189.

[6] *CIL.* vi. 1385.

barracks of the Misenates (p. 450) and of the equites singulares (p. 472) were not far away, it is a plausible suggestion that these brothels were on the southern slope of the hill, and that they were called **Summoenia** or **Summoenianae**,[1] because they were built, partially at least, under the old Servian wall.

In 59 A.D. Nero built on the Caelian a public market, the **macellum Magnum**,[2] which is shown on coins to have consisted of a building of two stories, with a central tholus, or domed structure, surrounded by columns. It was destroyed at some later date, and rebuilt about the end of the fourth century for public use, perhaps again as a market. A century later it was transformed into the church of S. Stefano Rotondo. Further changes were made in succeeding centuries, and of the original macellum of Nero the only remaining portions are the travertine foundations, part of the inclosure wall, and eight pilasters of the outer colonnade. The fourth-century structure was built on the original foundations, and appears to have preserved in general the form of Nero's building. It consisted of a two-storied circular colonnade, of twenty-two columns, which supported a domed roof. This was surrounded by an outer concentric colonnade of thirty-six columns, also two stories high. Outside of this was an ambulatory, 10 metres wide, divided into eight segments by rows of columns. The alternate segments were inclosed by an outer wall.

The **Antrum Cyclopis** of the Regionary Catalogue would appear to have been a grotto in the side of the hill, which was probably built up in some way. It gave its name to a vicus.

**Private Houses**. — Under the empire, the Caelian became a favorite residential quarter for the rich,[3] and the excavations [4]

---

[1] Mart. i. 34; iii. 82; xi. 61.

[2] Dio Cass. lxi. 18; *CIL*. vi. 1648, 9183; Cohen, *Nero*, 126–130; *Mon. d. Lincei*, i. 503–507; *Mitt*. 1892, 297–299; Gilbert, III. 238; Jordan, I. 3. 237–238; Altmann, *Rundbauten*, 75–76.

[3] Cf. Gilbert, III. 348–349; Mart. xii. 18. 4.           [4] *NS*. 1885, 66.

of recent years, particularly those carried on within the area now occupied by the villa Casali and the Ospedale Militare, have brought to light many remains and inscriptions belonging to their houses.[1] They occupied the central part of the hill, on both sides of the rivus Herculaneus from the castra Peregrina east.

Among them were the houses of **Q. Aurelius Symmachus**,[2] the famous statesman and orator of the fourth century, and of **C. Stertinius Xenophon**,[3] the physician of Claudius. Near by were the residences of the **Pisones**[4] and **Valerii**,[5] as well as many others. Here, too, was some sort of a pleasure resort of Domitian's, the **Mica Aurea**,[6] and the basilica **Hilariana**,[7] of which nothing more is known. The house of **Mamurra**[8] was celebrated as the first in which the walls were lined with marble.

The most famous of all these houses is that which belonged to the **Laterani**, called by Juvenal [9] *egregiae Lateranorum aedes*. In 65 A.D. Plautius Lateranus was executed by Nero for having joined in the conspiracy of Piso, and all his property is supposed to have been confiscated, including the house, which then remained in the possession of the emperors until Severus restored it to T. Sextius Lateranus.[10] It must have fallen again into imperial hands, for Constantine presented it to Pope Miltiades in 313 A.D., after which time it continued to be the official residence of the popes until it was destroyed by the gradual enlargement of the great church of St. John Lateran.

---

[1] For a list of these houses, see Richter, *Top.*[2] 338–339.

[2] Symm. *Epist.* iii. 12, 88; vii. 18, 19; *CIL.* vi. 1699.

[3] Pl. *NH.* xxix. 7–8; *CIL.* vi. 8905; xv. 7544; *BC.* 1886, 104.

[4] Cic. *in Pis.* 61; *CIL.* xv. 7513.

[5] *CIL.* vi. 1684–1694; *BC.* 1890, 288–292; Jordan, I. 3. 240. For the interesting excavations recently made on the site of this house, see *NS.* 1902, 283–284; *BC.* 1902, 74–78, 145–163; *CR.* 1905, 328.

[6] *Chronogr. a. 354.* p. 146; *Not.* Reg. ii (Mart. ii. 59? Cf. Jordan, I. 3. 252).

[7] *BC.* 1890, 18–25, 78; *Mitt.* 1891, 109–110.

[8] Pl. *NH.* xxxvi. 48.          [9] x. 17.

[10] Tac. *Ann.* xv. 49, 60; Vict. *Epit.* 20; Jul. Cap. *Vit. M. Ant.* 1; Gilbert, III. 349; Jordan, I. 3. 243–245.

Some of its ruins[1] have been discovered beneath the choir of the church, at depths varying from 7.50 to 13 metres, and consist principally of a series of apartments connected by a porticus and adorned with rows of columns, statues, and other works of art. Lead pipes of the second century, inscribed with names of members of the Laterani family, are thought by some to prove that the house itself did not pass out of the possession of its original owners until the following century. The obelisk in the piazza was brought from the Circus Maximus (p. 408), and the statue of Marcus Aurelius, now on the Capitol, stood here until the year 1538. Marcus Aurelius[2] himself was born in the house of the Annii which was near that of the Laterani.

A very interesting house, of a rather late period, is that of St. John and St. Paul (domus sctt. Iohannis et Pauli), recently discovered beneath the church of SS. Giovanni e Paolo.[3] This house, in which these two saints are reported to have been martyred, is a private dwelling of the second century, which was enlarged and rebuilt in the third and fourth, and over which the basilica was erected in the fifth. The enlargement consisted for the most part in connecting two houses, which had been separated by a narrow street. In the excavated portion upward of thirty rooms have been opened up, among them a cavaedium with five rows of three rooms each on its south side, bath-rooms, storerooms, and stairways. The house had three stories, traces of which may be seen on the left of the clivus Scauri (via di SS. Giovanni e Paolo). There is an arcade below, and rows of windows in the two upper stories. The atrium and adjacent apartments probably occupy most of that portion of the house which has not yet been excavated.

---

[1] *Ann. d. Ist.* 1877, 332–384.        [2] Jul. Capit. *Vit. M. Ant.* 1; *CP.* 1909, 195.
[3] *NS.* 1887, 532; 1890, 79–80, 150; 1891, 161–162; 1892, 264; *BC.* 1887, 321–322; 1892, 65; 1909, 122–123; *Mitt.* 1889, 261–262; 1891, 107–108; 1892, 297; *AJA.* 1890, 261–285, pl. xvi, xvii; 1891, 25–37, pl. iv–vi.

# CHAPTER XVII.

## THE ESQUILINE. REGIONS III, IV, V.

**The Esquiline district**[1] included the two spurs of the Esquiline hill, the Oppius and the Cispius; the Carinae[2] or western, and the Fagutal or northwestern, slope of the Oppius; the Subura, the valley between the Oppius and the Cispius; and the campus Esquilinus[3] or wide plateau east of the Servian wall which was afterward region V. Esquiliae or mons Esquilinus usually denoted the whole hill with its two spurs and the plateau behind (p. 40).

In the organization of Augustus this district was divided into three regions. Region III included the Colosseum valley and was bounded by the street which connected this valley with the porta Caelemontana (the modern via dei SS. Quattro), by the Servian wall, the clivus Suburanus and the Subura, and probably by the vicus Cuprius. Region IV lay north of III, and was bounded on the other sides by the Sacra via, the Forum, the forum of Nerva, and the vicus Patricius. Between the forum of Nerva and the vicus Patricius, the boundary seems to have described a wide curve. Region V lay east of the Servian wall, from the street between the porta Caelemontana and the porta Asinaria on the south to the castra Praetoria on the north. A large part of this region was known during the republic as the pagus Montanus,[4] a reminiscence of its earlier organization as a canton; and its northern section, between the Servian and Aurelian walls and adjacent to the castra

---

[1] Jordan, I. 3. 254 ff.
[2] Varro, *LL*. v. 47; Gilbert, II. 62; Jordan, I. 3. 262–265.
[3] Cic. *Phil*. ix. 17; Strabo, v. 3.9 (237); Suet. *Claud*. 25.
[4] *CIL*. vi. 3823; Jordan, I. 1. 184; Gilbert, I. 169.

Praetoria, was called the campus Viminalis sub aggere.[1] Near the porta Esquilina was the open area of the forum Esquilinum,[2] probably inside rather than outside the wall.

**Ancient Necropolis.** — In very early times a vast necropolis[3] spread over the Esquiline, from the modern villa Spithoever and the Treasury building to the piazza Vittorio Emanuele. Within this area tombs have been discovered of two successive types. The earliest and most numerous are *putei*, or graves cut in the tufa rock, from 2 to 4 metres in length, in which the bones of the dead were laid, together with various articles of furniture and personal equipment. Those of the second type contain stone receptacles, monolithic except for the lids, or else made of several slabs, like small boxes. These tombs have been found in other places, but especially in the via Napoleone III and the piazza Vittorio Emanuele. It seems clear, therefore, that during the first period of the iron age the inhabitants of this district dug both trench-tombs for burial and well-tombs for ashes. The Servian wall was built directly across the necropolis and over the tombs themselves.

During the later republic this district, outside the Servian wall and extending as far as the amphitheatrum Castrense, was used as a cemetery, and divided into two zones. The first, where the poor, slaves, and malefactors were buried, and which was in a sense a Potter's Field, is said to have occupied a space 1000 feet long and 300 wide,[4] just outside the agger of Servius near the porta Esquilina. This was also the place of public executions[5] during the republic. Under the empire, executions may have taken place near the Sessorium (p. 469),

---

[1] *Not.* Reg. v; Jordan, I. 3. 342; II. 129.

[2] App. *Bell. Civ.* i. 58; *CIL.* vi. 2223, 9179–9180; Jordan, I. 3. 317–318; Richter, *Top.*[2] 332.

[3] *BC.* 1874, 46–53; 1885, 39–50; 1896, 5–60; 1898, 137–140; *Ann. d. Ist.* 1879, 253–299; 1880, 265–342; 1882, 5–58; *Bull. d. Ist.* 1885, 72–77; Jordan, I. 3. 261, 265–270; Pinza, *Mon. d. Lincei*, xv. 43–247.

[4] Hor. *Sat.* i. 8. 8–13.       [5] Tac. *Ann.* ii. 32; Suet. *Claud.* 25.

just north of S. Croce in Gerusalemme. In this part of the cemetery the tombs were rectangular pits, from 4 to 5 metres in length and unconnected with each other, arranged in rows which ran north and south. They were called *puticuli*,[1] and were made of blocks of lapis Gabinus. Into them the bodies were thrown promiscuously. In the via Napoleone III, besides the ancient tombs, a large number of these of later date was found, filled with matter containing bones, ashes, and organic débris. The average depth of soil above these tombs was from 6 to 8 metres. Traces have also been found of a stone channel, which is thought by some to have surrounded this part of the cemetery and to have formed a definite boundary. Adjacent to this cemetery was the lucus Libitinae,[2] or grove of Venus Libitina, where that goddess was worshipped.

Beyond this zone lay the second, in which a better class of Romans — mechanics, tradesmen, and freedmen — were buried, and occasionally men of rank, as C. Pansa, Sev. Sulpicius, Horace, and Maecenas.[3]

The natural result of all this was the creation of an intolerable nuisance. This part of the Esquiline came to be known as the *atrae Esquiliae*,[4] and was a menace to the health of the whole city until it was reclaimed by Maecenas.

**Streets.** — A good deal is known about the ancient system of streets in this district from other evidence, and especially from the discovery of much of the ancient pavements. The main artery of communication between the Esquiline and the rest of the city was the Argiletum[5] (p. 173), which ran northeast from the Forum through the later forum Transitorium, and

---

[1] Varro, *LL.* v. 25; Fest. *Epit.* 216; Comm. Cruq. *ad* Hor. *Sat.* i. 8. 10; Gilbert, III. 310–311.

[2] Dionys. iv. 15; Plut. *Quaest. Rom.* 23; Asc. *in Mil.* p. 34; *CIL.* vi. 9974, 10022; *BC.* 1905, 207–208.

[3] Cic. *Phil.* ix. 17; Suet. *Vit. Hor.;* Jordan, I. 3. 270–271.

[4] Hor. *Sat.* ii. 6. 32.     [5] *BC.* 1880, 98–102.

its continuation the Subura. The beginning of the Subura, between the spurs of the Oppius, the Cispius, and the Viminal, was called the **Primae Fauces**,[1] and its upper part, where it ascended the hill to the porta Esquilina, was called the **clivus Suburanus**.[2] The ancient pavement of this thoroughfare has been found along the line of the via di S. Lucia in Selci, the via di S. Martino, and the via di S. Vito. Outside the porta Esquilina this road divided into the via Tiburtina and the via Praenestina. At the west end of the Cispius the **vicus Patricius**,[3] a name of doubtful origin, branched off from the Subura to the north, and extending to the porta Viminalis formed the boundary between regions IV and VI. The pavement of this street lies very near the via Urbana. A second street led from the northwest corner of the basilica of Constantine straight up the Carinae to the summit of the Oppius, and its pavement is beneath that of the via di S. Pietro in Vincoli. The ancient name of this street is uncertain, but it may have been the **clivus Orbius**[4] (Urbius), which was also called the **vicus Sceleratus**,[5] from the legend that here Tullia drove over the body of her murdered father.

Another street, the **vicus Cuprius**,[6] started near the Colosseum and ran north across the slope of the Carinae to the Subura. This vicus, at its highest point, is said to have crossed the clivus Orbius; and in fact the pavement of an ancient street, which corresponds with what is known of the vicus Cuprius, does cross the clivus Orbius below the height of S. Pietro in Vincoli and coincides quite closely with the via del Cardello.

From the Colosseum valley two streets led east. The more

---

[1] Mart. ii. 17. 1.  [2] Mart. v. 22. 5.

[3] Fest. 221, 351; Mart. vii. 73. 2; x. 68. 2; Jordan, *FUR.* 9; *CIL.* vi. 1775; *Bull. Crist.* 1867, 57; Gilbert, II. 358; III. 357; Jordan, I. 3. 339.

[4] Fest. 182; Solin. i. 25; Liv. i. 48; Dionys. iv. 39; Jordan, I. 3. 258; Pais, *Legends*, 273–274.

[5] Varro. *LL.* v. 159; Fest. 333; Gilbert, I. 186–191.

[6] Varro, *LL.* v. 159; Liv. i. 48; Dionys. iii. 22; Gilbert, I. 187–189.

northerly coincides closely with the modern via Labicana, and can be traced across the Esquiline to the porta Maggiore. The other street is that which formed the boundary between regions II and III (probably the via Maior[1] of the twelfth century), coinciding closely with the via dei SS. Quattro and via S. Giovanni in Laterano. This led to the porta Caelemontana and on to the porta Asinaria.

As the wall and agger of Servius gradually fell into decay and the moat was filled up, houses began to be erected on this new ground and streets to be laid out on both sides of the wall parallel to it. The pavement of one of these streets has been discovered for the entire distance between the porta Caelemontana and the northwest corner of the piazza Vittorio Emanuele, just outside the porta Esquilina, at an average depth of 5 to 6 metres below the modern level. The ancient name of this street is not known, but after the seventh century it was called the via Merulana,[2] a name which has now been transferred to the new avenue which leads from S. Maria Maggiore to the Lateran. This ancient street was probably the principal thoroughfare between the north and south parts of the Esquiline.

Besides these streets, the line of which is partially determined, there was a clivus Pullius,[3] leading from the Subura south to the Oppius; a vicus Sandaliarius,[4] which probably opened into the Argiletum and corresponds to the via del Colosseo; and a street[5] of unknown name, which branched off toward the east from the vicus Cuprius. The vicus Iovis Fagutalis[6] must

---

[1] Jordan, I. 3. 242; II. 352–353; Hülsen, *La Pianta di Roma dell'Anonimo Einsidlense*, 406. Via Maior, or via Papalis, appears to have been applied to a continuous line of streets from the pons Aelius to the porta Asinaria.

[2] *Mon. d. Lincei*, i. 552–553; Jordan, I. 3. 351.

[3] Varro, *LL.* v. 158; Solin. i. 26; *BC.* 1891, 342; Jordan, I. 3. 257; II. 254; Gilbert, I. 164; III. 352; *Bull. Crist.* 1863, 23.

[4] Suet. *Aug.* 57; Gell. xviii. 4; *CIL.* vi. 448; BC. 1877, 162–163; 1890, 132; *RhM.* 1894, 630; Jordan, I. 3. 329.

[5] Richter, *Top.*[2] 311; *NS.* 1884, 396.     [6] *CIL.* vi. 452.

have been on the Fagutal; and the vicus Summi Choragi [1] evidently derived its name from that building (p. 334). The Corneta [2] was between the Sacra via and the Macellum. The vicus Sabuci [3] was somewhere in region III; and the clivus Bassilli [4] probably branched off to the north from the via Tiburtina. Of the vicus Africus [5] nothing is known except that it was on the Esquiline.

## REGION III. [6]

**Temples and Shrines.** — The temple which gave its name to this region was that of Isis, [7] which was also dedicated to Serapis, like that in the campus Martius; but nothing is known of the date of its building or of its history. On the relief of the Haterii (Fig. 2) an arch, spanning the street that nearly coincides with the via Labicana, is marked arcus ad Isis, and on the line of this street, near the church of SS. Pietro e Marcellino, the remains of a temple, decorated in Egyptian style, were discovered in the seventeenth century. Other Egyptian remains have been found in this region as far north as the via Buonarotti, so that the exact site of the temple is a matter of dispute. It was probably near SS. Pietro e Marcellino.

At the crossing of the vicus Cuprius and the clivus Orbius stood the Dianium, a shrine of Diana, which is mentioned only once [8] and had disappeared in Livy's time. Plutarch [9] speaks of a temple of Diana in the vicus Patricius, but nothing more is known of it, nor of the temple of Bellona Rufilia, [10] which stood *ab Isis Serapis.*

---

[1] Jordan, *FUR.* 7.

[2] Varro, *LL.* v. 152; Gilbert, III. 209; Jordan, I. 3. 1.    [3] *CIL.* vi. 801.

[4] *BC.* 1890, 335; *Mitt.* 1891, 112.    [5] Varro, *LL.* v. 159.

[6] The Colosseum and attached buildings, although falling within this region, have been already described, pp. 324–335.

[7] *Not.* Reg. iii; Treb. Poll. *Vit. Trig. Tyr.* 25; *NS.* 1888, 626; *BC.* 1887, 132–134; 1889, 37–39; *Mitt.* 1889, 279–280; Lanciani, *Ruins,* 360; Jordan, I. 3. 304.

[8] Liv. i. 48.    [9] *Quaest. Rom.* 3.    [10] *CIL.* vi. 2234.

Near the Tigillum Sororium were two altars, dedicated to Iuno Sororia and Ianus Curiatius,[1] on which from early times expiatory sacrifices had been made. These altars were undoubtedly connected with the expiation of Horatius.

**Other Public Buildings.** — Tradition said that the surviving Horatius was compelled to pass beneath a wooden cross-bar supported by two vertical posts, in expiation of the murder of his sister.[2] This yoke was called the Tigillum Sororium, and was probably in reality an ancient Janus-gate, with which the Horatius legend became connected. It appears to have stood at a place where two roads crossed, *ad compitum Acili*,[3] perhaps on the vicus Cuprius (p. 447), — at any rate somewhere on the southwest slope of the Oppius.

Directly east of S. Clemente, the site of the imperial mint is marked by the discovery of inscriptions relating to the **Moneta,** or **Moneta Caesaris**, and to its officials, the *monetarii*.[4] The mint had apparently been transferred hither from the temple of Iuno Moneta on the Capitoline. Between the thermae Traianae and S. Clemente were the **castra Misenatium**,[5] the barracks occupied by the sailors detailed for service in the city from the imperial fleet stationed at Misenum. The site is known only from inscriptions and a fragment of the Marble Plan. Between these barracks and S. Clemente was the **Summum Choragium** (see p. 334), and still farther east on the same street was the **ludus Magnus**,[6] or principal training school for gladi-

---

[1] Fest. 297; *Epit.* 307; Dionys. iii. 22; Schol. Bob. *ad* Cic. *pro Mil.* 2.

[2] Dionys. iii. 22; Fest. 297; *Epit.* 307; Liv. i. 26; Auct. *de Vir. Ill.* 9; Gilbert, I. 178–179; II. 55–58; *BC.* 1890, 128–129; *Mélanges*, 1908, 244.

[3] Pl. *NH.* xxix. 12; *Hemerol. Arv. Kal. Oct.;* Jordan, I. 3. 322; II. 100; Gilbert, I. 182, 191.

[4] *Not.* Reg. iii; *BC.* 1891, 343; *CIL.* vi. 42–44, 791, 1647; Gilbert, III. 185.

[5] Jordan, *FUR.* 5; *CIL.* vi. 1091; Jordan, I. 3. 301; II. 116; Gilbert, III. 200; *Ann. d. Ist.* 1862, 64; *BC.* 1891, 193.

[6] *Not.* Reg. iii; Herodian. i. 16; Jordan, *FUR.* 4; *CIL.* vi. 1645, 1647, 7659, 10164–10170; Gilbert, III. 332.

ators, and probably the ludus Dacicus,[1] a similar school for Dacians. In the vineyard of the monks of S. Pietro in Vincoli inscriptions[2] have been found relating to a ξυστικὴ σύνοδος τῶν περὶ τὸν Ἡρακλέα ἀθλητῶν or *curia athletarum*, evidently the headquarters of some organization of athletes. This hall was undoubtedly in the neighborhood of the thermae Traianae; but whether it can be identified with the basilica-shaped hall just north of these thermae, as some believe, is entirely uncertain.

The porticus Liviae,[3] fronting directly on the clivus Suburanus, was built by Augustus on the site previously occupied by the house of Vedius Pollio. This house,[4] which had become famous for its luxury and magnificence, was left by will to Augustus by Pollio, who died in 15 B.C.; but the emperor tore it down at once, in order to show his disapproval of such private residences, and erected the porticus in its place. This was not finished and dedicated to Livia until 7 B.C.[5] It was the most important porticus in the city, after those of the campus Martius, and much frequented.[6] Its site and general plan are known to us from three fragments of the Marble Plan,[7] and from drawings made in the sixteenth century of the ruins which were then visible. It was rectangular in shape, about 115 metres long and 75 wide, and consisted of an outer wall and a double row of columns within. In each of the long sides were three niches, the central one square, the others semicircular. There was also a semicircular apse on the south side. The entrance was on the north, where there was a flight of steps 20 metres wide leading down to the clivus Suburanus. In the centre of the area was something which appears to have

---

[1] *Not.* Reg. iii.

[2] *BC.* 1891, 185–209; *CIL.* vi. 10153–10154; *Inscriptiones Graecae Siciliae et Italiae*, 1102–1110.

[3] *BC.* 1886, 270–274; *Mitt.* 1889, 78–79.

[4] Dio Cass. liv. 23; Ov. *Fast.* vi. 639–644.

[5] Dio Cass. lv. 8; Suet. *Aug.* 29.

[6] Ov. *Ars Am.* i. 71; Strabo, v. 3. 8; Pl. *NH.* xiv. 11; Gilbert, III. 253.

[7] Jordan, *FUR.* 10, 11, 109.

been a fountain.   An aedes Concordiae[1] built by Livia was connected with the porticus, but it was probably outside the inclosure rather than within it.

The office of *praefectus urbi* became permanent during the reign of Tiberius, and thenceforth one of the most important in the empire.   The general offices, Praefectura Urbana,[2] of this prefecture were west of the thermae Traianae, within the area now bounded by the vie di S. Pietro in Vincoli, della Polveriera, and dei Serpenti.   The identification of this site is rendered possible by inscriptions, although no trace of the building itself remains.   It dated from the early empire, and contained at least three parts — the *scrinia* or archives, the *secretarium* or prefect's office, and the *tribunalia* where he gave his decisions.   The secretarium was called secretarium Tellurense, which indicates that the building stood *in Tellure*, or in the vicus Tellurensis, near the temple of Tellus.   The inscriptions also indicate that adjacent to the Praefectura was a porticus,[3] in which copies of the edicts, preserved in the archives, were set up for public inspection ; and this porticus may be identical with the porticus thermarum Traianarum mentioned in another inscription.[4]

The domus Aurea[5] of Nero, as has already been said (p. 72), spread over a large part of the Esquiline.   It was evidently a large park,[6] containing various buildings of the greatest magnificence and many treasures.   The most extensive existing remains are beneath and just east of the thermae Traianae. That part which is beneath the thermae is built of opus latericium covered with stucco, and consists of a series of parallel

---

[1] Ov. *Fast.* vi. 637 ; Jordan, I. 3. 315.

[2] *BC.* 1892, 19–37 ;  *Mitt.* 1893, 298–302 ;  *RhM.* 1894, 629–630.

[3] *BC.* 1891, 342–358.

[4] *Athen. Mitt.* 1891, 267–279 ;  *CIL.* iii. 12336.

[5] *Mélanges*, 1891, 161–167 ; Jordan, I. 3. 273–279 ; A. Profumo, *Le Fonti ed I Tempi dello Incendio Neroniano*, Rome, 1905, 423–431.

[6] Suet. *Nero*, 31 ;  *Otho*, 7 ;  Dio Cass. lxv. 4 ;  Tac. *Ann.* xv. 39, 42 ; Pl. *NH.* xxxiii. 54 ; xxxiv. 84 ; xxxv. 120 ; xxxvi. 37 ; Gilbert, III. 179–180.

chambers opening north and south into courts surrounded with colonnades. In the centre of the north peristyle is a fountain, and along its north side a cryptoporticus. The wall-paintings that were found in these chambers [1] in the fifteenth century afterward inspired Raphael to paint his famous frescoes in the loggia of the Vatican and in the villa Madama. A few traces of them still remain, and also of others discovered in 1813 in the cryptoporticus.

The ruins of the domus Aurea just east of the thermae, generally known as Le Capocce or Le Sette Sale, belong to a piscina, or reservoir. This building is rectangular except on the east where it is curved, and consists of nine parallel chambers lined with waterproof cement. Originally there was a second story, as in the piscina of the baths of Caracalla. The interior walls are pierced with openings, so arranged as not to be opposite each other.

**Thermae.** — We are told that when the Colosseum was dedicated, Titus built the thermae Titianae near by with great speed, and celebrated their completion with magnificent games.[2] These baths were still used in the fourth century;[3] and in the sixteenth so much of them was visible that drawings could be made. After that time they were almost totally destroyed, and it is only within recent years that a few meagre remains have come to light. They are situated just west of the thermae Traianae, on the edge of the slope overhanging the Colosseum, and within the domus Aurea. A wide flight of steps led up from the paved area round the Colosseum to the thermae, which were about 18 metres above. Recent excavations have disclosed the ruins [4] of a sort of porticus

---

[1] *Mitt.* 1896, 213; *BC.* 1895, 174–181.

[2] Suet. *Tit.* 7; Dio Cass. lxvi. 25; Mart. *de Spect.* 2. 7; iii. 20, 15; *BC.* 1895, 110–115; Jordan, I. 3. 307–310.

[3] *Not.* Reg. iii; *CIL.* vi. 9797; *Chronogr. a. 354,* p. 146.

[4] *BC.* 1895, 117–127.

at the foot of this flight of steps, consisting of a row of six pilasters, adorned with half columns on travertine bases and originally connected by arches. This porticus may have belonged distinctively to the approach of the thermae, or to a porticus that surrounded a large part of the Colosseum area. In the fifth century the porticus was completely changed in appearance, and a Christian cemetery located here. The façade of the

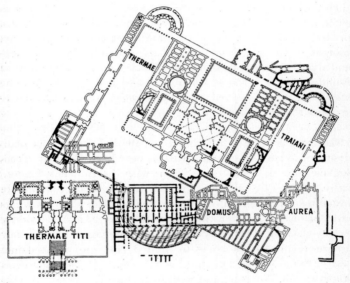

FIG. 87. — THE BATHS OF TITUS AND TRAJAN.

thermae was toward the north, and of this a small portion was found. These baths were the smallest of those known to us, measuring about 105 by 120 metres, and no actual buildings of the domus Aurea appear to have been destroyed to make room for them.

Nothing is known of the circumstances attending the building of the thermae Traianae. Trajan [1] erected them between the porticus Liviae and the thermae Titianae, thereby destroying or burying a considerable part of the domus Aurea. Our knowledge of their plan is based upon a small fragment of the Marble Plan,[2] on drawings of the sixteenth and eighteenth centuries, when enough of the building was left to admit of quite exact description, and on the very meagre remains which are now visible. They corresponded in general with the other thermae. The main building contained a rectangular frigidarium, a tepidarium, and a circular caldarium, with apodyteria or dressing-rooms, open courts or palaestrae at each end surrounded with colonnades, and the usual number of small baths and rooms for various purposes. This main building was surrounded on three sides, east, south, and west, by a peribolus which contained libraries, reading-rooms, gymnasia, and exedrae at the four corners. In the middle of the south side was a very large exedra, which served as a theatre. This exedra was built over that part of the domus Aurea already described (p. 452); and in order to provide sufficiently strong foundations for the cavea of the theatre, additional walls were built through the chambers of the domus Aurea, some corresponding with the walls of these chambers and others with the orientation of the baths themselves. The axis of the domus Aurea runs north and south, while that of the thermae runs northeast and southwest at an angle of 30° from the meridian. The extreme measurements of these baths are 340 metres in width and 330 in depth, or, excluding the exedral projections, 280 by 210 metres. The chief remains now visible belong to the exedrae at the northeast and southwest corners and to the east palaestra. These baths contained many works of art, some of which have been recovered, notably the Laocoon group.

---

[1] Pausan. v. 12. 4; Dio Cass. lxix. 4; *CIL.* vi. 1670, 8677, 8678, 9797; Gilbert, III. 297.

[2] Jordan, *FUR.* 109; *Mon. d. Lincei,* i. 484–485; *Mitt.* 1892, 302–304; Jordan, I. 3. 310–314.

**Private Houses.** — Besides the house of Vedius Pollio, another famous house in this region was that of **Pompeius**,[1] which stood *in Carinis* near the temple of Tellus, and was ornamented with *rostra*[2] that had been taken from captured pirate ships. After the death of Pompeius the house became the property of Antonius, and later of the imperial family. Tiberius lived in it before his accession;[3] and in the third century it belonged to the Gordiani.

Throughout the whole Esquiline district very many ruins of private dwellings have been found which can seldom or never be identified with any certainty.[4] In a few cases, the discovery of inscriptions gives the clew to the owners' names. Thus we know that the house of M. Servilius Fabianus[5] was south of the clivus Suburanus and just east of the porticus Liviae; that of Vettius Agorius Praetextatus and Fabia Paulina[6] was northeast of the porta Esquilina and outside the Servian wall; and that of Petronius Maximus[7] was destroyed by the building of the domus Aurea. The house of Bruttius Praesens in this region is singled out for mention in the *Notitia*, and was probably especially noteworthy. The emperor Balbinus[8] lived on the Carinae. Near Le Sette Sale (p. 453) are remains[9] of a tenement house called the insula Vitaliana, from its builder or owner.

The present church of S. Clemente is built over an earlier basilica, which, in its turn, rests upon a stratum of early imperial opus latericium; and beneath this is a great mass of opus quadratum of tufa. This belongs to the republican period and probably to some public building, not to a private house, but there is no clew as to its identity. Below the first basilica

---

[1] Suet. *de Gramm.* **15**; App. *Bell. Civ.* ii. 126; Vell. ii. 77; Cic. *de Har. Resp.* 49; Gilbert, III. 355.

[2] Cic. *Phil.* ii. 68; Jul. Cap. *Vit. Gord.* 3.      [3] Suet. *Tib.* 15.

[4] Cf., however, Lanciani, *Forma Urbis*, 23, 24, 30.

[5] *CIL.* vi. 1517.      [6] *CIL.* xv. 7563.      [7] *CIL.* vi. 1197–1198.

[8] Jul. Cap. *Vit. Maximi et Balbini*, 16.      [9] *BC.* 1895, 129; *CIL.* vi. 33893.

and behind the apse are the chambers of a house of the period before the Antonines, and among them a Mithraeum, or shrine of Mithras.[1]

## REGION IV.

This region took its name from the templum Pacis of Vespasian. The monumental structures in its southwest part, along the Sacra via, have been described in Chapter XII.

Its two principal streets, the Argiletum and the Subura, were perhaps the most crowded, noisy, and disreputable in the city. Certainly the reputation of the Subura [2] was of the very worst, as is amply testified by the evidence of literature. Retail business [3] of every description was carried on here; but the Argiletum seems to have been noted especially for its book and shoe shops,[4] while there is epigraphic and literary evidence for the presence in the Subura of crepidarii,[5] lanarii,[6] praecones,[7] ferrarii,[8] lintearii,[9] and impilarii,[10] and it was notorious for brothels and drinking shops.[11] In spite of this unsavory character, the Subura retained its importance, and no less a person than Julius Caesar lived in a house in this street, in which the grammarian Antonius Gnipho taught for a time.[12]

**Temples and Shrines.**— Except for the great temples on the Sacra via, buildings devoted to religious purposes were neither numerous nor important in this region. Probably the oldest temple was that of Tellus, situated on the west slope of the Carinae,[13] just west of the boundary of region III, on the site of the house of Sp. Cassius,[14] who was said to have been put to death for alleged treason in 485 B.C. In 270 B.C.

---

[1] *CIL.* vi. 748; *Bull. Crist.* 1870, 125 ff.

[2] Mart. xii. 18. 2; Juv. xi. 51.          [3] Mart. vii. 31.

[4] Mart. i. 3. 1; 117. 9; ii. 17. 3; cf. vicus Sandaliarius, p. 448.

[5] *CIL.* vi. 9284.      [7] *CIL.* vi. 1953.      [9] *CIL.* vi. 9526.

[6] *CIL.* vi. 9491.      [8] *CIL.* vi. 9399.      [10] *CIL.* vi. 33862.

[11] Mart. vi. 66. 1–2; xi. 61. 3.          [12] Suet. *Caes.* 46; *de Gramm.* 7.

[13] Dionys. viii. 79; Suet. *de Gramm.* 15.

[14] Cic. *de Domo*, 101; Val. Max. vi. 3, 1.

P. Sempronius Sophus vowed a temple to Tellus,[1] but the building which he erected was probably only an enlargement or rebuilding of a much earlier one. The area in front of the temple was dedicated to Ceres,[2] and the two goddesses were worshipped here together on December 13. The temple was restored by Q. Cicero, who had a house near by, about 54 B.C., and apparently some of the ground hitherto belonging to it fell into Cicero's hands.[3] The temple is mentioned in the fourth century, and while no remains have been found, it was undoubtedly situated just east of the via del Colosseo.[4] Near by were the horrea Chartaria,[5] or paper warehouses.

The temple of Iuno Lucina [6] was built in 375 B.C. It stood in a grove [7] on the slope of the Cispius, overlooking the Subura, and near the sixth chapel of the Argei. This would place it west of the church of S. Prassede, near the via dei Quattro Cantoni. Little is known of the later history of this temple, except that in 41 B.C. a murus Iunonis Lucinae [8] was either built or restored, and that the edifice itself continued to exist during the empire. The annual festival of the Matronalia [9] was celebrated here on March 1, and votive inscriptions to Juno have been found in the neighborhood.

In the vicus Sandaliarius was a statue of **Apollo Sandaliarius** [10] and a shrine dedicated by the *magistri* of that vicus to **Stata Fortuna**,[11] and in the vicus Patricius was a shrine of **Diana**.[12] In or near this same street was also a shrine and grove of **Mefitis**.[13]

---

[1] Flor. i. 14.   [2] Dionys. viii. 79; Liv. ii. 41; *CIL*. i[2]. pp. 336–337.

[3] Cic. *de Har. Resp.* 31; *ad Q. Fr.* ii. 3.7; iii. 1.14.

[4] *BC*. 1892, 19–37; *Mitt.* 1893, 299–302; Elter, *Forma Urbis*, i. 9; Gilbert, I. 193–195; Jordan, I. 3. 323–326.

[5] *Not.* Reg. iv.

[6] Varro, *LL*. v. 49, 50; Pl. *NH*. xvi. 235; Ov. *Fast.* ii. 435–436; iii. 247–248; *BC*. 1888, 394; 1889, 40; *Mitt.* 1889, 281.

[7] *BC*. 1905, 204–209.

[8] *CIL*. vi. 358; Eckhel, vii. 99.

[9] *CIL*. i[2]. p. 310.

[10] Suet. *Aug.* 57.

[11] *CIL*. vi. 761.

[12] Plut. *Quaest. Rom.* 3.

[13] Varro, *LL*. v. 49; Fest. 351.

In 1888, at the corner of the via S. Lucia in Selci (clivus Suburanus) and the via dei Quattro Cantoni a marble base was discovered, on which had stood a statue, and behind it part of an early travertine altar. On the base was an inscription recording the dedication in 10 B.C. of the statue to Mercurius.[1] This was one of the statues which Augustus erected at various points in the city with the money which the citizens presented to him on New Year's Day. The monument stood in a paved area, evidently the crossing of the clivus Suburanus and another street (the vicus Sobrius ? ),[2] and the statue was perhaps that of Mercurius Sobrius.[3] The older travertine altar was probably one of those which marked *compita*, and possibly replaced one of the older shrines of the Argei.

**Other Public Buildings**. — In the Subura was a tower, the turris Mamilia,[4] on which the inhabitants of the district, the Suburanenses, fastened the head of the horse which was sacrificed at the October festival, if they were successful in their annual contest with the Sacravienses (p. 41). The quarter immediately around this tower was called ad turrim Mamiliam.

An atrium Sutorium [5] is mentioned as being the place where the annual ceremony of the *tubilustrium* was observed; and while it is not even known in what part of the city this building was situated, it is natural to connect it with the headquarters of the shoe trade, and to place it in the Argiletum. As it is not mentioned after the first century, it may have stood on the site afterward occupied by the forum Transitorium.[6]

At the east end of the forum Transitorium and abutting against the apse of the forum of Augustus, are the remains of a curved wall, opening toward the Argiletum, which is prob-

---

[1] *BC.* 1888, 221–231; Suet. *Aug.* 57.

[2] Fest. 297; *Epit.* 296; *CIL.* vi. 9483.      [3] *CIL.* vi. 9714.

[4] Fest. 178, *Epit.* 131; Gilbert, II. 46, 94; *BC.* 1888, 398–399; *CIL.* vi. 33837.

[5] Varro, *LL.* vi. 14; Fest. 352; *CIL.* i². p. 313.

[6] Jordan, I, 2. 452; Gilbert, 1. 144.

ably the porticus Absidata[1] mentioned in the *Notitia*.    It formed
a species of pendant to the forum Transitorium.

The Roman markets, which had originally been held in the
Forum itself, were gradually removed to make room for more
important interests (p. 169).    The forum Cuppedinis,[2] or market
for delicacies, and the forum Piscarium,[3] or fish-market, were
in the district between the Sacra via and the Argiletum at
least as early as the third century B.C., and the general market[4]
must have been established there at about the same time.    In
210 B.C. the forum Piscarium was burned,[5] and a few years
later, in 179 B.C., M. Fulvius Nobilior built a new market-house,
the Macellum, and also his new basilica Aemilia between the
Macellum and the Forum.[6]    Into this Macellum the different
markets were brought together,[7] and thenceforth this name
displaced the earlier individual designations.    The building
consisted of a central tholus, surrounded by shops.[8]    It continued to be the principal market of Rome until Augustus
began to build other markets in different quarters of the city.
Its usefulness even for the Subura was greatly diminished by
the establishment of the macellum Liviae (p. 470), and it was
entirely removed at last to make room for the forum of Vespasian.    Near the Fauces Macelli,[9] the entrance to the market-house,
were the atria Licinia,[10] or auction rooms.

The only baths in this region of which we have any definite
knowledge were the balnea Naeratii Cerialis,[11] built by Naeratius
Cerialis, consul in 358 A.D.    They were situated in the square
now bounded by the vie Cavour, Manin, Farini, and the piazza

---

[1] *Mon. dei Lincei*, i. 530–532; Jordan, II. 99–100, 319; *Mélanges*, 1889, 350.
[2] Varro, *LL*. v. 146; Fest. 48; Donat. *ad* Ter. *Eun.* 256.
[3] Plaut. *Curc.* 474 ; Varro, *loc. cit.*
[4] Jordan, I. 2. 432–435; Gilbert, III. 207–209.
[5] Liv. xxvi. 27 ; xxvii. 11.                          [6] Liv. xl. 51.
[7] Varro, *LL*. v. 147; Plaut. *Pseud.* 168; Ter. *Eun.* 255–257.
[8] Varro, *ap.* Non. 448; Altmann, *Rundbauten*, 74.
[9] Cic. *Verr.* iii. 145; *pro Quinct.* 25.          [10] Cic. *pro Quinct.* 12.
[11] *CIL*. vi. 1744, 31916; *BC*. 1874, 84–88; 1905, 294–299.

dell' Esquilino, but the remains are too meagre to admit of any attempt at reconstruction. At the time when these baths were built, the area south of them now occupied by S. Maria Maggiore was called the Sicininum,[1] but no explanation of this name has been given.

Inscriptions[2] found at the corner of the via Mazzini and the via Carlo Alberto indicate that probably at this point there was a building called the castra Fontanorum, apparently the head-quarters of the *fontani* or *fullones*.[3] This guild erected statues and votive altars to Victoria, Diana, Hercules, and Minerva, in gratitude for its victory in some litigation with the *curatores aquarum*, between 226 and 244 A.D.

Near this point Junius Bassus, consul in 317 A.D., erected a basilica,[4] which was converted into the church of S. Andrea between 468 and 482. The church was destroyed in 1686.

**Private Houses.** — The excavations have brought to light evidence for the site and ownership of several private houses in this region, which is perhaps more definite than at some other points (cf. p. 456). The house of T. Flavius Tiberianus[5] was at the corner of the via Mazzini and via Napoleone III; that of L. Octavius Felix, near the railroad station; those of Geminia Bassa, Q. Munatius Celsus, and L. Naevius Clemens, just inside the porta Viminalis; and that of Naeratius Cerialis, close to his balnea. Near S. Martino ai Monti the remains of a large house of the fourth century were found,[6] among which was an aedicula, the lararium of the house, which contained a statue of Isis as Fortuna and busts of other divinities. Below and behind this aedicula was a Mithraeum, or square chamber dedicated to the worship of this oriental deity. On the wall was a relief of Mithras slaying the bull.

---

[1] *BC.* 1899, 230–233.
[2] *CIL.* vi. 70, 127, 266–268.
[3] *BC.* 1876, 139–140.

[4] *BC.* 1893, 89–104; *CIL.* vi. 1737.
[5] *CIL.* xv. 7453.
[6] *BC.* 1885, 27–38; *NS.* 1885, 67, 154.

In the old via Graziosa, which has now given way to the via Cavour, in the year 1848 a house was found which contained the wall paintings, representing landscapes from the Odyssey, which are now in the Vatican in the room of the Aldobrandini Nuptials.

## REGION V.

**Temples and Shrines.** — Buildings devoted to religious purposes were few and unimportant in this region. The temple of **Minerva Medica**,[1] dating from republican times, was probably situated west of the via Merulana in the via Curva, where in 1887 some ruins of tufa walls resembling *favissae* were found, together with hundreds of votive offerings, notwithstanding the fact that this site does not seem to agree with the order followed in the itinerary of the *Notitia*.

Just inside the porta Praenestina was a district known as ad Spem veterem,[2] the meeting place of several aqueducts (p. 93). This name was probably derived from an ancient temple of Spes, which is mentioned three times [3] in literature, and to which the via Gabina must have led from the porta Esquilina. Nothing more is known of this temple or its history.

Near the church of S. Eusebio many inscriptions [4] have been found which record dedications made by foreign soldiers, especially Thracians, to their native deities. These inscriptions mark the site of some shrine, perhaps one of **Mars** and **Hercules**.[5] Other inscriptions,[6] found near by, were dedicated to **Iuppiter Dolichenus** (cf. p. 416).

Lastly, the *Notitia* mentions a temple to **Hercules Sullanus**,[7]

---

[1] *CIL.* vi. 10133, 30980; *Not.* Reg. v; *BC.* 1887, 154–156, 192–200; 1888, 124–125; *Mitt.* 1889, 278; Jordan, I. 3. 353.

[2] Front. *de Aquis*, 5, 19, 20, 21, 65; Lanciani, *Acque*, 36; Herschel, *Frontinus*, 144; *CIL.* xv. 5929.

[3] Liv. ii. 51; Dionys. ix. 24; Lamprid. *Vit. Elag.* 13. Cf., however, Jordan, I. 3. 365.

[4] *CIL.* vi. 2797–2860, and freq.; *BC.* 1893, 261–271; 1894, 101–128, 225–240.

[5] *CIL.* vi. 2819.            [6] *CIL.* vi. 3698–3699.

[7] Jordan, I. 3. 359–360; II. 129; Altmann, *Rundbauten*, 81–83.

evidently erected by Sulla, perhaps for his victory over Marius on the Esquiline; and a shrine or temple of Isis Patricia.

**Water Works.** — The most characteristic features of this region were the aqueducts which crossed the Esquiline in various directions after having entered the city ad Spem Veterem, and the horti or parks. The aqueducts have been described in Chapter VI. There were nymphaea, great fountains, and piscinae or distributing stations, at various points throughout the region, and remains of many of them have been found. The most conspicuous of the nymphaea is that which stands southwest of the railroad tracks in the viale Principessa Margherita, in the ancient horti Liciniani (p. 467). These ruins[1] were known in the middle ages as the Terme di Galluccio or Le Galluzze, and after the beginning of the seventeenth century as Minerva Medica, having been erroneously identified with that temple. The *Notitia* mentions in region V a nymphaeum divi Alexandri, and it is still a disputed question whether this name belongs to the nymphaeum under consideration, or to another. The ruins consist of a decagonal hall of opus latericium, covered with a vaulted roof and surrounded on three sides with other chambers. In the interior of the hall are nine niches, besides the entrance; and above these are ten corresponding round-arched windows. The diameter of the hall is about 34 metres and the height was 33. The outside walls were covered with marble, and the interior richly decorated in a similar manner. Some of the pavement of porphyry has been found.

In the piazza Vittoria Emanuele are the remains of a great fountain, popularly known as I Trofei di Mario, which has sometimes been erroneously regarded as a castellum aquae. This ruin was called *Cimbrum* or *templum Marii* in the middle ages,[2] because in its niches were the trophies (*tropaea*) removed by Sixtus V in 1587, which are now on the balustrade of the

---

[1] *BC.* 1883, 17–18.    [2] *Mitt.* 1899, 255–259.

piazza del Campidoglio.  These trophies date from the time of Domitian, and therefore are not those erected by Marius on the Esquiline or elsewhere (p. 304).   We do not know how the name came to be transferred from one set of trophies to another which had nothing to do with the first.   The structure itself is of uncertain date but may belong to the time of Domitian.[1]   As it is a monumental fountain, standing at the angle between two streets, the via Tiburtina and the via Praenestina, it has been identified with the lacus Orphei,[2] mentioned in the *Notitia,* which was evidently a fountain named from a statue of Orpheus.   This fountain is fed by the aqua Iulia, and the existing ruins of brick-faced concrete indicate a high circular structure, perhaps 40 metres in diameter, with two stories and quite complicated in arrangement.   Around the interior of the halls on each floor were niches, and water probably flowed out from openings in the walls into a surrounding basin.

A third nymphaeum, which may have been the nymphaeum divi Alexandri, is reported[3] to have been found at the close of the fifteenth century in the villa Altieri, near the corner of the new streets, the via Bixio and the via Principe Eugenio.

**Horti**. — Horti, gardens or parks which were generally laid out by private individuals and afterward in most cases fell into the possession of the emperors, surrounded almost the entire city.   They were most numerous, however, in regions V and VII, and on the right bank of the river.   Credit for the development of this system is apparently due to Maecenas, who transformed the worst part of the Esquiline cemetery (p. 446) by partially levelling the agger, filling up the moat, and covering the area with earth to a depth about 6 metres, and then laid out the horti Maecenatis.[4]

---

[1] Jordan, I. 3. 349–350.

[2] Mart. x. 19. 6–7 ;  *Not.* Reg. v ;  Jordan, I. 3. 345 ;  II. 127, 495 ;  Lanciani, *Ruins*, 57.          [3] Vacca, *Memorie*, 109 ; Jordan, II. 128.

[4] Hor. *Sat.* i. 8. 7,  14, and  Schol. ;  Tac. *Ann.* xv. 39 ; Gilbert, III. 361–362; Jordan, I. 3. 346–347.

The extent[1] of these gardens is uncertain, and topographers
are not agreed as to whether they lay on both sides of the
agger and both north and south of the porta Esquilina.   Whatever may have been the original area laid out by Maecenas, in
their final shape the gardens probably stretched out on both
sides of the agger north of the gate, and also south of the
gate, but how far is only a matter of conjecture.   At the

FIG. 88.—THE SO-CALLED AUDITORIUM OF MAECENAS.

death of Maecenas these gardens became the property of Augustus.   Nero connected them with the domus Aurea, and viewed
the burning of Rome from the turris Maecenatiana,[2] a tower in
the gardens which was praised as *moles propinqua nubibus
arduis*.[3]   The gardens perhaps contained a swimming pool of
warm water.[4]

The ruins of one very curious building in these gardens still
remain.   It is the so-called **Auditorium Maecenatis**,[5] in the angle

---

[1] *B C*. 1874, 166–171.          [2] Suet. *Nero*, 38.          [3] Hor. *Od*. iii. 29. 10.
          [4] Dio Cass. lv. 7                    [5] *B C*. 1874, 137–165

between the via Merulana and the via Leopardi.  It is a hall
of opus reticulatum in the style of the beginning of the
empire, and built directly across the line of the Servian wall.
At the west end is a semicircular apse; the length of the hall
is 24.40 metres and its width 10.60.  Since the floor is 7
metres below the ancient level of the ground, the hall had to
be entered by an inclined plane.  The walls reach 6 metres
above this ancient ground level, and the roof was probably
vaulted.  In the apse are seven rows of curved steps, arranged
like the cavea of a theatre.  Above these steps in the apse are
five niches, and six more in each of the side walls of the hall.
All of these were beautifully painted with garden scenes and
landscapes, but the frescoes have almost entirely disappeared.
The pavement is of black and white mosaic.  While the purpose of this hall is entirely uncertain, it was probably not an
auditorium and may have been intended as a conservatory.[1]

Near the horti Maecenatiani were the horti Lamiani,[2] which
were probably laid out by L. Aelius Lamia, consul in 3 A.D.
The house of the Lamiae[3] was near the Trofei di Mario, and
the horti extended south from about this point, and east of the
ancient street (via Merulana) which separated them from the
gardens of Maecenas.  They became imperial property, and
Caligula's ashes were deposited here before being carried to
the mausoleum of Augustus.  With these horti were connected
the horti Maiani,[4] of which nothing further is known; but the
two are mentioned together as forming one whole, — horti
Lamiani et Maiani.  The area occupied by these gardens is
approximately bounded by the piazza Vittorio Emanuele, the
via Machiavelli, the via Bixio, the via Emanuele Filiberto, and

---

[1] *Bull. d. Ist.* 1875, 89.

[2] Suet. *Cal.* 59; Philo Jud. *de Virt.* ii. 597; *CIL.* vi. 8668; Gilbert, III. 362;
Jordan, I. 3, 347, where Hülsen regards the site of these gardens as entirely
uncertain; *BC.* 1907, 34.

[3] Cf. Hor. *Od.* i. 26; iii. 17; Val. Max. iv. 4. 8.

[4] Pl. *NH.* xxxv. 51; *CIL.* vi. 6152, 8668–8669.

the via Cairoli. Ancient writers describe the magnificence of the buildings and works of art within this area. Of the latter many have been found; but of the buildings themselves only insignificant remains, — rooms of opus reticulatum, a nymphaeum, and part of a porticus.

The horti Epaphroditiani, Pallantiani, and Torquatiani,[1] dating from the first century, were almost contiguous and are mentioned together. The horti Epaphroditiani, named probably after the freedman of Nero, lay north of the via Praenestina, within the area now bounded by the via Principe Eugenio, the via Mazzini, the via di S. Bibiana, and the piazza Vittorio Emanuele. The horti Pallantiani[2] were north of the horti Epaphroditiani and of the via di S. Bibiana, probably along the line of the via Tiburtina vetus, between the porta Esquilina and the porta Tiburtina. They were the property of Pallas, the freedman of Nero, and at his death were seized by Nero and added to the imperial domain. The horti Torquatiani are mentioned only once, but were probably south of the horti Epaphroditiani on the opposite side of the via Praenestina. They may have belonged to Torquatus Julius Silanus, who was killed and whose possessions were confiscated by Nero.

The horti Liciniani[3] belonged to the Licinian family, and are first mentioned in the third century, in connection with the emperor of that family, Gallienus, who made these gardens his favorite place of residence. They have been assigned conjecturally to the district between the via Praenestina and the later wall of Aurelian, from the horti Epaphroditiani east, which latter gardens they had perhaps absorbed. The remains of some nymphaea have been found within this area, but they are insignificant, except that described on page 463.

Horti Variani[4] is the name ordinarily given to a large park which extended south from the porta Praenestina to a point

---

[1] Front. de Aquis, 5, 19, 20, 68–69; BC. 1874, 53–54; Lanciani, Acque, 36–37; Gilbert, III. 362.

[2] Not. Reg. v.     [3] BC. 1874, 55; Jordan, I. 3. 358.     [4] Vop. Vit. Aur. 1.

considerably beyond the line of the Aurelian wall. The name
is derived arbitrarily from Varius, the father of Elagabalus.
These gardens certainly belonged to this emperor, but the
name given them in his biography [1] is horti Spei veteris, and it
is possible that the horti Variani were really on the Pincian.
Elagabalus is said to have built a temple here in honor of his
god Elagabalus ; [2] and within that part of the gardens which
lies outside the Aurelian wall remains of a circus are said to
have been found.    The fragments of an Egyptian obelisk, found
on the site of the supposed circus, mark the site of a sepulchral
monument of Hadrian's favorite, Antinous,[3] who, however, was
not buried here.    This obelisk now stands on the Pincian.
The Aurelian wall was built across these gardens, for remains
of walls connecting the two parts have been found, and the ruins
of buildings in the two sections have the same orientation.[4]
In the wall itself parts of structures of the third century are
embedded.

The horti Tauriani and horti Calyclani,[5] outside the Servian
wall and north of the porta Esquilina, appear to have extended
east toward the porta Tiburtina, and perhaps adjoined the
horti Pallantiani on the north.    Their limit on the west is
marked by two terminal stones discovered in the via Principe
Amadeo.    The horti Tauriani belonged to M. Statilius Taurus,[6]
consul in 44 A.D., whom Agrippina put to death in 53 A.D. in
order that she might get possession of the gardens.    Of the
horti Calyclani nothing is known.    In the neighborhood of
these gardens was a forum Tauri, and in the middle ages the
district was called Caput Tauri,[7] perhaps from the ox-skulls on
the frieze of the forum.    The porta Tiburtina was also called
porta Taurina,[8] which would seem to indicate that the gardens
extended as far as that gate.    Near the horti Tauriani were

[1] Lamprid. *Vit. Elag.* 13.        [2] Herodian. v. 6. 6.            [3] *Mitt.* 1896, 113–130.
[4] *Mon. d. Lincei*, i. 490–492.                      [6] Tac. *Ann.* xii. 59.
[5] *BC.* 1874, 57 ; 1875, 153 ; *CIL.* vi. 29771.        [7] *BC.* 1890, 280–283.
[8] Urlichs, *Codex Topographicus*, 115, 127–130, 150.

the horti Vettiani,[1] and probably the horti Scatoniani also,[2] but it is possible that this last name was applied to a part of the horti Vettiani.

The horti Lolliani[3] may be mentioned here, although they were not in region V, but on the boundaries of IV and VI south of the baths of Diocletian, as is shown by a travertine terminal stone discovered at the corner of the via Principe Umberto and the piazza delle Terme. These gardens probably belonged to Lollia Paulina, the defeated rival of Agrippina for the hand of Claudius. She was banished by Agrippina and her possessions confiscated.

All these gardens were probably preserved as parks until the downfall of the empire; but after that time they must have been largely converted into private property and built over, for almost the whole Esquiline was covered with streets in the early middle ages.

According to the *Notitia* the campus Viminalis sub aggere[4] was in region V, and must have extended along the east side of the agger, south of the vicus collis Viminalis. It is probable however that originally it also extended north of this line.

**Other Buildings.** — The Sessorium, a building[5] known in later times as the Palatium Sessorianum, was built before the Aurelian wall, and probably as early as the first century, when it is apparently spoken of as being near the spot where the execution of criminals took place (p. 445). The origin of the name is unexplained, but the building became an imperial residence in the fourth century and was a favorite home of Helena, the mother of Constantine. Its site is known, for the

---

[1] *CIL.* xv. 7563; Lanciani, *Syll. Aq.* 52.        [2] *CIL.* vi. 6281.
[3] *BC.* 1883, 220; *CIL.* vi. 31284; *Civiltà Cattolica*, 1883, 210.
[4] *Not.* Reg. v; *Arch. d. Soc. Romana di Storia Patria*, 1889, 199-207; *Mitt.* 1891, 113; Jordan, II. 129.
[5] Plut. *Galba*, 28; *Exc. Valesia*, 69; Comm. Cruq. *ad Hor. Epod.* 5. 100; *Sat.* i. 8. 11; Gilbert, III. 311; *Ann. d. Ist.* 1877, 371; *Mon. d. Lincei*, i. 490-492; Jordan, I. 3. 249.

church of S. Croce in Gerusalemme occupies one of the halls of the ancient palace. This rectangular hall, 34 metres long, 21 wide, and 20 high, resembled closely the templum Sacrae Urbis of Vespasian both in construction and scheme of decoration. It was converted into a church by Constantine, who added the apse at the east end, but the columns were not set up until the eighth century. North of the church, in the garden, are the remains of another hall of the Sessorium, consisting of an apse and the walls on each side. This hall was not destroyed until the sixteenth century.

North of S. Croce in the vigna Conti are the ruins of some thermae, including a piscina, which are known to have been restored by Helena after a fire [1] and are therefore called the thermae Helenae. Complete plans of these baths, made by Palladio and Sangallo in the sixteenth century, are in existence,[2] but the ruins themselves are very meagre.

The barracks of the cohors II vigilum [3] were in region V, and inscriptions found at the extreme south end of the piazza Vittorio Emanuele indicate their site.

Just outside the porta Esquilina and a little to the north was the macellum Liviae, or market built by Augustus and named after his wife.[4] Between the piazza Fanti and the arcus Gallieni the ruins of an open court surrounded with porticoes and shops have been found, which resembles a macellum; but the construction, of brick and opus reticulatum without ornament, dates from the time of Trajan, so that this was probably a later part of the macellum Liviae. Inscriptions [5] indicate restorations of this macellum in the fourth and fifth centuries, and it appears to have existed until the late middle ages.

The porta Esquilina, which may have opened into the forum

---

[1] *CIL*. vi. 1136; *B C*. 1907, 114–121.    [2] *B C*. 1896, 238.

[3] *CIL*. vi. 414, 1059; *Ann. d. Ist*. 1858, 279–284; Gilbert, III. 196.

[4] Dio Cass. lv. 8; *Not*. Reg. v; *Mon. d Lincei*, i. 531; Gilbert, III. 238; Jordan, I. 3. 344.

[5] *CIL*. vi. 1178, 1662.

Esquilinum (p. 445), disappeared with the wall, but in 262 A.D.
M. Aurelius Victor, praefectus urbi, erected on its site an arch,
dedicated to the emperor Gallienus.   This arcus Gallieni now
stands in the via di S. Vito, close to the church of the same
name.   The existing single arch is of travertine.   Its height
is 8.80 metres, its width 7.30, and its depth 3.50.   The piers
which support it are 1.40 metres wide and 3.50 deep, and
outside of them are two pilasters of the same depth, with
Corinthian capitals.   The entablature is 2 metres high, with

FIG. 89. — REMAINS OF THE AMPHITHEATRUM CASTRENSE.

the dedicatory inscription[1] on the architrave.   Beneath the
spring of the arch on each side is a simple cornice.   Drawings
of the fifteenth century show small side arches, but almost all
traces of them have disappeared.   The lower part of the arch
is buried beneath the earth, as the modern level is considerably
higher than the ancient.

South of S. Croce are the remains of another amphitheatre,
the amphitheatrum Castrense,[2] erected some time during the

[1] *CIL.* vi. 1106.

[2] *Not.* Reg. v ; Jordan, I. 3. 248 (where Hülsen explains the name as equivalent to ' Court-Amphitheatre ') ; *BC.* 1906, 73.

second century. The reason for the name is unknown, although it is sometimes explained as one given to the amphitheatre because it was built for the soldiers of the castra Praetoria, or for the foreign soldiers quartered in that region. When the Aurelian wall was built, the amphitheatre was utilized as a part of the line of fortification, the wall being joined to it in the middle of the east and west sides. The outer half of the building was thus made a projecting bastion, and the open arcades of the exterior were walled up. The inner half was evidently pulled down, so that little use can have been made of the edifice at that time. It was an elliptical building, with axes 88.5 and 78 metres in length. The exterior wall consisted of three stories of open arcades, adorned with pilasters with Corinthian capitals. The whole structure, including columns and capitals, was built of brick and brick-faced concrete. Drawings[1] of the sixteenth century represent all three stories, but since that time the upper one has entirely disappeared and all but a few fragments of the second. The cavea and the wall of the arena have also been destroyed, so that the remaining portion consists of the walled-up arcades of the lowest story.

In the via Tasso, just northwest of the Scala Santa, the remains[2] of the castra equitum singularium were found. The equites singulares were a select corps of cavalry, organized in the latter part of the first or at the beginning of the second century as a body-guard of the emperors. The meagre ruins of the barracks consisted principally of the wall of a large rectangular court in which were niches and in front of the niches inscribed pedestals. These inscriptions[3] have thrown much light upon the organization of the corps. The Notitia speaks

---

[1] Lanciani, *Ruins*, 386.

[2] *NS.* 1886, 12–21, 49–50; 1887, 139; 1891, 126–129; *BC.* 1885, 137–156; *Mitt.* 1889, 279; 1892, 300; Jordan, I. 3. 246.

[3] *CIL.* vi. 31138–31187; *Ann. d. Ist.* 1885, 235–291; *BC.* 1886, 124–147; 1906, 72–81.

of castra equitum singularium II, and an attempt has been made to identify the second of these barracks with some ruins found beneath the Corsini chapel of the Lateran, but without success.

According to Procopius, the **Vivarium**[1] was near the porta Praenestina. This appears to have been a rectangular inclosure in which wild beasts intended for use in the amphitheatre were kept. If Procopius is correct, the structure probably stood between the Aurelian wall and the via Labicana. In the middle ages, however, the castra Praetoria was called the Vivarium, and a building just south of it, the Vivariolum, and there is some further evidence in support of the view[2] that the Vivarium was there rather than at the porta Praenestina. On the whole, however, the latter is the more probable site.

**Tombs.** — Inside the porta Praenestina, on the north side of the old via Praenestina, during the laying out of new streets a number of burial-places have been found which have yielded a large store of inscriptions. Farthest from the gate, on the west of the viale Principessa Margherita, was the tomb of the Arruntii, **monumentum Arruntiorum,**[3] consisting of three columbaria, which probably belonged to L. Arruntius, consul in 6 A.D., and were designed for his family, freedmen, and slaves. Nearer the gate was another columbarium with three rooms, the **monumentum Statiliorum.**[4] One of the members of this family was M. Statilius Taurus, the owner of the horti Tauriani. In the immediate vicinity were several other columbaria,[5] all dating from the end of the republic or the early part of the first century. They were buried at a later time; but although the interiors were filled up, care was taken not to disturb the urns.

---

[1] *Bell. Goth.* i. 22–23; Jordan, I. 3. 365–367, 391–392.

[2] *CIL.* vi. 130; *BC.* 1876, 188; 1877, 93; Lanciani, *Storia degli Scavi,* ii. 247–249.

[3] *CIL.* vi. 5931–5960; Jordan, I. 3. 362.

[4] *CIL.* vi. 6213–6640; *BC.* 1880, 51–75.

[5] *CIL.* vi. 5961–6148, 6641–6790, and plan on page 982.

In this new stratum of earth later graves were made, and near the monumentum Statiliorum tombs of three periods were found, one above another.[1]   The earliest graves, of republican date, were 9.75 metres, the columbaria of the Augustan age 6.25 metres, and the graves of the third century from 2 to 3 metres, below the present level.

Close to the outer side of the porta Praenestina, in the angle formed by the via Praenestina and the via Labicana, is a most curious tomb, sepulchrum Eurysacis, which was built by a baker, M. Vergilius Eurysaces,[2] in the first century B.C.   The tomb is trapezoidal in shape, and built of concrete faced with travertine. It was once partially covered by a tower which flanked the gate, and the east side is almost demolished.   The other sides are largely composed of horizontal and vertical rows of stone cylinders, which possibly are designed to represent measures for grain.   Above them is a cornice and a frieze covered with reliefs which represent the various operations of bread-making.

---

[1] *NS.* 1880, 30.

[2] *CIL.* vi. 1958 ; E. Caetani–Lovatelli, *Passegiate nella Roma Antica*, Rome, 1909, 151–176.

# CHAPTER XVIII.

## THE VIA LATA AND THE PINCIAN HILL.
### REGION VII.

**Region VII** was bounded on the west by the via Lata (p. 125), which gave its name to the region and was included in it, and on the south and east, as far as the northwest corner of the Quirinal, by the Servian wall. From this point the line ran north, probably to the porta Pinciana, leaving the valley between the Pincian and the Quirinal in region VI. The north limit of the region in the time of Augustus is not known, but a stone [1] of Vespasian's pomerium (p. 68) has been found west of the porta Pinciana, showing that the region extended to this point two centuries before the building of Aurelian's wall. As already remarked, the substructures of the Pincian on the north and east were made a part of Aurelian's line of defence. The north part of region VII was the collis hortulorum,[2] or mons Pincius, as it was afterward called from the gens Pincia which dwelt there.[3] Down to the third century it is probable that only the south part of this region was built up, but that part was thickly inhabited.[4]

Between the via Lata and the eastern limits of the region, where the via Salaria vetus ran north to the porta Pinciana, there must have been several cross-streets like those north and south of the campus Agrippae, but none of these have been identified.

---

[1] *CIL*. vi. 31538 a.  [2] Suet. *Nero*, 50.

[3] *CIL*. vi. 1754; Cassiod. *Var*. iii. 10; *Mitt*. 1889, 269–270.

[4] Jul. Cap. *Vit. Gord*. 32; *Not*. Reg. vii; Richter, *Top*.[2] 260; Gilbert, III. 373–374.

**Temples and Shrines.**— We know very little of temples in this region, and probably they were few in number. The most important was the great temple of the Sun, templum Solis Aureliani, built by Aurelian after his return from the east in 273 A. D., and famous for its magnificence.[1] The temple was surrounded with a porticus, in some part of which were stored the *vina fiscalia*, which had been brought from the Ciconiae (p. 342).[2] This temple is mentioned in the fourth century as being *in campo Agrippae*.[3] By some it has been identified with the ruins [4] in the gardens of the palazzo Colonna (p. 492); by others [5] it is placed in the area bounded by the Corso, the via Claudio, and the via Frattina, all of which correspond to ancient streets. Here have been found peperino walls, granite columns, and architectural remains, and drawings of the sixteenth century represent here a structure which the supporters of this view assert to be a temple. These plans show two adjacent inclosures, one with curved ends, 90.50 metres in length and 42.70 in width, and the other rectangular, 126 metres long and 86.38 wide. Without further discussion it may be said that there is insufficient evidence for the hypothesis that these plans and ruins belong to a temple, and therefore the site of the temple of the Sun must be sought for elsewhere, although near the campus Agrippae. It is possible that the ruins just described may belong to porticoes in the horti Largiani,[6] which are said to have been in this region.

The Regionary Catalogue mentions templa duo nova Spei et Fortunae,[7] but nothing further is known of them. An inscription [8] belonging to a sacellum Silvani was found on the Pincian

---

[1] Vop. *Vit. Aur.* 1, 10, 25, 28, 35, 39; *Vit. Tac.* 9; Aur. Vict. *Caes.* 35; Eutrop. ix. 15.

[2] Vop. *Vit. Aur.* 48; cf. *CIL.* vi. 1785.

[3] *Chronogr. a. 354*, p. 148.　　　　　　[4] *BC.* 1894, 297–307; 1895, 94–101.

[5] *Mitt.* 1888, 98; *RhM.* 1894, 393–396; *BC.* 1895, 39–59; Jordan, I. 3. 453-456; *NS.* 1908, 231–233.

[6] *Not.* Reg. vii.　　　　　　　　[7] Jordan, II. 7–8.

[8] *CIL.* vi. 623; *Bull. d. Ist.* 1868, 119.

in the horti Aciliorum.   In 1794 the foundation of the porticus
of an octostyle temple [1] fronting on the via Lata, and also a
portion of the cella wall, were found at the corner of the Corso
and the via Condotti.   The columns were of red granite, and
the bases, steps, and capitals of marble.   No clew exists for
the identification of this temple, and the same is true of other
ruins [2] not far distant, which may belong to a temple.   These
lie beneath the church of S. Giovannino in Capite, at the corner of the via della Mercede and the via del Moretto, and are
the remains of travertine walls, 10 and 6 metres long, which
form the sides of the northwest corner of some building in
which a sanctuary of Mithras had been established in the
fourth century.

**Other Buildings.** — The building activity displayed by
Agrippa in the campus Martius extended across the via Lata,
and the campus Agrippae,[3] laid out by Agrippa and finished and
dedicated by Augustus in 7 B.C., was the topographical centre
of the region.   This campus, which was a beautiful park and
a favorite promenade of the Romans, extended from the line
of the aqua Virgo on the south at least as far as the via Claudio
on the north, and from the via Lata to the slope of the Quirinal,
although its boundary on the east is quite uncertain.   The
west side of the campus was occupied by the porticus Vipsania
or Polae, named from the sister of Agrippa, by whom it had
been commenced.[4]   It was finished and opened by Augustus.
This porticus [5] extended along the via Lata from a point not
very far from the north end of the Saepta, of which it formed
a practical continuation, although on the opposite side of the
street.   It also resembled the Saepta closely in size and con-

---

[1] *BC.* 1894, 292–293.                    [2] *BC.* 1894, 293–296.
[3] Dio Cass. lv. 8;  Gilbert, III. 245–247.
[4] Tac. *Hist.* i. 31;  Mart. i. 108. 3;  iv. 18. 1;  Plut. *Galba*, 25;  Pl. *NH.* iii. 17;
Dio Cass. *loc. cit.*
[5] *BC.* 1887, 146–148;  1892, 275–279;  1895, 46–48.

struction (p. 384). In it was a map of the world[1] prepared by order of Agrippa. The porticus appears to have undergone changes in later times, as part of the remains date from the Flavian emperors, and in the second century the intercolumnar spaces were closed up with brick-faced walls, thus making rows of separate chambers. The edifice existed in the fourth century, when it is mentioned by the corrupted name of porticus Gypsiani.[2] At various points in the area covered by the porticus remains have been found of semicircular arches with travertine pillars and pilasters with Doric capitals, and of a travertine pavement and cipollino columns with Corinthian capitals.

In the Regionary Catalogue, in connection with the porticus Gypsiani, is mentioned a porticus Constantini,[3] but nothing further is known about it and there are no indications as to its exact location. It is possible that this was the name given to part of the porticus surrounding the statio cohortis I vigilum (see below).

In documents[4] of the fourth century mention is also made of certain castra as *in campo Agrippae*, which must refer to the castra Urbana, or barracks of the *cohortes urbanae*. Near these barracks was the forum Suarium,[5] or pork market. The trade in pork seems to have become even more important under the empire than in earlier times, and there are indications that the superintendence of this market was in the hands of an officer of the cohortes urbanae. The site of the castra and of the forum Suarium was probably north of the campus Agrippae, between it and the horti Lucullani.

Between the Saepta and the base of the Quirinal the remains of an extensive structure were found in the seventeenth cen-

---

[1] Pl. *NH.* iii. 17.      [2] *Not.* Reg. vii.

[3] *BC.* 1887, 146; *Ann. d. Ist.* 1858, 279; *Mon. d. Lincei,* i. 474–475; Gilbert, III. 252.

[4] *Not.* Reg. vii; *Chronogr. a. 354,* p. 148.

[5] *Not.* Reg. vii; *CIL.* vi. 1156, 3728, 9631; *BC.* 1895, 48–49; Gilbert, III. 199.

tury. This is represented on the Marble Plan,[1] and was the statio cohortis I vigilum [2] as well as the headquarters of the praefectus vigilum. It was a rectangular building, with its main axis extending due north and south at an angle of 18° with the via Lata, and divided into three parts, each of which consisted of a central court surrounded by a porticus and rows of chambers. Some of these rooms showed signs of having been luxuriously furnished and decorated. The entire area is now covered with modern buildings.

**Arches.** — There were at least four arches erected on the via Lata which belonged to region VII. Just north of the Saepta the via Lata was crossed by the aqua Virgo, and here Claudius built a triumphal arch, the arcus Claudii,[3] in commemoration of his victories in Britain in 51–52 A.D. The arch formed part of the aqueduct, and seems to have been in ruins as early as the eighth century. Coins[4] of the period represent an arch commemorating these victories of Claudius, which is surmounted by an equestrian statue and trophies. Portions of the travertine foundations and inscriptions[5] dedicated to other members of the imperial family have been found, together with some fragments of sculpture of which all traces have been lost.[6]

Farther north and close to the ara Pacis was an arch over the via Flaminia, the arcus Hadriani,[7] which stood until 1662, when it was removed by Alexander VII in order that the Corso might be widened. The foundation of one of the piers has been found beneath the palazzo Fiano, 2.34 metres below the level of the Corso. From the sixteenth century it bore the

---

[1] Jordan, *FUR.* 36.

[2] *CIL.* vi. 233, 1056, 1092; *Ann. d. Ist.* 1858, 267–278; *BC.* 1894, 287–291; Gilbert, III. 196; Jordan, I. 1. 308; 3. 461.

[3] *CIL.* vi. 920; Jordan, I. 3. 468–469; II. 418; Gilbert, III. 190; *BC.* 1878, 14–21; *Mon. d. Lincei,* i. 478.

[4] Cohen, *Claud.* 16.     [5] *CIL.* vi. 921–923.     [6] *PBS.* iii. 215–223.

[7] *BC.* 1891, 18–23; 1896, 239–246; *Mitt.* 1892, 315; 1893, 304; Jordan, I. 3. 465–467.

name of arco di Portogallo.   Two of the reliefs[1] from this arch
have been found, and are now in the palazzo dei Conservatori.
They belong to the period of Hadrian, and the arch itself is
usually ascribed to that emperor; but descriptions written
before its destruction seem to lend some support to the view
that the structure itself was of late date, perhaps even later
than Constantine, and that it was adorned with sculpture from
much earlier buildings.   One of the reliefs represents the
apotheosis of an empress, either Plotina the wife of Trajan or
Sabina the wife of Hadrian.

The arcus Diocletiani (Novus)[2] spanned the via Lata south of
the arcus Claudii and directly in front of the modern church
of S. Maria in via Lata.   It was probably built by Diocletian
and Maximian in 301 A.D., and stood until the time of Inno-
cent VIII (1488–1492).   The fragments of a relief[3] found near
this site and now preserved in the villa Medici, which represent triumphal scenes, probably belonged to this arch.

In the *Mirabilia* mention is made of an arcus Manus Carneae,[4]
near the church of S. Marco.   Recently a very clever attempt
has been made to identify this arch with that represented on
one of the reliefs in the palazzo dei Conservatori which pictures the entry of Marcus Aurelius into Rome, and to ascribe
its erection to Domitian.

In the gardens of the house, No. 12 via del Nazareno, is
another arch in the line of the aqua Virgo, which spanned an
ancient street, and is also called arcus Claudii.[5]

**Horti**. — The horti Lucullani, laid out by L. Licinius Lucullus[6]
about 60 B.C., were on the southern slope of the Pincian, for

---

[1] Helbig, *Führer durch die Museen Roms*, 2d ed. 564, 565; Strong, *Sculpture*, 236–238; *PBS.* iv. 258–263; v. 180.

[2] *BC.* 1895, 46; Jordan, I. 3. 469–470; II. 7, 102, 417.

[3] Matz-Duhn, *Antike Bildwerke*, 3525; *CIL.* vi. 31383; *PBS.* iii. 271.

[4] *Mon. d. Lincei*, i. 550; *PBS.* iii. 259–261, 269–271.

[5] *CIL.* vi. 1252; *Mon. d. Lincei*, i. 455.

[6] Front. *de Aq.* 22; Tac. *Ann.* xi. 1, 32, 37; Plut. *Lucull.* 39; Gilbert, III.
377; *BC.* 1891, 153–155.

the most part between the modern via del Tritone, the via due Macelli, and the via di Porta Pinciana.  In 46 A.D. they belonged to Valerius Asiaticus, but were coveted by Messalina, who compelled the owner to commit suicide.  After that time the gardens belonged to the imperial family.  They contained a palace and the usual porticoes, libraries, and similar buildings, of which only the most meagre traces now remain — some walls and bases of columns in the via Sistina and the via due Macelli, mosaic pavement in the via Gregoriana (No. 46), etc.

The northern and highest part of the Pincian was occupied by the horti Aciliorum,[1] which extended from the church of S. Trinità dei Monti beyond the slopes of the hill into the grounds of the villa Borghese, and on the east probably as far as the porta Pinciana.  We do not know the precise date when they were laid out, but they belonged to the Acilii Glabriones as early as the first century, and in the fourth to Petronius Probus, being one of the few gardens which had not then fallen into the hands of the emperors.  They were inclosed on the north, west, and east by supporting walls and terraces, built along the slope of the hill.  This wall on the east and north was utilized by Aurelian in his line of defence, part of it being rebuilt, but a considerable portion on each side of the extreme northeast angle was left in its original form.  Even these substructures have been somewhat altered in modern times by additional buttresses, but their original construction can be seen.  The wall is built of opus reticulatum, in a series of lofty arcades with massive intervening piers.  On the west side of the hill there were two lines of terraces, supported by walls, of which nothing but the slightest traces remain.  Just north of S. Trinità the ruins of a great hemicycle have been found, which opened toward the west, and from which flights of steps led down to the plain below.  Beneath the modern casino is a

---

[1] *CIL*. vi. 623; *BC*. 1891, 132–155.

piscina, divided into two sections and connected with a reservoir by tunnels 80 metres long. This reservoir is formed of galleries cut in the rock, about 2 metres wide and a little more than 2 metres high, which intersect each other at right angles. East of the hemicycle, near the sharp angle in the Aurelian wall, is a mound called Il Parnasso or Belvedere di villa Medici, built on the ruins of an ancient octagonal structure, once thought to be a temple, but really a nymphaeum belonging to the extensive water works of the gardens. The buildings of the palace and its various annexes extended along the west brow of the hill, from the villa Medici to S. Maria del Popolo, where their ruins were discovered in 1812. Under the north slope of the hill, near S. Maria del Popolo and also near S. Trinità, wine cellars, excavated in the rock and containing rows of amphorae, have been found.

The **horti Pompei** [1] seem to have been either at the foot of this hill or to have extended up its western slope. On the northwestern slope was the **monumentum Domitiorum**,[2] or family tomb of the Domitii, in which Nero's ashes were placed, and it is probable that this tomb stood in a park belonging to the Domitii.

Of the other monuments in this region mentioned in the *Notitia* — the **lacus Ganymedis, nymphaeum Iovis**,[3] **aedicula Capraria**,[4] **equi Tiridatis regis Armeniorum, Mansuetae**, and **lapis pertusus** — nothing is known.

**Tombs.** — There were tombs on the via Flaminia, at points which marked the successive limits of the city. The oldest is the **sepulchrum Bibuli**,[5] at the base of the Capitoline close to the approach to the monument of Vittorio Emanuele. This tomb was just outside the porta Fontinalis, and was erected in the last century of the republic by decree of the senate, in honor

---

[1] Plut. *Pomp.* 44; *CIL.* vi. 6299; cf. Asc. *in Mil.* 67; Jordan, I. 3. 492.

[2] Suet. *Nero*, 50.   [4] Gilbert, III. 377.

[3] *BC.* 1887, 144–145.   [5] *CIL.* vi. 1319; Jordan, I. 1. 207.

of C. Publicius Bibulus, a plebeian aedile.   The façade is of
travertine, with a massive base supporting four Tuscan pilasters with an entablature.   The frieze is decorated with reliefs
of garlands, rosettes, and ox-skulls.   Between the pilasters
were windows, and the inscription is on the dado.

The tombs of the later period begin at the piazza del Popolo
and extend beyond the porta Flaminia.[1]   The foundations of
two of them, which seem to be as early as the end of the republic, have been found beneath the churches of S. Maria dei
Miracoli and S. Maria in Montesanto, at the very end of the
Corso.   Immediately outside the porta del Popolo were the
tombs of the gens Gallonia[2] and of L. Nonius Asprenas,[3] consul in
29 A.D. ; of the gens Benina and of Publius Aelius Gutta Calpurni-
anus,[4] a celebrated charioteer of the time of Hadrian or the
Antonines.

**Private Houses.** — Few inscriptions relating to private houses
have been found in this district, but there is epigraphic evidence
for the existence of a domus Postumiorum[5] on the Pincian, between the horti Lucullani and the horti Aciliorum, and of a
house belonging to a certain T. Sextius Africanus,[6] in the via
del Babuino, at the corner of the via del Gesù Maria.   Two inscriptions[7] on the collars worn by slaves mention a physician
Gemellinus and a certain Flavius in the via Lata.   M. Messala
Corvinus[8] also had a park or house on this hill.

---

[1] B C. 1877, 184–195;  1880, 169–182;  1881, 174–188.

[2] CIL. vi. 31714.

[3] CIL. vi. 31689.

[7] Richter, Top.² 260;  CIL. xv. 7186, 7187.

[8] CIL. vi. 29789;  B C. 1889, 208.

[4] CIL. vi. 10047.

[5] RhM. 1894, 390.

[6] Gilbert, III. 375.

# CHAPTER XIX.

## THE QUIRINAL AND THE VIMINAL. REGION VI.

This region, lying between the imperial fora, the east boundary of region VII, and the northwest boundary of region IV, comprised the Viminal, the Quirinal, the valley between the Quirinal and the Pincian, and the lower slope of the latter hill. The different divisions of the Quirinal, the earliest name for which is said to have been Agonus or Agonius,[1] have been described on page 16, and the corresponding gates in the Servian wall on page 49. The region took its name from its principal street, the **Alta Semita**, which ran northwest along the ridge of the Quirinal to the porta Collina. This street corresponded exactly with the modern via del Quirinale and via Venti Settembre from the piazza del Quirinale east, and the ancient pavement lies at an average depth of 1.83 metres below the present level.[2] Beyond the junction of the vicus Longus, this street was probably called the **vicus portae Collinae**.[3]

The second most important street in the region was the **vicus Longus**,[4] which traversed the valley between the Quirinal and the Viminal, and joined the Alta Semita inside the porta Collina, very near where the via Quintino Sella runs into the via Venti Settembre. The pavement of the vicus Longus has been found on a line that crosses the via Nazionale at an angle of 20° near the Banca d'Italia, at various points between the bank and the baths of Diocletian, a distance of one kilometre.

---

[1] Fest. *Epit.* 10, 254.

[2] *BC.* 1889, 332; *RhM.* 1894, 387; Gilbert, III. 368.

[3] *CIL.* vi. 450.

[4] Fest. 237; Liv. x. 23; Val. Max. ii. 5. 6; *CIL.* vi. 9736, 10023; *RhM.* 1894, 382–384; Gilbert, III. 368.

A considerable part of the northeast section of this street was destroyed by the erection of these baths.

A third street, running in the same general direction, was the vicus collis Viminalis,[1] which extended along the ridge of the Viminal to the porta Viminalis. It is not represented by any modern street, but its pavement has been found along a line from the via Napoli through the porta Chiusa to the porta Viminalis.

The practical continuation of the Alta Semita from the south end of the Quirinal ridge down to the imperial fora was the vicus laci Fundani,[2] which seems to have corresponded in general with the present via del Quirinale. It derived its name from the lacus Fundani,[3] a fountain which could not have been far from the Cati fons (p. 19). Near the lacus Fundani was probably the temple of Hercules Fundanius.[4]

Communication between the Alta Semita and the vicus Longus was effected by three cross-streets,— the clivus Salutis or Salutaris, the clivus Mamuri, and a street called ad Malum Punicum. The first of these[5] derived its name from the hill on which it was, the collis Salutaris, and corresponded in general with the via della Consulta. Its pavement[6] has been found at a depth of 18 metres below the new public gardens, at the corner of the via della Consulta and the via Venti Settembre, and at the lower end under the Banca d' Italia. The clivus Mamuri,[7] named from the statua Mamuri,[8] was probably just east of S. Vitale and S. Andrea di Monte Cavallo. The third street, ad Malum Punicum,[9] probably corresponded with the via delle Quattro Fontane. The vicus Insteius or Insteianus,[10]

---

1 *CIL.* vi. 2227–2228; *BC.* 1874, 199.

2 *CIL.* vi. 1297; *RhM.* 1894, 401–403.

3 Tac. *Hist.* iii. 69; Placidus, p. 29; *CIL.* vi. 9854.

4 *CIL.* vi. 311; Vop. *Vit. Tac.* 17.

5 Symm. *Epist.* v. 54; *BC.* 1889, 387; 1890, 11; *RhM.* 1894, 405.

6 *BC.* 1886, 187.    7 *RhM.* 1894, 405, 417.    8 *Not.* Reg. vi; Gilbert, III. 370.

9 Suet. *Dom.* 1; *RhM.* 1894, 399, 401; *BC.* 1889, 383.

10 Varro, *LL.* v. 52; Liv. xxiv. 10.

mentioned in the description of the Argei, seems to have ascended the hill near the porta Fontinalis, but to have been destroyed by the building of the imperial fora.    The street called ad Tonsores [1] was near the temple of Flora, and its position is therefore dependent upon the site assigned to that edifice (p. 489).    Another street, ad Tres Fortunas,[2] was evidently near those temples (p. 490) and may possibly be identified with an ancient street running south from the campus Sceleratus, nearly parallel to the Servian agger, on which remains of houses have been found.

The principal open space in this region was between the castra Praetoria and the Servian agger, north of the vicus collis Viminalis.    A large part of this area was afterward used as a drill ground by the praetorian cohorts, and was perhaps called the campus cohortium Praetoriarum.[3]    The campus Sceleratus [4] was an open area, immediately inside the Servian wall southwest of the porta Collina, where Vestal Virgins who had broken their vow of chastity were buried alive.

Two names occur in the Regionary Catalogue, probably of buildings, but which also designated localities, perhaps open squares.    These were the Gallinae Albae and the Decem Tabernae,[5] the latter plainly a sort of bazaar.    Both were on the south part of the Viminal, in the vicinity of S. Lorenzo in Panisperna. Of the area Candidi mentioned in the *Notitia*, nothing is known, but it is conjecturally placed near S. Pudenziana.[6]

**Temples and Shrines**. — There were many places of worship on the Quirinal, as was to be expected from its early settlement.    Before the great temple was built on the Capitoline to Jupiter, Juno, and Minerva, there was a temple on the Quirinal dedicated to these same gods and called the Capitolium,

---

[1] *Mitt.* 1891, 341; *BC.* 1893, 187; *CIL.* xv. 7172.
[2] Jordan, I. 3. 382.                [3] Tac. *Ann.* xii. 36; Jordan, I. 3. 384.
[4] Serv. *ad Aen.* xi. 206; Liv. viii. 15; Dionys. ii. 67; Plut. *Numa*, 10.
[5] *Not.* Reg. vi; *RhM.* 1894, 417; *Mitt.* 1892, 307.          [6] *RhM. loc. cit.*

but known in historical times as the **Capitolium vetus** [1] or **antiquum**, to distinguish it from the other. We know nothing of the history of the temple building, except that it existed throughout the empire. The discovery of dedicatory inscriptions,[2] placed in the temple by certain cities of Asia Minor during the Mithradatic wars, and other known facts in the topography of the Quirinal, make it certain that it stood north of the Alta Semita, but whether west or east of the modern via delle Quattro Fontane is uncertain.[3] Besides its Capitolium, the original Quirinal settlement possessed an **Auguraculum** [4] on the south point of the hill, the collis Latiaris, which corresponded to the auguraculum on the Arx of the Capitoline.

A second very ancient temple on the Quirinal was that of the Sabine deity, **Semo Sancus** or **Dius Fidius**.[5] Tradition ascribed the building of this temple to Titus Tatius, and it was said to have contained such ancient documents as the treaty with Gabii, and the household implements of Tanaquil. According to another form of the tradition,[6] it was built by Tarquinius Superbus, and dedicated by Sp. Postumius in 466 B.C. Possibly an earlier edifice was only restored by Postumius. The temple undoubtedly stood on the slope of the hill just north of the porta Sanqualis,[7] between the sharp turn of the via Nazionale and the via del Quirinale, where inscriptions [8] have been found, and three fragments of concrete foundations which may possibly have belonged to it.

---

[1] Varro, *LL*. v. 158; Mart. v. 22; vii. 73; Gilbert, II. 84–89; III. 371; Jordan, I. 3. 411.

[2] *CIL*. vi. 373, 374, 30927; *BC*. 1887, 251.

[3] *RhM*. 1884, 408–409; Jordan, I. 3. 395.

[4] Varro, *LL*. v. 52; Jordan, II. 264; Gilbert, I. 274.

[5] Tertull. *ad Nat*. ii. 9; Ov. *Fast*. vi. 213–218; Dionys. iv. 58; Pl. *NH*. viii. 194; Gilbert, I. 275–280; III. 370–371; Jordan, I. 3. 400–402.

[6] Dionys. ix. 60.

[7] Fest. 345; Liv. viii. 20; *RhM*. 1894, 409; *BC*. 1881, 5; 1887, 8; *Mitt*. 1889, 274.

[8] *CIL*. vi. 568, 30994.

The temple of **Quirinus** represented perhaps the oldest cult in this part of the city. Its establishment[1] was ascribed to Numa, and the name was said to have been given to the porta Quirinalis, and presumably to the hill itself, because of a shrine of Quirinus which was near the gate. The builder of the actual temple of Quirinus is said to have been L. Papirius Cursor,[2] in 293 B.C., although an assembly of the senate is said to have been held in this temple in 435 B.C. In 206 B.C.[3] the temple was injured by lightning, and it was burned in 49 B.C., but soon rebuilt.[4] A final restoration was completed by Augustus in 16 B.C.,[5] and this structure lasted at least as long as the empire. It is described[6] as being dipteral, octostyle, with a pronaos and a porch in the rear. It had seventy-six columns in all, two rows of fifteen each on the sides and a double row of eight at each end, and was surrounded by a porticus.[7] Augustus's restoration occupied the site of the temple of Papirius, and this has been determined, by the finding of inscriptions,[8] to be north of the Alta Semita, but whether in the very centre of the royal gardens or in their eastern part is a disputed point. It is also uncertain whether or not this temple stood on the site of the original **sacellum Quirini**,[9] which was near the porta Quirinalis. Next to his temple Papirius set up the first **solarium horologium**[10] in Rome, and just west of it was the **pulvinar Solis**, a shrine dedicated to the sun.[11] Little is known of this, except that it was in existence during the first centuries before and after Christ.

The worship of **Salus**[12] existed at a very early date on the

---

[1] Cic. *de Legg.* i. 3; Dionys. ii. 63; Fest. 254; Varro, *LL.* v. 51; Gilbert, I. 280; III. 370; *CIL.* i². pp. 310, 320; *Hermes*, 1891, 137–144.

[2] Liv. iv. 21; x. 46; Ov. *Fast.* ii. 511; vi. 795–796.    [3] Liv. xxviii. 11.

[4] Dio Cass. xli. 14; xliii. 45.    [5] *Mon. Anc.* iv. 5; Dio Cass. liv. 19.

[6] Vitr. iii. 2. 7.    [7] Mart. xi. 1. 9.

[8] *BC.* 1889, 336–339, 379–391; *RhM.* 1894, 405–406; Jordan, I. 3. 409-410.

[9] Pl. *NH.* xv. 120; Fest. 255; *Hermes*, 1891, 139; *Mitt.* 1891, 119.

[10] Pl. *NH.* vii. 213.    [11] Quint. i. 7. 12.

[12] Liv. ix. 43; x. 1; xxviii. 11; Gilbert, III. 371.

Quirinal, one part of which, the collis Salutaris, derived its name from this cult. Some shrine must therefore have stood here in earlier times, although Roman historians state that the temple was vowed in 311 and dedicated in 303 b.c. by C. Junius Bubulcus. It was famous for the paintings [1] by Fabius Pictor with which it was adorned, and although the edifice was injured by lightning in 276 and in 206 b.c., the paintings were preserved until it was burned in the reign of Claudius. The temple was restored and was in existence in the fourth century. No traces of the building have come to light, but it was near the temple of Quirinus and the house of Atticus (p. 503), and probably on or near the clivus Salutis.[2] Therefore, of the two conjectural sites, one just east of the via delle Quattro Fontane and the other at the west end of the royal palace, the latter is the more probable.

The cult of **Flora** was of ancient Sabine origin and was established on the Quirinal, where Titus Tatius is said to have erected an altar.[3] Nothing is known of the date of the building of the temple as it existed in historical times, or of its history, except a possible restoration by the younger Symmachus in the fourth century; nor is its site at all certain. We are told that a clivus led up to the Capitolium vetus from the temple of Flora, and that it was not far from the temple of Quirinus; but it is claimed that two sites conform to this statement, one outside the Servian wall at the foot of the Quirinal, near the piazza Barberini, and the other just below the Capitolium vetus, between it and the street ad Malum Punicum, the modern via delle Quattro Fontane. The street on which the temple stood was called Pila Tiburtina.[4]

---

[1] Val. Max. viii. 14. 6; Pl. *NH.* xxxv. 19; *BC.* 1889, 340; Helbig, *Führer,* i². 421.

[2] Cic. *ad Att.* iv. 1; xii. 45; *RhM.* 1894, 404; *BC.* 1873, 227.

[3] Varro, *LL.* v. 158; Vitr. vii. 9. 4; Mart. v. 22; vi. 27; Gilbert, I. 287; *BC.* 1893, 189; *Bull. Crist.* 1868, 55; *RhM.* 1894, 407; Jordan, I. 3. 412.

[4] Mart. v. 22. 3; *RhM.* 1894, 397; Jordan. I. 3. 426–427.

On the Quirinal side of the vicus Longus was a sacellum Pudicitiae Plebeiae,[1] said to have been built by a certain Virginia of patrician birth, who had married a plebeian consul, L. Volumnius, and had therefore been excluded from participation in the worship of the goddess Pudicitia Patricia in the forum Boarium. The shrine certainly dated from the time of the struggle between the orders. At the highest point of the vicus Longus there was also a temple of Febris.[2]

Near the porta Collina were three temples of Fortuna, Tres fortunae,[3] to which the vicus ad Tres Fortunas (p. 486) probably led. These temples seem to have formed a sort of cult-unit, although they were built at different times and their festivals occurred on different days. According to the calendar, one was called the temple of Fortuna Publica Citerior, another that of Fortuna Primigenia, and the third, of Fortuna Publica populi Romani Quiritium Primigenia. This last was vowed in 204 B.C. by P. Sempronius Sophus and dedicated in 194 by Q. Marcius Ralla. One of these is mentioned by Vitruvius as an illustration of a temple in antis. The podium and foundations of one of the other two were probably discovered[4] in 1881–1882, just inside the Servian agger, at the corner of the via Flavia and the via di Servio Tullio. Somewhere on the Quirinal, but apparently without connection with these three temples, was an altar to τύχη εὐελπις.[5]

Outside the porta Collina, and probably west of the via Salaria, was a temple of Venus Erycina,[6] which was vowed in 184 B.C. by the consul L. Porcius Licinus during his Ligurian campaign, and dedicated three years later. It was surrounded

---

[1] Liv. x. 23.  [2] Val. Max. ii. 5. 6.

[3] Vitr. iii. 2. 2; Ov. *Fast.* iv. 375; v. 729; Liv. xxix. 36; xxxiv. 53; xliii. 13; *CIL.* i². pp. 315, 319, 335; vi. 3679, 3681; Gilbert, III. 372; Jordan, I. 3. 413–414.

[4] *BC.* 1873, 201–211, 233, 243, 248.

[5] Plut. *de Fort. Rom.* 10.

[6] Ov. *Fast.* iv. 871; *Rem. Am.* 549; Liv. xxx. 38; xl. 34; Strabo, vi. 2. 5 (272); App. *Bell. Civ.* i. 93; Gilbert, III. 91; *Mitt.* 1889, 270–275; 1892, 32–80; Helbig, *Führer*, ii². 118; Jordan, I. 3. 415–416.

by a porticus, and lasted as long as the empire. It has been suggested that this temple may possibly be identified with that of Venus hortorum Sallustianorum (p. 502).

Near the temple of Venus Erycina was the temple of **Honos**, of which nothing is known except that it dated from republican times, and that its erection necessitated the removal of numerous tombs.[1]    The discovery of an inscription from this temple shows that it stood a short distance inside the agger of Servius, under the east wing of the Treasury building.

A third temple in this immediate neighborhood outside the porta Collina was that of **Hercules**,[2] which was built before the second Punic war, as Hannibal is said to have approached the city *ad portam Collinam usque ad Herculis templum.*    There are, however, no indications as to its exact distance from the gate.    Somewhere outside the porta Viminalis was a sacellum **Deae Neniae**, but this is mentioned only once.[3]

Besides the temples already described, there were two altars in this region, belonging to the republican period.    One, the **ara Iovis Vimini**,[4] is the only shrine known to us on the Viminal proper.    It belonged to a very early period, as it is mentioned in connection with the Argei, and was dedicated to the worship of Jupiter as tutelary divinity of the Viminal hill.    The second altar, the **ara Vermini**,[5] was found when the débris of the agger between the porta Collina and the porta Viminalis was removed.    It was erected in the first century B.C. by the duumvir A. Postumius, in accordance with a lex Plaetoria. This altar, now in the Museo degli Orti Botanici, is 0.75 metre square and 1.03 metres high.    In shape it resembles that found on the Palatine (p. 140), dedicated to an unknown deity.

The only temple in region VI which is known to have

---

[1] Cic. *de Legg.* ii. 58; *CIL.* vi. 3692; *BC.* 1873, 229; *Bull. d. Ist.* 1873, 90.

[2] Liv. xxvi. 10; Gilbert, III. 92; *Mitt.* 1891, 114; *CIL.* vi. 30899.

[3] Fest. *Epit.* 163.        [4] Varro, *LL.* v. 51; Fest. 376; Gilbert, I. 271.

[5] *CIL.* vi. 31057; *BC.* 1876, 24–28; 1898, 164–165; *Jahreshefte d. oest. arch. Instituts,* 1903, 142; Lanciani, *Ancient Rome,* 52.

been erected during the imperial period was that of Serapis, mentioned in the Regionary Catalogue. Sufficient epigraphic evidence [1] has been found to prove that Caracalla built the temple, but its site is not indicated. It has been identified by some [2] with the temple which stood on the site of the Colonna gardens; while others [3] think that this latter edifice was the famous temple of the Sun, which was built by Aurelian (p. 476). This latter hypothesis is, however, untenable.

Of the great temple in the Colonna gardens considerable ruins were still standing in the sixteenth and seventeenth centuries, especially of one corner of the front wall of the cella and of the pediment, which was known as the Torre Mesa, Torre di Mecenate, or Frontispizio di Nerone. Drawings and plans of that time give a fairly satisfactory idea of the structure. It stood on the edge of the hill, on the west side of the present via della Consulta. It extended due east and west, and from the platform at the rear of the cella a great flight of steps led down to the valley some 20 metres below. This flight was curiously built, being divided into double narrow rows of steps on each side of a central space. The temple area was surrounded with a wall containing niches, but not with the usual porticus. The cella was built of peperino lined with marble, and was surrounded by marble columns in front and on the sides. The shafts of these columns were 17.66, the capitals 2.47, and the entablature 4.83 metres in height. The corner of the cornice now lying in the Colonna gardens is the largest architectural fragment in Rome, its dimensions being $3.70 \times 2.80 \times 3.90$ metres, and its weight 100 tons. Another fragment of the architrave and frieze measured $5 \times 2.50 \times 1.60$ metres. The material of the steps was used to build the steps of Aracoeli in 1348.

In commemoration of the great fire of Nero, and also *incendio-*

---

[1] *CIL.* vi. 570–574.

[2] *RhM.* 1894, 392–396; *BC.* 1895, 39 ff.; Jordan, I. 3. 421–423.

[3] *BC.* 1894, 285; 1895, 81.

*rum arcendorum causa*, Domitian erected a certain number of altars, **arae incendii Neroniani**, on which annual sacrifices were offered to Vulcan.   Three inscriptions relating to these altars have been found but exist only in copies.   One of the altars was on the Aventine (p. 410) and has disappeared, but another was found in 1889 on the Quirinal.   It stood in an area paved with travertine, on the south side of the Alta Semita,[2] opposite the temple of Quirinus, and close to the modern church of S. Andrea.   Three steps led up from this area to the higher level of the Alta Semita.   They have been traced for a distance of 35 metres, and are partially visible in the modern wall.   Along the front of the area, close to the lower step, was a row of travertine cippi, 1.40 metres in height, 0.80 × 0.50 in depth and width, and 2.50 apart, of which three were found *in situ*, two whole and one injured.   The altar itself was 2.75 metres back from the cippi, and was built of travertine, with a marble cornice.   It was 1.26 metres in height and 3.25 × 6.25 in breadth and length, and stood on a pedestal with two steps.   It is probable that there was one of these altars in each region.

Epigraphic evidence of four shrines of **Silvanus** has been found in region VI, — one [3] at the northwest corner of the thermae Diocletiani near S. Susanna, where there was also a Mithraeum ; [4] one [5] near the southwest side of the thermae; one[6] near the southeast corner of the thermae Constantinianae, under the Banca d' Italia, near which was also a Mithraeum ;[7] and the fourth in the gardens of Sallust.[8]

**Thermae.** — By far the largest building in region VI was the **thermae Diocletiani**, which were built by Diocletian and Max-

---

[1] *CIL*. vi. 826;  *Mitt*. 1891, 116–118;  1894, 94–97.

[2] *BC*. 1889, 331–335, 379 ff.                    [3] *CIL*. vi. 635.

[4] *CIL*. vi. 728, 3724.          [5] *CIL*. vi. 3716.          [6] *BC*. 1887, 102.

[7] *CIL*. vi. 726, 737, 31020–31022;  *NS*. 1887, 109.

[8] *CIL*. vi. 583, 640;  *BC*. 1887, 223;  1888, 402;  *Mitt*. 1889, 270.

imian, and dedicated in 305–306 A.D. after their abdication.[1]
These thermae, the largest in the empire, occupied an area
about 410 metres long and 400 wide, or, without the projecting
rooms, 356 by 316 metres, and could accommodate about three
thousand bathers at once.  The erection of so large a structure
on the Quirinal plateau necessitated the complete transformation of existing topographical conditions by the destruction of
the east part of the vicus Longus and the many buildings previously occupying its site, as well as by the construction of a
new ground level.[2]

The dedicatory inscription[3] has been preserved, with one
which records a later restoration, and we know that the baths
were in use as late as the fifth century.  After the fall of the
empire this great mass of buildings suffered from continual
destruction and transformation.  They were in a sad state of
ruin in the sixteenth century, when Michelangelo restored the
tepidarium as the church of S. Maria degli Angeli and constructed the cloisters in the east part of the building, which
are now the Museo delle Terme.  In recent years new streets
have been opened, and great buildings, like the Grand hotel,
the Massimi palace, and the Treasury, have been erected within the limits of the thermae.  The ruins have been built over
and occupied by various tenants, but are now to be entirely
converted into a national monument.  While the aspect of the
whole edifice has thus been rendered unrecognizable, some
parts have been fairly well preserved; and with the help of
early drawings it is possible not only to make out the original
plan, but also to reconstruct[4] the whole building in a reasonably
satisfactory manner.

In general plan these thermae did not differ from those of

[1] Treb. Pol. Vit. Trig. Tyr. 21; Vop. Vit. Probi, 2; Olympiodorus ap.
Photium, 80; Gilbert, III. 299; RhM. 1894, 388–389.

[2] BC. 1887, 181; CIL. xv. 7441.        [3] CIL. vi. 1130, 1131.

[4] E. Paulin, Les Thermes de Dioclétien, Paris, 1890, Fol. max.; Mitt. 1892,
308–311; Rivoira, Lombardic Architecture, I. 74–80.

Caracalla, and consisted of a vast inclosure or peribolus surrounding the baths proper. This building was rectangular in shape, 280 metres wide and 160 deep, and its main axis ran northeast-southwest. Its exterior was built in two stories of arcades and pilasters, the lower of the Ionic, the upper of the composite Corinthian order. In the centre of the east

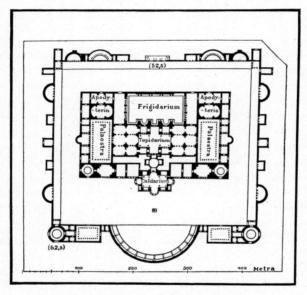

FIG. 90. — PLAN OF THE BATHS OF DIOCLETIAN.

side was the frigidarium, an enormous open hall that contained the piscina, or swimming pool, with two semicircular niches on the west side. At each end of this hall were vestibules, separated from it by rows of columns, and beyond them large dressing rooms, or apodyteria. There were four entrances on the east side, which was the front, two into the two vestibules and two into the apodyteria beyond. There was therefore no direct entrance into the frigidarium from without, as in the thermae of Caracalla. Behind the frigidarium was the great hall of the tepidarium, 65 metres wide and 25 deep, with a vaulted roof supported on eight monolithic columns of gray granite. In the piers at the four corners of the hall were small baths. This hall forms the transept of the church of S. Maria degli Angeli, but the floor of the church is 2 metres above the ancient level, so that the bases of the columns are entirely covered, and the apparent bases are only rings. Between the tepidarium and caldarium was a circular hall, which now serves as the vestibule of the church. The caldarium itself projected out from the west side of the building and has been destroyed. In the centre of the north and south sides were two large open palaestrae, surrounded with colonnades above which there were galleries. Besides these principal halls, there were very many other apartments of all sizes for the numerous purposes of the baths, — dressing, anointing, bathing, and exercising. In the building there are said to have been nearly thirty-two hundred seats of polished marble. The edifice was built of concrete and brick and lined with stucco and marble, the slabs of which were fastened to the walls with bronze hooks. There is no doubt that the whole structure was magnificently decorated, but it probably was not especially rich in works of art.

Around the peribolus were small rectangular halls and semicircular exedrae, which were used as reading and lecture rooms, gymnasia, and lounging rooms. In the centre of the west side was a very large exedra equipped as a theatre. The lines of this exedra are preserved in the piazza delle Terme, where the modern buildings stand on the curve of its circumference. At the northwest and southwest corners of the peribolus were circular halls of which the exact purpose is not known. That at the northwest corner is well preserved and has been dedicated as the church of S. Bernardo. In the ruins of the other a prison has been established. During the fourth century, the bibliotheca Ulpia which Trajan had established in his forum (p. 289) was transferred to these thermae.

The piscina, or reservoir of the baths, fed by the aqua Marcia, was outside the peribolus, on the south side. Being in the angle between the baths and the vicus collis Viminalis it was trapezoidal in shape, 91 metres long, with an average width of 16 metres. The vaulted roof was supported by forty-five square piers of masonry.[1] Considerable remains of this piscina existed until 1860, and the last vestiges above ground were not destroyed until 1876.[2] At the northeast corner of the thermae was the piscina aquarum Marciae Tepulae Iuliae, which was discovered in building the foundations of the Treasury.

The thermae Constantinianae, the last great baths of Rome, were built by Constantine; but aside from this fact we know nothing of their history, except that at some later time they were restored by a certain Petronius Perpenna, prefect of the city.[3] The ruins, which were standing in the seventeenth century, were destroyed to make room for the palazzo Rospigliosi, and although in the process of building the via Nazionale and the Teatro Drammatico portions of them have been found, there is nothing now remaining but the most meagre fragments.

Only an irregular space,[4] between the vicus Longus, the Alta Semita, the clivus Salutis, and the vicus laci Fundani, was available for these baths, and as it was also on a side hill it was necessary to make an artificial level, and remains of houses of the second, third, and fourth centuries have been found buried beneath the foundations. As a result of these conditions these thermae differed from all others in Rome. Our knowledge of them is derived from drawings of archi-

---

[1] Lanciani, *Acque*, 96.

[2] For more recent excavations, cf. *BC*. 1906, 106–107; *NS*. 1906, 120.

[3] Aur. Vict. *Caes*. 40; *CIL*. vi. 1750; Jordan, I. 3. 438–441; II. 526–528; Gilbert, III. 300.        [4] *RhM*. 1894, 389–392.

tects of the sixteenth century. They extended due north and south, and as the main building occupied all the space between the streets on the east and west, the ordinary peribolus was replaced by an inclosure which extended across its front and was bounded on the north by a curved line. The palazzo della Consulta now occupies this curved quasi-peribolus. The

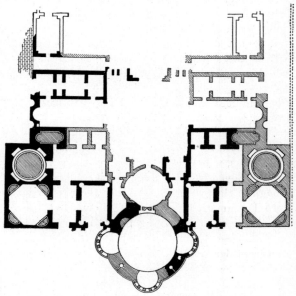

FIG. 91 — PLAN OF THE BATHS OF CONSTANTINE.

frigidarium was in the middle of the north side, and back of it the tepidarium and the caldarium, both circular in shape. Owing to the narrowness of the space, the ordinary succession of three anterooms on each side of the caldarium was not possible, and these rooms were grouped differently.

During the excavations [1] on this site some notable works of

---

[1] *RhM.* 1894, 423 n.; *CIL.* vi. 1148–1150; Lanciani, *Ancient Rome*, 297 ff.

art have been found, such as the Dioscuri on the Quirinal and
the statue of Constantine in the Lateran, which undoubtedly
came from the thermae.  Besides these thermae, balnea Stephani
are mentioned,[1] probably near the house of Martial, and a
lavacrum Agrippinae [2] occurs in inscriptions on lead pipes.

**Other Buildings.** — The castra Praetoria,[3] or barracks of the
praetorian cohorts, were built by Tiberius in the extreme
northeastern part of the city, just beyond the inhabited district.
These barracks were constructed on the well-known model of
a fortified Roman camp, and formed a rectangle 440 metres
long and 380 wide.  The walls were furnished with battlements and turreted gates, the masonry being brickwork of the
best period.  Aurelian incorporated the castra in his line of
fortification, which joined the castra at the northwest corner
and again at the middle of the south side.  The north and east
wall of the castra thus formed the continuation of the Aurelian
wall; but as it was not sufficiently high, its height was
increased not only by an addition at the top, but also by dig-
ging away the soil at its base on the outside to a depth of 3.50
metres, thus laying bare the foundations.  Constantine dis-
mantled the barracks by destroying the wall on the inner sides,
toward the city.  The original wall on the north and east sides
can be distinguished from the additions of Aurelian by the
difference in brickwork and by the outline of the battlements.
The gates on these two sides, which were walled up by Aurelian, can also be seen.  All round the inside of the wall were
rows of chambers occupied by the soldiers, some of which have
been excavated.  They are 4 metres in height and 4.40 in
width, built of opus reticulatum and lined with stucco.  Above
them was a vaulted corridor 7.70 metres high, and over that a

---

[1] Mart. xi. 52. 4; xiv. 60.          [2] *CIL.* xv. 7247; Jordan, I. 3. 375.
[3] Suet. *Tib.* 37; *Nero*, 48; Tac. *Ann.* iv. 2; *Hist.* iii. 84; Schol. Juv. x. 95;
Pl. *NH.* iii. 67; *BC.* 1873, 5, 12; 1876, 176 ff.; 1877, 81; 1879, 36; 1880, 82; Gilbert, III. 198–199; Jordan, I. 3. 385–390.

paved walk for the guards.  This form of construction probably surrounded the whole area of the castra, but all traces of
the west side, and almost all of the south side except some
foundations, have disappeared.  Many fragments [1] of lead water
pipes have been found, which show the care expended by
successive emperors, Marcus Aurelius, Severus, Caracalla, and
others, on the water supply of the barracks.  The principal
gate, porta Praetoria, was on the north side ; the porta principalis dextra and the porta principalis sinistra on the west and
east sides respectively.

According to the statements of certain writers of the renaissance, an arch dedicated to Gordianus III stood inside the
castra Praetoria. [2]  Although there is no further evidence for
this arch except some architectural remains found at some distance from its supposed site, its existence has been generally
admitted and complete restorations attempted.  Very recently, however, the statements referred to have been dis-
credited, and the provenience of the fragments disputed. [3]  In
the north part of the castra was an ara Fortunae Restitutricis, [4]
the inscription of which was found on the spot; and it is probable that there were several such altars to various divinities
within the precinct.  Modern barracks now occupy the area of
the old castra.

The wide open space (p. 486) in front of the castra was undoubtedly devoted to the use of the praetorians, for no traces
of buildings have been found there, except of some few shrines
and altars.  The ruins of two such shrines have been found
between the via Montebello, the via Goito, and the via Gaeta. [5]
One was a small temple 10 metres wide and 16 long, which
stood in the midst of a paved inclosure.  It contained inscribed
lists, *laterculi*, of the soldiers who had dedicated it.  The other
was a smaller aedicula with four columns in front, which was

---

[1] *CIL.* xv. 7237–7244.      [2] *BC.* 1873, 103, 234; cf. *Mon. d. Lincei.* i. 550.
[3] Jordan, I. 3. 390–391.      [4] *CIL.* vi. 30876 ; *BC.* 1888, 401.
[5] *BC.* 1873, 103, 234; 1877, 21; 1878, 263; *CIL.* vi. 31383, 32523–4, 32622–4.

dedicated by the same soldiers. Of this temple fragments of the cornice, and of a frieze decorated with ox skulls, were found.

The statio cohortis III vigilum, or barracks of the watchmen on duty in regions IV and VI, was probably just inside the porta Viminalis, near the southeast corner of the thermae Diocletiani, but the evidence, which is epigraphic, is scanty.[1] Between the temples of Flora and Quirinus were the officinae minii,[2] or mills for the working of the cinnabar brought from Spain. Assuming that the temple of Flora was near the piazza Barberini (p. 489), these officinae were probably at the foot of the hill, near the present via Rasella.

**Horti Sallustiani**. — Although within the limits of region VI, these gardens, with the horti Lucullani and horti Aciliorum, formed the northern group of parks, just as those on the Esquiline formed the southern. They occupied the northwest slope of the Quirinal, the southeast slope of the Pincian as far as the via Salaria vetus, and the valley between, extending nearly to the line of the Aurelian wall in one direction and to the campus Agrippae in the other. They were laid out by the historian Sallust,[3] who lavished upon them the great wealth which he had amassed in Numidia, and they continued in the possession of the family of the Sallustii until the reign of Tiberius. After that time they were a favorite residence of the emperors, especially Nero, Vespasian, and Nerva, and later Aurelian.[4] In 410 A.D. they were sacked by the Goths under Alaric.[5] It is probable that these gardens were on the whole

---

[1] *CIL.* vi. 3761; *BC.* 1873, 250; 1876, 107; *RhM.* 1894, 417 n.; Lanciani, *Acque*, 286; Jordan, I. 1. 309; II. 122.

[2] Vitr. vii. 9. 4; *BC.* 1889, 379; *RhM.* 1894, 407.

[3] Dio Cass. xliii. 9; Ps.-Cic. *Resp. in Sall.* 19; Tac. *Ann.* iii. 30; *CIL.* vi. 8670–8672, 9005; Gilbert, III. 375–376; Jordan, I. 3. 430–436.

[4] Tac. *Ann.* xiii. 47; Dio Cass. lxvi. 10; Vop. *Vit. Aurel.* 49; *Chronogr. a. 354*, p. 146.

[5] Procop. *Bell. Vand.* i. 2.

the most magnificent in Rome.　Many works of art have been found within the ruins, as well as the obelisk which now stands in the piazza di S. Trinità dei Monti.

Within the gardens were many buildings of various kinds, of some of which architectural fragments have been found, but usually not such as to admit of identification.　Several inscriptions prove the existence of a temple of **Venus hortorum Sallustianorum**,[1] and an attempt has been made to identify this temple with a round structure near the porta Salaria, the ruins of which were discovered in the sixteenth century and described by architects of the time.[2]　This structure, however, was not a temple, but rather a nymphaeum, connected with the elaborate system of water supply installed in the gardens.　The remains of three piscinae belonging to this system have been found,[3] one on the north side of the vicus portae Collinae (via Venti Settembre) opposite the Treasury, one in the vicolo di S. Niccolò da Tolentino, and the third under the casino Aurora in the via Ludovisi; also a number of lead water pipes inscribed with the names of Nero, Alexander Severus, and Valentinian.[4]

Aurelian constructed a **porticus Miliarensis**[5] — a name which should mean a porticus one thousand *passus* in length —within these gardens, and this is frequently located on the north side of the vicus portae Collinae, but without convincing evidence. A porticus of this length must have run about the gardens in various directions.

Before the destruction of the villa Ludovisi that occupied this district and the construction of the new Ludovisi quarter, many more vestiges of the ancient gardens remained, notably the ruins of substructures of a great building, perhaps a Hippodromus, built against the slope of the Quirinal south of the via Sallustiana.　During the process of transformation a porticus

---

[1] *CIL*. vi. 122, 32451; *BC.* 1885, 162.

[2] *BC.* 1888, 3–11; *Mitt.* 1889, 270–274; 1892, 313; *Mélanges*, 1891, 167–170.

[3] Gilbert, III. 376, and references there given.

[4] *CIL*. xv. 7249, 7250, 7259.　　　　[5] Vop. *Vit. Aur*, 49.

with travertine columns was found between the via Sallustiana and the via Boncompagni. At present the only ruins visible are at the end of the via Sallustiana, where the ancient level is far below the modern. These ruins are those of a nymphaeum containing an octagonal hall with niches and lined with marble, and of an adjacent large building, probably a place of residence, with apartments rising to a height of four stories.

In the fourth century the historian Obsequens[1] speaks of certain horti Caesaris *ad portam Collinam* as existing in the year 17 B.C., and these may have formed part of the horti Sallustiani.[2]

**Private Houses.** — In no other section of the city have indications of private houses been found in such numbers. In most cases the evidence comes from inscriptions, generally from those on water pipes, and must be used with caution in determining the exact location of a house, as pipes belonging to one man might extend to a considerable distance beyond his house. The names indicate that this section was largely inhabited by rich and influential families. T. Pomponius Atticus,[3] the friend of Cicero, lived on the Quirinal near the temples of Salus and Quirinus. His house was old-fashioned in its appointments, but provided with a delightful garden. An inscription[4] of 101 A.D. shows that the house of T. Pomponius Bassus, *curator alimentorum* under Trajan, was at the southeast corner of the Alta Semita and the clivus Salutis, and there is every reason to believe that this had been the site of the house of the Pomponii from the first. Martial lived[5] in a tenement in the street called ad Pirum, and later[6] in his own house in the street that led from the temple of Flora to the Capitolium vetus; but neither site can be definitely located. Vespasian

---

[1] 71 (131).    [2] Ps.-Cic. *Resp. in Sall.* 19.

[3] Cic. *ad Att.* iv. 1; xii. 45; *de Legg.* i. 3; Nepos, *Att.* 13.

[4] *CIL.* vi. 1492; *BC.* 1889, 380; *RhM.* 1894, 397, 399, 403.

[5] Mart. i. 108. 3, 117. 6; *RhM.* 1894, 396–397.

[6] Mart. v. 22. 3; x. 58.

lived in a house in the street ad Malum Punicum,[1] and his
brother Flavius Sabinus near by.

A glance at Lanciani's map [2] will show the number of houses
of which pipes have been found,[3] but the exact position of
only a small part of these is assured. Of this small number
may be mentioned those of Vulcacius Rufinus, [4] uncle of the .
emperor Julian, under the Ministero della Guerra, and that
of the gens Nummia [5] just east of it; that of T. Aelius Naevius
Antoninus Severus,[6] in the via Nazionale near the palazzo
dell' Esposizione, and that of Aemilia Paulina Asiatica,[7] under
this building; those of L. Cornelius Pusio [8] and C. Articuleius
Germinianus,[9] near the Banca d' Italia; that of a certain Cornelia Tauri f. T. Axi (uxor),[10] in the via Nazionale, east of the
via dei Serpenti; that of Alfenius Ceionius Iulianus Carmenius,[11]
in the villa Barberini; and that of Q. Valerius Vegetus,[12] near
the Ministero della Guerra. Near the Teatro Drammatico was
the house of Narcissus,[13] the famous freedman of Claudius.

**Tombs.** — Domitian was born in 51 A.D. in the house of his
father Vespasian, and after becoming emperor he erected on
this spot a temple to the gens Flavia,[14] which was to be the
mausoleum of the family. In this mausoleum were deposited
the remains of the three Flavian emperors, and the edifice
existed in the fourth century, although nothing is known of its

---

[1] *CIL*. vi. 29788; Suet. *Dom*. 1.             [2] Nos. ix, x, xvi, xvii.

[3] *CIL*. xv. 7235–7913; *RhM*. 1894, 384; *BC*. 1889, 379 ff.

[4] *BC*. 1884, 45; 1885, 17–22; *RhM*. 1894, 385.

[5] *CIL*. vi. 1748; *BC*. 1885, 5–10; 1886, 18–25; *RhM*. 1894, 386.

[6] *BC*. 1881, 15; Kaibel, *Inscriptiones Graecae*, 1071; *CIL*. vi. 1332, 9147;
*RhM*. 1894, 385–386.

[7] *CIL*. xv. 7380; *Mitt*. 1889, 276.

[8] *Mitt*. 1892, 197–203; *NS*. 1893, 194; *RhM*. 1894, 386.

[9] *RhM*. 1894, 386.             [10] *BC*. 1880, 327; 1881, 15; *RhM*. 1894, 386.

[11] *CIL*. vi. 1675; *BC*. 1884, 43; *RhM*. 1894, 387.

[12] *CIL*. xv. 7558.

[13] *CIL*. xv. 7500. Cf., however, Jordan, I. 3. 421.

[14] Suet. *Dom*. 1, 5, 15, 17; Stat. *Silv*. iv. 3. 18; Mart. ix. 1. 8, 3. 12, 34. 2.

intervening history.  Its site,[1] as already indicated (p. 504),
was south of the Alta Semita, in or near the street ad Malum
Punicum (via delle Quattro Fontane).

Just outside the porta Salutaris, at the upper end of the
present via Dataria, was found a tomb of republican date belonging to the Sempronii.[2]  This tomb was built of travertine
and ornamented with a Greek frieze.  Its discovery in 1866
assisted materially in determining the position of the porta and
clivus Salutaris.

In the seventeenth century the large marble tomb of a certain Octavia,[3] wife of Appius, was found on the east side of
the via Salaria vetus, at the corner of the present via di porta
Pinciana and the via Sistina; inside the porta Salaria on the
east side of the via Salaria nova, in the grounds of the villa
Buonaparte, the tomb of the Calpurnii;[4] just outside this gate
and partially covered by its towers, the tombs of Cornelia
Scipionis f. Vatieni (uxor)[5] on the north side, and of Q. Sulpicius Maximus[6] on the south; and under the tower of the porta
Nomentana, the tomb of a Q. Haterius.[7]

Outside the Aurelian wall, between the via Salaria and the
via porta Pinciana, was a necropolis of the last century of
the republic and the first two of the empire, where the freedmen
and slaves of more than twenty of the great families of Rome,
and also the soldiers of the praetorian guard, were buried.   Inscriptions by the hundreds have been found in this cemetery
for two centuries, and the growth of the city in this region during the last twenty years has resulted in the discovery of un-
usually large numbers, as well as of many columbaria.[8]  These

---

[1] BC. 1889, 383;  RhM. 1894, 399–400;  Mitt. 1891, 120;  Altmann, Rundbauten,
88;  PBS. iii. 243.

[2] BC. 1876, 126;  RhM. 1894, 411;  CIL. vi. 26152.     [3] CIL. vi. 23330.

[4] BC. 1885, 101;  Bull. d. Ist. 1885, 9–13, 22–30;  CIL. vi. 31721–31727.

[5] CIL. vi. 1296.       [6] CIL. vi. 33976.       [7] CIL. vi. 1426.

[8] NS. 1886–1907 passim;  BC. 1886, 401 ff.;  1897, 57 ff., 276 ff.;  1899, 63 ff.,
152 ff., 263–269;  1902, 81–92;  1905–1908 passim;  Mitt. 1891, 124.

columbaria are regularly built of opus reticulatum, and correspond in orientation with the via Salaria. Outside the porta Nomentana were the columbaria of the Aelii and Domitii, and other tombs. Traces of another necropolis [1] have recently been found between the via delle Finanze and the via S. Susanna.

---

[1] *NS*. 1907, 505-520.

# CHAPTER XX.

## THE TRANSTIBERINE DISTRICT. REGION XIV.

**The right bank of the Tiber** was originally in the possession of the Etruscans, in particular of the inhabitants of Veii, and the name ripa Veientana,[1] which during the empire seems to have been applied to that part of it north of the pons Aurelius, was probably in use from very early times. The whole district between the lower reaches of the Tiber and the more restricted limits of Veientine territory was known to the Romans as ager Vaticanus,[2] a name for which no satisfactory explanation has been found, although it may possibly have been derived from that of some early town, Vaticum or Vatica. The ridge that runs north and south along the river through this ager Vaticanus was called from earliest times Ianiculum, or the Janus-city (p. 16). It extended from a point opposite the extreme southern limit of the city to monte Mario, the division between the modern monte Vaticano and the ridge being artificial[3] and due to the removal of the vast amount of clay which has been dug here for many centuries. By the end of the republic the term mons Vaticanus,[4] or its plural montes Vaticani, had come to be employed as synonymous with Ianiculum, but there is no evidence that mons Vaticanus was used as a specific name for any part of the ridge.

The level ground between this ridge and the river was called Vaticanum,[5] until Caligula built his circus where St. Peter's

---

[1] *BC.* 1887, 15; *Mitt.* 1889, 286–287; *CIL.* vi. 31547, 31555; Jordan, I. 3, 651.

[2] Cic. *de Leg. agr.* ii. 96; Liv. x. 26; Gell. xvi. 17; *RhM.* 1891, 112–138; *BC.* 1908, 23–26.

[3] *BC.* 1892, 288.

[4] Cic. *ad Att.* xiii. 33; Hor. *Od.* i. 20. 7; Juv. vi. 344.    [5] Pl. *NH.* xviii. 20.

now stands. Thenceforth Vaticanum seems to have been gradually restricted to this circus and its immediate surroundings.[1] That part of the plain which is inclosed in the great bend of the Tiber, opposite the forum Boarium, was known as the pagus Ianiculensis,[2] a reminiscence of its earlier corporate existence (cf. pagus Montanus, p. 444).

This Transtiberine district was one of the earliest parts of the ager Romanus, and until the later times of the republic it preserved an almost purely suburban character. The prata Quinctia,[3] or four acres which belonged to Cincinnatus opposite the Navalia, were cultivated even in the reign of Augustus, as were also the prata Mucia.[4] Even in the fourth century we are told that the right bank was called Codeta[5] because bushes grew there in form like mares' tails. The district did not form a part of the Servian city, but the building of the pons Sublicius necessitated some sort of fortification on the right bank of the river; and, in fact, remains[6] of opus quadratum, like that of the Servian wall, have been found just opposite the forum Boarium. When the pons Aemilius was built, a sort of viaduct of tufa was constructed from it to the Janiculum, fragments of which have been found.[7] The road appears to have been 20 Roman feet in width. Augustus included trans Tiberim in the city, and made it the fourteenth region. Its boundaries are quite uncertain, but it must have included much more than was afterward brought within the Aurelian wall, and probably extended from the horti Agrippinae south as far as the Aventine. The line of the Aurelian wall has already been described (p. 66).

The earliest population of the right bank seems to have been made up for the most part of fishermen, tanners, and

---

[1] Pl. *NH.* xvi. 201; xxxvi. 74; Suet. *Claud.* 21.
[2] *CIL.* vi. 2219–2220; Gilbert, II. 176–177.
[3] Liv. iii. 26; Pl. *NH.* xviii. 20.    [5] Fest. *Epit.* 58; Jordan, I. 3. 624.
[4] Liv. ii. 13; Dionys. v. 35.    [6] *NS.* 1880, 226, 468.
[7] *BC.* 1889, 475–476; 1890, 6–9, 57–65; *Mitt.* 1891, 145–158.

potters. To the importance of the first the *ludi piscatorii*[1]
bear witness. The Coraria,[2] or tanners' quarter, existed down
to the fourth century. Many remains of the shops of the
potters[3] have been found on the bank, especially near the
Ospizio di S. Michele, and the clay pits have already been
referred to. Other trades[4] followed these; and under the empire the larger part of the district was covered with a network of narrow streets and crowded houses and shops, and
inhabited by a population decidedly doubtful in character.

A short distance below the porta Aurelia were the molinae,[5] or
public mills, driven by the aqua Traiana, which continued in
use until the sixth century.

There were also docks and horrea[6] on this side of the river,
for mounds of broken amphorae and doliola, like those of
monte Testaccio, have been found in the Prati di Castello, —
the name formerly given to the fields north and east of the
Vatican, — while the church of S. Francesco a Ripa stands
upon a similar mound.[7] During the excavations in the villa
Farnesina, an inscription[8] belonging to the cellae vinariae
nova et Arruntiana was found beneath a pile of broken wine
jars, and afterward the warehouse itself (p. 516) was discovered.

Our information as to the growth and appearance of the
Transtiberine district before the end of the republic is very
meagre; but after that date it developed along two lines, — one
that already described, and the other, that which was suggested
to the rich Romans by the natural beauty of the ridge of the
Janiculum. This gave rise to the formation of a series of
gardens and parks, which belonged both to private individuals
and to the emperors.[9]

---

[1] Fest. 210, 238; Ov. *Fast.* vi. 237–240.

[2] *Bull. d. Ist.* 1871, 161–170; *BC.* 1887, 3–7; *Mitt.* 1889, 288–289; Gilbert,
III. 447; *CIL.* vi. 1117–1118.

[3] Cf. Juv. vi. 344; Pl. *NH.* xxxv. 163.      [4] *NS.* 1887, 17.

[5] Not. *Reg.* xiv; Procop. *Bell. Goth.* i. 19; Jordan, I. 3. 648.

[6] *BC.* 1889, 359; *NS.* 1884, 392.      [7] *Ann. d. Ist.* 1878 186–187.

[8] *CIL.* vi. 8826; *NS.* 1878, 66.      [9] Jordan, I. 3, 628–630.

**Temples and Shrines.** — Tradition assigned the earliest cults in this district to the time of Numa, who was said to have been buried near the altar of Fons or Fontus,[1] a son of Janus. To this period also belongs the lucus Furrinae,[2] in which C. Gracchus was killed.

Very recent excavations have shown that this grove covered the site of the present villa Sciarra on the Janiculum. Part of the inclosing wall of the lucus has been found, its sacred spring, and remains of a temple of Iuppiter Heliopolitanus and other Syrian deities whose worship was established here during the empire. Most of the dedicatory inscriptions date from 175–185 A.D., and the remains of the earlier temple belong to about the same period, while those of later date indicate a restoration about the end of the third century. Among the fragments of sculpture that have been found are statues of Hades, Bacchus, and an Egyptian king of about the thirtieth dynasty.

The temple of Fors Fortuna stood at the first milestone on the via Portuensis, and was ascribed to Servius Tullius,[3] as well as another temple[4] of the same goddess at the sixth milestone, in the grove of the Arval Brethren. In 293 B.C. Sp. Carvilius built a temple to Fors Fortuna *prope aedem eius deae ab rege Servio Tullio dedicatam,*[5] but it is uncertain which of the two earlier temples is referred to. Again, in 17 A.D., still another temple to this goddess was erected in the horti Caesaris, and therefore close to the first ascribed to Servius.[6] In this

---

[1] Liv. xl. 29; Cic. *de Legg.* ii. 56; *de Nat. Deor.* iii. 52; Arnob. iii. 29.

[2] Cic. *ad Q. Fr.* iii. 1; Auct. *de Vir. Ill.* 65; Plut. *C. Gracch.* 17; *BC.* 1905, 216; 1907, 45–81; 1909, 97–106; *Mitt.* 1907, 225–254; *Mélanges,* 1908, 283–336; 1909, 1–80, 238–268; *CQ.* 1908, 148–149; *Arch. Anz.* 1909, 130.

[3] Varro, *LL.* vi. 17; Plut. *de Fort. Rom.* 5; Donat. *Phorm.* v. 6. 1; Gilbert, II. 393; III. 450–451; Jordan, I. 3. 644.

[4] *Hemer. Amit. viii. Kal. Iul.;* *CIL.* i². p. 320; Ov. *Fast.* vi. 783; *CIL.* vi. 167–169; *BC.* 1904, 317–324.

[5] Liv. x. 46.

[6] Tac. *Ann.* ii. 41; Plut. *Brut.* 20. (This was not a restoration of the earlier temple.)

neighborhood many small votive offerings in bronze have been found.[1] The ruins of a concrete podium faced with peperino, with architectural fragments, which were discovered in 1861, may perhaps belong to the temple of Servius.[2]

Where the railroad station of Trastevere now stands, a shrine was discovered,[3] cut in the tufa rock and dedicated to Hercules, who is represented as reclining. In front of the shrine were two altars, exactly alike. This shrine was undoubtedly that of **Hercules Cubans**,[4] and probably gave its name to a vicus, as we may infer from the vicus statuae Valerianae[5] near by. The same is probably true of another monument mentioned only in the *Notitia*, the **Caput Gorgonis**.[6] It has been suggested[7] that the Gorgon represented the ancient Furrina, and that the vicus led from the Tiber to the lucus Furrinae.

Near the church of S. Cecilia was a sacellum **Bonae Deae**,[8] and near Caligula's circus a temple of the **Magna Mater**.[9] This temple was also called **Frigianum** (Phrygianum), and must have been one of the most important seats of the cult of Cybele, for an inscription[10] found in Lyons shows that a similar sanctuary there was called Vaticanum.

Of the shrines dedicated to the **Corniscae**[11] and to **Iuppiter Dolichenus**[12] nothing further is known.

**Horti.** — The most distinctive feature of the Transtiberine region was the gardens, which extended from the bank of the river opposite monte Testaccio along the ridge of the Janiculum to the mausoleum of Hadrian. The most southern were

---

[1] *NS*. 1888, 229; *Mitt*. 1889, 290–291.

[2] *BC*. 1884, 26–27; *Ann. d. Ist*. 1860, 415–418.

[3] *NS*. 1889, 243–247; *BC*. 1890, 9; *Mitt*. 1891, 149; 1892, 331.

[4] *Not*. Reg. xiv.

[5] *Bas. Cap*. Reg. xiv. 12; *BC*. 1891, 342, 357; *Not*. Reg. xiv; *CIL*. vi. 31893.

[6] *Not*. Reg. xiv.         [7] *Mitt*. 1907, 250.         [8] *CIL*. vi. 65–67, 75.

[9] *CIL*. vi. 497–504; *Not*. Reg. xiv; Gilbert, III. 113; *RhM*. 1891, 132.

[10] *CIL*. xiii. 1751.      [11] *CIL*. vi. 96; Fest. *Epit*. 64.      [12] *CIL*. vi. 415.

the horti Caesaris,[1] which extended from a point near the porta Portuensis south along the via Portuensis, and contained within their limits the temple of Fors Fortuna, which was one mile from the porta Portuensis. These gardens were left by Caesar to the Roman people, and were thereafter public property. There is no later mention of them ; but remains of works of art as well as of buildings have frequently been found [2] within these limits.

North of the horti Caesaris were the horti Getae,[3] which perhaps lay on the ridge and the east slope of the Janiculum, covering the ground now occupied by the villa Corsini, the villa Lante, and perhaps part of the convent of S. Onofrio. These gardens were probably constructed by Severus,[4] under the name of his youngest son, and some remains of works of art and buildings have been found in this district.

At the foot of the slope beyond S. Onofrio were the horti Agrippinae, which occupied the present site of St. Peter's and extended to the Tiber, from which they were separated by a portico. These gardens were owned by Agrippina,[5] and at her death in 33 A.D. came into the possession of her son Caligula. Thenceforth they were a part of the imperial property, a favorite resort of later emperors, especially of Nero and Elagabalus, and appear to have been commonly known as the horti Neronis.[6]

The north boundary of the horti Agrippinae appears to have been the via Cornelia, and from this street east extended the horti Domitiae,[7] which belonged to Domitia, either the sister of Nero's father, or the daughter of Corbulo and wife of Domitian. Both these gardens were probably often included under

---

[1] Cic. *Phil.* ii. 109; Hor. *Sat.* i. 9. 18; Tac. *Ann.* ii. 41; Dio Cass. xliv. 35.

[2] *BC.* 1884, 25–30; 1887, 90–95; *Ann. d. Ist.* 1860, 415–450.

[3] *Not.* Reg. xiv; Jordan, I. 3, 649, 656.     [5] Sen. *de Ira*, iii. 18.

[4] Spart. *Vit. Sev.* 4.     [6] Tac. *Ann.* xv. 39, 44.

[7] Jul. Cap. *Vit. Anton.* 5; Vop. *Vit. Aurel.* 49; *Not.* Reg. xiv; *CIL.* vi. 16983; Jordan, I. 3. 662–663.

the term horti Neronis.  When the palazzo di Giustizia was built, their eastern boundary was found to coincide with the axis of the new structure, and on the west of this line many monumental remains of opus reticulatum and marble were discovered.[1]  Before the great changes effected since 1870 in this part of the city, the north portion of this park was represented by the Prati di Castello.

There were many other gardens in this region.  Cicero mentions those of Drusus,[2] Cassius, Lamia,[3] Clodia,[4] Silius,[5] and Scapula,[6] some of which he thought of buying; Galba had his own on the via Aurelia;[7] and those of M. Regulus[8] were probably near by.  One inscription[9] records the horti Aboniani.  The horti Antoniani[10] were near those of Caesar.

**Other Buildings.** — In the transtiberine region Augustus constructed a naumachia, the naumachia Augusti, and between it and the river he laid out a grove, the nemus Caesarum.[11]  This naumachia was 1800 Roman feet (536 metres) long, and 1200 (357) wide, and was supplied with water by the aqua Alsietina, built by Augustus for this purpose (p. 98).  It was used by Nero and Titus,[12] but fell into disuse later, for in the time of Alexander Severus only traces of it remained.[13]  The pons Naumacharius,[14] which was restored by Tiberius after a fire, must have been a bridge across this naumachia.  It has been generally supposed that the naumachia of Augustus was situated opposite the Aventine, in the district between S. Cosimato and S. Francesco a Ripa, but a much stronger case can be made out

---

[1] *BC.* 1889, 173–178, 445–446.

[2] *Ad Att.* xii. 21, 23, 25.

[3] *Ad Att.* xii. 21.

[4] *Pro Cael.* 36.

[5] *Ad Att.* xii. 26, 27.

[6] *Ad Att.* xii. 37.

[7] Suet. *Galba*, 20 ; Tac. *Hist.* i. 49.

[8] Pl. *Epist.* iv. 2.

[9] *CIL.* vi. 671.

[10] *CIL.* vi. 9990–9991 ; Dio Cass. xlvii. 40.

[11] *Mon. Anc.* iv. 43–44; Tac. *Ann.* xii. 56; xiv. 15; Suet. *Aug.* 43; *Tib.* 72; Gilbert, III. 334–335.

[12] Suet. *Nero*, 12; *Tit.* 7; Dio Cass. lxi. 20; lxvi. 25.

[13] Dio Cass. lv. 10.

[14] Pl. *NH.* xvi. 190, 200.

for the site between the villa Lante and the Lungara, just north
of the villa Corsini.[1]   Domitian built a second naumachia[2] on
the west side of the river, and Philippus Arabs still a third,[3]
although this may perhaps have been only a restoration of that
of Augustus.   It is probable that the naumachia of Domitian
was situated northwest of the mausoleum of Hadrian, in the
district called regio naumachiae in the middle ages, where
remains of such a structure have been found.[4]

At the monte de' Fiori, near the church of S. Crisogono, is
the excubitorium cohortis VII vigilum, which was discovered in
1866.   The building, which appears to have been originally a
large private house, belongs to the second century, and on its
walls are many graffiti, dating from 215 to 245 A.D. and containing much information with regard to the organization of
the corps.[5]   The portion excavated consists of a central atrium
with mosaic pavement and a hexagonal fountain, and adjacent
apartments, among them a lararium and a balneum.

The castra Lecticariorum,[6] or headquarters of the guild of
litter-carriers, were perhaps in this neighborhood, and nearer
S. Maria in Trastevere the castra Ravennatium,[7] or barracks of a
detachment of sailors from the imperial fleet stationed at
Ravenna (cf. p. 450).   No trace of these castra has been found
except inscriptions.[8]

In the horti Agrippinae, Caligula built the circus Vaticanus,[9]
sometimes called the circus Gai et Neronis,[10] as it was conspicu-

---

[1] Jordan, I. 3, 640–642, 652–656.

[2] Suet. *Dom.* 4–5; Dio Cass. lxvii. 8.        [3] Aur. Vict. *Caes.* 28.

[4] Jordan, I. 3. 660; II. 328, 430; Hülsen, *Il Gaianum e la Naumachia
Vaticana, Diss. d. Pont. Accad. Romana,* 1902, 355–379.

[5] *Bull. d. Ist.* 1867, 8–12 (building), 12–30 (inscriptions); *Ann. d. Ist.* 1874,
111–163 (insc.); *CIL.* vi. 2998–3091; Jordan, I. 1. 309; Gilbert, III. 197.

[6] *Not.* Reg. xiv; *CIL.* vi. 8872–8876; Gilbert, III. 184; Jordan, I. 3, 669.

[7] *Mirab.* 10.                    [8] *CIL.* vi. 3148–3162.

[9] Suet. *Cal.* 54; *Claud.* 21; *Nero,* 22; Dio Cass. lix. 14; Tac. *Ann.* xiv. 14;
Pl. *NH.* xvi. 201; Gilbert, III. 320; Hülsen, *Il Circo di Nerone al Vaticano,*
reprinted from *Miscellanea Ceriani,* Milan, 1910, 256–278.

[10] Pl. *NH.* xxxvi. 74.

ously identified with the orgies of the latter emperor.    The
south wall of the first basilica of St. Peter's coincided with the
north wall of this circus.    The *carceres* were at the east end of
the circus, toward the Tiber, and were flanked by two towers,
placed unsymmetrically.    On the spina, Caligula erected the
obelisk[1] from Heliopolis, obeliscus Vaticanus, which now stands
in front of St. Peter's.    It is of red granite, a monolith 25.36
metres in height, without hieroglyphics, and was moved from
its ancient to its present site in 1586, having stood erect from
the time when it was brought to the city.

Whether the name Gaianum,[2] found in the Regionary Catalogue, was ever applied to the circus of Caligula, is doubtful.
It is, on the contrary, very probable that this was the name of
an open space south and southwest of the naumachia of Domitian,
round which the statues of famous charioteers were erected.[3]

We know the names of baths, the balnea Ampelidis and Prisci
and Dianae ;[4] of a campus, the campus Bruttianus ;[5] and of a street,
the Mica Aurea[6] (cf. p. 442), but none of these can be located.

In widening the channel of the Tiber within the grounds of
the villa Farnesina some interesting buildings were discovered,[7]
which have since been destroyed.    The farthest north of these
was a private dwelling of the first century, with a cryptoporticus
and various rooms in which excellent specimens of wall-paintings were found.    These paintings are now in the Museo delle
Terme, together with stucco ceilings in relief.    South of this
house was a rectangular structure, the first story of which consisted of vaulted store-rooms, and the second of a complex of
courts surrounded by long porticoes, of many of which the
columns were found.    The building in general resembled the

---

[1] Pl. *NH*. xvi. 201 ; *CIL*. vi. 882 ; Gilbert, III. 194.

[2] Dio Cass. lix. 14 ; *BC*. 1896, 248–249 ; Jordan, I. 3. 662.

[3] See Hülsen's work, quoted on p. 514, note 4.

[4] *Not*. Reg. xiv.                    [5] *Not*. Reg. xiv.

[6] *BC*. 1889, 392–399 ; *Mitt*. 1891, 148.

[7] *NS*. 1878, 66 ; 1879, 15, 40, 68 ; 1880, 127–142, pl. iv. ; 1884, 238 ; *BC*. 1900,
321–341.

horrea, and was called the cellae vinariae nova et Arruntiana (p. 509). It was cut through by the Aurelian wall when that was built.

Between these two buildings was another, of trapezoidal shape, which may have been the schola of the *collegium Liberi patris et Mercuri negotiantium cellarum vinariarum novae et Arruntianae Caesaris (nostri)*.

South of the Aurelian wall and close to it was found the tomb of C. Sulpicius Platorinus,[1] who was *triumvir monetalis* in 18 B.C. The tomb itself was rectangular, 7.44 metres long and 7.12 wide, with the entrance on the west. The stylobate and front part of the walls were of travertine, the inner walls of brick-faced concrete. The pavement was of white mosaic. In the niches were cinerary urns with inscriptions, and on the pavement were found two statues of heroic size and a bust. Remains of ancient columbaria have recently been found [2] on the via Portuensis, near the railway station of Trastevere.

**Mausoleum Hadriani**. — In the horti Domitiae, Hadrian began the erection of his famous mausoleum,[3] also called moles Hadriani or Hadrianeum, and sepulcrum Antoninorum, which was not finished until 139 A.D. At the same time he constructed the pons Aelius. When the Aurelian wall was restored by Honorius, the mausoleum was connected by short walls with the north end of the pons Aelius and the fortifications on the left bank,[4] and converted into the chief fortress of the city, which it has continued to be until very recently. In 590 A.D., during a plague, Gregory the Great is said to have beheld the archangel Michael sheathing his sword above the fortress. A chapel was therefore dedicated to the archangel on the mau-

---

[1] *NS.* 1880, 129–138; 1883, 372; 1896, 468; *BC.* 1880, 136; *Mitt.* 1889, 286; *CIL.* vi. 31761–31768 a.

[2] *BC.* 1908, 98–101.

[3] Spart. *Vit. Hadr.* 19; Jul. Cap. *Vit. Ant. Pii*, 5; Procop. *Bell. Goth.* i. 22; Gilbert, III. 308–309; Jordan, I. 3, 663–667; II. 426–428, 433–434.

[4] *Mon. d. Lincei*, i. 444–449; *Mitt.* 1892, 329.

soleum and a statue erected, probably about 610, since which
time the building has borne the name of Castel S. Angelo.

The structure has undergone extensive changes and many
additions have been made during the past centuries, but with
the help of medieval drawings and recent excavations, its

Fig. 92.—The Castle of S. Angelo.

original form can be partially [1] made out.    The lower part was
a rectangular foundation or podium 84 metres square and
about 10 high, built of concrete with travertine walls, which
was faced with blocks of white marble.    The outer surface

[1] *BC.* 1888, 129–131 ; 1893, 22–25; *NS.* 1892, 412–428 ; *Mitt.* 1891, 137–145;
1893, 321–324; Borgatti, *Castel S. Angelo*, Rome, 1890 ; Rodocanachi, *Le
Chateau Saint-Ange*, Paris, 1909.

was decorated with Corinthian pilasters and an entablature, the frieze of which was adorned with garlands and ox-skulls in relief.   A fragment of one of the Corinthian capitals is in the Museo delle Terme.   Around this foundation was a rather wide avenue, inclosed by a low wall and a line of travertine pillars, between which were bronze gratings.   On the tops of the pillars were bronze peacocks.   The entrance was in the centre of the side toward the river, directly opposite the head of the bridge, between which and the inclosing grating there was a street running along the river bank.   The opening through this inclosing grating and the wall was triple, after the manner of a triumphal arch, the central passage being 2.40 metres wide, and the others 2.10.   Over the entrance, set in the wall of the podium, was the sepulchral inscription of Hadrian; and on each side of the entrance was a row of eight inscriptions, commemorating other members of the imperial family, while that of Commodus was set above this row on the left.   Of these eighteen inscriptions,[1] twelve have been found.   This great foundation is for the most part below the present level or concealed by later masonry.

On this square base stood a circular mass 64 metres in diameter and 21 high, made of concrete inclosed in walls of travertine and peperino, which was faced with Parian marble.   This facing was probably made of rectangular blocks, and above the entablature was a row of statues encircling the entire building. This cylindrical portion forms the principal part of the modern fortress; but of the decoration nothing but some fragments of the marble facing remains.   Above the centre of the drum rose a small base, probably cylindrical, which supported a statue of Hadrian in a quadriga.   The colossal heads of Hadrian and Antoninus now in the Vatican undoubtedly belonged to the adornment of the mausoleum, but we do not know just where they were placed.

---

[1] *CIL.* vi. 984–995.

From the outer entrance in the square base, an inclined way led straight into the mass for about 16 metres to a vaulted vestibule, in which was a niche where a statue of Hadrian must have stood.    From this vestibule a passage more than 9 metres high and 3 wide led upward in a spiral round the whole drum, until it reached a point directly over the vestibule. Thence it led straight into the principal sepulchral chamber in the upper part of the drum.    This passage was lined with marble and paved with mosaic.    The sepulchral chamber was

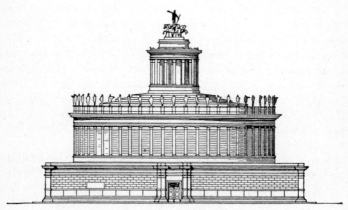

FIG. 93. — THE MAUSOLEUM OF HADRIAN RESTORED.

9 by 8 metres in area and 12 metres high, constructed of blocks of peperino and travertine and lined with the most precious marbles.    In each of the four sides of the chamber were niches containing sarcophagi.    The lid of a porphyry sarcophagus found here is now used as the baptismal font in St. Peter's, but the sarcophagus itself has disappeared.    In this chamber were the ashes of Hadrian and probably of his wife Sabina, and of Aelius Caesar.    From this chamber, and also from the spiral passage, air ducts were cut through to the outside of the drum, and provision was also made for drainage.    The square

rooms immediately above the central chamber have recently been shown to be ancient, and were doubtless also sepulchral chambers. In this mausoleum were probably buried all the emperors and members of their immediate families, from Hadrian to Severus and his sons.[1]

Many traces of tombs have been found along the streets which ran west and northwest from the pons Aelius; and between 1492 and 1503 a pyramid,[2] meta **Romuli**, which stood at the corner of the Borgo Nuovo and the vicolo dei Penitenzieri, was removed by Alexander VI. This pyramid was regarded by some as a tomb of Romulus, and by others as that of Scipio Africanus. Another sepulchral monument, shaped something like an obelisk, and known in the middle ages as the **obeliscus Neronis**, or **terebinthus Neronis**,[3] was situated not far from the pyramid, and was destroyed at about the same period.

---

[1] Spart. *Vit. Sev.* 19, 24; Jul. Cap. *Vit. Opil. Macrin.* 5; Dio Cass. lxxvi. 15; lxxviii. 9, 24.

[2] Jordan, I. 3. 659; II. 405–406; *BC.* 1908, 26–30.

[3] *Mon. d. Lincei*, i. 525–527.

# INDEX.

521

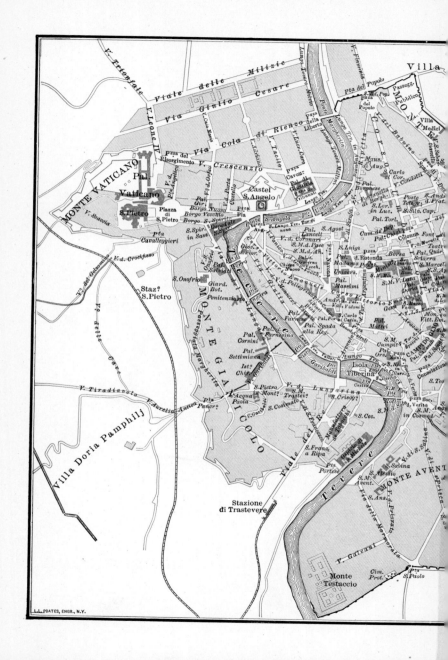

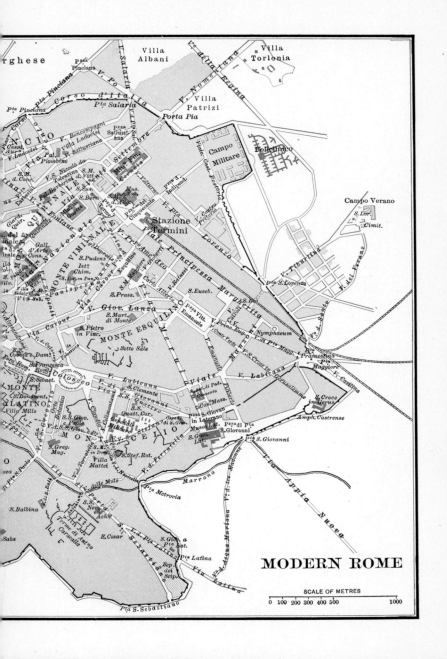

MODERN ROME

SCALE OF METRES

0   100  200 300 400 500          1000

6